ENCYCLOPEDIA OF THE
UNITED STATES
CABINET

ENCYCLOPEDIA OF THE
UNITED STATES
CABINET

VOLUME ONE

MARK GROSSMAN

A B C ☵ C L I O

SANTA BARBARA, CALIFORNIA   DENVER, COLORADO   OXFORD, ENGLAND

Library of Congress Cataloging-in-Publication Data

Grossman, Mark.
  Encyclopedia of the United States cabinet / Mark Grossman.
      p. cm.
Includes bibliographical references and index.
  ISBN 0-87436-977-0
  1. Cabinet officers—United States—Biography—Encyclopedias. 2.
Cabinet officers—United States—History—Encyclopedias. 3. United
States—Politics and government—Encyclopedias. I. Title.
  E176 .G89 2000
  352.24'092'273—dc21
                                                00-011925

06 05 04 03 02 01 00 10 9 8 7 6 5 4 3 2 1

ABC-CLIO, Inc.
130 Cremona Drive, P.O. Box 1911
Santa Barbara, California 93116–1911

This book is printed on acid-free paper ∞.

Manufactured in the United States of America

CONTENTS

VOLUME 3

PREFACE

The budget should be balanced, the Treasury should be refilled, public debt should be reduced, the arrogance of officialdom should be tempered and controlled, and the assistance to foreign lands should be curtailed lest Rome become bankrupt." So wrote the Roman orator Cicero on the powers he saw fit for government. The United States Constitution does not mention a cabinet—in fact, it does not even broach the subject of close advisers to the president. A cabinet based on the British model—which includes a foreign minister, a home minister, and a chancellor of the exchequer (treasury)—was the idea first advanced by the founding fathers during the Constitutional Convention in 1787. The "cabinet" as an institution predated the United States. Early in the fifteenth century, the English Privy Council sat as a group of advisers to the king. They met in the king's royal chamber or cabinet and came to be known as the Cabinet Council. At first, this group of advisers had no official standing or special authority. In time, they came to be under not the king but the prime minister, who came to control more of the nation's business under the system that evolved in the eighteenth century with the rise of parliamentary control. Since 1780, the number of people sitting in the prime minister's cabinet has been fixed, with all of the heads of the major departments sitting to advise the prime minister. Thus, these ministers are accountable to the Parliament. Whereas ministers in the British cabinet are members of Parliament themselves, in the

United States cabinet members cannot be members of Congress. A cabinet officer in the United States may speak to the Congress only when asked to appear before a committee or special hearing.

Under the Constitution that created the U.S. government in 1787, Congress was given the power to establish executive department agencies, which supplanted the numerous boards and advisers instituted under the Articles of Confederation. In 1789, Congress created the Departments of State, Treasury, and War and the Office of the Attorney General, later called the Department of Justice. President George Washington, to receive advice on matters relating to these executive departments, named five men to these offices—Edmund Randolph as attorney general, Thomas Jefferson as secretary of state, Samuel Osgood as postmaster general, Henry Knox as secretary of war, and Alexander Hamilton as secretary of the treasury. (The Post Office Department was initially situated in the Department of State and was not qualified as a full cabinet agency until the administration of Andrew Jackson, in 1829. Further, it was not until 1798 that the Navy Department was established, with Benjamin Stoddert appointed as the first secretary.) These men conducted affairs dealing with these offices, presented opinions and advice both to the president and to Congress, and issued annual reports on the status of their particular departments.

Over the years, Congress has created new agencies specifically to oversee such national matters as land management (Interior), agriculture, commerce, labor, health, education, welfare, human services, housing and urban development, energy, and veterans affairs. By 1989, through retraction (for instance, melding the departments of War and Navy into the Department of Defense, and the decision in 1971 to make the Post Office Department a separate government entity, the United States Postal Service) and growth, the cabinet had expanded to fourteen departments.

The cabinet has been a springboard to higher office. Of the forty-one men who have been in the White House as of this writing, eight had previously served in the cabinet (Jefferson, Madison, Monroe, John Quincy Adams, Van Buren, Buchanan, Taft, and Hoover); of these, six served as secretary of state (Taft was also a secretary of war and Hoover a secretary of commerce). Of the nine American politicians who have won the Nobel Peace Prize, five have been cabinet members. Cabinet members are also remembered in their home states: by law, each state is allowed to send, to be exhibited in Statuary Hall in the Capitol in Washington, D.C., two statues of their citizens "illustrious for their historic renown or for distinguished civic or military services." Of the ninety-five statues in the collection (five states have sent only one statue), twelve served at some point in their careers in the cabinet. Thus the history of these men and women *is* the story of our nation; their lives and service, more than most, helped shape the United States.

And while presidents to a great extent have leaned upon their cabinet members for advice, on the whole they have dismissed these men and, more recently, women and their recommendations with amazing haste. Presidential biographies (and, to a large extent, autobiographies) barely mention these cabinet secretaries, except for those who had been close to the president prior to their service. Calvin Coolidge, in his 1929 tome, *The Autobiog-*

raphy of Calvin Coolidge (New York: Cosmopolitan Book Corporation), explains in the barest terms how the cabinet met "at ten-thirty on Tuesdays and Fridays" and that "each member was asked if he had any problem he wished to lay before the President." The particulars of each secretary are not discussed. An NBC News report just after Ronald Reagan assumed the presidency in 1981 remarked that he met with and accepted the advice of his cabinet officers more than any other president in recent history. The degree of cooperation in any given administration is not known until long afterward, when some autobiographies by, and biographies of, the numerous secretaries are finally published.

As a student of and writer on American history, I am always on the lookout for gaps in the literature. The need for a comprehensive work with complete biographies of every person who ever served in the U.S. cabinet was one of the areas I targeted when I began my writing career in 1987. Two years later, I took an interest in the selection of a cabinet officer when I wrote my-then U.S. senator, Bob Graham of Florida, of my support for the confirmation of John Tower as secretary of defense. And although Tower failed in his nomination, I became fascinated with the men and women who had sat in the cabinet since the start of the U.S. government, including those departments that no longer exist (the Departments of War and the Navy, the Department of Commerce and Labor, and the Post Office Department). I began research into this particular work more than seven years ago, when publishing a comprehensive encyclopedia became more and more possible. My starting point was the research for my 1994 book, *The ABC-Clio Companion to the Environmental Movement*, in which I profiled the lives of most, but not all, of the secretaries of the interior, and this material was eventually expanded into the present volumes. My original work has been complemented by more extensive research into all of the cabinet secretaries, including examinations of their annual reports, personal correspondence, and other materials, such as newspapers and other contemporary documents. Visits to numerous libraries and other archival institutions across the United States, as well as to England in 1996 and 1999, and years of documentation and communication with several former cabinet officers, augmented my research.

The first and best means of finding the thoughts and personal opinions and positions of each cabinet secretary was to examine both their official and personal correspondence and the annual reports of the respective departments. While much of the official correspondence was found to be unhelpful, consisting almost entirely of letters regarding personal matters, commissions, and other agency duties, the personal correspondence was often of great interest, and several letters and other pieces of communication that could legally be used have been quoted in many of the biographies contained herein. However, many private papers of varied cabinet officers, particularly during the eighteenth and nineteenth centuries, were mainly requests for information or, in the cases of the war and navy secretaries, letters to soldiers announcing their commissions.

The annual reports, however, have been used to a great extent to render an important examination of each cabinet secretary's duties of that report year, providing analysis of policy changes and other administrative efforts. Unfortunately, many of the annual reports of the first years of the original cabinet departments are hard to find; they were not issued by Congress or the department as reports, as they are today, but as part of a president's message to Congress, which was submitted in writing and not delivered in person as is the case now. In 1813, the House of Representatives (followed soon after by the Senate) passed a resolution calling for the publication of all

reports of Congress and the executive departments after that time. These documents can now be found in their original form if one is lucky to live near a library with such a rich and ancient collection. The U.S. government, however, has also released these reports in a microfiche edition called the *U.S. Serial Set.* Starting with the Fifteenth Congress (1817), all congressional documents can be found in this collection. In 1831, Congress resolved to publish all documents prior to the 1817 date in another publication. From 1832 until 1861 Gales and Seaton, then the official printer of Congress, released 38 volumes of these earlier documents prior to 1817 in the series called the *American State Papers.* Filed into ten "classes" (i.e., Foreign Relations [class I], Indian Affairs [class II], etc.), these documents are invaluable for the researcher to locate and investigate the goings-on of the executive departments in the first years of the Republic, not just through annual reports but reports on other matters, including foreign policy, war-making, internal affairs, and governmental affairs. Many of the early annual reports (War, Navy, Post Office) come from this collection, as well as other important documents dealing with policymaking and other matters. Numbered identification of these documents, whether from the *U.S. Serial Set* or the *American State Papers,* is provided in both the "reference" sections following each biography, as well as in the bibliography section. A reference to "IV:I:57" means Class IV, volume I, page 57 of that particular class of paper.

Extensive research was conducted through newspapers from every major American city, including New York, Washington, D.C., Chicago, Baltimore, Los Angeles, and other papers from smaller cities. While more than 2,000 references to specific newspaper articles were used, for reasons of space and clarity these have not been cited individually.

The eight years between the first researches of this book and its ultimate completion saw the change of several cabinet officers, allowing me to write about the end of their service, as well as the introduction of new officers who are profiled here in depth for the first time. In fact, as this book was going to press, five present and former cabinet officers were in the news: the resignation of Secretary of Commerce William Daley and his replacement by former Representative Norman Y. Mineta; the resignation of Secretary of Veterans Affairs Togo West and his replacement by Deputy Secretary Hershel Gober; and the clearing of Secretary of the Interior Bruce Babbitt by an independent counsel on allegations that he lied to Congress.

A note of caution: In utilizing vast numbers of sources, including books, documents, and newspapers, I have discovered that the dates of swearing in, resignation, and other dates of service may vary from source to source. Thus I spent some time in trying to resolve the conflict over these apparent disparities. Any and all errors in fact are mine and mine alone.

An additional note: Veteran watchers of the president's State of the Union address may note that all of the cabinet secretaries save one are always in attendance. This missing member is customarily far away from the Capitol, where the president, vice president, Speaker of the House, and Senate president *pro tempore* are all in one place, in case there is a horrible accident and all in line for succession to the presidency are somehow killed. This custom first came about in 1947, when Congress passed an act establishing the order of succession. With the passage of various amendments, including one in 1988, the statute for succession now reads: "If, by reason of death, resignation removal from office, or failure to qualify, there is no president *pro tempore* to act as president, then the officer of the United States who is highest on the following list, and who is not under any disability to discharge the powers and duties of president shall act as

president; the Secretaries of State, treasury, defense, attorney general; secretaries of interior, agriculture, commerce, labor, health and human services, housing and urban development, transportation, energy, education" (Act of 18 July 1947, amended 9 September 1965, 15 October 1966, 4 August 1977, 27 September 1979, and 1988).

The order of succession is thus:

1. The Vice President
2. The Speaker of the House
3. The President *pro tempore* of the Senate
4. Secretary of State
5. Secretary of the Treasury
6. Secretary of Defense
7. Attorney General
8. Secretary of the Interior
9. Secretary of Agriculture
10. Secretary of Commerce
11. Secretary of Labor
12. Secretary of Health and Human Services
13. Secretary of Housing and Urban Development
14. Secretary of Transportation
15. Secretary of Energy
16. Secretary of Education
17. Secretary of Veterans Affairs

I would like to thank all the people who helped to make this work a reality in the more than eight years it took to compose, from the beginnings of research until its publication: Todd Hallman and Susan McRory at ABC-CLIO, who saw this project through its birth pangs, evolution, and final editing and publication; the staff of the Broward County Main Library in Fort Lauderdale, Florida, where I began the introductory work on this book in 1992; John E. White, head of the Public Services Staff, and the rest of the staff of the Wilson Library at the University of North Carolina at Chapel Hill, all of whom were incredibly patient with me when I visited their institution in 1993 and allowed copies to be made of several collections, including the papers of the Thompson Family (relating to Secretary of the Interior Jacob Thompson), Christopher Gustavus Memminger, John de Berniere Hooper, and fragments of the Thomas Bragg Diary (1861–1862), all in the Southern Historical Collection; the staff of the British Library in London, both at the original building at the British Museum during my trip there in 1996 and at the new location at St. Pancras when I was in London in 1999, both places for major research into the vast subject of the initial history of the British cabinet, and official reactions of the British government to American foreign policy; the staff of the Main Reading Room, Newspaper Reading Room, and Manuscript Division of the Library of Congress, without whose help in my six visits to their institution, 1992–1997, the completion of this work would not have been possible; the staff of the National Archives in Washington, D.C., who granted me access to thousands of papers dealing with the public correspondence of various cabinet officials; the staff of Columbia University in New York, for their work in helping me to find and copy many rare works on various American historical figures located in their archives; the curators of the New-York Historical Society, who helped me delve into their substantive collections to find letters to and from various cabinet officers; my friend Melanie Yolles, in the Manuscript and Rare Books Division of the New York Public Library, who always has a smile on her face when I visit that hallowed institution and who helped me access many collections that dealt with cabinet officers; the caretakers of the Trinity Churchyard in New York City, where Alexander Hamilton and Albert Gallatin are buried and where I was allowed close access to photograph and copy the inscriptions on their gravestones; the terrific staff of the Natural Resources Library at the Department of the Interior; Mr. Don Clemmer, of the Ralph Bunche Library

of the U.S. Department of State, for allowing me to photocopy literally tens of thousands of pages from the incredible number of historical works in the library's rich and fantastic collection; Mr. Michael Conklin, of the Department of Treasury Library in Washington, D.C., who helped me meander and copy my way through that rarely used, but valuable, archive; Mr. Mark Feldt, of the Justice Department's main library in Washington, D.C., for allowing me access and the ability to copy hundreds of books and reports in that department's archives; the staff of the University of London, who allowed me unlimited access to their libraries' archives during my visit to London in 1996; Mr. Robert A. McCown, Manuscripts Librarian at the University of Iowa Libraries, the University of Iowa, Iowa City, for his help in accessing a letter from Richard Rush to Alexander James Dallas; the staff of the Arizona Department of Library, Archives, and Public Records in the State Capitol in Phoenix, for their aid in accessing papers and documents on Bruce Babbitt during his time as governor of that state; Richard Baker in the U.S. Senate Historical Office, whose assistance on several matters involved in this work were both a blessing and invaluable; Mr. Jeffrey D. Marshall, University Archivist and Curator of Manuscripts at the Bailey-Howe Library, at the University of Vermont at Burlington, for his help in accessing and copying almost a hundred letters from the Jacob Collamer Papers; the staff of the University of Nevada at Las Vegas, who assisted me in working my way through their incredible collections, most notably the microforms and Government Documents areas, in my four visits there; Gary V. Parker, III, of the Education Library of Peabody College at Vanderbilt University in Nashville, Tennessee, for his aid in obtaining a hard-to-get thesis on Aaron V. Brown; Librarian Rob Kennison and the staff at the Lawrence Public Library in Lawrence, Kansas, for supplying information on John

Palmer Usher; the staff of the Department of Labor library, where I was able to access hard-to-find works on the early years of that agency; the staff of Arizona State University, where I spent countless weeks copying from their microforms and government documents collections, as well as their general collections, one of the best I have ever seen; the staff of American University, where I went to on my six visits to Washington, D.C., to copy hundreds of books and articles; the staff of the Catholic University of America in Washington, D.C., where I found in their rarely used library hundreds of ancient works and dissertations; the staff of Georgetown University in Washington, D.C., who allowed me access to meander through their fantastic collections of books, articles, and dissertations; the wonderful help I received from Cecil Andrus, secretary of the interior under Jimmy Carter, Andrew Card, secretary of transportation under George Bush, and Barbara Hackman Franklin, secretary of commerce under George Bush, all of whom answered my questions and gave statements that have been used in their biographies (and thanks to Andy for his yearly Christmas cards!); the wonderful staff of the Public Record Office, Kew, England, for their marvelous and fulfilling help in accessing numerous documents and other works on British foreign policy matters, including the papers of the British Foreign Office and several British foreign ministers; Mr. John Pusey and the staff of the new and old Bodleian libraries at Oxford University in Oxford, England, who allowed me unlimited access to their documents and other works on British foreign policy; the interlibrary loan offices of the State College Library at Jacksonville, Alabama, and the Mid-Continent Public Library in Claycomo, Missouri; the countless hundreds of unnamed libraries across the United States who assisted me with interlibrary loan requests, shipping books, articles, and microfilms to me for my perusal and use; and finally to Bill, Steve, and Barbara and all of the wonderful staff of the Maricopa County Library in Phoenix, without whom this work would never have been completed.

Mark Grossman
30 August 2000

CHRONOLOGICAL LIST OF CABINET MEMBERS

AGRICULTURE

Norman Jay Colman (1889), 4
Jeremiah McLain Rusk (1889–1893), 6
Julius Sterling Morton (1893–1897), 7
James Wilson (1897–1913), 8
David Franklin Houston (1913–1920), 10
Edwin Thomas Meredith (1920–1921), 12
Henry Cantwell Wallace (1921–1924), 13
Howard Mason Gore (1924–1925), 15
William Marion Jardine (1925–1929), 16
Arthur Mastick Hyde (1929–1933), 17
Henry Agard Wallace (1933–1940), 18
Claude Raymond Wickard (1940–1945), 20
Clinton Presba Anderson (1945–1948), 21
Charles Franklin Brannan (1948–1953), 23
Ezra Taft Benson (1953–1961), 24
Orville Lothrop Freeman (1961–1969), 26
Clifford Morris Hardin (1969–1971), 28
Earl Lauer Butz (1971–1976), 29
John Albert Knebel (1976–1977), 30
Robert Selmer Bergland (1977–1981), 30
John Rusling Block (1981–1986), 31
Richard Edmund Lyng (1986–1989), 33
Clayton Keith Yeutter (1989–1991), 34
Edward Rell Madigan (1991–1993), 35
Alphonso Michael Espy (1993–1994), 36
Daniel Robert Glickman (1995–), 37

ATTORNEY GENERAL/JUSTICE

Edmund Jenings Randolph (1789–1794), 41
William Bradford, Jr. (1794–1795), 44
Charles Lee (1795–1801), 45
Levi Lincoln (1801–1804), 46
John Breckinridge (1805–1806), 47
Caesar Augustus Rodney (1807–1811), 48
William Pinkney (1811–1814), 49
Richard Rush (1814–1817), 51
William Wirt (1817–1829), 53
John MacPherson Berrien (1829–1831), 54
Roger Brooke Taney (1831–1833), 55
Benjamin Franklin Butler (1833–1838), 57
Felix Grundy (1838–1840), 57

Henry Dilworth Gilpin (1840–1841), 59
John Jordan Crittenden (1841), 60
Hugh Swinton Legaré (1841–1843), 61
John Nelson (1843–1845), 62
John Young Mason (1845–1846), 63
Nathan Clifford (1846–1848), 63
Isaac Toucey (1848–1849), 65
Reverdy Johnson (1849–1850), 66
John Jordan Crittenden (1850–1853), 67
Caleb Cushing (1853–1857), 67
Jeremiah Sullivan Black (1857–1860), 70
Edwin McMasters Stanton (1860–1861), 71
Edward Bates (1861–1864), 73
James Speed (1864–1866), 75
Henry Stanbery (1866–1868), 76
William Maxwell Evarts (1868–1869), 77
Ebenezer Rockwood Hoar (1869–1870), 79
Amos Tappan Akerman (1870–1872), 81
George Henry Williams (1872–1875), 82
Edwards Pierrepont (1875–1876), 83
Alphonso Taft (1876–1877), 84
Charles Devens (1877–1881), 85
Isaac Wayne MacVeagh (1881), 86
Benjamin Harris Brewster (1881–1885), 87
Augustus Hill Garland (1885–1889), 88
William Henry Harrison Miller (1889–1893), 89
Richard Olney (1893–1895), 90
Judson Harmon (1895–1897), 93
Joseph McKenna (1897), 94
John William Griggs (1898–1901), 95
Philander Chase Knox (1901–1904), 96
William Henry Moody (1904–1906), 98
Charles Joseph Bonaparte (1906–1909), 98
George Woodward Wickersham (1909–1913), 98
James Clark McReynolds (1913–1914), 99
Thomas Watt Gregory (1914–1919), 101
Alexander Mitchell Palmer (1919–1921), 102
Harry Micajah Daugherty (1921–1924), 103
Harlan Fiske Stone (1924–1925), 105
John Garibaldi Sargent (1925–1929), 107
William DeWitt Mitchell (1929–1933), 108
Homer Stillé Cummings (1933–1939), 110

Walter Forward (1841–1843), 787
John Canfield Spencer (1843–1844), 788
George Mortimer Bibb (1844–1845), 788
Robert James Walker (1845–1849), 790
William Morris Meredith (1849–1850), 792
Thomas Corwin (1850–1853), 794
James Guthrie (1853–1857), 796
Howell Cobb (1857–1860), 798
Philip Francis Thomas (1860–1861), 802
John Adams Dix (1861), 804
Salmon Portland Chase (1861–1864), 806
William Pitt Fessenden (1864–1865), 809
Hugh McCulloch (1865–1869), 811
George Sewall Boutwell (1869–1873), 813
William Adams Richardson (1873–1874), 816
Benjamin Helm Bristow (1874–1876), 818
Lot Myrick Morrill (1876–1877), 820
John Sherman (1877–1881), 821
William Windom (1881), 825
Charles James Folger (1881–1884), 827
Walter Quintin Gresham (1884), 828
Daniel Manning (1885–1887), 828
Charles Stebbins Fairchild (1887–1889), 829
William Windom (1889–1891), 831
Charles Foster (1891–1893), 831
John Griffin Carlisle (1893–1897), 833
Lyman Judson Gage (1897–1902), 835
Leslie Mortimer Shaw (1902–1907), 836
George Bruce Cortelyou (1907–1909), 838
Franklin MacVeagh (1909–1913), 838
William Gibbs McAdoo (1913–1918), 839
George Carter Glass (1918–1920), 842
David Franklin Houston (1920–1921), 844
Andrew William Mellon (1921–1932), 844
Ogden Livingston Mills (1932–1933), 847
William Hartman Woodin (1933), 848
Henry Morgenthau, Jr. (1934–1945), 850
Frederick Moore Vinson (1945–1946), 852
John Wesley Snyder (1946–1953), 854
George Magoffin Humphrey (1953–1957), 856
Robert Bernerd Anderson (1957–1961), 858
Clarence Douglas Dillon (1961–1965), 860
Henry Hammill Fowler (1965–1968), 862
Joseph Walker Barr (1968–1969), 864
David Matthew Kennedy (1969–1971), 865
John Bowden Connally, Jr. (1971–1972), 866
George Pratt Shultz (1972–1974), 869
William Edward Simon (1974–1977), 869
Werner Michael Blumenthal (1977–1979), 870
George William Miller (1979–1981), 873
Donald Thomas Regan (1981–1985), 874
James Addison Baker III (1985–1988), 876
Nicholas Frederick Brady (1988–1993), 878
Lloyd Millard Bentsen, Jr. (1993–1994), 879

Robert Edward Rubin (1995–1999), 882
Lawrence Henry Summers (1999–), 883

VETERANS AFFAIRS
Edward Joseph Derwinski (1989–1993), 890
Jesse Brown (1993–1997), 891
Togo Dennis West, Jr. (1997–2000), 892
Hershel W. Gober (2000–), 893

WAR
Henry Knox (1789–1795), 898
Timothy Pickering (1795–1796), 899
James McHenry (1796–1800), 899
Samuel Dexter (1800–1801), 900
Henry Dearborn (1801–1809), 901
William Eustis (1809–1812), 903
John Armstrong, Jr. (1813–1814), 904
James Monroe (1815), 905
William Harris Crawford (1815–1816), 905
John Caldwell Calhoun (1817–1825), 907
James Barbour (1825–1828), 909
Peter Buell Porter (1828–1829), 910
John Henry Eaton (1829–1831), 911
Lewis Cass (1831–1836), 913
Benjamin Franklin Butler (1836–1837), 915
Joel Roberts Poinsett (1837–1841), 915
John Bell (1841), 916
John Canfield Spencer (1841–1843), 917
James Madison Porter (1843–1844), 918
William Wilkins (1844–1845), 919
William Learned Marcy (1845–1849), 920
George Walker Crawford (1849–1850), 922
Charles Magill Conrad (1850–1853), 923
Jefferson Finis Davis (1853–1857), 924
John Buchanan Floyd (1857–1861), 926
Joseph Holt (1861), 927
Simon Cameron (1861–1862), 927
Edwin McMasters Stanton (1862–1867), 928
Ulysses S. Grant (1867–1868)
Lorenzo Thomas (1868)
John McAllister Schofield (1868–1869), 928
John Aaron Rawlins (1869), 930
William Worth Belknap (1869–1876), 930
Alphonso Taft (1876), 931
James Donald Cameron (1876–1877), 932
George Washington McCrary (1877–1879), 933
Alexander Ramsey (1879–1881), 934
Robert Todd Lincoln (1881–1885), 935
William Crowninshield Endicott (1885–1889), 936
Redfield Proctor (1889–1891), 937
Stephen Benton Elkins (1891–1893), 938
Daniel Scott Lamont (1893–1897), 940
Russell Alexander Alger (1897–1899), 941
Elihu Root (1899–1904), 942

ABBREVIATIONS

ASP   *American State Papers*

DAB   *Dictionary of American
Biography*

DOJ   Department of Justice

GPO   Government Printing Office

HEW   Health, Education, and Welfare

HHS   Health and Human Services

HUD   Housing and Urban
Development

NCAB   *National Cyclopedia of
American Biography*

UNITED STATES CABINET

AGRICULTURE

━━━➤●◄━━━

In his farewell address on 7 December 1796, George Washington asked Congress to establish a federal board of agriculture to disseminate agricultural information and improve the nation's agronomy. In January 1797, a congressional committee proposed Washington's plan, but it never came up for a vote. In 1819, in an effort to establish a domestic agriculture industry, Secretary of the Treasury William H. Crawford sent notices to consuls abroad to send back to the United States seeds of native plants in the countries where they were stationed. It was not until 1836 that the commissioner of patents, Henry L. Ellsworth, began to distribute seeds to farmers. Three years later, after seeing the results of Ellsworth's efforts, Congress appropriated $1,000 for Ellsworth's office to compile agricultural statistics and undertake agricultural studies in addition to distributing seeds.

In 1861, almost sixty-five years after Washington's initial appeal, President Abraham Lincoln took up George Washington's proposal and again asked Congress to enact a federal agricultural board, and on 15 May 1862, Lincoln signed into law the act establishing the Department of Agriculture. It did not have cabinet status, however. Instead, the department was headed by a commissioner of agriculture; among the men who served as commissioners were Isaac Newton (served 1862–1867), John W. Stokes (served 1867), Horace Capron (served 1867–1871), Frederick Watts (served 1871–1877), William G. Le Duc (served 1877–1881), George B. Loring (served 1881–1885), and Norman J. Colman (served 1885–1889). Colman's chief accomplishment, while he was commissioner, was the Hatch Act, supported and passed by Congress in 1887, which allowed for federal grants to agricultural research stations, and which formed a compact between the Agriculture Department and the nation's land grant colleges.

Under the Act of Congress of 9 February 1889, the Department of Agriculture was elevated to the cabinet, the eighth such department; in the enactment, Congress stated: "There shall be at the seat of government a Department of Agriculture, the general design and duties of which shall be to acquire and to diffuse among the people of the United States useful information on subjects connected with agriculture, rural development, aquaculture, and human nutrition, in the most general and comprehensive sense of those terms, and to procure, propagate, and distribute among the people new and valuable seeds and plants."

Norman Colman was named the first secretary, although the Senate did not confirm him, and he left the cabinet just two weeks later. His successor was Jeremiah M. Rusk, a Civil War veteran and former governor of Wisconsin. Rusk organized the department, dividing it into an executive department, under the control of the secretary, and a scientific department, under the direction of the assistant secretary. In his message to Congress of 3 December 1889 President Benjamin Harrison said, "The creation of [the] . . . Department of Agriculture, by the act of February 9, last, was a wise and timely response to a request which had long been respectfully urged by the farmers of the country. . . . But much remains to be fairly done to perfect the organization of the Department so that it may fairly realize the expectations which its creation excited."

In his 1891 annual report, Rusk called for a departmental system for inspecting the entire American food system. More importantly, however, Rusk was faced with a boycott of American meat by the European powers, a resistance that ended, after two years, through congressional action. It was under Rusk's successor, J. Sterling Morton, that the official seal of the department was created in 1894—a national shield, embracing a shock of corn and a plow and surrounded by numerous stars. Around the shield is the motto, "Agriculture is the foundation of manufacture and economy." Morton oversaw an increase in department appropriations and spending, the establishment of the Section of Foreign Markets to encourage the sale of American products abroad, and funding for department nutrition studies.

During the tenure of the fourth secretary, James Wilson, the number of department employees went from 2,444 to 13,858, and the department's annual budget rose from $3,636,264 to $21,103,646. Wilson, the first secretary from Iowa, served for sixteen years, from 6 March 1897 to 5 March 1913, through the McKinley, Roosevelt, and Taft administrations, the longest cabinet tenure in American history. Wilson expanded the department, brought together the interests of agriculture, capital, and labor with the formation of the U.S. Industrial Commission in 1898, and established experiment stations, called for under the Hatch Act. The tenures of the fifth and sixth secretaries, David F. Houston and Edwin T. Meredith, coincided with World War I and calls to expand the production of food for domestic consumption and export, particularly to Allied nations in need of supplies. The end of the war brought a decline in agricultural prices. Congress enacted the Smith-Lever Act on 8 May 1914, while Houston was secretary. The act provided for the cooperative administration of extension work by the department and state agricultural colleges and resulted in the establishment of the Cooperative Extension Service within the department.

Under Secretary Henry C. Wallace (served 1921–1924), the Clarke-McNary Act and the Agricultural Credits Act of 1923 were signed, although Wallace's project, the McNary-Haugen Farm Bill, was vetoed by Presidents Warren G. Harding and Calvin Coolidge. Secretaries William M. Jardine and Arthur M. Hyde dealt with continuing erosion in farm income at the time leading up to the Great Depression in 1929. Under Henry C. Wallace's son, Henry A. Wallace (served 1933–1941), the department responded to the Great Depression by overseeing congressional enactment of the Agricultural Adjustment Act, which for the first time gave the department the right to provide economic assistance to cash-strapped farmers, and established the Soil Conservation Service and the Rural Electrification Administration. The staff in the department rose from 27,000 in 1932 to 106,000 in 1937. Wallace's successor, Claude Wickard, oversaw the agricultural portion of the Lend-Lease Act, in which commodities were sent to Great Britain and other Allies before the United States became involved in World War II.

In 1954, under Secretary Ezra Taft Benson (served 1953–1961), Congress established the Agricultural Trade Development and Assistance Act (Public Law 480), also known as Food for Peace, in which the United States used food and food credits for goodwill overseas, as well as disposing of surplus farm crops. Benson also launched the department's first comprehensive rural development program and oversaw the enactment of the Poultry Inspection Act in 1957. Although Congress authorized Secretary Benson to establish a food stamp program, this was not fully implemented until the tenure of his successor, Orville L. Freeman (served 1961–1969). Under Freeman, Congress enacted the Area Redevelopment Act of 1961, which approved monies for use in bringing jobs to rural areas with high unemployment, as well as the 1962 Farm Bill. Freeman's proposal to rename the department as the Department of Food, Agriculture, and Rural Affairs was not carried out. Clifford M. Hardin (served 1971–1973) tried to carry out a plan of consolidating the department into a new department of community development, economic affairs, natural resources, and human resources, but there was resistance from farmers' groups, and this plan failed as well. Hardin's successor, Earl L. Butz, oversaw congressional enactment of the Agriculture and Consumer Protection Act, which changed the department's mission from controlling the production of commodities to overseeing their marketing and salability.

The late 1970s saw a shift in the power of the department, as the Farm Bill of 1977, as well as those passed in 1981, 1985, and 1990, changed the way the department did its business. Through the tenures of Secretaries John Block (served 1981–1986), Richard Lyng (served 1986–1989), Clayton Yeutter (served 1989–1991), and Edward Madigan (served 1991–1993), the department used new powers to enforce food safety regulations and, in the 1990s, established new guidelines for healthy nutrition. In 1993, former Representative Michael Espy became the first African American to serve as secretary, but his tenure was marred by allegations of corruption, and he was forced to resign after less than two years as secretary. He was later acquitted of charges of taking gifts in his official capacity as secretary from corporations doing business with the department. His successor, former Representative Daniel Glickman of Kansas, worked to end outbreaks of disease in food and instituted a new policy regarding healthy foods.

When the Department of Agriculture was established in 1862, it occupied six rooms in the basement of the Patent Office Building, now known as the Civil Service Building. After the end of the Civil War, a cattle yard used by the Union Army at what is now the area between Independence and Constitution Avenues and Twelfth and Fourteenth Streets was transferred to the department to be used as an experimental garden. In 1863, Commissioner Isaac Newton asked Congress for funds to construct new quarters; in 1867, Congress appropriated $100,000 for a new building, which was finished the following year. Historian James M. Goode wrote, "By 1868 [the department], with a staff of seventy-two, was able to occupy its new headquarters on the Mall, some thirty yards north of the present Agriculture Building." However, this structure was not sufficient for department operations. In the first report of the department as a cabinet-level agency, for 1889, Secretary Jeremiah Rusk wrote, "I found clerks crowded into rooms and subject to discomforts and inconveniences. I have found two branches of two distinct divisions crowded into one small room; records and books lying upon open tables and chairs for want of sufficient wall space to accommodate cases for their proper care and preservation; the chemical laboratory crowded into a damp, illy ventilated, and wholly unsuitable basement, originally intended no doubt for storage purposes, and its work in certain investigations restricted because of the offensive fumes from such analyses, and because of the dangers to human life and limb from explosions of gases and other causes; and, in a word, there was a complete want of that systematic and orderly conduct of the public business which ought to obtain in every well-conducted office." It was not until the early part of the twentieth century that new additions were constructed, completed in 1907; these were supplemented by the construction of the main administration building, completed in 1930. This building is now known as the Jamie Whitten Department of Agriculture Building, named in honor of Representative Jamie Lloyd Whitten of Mississippi, who served in the U.S. House from 1941 to 1995.

According to the *United States Government Manual 1996/1997,* "The Department . . . works to improve and maintain farm income and to develop and expand markets abroad for agricultural products. The Department helps to curb and to cure poverty, hunger, and malnutrition. It works to enhance the environment and to maintain production capacity by helping landowners protect the soil, water, forests, and other natural resources. Rural development, credit, and conservation programs are key resources for carrying out national growth policies. . . . The Department, through inspection and grading services, safeguards and ensures standards of quality in the daily food supply." Agencies under the Department of Agriculture's control include the Forest Service, the Conservation Service, the Farm Service Agency, the Rural Utilities Service, the Food Safety and Inspection Service, and the Agricultural Research Service.

References: Baker, Gladys L., et al., *Century of Service: The First 100 Years of the United States Department of Agriculture* (Washington, DC: GPO, 1963); Barnett, Claribel R., "Newton, Isaac," in *DAB* 7: 472–473; *First Report of the Secretary of Agriculture, 1889* (Washington, DC: GPO, 1889), 8; Goode, James M., *Capital Losses: A Cultural History of Washington's Destroyed Buildings* (Washington, DC: Smithsonian, 1982), 316; *United States Government Manual 1996/1997* (Washington, DC: GPO, 1996), 110.

NORMAN JAY COLMAN
1827–1911

Norman Colman was the last commissioner of agriculture and the first secretary of agriculture. He was a staunch advocate of horticulture and agronomy and was the editor and owner of one of the nation's most prestigious journals on agriculture in the late nineteenth century, *Colman's Rural World.* The son of Hamilton Colman and Nancy (née Sprague) Colman, Norman Colman was born on his family's farm near Richfield Springs, New York, on 16 May 1827. He re-

ceived a limited education while working on the farm. At the age of 20, Colman moved to Louisville, Kentucky, and studied law at the University of Louisville, from which he received a law degree. He then moved to New Albany, Indiana, where he began a law practice with Michael C. Kerr, a local politician. Although he was elected as a district attorney, Colman decided not to continue in law, and he resigned his office and moved to St. Louis, Missouri, where he bought a farm. He remained politically active and was elected as an alderman in that city.

Colman also became a leading voice for agriculture in Missouri, purchasing, in 1855, the journal, *Valley Farmer,* and establishing, in 1856, the St. Louis Nursery. He lectured on farm problems and helped raise circulation of his journal to 10,000 by 1860. Over the next thirty years, Colman became a unique American voice on behalf of agriculture, helping to found the St. Louis Agricultural and Mechanical Association in 1856 and the Missouri State Horticultural Society in 1859. In 1860, Colman was an unsuccessful nominee for a seat in the state House of Representatives. When the Civil War broke out in 1861, Colman, a Democrat, volunteered for service in the Union Army and was assigned as a lieutenant colonel in the Eighty-fifth Regiment of the Enrolled Missouri Militia. After the war, because he had been loyal to the Union, he was allowed to run for political office and was elected to the state House in 1866. Colman was a staunch advocate for agricultural interests and for the rights of former Confederates. In 1868, he was nominated for lieutenant governor of Missouri, but lost. In 1874, he tried to win his party's nomination for governor, but won the lieutenant governor's nomination instead. He was elected and served under Republican Governor Joseph W. McClung. It was the last elected office Colman would hold. Following the Civil War, but before he reentered politics, Colman revived his journal, renaming it *Colman's Rural World and Valley Farmer*. He became one of the nation's leading voices on agricultural matters.

In 1884, New York Governor Grover Cleveland became the first Democrat elected president since the end of the Civil War. At that time, Cleveland named Colman as the sixth commissioner of agriculture, replacing George Bailey Loring. Colman served from 3 April 1885 until 15 February 1889; during this time, he authored and oversaw the congressional enactment of the Hatch Experiment Station Act on 2 March 1887, which provided federal grants for agricultural experiment stations across the United States while at the same time assisting land grant colleges established under the Morrill Act. Historian Bruce Seely wrote, "Colman proved a politically skillful administrator who balanced patronage with competence. As always, he supported practical programs but recognized the value of scientific research. He attempted to replace seed distribution as the department's main activity with programs like the campaign to combat an outbreak of pleuropneumonia among cattle after 1885. During his tenure, the division of entomology was strengthened, and a vegetable pathology section, a division of pomology, and a division of economic ornithology and mammalogy were created." In his final report as commissioner, dated 1 December 1888, Colman noted, "The Department has continued its efforts to apply the latest results of scientific discovery to agricultural practice. Its aim is ever practical, in the direction of economy and variety in production, through the union of science and experiment and the advance of rural education."

On 15 February 1889, two weeks before Cleveland left office, Congress acted on a long-standing recommendation and elevated the Department of Agriculture to cabinet-level status, the first such elevation since the Department of the Interior was moved in 1849, and Colman officially became the first secretary of agriculture, although Cleveland did not send his name to the Senate for confirmation. Colman served as secretary from 15 February 1889 until 4 March 1889, a period of little more than two weeks.

After leaving office, Colman retired to his home, continuing his agricultural pursuits, as well as editing *Colman's Rural World*. He died in Plattsburg, Missouri, on 3 November 1911, at the age of 84.

References: "Colman, Norman J.," in *NCAB* 5: 165–166; *Report of the Commissioner of Agriculture, 1888* (Washington, DC: GPO, 1889), 7; Seely, Bruce E., "Colman, Norman Jay," in John A. Garraty and Mark C. Carnes, gen. eds., *American National Biography* (New York: Oxford University Press; 24 vols., 1999), 5: 261–262; Shoemaker, Floyd Calvin, "Colman, Norman Jay," in *DAB* 1: 314–315; Smith, William Henry, *History of the Cabinet of the United States of America, from President Washington to President Coolidge* (Baltimore: Industrial Printing, 1925), 482; Summers, Floyd G., "Norman J. Colman, First Secretary of Agriculture," *Missouri Historical Review* 19 (April 1925), 404–408.

JEREMIAH MCLAIN RUSK
1830–1893

Historians Homer Socolofsky and Allan Spetter call Jeremiah Rusk the classic example of a self-made man. The first person confirmed as secretary of agriculture, he spent much of his tenure convincing European nations that American meat products were safe for consumption. Rusk was born on his parents' farm in Deerfield Township, Ohio, on 17 June 1830, the son of Daniel Rusk and Jane (née Faulkner) Rusk. He received a limited education, spending much of his time helping out on the family farm. At 23, he relocated to Wisconsin and bought his own farm. Rusk served in a number of local offices, including as a member of the Wisconsin state legislature in 1862. He then served with the Twenty-fifth Wisconsin Volunteers during the Civil War, rising to the rank of lieutenant colonel. He was cited for bravery for his actions at the Battle of the Salkehatchie River in South Carolina.

After the war, Rusk returned to his farm. He also served as the bank controller for the state for two terms (1865–1869). In 1870, he was elected to the U.S. House of Representatives, where he served as a Republican for three terms—from 1871 to 1877. President James Garfield offered him the post of U.S. minister to Paraguay and Uruguay, as well as ambassador to Denmark, but he declined. When Republican Governor William E. Smith announced his retirement, Rusk's name was entered, by the Republicans, for the nomination, and Rusk won. He was reelected in 1884 and 1886. Senator Benjamin Harrison of Indiana, following his election as president in 1888, named Rusk as his secretary of agriculture. Rusk served for the entire four years of Harrison's administration, until 4 March 1893. One of his first actions as secretary was to establish the department's Office of Fiber Investigations to encourage an American fiber industry. On 30 August 1890, the Congress enacted the Meat Inspection Act, which, for the first time, allowed the department to inspect salted pork and bacon, inspect live animals for export, and quarantine imported animals. This act came about because of fears on the part of European nations that American pork was diseased with trichinosis, initiating a boycott. The ending of the boycott was perhaps Rusk's most important accomplishment in office. Rusk was criticized for the threefold increase in Agriculture Department appropriations during his tenure. In his defense, Rusk stated, "I have already called attention in my last annual report to the fact that any one making a fair estimate of the expenditures of this department will recognize that nearly $900,000 appropriated for the United States Weather Bureau is not an increase of expense, having simply been a transfer from one appropriation to another. . . . Another point to be considered is that under the Hatch Bill providing for experiment stations in every State in which there was established an agricultural college, there has been a steady increase, provided by law, and aggregating over the past year more than $700,000, over which the head of the department exercises no control whatever, the same being included under the appropriations for the Department of Agriculture simply as a matter of convenience to the accountants of the Treasury."

Jeremiah Rusk lived less than a year after leaving his position. He returned to Viroqua, Wisconsin, where he died on 21 November 1893 at the age of 63. He was interred in Viroqua Cemetery. Rusk County, Wisconsin, was named in his honor in 1905.

References: "Rusk, Jeremiah M.," in Robert Sobel and John Raimo, eds., *Biographical Directory of the Governors of the United States, 1789–1978* (Westport, CT: Meckler Books; 4 vols., 1978), 4: 1734–1735; Smith, William Henry, *History of the Cabinet of the United States of America, from President Washington to President Coolidge* (Baltimore: Industrial Printing, 1925), 482–483; Socolofsky, Homer E., and Allan B. Spetter, *The Presidency of Benjamin Harrison* (Lawrence: University Press of Kansas, 1987), 26.

JULIUS STERLING MORTON

1832–1902

Julius Morton was a noted agricultural expert and the founder of Arbor Day. He became the first of three Nebraskans to hold the office of secretary of agriculture. Born in the village of Adams, New York, on 22 April 1832, he was the son of Julius Dewey Morton and Emeline (née Sterling) Morton. When Morton was 2, the family moved west, settling first in Monroe, Michigan, and then Detroit. Morton attended local schools and spent two years at the University of Michigan. He received a bachelor's degree from Union College in Schenectady, New York, in 1856, although it does not appear that he ever attended that college. In 1854, Morton moved to Bellevue, Nebraska, then Nebraska City, where he became the editor of the pioneer newspaper, *Nebraska City News*. Over the next several years, he used his home, Arbor Lodge, as the center of a movement for horticulture in Nebraska. At the Nebraska State Fair in 1869, Morton, along with other horticulturists, formed the Nebraska State Horticulture Society. In 1872, Morton delivered an address that called for a national day in which people would plant trees. This day, later placed on Morton's birthday of 22 April, has become known as Arbor Day.

In politics, Morton was elected as a member of the Nebraska territorial legislature, was appointed secretary of the territory by President James Buchanan in 1860, and was acting governor between the tenures of Territorial Governors Samuel W. Black and Algernon Sidney Paddock. In 1866, he was the Democratic candidate to become the first state governor of Nebraska, but he was defeated by Republican David C. Butler.

In 1892, President Grover Cleveland was elected to a second nonconsecutive term. On 3 February 1893, the *New York Times* reported that Cleveland had offered Governor Horace Boies of Iowa the post of secretary of agriculture. The *New York Times* editorialized that "the Governor stands closer to the farmers in the Nation than any other man in public life today, and Mr. Cleveland could not have chosen wiser than he has done in selecting him to represent the great agricultural interests in this Cabinet." However, on 17 February 1893, Cleveland announced that Morton would receive the nomination. Morton was confirmed as the third secretary, and he served until the end of the second Cleveland administration in March 1897. Morton turned the department into a major force for American agricultural products overseas and in the United States. Gladys Baker, an Agriculture Department historian, wrote in 1963, "When Morton became Secretary of Agriculture in 1893, the economic condition of agriculture and the Nation made it easy for the Secretary to follow his conservative convictions. Agriculture was in a difficult economic situation, while the general economy was heading into the Panic of 1893 and a subsequent depression especially adverse to farmers. . . . When the Secretary took office, he found that the regulations of the Civil Service Commission restricted his authority to hire and fire employees. He was very critical of the 'classified service' and the Commission in his first annual report. However, Morton came gradually to realize that the most promising means of attaining greater efficiency in the public service in the Department was the further extension of the classified service. On 10 June 1896, a sweeping order of the President placed all employees of the Department except the private Secretary and manual laborers under civil service rules."

In the first annual report, for 1893, Morton wrote, "Although [the boycott against pork products] was repealed two years ago . . . we are still very far from having regained the trade in pork products which we had with Germany and France prior to the enforcement of their prohibitory laws. The lesson gained . . . is, that the people of this country are to be much benefited by the diversification of agricultural exports and by their entrance to all the countries of the globe which it is in our power to supply with any product that the varied soil and climate of this vast country will enable us to grow at a profit." In his 1894 report, he reiterated, "There is nothing of greater or more vital importance to the farmers of the United States than the widening of the markets for their products. . . . Therefore, the relation of supply to demand is the creator of prices and the sole regulator of values. Holding such views, the Secretary of Agriculture has carefully studied and enumerated the demand for American agricultural products in the principal markets of the world." Morton secured congressional appropriations for Farmer's Bulletins issued by the Department of Agriculture.

After leaving office, Morton returned to Nebraska, where he began to edit *The Illustrated History of Nebraska,* completed after his death by Albert Watkins, and he published the *Conservative,* a journal that dealt with economic and political issues. Morton died at his home in Nebraska City on 27 April 1902, five days after his seventieth birthday. He was buried in the Wyuka Cemetery in Nebraska City. Arbor Day, a national holiday, is now celebrated on 22 April, Morton's birthday. After his death, the Arbor Day Memorial Foundation was established.

References: Baker, Gladys L., et al., *Century of Service: The First 100 Years of the United States Department of Agriculture* (Washington, DC: Department of Agriculture, 1963), 34–35; Clepper, Henry, "Morton, Julius Sterling," in Richard H. Stroud, ed., *National Leaders of American Conservation* (Washington, DC: Smithsonian, 1985), 273; Hicks, John Donald, "Morton, Julius Sterling," in *DAB* 7: 257–258; "Morton, Julius Sterling," in *NCAB* 6: 487–488; Olson, James C., "Arbor Day: A Pioneer Expression of Concern for the Environment," *Nebraska History* 53: 1 (Spring 1972), 1–14; *Report of the Secretary of Agriculture, 1893* (Washington, DC: GPO: 1894), 48; *Report of the Secretary of Agriculture, 1895* (Washington, DC: GPO 1895), 5.

JAMES WILSON
1835–1920

James Wilson remains the longest-serving cabinet secretary in the history of the American cabinet—sixteen years. During his tenure, there was a massive expansion of the department into the modern agency of today, with cooperative extension work and the promotion of agriculture being extended. Wilson is the only secretary of agriculture not born in the United States. He was born in Ayrshire, Scotland, on 16 August 1835, the son of John Wilson and Jean (née McCosh) Wilson, who emigrated to the United States in 1851, when their son was 16. They initially settled in Norwich, Connecticut, but, in 1855, moved to a farm near the village of Traer, Iowa. Wilson attended the public schools of rural Iowa, then entered Iowa (now Grinnell) College. Wilson left college early and went to work on either his own farm or his father's farm, becoming an expert in agriculture, especially the areas of livestock feeding and raising purebred animals. He also taught school for a time.

Wilson entered politics and, in 1866, he was elected as a Republican to a seat in the Iowa state House of Representatives; he served as Speaker from 1870 to 1871. From 1870 to 1874, he served as regent of the state university. In 1872, Wilson was elected to a seat in the U.S. House of Representatives, serving from 4 March 1873 to 3 March 1877. He was a member of the Committee on Agriculture and the Committee on Rules. To distinguish him from Senator James Falconer Wilson, also of Iowa, Representative James Wilson was nicknamed "Tama Jim." In 1876, he refused to run for reelection and, instead, returned to Iowa and his farm. In 1878, Governor Buren R. Sherman of Iowa named him as a member of the Iowa Railway Commission, on which he sat until 1883. In 1882, he was again elected to the U.S. House of Representatives, and served a two-year term, leaving office on 3 March 1885. In 1891, Wilson, back in Iowa, was named as director of the agricultural experiment station and professor of agriculture, at the Iowa Agricultural College at Ames. He remained there until 1897.

In 1896, Representative William McKinley of Ohio was elected president of the United States. According to biographer Louis Bernard Schmidt, a bitter rivalry arose between the Iowa factions of Senator Albert Cummins and Lieutenant Governor John Albert Tiffin Hull over a cabinet spot—Cummins wanted to be attorney general and Hull wanted the War portfolio. H. G. McMillan, the chairman of the state Republican Party, asked Henry Cantwell Wallace, a well-known agricultural expert in Iowa (who later served as secretary of agriculture for Warren G. Harding and Calvin Coolidge) for a recommendation. Wallace advocated that both men drop out in exchange for Wilson to be named as secretary of agriculture. Both men agreed and Wilson accepted the cabinet post. McKinley biographer Margaret Leech wrote that "McKinley was not intimate with Wilson—their service in Congress had coincided by only one term—but he knew that this was a good appointment, and he was happy to make it. In Wilson, he found a wise counselor and a steady and compassionate friend."

In his sixteen years as agriculture secretary, Wilson made the Department of Agriculture one of the greatest departments in the world in the area of soil investigation, farm management, land cultivation, and forest conservation. Wilson shaped the Department of Agriculture from a small bureau that dwelt on farm statistics to one that embraced all areas of agriculture, horticulture, farming, and plant and animal studies. Biographer Louis Schmidt stated, "In the management of the department of agriculture he began with two cardinal rules: to find the best markets for the products of the farm and to induce and teach the farmers to raise the very best examples of the articles that the markets wanted."

In his first annual report, Wilson outlined what he felt to be the department's objectives: "The Department of Agriculture was organized to help farmers to a better knowledge of production and its tendencies at home and abroad, so as to enable them to intelligently meet the requirements of home and foreign markets for material that may be profitably grown or manufactured on American farms. It was also intended that the Department should organize a comprehensive system of means by which the sciences that relate to agriculture should become familiar as household words among our farmers." In his 1901 annual report, Wilson wrote, "The Department of Agriculture has reached farther into sympathy with the industries of the people during the past year. It has identified itself more intimately with the experiment stations of the several States and Territories and what pertains to the interests of their people. It has gone farther in foreign lands to find many things that will be valuable to our producers. This grouping of related sciences into Bureaus has economized time and contributed to efficiency. The process could be advantageously extended to other Divisions and Offices that are growing beyond their present environment." Expenditures for the Department of Agriculture were six times in 1913, when he left office, what they had been in 1897; staff went from 2,444 total employees in 1897 to 2,815 in Washington and an additional 11,043 in the field by 1913. But there was also sizing down. When he assumed office, for instance, plant research was conducted by several bureaus inside the department; his order resulted on 1 July 1901 in the consolidation of these bureaus into the Bureau of Plant Industry. Legal matters inside the department were also standardized; on 17 June 1905, Wilson ordered that all legal activities be undertaken by a solicitor of the department, and he named George P. McCabe to that office. Overall, Wilson took varied departments and bureaus and set them to work in each specific area of expertise: plant and animal life, soils, nutrition, and chemical research.

Wilson's long tenure brought him wide acclaim during his last years in office. *World's Work,* a major opinion magazine of the time, exclaimed in an 1909 editorial when President William Howard Taft was considering replacing Wilson as agriculture secretary, "During [Wilson's] administration of the Department, it has become the most various in its activities and the most efficient organization of its kind in the world; and it is of direct help to a larger number of persons than any other department of the government, except the Post Office." Wilson remains the only man to serve in the cabinets of three successive presidents—McKinley, Roosevelt, and Taft.

After leaving office in March 1913, Wilson returned to Iowa, where the governor, George W. Clarke, named Wilson to serve as an investigator, with noted farm expert Henry Cantwell Wallace, to study farm conditions in Great Britain. James Wilson died on his farm on 26 August 1920, at the age of 85, and was buried in the Buckingham Cemetery in Traer. He was memorialized as the man who changed the face of farming in the United States.

References: Annual Reports of the Department of Agriculture for the Fiscal Year Ended June 30, 1897: Report of the Secretary of Agriculture. Miscellaneous Reports (Washington, DC: GPO, 1897), 5; *Annual Reports of the Department of Agriculture for the Fiscal Year Ended June 30, 1901: Report of the Secretary of Agriculture. Departmental Reports* (Washington, DC: GPO, 1901), 9; "A Cabinet Record without Precedent," *World's Work* 17: 4 (February 1909), 11189; Leech, Margaret, *In the Days of McKinley* (New York: Harper & Brothers, 1959), 106; Schmidt, Louis Bernard, "Wilson, James," in *DAB* 10: 330–331; Wilcox, Earley Vernon, *Tama Jim* (Boston: Stratford, 1930).

DAVID FRANKLIN HOUSTON
1866–1940

Davidavid Houston served as Woodrow Wilson's secretary of agriculture and secretary of the Treasury. Houston came to office with little experience in the area of agriculture or finance. The son of William H. Houston, a farmer and market owner, and Cor-

nelia Anne (née Stevens) Houston, David F. Houston was born in the village of Monroe, North Carolina, on 17 February 1866.

Houston attended schools in South Carolina, then graduated from the University of South Carolina with a bachelor of arts degree in 1887. He took one year of graduate study before leaving to serve as the superintendent of schools in Spartanburg, South Carolina, from 1888 to 1891. In 1891, he left South Carolina for graduate study in political science and economics at Harvard, receiving a master's degree in 1892.

Houston then went to the University of Texas, where, from 1894 to 1902, he was a professor of political science. He served as dean of the faculty from 1899 to 1902. In 1902, he left the University of Texas when he was selected as president of the Agricultural and Mechanical College of Texas (now Texas A & M University at College Station). In 1905, he was elected president of the University of Texas; in 1908, he was elected as chancellor of Washington University in St. Louis, Missouri, and, during the next four years, he helped turn Washington University into one of the premier universities of the American Midwest.

In December 1911, Houston met Governor Woodrow Wilson of New Jersey—the two men were brought together by Colonel Edward House, a close Wilson aide who had known Houston in Texas. In 1912, Wilson won the Democratic presidential nomination and then the presidential election. Houston wrote in his memoirs that "the President-elect wanted me in his Cabinet, that his plans would be thrown out of gear if I declined, and that I must accept." Houston replied that he would take the Agriculture position for two years, after which he would retire. Wilson agreed, and Houston accepted. He wrote, "I felt greatly honoured to be asked to join the President's Cabinet and serve as Secretary of Agriculture, but for financial reasons it was a serious business for me to go to Washington in such a capacity." Prior to the announcement of Houston's selection, however, there was speculation on other names for Agriculture: Henry Jackson Waters, president of Kansas State College; Charles Dabney, a former assistant secretary of agriculture; and Walter Hines Page, editor of *World's Work,* a major opinion journal. It was not until Houston was seen riding in the inaugural parade that his selection became known; he was confirmed and sworn in as the fifth secretary of agriculture on 5 March 1913.

Houston served not two years, but nearly seven years. During this period, World War I began, and Houston oversaw increased production of food for domestic and foreign consumption. In his first annual report in 1913, Houston called on the department to emphasize not just production of foodstuffs, but to address "the broader economic problems of rural life." In 1914, he was able to have Congress enact the Agricultural Education Extension Act, which Wilson signed into law on 8 May 1914. Wilson later wrote to Representative Asbury Francis Lever, chairman of the House Committee on Agriculture, "Greatly increased provision has been made, through the enactment of the co-operative agricultural extension act, for conveying agricultural information to farmers, and for inducing them to apply it. This piece of legislation is one of the most significant and far-reaching measures for the education of adults ever adopted by any Government."

Biographer Arthur S. Link wrote, "Traditionally, the Department of Agriculture had emphasized improved methods of production; Houston gave more emphasis to other aspects of agriculture, especially to the problems of prices, marketing, and distribution." In his last report as secretary of agriculture, Houston wrote about the impact not just of American troops and materiel to the war effort in Europe, but of food in the postwar needs of all countries: "America had again to assist in saving Europe and herself by supplying food, and that in great abundance. It was estimated that Europe would need to import 20 million tons of bread grains alone, and that of this quantity 11 million must come from the United States. It was obvious also that she would call for large imports of meats and fats, and that for months, until

shipping expanded again, most of these must be obtained in the United States. This burden America was able to assume because of the achievements of the farmers."

When Secretary of War Lindley Garrison resigned in 1916, Houston and Secretary of the Interior Franklin K. Lane were considered to fill the vacancy; on 15 February 1916, the *New York Times* wrote that Wilson was inclined to name Houston to the post. After much consideration, however, Newton D. Baker was finally selected. However, when Secretary of the Treasury Carter Glass resigned to take a seat in the U.S. Senate, Houston was the leading candidate. The *New York Times* praised Houston's service as secretary of agriculture following his selection on 27 January 1920.

During his service as the forty-eighth secretary of the Treasury, from 2 February 1920 until 4 March 1921, Houston tried to steady the department during troubled times. The war had ended a year earlier, and Wilson had just suffered a stroke, leaving the administration shaken. Houston biographer Robert Herren explained, "Because the war had ended and government outlays were rapidly failing, Houston's tenure at the Treasury was not concerned with new large-scale borrowing. Although there was no new borrowing, Houston's Treasury had to refinance maturing debt and began plans to retire the debt. Houston differed from his predecessors—William Gibbs McAdoo and Carter Glass—by floating the debt at market rates rather than at preferential rates. To retire the debt, Houston wanted to restrain government spending—he convinced Wilson to oppose the Soldier's Bonus Plan—and to keep tax revenues high. He supported some tax reform: ending the excess profits tax, the tax surcharge, and several excise taxes."

After leaving the government, Houston served as president of Bell Telephone Securities Co., vice-president of the American Telephone & Telegraph Company, and president of the Mutual Life Insurance Corporation of New York. Houston died in New York City, on 2 September 1940, at the age of 74.

References: Commager, Henry Steele, ed., *Documents of American History* (New York: Appleton-Century-Crofts, 1949), 295; Herren, Robert Stanley, "David F. Houston," in Bernard S. Katz and C. Daniel Vencill, eds., *Biographical Dictionary of the United States Secretaries of the Treasury, 1789–1995* (Westport, CT: Greenwood, 1996), 203; Houston, David F., *Eight Years with Wilson's Cabinet, 1913 to 1920. With a Personal Estimate of the President* (Garden City, NY: Doubleday, Page; 2 vols., 1926), 1: 12, 14, 202–208; Link, Arthur S., "Houston, David Franklin," in *DAB* 2: 321–322; Payne, John Wesley, Jr., "David F. Houston: A Biography" (Ph.D. dissertation, University of Texas, 1953), 3–6; "Report of the Secretary," in *Yearbook of the United States Department of Agriculture [for the Year 1913]* (Washington, DC: GPO 1914), 26; "Report of the Secretary," in *Yearbook of the United States Department of Agriculture [for the Year 1919]* (Washington, DC: GPO 1920), 10.

EDWIN THOMAS MEREDITH

1876–1928

Edwin Meredith was just 43 when named as Woodrow Wilson's secretary of agriculture in January 1920, the youngest man named to Wilson's cabinet. Meredith was also known as a successful farm journalist. The son of Thomas Oliver Meredith, a farm implement salesman, and Minerva (née Marsh) Meredith, Edwin Meredith was born in Avoca, Iowa, on 23 December 1876. When Meredith was still a child his father sold his business and moved to a farm in Mame, Iowa. In 1892, Meredith was sent to live with his grandfather Thomas Meredith in Des Moines. At the time, Thomas Meredith was a famed journalist and the founder of the reformist newspaper, *Farmer's Tribune.* The paper was edited by General James B. Weaver of Virginia, who served as the vice-presidential candidate of the Populist or People's Party in 1892, and the paper became the official organ of the party in Iowa. Two years later, Meredith took over as general manager of the newspaper; however, its influence, like that of the Populist Party,

waned in Iowa. Meredith's grandfather sold his half of the company in 1896, and Meredith sold his ownership in 1904.

In 1902, however, Meredith started printing *Successful Farming* and by 1908, he had over 100,000 subscribers. He transformed it into one of the most successful agricultural journals in the history of the United States, rivaling Henry Wallace's *Wallaces' Farmer* in scope and influence. Meredith served as vice-president and president of the Agricultural Publishers Association.

Meredith became a Democrat after the collapse of the Populist Party and, in 1912, was a supporter of Governor Woodrow Wilson of New Jersey, the Democratic presidential candidate. Meredith ran unsuccessfully for a U.S. Senate seat in 1914 and for governor two years later. In 1915, he was named to the board of directors for the Chamber of Commerce of the United States. In 1917, at the urging of President Wilson, Meredith served on the American Labor Mission, a commission that traveled to England to study labor conditions in England, France, and Italy. In 1918, Wilson named him to the Treasury Department's Advisory Committee on Excess Profits.

Wilson accepted the resignation of his secretary of the treasury, Carter Glass, in January 1920. To replace Glass at Treasury, Wilson named Secretary of Agriculture David F. Houston and to replace Houston at Agriculture, he nominated Meredith. Meredith was confirmed unanimously on 31 January 1970 as the sixth secretary of agriculture; knowing that Wilson's term had little more than a year to go, Meredith's duty was in a caretaker capacity. Despite this, he devised a plan for farm relief to assist farmers hit hard by the postwar economic slowdown. Meredith's plan had little chance of passing because Wilson's administration was coming to an end.

In an article he wrote for the *North American Review,* Meredith explained, "Agriculture is fundamental, and it follows that we are anxious to keep upon the farms a contented, prosperous citizenship, giving them an American standard of living, which means cost of production enough to keep the children in school. Why, then, should we permit the small exportable surplus of our agricultural products to come in competition in Liverpool with the Russian peasant's wheat, with wheat from the Balkan States, with Australian wool, permitting the sale of this small per cent to force a price which bankrupts our farmers by so greatly reducing the price of the large portion we consume in this country? If the law of supply and demand is the controlling factor, why should we not give some attention to the question of our domestic needs; the amount that the world will accept from us at cost of production plus a reasonable profit, and then in some way regulate the production to meet the demand?"

After leaving office in March 1921, Meredith returned to publishing, purchasing *Dairy Farmer* and launching *Fruit, Garden and Home* (now known as *Better Homes and Gardens*). However, he remained involved in politics and, in 1923, joined a group of dry Democrats, who favored Prohibition, and supported former Secretary of the Treasury William Gibbs McAdoo for president. Meredith went to the party's National Convention in New York with firm backing for McAdoo. However, the nomination went to former Solicitor General John W. Davis. Davis then offered the vice-presidential nomination to Meredith, who declined. Meredith waited until after Davis's defeat in November to warn dry Democrats that New York Governor Al Smith, a wet Democrat—against Prohibition—was the leading contender for the 1928 nomination. In late 1927, Meredith offered to oppose Smith. However, when the Iowa state party met, Meredith was in Johns Hopkins Hospital in Baltimore recovering from high blood pressure. The party endorsed Smith. Meredith returned to Iowa, but his condition worsened. On 17 June 1928, Meredith died at the age of 51.

References: Allen, Lee N., "The McAdoo Campaign for the Presidential Nomination in 1924," *Journal of Southern History* 29 (May 1963), 226–227; Baker, Gladys L., et al., *Century of Service: The First 100 Years of the United States Department of Agriculture* (Washington, DC: GPO, 1963), 97–101; Burner, David, "The Democratic Party in the Election of 1924," *Mid-America* 46 (April 1964), 100–102; "Edwin T. Meredith: Eminent Iowan," *Annals of Iowa* 29: 8, 3d series (April 1949), 569–588; Meredith, Edwin Thomas, "Business and Agriculture," *North American Review* 214: 791 (October 1921), 464; "Meredith, Edwin Thomas," in *NCAB* 16: 32–33; Stratton, David H., "Splattered with Oil: William G. McAdoo and the 1924 Democratic Presidential Nomination," *Southwestern Social Science Quarterly* 44 (June 1963), 74.

HENRY CANTWELL WALLACE
1866–1924

Henry Cantwell Wallace is one of only two men who served in the same cabinet position as their sons (the other was Secretary of War Simon Cameron and his son James Donald Cameron). Wallace was a noted agricultural expert, who edited *Wallaces' Farmer* magazine; he served for more than three and a half years as secretary of agriculture in the cabinets of Presidents Warren G. Harding and Calvin Coolidge. Born in Rock Island, Illinois, on 11 May 1866, Wallace was the son of Henry Wallace, a farmer and agricultural expert, and Nannie (née Cantwell) Wallace. However, soon after Wallace was born, his father moved his family to a farm in Adair County, Iowa.

When he became 18, Wallace took over control of his family's 320-acre farm, but after realizing that he needed a proper education in how to farm, he sold off his farm equipment and attended Iowa State College of Agriculture; Wallace was awarded a bachelor of science in agriculture degree in 1892. He became an expert in dairying and, after graduation, was accepted as an assistant professor of agriculture, serving for three years under the tutelage of James Wilson, an Iowa farmer himself who later went on to serve as secretary of agriculture.

From 1893 to 1895, Wallace served as editor of two farm journals, *Creamery Gazette* and *Farm and Dairy*. In 1895, his father and his brother John joined him and the two magazines were merged into *Wallaces' Farmer,* which soon became one of the most influential farm journals of opinion and advice. Wallace remained a contributor to the magazine, even while he was serving in the cabinet.

Following the end of World War I, Wallace saw that farmers nationwide, but particularly in the farm belt, were going bankrupt due to the low prices the world was willing to pay for food because of the economic slowdown. He worked, from 1917 to 1920, applying for relief for farmers, achieving limited success with the Democratic administration of Woodrow Wilson. However, after Wilson left office, Wallace was named as secretary of agriculture, in 1920, and he was able to accomplish much more for the farmers. Wallace, a Republican, had written to Warren G. Harding prior to his election as president, requesting assistance for the starving farmers of the nation. Harding replied, "If the verdict of Tuesday is what we are expecting it to be I shall very much want your assistance in making good the promises which we have made to the American people."

It is doubtful that Wallace was looking for a political appointment when he wrote to Harding—nonetheless, when Harding assembled his cabinet, he selected Wallace for the Agriculture portfolio. Harding biographer Francis Russell wrote, "As Secretary of Agriculture Harding picked the competent if temperamental Iowa farmer, conservationist, and editor, Henry C. Wallace. Wallace was a farmer's farmer. . . . Through his paper and the Cornbelt Meat Producers Association, of which he was secretary for fourteen years, Wallace exerted a large influence among the various farm organizations and became a recognized leader of the agricultural interests. For the farm belt he seemed a promise that the Republican platform pledges of farm relief meant something. Although he considered Harding 'sporty' rather than steady he thought he 'seemed willing to listen to reason in the farm cause.'"

Wallace was confirmed by the Senate on 4 March 1921, and he took office as the sev-

enth secretary of agriculture. Immediately, he set to work to improve the lot of the farmer, not just making sure that government protected production efficiency but he assisted in gaining new markets for farmers. He wrote that he was to further "good farming and good thinking on problems connected with food production and distribution." Biographer Russell Lord wrote, "Under his firm and quiet hand the Department was humming along evenly in its thousands of somewhat sequestered ways of applied physical research. . . . Harry Wallace handled warring aides in the same sure, confident manner . . . assigning able men to important chiefships or special assignments, sparking them with ideas to supplement their own, then crediting the whole result, of it came out right, to them; or backing them up, silently and steadily, if it didn't." Gladys Baker, in a history of the department, added, "Publication of a special series of five yearbooks to assist farmers in solving urgent problems began in 1921. The yearbooks from then through 1925 dealt with economic aspects of agriculture as they related to grains, livestock, fibers, dairy products, tobacco, forestry, forage resources, land utilization and tenure, highways, credit, taxation, the poultry industry, weather forecasting, and fruits and vegetables."

In December 1921, following a recommendation from Wallace, President Harding called for a national agricultural conference, which opened in Washington on 23 January 1922. Harding said to those assembled, "This conference would do the most lasting good if it would find ways to impress the great mass of farmers to avail themselves of the best methods. . . . In the last analysis, legislation can do little more than give the farmer the chance to organize and help himself."

Under Wallace's leadership, Congress enacted the Agricultural Credits Act of 1923, which established federal credit banks in twelve federal districts to loan needed funds to farmers. Wallace also backed the passage of the McNary-Haugen Farm Bill, though Harding and then his successor, Calvin Coolidge, vetoed it. Wallace was with President Harding during a trip to Alaska and California when the president died suddenly on 2 August 1923. Wallace was reappointed to the cabinet by President Coolidge.

On 25 October 1924, Wallace died at the age of 58 and was buried in Des Moines. After his death, his work, *Our Debt and Duty to the Farmer* was published, with a chapter written by his son, Henry Agard Wallace, who succeeded him as editor of *Wallaces' Farmer* and, in 1933, as secretary of agriculture.

See also Henry Agard Wallace.

References: Baker, Gladys L., et al., *Century of Service: The First 100 Years of the United States Department of Agriculture* (Washington, DC: GPO: 1963), 102; Clark, Olynthus B., "Keeping Them on the Farm: The Story of Henry C. Wallace," *Independent* 3765: 105 (2 April 1921), 333, 355–357; Kirkendall, Richard S., *Uncle Henry: A Documentary Profile of the First Henry Wallace* (Ames: Iowa State University Press, 1993), 9; Lord, Russell, *The Wallaces of Iowa* (Boston: Houghton Mifflin, 1947), 2–3, 223–224; Russell, Francis, *The Shadow of Blooming Grove: Warren G. Harding in His Times* (New York: McGraw-Hill, 1968), 434; Schmidt, Louis Bernard, "Wallace, Henry Cantwell," in *DAB* 10: 370–371; Winters, Donald L., "Ambiguity and Agriculture Policy: Henry Cantwell Wallace As Secretary of Agriculture," *Agricultural History* 64 (Spring 1990), 191–198; Winters, Donald L., *Henry Cantwell Wallace, As Secretary of Agriculture, 1921–24* (Urbana: University of Illinois Press, 1970).

HOWARD MASON GORE
1877–1947

Howard Gore succeeded the popular Henry C. Wallace as secretary of agriculture, but served in the cabinet for only four months. The son of Solomon Gore, a farmer, and Marietta Payne (née Rogers) Gore, Howard Gore was born in Clarksburg, West Virginia, on 12 October 1877. Gore attended local public schools, while also working on his father's farm. He entered West Virginia University (now the University of West Virginia) in 1896, and earned his bachelor's degree in agriculture four years later. He re-

turned to farming, becoming the owner of several hog and cattle farms with his brothers; over the years, the men formed their own businesses, W. F. Gore and Brothers and H. M. Gore and Brothers. From 1912 to 1916, Howard Gore served as president of the West Virginia Livestock Association and president of the Virginia Hereford Breeders Association, from 1918 to 1921. During World War I, he served as assistant food administrator for West Virginia and, in 1918, was named as assistant U.S. food administrator under Herbert Hoover. Gore also worked in the Bureau of Animal Husbandry.

On 17 September 1923, Gore was named by President Calvin Coolidge as assistant secretary of agriculture, serving under Secretary Henry C. Wallace. On 25 October 1924, Wallace died and on 22 November 1924, Gore was nominated to succeed Wallace as secretary of agriculture. Gore was confirmed on 4 December 1924; he remained in office only until 4 March 1925, when he resigned, having been elected governor of West Virginia. There is little record of anything Gore did as secretary; department historian Gladys Baker wrote that "in effect, his was only an interim appointment." Gore served a single four-year term as governor of West Virginia, 1925 to 1929. Gore left office on 4 March 1929. In 1928, he had been an unsuccessful Republican candidate for the U.S. Senate. However, in 1931, his successor as governor, William G. Conley, named him as West Virginia commissioner of agriculture, and he served until 1933. He then was a member of the West Virginia Public Service Commission. He was attending a meeting of that organization in Clarksburg on 13 June 1947 when he became ill. A week later, on 20 June, Gore died, at the age of 69.

References: Baker, Gladys L., et al., *Century of Service: The First 100 Years of the United States Department of Agriculture* (Washington, DC: GPO 1963), 122–123; "Gore, Howard Mason," in *NCAB* 35: 239, B: 45; "Gore, Howard Mason," in Robert Sobel and John Raimo, eds., *Biographical Directory of the Governors of the United States, 1789–1978* (Westport, CT: Meckler Books, 4 vols., 1978), 4: 1704.

WILLIAM MARION JARDINE
1879–1955

William Jardine served as secretary of agriculture for the entire four years of President Calvin Coolidge's elected term, 1925 to 1929. The son of William Jardine, a farmer, and Rebecca (née Dudley) Jardine, Jardine was born in Malad Valley, Idaho, on 16 January 1879. He attended school sporadically, instead, working on his family's farm. At 17, he left the farm and moved to Big Hole, Montana, where he earned a living as a dairy helper and cutting down trees for wire poles. In 1899, at the age of 20, Jardine moved to Logan, Utah, where he enrolled in the Agricultural College of Utah. In 1904, he earned a bachelor of science degree in agriculture and went to work at the school as an assistant in agronomy, advancing to instructor, and finally professor in 1906.

In 1907, Jardine moved to Washington, D.C., when he was hired as an assistant cerealist at the U.S. Department of Agriculture studying grain problems; he discovered new ways to grow disease-resistant wheat. In 1910, he became an agronomist at the Kansas State Agricultural College in Manhattan, Kansas, and, two years later, was hired as a lecturer in agricultural problems at the Michigan Graduate School of Agriculture. He returned to Kansas State Agricultural College and was acting director of the experiment station, then professor of agronomy, and, in 1918, president of the college. In 1924, following the death of Secretary of Agriculture Henry C. Wallace, President Calvin Coolidge nominated Howard M. Gore, but Gore was elected governor of West Virginia a month after taking office. In late 1924, Jardine was a member of the president's agricultural conference, which assembled in Washington, D.C., in November 1924. Jardine was confirmed by the Senate and took office as the ninth secretary of agriculture; he remained a member of the agricultural conference; the group reported to Coolidge early in 1925 on the status of livestock and on recommendations for congressional legislation. Although he was firmly against passage of the McNary-Haugen Farm Relief Act, Jardine did support a program of commodity cooperatives and corporations, which were to be owned by a federal farm board, enacted under the Agricultural Marketing Act of 1929.

One of the president's conference recommendations, to expand bureaus inside the Department of Agriculture, was implemented by Jardine when he established a cooperative-making division as a research bureau, and he centralized all regulatory oversight under one bureau. Jardine also oversaw the implementation of the Purnell Act, enacted on 24 February 1925, which authorized funds for research by state experiment stations. On 22 May 1928, Congress passed the McSweeney-McNary Act, which called for a program of forestry research to provide for a supply of timber and other forestry products. Finally, under Jardine, Congress authorized money to complete construction on the so-called South Building of the Agriculture Department, which was finished in 1937.

After leaving office, in March 1929, Jardine returned to Kansas, but, in July 1930, he was appointed by President Herbert Hoover as the U.S. minister to Egypt. Jardine served in this position until 5 September 1933. After returning to the United States, Jardine served for a short time as the temporary state treasurer of Kansas, named by Governor Alf Landon. In 1934, he was named president of the Municipal University of Wichita (now Wichita State University) in Kansas. During World War II, Jardine was asked by the government to give advice on matters that would assist in food production. He retired from the college in 1949.

Jardine died in San Antonio, Texas, on 17 January 1955, one day after his seventy-sixth birthday.

References: Baker, Gladys L., et al., *Century of Service: The First 100 Years of the United States Department of Agriculture* (Washington, DC: GPO, 1963), 123–129; "Jardine, William Marion," in *NCAB* A: 14–15; Saloutos, Theodore, "Jardine, William Marion," in *DAB* 5: 364–365.

ARTHUR MASTICK HYDE

1877–1947

Arthur Hyde served for two years as secretary of agriculture during the Great
Depression; he was also governor of Missouri for a term. Born in Princeton, Missouri,
on 12 July 1877, Hyde was the son of Ira
Barnes Hyde, an attorney, and Caroline
Emily (née Mastick) Hyde. Hyde attended
local schools in Princeton, except for two
years following his mother's death in 1889,
when he lived with an aunt in Ohio. He studied for two years at the Oberlin Academy in
Oberlin, Ohio, before he entered the University of Michigan in 1895, earning a bachelor's
degree four years later. He was awarded a
law degree from the University of Iowa in
1900 and was admitted to the Missouri bar
the following year; he entered into a law
practice with his father until 1915, when he
opened his own office in Trenton.

Hyde became a leading attorney and a
civic leader. He was elected mayor of Princeton in 1908 and was reelected in 1910. He
also became a wealthy businessman, with
banks, lumber businesses, farming businesses, and an automobile distributorship.
He was a Republican, but left in 1912 to become a Progressive candidate for Missouri attorney general; he was defeated. He returned
to the regular Republican Party and was
nominated for governor of Missouri in 1920.
He defeated Democrat J. Atkinson by more
than 140,000 votes out of some 1.3 million
cast and served from 10 January 1921 to
12 January 1925. Constitutionally unable to
serve more than one term, Hyde left office,
serving as president of the Sentinel Life Insurance Company from 1927 to 1928.

In 1928, Secretary of Commerce Herbert
Hoover was elected president of the United
States; he selected Arthur M. Hyde for secretary of agriculture. *Collier's* magazine noted,
"He isn't a dirt farmer nor yet a scientific agriculturist. He is a politician who knows more
about farmers than farming." Confirmed by
the Senate on 5 March 1929, Hyde became
the tenth secretary of agriculture, serving for
the four years of Hoover's administration,
until 4 March 1933.

Because the Great Depression hit the
country just months into his tenure, hitting
farmers as hard as other working people,
Hyde became immersed in trying to assist the
agricultural economy. Under the Agricultural
Marketing Act of 1929, the Federal Farm
Board was established; Hyde was a member.
Hoover biographer Martin Fausold wrote, "In
the Agriculture Department's 1930 annual report to the president, . . . Hyde, though he
was intensely jealous of the independent
Farm Board set up by the Agricultural Marketing Act, contemplated its ability to provide multifaceted farm relief. Secretary Hyde
emphasized particularly the following functions of the Farm Board, which had a re-
volving fund of $500 million: 'Strengthening
the bargaining power of producers and increasing the efficiency of their marketing
operations through the development of effective cooperative-selling associations, stabilizing corporations, and clearing houses.'
Next came a call for 'stabilizing the supply of
agriculture products and minimizing fluctua-
tions in prices by preventing surplus production in so far as possible, and by effective
distribution of surpluses once produced.'"

Department historian Gladys Baker wrote,
"A Federal Drought Relief Committee,
headed by the Secretary of Agriculture, was
established in 1930. In addition to recommending loan policies, it aided stricken
counties in obtaining reduced railroad rates
for shipments of hay, feed, and water. Measures taken for alleviating the economic depression, such as increased road construction, were emphasized in drought areas. In
his 1931 report, Secretary Hyde pointed out
the need for curtailing acreage and livestock
breeding, and urged that this be done by voluntary concerted action. The Department issued a special outlook report in the fall of
1930, urging farmers to reduce their acreage
of cotton. However, previous experience
with such pleas and the problems faced by
the Federal Farm Board indicated that such

efforts were ineffectual. Voluntary concerted effort was a useful tool, but it was not a remedy for a desperate situation." The Depression overwhelmed all of Hoover's administration and Hoover was turned out of office in the election of 1932.

Hyde returned to Trenton, Missouri, where he practiced the law for the remainder of his life. He died of cancer in New York City on 17 October 1947, at the age of 70.

References: Baker, Gladys L., et al., *Century of Service: The First 100 Years of the United States Department of Agriculture* (Washington, DC: GPO, 1963), 141; Fausold, Martin L., *The Presidency of Herbert Hoover* (Lawrence: University Press of Kansas, 1985), 106–107; Holman, Charles W., "The Farm Board at Work," *World's Work* 58: 10 (October 1929), 81–86; "Hyde, Arthur Mastick," in Robert Sobel and John Raimo, eds., *Biographical Directory of the Governors of the United States, 1789–1978* (Westport, CT: Meckler Books, 4 vols., 1978), 2: 861–862; Mitchell, Franklin D., "Hyde, Arthur Mastick," in *DAB* 2: 415–417.

HENRY AGARD WALLACE
1888–1965

Henry A. Wallace was a noted agricultural expert who came from a long line of farmers. He served as secretary of agriculture, vice-president of the United States, and secretary of commerce, all from 1933 to 1946; two years later, he ran for the presidency on the Progressive ticket, with a platform of friendship with the Soviet Union. Wallace was brash and outspoken, and his liberalism cost him the vice-presidency and the presidency. He was also one of the towering figures of the twentieth century. Born in Orient, Iowa, on 7 October 1888, he was the son of Henry Cantwell Wallace, the editor of *Wallaces' Farmer,* and Carrie May (née Brodhead) Wallace. When Wallace was four, the family moved to Ames, Iowa, where his father finished his education at the Iowa

State College of Agriculture and Mechanical Arts. Wallace was influenced by his mother's interest in plant growing and his visits with George Washington Carver, a leading agronomist. Carver left Ames to serve as chair of the Department of Agriculture at Tuskegee Institute in Alabama in 1896, but his influence over Wallace was a key event in his life. When he was 15, in 1903, Wallace was already conducting experiments. He attended Iowa State College and received a bachelor of science degree in animal husbandry in 1910; he returned to the farm, where he carried out numerous experiments, including corn yield and corn quality studies; in 1926, he formed the Hi-Bred Corn Company, which marketed the first hybrid corn for commercial sale.

Wallace used statistics to plan crop yields and hog sales; when he lectured on the subject at Iowa State, his work encouraged the school to start a biometrics laboratory in order to teach Wallace's methods. Wallace saw the Depression hit the nation's farms just after World War I. Many historians blame the Depression on low prices and massive surpluses. Wallace argued in his first book, *Agricultural Prices* (1920), that farming needed to be based on production costs and not the free market. In *Wallaces' Farmer,* he began a campaign to rid farmers of surpluses; using the phrase "less corn, more clover, more money," he called for a government campaign to enact price supports and production quotas.

Following the election of Governor Franklin D. Roosevelt of New York as president, Wallace was asked to meet with Roosevelt at the president-elect's retreat in Warm Springs, Georgia, in December 1932. Roosevelt biographer Ted Morgan explains, "Roosevelt wanted [Wallace] because he was a respected leader of the Midwestern agricultural movement, had ideas on crop curtailment that jibed with his own, and was a link with the other Republicans who had voted for him." And although future Secretary of the Treasury Henry Morgenthau, Jr., desired the post, it ultimately went to Wallace, only the second man to serve in the same cabinet position as his father. Wallace had been, like his father and grandfather before him, a Republican, but in 1928 he left the party for the Democrats and supported New York Governor Al Smith for president. On 4 March 1933, Wallace was confirmed as the eleventh secretary of agriculture.

He immediately put his plan for limiting production into force; even before taking office, he convened an agricultural summit and drafted, with Assistant Secretary of Agriculture Rexford Tugwell, a major piece of legislation for Congress to consider—the Agricultural Adjustment Act (AAA) of 1933. Wallace directed that fields be plowed under, surplus hogs and cattle be slaughtered, and subsidies be provided to farmers. Prices on commodities rose. However, in 1936 the U.S. Supreme Court held that the AAA was unconstitutional, as the federal government could not direct agriculture in the nation. Wallace drafted a new law that Congress quickly passed—the Soil Conservation and Domestic Allotment Act of 1936—that supplemented the 1935 Soil Conservation Act, allowing government regulation in the area of soil conservation, thus passing constitutional scrutiny.

In 1940, President Roosevelt, running for an unprecedented third term, angered his vice-president, John Nance Garner, who thought Roosevelt should retire after two terms, so Roosevelt then selected Wallace as his running mate. Wallace was sworn in as the thirty-third vice-president on 20 January 1941. During his four years as vice-president, Wallace served as chairman of the Economic Defense Board to coordinate national economic plans in the event of war, as well as chairman of the Supply Priorities and Allocations Board, giving Wallace wide-ranging powers to control the national economy. When the United States entered the war in December 1941, Wallace found himself at odds with cabinet secretaries, especially Secretary of Commerce Jesse H. Jones. This feud had unintended consequences: it forced Roosevelt to realize that these two men could not get along, despite his best efforts. He ordered a truce, but when Wallace's aide

Milo Perkins wrote a caustic and stinging critique of Jones and his wartime work, Roosevelt forced Jones out of the cabinet and, in 1944, dropped Wallace as vice-president, replacing him with Senator Harry S Truman of Missouri. Wallace in his speech before the Democratic National Convention, declared: "The future belongs to those who go down the line unswervingly for the liberal principles of both political and economic democracy regardless of race, color, or religion. In a political, educational, and economic sense there must be no inferior races. . . . The future must bring equal wages for equal work regardless of sex or race."

After Roosevelt's fourth election victory, he named Wallace as secretary of commerce. As the tenth secretary of commerce, from 1941 until 1946, Wallace advocated closer relations between the United States and the Soviet Union as the cure to the mutual suspicion between the two countries. He also supported trade agreements with labor clauses that could open the world for U.S. trade. In his book, *Sixty Million Jobs* (1945), he outlined a plan of action that he felt would result in full employment. Perhaps his most controversial stand as secretary of commerce came when he called on Truman to share American atomic bomb technology with the Soviets to show good faith. But as the Truman administration took a firmer and harder stand against the Soviets, Wallace derided the policy.

In July 1946, Wallace sent Truman a twelve-page letter outlining his concerns. When Wallace did not get a satisfactory answer, he aired his views in a speech at New York's Madison Square Garden on 12 September 1946, challenging the American government just as Secretary of State James Byrnes was negotiating with the Soviets in Paris over military forces in Europe. The uproar over the speech caused Truman to demand Wallace's resignation on 20 September. However, Truman had seen Wallace's remarks prior to their delivery and had not objected to them. Wallace did not regret that his position had cost him his job. "Winning the peace is more important than high office," he said in an interview. "I intend to carry on the fight for peace."

Wallace moved to New York and became the editor of the *New Republic,* a left-wing opinion magazine. In December 1947, Wallace formed the Progressive Party and declared his candidacy for president of the United States. He named Senator Glen H. Taylor of Idaho as his running mate. Wallace was also backed by communists in the United States; he was beset by charges that he was a Communist dupe. After the election loss, he faded from view, breaking with the Progressive Party in 1950 over its support of the North Korean invasion of South Korea. He returned to his first love, farm science. He supported the candidacy of General Dwight D. Eisenhower in 1952, as well as that of President Lyndon B. Johnson in 1964.

In early 1964, Wallace developed Lou Gehrig's disease. Yet he worked on his experiments until weeks prior to his death, as well as keeping detailed notes on his illness to help future generations. Wallace died in Danbury, Connecticut, on 18 November 1965, at the age of 77.

References: Baker, Gladys L., et al., *Century of Service: The First 100 Years of the United States Department of Agriculture* (Washington, DC: GPO, 1963), 102; Kirkendall, Richard S., "The Second Secretary Wallace," *Agricultural History* 64 (Spring 1990), 199–206; ———, *Uncle Henry: A Documentary Profile of the First Henry Wallace* (Ames: Iowa State University Press, 1993), 9; Kirschner, Don S., "Henry A. Wallace as Farm Editor," *American Quarterly* 17: 2 (Summer 1965), 187–202; Lord, Russell, *The Wallaces of Iowa* (Boston: Houghton Mifflin, 1947), 2–3; *Meet Henry Wallace: An Illustrated Biography of the New Party Candidate including His Own Statements on All Important Issues* (New York: Boni & Gaer, 1948); Morgan, Ted, *FDR: A Biography* (New York: Simon & Schuster, 1985), 370; Schapsmeier, Edward L., and Frederick H. Schapsmeier, *Henry A. Wallace of Iowa: The Agrarian Years, 1910–1940* (Ames: Iowa State University Press, 1968); Schmidt, Louis Bernard, "Wallace, Henry Cantwell," in *DAB* 10: 370–371; Stevens, Donald G., "Organizing for Economic Defense: Henry Wallace and the Board of Economic Warfare's Policy Initiatives, 1942," *Presidential Studies Quarterly* 26: 4 (Fall 1996), 1126–1139; "Wallace, Henry Agard," in Maxine Block, ed., *Current Biography: Who's News and Why, 1940* (New York: H. W. Wilson, 1940), 835–838; White, Graham, and John Maze, *Henry A. Wallace: His Search for a New World Order* (Chapel Hill: University of North Carolina Press, 1995).

CLAUDE RAYMOND WICKARD
1893–1967

President Franklin D. Roosevelt named Claude Wickard as secretary of agriculture, in September 1940, to replace Henry Wallace. Born on his family's farm near Camden, Indiana, on 28 February 1893, Wickard was the son of Andrew Jackson Wickard, a farmer, and Iva Lenora (née Kirkpatrick) Wickard. Wickard attended schools in Delphi, Indiana, at the same time assisting his father in the operation of the farm. In 1911, he went to Purdue University and, in 1915, received a bachelor of science degree in agriculture. He then returned to the family farm to apply his studies on farm operations, including soil conservation and crops that raised the nutrient levels in the earth. Because of his farming success, Wickard was named, in 1927, as a Master Farmer of Indiana by *Prairie Farmer* magazine. In 1932, he was elected, as a Democrat, to the Indiana state Senate for a single term. The following year, he was named to serve in the new Agricultural Adjustment Administration (AAA) as assistant chief of the corn and hog section. The AAA was established under President Franklin D. Roosevelt's New Deal economic program that was launched to combat the Depression. In 1936, when the U.S. Supreme Court found that the AAA violated the Constitution, Congress established a new agency that could pass constitutional muster, and Wickard was named as assistant director, and then director, of the North Central Division of the new AAA, which encompassed the so-called corn-belt states, including Indiana. Although he was never credited, he was responsible for several agricultural programs that were adopted by the Department of Agriculture in Washington.

Wickard's effective handling of corn-belt farm problems led President Roosevelt to name him as undersecretary of agriculture in January 1940, under Secretary Henry A. Wallace. When Wallace was nominated as Roosevelt's running mate for the 1940 election, Wickard was nominated to fill the impending vacancy on 19 August 1940, the same day that Wallace's nomination became official. Four days later Wickard was confirmed by the Senate, and he took office as the twelfth secretary of agriculture, announcing that he intended to continue Wallace's policies. In 1933, Wallace had encouraged farmers to plow under some crops to create scarcity and drive up prices; in 1940, Wickard, sensing war was coming, encouraged farmers to increase their production to augment foreign and domestic supplies. When war did come, Wickard offered a series of proposals to conserve farm and forest lands. In 1944, he said, "We are at the crossroads in our history so far as our natural resources are concerned. Either we take the uphill road to conservation and restoration, or the downhill road to further exploitation and eventual ruin."

In September 1941, Wickard announced a major three-step program for the department, which entailed meeting the needs of the American people as to food and other commodities, supplying Great Britain and other Allies with shipments of similar commodities, and laying stock of these supplies for the period after the end of the war when European refugees and other starving millions would need American assistance. In December 1942, Wickard convinced Roosevelt to name him as U.S. food administrator, but Wickard mishandled the job through a series of disastrous appointments and was forced to cede the agency after just four months. For political reasons, however, Roosevelt retained him as secretary of agriculture.

On 12 April 1945, President Roosevelt died. On 22 May 1945, President Harry S Truman called in Wickard, Secretary of Labor Frances Perkins, and Attorney General Francis Biddle and asked all three for their resignations. Wickard was offered several other posts, and he took over as administrator of the Rural Electrification Administration (REA), which was established to provide federally-funded electrical power to those people who had none. When he took over as head of the REA, 45 percent of people on farms had electric power. When he left that office in January 1953, this number had risen to 88 percent. Wickard retired to his farm in Indiana. He ran, as a Democrat, for the U.S. Senate in 1956 to unseat Senator Homer Capehart, a Republican, but lost. On 29 April 1967, Wickard was killed in a car accident. He was 74 years old.

References: Albertson, Dean, "Wickard, Claude Raymond," in *DAB* 8: 699–700; Baker, Gladys L., et al., *Century of Service: The First 100 Years of the United States Department of Agriculture* (Washington, DC: GPO, 1963), 282–283; "Wickard, Claude Raymond," in Maxine Block, ed., *Current Biography: Who's News and Why, 1940* (New York: H. W. Wilson, 1940), 867–868; "Wickard, Claude Raymond," in *NCAB* F: 26–27.

CLINTON PRESBA ANDERSON
1895–1975

Clinton Anderson was a maverick in the U.S. Senate, best remembered for being the architect of some of the most far-reaching conservation measures passed by Congress. The son of Andrew Jay Anderson and Hattie Belle (née Presba) Anderson, Anderson was born in the town of Centerville, South Dakota, on 23 October 1895. Anderson attended the public schools of the area, then went to the Dakota Wesleyan University, from 1913 to 1915, then spent a year at the University of Michigan at Ann Arbor, but he never received a degree (Dakota Wesleyan awarded him an honorary degree in 1933). He tried to enlist in the U.S. Army, but was turned down because of a lung condition. Instead, he moved to Albuquerque, New Mexico, to recover his health. Anderson became a newspaper reporter for the Albuquerque *Journal,* and served as its editor from 1918 to 1922. He also became involved in the insurance business, working as the manager of the insurance department of the New Mexico Loan and Mortgage Company. In 1925, he started his own insurance business.

Anderson, a Democrat, was named, in 1933, as the state treasurer by Governor Andrew W. Hockenhull. In 1934, Governor Hockenhull put Anderson in charge of the New Mexico Relief Administration, and Anderson helped make the agency financially viable by demanding that people work for their government assistance if they could. He was then named as field representative of the national bureau, the Federal Emergency Relief Administration in 1935, and, in 1936, he was promoted to chairman and executive director of the Unemployment Compensation Commission, where he served until 1938. Anderson was named, in 1939, as managing director of the U.S. Coronado Exposition Commission, a celebration that commemorated the explorations in the American Southwest of Don Francisco Vásquez de Coronado (1510–1554). In 1940, Anderson was elected to the U.S. House of Representatives as New Mexico's representative-at-large, serving from 3 January 1941 until his resignation on 30 June 1945. He was a member of the House Appropriations Committee and the House Ways and Means Committee.

Although a liberal, Anderson did not blindly support the policies of President Franklin D. Roosevelt. He differed with the president, for instance, on neutrality in the war in Europe and on increasing the debt limit, and he voted to override Roosevelt's veto of an antistrike bill. When Roosevelt died and his vice-president, Harry S Truman, succeeded him, Anderson backed Truman's veto of farm-draft deferment legislation. This may have influenced Truman when he fired Secretary of Agriculture Claude Wickard in May 1945, although in his memoirs Truman wrote that it was Wickard who wanted out of

the cabinet. Truman wrote. "The appointment of a new Secretary of Agriculture became necessary when I appointed Claude Wickard to be head of the Rural Electrification Administration. He had told me he would like to be head of the REA and did not want to remain any longer as Secretary of Agriculture. I was very much surprised that he asked for the new office, and I gave it to him because I knew he was well fitted for it. . . . Clinton Anderson was on the special committee of the House of Representatives to investigate food shortages and had been instrumental in the passage of a great deal of legislation in the House. I invited him to breakfast at the White House one morning and asked him if he would consider being Secretary of Agriculture, and he accepted."

Confirmed on 1 June 1945, Anderson became the thirteenth secretary of agriculture, serving until 10 May 1948. Implementing President Truman's Nine Point Famine Relief Program for starving nations, Anderson ordered that domestic wheat supplies be conserved and combined into a concerted effort to assist in European relief, which at the same time diminished livestock grain supplies nationwide. Department historian Gladys Baker wrote, "Upon taking his oath of office as Secretary, Clinton Anderson stated that his immediate concern would be with four chief problems fundamental to a sound food program . . . : 1) Abundant production to meet wartime requirements; 2) the guarantees farmers needed from government to get greater production; 3) the necessary action to make good on the promises of government to farmers; and 4) improvements in distribution so that supplies might be shared more fairly by everyone."

At the time that Anderson's appointment was announced, Truman indicated that he was moving the War Food Administration, set up to assist food supply movement during World War II, into the Department of Agriculture. He also named Anderson as War Food administrator, replacing Marvin Jones. Thus the major government offices dealing with food were unified under one person and one office. Anderson's impact at the Department of Agriculture was minimal; he served less than three years.

On 10 May 1948, Anderson resigned from the cabinet to enter the Democratic primary for a seat in the U.S. Senate. Anderson later wrote that Truman offered him the opportunity of remaining in the cabinet and also serving as chairman of the Democratic National Committee; but, in fact, Anderson was quite ill. He approached Truman in 1947 to ask to leave. He wrote in his memoirs, "Mr. Truman . . . was quite insistent that I remain in the cabinet. He felt that my departure would make it appear he was being deserted by all his old friends. I agreed to stay but said I would resign after election day. He accepted the alternative as reasonable, and I looked forward to another year at the Agriculture Department, then to going home."

Instead, Anderson went back to New Mexico and, after Senator Carl Hatch indicated he would not seek reelection in 1948, Anderson entered the race to succeed him. He won the primary and was elected, serving until his resignation in 1973. In more than two decades in the Senate, Anderson became a major influence in the areas of space exploration, atomic energy, and conservation. He served as chairman of the Joint Committee on Atomic Energy, the Joint Committee on Construction of Building for the Smithsonian, the Joint Committee on Navajo-Hopi Indian Affairs, the Special Committee on the Preservation of Senate Records, the Committee on Interior and Insular Affairs, the Special Committee on National Fuel Policy, and the Committee on Aeronautical and Space Sciences.

Anderson's biggest impact came in the area of natural resources and conservation. As chairman of the Senate Interior Committee from 1961 to 1963, he was the Senate's leading adherent and promoter for natural resources, wilderness protection, and outdoor recreation legislation. With Representative Wayne Aspinall of Colorado, Anderson helped sponsor or get Congress to enact the Wilderness Act, the Land and Water Conservation Fund Act, the Outdoor Recreation Act, and the Public Land Law Review Commis-

sion. Secretary of the Interior Stewart L. Udall said that the Eighty-eighth Congress (1963–1964) "wrote brilliant new chapters and established wholesome new principles." Historians credit the influence of Clinton Anderson in the Senate for these measures that inaugurated the environmental movement.

In 1972, Anderson, at 77 years old, declined to run for reelection; he retired to his home in Albuquerque. On 11 November 1975, he suffered a stroke and died at the age of 80.

References: Anderson, Clinton P., with Milton Viorst, *Outsider in the Senate: Senator Clinton Anderson's Memoirs* (New York: World Publishing, 1970), 85–86; "Anderson, Clinton P(resba)" in Anne Rothe, ed., *Current Biography 1945* (New York: H. W. Wilson, 1945), 5–8; Baker, Gladys L., et al., *Century of Service: The First 100 Years of the United States Department of Agriculture* (Washington, DC: GPO, 1963), 332; Baker, Richard A., "The Conservation Congress of Anderson and Aspinall, 1963–64," *Journal of Forest History* 29: 3 (July 1985), 104–119; Baker, Richard Allan, *Conservation Politics: The Senate Career of Clinton P. Anderson* (Albuquerque: University of New Mexico Press, 1985); Truman, Harry S, *Memoirs by Harry S. Truman: Year of Decisions* (New York: New American Library, 1955), 362–363; Walker, J. Samuel, "The Confessions of a Cold Warrior: Clinton P. Anderson and American Foreign Policy, 1945–1972," *New Mexico Historical Review* 52 (April 1977), 117–134.

CHARLES FRANKLIN BRANNAN
1903–1992

Charles Brannan's plan for agriculture, known as the Brannan Plan, highlighted his four-and-a-half-year tenure as secretary of agriculture. Brannan was an agriculturist since his college days, and became a worker for the New Deal programs established by President Franklin D. Roosevelt. Born in Denver, Colorado, on 23 August 1903, he was the son of John Brannan, an electrical engineer, and Ella Louise (née Street) Brannan. After attending Denver schools, he received an education at the University of Denver, earning a law degree in 1929. Brannan was admitted to the Colorado bar in 1929 and worked in Denver, specializing in mining and irrigation law. In 1935, he was appointed by President Franklin D. Roosevelt as assistant regional counsel for the Resettlement Administration, a New Deal economic agency inside the Department of Agriculture. In 1937, Brannan was promoted to regional attorney in the office of Solicitor in the Department of Agriculture, where he assisted in forming irrigation districts for farmers in distress from the Depression. In November 1941, Brannan was named as regional director of the Farm Security Administration, another New Deal agency, covering the states of Colorado, Montana, and Wyoming. He assisted in granting loans and credits for farmers. He also served, for several months during 1944, as assistant administrator of the Farm Security Administration. On 21 June 1944, Brannan was named by President Roosevelt as assistant secretary of agriculture, serving under Secretary Claude Wickard and then Secretary Clinton P. Anderson. He assisted both men in congressional strategy and carrying out internal department policy.

Secretary Anderson resigned on 10 May 1948; President Truman waited nearly two weeks before naming Brannan to the vacancy on 23 May. Brannan was confirmed on 28 May as the fourteenth secretary of agriculture. During his tenure, which lasted until the end of the Truman administration on 20 January 1953, Brannan supported the Truman farm administration program. Historian Todd Swanstrom wrote, "In 1949 Brannan presented the Administration's controversial farm program. The proposal . . . was a major departure from previous agricultural policies. It was designed to maintain farm income at record wartime levels while letting supply and demand determine the market price of commodities. Working with Roosevelt's program of restricting production and marketing to maintain prices, Brannan proposed direct payments to farmers when prices fell below support levels. He recommended guaranteeing farmers a secure income based on the average cash receipts for the first 10 of the last 12 years. This had the effect of guaranteeing high, rigid price supports at from 90% to 100% of parity." Senator Clinton Anderson led the fight in the Senate against the plan. Instead, with Senator Albert Gore, Sr., of Tennessee, he sponsored the Gore-Anderson bill, which replaced the rigid plan with a sliding one. Despite the legislative loss, Brannan continued to advocate his plan, until accusations by his political enemies of using department funds to pay for a political cause diverted his energies. An investigation cleared Brannan in 1950.

After leaving office, Brannan returned to private law practice and, for several years, served as general counsel for the liberal National Farmers Union. In 1962, Secretary of Agriculture Orville Freeman named him as a member of a committee to study the effectiveness of farm programs. Brannan died on 2 July 1992, seven weeks before his ninetieth birthday.

References: "Brannan, Charles F(ranklin)," in Anne Rothe, ed., *Current Biography 1948* (New York: H. W. Wilson, 1948), 57–59; Christenson, Reo M., *The Brannan Plan: Farm Politics and Policy* (Ann Arbor: University of Michigan Press, 1959), 18–23; Kunze, Joel, "Brannan, Charles Franklin," in Richard S. Kirkendall, ed., *The Harry S Truman Encyclopedia* (Boston: G. K. Hall, 1989), 35–36; Swanstom, Todd, "Brannan, Charles F(ranklin)," in Eleanora Schoenebaum, ed., *Political Profiles: The Truman Years* (New York: Facts on File, 1978), 51–53.

EZRA TAFT BENSON
1899–1994

E zra Benson is remembered chiefly for his leadership of the Church of Jesus Christ of Latter-Day Saints (the Mormons). He served as the secretary of agriculture during the eight years of the Dwight D. Eisenhower administration, from 1953 to 1961. Born on his family's farm in Whitney, Idaho, on 4 August 1899, Benson was the son of George Taft Benson, a farmer, and Sarah (née Dunkley) Benson. Benson grew up on his family's farm and received a private and public school education. In 1914, Benson entered the Oneida Stake Academy, in Preston, Idaho and graduated in 1918. He had just started attending classes at the Utah State University when he was drafted into the U.S. Army during the last months of World War I. He returned to the United States and then went to England on a church mission until 1921.

When Benson returned, he enrolled at Brigham Young University and graduated, in 1926, with a bachelor's degree with honors in animal husbandry and a minor in agronomy. He then moved to Iowa, where he entered Iowa State College and received a master's degree in agricultural economics in 1927. He returned to his family's farm and, in 1929, was named as agricultural agent for Franklin County, Idaho, assisting local farmers with new grain introduction and advice from specialists. In 1930, he was promoted to agricultural economist and marketing specialist at the University of Idaho's Extension Division.

In 1938, he left his agricultural work when called by the Mormon Church to be stake president. In 1939, Benson moved to Washington, D.C., when he was offered the position of executive secretary of the National Council of Farmer's Cooperatives; he traveled the United States and became more acquainted with the everyday problems of farmers. He also served as president of the Mormon Church's Washington, D.C., stake. On 1943, Mormon President Heber J. Grant called Benson to become one of the Church's Quorum of Twelve Apostles, and he was ordained by Grant. In 1945, following the end of World War II, the new Mormon president, George Albert Smith, sent Benson to war-ravaged Europe to coordinate relief efforts. Benson saw the destruction caused by war, and the rise of communism, which he fought for the remainder of his life.

He spent a year in Europe coordinating relief; in 1946, he also served as a delegate to the first International Conference of Farm Organizations held in London. When he returned to the United States, Benson served, until 1950, as director of the Farm Federation.

Following the election of General Dwight D. Eisenhower as president in 1952, Benson was approached about serving in the cabinet as secretary of agriculture. Benson later related how he was offered the position; he put forward several reasons why he should not be named. " 'I come from a state that is usually considered rather unimportant agriculturally. Even my original native state of Idaho is not one of the leading agricultural states. It's been the custom to select the Secretary of Agriculture from the big farm belt of the Middle West. What's going to be the reaction is you select a man from Utah to be your Secretary of Agriculture when we've only got about 3 per cent of our state land area under cultivation? . . .' Finally, I said, 'And I wonder about the wisdom of calling a clergyman, a Church official, to be a Cabinet member. What will be the reaction from other religious groups, from people generally?' . . . The General mulled that over for a few seconds: 'We've got a job to do. I didn't want to be President, frankly, when the pressure started. But you can't refuse to serve America. I want you on my team, and you can't say no.'"

After being confirmed by the Senate on 21 January 1953, Benson took office as the fifteenth secretary of agriculture and served until the end of the Eisenhower administration, through two full terms, on 20 January 1953. In his *General Statement on Agricultural Policy,* Benson wrote, "The supreme test of any government policy, agricultural or other, should be: 'How will it affect the character, morale, and well-being of our people? . . . A completely planned and subsidized economy weakens initiative, discourages industry, destroys character, and demoralizes the people." Benson had many critics, particularly those who did not agree with his belief that no real American wants to be subsidized, and toward that end he advocated flexible price supports for farming products. But Benson was also a staunch anticommunist, and in many speeches as secretary, he spoke out on the evils of the Communist way of life.

After leaving office, Benson became a leader in the Mormon Church; in 1985, at age 86, he was named the thirteenth president of the church. In the last decades of his life, he wrote several books, including *Cross Fire* (1962), which was a history of his service in the cabinet. Benson died at his home in Salt Lake City on 20 May 1994 at the age of 94. In 1997, he was inducted into the Idaho Hall of Fame. The Ezra Taft Benson Agriculture and Food Institute at Brigham Young University was named in his honor.

References: Benson, Ezra Taft, *Cross Fire: The Eight Years with Eisenhower* (Garden City, NY: Doubleday, 1962), 5–12, 602; "Benson, Ezra Taft," in Marjorie Kent Candee, ed., *Current Biography 1953* (New York: H. W. Wilson, 1953), 64–66; Benson, Reed A., and Sheri L. Dew, "Benson, Ezra Taft," in Daniel H. Ludlow, ed., *Encyclopedia of Mormonism* (New York: Macmillan, 5 vols., 1992), 1: 100–104; Pach, Chester J., Jr., and Elmo Richardson, *The Presidency of Dwight D. Eisenhower* (Lawrence: University Press of Kansas, 1991); Schapsmeier, Edward L., and Frederick H. Schapsmeier, *Ezra Taft Benson and the Politics of Agriculture: The Eisenhower Years, 1953–1961* (Danville, IL: Interstate Printers, 1975).

ORVILLE LOTHROP FREEMAN

1918–

Orville Freeman was the governor of Minnesota when selected by President-elect John F. Kennedy to serve as his secretary of agriculture. A leader in his home state's Farmer-Labor Party, he later became one of only three cabinet secretaries to serve in both the Kennedy and Johnson administrations. The son of Orville Freeman and Frances (née Schroeder) Freeman, Freeman was born on 9 May 1918 in Minneapolis,

Minnesota. Freeman attended local schools in Minneapolis then the University of Minnesota, earning a bachelor of arts degree in 1940.

Freeman began the study of the law at that university's law school in 1941, but when the United States entered World War II he left school and volunteered for service, entering the U.S. Marine Corps as a second lieutenant and was in the Pacific Theater of Operations with the Third Marine Division, including on Guadalcanal and on the Bougainville Islands. After being wounded, he was sent, for the remainder of his duty, to help administer a veterans' rehabilitation program in Washington, D.C. In 1945, he was discharged with the rank of major. He continued in the Marine Corps Reserve, rising to the rank of lieutenant colonel. He returned to the University of Minnesota and was awarded his law degree in 1946.

Freeman practiced law, for a time, in Minneapolis with the firm of Larson, Loevinger, Linquist, & Freeman; he was involved in politics as well. In 1945, Minneapolis Mayor Hubert H. Humphrey appointed Freeman as his assistant in charge of veterans' affairs for the city. Freeman also joined the Democratic-Farmer-Labor Party (DFL). In 1944, farmers upset with the political system in the state joined with Democrats to form the Minnesota DFL. Freeman became a member of this coalition and became a member of the Hennepin County Central Committee in 1946. In 1948, he was named as chairman of the state party and assisted Humphrey in the latter's successful campaign for the U.S. Senate that year. In 1950, Humphrey forces in the state tried to get Freeman nominated for governor; instead, he got a nomination for state attorney general, but lost. Two years later, Freeman was nominated for governor, but lost to Republican C. Elmer Anderson by 160,000 votes out of some 1.4 million cast. In 1954, however, Freeman defeated Anderson by 70,000 votes, and became governor in January 1955.

After losing a reelection bid to Republican Elmer Lee Anderson in 1960, Freeman was selected by President-elect John F. Kennedy as his secretary of agriculture. Senator Hubert Humphrey had tried to capture the 1960 Democratic presidential nomination but failed, and Freeman had given his support to Senator Kennedy. When Kennedy announced his selection of Freeman, he said of farm conditions in the United States, "I said on many occasions during the campaign that I consider the sharp decline in agricultural income to be the number one domestic problem that the country faces. The decline in agricultural income affects adversely not only the farm families of the United States, but it affects our entire economy. There is a close relationship between the decline of farm income and the recession of 1958 and the slowdown in the economy in 1960. . . . The country cannot be prosperous unless all groups within our borders are prosperous. . . . This administration is going to work vigorously in attempting to improve the position of the American farmer."

Confirmed by the Senate on 21 January 1961, Freeman took office as the sixteenth secretary of agriculture. He served throughout Kennedy's administration and that of Kennedy's successor, Lyndon B. Johnson. Through his eight years of service, ending on 20 January 1969, Freeman coordinated all of the Kennedy and Johnson administration agriculture programs. Freeman urged President Kennedy to sign an executive order to expand the department's program of food distribution to poverty-stricken Americans, under which Freeman claimed that "we are providing essential food for those who need it and at the same time assisting American farmers by action that will help to decrease our agricultural surplus."

Freeman established a food stamp program for poor people to use to purchase government supplies of food and, after a Senate committee headed by Senator Hubert Humphrey recommended a Food for Peace Program as part of American foreign policy, Freeman instituted such a plan. Freeman also expanded the Agricultural Trade Development and Assistance Act of 1954 that provided federal aid to schools for nutritious meals. Historian Joseph Holub wrote, "Under Freeman, the Department of Agriculture expanded its sphere of activity. His 'rural renewal' proposals were designed to keep the rural unemployed from flooding the crowded urban labor market by creating non-farm employment opportunities in the countryside. The Area Redevelopment Act of 1961 authorized federal money for the creation of new businesses and new uses of land and for vocational training in rural areas of chronic unemployment. Parts of the 1962 farm bill expanded government food donations programs at home and abroad and provided federal aid to farmers who converted crop land top non-farm income producing uses. The Food for Peace program disposed of large amounts of the U.S. farm surplus abroad and, as supporters pointed out, substituted food for the U.S. dollar as a form of foreign aid." One of Freeman's key proposals was to rename the department the Department of Food and Agriculture, or the Department of Food, Agriculture, and Rural Affairs, but Congress did not make the change.

Freeman left office in January 1969, having served one of the longest tenures in the history of the Agriculture Department. He joined EDP Technology International, Inc., as its president. In 1981, Freeman was named as chairman of the board of the Business International Corporation. He became a partner of the Minneapolis law firm of Popham, Haik, Schnobrich, & Kaufman in the 1990s.

References: Baker, Gladys L., et al., *Century of Service: The First 100 Years of the United States Department of Agriculture* (Washington, DC: GPO, 1963), 403–405; "Freeman, Orville L(othrop)," in Marjorie Kent Candee, ed., *Current Biography 1956* (New York: H. W. Wilson, 1956), 192–193; "Freeman, Orville Lothrop," in Robert Sobel and John Raimo, eds., *Biographical Directory of the Governors of the United States, 1789–1978* (Westport, CT: Meckler Books; 4 vols., 1978), 2: 794; Heller, Deane, and David Heller, *The Kennedy Cabinet: America's Men of Destiny* (Derby, CT: Monarch Books, 1961), 131; Holub, Joseph C., "Freeman, Orville L(othrop)," in Nelson Lichtenstein, ed., *Political Profiles: The Kennedy Years* (New York: Facts on File, 1976), 163–166.

CLIFFORD MORRIS HARDIN
1915–

Clifford Hardin was serving as chancellor of the University of Nebraska when selected by President-elect Richard M. Nixon to be secretary of agriculture. A specialist in agricultural issues, he was deeply involved, for many years, with the issue of world hunger. Born on his family's farm near Knightstown, Indiana, on 9 October 1915, Hardin is the son of James Alvin Hardin, a farmer, and Mabel (née Macy) Hardin. During the Depression, Clifford's father left the farm to work in Florida, leaving his son to care for the family. In high school he earned a 4-H Club scholarship to Purdue University, where he earned a bachelor's degree in agriculture in 1937; after taking courses in agricultural economics at Purdue, he was awarded a master of science degree. He finished his education at the University of Chicago and then received his Ph.D. degree from Purdue in 1941.

At the same time that he was completing his higher education, Hardin was serving as an assistant teacher at Purdue from 1937 to 1941; after gaining his Ph.D., he joined the faculty of the University of Wisconsin as a professor in agricultural economics, moving, in 1944, to Michigan State College. In 1947, Hardin began to work on a series of activities to help solve the problem of world hunger, including assisting in sending food to post–World War II Japan. He helped found agricultural programs and set up the University of the Ryukyus in Japan. In 1954, Hardin left Michigan and became the chancellor of the University of Nebraska. In his more than fourteen years there, he served on several governmental committees, including President John F. Kennedy's Clay Committee to study the American foreign food aid program, and he was a member of the National Science Foundation under President Lyndon B. Johnson.

Hardin was selected, following the 1968 election, by President-elect Richard M. Nixon as secretary of agriculture. In presenting Hardin as a member of his new cabinet on 11 December 1968, Nixon said that he wanted Hardin "to speak for the farmers to the President, instead of speaking for the President to the farmers." Confirmed on 20 January 1969, as the seventeenth secretary of agriculture, Hardin served for nearly three years, until 17 November 1971. He established the department's Food and Nutrition Service and worked to get Congress to enact the Agriculture Act of 1970, which blended his proposals for world price rates for commodities with those backed by farmers, who wanted higher grain prices.

Historian Andrew Eiler, in a biography of Hardin, explained that Hardin's lack of friends in Congress and opposition to his policies on price supports from liberal farm groups made his tenure almost impossible. Perhaps Hardin's defining moment came when he tried to carry out Nixon's plan of consolidating numerous cabinet agencies: the operation hinged on dividing the responsibilities of the Department of Agriculture into a new Department of Community Development, Economic Affairs, Natural Resources and Human Resources. When farmers complained and Congress balked, the plan collapsed.

On 11 November 1971, Hardin offered his resignation so that Nixon could gain the support of more farmers; Nixon named Earl L. Butz as his replacement. Hardin left office six days later. He then became the chairman of the Ralston-Purina Corporation in St. Louis, Missouri. The Clifford Hardin Nebraska Center for Continuing Education at the University of Nebraska at Lincoln has been named in his honor.

References: Eiler, Andrew, "Hardin, Clifford M(orris)," in Eleanora W. Schoenebaum, ed., *Political Profiles: The Nixon/Ford Years* (New York: Facts on File, 1982), 271–274; "Hardin, Clifford M(orris)," in Charles Moritz, ed., *Current Biography 1969* (New York: H. W. Wilson, 1969), 192–194.

EARL LAUER BUTZ
1909–

Earl Butz served under Secretary of Agriculture Ezra Taft Benson during the Eisenhower administration and replaced Secretary Clifford M. Hardin to serve as President Richard M. Nixon's eighteenth secretary. Born on his family's farm near the village of Albion, Indiana, on 3 July 1909, he is the son of Harman Lee Butz, a farmer, and Ada Tillie (née Lower) Butz. Butz initially sought to enter the ministry, later deciding to follow his father and become a farmer. He attended Purdue University in Indiana on a scholarship from the 4-H Club, and he earned a bachelor of science degree in agriculture in 1932. He worked for a year on his family's farm, then returned to Purdue to take up graduate studies and earned a Ph.D. degree in agricultural economics in 1937, becoming the first person to earn such a degree from Purdue. He remained at Purdue as an instructor in agriculture, as well as policy, statistics, finance, and management of agriculture. In 1946, he became the head of the department. From 1942 to 1951, he also served as a researcher for the Brookings Institution in Washington, D.C. During this period he wrote on agricultural matters, including *The Production Credit System for Farmers* (1944) and *Price Fixings for Food Stuffs* (1952).

In 1954, Butz took leave from Purdue when Secretary of Agriculture Ezra Taft Benson named him as assistant secretary of agriculture in charge of marketing and foreign agricultural aid programs, which were administered by the department. Butz returned to Purdue in 1957 and, in 1967, was named as dean of the School of Continuing Education as well as vice-president of the Purdue Research Foundation. In 1968, he attempted, but failed, to gain the Republican gubernatorial nomination in Indiana.

On 11 November 1971, Secretary of Agriculture Hardin resigned, and Nixon named Butz as his successor. Butz was confirmed as the eighteenth secretary on 2 December 1971 by a vote of 51 to 44; he served until 4 October 1976, during which time he applied his conservative philosophies to the department. Historian John D'Emilio wrote, "Although he favored a return to free market forces and a minimum of federal support for agriculture, Butz released agricultural appropriations impounded by the Nixon administration. In December [1971] he announced the purchase of large amounts of corn and other grains on the open market to bolster farm prices. He also increased the subsidies paid to farmers to retire land from production and raised environmental conservation payments. In a gesture to congressional liberals he announced in January 1972 a reversal of planned cutbacks of $200 million in the food stamp program. . . . Butz advocated improved income levels for the nation's farmers. In a February 1972 tour of farm states, he opposed controls on farm prices and blamed middlemen for rising food costs."

Butz also helped sell at least $750 million in wheat, corn, and other surplus grains to the Soviet Union, all of which boosted farm income but raised costs in the United States, leading to increased inflation and criticism for Butz, as well as an investigation of charges he helped cronies profit from the Soviet deal, but Butz was cleared by the General Accounting Office of any wrongdoing. Although he was never personally charged, a corruption scandal inside the department in 1974 and 1975 led to fifty indictments of grain inspectors for bribe-taking. Butz remained in his job even after President Nixon resigned in August 1974. However, Butz clashed with Nixon's successor, Gerald R. Ford, when he attempted to sell $500 million in grain to the Soviets but was overruled by Ford because of inflationary threats.

Butz's tenure as secretary of agriculture ended suddenly during the 1976 general election. In September, former White House counsel John Dean told *Rolling Stone* magazine that a high administration official had told an off-color joke that denigrated blacks. When another magazine, days later, attributed the quote to Butz, he apologized. However, the damage was done and on 4 October 1976 Ford asked for his resignation. Butz returned to Purdue, where he taught and continues to serve as dean emeritus of agriculture. In 1981, he pleaded guilty to income tax invasion and was sentenced to thirty days in jail, all of which was suspended. In 1999, Butz donated $1 million to the Purdue University Agriculture Economics Department.

References: "Butz, Earl L(auer)," in Charles Moritz, ed., *Current Biography 1972* (New York: H. W. Wilson, 1972), 65–68; D'Emilio, John, "Butz, Earl L(auer)," in Eleanora W. Schoenebaum, ed., *Political Profiles: The Nixon/Ford Years* (New York: Facts on File, 1982), 102–104.

JOHN ALBERT KNEBEL
1936–

John Knebel served as the nineteenth secretary of agriculture for a period of only two and a half months; he served in a caretaker position until the end of the Ford administration. Born in Tulsa, Oklahoma, on 4 October 1936, Knebel graduated from the U.S. Military Academy at West Point in 1959, then served for four years in the U.S. Air Force. He received his master's degree from Creighton University in Omaha, Nebraska, in 1962 and his law degree from American University in Washington, D.C., three years later. He was admitted to the bar and joined the Washington, D.C., law firm of Howrey, Simon, Baker, and Murchison, where he remained until 1968. From 1963 to 1964, Knebel was the legislative assistant for Congressman J. Ernest Wharton of New York, and, in 1969, he was named as assistant counsel for the Committee on Agriculture in the U.S. House. On 1 March 1971, Knebel was named by President Richard M. Nixon as general counsel for the Small Business Administration, serving until January 1973, when he became general counsel for the Department of Agriculture. In December 1975, he was named by President Gerald R. Ford as deputy secretary of agriculture and, following the resignation of Secretary Earl Butz on 4 October 1976, he served for one month as secretary ad interim. On 4 November, Ford announced Knebel's appointment as secretary, a recess one because the Senate had ended its session. Knebel served only until 20 January 1977, because Ford was defeated in the election. During this short period, he is best remembered for his statement on 13 October announcing a large wheat sale to the Soviet Union, assisting American farmers who were suffering from a drought.

After leaving office, Knebel returned to practicing law with Brownstein, Zesdman, Shomev, and Chase in Washington, D.C. He served as president of the American Mining Congress from 1986 until 1997 and then became executive vice-president of operations for the National Association of Broadcasters.

References: Henry, Diane, "John Albert Knebel: Acting Secretary of Agriculture," *New York Times,* 5 October 1976, 32.

ROBERT SELMER BERGLAND
1928–

Robert Bergland became, in 1977, the first farmer to serve as secretary of agriculture since Claude Wickard left office in 1945. A longtime Minnesota politician who served in Congress from 1971 to 1977, Bergland was one of only five cabinet members to serve throughout the administration of President Jimmy Carter. Born in Roseau, Minnesota, on 22 July 1938, Bergland is the son of Selmer Bennett Bergland, a garage mechanic, and Mabel (née Evans) Bergland. Bergland attended local schools in Roseau, then entered the Minnesota School of Agriculture in St. Paul and completed a two-year agricultural program in 1948. He became a field representative for the National Farmers Union. In

1950, Bergland purchased a farm and, at the same time, entered politics by going to work, first, as secretary, and then as county chairman, of the Minnesota Democratic-Farmer-Labor Party, a coalition of Democrats and farmers. When prices for commodities plummeted, he was forced to work odd jobs, including as a logger and as a policeman.

In March 1961, Secretary of Agriculture Orville L. Freeman named Bergland as chairman of the Minnesota Agricultural Stabilization and Conservation Service, an arm of the U.S. Department of Agriculture. He served in this position until January 1963, when he was promoted to Midwest regional director of the service, where he worked until 1968. He resigned to run a campaign for a U.S. House seat, losing to Republican Odin Langen. Two years later, however, Bergland again ran against Langen, won, and took office in January 1971. He served until 22 January 1977, during which time he served on the House Committee on Agriculture's subcommittees for Conservation and Credit, and Livestock, Grains, Dairy, and Poultry.

In 1976, Georgia Governor Jimmy Carter was elected president. In selecting his secretary of agriculture, he lobbied Bergland, who agreed to give up his House seat to serve in the cabinet. Officially named as secretary on 20 December 1976, he told reporters, "I will be the farmer's advocate." Nominated and confirmed on 20 January 1977, Bergland took office three days later as the twentieth secretary of agriculture. His tenure, which lasted until the end of the Carter administration on 20 January 1981, was marked by a fight to maintain price supports for farm commodities. Bergland also undertook the first department-wide study of the structure of agricultural in the United States; he downsized the department by abolishing 10 percent of the advisory committees; revised the food stamp program to assist 2.5 million needy people, while cutting benefits for the less needy; and dealt with the issue of small farms in his landmark report, *A Time to Choose,* in which he wrote that "unless present policies and programs are changed so that they counter, instead of reinforce or ac-

celerate the trends towards ever-larger farming operations, the result will be a few large farms controlling food production in only a few years." But when Carter imposed a grain embargo on the Soviet Union in 1980, grain prices in the United States plummeted, hurting farmers; Bergland was considered responsible. The problems caused by low prices only got worse, causing numerous farm failures and possibly contributing to Carter's reelection loss later that year. After leaving office, Bergland became the president of Farmland World Trade, an international trade firm associated with Farmland Industries of Kansas City, Missouri. He left this position in 1983, when he was appointed as general manager of the National Rural Electric Cooperative Association, where he remained until his retirement in 1993. In 1997, he was elected to the University of Minnesota Board of Regents. He now lives on his family's farm in Roseau, Minnesota.

References: "Bergland, Bob," in Charles Moritz, ed., *Current Biography 1977* (New York: H. W. Wilson, 1977), 51–54; Robbins, William, "Robert Selmer Bergland," *New York Times,* 21 December 1976, 24; U.S. Department of Agriculture, *A Time to Choose: Summary Report on the Structure of Agriculture* (Washington, DC: Department of Agriculture, 1981).

JOHN RUSLING BLOCK
1935–

John Block was the first agribusinessman to serve as secretary of agriculture. He was an experienced agriculture advocate who called on the free market to solve the problems of the American farmer. Born in Galesburg, Illinois, on 15 February 1935, Block was the son of Julius Block, a farmer, and Madeline Block. He grew up on his father's farm in Knox County, near Galesburg. Block considered attending Northwestern University to study speech and drama, but instead entered the U.S. Military Academy at West Point and, after his graduation in 1957, served in the U.S. Army for three years as a platoon leader in the 101st Airborne Division at Fort Benning, Georgia. In 1960, he returned to his family's farm and, over the next twenty years, expanded it from 312 acres to more than 3,000 acres.

In 1977, Block was named by Illinois Governor James R. Thompson, Jr., as state secretary of agriculture. Over the next three years, he became a national leader in agriculture, calling attention to soil erosion on farms and traveling overseas to open world markets for soybeans and corn.

In 1980, Block formed Farmers for Reagan, which backed the campaign of Republican presidential nominee Ronald Reagan. Reagan wanted to name his friend Richard Lyng secretary of agriculture, but Senator Robert J. Dole of Kansas convinced the president-elect to select Block. "I didn't meet him until after the election," Dole later said in an interview, "but my gut feeling was that here was a real, live, active producer. He's an outstanding farmer and I get that reaction from Governor Thompson, farm bureaus, and radio farm newscasters. . . . He's another fresh face—no retread. And he's out there on the farm, not for publicity, either. He runs a farm." On 22 December 1980, Reagan selected Block.

The following day, the secretary-designate held a press conference in which he stated that food would be used as a weapon by the new administration to assist in world stability. Block said, "I believe food is now the greatest weapon we have for keeping peace in the world. It will continue to be for the next 20 years, as other countries become more dependent on American farm exports and become reluctant to upset us." However, in his confirmation hearings, he said that boycotts using food should be done as a last resort and pledged to end the grain embargo of the Soviet Union, imposed by his predecessor, Secretary Bob Bergland.

Block was confirmed by the Senate on 22 January 1981, by a vote of 98 to 0, and was sworn in as the twenty-first secretary of agriculture. He oversaw the largest spending on agriculture in the nation's history—outlays were $68.2 billion (they had been $16.8 billion in the five total years before he took office). It was a period of dwindling exports and rising prices—the number of farms in this period dropped 15 percent, from 2.5 million to fewer than 2.2 million nationwide—caused mostly by the high American dollar overseas, a new ability for countries that had earlier relied on American farm imports to adequately feed themselves, and the high price of technological improvements on farms. Block called upon Congress to end the price-support system, claiming that it blocked farmers from standing on their own. In order to end this system, Block authored the 1985 Farm Bill, which was passed by Congress, lowering the prices the government would pay farmers for their major crops. Block saw this as the chief way to end price supports.

On 7 January 1986, Block announced he was resigning, after his own family farm had suffered from recessionary times and had cost him millions of dollars. On his resignation Reagan wrote "Yours has been a challenging assignment, and you have handled it with great distinction. We have come a long way together. Following up on our campaign promise, we removed the grain embargo and stuck to it. The consistency of our policy has helped the American farmer to win back markets some had thought we might have lost for good. And, beyond that, our farsighted export initiatives have helped to create new markets abroad for our agricultural producers. Through our PIK [payment in kind] program we made headway in reducing the economic stress being felt in rural America. . . . I'm especially proud, and you should be too, of the 1985 Farm Bill that starts getting government out of the way, so that enterprise and innovation can have free play. . . . I believe that our Farm Credit legislation has done much to restore the integrity of the farm credit system and provide lower interest rates for farmers, another of our goals and promises."

After leaving office, Block became the president of Food Distributors International, a lobbying group in Falls Church, Virginia, which represents the wholesale grocery and food service distribution industry in the United States, Canada, and overseas.

References: "Block, John R(usling)," in Charles Moritz, ed., *Current Biography 1982* (New York: H. W. Wilson, 1982), 37–40; De Witt, Karen, "Agriculture: John Rusling Block," *New York Times,* 23 December 1980, A12.

RICHARD EDMUND LYNG
1918–

R ichard Lyng is a native Californian and an agribusinessman who was Governor Ronald Reagan's state agriculture director. He later served as assistant secretary of agriculture under President Richard M. Nixon and secretary of agriculture under President Reagan. Richard Lyng, the son of Edmund John Lyng, a farmer, and Cecilia (née McGrath) Lyng, was born in San Francisco, California, on 29 June 1918. Lyng attended public schools in Modesto, then went to Notre Dame University in Indiana, graduating with a Ph.B. degree summa cum laude in 1940. He then returned to Modesto, where he worked for his father's business, the Ed J. Lyng Company, which grew and processed beans and seeds; Lyng served as president from 1949 to 1967. He also was president of the California Seed Association in 1953. During World War II, Lyng volunteered for service in the U.S. Army and was sent to the Pacific theater; he saw action on Guadalcanal and the Bougainville Islands and, in 1945, was discharged with the rank of second lieutenant.

A Republican, Lyng ran, unsuccessfully, for a seat in the California state Senate in 1966 and never sought public office again. In 1967 Lyng was asked by California Governor Ronald Reagan to serve as director of the state Department of Agriculture. His work was prized by both Reagan and the employees of the department. Two years later, in February 1969, Lyng was named by President Richard M. Nixon as assistant secretary of agriculture for marketing and consumer services, serving from 3 March 1969 until 23 January 1973 under Secretaries Clifford M. Hardin and Earl L. Butz. He also served, during this period, as director of the Commodity Credit Corporation, an agency within the Agriculture Department that helped stabilize farm prices and provided farmers with income support. One of Lyng's chief tasks was to enforce the 1967 Wholesome Meat Act and oversee the U.S. government's food aid program nationally, helping to introduce new measures to unify food stamp regulations nationwide. After leaving office, Lyng was named as president of the American Meat Institute, but remained in politics when he served as the head of Farmers for Ford in 1976, advocating the election of President Gerald R. Ford.

In 1980, when former Governor Reagan entered the race for the Republican presidential nomination, Lyng joined his campaign and, in the general election, served as codirector of the campaign's farm and food committee. After Reagan's victory, Lyng was the top choice for secretary of agriculture, but Senator Robert J. Dole of Kansas requested that a midwesterner be named to the position, and John R. Block was named as secretary, and Lyng was given the position of deputy secretary. Serving as the department's traveling lobbyist, Lyng spoke with farmers nationwide to get an understanding of their problems and how the Department of Agriculture could assist them. In January 1985, Lyng announced his resignation from the department. He remained in Washington, D.C., however, with William Lesher, another top Department of Agriculture official, and founded Lyng and Lesher, Inc., a lobbying group involved in agricultural matters.

On 7 January 1986, Secretary Block announced his resignation to return to private business. Lyng was chosen to succeed Block, and, on 29 January 1986, Reagan named

Lyng as the new secretary of agriculture, making him, at 67, the oldest man to ever hold that position. In his confirmation hearings, Lyng told the Senate that he wanted to use the power of the department to open trade with foreign countries that had prohibited certain American commodities. Lyng was confirmed on 6 March 1986 by a vote of 95 to 2 and took office as the twenty-second secretary of agriculture. Lyng was involved in sending surplus wheat stocks to the Soviet Union and working on removing trade barriers put up by the European Economic Union. Lyng's tenure is remembered for his composed style under pressure. He served until the end of the Reagan administration, on 20 January 1989.

References: "Lyng, Richard E(dmund)," in Charles Moritz, ed., *Current Biography 1986* (New York: H. W. Wilson, 1986), 322–325.

CLAYTON KEITH YEUTTER

1930–

Since his early days at the University of Nebraska at Lincoln, when he was honored as an outstanding student in animal husbandry, Clayton Yeutter wanted to be the secretary of agriculture. Born in Eustis, Nebraska, on 10 December 1930, he attended local schools and then earned a bachelor of science degree with high distinction from the University of Nebraska at Lincoln in 1952. He joined the U.S. Air Force in 1952 and remained in the service for five years, first as an airman and then receiving a direct commission in medical administration; he was discharged in 1957, but remained in the active reserve until 1977. After leaving the military in 1957, he entered the University of Nebraska Law School, which awarded him his law degree in 1963. He completed his education by earning a Ph.D. in agricultural economics from the University of Nebraska at Lincoln in 1966. From 1957 to 1975, Yeut-

ter operated a 2,500-acre ranch in central Nebraska. He also served as a faculty member of the University of Nebraska's Department of Agricultural Economics from 1960 to 1966 and practiced law in Lincoln from 1963 to 1968. He served as an executive assistant to Nebraska Governors Frank B. Morrison and Norbert T. Tieman from 1966 to 1968.

In the 1970s, Yeutter held a number of positions within the Nixon and Ford administrations. He served as the administrator of the Consumer and Marketing Service in the Department of Agriculture from October 1970 to December 1971, as regional director for the Committee to Reelect the President in 1972, as assistant secretary of agriculture for Marketing and Consumer Services from January 1973 to March 1974, as assistant secretary of agriculture for International Affairs and Commodity Programs from March 1974 to June 1975, and as deputy special trade representative from June 1975 until January 1977. After leaving office, he went to work as the president and chief executive officer of the Chicago Mercantile Exchange. Yeutter oversaw the building of Mercantile Exchange into one of the largest private-sector financial institutions in the world.

In 1985, President Ronald Reagan named Yeutter as the U.S. trade representative, in charge of handling trade issues for the U.S. government and coordinating trade policies with the executive departments. In this position, he worked to arrange the 100-nation Uruguay Round of GATT (General Agreement on Tariffs and Trade) talks, as well as leading the American delegation in talks to finalize a U.S.-Canada free trade agreement and pushing the 1988 Trade Bill though Congress.

On 14 December 1988, President-elect George Bush named Yeutter as the secretary of agriculture. Yeutter was reluctant to take the position, saying he was "burned out" after years of working on trade, but serving as the head of the Agriculture Department had been his dream, and he accepted the appointment. Confirmed by the Senate, by a unanimous vote on 8 February 1989, he was sworn in, eight days later, as the twenty-third secretary of agriculture. His tenure only lasted until 1 March 1991, but in that time he was key in pushing the landmark 1990 Farm Bill though Congress.

On 25 January 1991, Yeutter resigned to become chairman of the Republican National Committee, effective 1 March. President Bush wrote to him, "You have worked tirelessly toward our mutual goal of further opening the world's markets to increase their opportunities in global trade. . . . The success of American agriculture is the envy of the world. It is, therefore, fitting and commendable that you and the Department of Agriculture have taken a leading and critical role in assisting Eastern Europe in its transition to a market-oriented economy. . . . I commend you for your tremendous effort in successfully negotiating the 1990 Farm Bill of which we can both be proud. It is a market-oriented bill that keeps our farmers competitive, keeps our rural areas environmentally sound, and lets farmers make more of their own production decisions. It also encourages crucial agricultural research and ensures a safe and wholesome food supply for all Americans. . . . I am also grateful for your many other important accomplishments, including supporting the development of alternative fuels; encouraging rural economic development; increasing opportunities for minorities and women at USDA; boosting the Women, Infants and Children and other food programs for those in need; and bringing balance and good common sense to a number of delicate food safety and environmental issues."

Following Bush's reelection defeat in 1992, Yeutter stepped down as head of the Republican National Committee. He presently practices law with the Washington, D.C., law firm of Hogan and Hartson.

References: "Yeutter, Clayton Keith," in Robert Sobel, ed.-in-chief, *Biographical Directory of the United States Executive Branch, 1774–1989* (Westport, CT: Greenwood, 1990), 399–400.

EDWARD RELL MADIGAN
1936–1994

A moderate Republican in the U.S. House of Representatives, Edward Madigan, the minority leader on the House Agriculture Committee, was responsible for developing the 1985 Farm Bill, a landmark piece of agricultural legislation. For this work, he was chosen as the secretary of agriculture by President George Bush. Born in Lincoln, Illinois, on 13 January 1936, Madigan was the son of Earl T. Madigan, a local entrepreneur, and Theresa (née Loobey) Madigan. Madigan attended local schools, then earned his A.A. degree in business from Lincoln Junior College in Illinois in 1955. He entered his family's business then he served on the Lincoln Board of Zoning Appeals from 1965 to 1969. A moderate Republican, he served in the state House of Representatives from 1967 to 1972 and, in 1972, was elected to a seat in the U.S. House of Representatives, serving from 3 January 1973 until 8 March 1991. He spent sixteen of his eighteen years in Congress as a member of the House Agriculture Committee and, from 1983 to 1991, was the ranking Republican. In 1989, he lost a chance for election as Republican whip. He helped coauthor the Railroad Deregulation Act of 1980; he was best known for his work on agricultural matters, authoring the farm bills of 1985 and 1990 and opposing a strengthening of the Farm Credit System Act supported by the Reagan administration to assist needy farmers with government-backed loans.

In mid-January 1991, Secretary of Agriculture Clayton Yeutter prepared to resign, and Madigan sought the vacancy, even though Bush was considering Senator Rudy Boschwitz from Minnesota. Bush selected Madigan on 25 January 1991. Confirmed on 7 March 1991 by a vote of 99 to 0, Madigan took office on 12 March 1991 as the twenty-fourth secretary of agriculture and served in that position until the end of the Bush administration on 20 January 1993. He was key in getting the drug company Bristol-Myers-Squibb, the maker of Taxol, a cancer drug made from the Pacific yew tree, to preserve the remaining trees and cooperate with a Department of Agriculture program, funded partially by the government and partially by the company, to determine the number of trees that stood and how they could be harvested thoughtfully.

In February 1992, Madigan announced new rules regarding water quality projects, including adding $6.75 million authorized by the 1990 Farm Bill to projects that implemented Water Quality Incentive Practices under the department's Agricultural Conservation Program. As part of the 1990 Farm Bill, Madigan also announced that under the Wetlands Reserve Program, eight states would get funding to start wetlands preservation and management. He said, "Wetlands are critical for the protection and enhancement of habitat for migratory birds and other wildlife, improving the hydrology of our nation's water supplies, and storing flood waters. It is more important now than ever that our wetlands be preserved for future generations." In the 1991 Agriculture Department Yearbook, he stated, "Taking care of our environment must be a cooperative effort to conserve the land, water, and air in a way that will best sustain the earth and all its people. The environment is everyone's business."

Madigan did disagree with Secretary of Health and Human Services Louis W. Sullivan over rules promulgated by the Food and Drug Administration (FDA). Under the Nutrition Labeling and Education Act of 1990, the FDA had until November 1992 to develop new rules regarding the labeling of food; Madigan agreed to have the Department of Agriculture cooperate to get one federal standard. However, Madigan did not agree with the program established by the FDA, and President Bush had the two men meet in a summit to straighten out any inconsistencies.

Madigan completed his tenure in January 1993. A year after leaving the government, Madigan was diagnosed with lung cancer.

On 7 December 1994, he died at the age of 58. In his memory, Congress established, as part of Title II of the Federal Agricultural and Improvement Reform Act of 1996, the Edward Madigan U.S. Agricultural Export Excellence Award, to honor entrepreneurial efforts to promote American agricultural exports. In 1996, Congress honored Madigan by naming the post office in his hometown of Lincoln as the Edward Madigan Post Office.

References: "Madigan, Edward R.," in Charles Moritz, ed., *Current Biography 1992* (New York: H. W. Wilson, 1992), 369–373; *The U.S. Department of Agriculture Yearbook for 1991* (Washington, DC: GPO, 1992), 4; United States Congress, House, Committee on Agriculture, *Reorganization of the U.S. Department of Agriculture: Hearing Before the Committee on Agriculture, House of Representatives, One Hundred Second Congress, Second Session, June 23, 1992* (Washington, DC: GPO, 1992).

ALPHONSO MICHAEL ESPY
1953–

Michael Espy was the first African American to serve as secretary of agriculture and, in August 1997, the first person to be indicted for crimes committed while secretary. The son of Henry Espy and Willie Jean (née Huddleston) Espy, Mike Espy was born in Yazoo, Mississippi, on 30 November 1953 into a well-to-do family. Espy finished his primary education in Yazoo and attended Howard University in Washington, D.C., receiving his bachelor's degree in political science in 1975; he then attended Santa Clara Law School in California, receiving a law degree in 1978. He returned to Mississippi and joined Central Mississippi Legal Services as managing attorney for two years. In 1980, he entered the political realm when he was named as assistant secretary for public lands for the state of Mississippi. He later served, from 1984 to 1985, as assistant attorney general for consumer protection in that state.

Based on the 1980 census, the Justice Department redrew district lines in Mississippi, creating a district with a substantial African American vote. Espy ran in the Democratic primary for the seat against two white opponents and won the party's nomination; he then defeated the incumbent congressman, Representative Webb Franklin, and when he entered Congress in January 1987, became the first African American to represent Mississippi since John Roy Lynch, and the only African American to represent a rural district with a white majority. Despite being a liberal Democrat, Espy supported the death penalty and funding for the Contras, anticommunist rebels in Nicaragua; he even appeared in an ad for the National Rifle Association. He served as a leading member on the Agriculture and Budget Committees. As a member of the Congressional Black Caucus, he worked with the Reagan administration to secure microenterprise loans for poor farmers in his district, and supported efforts to help welfare recipients gain loans from banks to start small businesses, calling for an attitude of self-reliance.

In 1992, Espy was reelected and expected to be named either chairman of the House Agriculture Committee or to a seat on the House Appropriations Committee. When neither position came, he instead lobbied for a position in the administration of Arkansas Governor Bill Clinton, who had just been elected president. Espy wanted to be named secretary of housing and urban development, but when that position went to San Antonio Mayor Henry Cisneros, Espy was offered Agriculture; he accepted, becoming the first southerner as well as the first black named to the post. After being confirmed on 21 January 1993, he took office as the twenty-fifth secretary of agriculture. During his short tenure, he battled to rid the department of racism against black farmers, advocated modernizing the department's meat inspection program in the wake of a series of deaths from tainted hamburger, and offered assistance to farmers whose crops were destroyed by 1993 floods in Iowa.

However, Espy was accused of accepting gifts from several corporations doing business with the department. In September 1994, an independent counsel, Donald Smaltz, was assigned to investigate whether Espy had violated any law. When details of his gift-taking were made public, he announced his resignation, on 2 October 1994, to take effect at the end of the year. From that time until August 1997, Smaltz pursued more than a dozen separate cases against companies and lobbyists that had given money and gifts to Espy. In August 1997, Espy was indicted on thirty-nine counts of corruption, although one count was later dismissed. His trial began in October 1998, and, after Judge Ricardo Urbina threw out an additional eight charges, Espy was acquitted of the remaining thirty charges on 2 December 1997.

References: "Espy, Mike," Judith Graham, ed., *Current Biography 1993* (New York: H. W. Wilson, 1993), 183–187; "Mike Espy: Agriculture," in Jeffrey B. Trammell and Gary P. Osifchin, eds., *The Clinton 500: The New Team Running America, 1994* (Washington, DC: Almanac Publishing, 1994), 91; Ragsdale, Bruce, and Joel D. Treese, *Black Americans in Congress, 1870–1989* (Washington, DC: GPO, 1990), 49–50; Rosen, Isaac, "Mike Espy," in *Contemporary Black Biography* (Detroit, MI: Gale Research, 13 vols., 1992–1997), 6: 87–90.

DANIEL ROBERT GLICKMAN
1944–

Daniel Glickman was a longtime congressman from Kansas who spent much of his time fighting for farm subsidies and helping shape major farm bills passed by Congress in the late 1980s and early 1990s. Born in Wichita, Kansas, on 24 November 1944, he attended public schools there, then entered the University of Michigan, where he earned a bachelor of arts degree in 1966; he entered George Washington University in Washington, D.C., and received his law degree in 1969. Glickman was admitted to the District of Columbia bar in 1969 and was hired as a trial attorney for the U.S. Securities and Exchange Commission, serving until 1970. In 1970, he returned to Wichita and became an officer in Glickman, Inc., his family's metal recycling company. In 1971, Glickman opened a law practice in Wichita, remaining there until 1977 as a member of the firm of Sargent, Klenda, and Glickman.

In 1976, Glickman ran as a Democrat for a seat in the U.S. House of Representatives from Kansas' Fourth District. Elected, he served from 1977 until he left office in 1995. As a representative from an important farm state, Glickman served as a member of the House Agriculture Committee, including six years as chairman of the Subcommittee on General Farm Commodities and its predecessor, the Subcommittee on Wheat, Soybeans, and Feed Grains. He was a key promoter of the Farm Bills of 1977, 1981, 1985, and 1990. He also served as chairman of the Permanent Select Committee on Intelligence in the 103d Congress.

In 1994, Glickman was defeated by Republican Sam Brownback. Following the resignation of Secretary of Agriculture Espy, Glickman was named, on 28 December 1994 as Espy's successor. Others considered for the vacancy included Deputy Secretary of Agriculture Rick Rominger and Representative E. (Kika) de la Garza of Texas. Despite going before a Senate Agricultural Committee controlled by Republicans, Glickman won easy confirmation and was sworn in as the twenty-sixth secretary of agriculture on 30 March 1995. In the five years he has been in office, Glickman has revolutionized the department—modernizing its field office structure nationwide, cutting department expenses by $4 billion by eliminating 13,000 positions, and cutting the number of department agencies from forty-three to thirty.

Glickman also has overseen the implementation of a new meat and poultry inspection system, the Pathogen Reduction and Hazard Analysis of Critical Control Points Rule, after a series of incidents with foodborne diseases. He has spotlighted the problems of small and socially disadvantaged farmers, particularly those in rural communities; has attempted to prevent the rise of agribusiness from adversely affecting them; and has helped initiate a new school lunch and breakfast program for schools nationwide. In his 1997 annual report, called *A Change for the Better,* Glickman wrote of the department and his policies, "In 1997, USDA made significant strides in advancing the fight against hunger, taking America's conservation efforts to new levels, modernizing and improving food safety, and creating a new day for civil rights at USDA. . . . We worked to expand trade, enhanced opportunities for family farmers; protected our natural resources; fed hungry children and families in need; made food recovery a national priority; instituted a sweeping overhaul of meat and poultry inspections; made scientific discoveries that help farmers, ranchers and all Americans; protected crops and livestock from diseases and pests; and helped farmers and ranchers do their work in a more sustainable way. . . . As the department of rural America, we improved living standards in our rural communities by helping create jobs, improve housing, strengthen education, and assure wider availability of safe running water and quality health care."

References: Biographical information courtesy of the Department of Agriculture; *A Change for the Better: 1997 Report of the Secretary of Agriculture* (Washington, DC: GPO, 1998), 2–3.

ATTORNEY GENERAL/JUSTICE

The attorney general, appointed by the president and confirmed by the Senate, is the head of the Department of Justice, which administers through the courts the laws that Congress enacts. The Department of Justice now has oversight over thirty-eight divisions and bureaus; some of the most recognizable are the Office of the Solicitor General (who argues cases before the Supreme Court), the Federal Bureau of Investigation (FBI), the Drug Enforcement Administration (DEA), and the Civil Rights Division.

Under the colonial system, each individual colony had an attorney general, appointed and sanctioned by the English Crown, who handled legal matters. Thus, when the United States achieved independence and a federal governmental system was established, the need for a similar national post was evident. Under the Judiciary Act of 24 September 1789, Congress provided that "the supreme court shall appoint a meet person, learned in the law, to act as Attorney General for the United States, and shall swear him to a faithful execution of his office." The act also set the annual salary of the attorney general at $1,500, compared with $3,500 for the secretaries of state and treasury and $3,000 for the secretary of war. A history of the department explains, "In providing for the appointment . . . it is evident that Congress was thinking more in terms of a legal counselor for the government—an official to interpret and expound the law—than of an official [to] . . . punish those who transgressed the law."

When the time came to name the first man to hold this position, President George Washington appointed Edmund Randolph, who during the Revolutionary War had been Washington's personal attorney and close aide. Randolph did not hold cabinet status; however, portraits of Washington's cabinet included Randolph, and the attorney general was henceforth recognized as a part of the cabinet. In England, the attorney general has never sat as a member of the cabinet; in 1818, former Attorney General Richard Rush found this situation absurd. While visiting London, he wrote, "In the complicated and daily workings of the machine of free government throughout a vast empire, I could still see room for the constant presence of the attorney general in the cabinet."

Opening the office of the attorney general was no easy feat for Edmund Randolph. Setting up shop in New York, then the seat of the American government, in February 1790, he discovered that Congress had appropriated no funds for assistants, and all labor was to be accomplished by him alone. In his letter asking Randolph to accept the assignment, Washington wrote that the work would "confer preeminence" upon the holder; however, to supplement his income, Randolph became the first of twenty-two attorneys general to perform private law work outside the sphere of the public office. This practice was ended by the twenty-third attorney general, Caleb Cushing, in 1853.

Randolph helped to move the office when the federal government moved its seat from New York to Philadelphia in 1794; Charles Lee, the third attorney general, oversaw its final transfer to Washington in 1800. By this time, the salary for the office had increased to $3,000 per annum, but still no funds for clerks had been allotted. This changed in 1818, when Attorney General William Wirt was given $1,000 for a single clerk and an additional $500 for office space and "incidental expenses." It would not be until 1853, under Caleb Cushing, that Congress raised the salary of the attorney general to $8,000 a year, which was commensurate with the other cabinet officers.

Until a permanent home on Pennsylvania Avenue was constructed in 1934, the attorney general was never situated in one fixed location. Congress had assumed that the attorney general, whose main duty was to argue the government's side in cases before the Supreme Court, would be assigned an office next to the courtroom, then located in the Capitol building. In 1822, Wirt oversaw a move into an office on the second floor of the old War Department building, where the office would remain until Felix Grundy moved it in 1839 to the second floor of the Treasury building. As the office's workload continued to grow, it was forced to find newer and bigger quarters.

After another move in 1861, Attorney General Edward Bates requested that Congress establish a permanent department with control over district attorneys in the United States and create the office of assistant attorney general. In 1870 Congress enacted a bill that established the Department of Justice, and the new office was constituted on 1 July of that year with a budget of $67,320. The action also created the office of solicitor general, now the second highest ranking officer in the department, who argues the federal government's position in cases before the Supreme Court. Control and supervision of federal prisons and their prisoners were transferred to the new department, and in 1879, Congress appropriated moneys for the attorney general to find, investigate, and prosecute criminal acts and conferred the authority to seize records and other official documents. By an act of 19 January 1886, the attorney general was placed fourth in the line of succession if the president or vice-president was removed from office or died.

Although it had achieved full department status in 1870, the agency's operations still lacked a permanent headquarters, despite repeated requests in the attorney general's annual reports to Congress. The Department of Justice's offices continued to wander among several buildings in downtown Washington, including the old Freedmen's Bank Building from 1882 until 1899 (which ended when that structure was declared unfit for human occupancy) and the Palmer House Hotel from 1899 until 1917 (an unusual location for a department of 260 employees). On 3 July 1930, Congress finally appropriated $10 million to build a permanent headquarters for the department between Constitution and Pennsylvania Avenues and 9th and 10th Streets. Constructed under Attorneys General John G. Sargent (who reviewed the plans before the money was appropriated), William D. Mitchell, and Homer S. Cummings, the building was first occupied on 1 September 1934, dedicated on 25 October of that year, and officially completed in 1935.

After the completion of the building, the department continued to grow. Having survived the scandals of Teapot Dome (which brought down Attorney General Harry M. Daugherty) and Watergate (in which former Attorney General John Mitchell served a prison term), it saw a father and son (Tom Clark and Ramsey Clark) serve, as well as the first woman, Janet Reno.

More men from the attorney general's office have gone on to serve on the U.S. Supreme Court than from any other cabinet agency—a total of ten. These included Edwin M. Stanton, who accepted an appointment to the Court and was confirmed but died before he could take his seat, as well as Roger B. Taney, Nathan Clifford, Joseph McKenna, and Harlan Fiske Stone (Taney and Stone served as Chief Justice). George Henry Williams was named as chief justice in 1874 but was not confirmed.

As in the other cabinet-level departments in the federal government, turnover has always been a concern. Since its inception in 1789, seventy-eight men and women have held the position, a rate of one new attorney general every thirty-two months. Of the original cabinet offices still in existence (including Treasury and State), there have been more attorneys general than any other office. In cabinet meetings, the attorney general, holding to long-standing protocol, sits fourth from the president, after the secretary of state, the secretary of defense, and the secretary of the treasury.

References: Easby-Smith, James S., *The Department of Justice: Its History and Functions* (Washington, DC: W. H. Lowdermilk, 1904), 4; Huston, Luther A., *The Department of Justice* (New York: Frederick A. Praeger, 1967); Rush, Richard, *Memoranda of a Residence in the Court of London* (Philadelphia: Carey, Lea & Blanchard, 1833), 63 (Rush letter); *200th Anniversary of the Office of Attorney General, 1789–1989* (Washington, DC: Department of Justice, 1990); Vasaio, Antonio, *The Fiftieth Anniversary of the U.S. Department of Justice Building, 1934–1984* (Washington, DC: GPO, 1985).

EDMUND JENINGS RANDOLPH
1753–1813

Born into privilege and wealth, for most of his life, Edmund Randolph served his nation, including as an aide-de-camp to General George Washington during the American Revolutionary War, as the first attorney general of the state of Virginia, and, from 1789 to 1794, as the nation's first attorney general. The son of John Randolph, a noted Virginia lawyer, and Ariana (née Jenings—the most common spelling—or Jennings) Randolph, Edmund Jenings Randolph was born at his father's estate, Tazewell Hall, in Williamsburg, Virginia, on 10 August 1753. Edmund Randolph attended the College of William and Mary, and then studied law under his father. At the beginning of the American Revolution, John Randolph, a staunch Tory, took his family to England, where he died in 1784. When his father left for England, Edmund Randolph remained in America to serve the colonial cause, becoming a loyal and trusted confidante to General George Washington.

In 1774, his cousin Thomas Jefferson retired from the practice of law and asked Randolph to take over his office. Later that year, Randolph was named as the clerk of the Committee on Courts and Justice by the House of Burgesses, the legislature of the Virginia colony. When the war broke out, he was appointed by the Continental Congress as deputy muster master general of the Continental Army for the Southern District, serving from 1775 until 1776. During that period, he served as Washington's aide-de-camp. Randolph resigned his military post when he was elected (at the age of 23) to represent Williamsburg, at the Fifth Virginia convention, which drew up a state constitution for Virginia.

Under the new state constitution, Randolph was named as the state's first attorney general, positioned to carry out its laws and legal functions. He served in this post until 1786. During this same period, he was elected as a delegate to the Continental Congress from Virginia (1779–1786). In 1786 he was elected governor of Virginia. In this capacity, he was sent to Philadelphia as a member of the Virginia delegation (among whose other members were Jacob McClurg, George Mason, and George Washington) to the Constitutional Convention. On 29 May 1787, Randolph presented the Virginia Plan, which laid out a broad outline for a strong federal government composed of three branches—executive, judicial, and legislative—that held sway over all of the states and could enact and carry out laws. This blueprint, which was argued over for months, eventually became the foundation for the U.S. Constitution, which was signed on 17 September 1787. However, Randolph, along with fellow Virginian George Mason, was not pleased with the revisions to his original plan and did not sign the final document. In a letter, he said that the document was "the fætus of monarchy" and was "a unity in the Executive magistracy." He demanded that a bill of rights be included and published a *Letter . . . on the Federal Constitution* (1787) denouncing the document. Nonetheless, when time came for state ratification, Randolph asked the state legislature to approve the U.S. Constitution.

With the formation of the federal government and the election of George Washington as the first president, a cabinet of advisers was needed. To fill the position of attorney general, Washington asked John Marshall, considered one of the judicial luminaries in the young nation, but Marshall refused the honor. The president then reached out to a man whose abilities he knew well: Edmund Randolph. Randolph served as attorney general from 26 September 1789 to 27 January 1794. In this capacity, he issued only eight official opinions and his first annual report, issued on 31 December 1790, is only one page long.

Perhaps this lack of published output is evidence that Randolph despised the position in which he served. He was disappointed in the lack of cabinet rank and the pittance of a salary—a mere $1,500 a year—which forced him to continue his private practice as well as the government position. Historian Moncure Conway quotes Randolph that as attorney general he regarded himself as "a sort of mongrel between the State and U.S.; called an officer of some rank under the latter, and yet thrust out to get a livelihood in the former." Randolph saw the position as a mere legal adviser to the president, at his beck and call. And because Washington was such an independent figure, he knew that he would be called upon few times if any. On 27 January 1794, Randolph resigned as the first attorney general to become the second secretary of state, succeeding Thomas Jefferson.

According to a history of that department, Randolph directed the negotiation of the Treaty of San Lorenzo (1795), a peace treaty between the United States and Spain. Yet it was the negotiations over the Jay Treaty that cost Randolph his office. This treaty was officially entitled, "Treaty of Amity, Commerce, and Navigation, Between His Britannic Majesty and The United States of America, Conditionally Ratified By the Senate of the United States, at Philadelphia, June 24, 1795." In the years since the founding of the republic, the United States had had numerous disagreements with Great Britain over the Treaty of Paris of 1783, which had ended the American Revolutionary War, especially with regard to restriction and regulation of trade. Randolph demonstrated these problems in a report to Congress entitled "Foreign Aggressions of American Commerce," in which he explained, "On my succession to the Department of State, I found a large volume of complaints, which the notification had collected, against severities on our trade, various in their kind and degree. Having reason to presume, as the fact has proved, that every day would increase the catalogue, I have waited to digest the mass, until time should have been allowed for exhibiting the diversified forms in which our commerce has hourly suffered. Every information is at length obtained which may be expected. . . . The sensations excited by the embarrassments, danger, and even ruin, which threaten our trade, cannot be better expressed, than in the words of the committee in Philadelphia: 'On these cases, which are accompanied by the legal proofs, the committee think it unnecessary to enlarge, as the inferences will, of course, occur to the Secretary; but they beg leave to be permitted to state other circumstances, which, though not in legal proof, are either of such public notoriety as to render legal proof unnecessary, or so vouched to the committee as to leave them in no doubt of the truth of them.' " At first, Treasury Secretary Alexander Hamilton was chosen to negotiate an end to the differences with the British, but Randolph chose to use Chief Justice John Jay of the Supreme Court as the negotiator. However, Randolph had taken the position that Jay should resign from the Court if he wanted such a diplomatic mission.

The resulting treaty of friendship between the United States and Britain was met with bitterness by the French, who saw in it an age of more intimate relations between England and America. To calm the French, Randolph secretly held talks with the French minister plenipotentiary, Joseph Fauchet. These dispatches came into the hands of George Hammond, the British minister plenipotentiary to the United States. On 20 August 1795, Washington confronted Randolph with the messages, which implied that he could be bribed with French funds: the letters apparently alluded to "some thousands of dollars." Randolph, shocked at the release of the dispatches, went home and offered his resignation. In his resignation letter to the president, he explained that the situation was not as it seemed and that he would submit his bank's account figures for examination. Fauchet, embarrassed, immediately apologized, declaring that he had not meant to impugn Randolph's honor; Randolph, to counter his critics, composed *A Vindication of Mr. Randolph's Resignation,* which was published in leaflet form.

After his retirement, Randolph returned to the practice of law, becoming once again a leading Virginia attorney. During these final years, he drafted a history of his native state. In 1807, he acted as senior counsel for Aaron Burr in his treason trial, obtaining an acquittal for the former vice-president. On 12 September 1813, at 60 years of age and suffering from various maladies, Randolph visited his friend Nathaniel Burwell at a nearby residence. There he collapsed and died. Randolph was buried in the Old Chapel Cemetery in Millwood, Virginia.

References: Anderson, Dice R., "Randolph, Edmund" in *DAB* 8: 353–355; *The Attorney Generals of the United States, 1789–1985* (Washington, DC: Department of Justice, 1985), 2; Conway, Moncure Daniel, *Omitted Chapters of History, Disclosed in the Life and Papers of Edmund Randolph* (New York and London: G. P. Putnam's Sons, 1888), 135; Farrand, Max, ed., *The Records of the Federal Convention of 1787* (New Haven, CT: Yale University Press; 3 vols., 1911), 1: 20–22, 66; "Foreign Aggressions on American Commerce," Report No. 83, 3d Cong., 1st sess. (1794), in Walter Lowrie and Matthew St. Clair Clarke, eds., *ASP,* Foreign Affairs (Class I), 1: 423–424; Hall, Benjamin F., et al., comps., *Official Opinions of the Attorneys General of the United States* (Washington, DC: Robert Farnham; 43 vols., plus annual updates, 1852–1996), 1: 2–38; Reardon, John J., *Edmund Randolph: A Biography* (New York: Macmillan, 1974); *The Secretaries of State: Portraits and Biographical Sketches,* Department of State Publication 8921 (Washington, DC, November 1978), 7; *A Vindication of Mr. Randolph's Resignation* (Philadelphia: Samuel H. Smith, 1795).

WILLIAM BRADFORD, JR.
1755–1795

An intimate of George Washington, whose counsel was accorded special respect by the general and president, William Bradford was chosen to succeed Edmund Randolph when Randolph was promoted to secretary of state. Very little is known of Bradford's life. A noted jurist, he was born in Philadelphia on 14 September 1755, the son of William Bradford, a colonial printer and Rachel (née Budd) Bradford. The new appointee had received his bachelor's and master's degrees from Princeton College in 1772 and 1775, respectively, and then studied law under Edward Shippen, who later served as chief justice of the Pennsylvania Supreme Court.

Bradford volunteered as a private in the Revolutionary Army in 1776, and soon advanced through the ranks to colonel. On 10 April 1777 he was elected to a seat in the Continental Congress, but declined in order to remain with the army, spending the cold years of 1777–1779 in Valley Forge, White Plains, and Fredericksburg. When health problems forced him to resign his commission on 1 April 1779, he returned to his legal studies and was admitted to the bar in 1779. Only 25, he was soon asked to succeed Jonathan Sergeant as attorney general of the Commonwealth of Pennsylvania, where he served for eleven years. Biographer James Ballagh writes, "His contemporaries considered him a lawyer of high tone, eloquent, and of great purity of life and purpose." On 22 August 1791, he was elevated to the Pennsylvania State Supreme Court by Governor Thomas Mifflin, holding that post until 1794.

On 27 January 1794, Attorney General Edmund Randolph resigned his office to become secretary of state, and, apparently upon the recommendation of Alexander Hamilton, Bradford was offered the open spot, which he accepted the following day. During his tenure, he was named as a commissioner to settle the Whiskey Rebellion, an insurrection by farmers over the U.S. government's plan to tax whiskey, and it was upon his recommendation that Washington sent a force to "secure the execution of the laws," firmly establishing the federal government's national authority.

Bradford was already ill when appointed attorney general, but it was the controversy over the legal ramifications over the Fauchet incident that probably overtaxed his health. The incident involved allegations that the then-secretary of state, Edmund Randolph, was receiving bribes from the French minister. The scandal was unprecedented and the president spent considerable time asking Bradford's opinion on the matter. On 23 August 1795, three days after Randolph resigned as secretary of state as a result of the allegations, Bradford succumbed to a fever at Rose Hill, the estate of his father-in-law, Elias Boudinot, in New Jersey. He was one month shy of his fortieth birthday. His remains were laid to rest in St. Mary's Churchyard, Burlington, New Jersey. Because of his short tenure of only nineteen months, he did not offer many official opinions and histories of the Department of Justice discuss him only in passing references. However, Bradford County, Pennsylvania, was named in his honor.

References: *The Attorney Generals of the United States, 1789–1985* (Washington, DC: Department of Justice, 1985), 4; Ballagh, James Curtis, "Bradford, William" in *DAB* 1: 566; Hinsdale, Mary Louise, *A History of the President's Cabinet* (Ann Arbor, MI: George Ware, 1911); Miller, John C., *The Federalist Era, 1789–1801* (New York: G. Braziller, 1962); Smith, William Henry, *History of the Cabinet of the United States of America, From President Washington to President Coolidge* (Baltimore: Industrial Printing, 1925), 320.

CHARLES LEE
1758?–1815

The third attorney general, serving in the cabinets of George Washington and John Adams, Charles Lee followed in the footsteps of William Bradford. He was born in 1758 (records are sketchy but one source believes that it was July of that year) in Fauquier County, Virginia, the son of Henry Lee and Mary (née Grymes) Lee. Among Charles Lee's brothers were the famed Revolutionary War general "Light-Horse" Harry Lee and Richard Bland Lee, a longtime Virginia politician who served in the House of Delegates and in the first Congress to meet in 1789. His nephew was Robert Edward Lee (son of Harry), famed Confederate general during the Civil War. In 1770, when he was about 12 years old, Charles Lee was allowed to enter the College of New Jersey (now Princeton University) because of his academic skills, and received a B.A. degree five years later.

From 1777 until 1789, Lee served as a "naval officer of the South Potomac" and, because of his friendship with George Washington, was named as collector of the port of Alexandria in 1789, serving until 1793. He studied law in the office of Jared Ingersoll, a member of the Constitutional Convention, and was admitted to the bar in June 1794. After leaving the port collector's post, he served in the General Assembly of Virginia from Fairfax County. During his term he was a staunch opponent of pro-French policies and an ardent supporter of President George Washington. On 19 November 1795, the president approached Lee to take the post of attorney general. Historian Jared Sparks indicates that Washington had earlier offered the spot to John Marshall, who refused on the grounds that the position would injure his private law practice, and a "Colonel Innes," of Virginia, who also declined. Lee accepted eleven days later, and served until 4 March 1801.

When difficulties arose between the United States and France, while France was at war with Britain, Lee was an indefatigable opponent of conciliation toward France. A history of the Department of Justice relates, "[Lee] proposed a declaration of war, an embargo on French shipping, revocation of the exequaturs of French consuls, the opening of America ports to British privateers, and the arming of American merchant ships." Any or all of these actions would surely have brought the United States directly into the war, but Washington's "prudence and policies" prevailed, and in 1800, a "treaty of peace and friendship" was negotiated with France. Although Lee remained as attorney general when John Adams ascended to the presidency, and served throughout the second president's term, he issued a mere twenty opinions.

The Federalists were turned out of office in the election of 1800, and Lee prepared to leave government and return to his private practice. Under the newly-passed Judiciary Act of 1800, however, President Adams appointed Lee as a judge of one of the new circuit courts, which were later eliminated when Congress repealed the act in 1802. Slandered as a "midnight judge" because his nomination came on 3 March 1801, the day before Adams was to leave office, Lee retired from the judgeship in 1802. President Thomas Jefferson later offered Lee the post of Chief Justice of the U.S. Supreme Court, but he declined.

In 1803, Lee was offered the opportunity to avenge the "midnight judge" label. He was asked to represent several men who had received commissions from Adams on his last day in office but had been refused by the incoming administration. One of the litigants, William Marbury, sued James Madison, the secretary of state, to deliver the commissions. Lee argued the case before the Supreme Court. In the Supreme Court's decision, Chief Justice John Marshall held that Madison could not be forced to deliver the commissions. This action is historically considered to have established the doctrine of judicial review. In 1805, Lee served as defense counsel for Associate Justice Samuel Chase in his impeachment hearings before the U.S. Senate, and, in 1806, Lee acted as defense counsel in the treason trial of Vice-president Aaron Burr in Richmond, Virginia. Ironically, Chief Justice Marshall sat as the trial judge (he was on circuit). The jury returned after twenty-five minutes of deliberation to acquit Burr, who fled to Europe to escape irate mobs.

Lee retired to his home in Fauquier County, Virginia, near Warrenton, for the final decade of his life. He died there on 24 June 1815.

References: *The Attorney Generals of the United States, 1789–1985* (Washington, DC: Department of Justice, 1985), 6; Kurtz, Stephen G., *The Presidency of John Adams: The Collapse of Federalism, 1798–1800* (Philadelphia: University of Pennsylvania Press, 1957); Robb, Arthur, "Biographical Sketches of the Attorneys General" (Unpublished essay DOJ, Washington, DC, 1946), 3; Smith, William Henry, *History of the Cabinet of the United States of America, From President Washington to President Coolidge* (Baltimore: Industrial Printing, 1925), 320; Sparks, Jared, ed. "Choice of Marshall for Attorney Generalship" in *The Writings of George Washington* (Boston: Ferdinand Andrews; Russell, Odiorne and Metcalf; and Hilliard, Gray; 12 vols., 1833–1839), 11: 62; *200th Anniversary of the Office of Attorney General, 1789–1989* (Washington, DC: Department of Justice, 1990), 19; Woodfin, Maude H., "Lee, Charles" in *DAB* 6: 101–102.

LEVI LINCOLN
1749–1820

L evi Lincoln was one of the leading jurists of his day, and the first attorney general appointed during the post-Federalist era. He was born in Hingham, Massachusetts, on 15 May 1749, the son of Enoch Lincoln, a farmer, and Rachel (née Fearing) Lincoln. After attending common schools, he was apprenticed as a blacksmith, but his love of books convinced his father to send him to college. Levi Lincoln entered Harvard College to study theology, but after hearing John Adams speak in Boston on the law he took to the study of that profession. He began his law studies in Newburyport after graduating from Harvard in 1772 and continued in the Northampton office of Joseph Hawley. Lincoln opened his own practice in Worcester in 1775.

Lincoln served for a brief time in the militia during the Revolutionary War, seeing action at Lexington with the Minutemen. After the war he returned to Worcester, where he acted as a judge of probate from 1777 until 1781 and served in other legal offices, including county prosecutor and clerk of the courts. He was a delegate to the Massachusetts State Constitutional Convention in 1779 and was elected as a delegate to the Continental Congress in 1781, but he refused to serve. During this period Lincoln worked on several little-known but highly important cases in the history of American jurisprudence: *Quork Walker v. Nathaniel Jenison, Nathaniel Jenison v. John Caldwell,* and *The Commonwealth v. Nathaniel Jenison.* In these cases, he and attorney Caleb Strong argued that slavery was illegal in Massachusetts under the national Bill of Rights. The state supreme court found in their favor, making their arguments the first recognized court cases striking down slavery as unconstitutional.

Lincoln served as a delegate to the Massachusetts House of Representatives in 1796 and the State Senate from 1797–1798. Lincoln was elected to the U.S. House of Representatives in 1800. His term was cut short when he was appointed attorney general by President Thomas Jefferson on 5 March 1801. President Jefferson initially nominated Theophilus Parsons, who was then chief justice of the Supreme Judicial Court of Massachusetts. Parsons refused the honor, *after* being confirmed by the Senate (one of the few nominees to decline after completing the confirmation process). Jefferson then offered the office to Lincoln, who accepted and was confirmed. Although Lincoln served through Jefferson's entire first term, 5 March 1801 until 3 March 1805, constituting one of the longest tenures up until that time, little has been written about him, even in department histories.

After leaving the cabinet, Lincoln was elected to the Massachusetts Governors' Council in 1806 and, in 1807, was elected as lieutenant governor of the state. In 1808, upon the death of Governor James Sullivan, he ascended to the governorship, where he served until he ran unsuccessfully for a term of his own in 1809. He was subsequently elected again to the Governors' Council, serving from 1810 to 1812.

On 13 September 1810, Supreme Court Justice William Cushing died, and former President Jefferson, writing to President Madison on a selection to fill the seat, spoke of his former attorney general's integrity and character. Madison offered the vacancy to Lincoln, but the jurist refused the honor because his eyesight was declining and he did not think he could handle the workload. Levi Lincoln spent his final years in retirement on his farm in Worcester, Massachusetts. He died there on 14 April 1820, a month shy of his seventieth birthday, and was interred in Rural Cemetery in Worcester. His son, also named Levi Lincoln (1782–1868), served as governor of Massachusetts from 1825 to 1834.

References: Ford, Paul Leicester, ed. *The Writings of Thomas Jefferson: Collected* (New York: G. P. Putnam's Sons; 10 vols., 1892–1899), 9: 282–284; "Lincoln, Levi" in Sobel, Robert, and John Raimo, eds., *Biographical Directory of the Governors of the United States, 1789–1978* (Westport, CT: Meckler Books; 4 vols., 1978), 2: 694; Parsons, Theophilus, *Memoir of Theophilus Parsons* (Boston: Ticknor and Fields, 1859) Robb, Arthur, "Biographical Sketches of the Attorneys General" (Unpublished essay DOJ, Washington, DC, 1946), I; Smith, William Henry, *History of the Cabinet of the United States of America, From President Washington to President Coolidge* (Baltimore: Industrial Printing, 1925), 320–321; *The Attorney Generals of the United States, 1789–1985* (Washington, DC: Department of Justice, 1985), 8; *Who Shall Be Governor?: The Contrast, Containing Sketches of the Characters and Public Services of the Two Candidates [Christopher Gore and Levi Lincoln] for the office of Chief Magistrate of the* *Commonwealth of Massachusetts* (Worcester, MA: *Spy* Office, 1809).

JOHN BRECKINRIDGE
1760–1806

John Breckinridge was known as one of the finest jurists of his day, and his skill was rewarded by appointment as the fifth attorney general. Born near Staunton, Virginia, on 2 December 1760, John Breckinridge was the son of Robert Breckinridge and Lettice (née Preston) Breckinridge. Little is known of his early life, but one known instance is quite remarkable. At the age of 19, while still a student at William and Mary College, he was elected to the Virginia legislature. Because he was too young, he was not admitted; yet his constituents reelected him, and he was again refused. When he was elected a third time, the legislators made an exception and allowed him to take his seat. He studied the law after leaving college, and was admitted to the Virginia bar in 1785. He then opened a practice in Charlottesville. That same year, he married May Hopkins "Polly" Cabell, the daughter of a state senator. He was elected to the U.S. Congress, but refused because he decided to move his family to Kentucky.

The family settled in Lexington, and Breckinridge soon became one of the leading attorneys in Kentucky. In 1798, he was elected to the Kentucky legislature, where he submitted the famous resolution declaring the right of all states to nullify federal actions deemed to be injurious. (Historians believe that Thomas Jefferson wrote the resolution and passed it on to Breckinridge.) In 1794, Breckinridge was an unsuccessful candidate for the U.S. Senate, but, in 1801, he was elected to that body and became an outspoken supporter of the policies of President Thomas Jefferson's administration. In fact, when Jefferson asked Congress for an amendment to acquire the Louisiana Purchase from France, Breckinridge was among those who advised him that he was already free to bargain under the treaty-making powers granted to the president by the Constitution.

When Attorney General Levi Lincoln resigned in March 1805, Secretary of the Navy Robert Smith asked to be moved to the vacant position. This request was granted pending the finding of a replacement. No successful nominee for the secretary of the navy was found and Robert Smith was asked to retreat to his former post. In a letter of 7 August 1805, Jefferson offered the attorney general position to Breckenridge. He stated he wanted Breckinridge in the cabinet "as your geographic position will enable you to bring into our councils a knowledge of the western interests and circumstances for which we are often at a loss and sometimes fail in our desires to promote them." Breckinridge accepted and was sworn in on 12 February 1806. However, Breckinridge biographer James Klotter writes, "In retrospect, it can be argued that Breckinridge erred in his move from the legislature. His senate leadership would be missed, and as attorney general he occupied a relatively minor office with no department to administer. He was 'an officer without an office, a legal advisor without a clerk, a prosecutor with no control over the district attorney.' The frustrations became apparent when, in early 1806, he argued six cases before the Supreme Court, winning only one. If he had hoped to influence Jefferson, Breckinridge faced a difficult task. The man from Monticello often kept his own counsel, and rumors spread that Jefferson's confidence in his appointee was waning. Only in his function as a liaison between the executive and legislative branches did Breckinridge find satisfaction, as various senators, as well as the president, sought his aid in drafting bills."

In the spring of 1806, Breckinridge returned home to Kentucky. His wife, inconsolable about his long absences, asked him to resign. Despite her pleas, Breckenridge was determined to return to Washington. While in Kentucky, however, he had caught a cold, and the trip sapped his always-precarious health. In October he collapsed from what may have been tuberculosis; his daughter Mary Ann remembered seeing him waste away to nothing. Breckinridge succumbed on 14 December 1806 at the age of 46. His original interment location was unknown; however, his remains were eventually laid to rest in the Lexington Cemetery in Lexington. Breckinridge County, Kentucky, is named in his honor. He was the grandfather of John Cabell Breckinridge, who served as vice-president of the United States, the Southern Democratic candidate for president in 1860, and Confederate secretary of war (1865) during the Civil War.

See also Breckinridge, John Cabell

References: *The Attorney Generals of the United States, 1789–1985* (Washington, DC: Department of Justice, 1985), 10; Harrison, Lowell Hayes, *John Breckinridge: Jeffersonian Republican* (Louisville, KY: Filson Club, 1969); Hinsdale, Mary Louise, *A History of the President's Cabinet* (Ann Arbor, MI: George Ware, 1911), 42–43; Klotter, James C., *The Breckinridges of Kentucky, 1760–1981* (Lexington: The University Press of Kentucky, 1986), 3–35; Smith, William Henry, *History of the Cabinet of the United States of America, From President Washington to President Coolidge* (Baltimore: Industrial Printing, 1925), 322–323; Starr, Harris Elwood, "Breckinridge, John" in *DAB* 2: 6.

CAESAR AUGUSTUS RODNEY
1772–1824

The public services of Caesar Rodney to his native land, which include his tenure as the sixth attorney general, were distinguished indeed. The son of Colonel Thomas Rodney (1744–1811), a Revolutionary War soldier and delegate to the Continental Congress from Delaware (1781), and Elizabeth (née Fisher) Rodney, Caesar Rodney was born in Dover, Delaware, on 4 January 1772. Rodney attended the University of Pennsylvania and graduated in 1789. He eventually studied law under Thomas B. McKean (who later served as governor of Delaware), and was admitted to the state bar in 1793. He then began a practice in Wilmington and New Castle.

In 1796, Rodney was elected to the Delaware House of Representatives, serving until 1802. A staunch supporter of Thomas Jefferson, Vice-president Rodney was induced to run in 1802 for a seat in the U.S. House against James A. Bayard, a member of an influential Delaware family who was the Federalist candidate. Rodney was elected, and served a single term. In January 1804, he was chosen as one of the House managers of the impeachment trial of Judge John Pickering of the U.S. District Court for New Hampshire and in December of that year served the same function for the impeachment trial of Supreme Court Justice Samuel Chase. There is no record of what he did after leaving the House in 1805. When Attorney General John Breckinridge died in office, President Jefferson offered the vacancy to Rodney, who accepted. He took office on 20 January 1807.

Although he served as attorney general throughout the remainder of the Jefferson administration and a portion of the Madison administration, Rodney's work in the office is little known. A history of the Justice Department relates that "Rodney did not have a distinguished record as Attorney General; but, in other capacities, stamped his name firmly on the annals of his times." Rodney resigned from the post on 5 December 1811. One historian, William Henry Smith, contends the resignation was "because the President nominated a candidate for a vacant place on the Supreme [Court] without consulting him."

Rodney apparently returned to his law practice. He served during the War of 1812 as a captain of artillery in the Delaware militia and was promoted at the end of the war to the rank of major. In January 1815 he was elected to the State Senate, where he served until November 1816. In 1817, President Monroe appointed him to a three-member commission (the other members were John

Graham and Theodorick Bland) investigating the new republics in South America.

An opponent of slavery within the United States, as well as the extension of the practice into the new territories, Rodney was elected to the U.S. House in 1820. He did not take his seat until December 1821, and the following month, the Delaware legislature elected him to the U.S. Senate. After just a year in the Senate, Rodney resigned to accept an offer from President James Monroe as minister plenipotentiary to Argentina, arriving in Buenos Aires on 14 November 1823. It was there that Rodney died on 10 June 1824 after a serious illness. He was buried in the English Churchyard in Buenos Aires, the only cabinet member interred outside the United States. He was 52 years old.

References: *The Attorney Generals of the United States, 1789–1985* (Washington, DC: Department of Justice, 1985), 12; Read, William T., *Biographical Sketch of Caesar Augustus Rodney* (Wilmington, DE: C. P. Johnson, 1853); Ryden, George H., "Rodney, Cæsar Augustus" in *DAB* 8: 82–83; Smith, William Henry, *History of the Cabinet of the United States of America, From President Washington to President Coolidge* (Baltimore: Industrial Printing, 1925), 323; *200th Anniversary of the Office of Attorney General, 1789–1989* (Washington, DC: Department of Justice, 1990), 19.

WILLIAM PINKNEY
1764–1822

Little of the life and services of our seventh attorney general, William Pinkney, is generally remembered, although law historian Charles Warren pronounced him "the undisputed head of the American bar." A distinguished attorney, considered in his time to be one of the finest in his field, he slipped into obscurity soon after his death. One of four children of Jonathan Pinkney, an English immigrant, and Ann (née Rind), William Pinkney was born in Annapolis, Maryland, on 17 March 1764. Because of his Loyalist sentiments during the Revolutionary War, Jonathan Pinkney's possessions were confiscated, forcing his son to leave King William School in Annapolis because he could not pay the tuition. Although William Pinkney apparently never received any additional formal education, he rose to become one of the nation's top attorneys. Biographer Arthur Robb does report, however, that Pinkney may have studied classical studies and medicine under a private tutor. He also studied the law under Samuel Chase, an eminent attorney who later became associate justice on the U.S. Supreme Court.

After being called to the Maryland bar in 1786, Pinkney opened a law office in Harford County. Two years later, he served in the state constitutional convention and, in 1789, was elected to a seat in the Maryland House of Delegates, where he served until 1792. He was then elected to the U.S. House of Representatives, but his seat was contested on the basis of residence eligibility. Although his appeal was successful, he ultimately refused to serve, instead taking a seat on the Executive Council of Maryland.

In 1796, President George Washington named Pinkney as one of the American commissioners to London to negotiate a treaty with Britain over boundaries with Canada (a pact now known as the Jay Treaty). A year after his return in 1804, Pinkney was named attorney general of Maryland. Shortly thereafter, President Thomas Jefferson chose him as minister plenipotentiary to Great Britain to end the impressment of American sailors by British ships, where he worked closely with Ambassador James Monroe. After 1807, when Monroe returned to the United States, Pinkney was the sole representative of the United States in London. The additional workload, combined with his ultimate failure to negotiate an end to the impressment controversy, led to nervous exhaustion and his resignation in early 1811. Pinkney returned to the United States a broken man.

On 11 December 1811, in reward for his years of service to his nation, President James Madison named Pinkney as the seventh attorney general of the United States, to replace the resigning Caesar A. Rodney. Little has been written of his tenure, except that as attorney general he drew up the declaration of war against Great Britain (War of 1812). One historian notes, "Not as Attorney General but in private practice, Pinkney was a busy lawyer before the Supreme Court, appearing as counsel in seventy-two cases." This scarcity of documentation continues throughout Pinkney's life; in fact, biographer William Henry Smith comments regretfully that: "During his life Pinkney was regarded as the first of American lawyers, even outranking Daniel Webster. He was also held to be the first of American orators. Unfortunately but few of his speeches have been preserved in their entirety." On 10 February 1814, Pinkney resigned and returned to his law practice full-time.

During the War of 1812, Pinkney, with the rank of major, commanded a militia of Maryland riflemen at the battle of Bladensburg, where he was severely wounded. In the February 1815 term of the U.S. Supreme Court, Pinkney appeared before the justices to deliver a speech on the issues involved in the celebrated shipping case *The Nereide*. Pinkney's remarks were so well-crafted, they inspired Chief Justice Marshall to later write, "With a pencil dipped in the most vivid colors, and guided by the hand of a master, a splendid portrait has been drawn, exhibiting this vessel and her freighter as forming a single figure, composed of the most discordant [contrary] materials, of peace and war. . . . So exquisite was the skill of the artist, so dazzling the garb in which the figure was presented, that it required the exercise of that cold investigating faculty which ought always to belong to those who sit on this bench, to discover its only imperfection: its want of resemblance."

Shortly after his argument in *The Nereide*, Pinkney was named U.S. minister to Russia and minister plenipotentiary to Naples, where he negotiated compensation for American ship losses. After two years in Naples and Moscow, Pinkney resigned and returned to the United States. Three years later, in 1819, he was elected to the U.S. Senate from Maryland, where he sat until his death. William Pinkney was three weeks shy of his sixty-eighth birthday when he died on 25 February 1822. He was buried in the Congressional Cemetery, Washington, DC.

References: The Attorney Generals of the United States, 1789–1985 (Washington, DC: Department of Justice, 1985), 14; Hinsdale, Mary Louise, *A History of the President's Cabinet* (Ann Arbor, MI: George Ware, 1911), 53; Robb, Arthur, "Biographical Sketches of the Attorneys General" (Unpublished essay DOJ, Washington, DC, 1946), 8; *Sketches of American Orators, by Anonymous, Written in Washington* (Baltimore: Fielding Lucas, Jr., 1816), 21–48; Smith, William Henry, *History of the Cabinet of the United States of America, From President Washington to President Coolidge* (Baltimore: Industrial Printing, 1925), 324–326; Warren, Charles, *History of the American Bar* (Boston: Little, Brown and Company, 1911), 259; Wheaton, Henry, *Some Account of the Life, Writings, and Speeches of William Pinkney* (New York: J. W. Palmer & Company, 1826), 5–13, 106–131.

RICHARD RUSH

1780–1859

Richard Rush was the son of one of the best-known Americans of the late eighteenth century. His own contributions to this country included service as attorney general, secretary of the treasury, and secretary of state *ad interim*. Rush, the son of Dr. Benjamin Rush, a noted colonial physician who signed the Declaration of Independence, was born on 29 August 1780 in Philadelphia, Pennsylvania. His mother, Julia Rush, was the daughter of Richard Stockton (1730–1781), who also signed the Declaration of Independence and was jailed for most of the Revolutionary War by the British. He was tutored at a young age by his father, and by the age of fourteen he entered the College of New Jersey, (now Princeton University), from which he graduated in 1797. He studied law in the offices of William Lewis in Philadelphia and, in 1800, was admitted to the Pennsylvania bar.

As a private attorney, Rush established his reputation when he defended William Duane, the editor of the *Aurora,* a journal, against charges that he had libeled Governor Thomas McKean. This case earned Rush prominence as a free-speech advocate. He was nominated for a seat in Congress, but he refused the honor. In January 1811, he was appointed attorney general of Pennsylvania and, within a year, in November, was named by President Madison as comptroller of the treasury.

During the War of 1812, the president put Rush forward as the administration speaker on war policy. His speech on 4 July of that year in Washington, while not considered his best, nonetheless tagged him as a rising star in the government. On 10 February 1814, following the resignation of Attorney General William Pinkney, President Madison asked Rush to fill the vacancy. Prior to this time no restrictions had been made on the place of residence of the attorney general; "it had been sufficient simply to appear before the Supreme Court when necessary." However, this time one of the conditions of appointment was that the attorney general must live in Washington. Rush accepted and served until 5 March 1817. Historians agree that Rush's most important contribution to the office was his oversight of the publication of *The Laws of the United States from 1789 to 1815.* This work was released in five volumes in 1815 and represents the first codification of the laws of the United States.

On 5 March 1817, under President James Monroe, Rush resigned as attorney general to accept an *ad interim* post as secretary of state until the actual appointee, American Ambassador John Quincy Adams, could wrap up business in London and return to the United States. During this appointment (5 March–22 September 1817), he signed one of the most important treaties in American history. In a series of letters to Sir Charles Bagot, the British Minister to the United States, Rush asked for a convention to end the use of armaments between their two nations on the U.S.-Canadian border. Their understanding, entitled an "Agreement Relating to Naval Forces on the American Lakes," was signed 29 April 1817. The convention, the first major treaty in history to have both sides in a conflict agree to disarm proportionately, made Rush one of the most successful secretaries of state, even though most histories of that department do not even mention his name. When Adams finally arrived to take up his post, he was so impressed with Rush's work that he recommended to the president that Rush be appointed as his replacement in London. Rush was named as minister plenipotentiary to the Court of St. James, and he sailed for London. He was 37 years old.

While John Quincy Adams had been disliked by much of British society, Rush was befriended and appreciated during his time in London. Many of the issues surrounding the treaty that ended the War of 1812, the Treaty of Ghent, were unresolved when Rush arrived, and he spent much of his time renegotiating portions of the pact with Lord Castlereagh, the British foreign minister, and his successor, George Canning. A treaty signed in 1818 established the border between the U.S. and British possessions in the western territories at the forty-ninth parallel and imposed joint control over the Oregon territory for a ten-year period. When General Andrew Jackson invaded Spanish Florida in 1818 and executed two British citizens, it was Rush who helped calm the British government and avoid a larger altercation. In his *Memoranda of a Residence in the Court of London,* written in 1833, Rush related that Castlereagh cautioned him that "war might have been produced by holding up a finger." A series of notes with Canning, and subsequent dispatches back to Secretary of State Adams and President Monroe, concluded with a series of principles outlined by Monroe, which have been labeled the Monroe Doctrine.

When Adams was elected president in 1824, he offered the post of secretary of the treasury to Rush, who accepted and served in that post from 7 March 1825 until 3 March 1829. In that period, writes Rush biographer Scott Fausti, "In order to protect American manufacturers, Rush specifically recommended raising import duties on all foreign wool and woolen goods, fine cotton goods, bar iron, and hemp. However, [he] favored the lowering of duties on imports he believed were staples of American life and that did not compete directly with domestic producers. He recommended the lowering of duties on cocoa, tea, coffee, and wines for the benefit of the American consumer." Rush was denounced during his tenure; Senator John Randolph of Virginia wrote that his appointment was the worst since Caligula made his horse a consul. Rush fought back, publishing a scathing article under the pen name "Julius" and demanding a duel with Randolph if the senator continued to make such remarks.

In 1828, President Adams sought reelection, and chose Rush as his running mate. The ticket was defeated, and Rush returned to private life on his estate outside of Philadelphia. In his final years, he brought the Smithson bequest to the United States to be used for the construction of the Smithsonian Institution and served for a short period as President James K. Polk's ambassador to France. His thoughts on this and his London mission were gathered by his son and published posthumously as *Recollections of a Residence at the English and French Courts,* (Philadelphia: J. B. Lippincott & Co., 1872).

Richard Rush died in Philadelphia on 30 July 1859, a month shy of his seventy-ninth birthday. He was buried in Laurel Hill Cemetery, Philadelphia.

References: *The Attorney Generals of the United States, 1789–1985* (Washington, DC: Department of Justice, 1985), 16; Fausti, Scott W., "Richard Rush" in Bernard S. Katz and C. Daniel Vencill, eds., *Biographical Dictionary of the United States Secretaries of the Treasury, 1789–1995* (Westport, CT: Greenwood, 1996), 303–310; Hargreaves, Mary, *The Presidency of John Quincy Adams* (Lawrence: University Press of Kansas, 1985), 49; Kruzel, Joseph, "From Rush-Bagot to START: The Lessons of Arms Control," in Charles W. Kegley and E. R. Wittkopf, eds., *The Global Agenda: Issues and Perspectives* (New York: Random House,

1988); Perkins, Dexter, "Rush, Richard," in *DAB* 8: 231–234; Rush, Richard, *Memoranda of a Residence in the Court of London* (Philadelphia: Carey, Lea & Blanchard, 1833), 120; Vasaio, Antonio, *The Fiftieth Anniversary of the U.S. Department of Justice Building, 1934–1984* (Washington, DC: GPO, 1985), 3–4; Willson, Beckles, *America's Ambassadors to England (1785–1928): A Narrative of Anglo-American Diplomatic Relations* (London: J. Murray, 1929), 138.

WILLIAM WIRT
1772–1834

Many consider William Wirt to be one of the greatest attorneys general ever to serve in the office. Historian William Henry Smith wrote in 1925, "There is a glamour about the name of William Wirt that has not been dissipated by the more than fourscore years that have passed since his death." Despite this attention, many of the facts of his life are in doubt. William Wirt, son of Swiss immigrant Jacob Wirt, a tavern owner, and Henrietta Wirt, a German immigrant, was born on 8 November 1772 in Bladensburg, Maryland. His father died when William Wirt was an infant, and his mother died when he was just eight. He was sent to a classical school in the Georgetown section of Washington, D.C., then part of Maryland. At the age of 17, he went to live as a tutor in the home of Benjamin Edwards, a leading Maryland citizen. In 1790, Wirt began the study of law at Montgomery Courthouse with William P. Hunt; later, he moved to Virginia, where he was admitted to the bar in 1792. He began a private law practice at Culpeper Court House, relocating to Richmond in 1799, then to Norfolk in 1803.

In 1795, Wirt became interested in the political scene. In 1800, he was elected as a clerk of the Virginia House of Delegates for three sessions, then in 1802 as chancellor of the eastern shore of Virginia. As clerk, he defended journalist James Thompson Callender against charges that he had published a libelous column on President John Adams. In 1807, he acted as government counsel in the treason trial of former Vice-president Aaron Burr. On 13 March 1816, he was appointed U.S. district attorney for Virginia by President James Madison.

In October 1817, President James Monroe, asked Wirt to take the position of attorney general. Wirt took office on 13 November 1817. According to biographer (and future secretary of the navy) John P. Kennedy, Wirt took the position with the stipulation that he be allowed to keep his private law practice and, if the need arose, be allowed to leave Washington for Baltimore, Philadelphia, or wherever his practice took him. Monroe agreed to this.

Wirt served from November 1817 until 3 March 1829, during the administrations of James Monroe and John Quincy Adams. His tenure ranks as the longest in the history of the office. On his first day in office, Wirt wrote on the flyleaf of a book, found years later in the justice department archives, "Finding on my appointment, this day, no book, document or papers of any kind to inform me of what has been done by any one of my predecessors, since the establishment of the Federal Government, and feeling strongly the inconvenience, both to the nation and myself, from this omission, I have determined to remedy it, so far as depends upon myself, and to keep a regular record of every official opinion I shall give while I hold this office, for the use of my successor." One historian relates, "Wirt's hand-kept records became the nucleus of a vast system that now makes use of every modern mechanical device to preserve official documents and correspondence."

As attorney general, Wirt served as the government's counsel in the celebrated cases of *McCulloch v. Maryland* and *Dartmouth College v. Woodward*. Although he was advised by President Adams that the action was not necessary, Wirt joined the rest of Adams's cabinet and resigned on the president's last day in office.

Resuming his private practice in Baltimore, Wirt remained out of the political scene for just two years. On 26 September 1831, the Anti-Masonic Party gathered (in the first political convention in American history) to nominate candidates for president and vice-president. The delegates nominated Wirt for president, with Amos Ellmaker of Pennsylvania as his running mate. The opposition candidates for the presidency were Andrew Jackson, who was running for reelection, and Henry Clay, the National Republican candidate. Many people tried to get Clay and Wirt to run on a unified ticket, but, despite their long friendship, Clay denounced the Anti-Masons and refused to negotiate with Wirt. In the end, Wirt's ticket drew heavily from Clay, throwing the election to Jackson. Wirt returned to his law practice, until his death two years after his unsuccessful presidential run. He died in Washington, on 18 February 1834 at the age of 72 and was buried in the Congressional Cemetery in Washington, D.C. Wirt County, West Virginia, is named in his honor.

It was not until 1849, fifteen years after his death, that Wirt's devotion to the attorney general's office became clear. In a letter to Congressman Hugh Nelson, then chairman of the House Judiciary Committee, Wirt had lamented that because there were no precedents for an attorney general to study, he might have issued an opinion that was wholly inconsistent with past opinions. Wirt asked that a record-keeping system be mandated by law, that a library of state statutes be established and maintained, and that future attorney generals be forced by law to give up their private practice to devote attention full time to the position.

Congress responded in some small ways to Wirt's criticisms: in 1818 he was provided a clerk and $500 for an office and stationery and his own salary was raised to $3,500 per year; in 1819 the salaries of his secretaries were raised; and in 1822, Wirt was given a office on the second floor of the old War Department building. Congress also authorized researchers to find the reports and opinions of the previous attorney generals and instructed that they be published as soon as possible. In 1841, seven years after Wirt's death, Congress issued the first volume (1471 pages long) of the *Official Opinions of the Attorneys-General,* of which Wirt's decisions filled over 500 pages.

References: *The Attorney Generals of the United States, 1789–1985* (Washington, DC: Department of Justice, 1985), 18; Kennedy, John Pendleton, *Memoirs of the Life of William Wirt* (Philadelphia: Lea and Blanchard; 2 vols., 1849), 1: 28–33, 192–195; Learned, Henry Barrett, "The Attorney-General and the Cabinet," *Political Science Quarterly* 24: 3 (1909), 447; Robb, Arthur, "Biographical Sketches of the Attorneys General" (Unpublished essay DOJ, Washington, DC, 1946), 12; Smith, William Henry, *History of the Cabinet of the United States of America, From President Washington to President Coolidge* (Baltimore: Industrial Printing, 1925), 326–329; *200th Anniversary of the Office of Attorney General, 1789–1989* (Washington, DC: Department of Justice, 1990), 21.

JOHN MACPHERSON BERRIEN
1781–1856

The tenth attorney general, who had little if any impact on the office, John Berrien was one of the cabinet officers who resigned in the midst of the infamous Eaton Affair of 1831. Berrien was born at Rocky Hill, near Princeton, New Jersey, on 23 August 1781, the son of John Berrien, a veteran of the Revolutionary War, and Margaret (née MacPherson) Berrien. Although Berrien moved with his parents to Georgia (a state with which he would be identified for the remainder of his life) when he was just a year old, he returned to New Jersey to attend Princeton College and graduated in 1796 at the age of 15. He returned to Savannah, studied law in the office of Joseph Clay, a federal judge, and was admitted to the Georgia bar in 1799, when he was 18 years old.

From 1799 until 1810, Berrien was a private attorney. In 1810, he was named as a judge of the Eastern District of Georgia, where he served until 1821. During the War of 1812, he was a captain in the volunteer army of the Georgia Hussars. He served as a state senator from 1822–1823, and, in 1824, was elected to the U.S. Senate. There, he was a supporter of Treasury Secretary William H. Crawford, and he pushed Crawford's name for president in 1824. When Andrew Jackson was elected, Berrien's friend John C. Calhoun of South Carolina was elected vice-president. At Calhoun's insistence President Jackson offered the attorney generalship to Berrien, who accepted. He took office on 9 March 1829. Berrien, along with Secretary of the Navy John Branch and Secretary of the Treasury Samuel Ingham, were designated "the Calhoun wing."

Little has been written about Berrien's activities as attorney general. His role in the Eaton Affair dominates his tenure. Conflicts arose among Calhoun's allies in the cabinet, which degenerated into scandal. (A full history of the Eaton affair can be found in the biography of Secretary of War John Eaton, 1829–1831.) When Jackson became aware of the problems, he forced Calhoun to resign as vice-president. Then, regarding Calhoun's supporters in the cabinet as spies, Jackson asked for, and received, their resignations on 22 June 1831 in the largest purge of the cabinet in history.

Berrien returned to private practice. In 1841, he was elected to the U.S. Senate from Georgia, serving until 1852. He then retired to his estate. John Berrien died on 1 January 1856, in Savannah, Georgia, at the age of 84, and was interred in the Laurel Grove Cemetery in that city. Berrien Counties in Georgia and Michigan are named in his honor.

References: *The Attorney Generals of the United States, 1789–1985* (Washington, DC: Department of Justice, 1985), 20; Brooks, Robert Preston, "Berrien, John MacPherson," in *DAB* 1: 225–226; Robb, Arthur, "Biographical Sketches of the Attorneys General" (Unpublished essay DOJ, Washington, DC, 1946), 14.

ROGER BROOKE TANEY
1777–1864

Roger Taney is remembered chiefly for his majority opinion in the landmark Supreme Court case *Dred Scott v. Sandford,* in which he held that slaves were not citizens under the Constitution. Yet as secretary of the treasury, he was involved in the Bank of the United States controversy and, as attorney general, was considered one of the finer legal minds to hold that position. Taney (pronounced "Taw-ney") was born on his father's tobacco plantation in Calvert County, Maryland, on 17 March 1777, the son of Michael Taney and Monica (née Brooke) Taney. Roger Taney attended Dickinson College in Carlisle, Pennsylvania, when he was 15 and graduated in 1795 as the valedictorian. He then went to Annapolis, Maryland, where he studied law under Jeremiah Townley Chase, a judge of the General Court of Maryland. Taney was admitted to the bar in 1799 and, as a favor to his father, returned to Calvert County to open his law office. He was elected to the state legislature, and after suffering defeat in his first reelection bid, moved to nearby Frederick. He was nominated in 1803 for the Maryland House of Delegates, but he was defeated.

In 1816, Taney was elected to the State Senate, serving a five-year term. He moved to Baltimore in 1823 and served as state attorney general in 1827. After asking for and receiving the resignation of Attorney General John M. Berrien, President Jackson appointed Taney to the position. He was confirmed by the Senate on 20 July 1831 and would serve in this post until 23 September 1833, when he resigned to take over the Treasury Department.

During his term as attorney general, Taney became caught up in the Bank of the United States controversy. Congress had chartered a national bank, but President Jackson refused to acknowledge it. Taney supported Jackson's position and drafted Jackson's veto message of the bill to recharter the bank. In the message, Taney disagreed with the argument that the Supreme Court's ruling in *McCulloch v. Maryland* settled the question of the constitutionality of the bank. He said that the authority of the Court must not be permitted "to control the Congress or the Executive when acting in their legislative capacities, but only have such influence as the force of their reasoning may deserve."

Because of the controversy, Secretary of the Treasury Louis McLane was moved over to the State Department, and William Duane was named to Treasury. When Jackson tried to move bank deposits out of the Bank of the United States, Duane resigned. Jackson then moved Taney over to the post, where he served without congressional consent from 23 September 1833 to 24 June 1834, during which time Taney tried unsuccessfully to mend the bank controversy. On 23 June 1834, Jackson formally nominated Taney for the Treasury post, but, angered by his work against the Bank of the United States, Congress rejected his nomination the following day by a 28–18 vote. Jackson sent the name of Levi Woodbury to the Senate, which confirmed him on 1 July 1834. Taney resigned and returned to his law practice in Maryland. After the resignation of Justice Gabriel Duvall of the Supreme Court, Taney's name was advanced for the vacant seat, but the Senate (still angered by the banking controversy) refused to vote on the nomination, effectively killing it. With the death of Chief Justice John Marshall on 4 July 1835, Jackson again nominated Taney. After a bitter struggle, the nomination was confirmed in a 29–15 vote on 15 March 1836, Taney was installed as the fifth Chief Justice of the Supreme Court—the first Catholic to hold that seat and the first of ten attorneys general to advance to the high court. His service, from 1836 until 1864, marks a tumultuous period in American history. It includes such landmark cases as *Charles River Bridge v. Warren Bridge* (1837), in which contracts between the state and private companies were held to be sacrosanct, and *Ex parte Merryman* (1861), in which Taney denied the right of presidents to sus-

pend the writ of habeas corpus. The most famous decision of the Taney Court was *Dred Scott v. Sandford* (1857). In this infamous decision he wrote: "They [blacks] had for more than a century before been regarded as beings of an inferior order and altogether unfit to associate with the white race, either in social or political relations; and so far inferior, that they had no rights which the white man was bound to respect; and that the negro might justly and lawfully be reduced to slavery for his benefit." The name of Roger Taney become synonymous with the Dred Scott case. Senator Charles Sumner, one of the greatest foes of slavery, said of him, "The name of Taney is to be hooted down [in] the pages of history. . . . He administered justice at last wickedly, and degraded the judiciary of the country, and degraded the age."

Taney died on Columbus Day, 1864 at the age of 77, after nearly twenty-eight years on the court and was buried in the St. John the Evangelist Cemetery in Frederick, Maryland. Taney County, Missouri, is named in his honor.

References: *The Attorney Generals of the United States, 1789–1985* (Washington, DC: Department of Justice, 1985), 22; Cushman, Clare, "Roger B. Taney," in Clare Cushman, ed. *The Supreme Court Justices: Illustrated Biographies, 1789–1995* (Washington, DC: Congressional Quarterly, 1995), 116–120; Lewis, H. H. Walker, *Without Fear or Favor: A Biography of Chief Justice Roger Brooke Taney* (Boston: Houghton Mifflin, 1965); Robb, Arthur, "Biographical Sketches of the Attorneys General" (Unpublished essay DOJ, Washington, DC, 1946), 15–16; Robbins, Ronald, and Bernard S. Katz, "Roger B. Taney," in Bernard S. Katz and C. Daniel Vencill, eds., *Biographical Dictionary of the United States Secretaries of the Treasury, 1789–1995* (Westport, CT: Greenwood, 1996), 349–354; Smith, Charles William, Jr., *Roger B. Taney: Jacksonian Jurist* (Chapel Hill: University of North Carolina Press, 1936), 4–21; Swisher, Carl Brent, *Roger B. Taney* (New York: Macmillan, 1935), 581–582; *200th Anniversary of the Office of Attorney General, 1789–1989* (Washington: Department of Justice, 1990), 24–25; Tyler, Samuel, *Memoir of Roger Brooke Taney, LL.D., Chief Justice of the Supreme Court of the United States* (Baltimore: J. Murphy, 1872); Warren, Earl, "Roger Brooke Taney: Fifth Chief Justice of the United States," *ABA Journal* 41: 6 (June 1955), 506.

BENJAMIN FRANKLIN BUTLER

1795–1858

Perhaps one of the most obscure men to hold the post of attorney general, Benjamin F. Butler, the twelfth man to occupy that office, was in his time a noted New York attorney and politician. He holds the distinction of being the only man to hold two cabinet positions at once, with full senate approval. He was born in Kinderhook Landing, New York, on 17 December 1795, the son of Medad Butler, a merchant, and Hannah (née Tyler) Butler. What schooling he had is barely known, except that one source calls it a "district school." According to historian Carl Swisher, attorney Peter Vivian Daniel was slated to become attorney general after Taney's resignation, but he declined "because of the difficult character of the office and the low compensation." President Andrew Jackson wanted a candidate who would support his position in the controversy over the Bank of the United States and chose Benjamin Butler. Jackson sent his nomination to the Senate on 15 November 1833, and Butler was confirmed. On 5 October 1836, Secretary of War Lewis Cass resigned, Jackson named Butler as secretary *ad interim*. The president had difficulty finding a permanent replacement and, rather than leave the post vacant, he sent Butler's name to the Senate. It confirmed him for this second position in 1836, with the stipulation that his tenure at War ran "during the pleasure of the President, until a successor, duly appointed, shall accept such office and enter upon the duties thereof." Butler held both the secretary of war and the attorney general positions until Van Buren named Joel Poinsett as the secretary of war in 1836. Although

Van Buren requested that he remain as attorney general, Butler resigned on 1 September 1838 and returned to New York with an appointment as U.S. attorney for the southern district of New York, where he served from 1838 to 1841 and again from 1845 to 1848. During this time he was also a professor of law at the University of New York. In 1845, he refused an offer from President James K. Polk to serve as secretary of war.

In his final years, Butler switched from the Democratic to the Republican Party because of his stand against slavery. He was in Paris, France, on 8 November 1858 when he suddenly died a month shy of his seventy-third birthday. He was buried in New York City.

References: The Attorney Generals of the United States, 1789–1985 (Washington, DC: Department of Justice, 1985), 24; Robb, Arthur, "Biographical Sketches of the Attorneys General" (Unpublished essay DOJ, Washington, DC, 1946), 17; Smith, William Henry, *History of the Cabinet of the United States of America, From President Washington to President Coolidge* (Baltimore: Industrial Printing, 1925), 332–333; Sobel, Robert, ed.-in-chief, *Biographical Directory of the United States Executive Branch, 1774–1971* (Westport, CT: Greenwood, 1971), 42–43; Swisher, Carl Brent, *History of the Supreme Court of the United States: The Taney Period, 1836–64* (New York: Macmillan, 1974), 18.

FELIX GRUNDY

1777–1840

Felix Grundy served fifteen months as the thirteenth attorney general, rising from a life of poverty to become the highest law officer in the land, and yet, little is known of his life. Born in Back Creek, a rural area of Berkeley County, Virginia (now West Virginia), on 11 September 1777. He was the son of George Grundy, an English emigrant, and Elizabeth Grundy. The family moved to Pennsylvania, then to Kentucky, when Felix was three. Felix Grundy's education was described as "meager." When his father died, sometime during his childhood, his mother instructed him for a time; however, after two of her other sons were killed by Indians, she sent him away to the Bardstown Academy. He studied the law under George Nicholas and, in 1797 at age 20, was admitted to the Kentucky bar.

In 1799, Grundy was elected to the state Constitutional Convention, and his work during the framing of the state constitution earned him high praise. The following year, he was elected to the Kentucky House of Representatives, resigning in 1806 to accept an appointment from Governor Christopher Greenup as a justice on the Kentucky Supreme Court of Errors and Appeals. Within a year he was promoted to chief justice but, finding the salary minuscule, he resigned in 1807 and moved to Nashville, Tennessee, to open a law practice. He defended mostly clients who faced execution; his skill in arguments before the jury resulted in only one execution in 165 cases, thereby "cheating the hangman of his due."

Still interested in politics, in 1811 he was elected to the U.S. House of Representatives for the first of two terms; he served on the prestigious Committee on Foreign Affairs. He refused to run for a third term and returned to Tennessee. In 1819 he was elected to the lower house of the state legislature where he served until 1825. In 1827, after two years away from politics, he ran for the U.S. Senate against John Bell, a member of the Tennessee senate but he lost. Although President Jackson did not get along with Grundy personally, when he named Senator John H. Eaton to his cabinet as secretary of war in 1829, he requested that Grundy fill Eaton's empty Senate seat. There, Grundy took a stand against Jackson and supported the state of South Carolina in its attempt to nullify federal tariff laws deemed injurious to the state. Perhaps in retribution, when Eaton resigned from the cabinet in 1831, Jackson supported him for reelection to his former senate seat in the next election. Grundy fought back, and the Tennessee legislature sent Grundy back for a full term. Nonetheless, his full Senate record reflects broad and deep support for the administration.

On 1 September 1838, Attorney General Benjamin Franklin Butler resigned, and President Martin Van Buren nominated Grundy to fill the position. Grundy was approved and served until 1 December 1839. There is little written about his tenure; even Justice Department histories barely mention him. His biographer, Joseph Howard Parks, states, "While a member of Van Buren's cabinet, Grundy was more of a political than a legal adviser. He spent more time and thought on how to carry the South, especially Tennessee, in 1840 than on questions of law. His legal reading had been limited, and he doubtless found the work of his new office rather dry and dull. He was better tempered to the excitement of a heated debate or a political campaign than to cold reasoning of legal opinions. . . . He had often been talked of for an appointment as postmaster general, but there is no evidence that he ever desired the office." His most notable achievement is that in 1839 he moved the attorney general's offices from the second floor of the old War Department building to the second floor of the Treasury building to expand the department's offices.

In 1839, James K. Polk was elected governor of Tennessee and the Democrats won the state legislature. They demanded that both their U.S. senators vote against the controversial Bank of the United States, and Senator Ephraim Hubbard Foster resigned in protest. The Tennessee legislature asked Grundy to be his replacement. Grundy obliged and resigned from the cabinet on 1 December 1839 to return to the Senate. Grundy came home during the election of 1840 to campaign for the Democrats. The rigors of travel during the campaign proved too much for him. While he was confined to bed at his home in Nashville, he was visited by former President Jackson, among others. Grundy did not recover and died on 19 December 1840 at the age of 53. He was buried in Mount Olivet Cemetery in Nashville. Grundy Counties in Illinois, Iowa, Missouri, and Tennessee are named in his honor.

References: Abernethy, Thomas P., "Grundy, Felix," in *DAB* 4: 32–33; *The Attorney Generals of the United States, 1789–1985* (Washington, DC: Department of Justice, 1985), 26; Caldwell, Joshua W., *Sketches of the Bench and Bar of Tennessee* (Knoxville, TN: Ogden Brothers, 1898); Parks, Joseph Howard, *Felix Grundy, Champion of Democracy* (Baton Rouge: Louisiana State University, 1940), 2–7, 318–339.

HENRY DILWORTH GILPIN

1801–1860

Henry Gilpin was the third of Martin Van Buren's three attorneys general. He was born 14 April 1801 in Lancaster, England. His father, Joshua Gilpin, a Philadelphia merchant, married Mary Dilworth, an Englishwoman in Europe; their son Henry was born at his mother's residence, one of only two attorneys general born outside of the United States (Francis Biddle, born in France, was the other). The Gilpins returned to the United States, but in 1811, they returned to England, and Henry was educated at the Hemel-Hempstead School near London. After graduating in 1816, he returned to the United States alone and entered the University of Pennsylvania, graduating in 1819.

Gilpin studied law in the office of Joseph Ingersoll, son of famed patriot Jared Ingersoll, and was admitted to the bar in 1822. He began a private law practice but at the same time devoted himself to literary matters; he published a second edition of John Sanderson's *Biography of the Signers of the Declaration of Independence* in 1828, while at the same time contributing articles to learned magazines such as the *Democratic Review.* His political pamphlet, *A Memorial of Sundry Citizens of Pennsylvania, Relative to the Treatment and Removal of the Indians,* which supported the government's Indian policy, earned him praise from George M. Dallas, the U.S. attorney for the eastern district of Pennsylvania. When Dallas resigned from the position to fill a seat in the U.S. Sen-

ate, President Andrew Jackson, on 20 December 1831, named Gilpin as his replacement. During his six years in the office he published a volume titled *Reports of Cases Adjudged in the District Court of the United States for the Eastern District of Pennsylvania, 1828–1836* (Philadelphia: P. H. Nicklin & T. Johnson, 1837). In 1837, President Martin Van Buren appointed him as solicitor of the Treasury, a post he held for three years.

On 1 December 1839, Attorney General Felix Grundy resigned, and, on 11 January 1840, Van Buren asked Gilpin to fill the vacant position. Gilpin served a little more than a year, from 11 January 1840 until the end of the Van Buren administration on 4 March 1841. In that time, he argued the government position in the *Amistad* case, in which slaves who had taken over a Spanish vessel transporting them to the United States had revolted and taken the ship to Massachusetts. Opposed in the arguments was former President John Quincy Adams. The court transcript relates one of Gilpin's arguments: "The judiciary act, which gives to this court its powers, so far as they depend on the legislature, directs that, on an appeal from the decree of an inferior court, this court shall render such judgment as the court below did, or should have rendered. It is to obtain from it such a decree in this case, that the United States present themselves here as appellants." On 9 March 1841, the Court held that the Africans could not be considered slaves and ordered their immediate freedom. Surprisingly, in the 1997 motion picture, *Amistad,* Gilpin is not portrayed.

Gilpin left office at the end of the Van Buren administration and settled in Philadelphia with his wife. His other non–law related publications included *Autobiography of Sir Walter Scott, Bart* (Philadelphia: Gihon & Smith, 1846) and the three-volume *Papers of James Madison, Purchased by Order of Congress* (Washington, DC: Langtree & O'Sullivan, 1840). Henry Gilpin died in Philadelphia on 29 January 1860 at the age of 58.

References: *The Attorney Generals of the United States, 1789–1985* (Washington, DC: Department of Justice, 1985), 28; Nichols, Roy F., "Gilpin, Henry Dilworth," in *DAB* 4: 315–316; Robb, Arthur, "Biographical Sketches of the Attorneys General" (Unpublished essay DOJ, Washington, DC, 1946), 19.

JOHN JORDAN CRITTENDEN
1787–1863

John Crittenden is the only man to serve as attorney general in separate appointments under two administrations; William Henry Harrison (1841) and Millard Fillmore (1850–1853). Born near Versailles, Kentucky, on 10 September 1787, the son of John Crittenden, a farmer who was a veteran of the Revolutionary War, Crittenden was sent to a school in Jessamine County, to prepare for college. He then began the study of law under George Mortimer Bibb, later secretary of the treasury (1844–1845). He finished his studies at the College of William and Mary in Virginia and, after graduating in 1807, was admitted to the Kentucky bar.

In 1809, although he was practicing in Kentucky, Illinois Territorial Governor Ninian Edwards named him as the territorial attorney general, and he held the post for a year. In 1811, Crittenden was elected to the Kentucky House of Representatives and was re-elected six times, serving as speaker in 1815 and 1816. During the War of 1812, he was a volunteer and aide-de-camp in the first division of the Kentucky militia, seeing action at the Battle of the Thames with General William Henry Harrison. In 1817, he was elected to the U.S. Senate to fill a vacancy caused by the resignation of Martin D. Hardin and left after the term ended in 1819. He was reelected to his state House seat again in 1825, serving for three one-year terms. In 1827, he was named as the U.S. attorney for Kentucky by President John Quincy Adams, but in 1829 was removed by President Andrew Jackson. In 1835, Crittenden was once again elected to the U.S. Sen-

ate, this time for a full six-year term. In 1841, he was widely considered a shoe-in for re-election to this safe seat.

Biographer Albert Kirwan related that following William Henry Harrison's election as president in 1840, he consulted with Daniel Webster and Henry Clay on cabinet selections, and it was Clay who wanted Crittenden, a fellow Kentuckian, as attorney general. Crittenden resigned his Senate seat and accepted the cabinet post as the fifteenth attorney general. Unfortunately, Harrison died one month after taking office, at the age of 68, plunging the nation into the first crisis of a vice-president ascending to the presidency. The new president, John Tyler, asked Crittenden to remain in office, but he resigned, to take effect 13 September. He never signed the annual report that year and had issued only thirteen official opinions, of which only one is considered noteworthy.

When Henry Clay resigned from the Senate in 1842 to begin his campaign for the presidency, the Kentucky legislature elected Crittenden to the vacant seat; he served until 1848. When he finished this term, he was asked by President Zachary Taylor to take a place in his cabinet, but he refused. Instead, he was elected governor of Kentucky, serving one half of his four-year term. On 22 July 1850, following the death of President Taylor, Attorney General Reverdy Johnson resigned. President Millard Fillmore offered the position to Governor Crittenden, who accepted, becoming the twenty-second attorney general. Little is known of this second tenure; a history of the Fillmore administration does not even mention Crittenden's selection. What is known is that during an illness of Secretary of State Daniel Webster, Crittenden served in the cabinet a third time by acting as secretary *ad interim*. A history of the Justice Department explains that Crittenden may be best remembered for advising President Fillmore that the Fugitive Slave Act of 1850 "did not conflict with the constitutional guarantee of habeas corpus." He left office at the end of the Fillmore administration, on 4 March 1853. Incoming President Franklin Pierce tried to get him to serve as attorney general in his administration, but Crittenden refused.

In 1854, Crittenden was, for the third time, elected to the U.S. Senate, this time serving until 1861. It was during this period that he made perhaps his greatest stamp on history. As the cauldron of sectional sentiment boiled, leading to the outbreak of the Civil War in late 1860, Crittenden used his Senate seat to try to head off conflict. On 18 December 1860, he introduced a series of resolutions, known as the Crittenden Compromise, composed of six proposed constitutional amendments and four suggested congressional proclamations, which both North and South might agree to and head off the threat of war. The compromise would have frozen in place slavery in the South, outlawed the practice in existing territories, and allowed it in new territories if the people of those territories voted for it. It also banned Congress from attempting to end slavery in any Southern state and called on the government to reimburse slaveowners for escaped slaves. Crittenden's compromise failed to gain support, particularly in the North, and the Civil War began just four months later. Two of Crittenden's sons fought in the conflict, on opposite sides. The *Baltimore American* editorialized on 12 January 1861, "We can scarcely conceive of a spectacle which has in it more of the moral sublime that this brave old man struggling for the salvation of his country. If 'pius Aeneas' excites our admiration in bearing old Anchises from the flames, how much more this venerable Father of the State struggling to rescue from the scorching blaze of sectional fury the precious deposit of the Constitution and the Union. Oh, 'old man eloquent,' a thousand blessing on thy venerable head! Surely the spirit of Henry Clay [who fashioned the Compromises of 1820 and 1850] has descended on Crittenden, the mantle of that Elijah has invested him with tenfold power. If this grandest structure of human wisdom shall survive the storm, the people of American will enshrine in their deepest hearts the name of this second Savior of his Country."

Although he was a Southerner, Crittenden apparently did not own slaves and did not believe in secession from the Union. He left the Senate in 1861 at the end of his term, but Unionists in Kentucky put his name up for a seat in the U.S. House of Representatives and Crittenden was elected. He did not finish the term. Sickly at the end of his long public career, Crittenden died on 26 July 1863 at the age of 75 and was buried in Frankfort Cemetery in Frankfort, Kentucky. Crittenden County, Kentucky, was named in his honor.

References: *The Attorney Generals of the United States, 1789–1985* (Washington, DC: Department of Justice, 1985), 30; Coleman, Mary Ann Butler, *The Life of John J. Crittenden, With Selections From His Correspondence and Speeches. Edited by his Daughter, Mrs. Chapman Coleman* (Philadelphia: J. B. Lippincott & Co.; 2 vols., 1871), 1: 13–15, 376–381; 2: 9–17; "Crittenden, John Jordan," in Robert Sobel and John Raimo, eds., *Biographical Directory of the Governors of the United States, 1789–1978* (Westport, CT: Meckler Books; 4 vols., 1978), 2: 519–520; Grayson, Beason Lee, *The Unknown President: The Administration of President Millard Fillmore* (Washington, DC: University Press of America, 1981); Kirwan, Albert D., *John J. Crittenden: The Struggle for the Union* (Lexington: University of Kentucky Press, 1962), 136–147; Robb, Arthur, "Biographical Sketches of the Attorneys General" (Unpublished essay DOJ, Washington, DC, 1946), 19; Smith, William Henry, *History of the Cabinet of the United States of America, From President Washington to President Coolidge* (Baltimore: Industrial Printing, 1925), 335.

HUGH SWINTON LEGARÉ
1797–1843

After service of less than two years, Hugh Legaré became the second attorney general to die in office, succumbing at the age of 46 (John Breckinridge also died in office at age 46). Yet in that short time he rendered 150 opinions, a startling and prestigious output compared to his predecessors. Hugh Swinton Legaré was born in Charleston, South Carolina, on 2 January 1797, the son of

Solomon Legaré and Mary (née Swinton) Legaré. Solomon Legaré died in 1797 "of a nervous fever" at the age of 29, when his son was an infant. Hugh Legaré was educated at home by his mother and later studied at several private schools, as well as the College of Charleston and South Carolina College.

After studying law under Mitchell King, Legaré went to Europe in 1818 and studied French in Paris and Roman law, natural philosophy, and mathematics at the University of Edinburgh. In 1820 he returned to South Carolina and took charge of his family's plantation on St. John's Island. That same year, he was elected to the lower house of the state legislature and reelected the following year, but he was defeated for a third term in 1822. He then opened a private practice, which lasted until he was elected once again to the state legislature, where he served for six years until 1830. That year, he was elected as state attorney general and, after arguing a case before the U.S. Supreme Court in 1832, was offered the post of American chargé d'affaires to Belgium by Secretary of State Edward Livingston. Following his four years in that position, he returned home to take a seat in the U.S. Congress, to which he had been elected. He was a vocal opponent of the Bank of the United States, and it was this stand that lost him a chance for reelection in 1838. He returned to the practice of law. In 1840, he campaigned for Whig presidential candidate William Henry Harrison.

Legaré was a close friend of Harrison's Vice-president, John Tyler. When Harrison died after just a month in office, Tyler became president. In September 1841, the entire cabinet resigned, and Tyler was forced to find replacements for the executive departments. He asked Legaré, who soon was installed as the sixteenth attorney general. Writes biographer Michael O'Brien, "As Attorney General, Legaré had two main responsibilities: to render opinions to government departments requiring legal advice and to appear before the Supreme Court. Of the former we have abundant published record; of the latter, little but the bare log of fifteen cases. He was thorough and minute in his

opinions. He did decline the entreaties of Cabinet officers to make the Attorney general a referee between departments, which had been [his predecessor William] Wirt's custom: 'The Attorney General's office is not a Court of Appeals,' he told the Secretary of the Treasury [Walter Forward] in March 1842. Otherwise he was energetic. Many opinions are not of permanent interest for the student of Legaré. Did distressed seamen have the right to aid from American consuls, under the provisions of the acts of 1792 and 1803? Did the president have the right to set aside the verdict of a decades-old courts-martial, if irregularities could be demonstrated?" Legaré served from 20 September 1841 until 20 June 1843.

When Daniel Webster resigned as secretary of state, Legaré served as secretary *ad interim* from 5 March 1843. He accompanied President Tyler to the unveiling of the Bunker Hill Monument in Boston on 17 June 1843; there he became ill and died three days later, at the age of 46.

References: The Attorney Generals of the United States, 1789–1985 (Washington, DC: Department of Justice, 1985), 32; Hamilton, Joseph Gregoire de Roulhac, "Legaré, Hugh Swinton," in *DAB* 6: 144–145; Legaré, Hugh Swinton, *Writings of Hugh Swinton Legaré, Late Attorney General and Acting Secretary of State of the United States* (Charleston, SC: Burges & James; 2 vols., 1845–1846), 1: v–ix; "Legaré, Hugh Swinton," in *NCAB* 5: 5; O'Brien, Michael, *A Character of Hugh Legaré* (Knoxville: University of Tennessee Press, 1985), 266–267.

JOHN NELSON
1794–1860

John Nelson is perhaps the most obscure of the seventy-eight people who have served as attorney general. He was born in Frederick, Maryland, on 1 June 1791. His father, Roger Nelson, became a general in the Continental Army during the American Revolution. John Nelson graduated from the College of William and Mary in Williamsburg, Virginia in 1811. He studied law and was admitted to the bar in 1813. He served in several local offices before being elected to the U.S. House of Representatives in 1821, serving a single term. In 1831 he was appointed as the American charge d'affaires to the Two Sicilies, as well as minister to the Court of Naples, where he served until 1832.

On 30 June 1843, Attorney General Hugh S. Legaré suddenly died; on 1 July, President John Tyler offered the vacancy to Nelson, who accepted, was confirmed, and served until the end of the Tyler administration, 4 March 1845. There is little record of his tenure as attorney general; several histories of the Justice Department merely list him as serving as attorney general.

After leaving office, Nelson seems to have disappeared, leaving no record or public writings. He died in obscurity in Baltimore, Maryland, on 8 January 1860 at the age of 68.

References: *The Attorney Generals of the United States, 1789–1985* (Washington, DC: Department of Justice, 1985), 34; "Nelson, John," in *NCAB* 5: 8; Robb, Arthur, "Biographical Sketches of the Attorneys General" (Unpublished essay DOJ, Washington, DC, 1946), 21; Smith, William Henry, *History of the Cabinet of the United States of America, From President Washington to President Coolidge* (Baltimore: Industrial Printing, 1925), 337.

JOHN YOUNG MASON
1799–1859

See Secretary of the Navy, 1844–1845, 1846–1849

NATHAN CLIFFORD
1803–1881

Although he served as the second of President James K. Polk's three attorneys general, little has been written of the year-and-a-half tenure of Nathan Clifford. He is better known as the second attorney general elevated to the U.S. Supreme Court, where he served from 1858 until his death in 1881. Clifford, the son of Nathaniel Clifford, a farmer, and Lydia (née Simpson) Clifford, was born in the village of Rumney, New Hampshire, on 18 August 1803. He attended local academies, including the Haverhill (New Hampshire) Academy, then studied the law in the office of Rumney attorney Josiah Quincy. In 1827 he was admitted to the New Hampshire bar and moved to the town of Newfield, in York County, Maine, to open a practice.

In 1830, when he was 27 years old, Clifford was elected as a Democrat to the lower house of the Maine state legislature, where he served four one-year terms, including the last two as Speaker. In 1834 he was elected as state attorney general, serving until 1838. The following year, he was elected to the U.S. House of Representatives, where he served two terms from 1839 until 1843. Defeat in the elections of 1843 sent Clifford back to Maine and his law practice. He would have remained a distinguished attorney in the state had he never risen any farther in politics. By 1846, however, that had all changed.

In September 1846, President James K. Polk was forced to shuffle his cabinet. Secretary of the Navy George Bancroft resigned, desiring a diplomatic post (he was named three days later as the American minister to the Court of St. James), and, on 9 September, Polk moved Attorney General John Young Mason, a former secretary of the navy in the Tyler administration, back to the Navy Department. According to Polk historian Paul Bergeron, "The top candidate [for a new attorney general] was Franklin Pierce of New

Hampshire . . . , but Pierce declined the honor. Meanwhile, Mason presided over both the Navy and the Justice departments. Near the end of September, Polk informed the cabinet that he was considering Nathan Clifford of Maine for appointment but that he wanted more information about him. Finally, on the thirtieth of the month, Polk wrote to Clifford, inviting him to accept the attorney generalship. Clifford responded affirmatively in a letter of 12 October. Three days later, an apparently eager Clifford arrived in Washington, ready to confer with the president and to receive his official commission; and on 17 October he attended his first cabinet meeting." Clifford was confirmed unanimously by the Senate.

His career seemed destined to be short. Several days before the new Supreme Court term opened in December, Clifford handed President Polk his resignation, saying that he was dissatisfied with the cabinet as a whole but not formally expressing a reason for such a bold act. Polk, in his diary, wrote, "I told him [that] if he resigned now it would be assumed by his political opponents that he was not qualified and would ruin him as a public man." Clifford then withdrew his resignation and went on to serve as attorney general until 17 March 1848. Supreme Court historians Joan Biskupic and Elder Witt explain, "During his service in the Polk cabinet, Clifford played a major role in mediating the many disputes between Polk and his Secretary of State, James Buchanan. Polk was vigorously pursuing his war with Mexico, while Buchanan advocated a more cautious policy. Buchanan liked and trusted Clifford." This friendship later led to political advancement for the New Englander.

As the war in Mexico came to an end, Polk named Clifford as a special commissioner to establish a treaty of peace between the United States and its neighbor to the south. Clifford's service produced a treaty that gave California to the United States. Clifford remained in Mexico City as the U.S. minister to Mexico until a new administration came to power in 1849, at which time Clifford returned to his law practice.

Following his dissenting opinion in the famed *Dred Scott* decision, which upheld the right to own slaves, Supreme Court Justice Benjamin R. Curtis resigned from the Court on 30 September 1857. President James Buchanan nominated Clifford to the vacancy on 9 December of that same year. Although he was considered by Northern senators to be a "doughface"—a Northerner who harbored Southern sympathies—the former attorney general nonetheless was confirmed, 26–23, on 12 January 1858 and took his seat on the high court, the second former attorney general to be elevated to the Court. In his twenty-three years as a justice, Clifford wrote no majority opinions, and as a result Clifford's role in Court history is negligible at best. Historian Charles Fairman wrote, "In his day Clifford was at once the most prolix and most pedestrian member of the Court." In his role as senior justice, Clifford did serve as the presiding member of the commission established in 1877 to decide the 1876 presidential election between Republican Rutherford B. Hayes and Democrat Samuel Tilden.

In 1880, Clifford suffered a serious stroke; however, he did not resign from the Court, hoping to hold out until a Democrat could occupy the White House and name a fellow Democrat to replace him on the court. He was not successful; Clifford died on 25 July 1881, a month short of his seventy-eighth birthday.

References: *The Attorney Generals of the United States, 1789–1985* (Washington, DC: Department of Justice, 1985), 38; Barnes, William Horatio, "Nathan Clifford, Associate Justice," in *The Supreme Court of the United States* (New York: Nelson & Phillips, 1875), 73–78; Bergeron, Paul H., *The Presidency of James K. Polk* (Lawrence: University Press of Kansas, 1987), 31; Biskupic, Joan, and Elder Witt, *Guide to the Supreme Court* (Washington, DC: Congressional Quarterly; 2 vols., 1997), 2: 889; Carson, Hampton Lawrence, *The History of the Supreme Court of the United States: With Biographies of All the Chief and Associate Justices* (Philadelphia: P. W. Ziegler, 1904), 77; Chandler, Walter, "Nathan Clifford: A Triumph of Untiring Effort," *American Bar Association Journal* 11 (January 1925), 57–60; Chase, Lucien

B., *History of the Polk Administration* (New York: George P. Putnam, 1850); Clifford, Philip Greely, *Nathan Clifford, Democrat (1803–1881)* (New York: G. P. Putnam's Sons, 1922), 3–5, 138–163; Currie, David P., *The Constitution in the Supreme Court: The First Hundred Years, 1789–1888* (Chicago: University of Chicago Press, 1985), 356.

ISAAC TOUCEY
1796–1869

Issac Toucey served as attorney general for less than a year and as secretary of the navy for four years, yet he may be better known for his service as governor of Connecticut from 1846 to 1847. Born in Newton, Massachusetts, on 5 November 1796, he was the son of Zalman Toucey, a farmer, and Phebe (née Boothe) Toucey. Isaac Toucey received a private education, studied law with Asa Chapman, who later became a leading Connecticut judge, and, in 1818, was admitted to the state bar. He began his practice of law in Hartford.

In 1821, Toucey was named the prosecuting attorney for Hartford County, serving until 1835. In that year, he was elected to the U.S. House of Representatives and served for two terms. In Congress, he was a member of the House Judiciary and Foreign Affairs Committees. Defeated for reelection in 1839, he returned to his law practice until 1842, when he was again named as Hartford County prosecuting attorney. In 1845, he was the unsuccessful Democratic candidate for governor of Connecticut; a year later in his second run for governor, despite receiving less than a majority of the popular vote, the legislature chose him as governor. Serving from 1846 until 1847, Toucey was noted for advocating an antibribery bill to try to halt state corruption. When he vetoed a popular measure backed by members of his own party for a bridge over the Connecticut River, he was refused renomination in 1847 and forced to leave the governorship. Soon after his term ended in 1848, he was approached by President James K. Polk to become attorney general.

On 18 March 1848, Attorney General Nathan Clifford resigned when he was nominated for the U.S. Supreme Court. President Polk then approached Toucey to fill the vacancy. The Connecticut attorney accepted and was sworn in on 29 June 1848 as the twentieth attorney general. He served as in the post from that date until the end of the Polk administration, 4 March 1849. During this period, he also served as acting secretary of state during a period of absence by Secretary of State James Buchanan. His period in office was so devoid of importance that Justice Department histories fail to name him at all.

In 1850, Toucey was elected to the upper house of the Connecticut legislature; two years later, he was elected to the lower house. That same year, he was elected to the U.S. Senate, where he served until 3 March 1857. In the Senate, Toucey was a Northerner with Southern sympathies. He spoke out in defense of the Fugitive Slave Law as "the law of the land," demanding that the government uphold it, and attacked those Republicans, most notably William Henry Seward and Charles Sumner, who said that a "higher law" allowed them to reject any law supporting slavery. With the election of former Secretary of State James Buchanan to the presidency, Toucey was asked to serve as the secretary of the navy in the new administration, mainly because of his support for slavery. Toucey accepted, resigned from the Senate, and took over the Navy Department on 6 March 1857. His tenure in that office lasted for the entire four years of Buchanan's reign. Toucey spent much of his time trying to get increased appropriations for building up what he considered to be an undersized navy. In his annual report for 1857, he wrote, "It is not the policy of our government to maintain a great navy in time of peace. It is against its settled policy to burden the resources of the people by an overgrown naval establishment. It is universally admitted to be inexpedient to endeavor to compete with other great commercial powers in the magnitude of their naval preparations. But it is the true policy of our government to take care that its navy, within its limited extent, should be unsurpassed in its efficiency and its completeness, and that our preparatory arrangements should be such that no event shall take us altogether by surprise."

As the nation became more divided by the issue of slavery, pushing the country ever closer to civil war, Toucey was charged with using his sympathy to the South by scattering many of the navy's ships so that they could not react to secession by the Southern states. A Senate investigation cleared him of any wrongdoing in 1864, but until that time he was condemned in his home state—his picture was even removed from the gallery of state governors. After leaving office, Toucey returned to Hartford, where he practiced law. He spent his final days caring for his wife, who was ill. Toucey died in Hartford on 30 July 1869 at the age of 72; he was buried in Cedar Hill Cemetery in Hartford.

References: *The Attorney Generals of the United States, 1789–1985* (Washington, DC: Department of Justice, 1985), 40; Chase, Lucien B., *History of the Polk Administration* (New York: George P. Putnam, 1850); Langley, Harold D., "Isaac Toucey," in Paolo E. Coletta, ed., *American Secretaries of the Navy* (Annapolis, MD: Naval Institute Press; 2 vols., 1980), 1: 302–318; Morse, Jarvis Means, "Toucey, Isaac," in *DAB* 9: 600–601; "Toucey, Isaac," in Robert Sobel and John Raimo, eds., *Biographical Directory of the Governors of the United States, 1789–1978* (Westport, CT: Meckler Books; 4 vols., 1978), 1: 170.

REVERDY JOHNSON
1796–1876

Reverdy Johnson, according to a history of the Justice Department, "was one of the most unusual men to occupy the office. His services as Attorney general were not noteworthy, but his other activities during a na-

tional career stamped him as a foremost lawyer, diplomat, and citizen." Johnson, the son of John Johnson, an immigrant from England and Maryland state legislator, and Deborah (née Ghieselen) Johnson, of Huguenot descent, was born in Annapolis, Maryland, on 21 May 1796. He attended St. John's College in Annapolis, from which he graduated in 1811. He then began the study of law, first with his father and then with a judge known only by the last name of Stephen. In 1816, at the age of 20, Johnson was admitted to the state bar.

Johnson started a private law practice in Upper Marlborough, the county seat of Prince George's County, Maryland, but a year later moved to Baltimore, where he soon became a noted lawyer. He served two single-year terms (1821, 1826) as a Maryland state senator but resigned when the duties of the office infringed on his law practice. Elected to the U.S. Senate in 1844, he served until 7 March 1849, when President Zachary Taylor selected him as his attorney general. Of his tenure, which lasted until 20 July 1850, biographer Bernard Steiner writes, "In general he believed in following the doctrine of *stare decisis* with reference to the opinions of his predecessors, though he decided differently from them, when he saw good cause to do so."

He was soon caught up in a serious scandal that historians claim almost got him fired from the cabinet. Secretary of War George W. Crawford had been the attorney for a claim of a ship against the United States government. Johnson offered an opinion in which he said that the lawyer for the case, after winning half of the award, was deserving of interest from the government. Crawford received an additional $94,000 on this opinion. Johnson later said that he had had no idea that Crawford was the lawyer in the case; nonetheless, historian Bernard Steiner claims that had he not died on 2 July 1850, President Taylor would have fired him for the slip. Following Taylor's death, Johnson, as well as the rest of the cabinet, offered his resignation to President Millard Fillmore and left office on 20 July 1850.

Johnson's career after he left government was involved with law and diplomacy. He was sympathetic with the Southern cause and represented the slaveowning defendant before the Supreme Court in the famed *Dred Scott* case, which upheld the right to own slaves. When the Civil War seemed certain to break out, he served as a member of a peace conference held in Washington in early 1861. That same year, he was elected to the Maryland House of Representatives, where he urged the state not to secede. Johnson apparently saw secession as treason, and he later supported President Abraham Lincoln's suspension of the writ of *habeas corpus*. Elected to the U.S. Senate in 1862, he did not take his seat until 1863 because he was sent to New Orleans on President Lincoln's behalf to investigate complaints lodged by foreign consuls against the city's military commander, General Benjamin F. Butler. He served on the Committee of Fifteen, which established a program of postwar reconstruction, and voted to find President Andrew Johnson not guilty in his impeachment trial. He resigned his seat in 1868 to replace Charles Francis Adams as the American minister to Great Britain, where he served until 1869. On his return to the United States, much of his law practice dealt with defending clients accused of treason against the United States during the war and members of the Ku Klux Klan. He also served as the attorney for a man accused of preventing freed blacks from voting (*United States v. Cruikshank* [1875]).

On 10 February 1876, while arguing a case before the Maryland Court of Appeals in Annapolis, Johnson suffered an accidental fall and died from his injuries. He was 79 years old.

References: The Attorney Generals of the United States, 1789–1985 (Washington, DC: Department of Justice, 1985), 42; Robb, Arthur, "Biographical Sketches of the Attorneys General" (Unpublished essay DOJ, Washington, DC, 1946), 25; Steiner, Bernard C., *Life of Reverdy Johnson* (Baltimore: Norman Remington, 1914), 1–5, 34–37; *200th Anniversary of the Office of Attorney General,*

1789–1989 (Washington, DC: Department of Justice, 1990), 25; Williams, Mary Wilhelmine, "Johnson, Reverdy," in *DAB* 5: 112–114; Willson, Beckles, *America's Ambassadors to England (1785–1928): A Narrative of Anglo-American Diplomatic Relations* (London: J. Murray, 1929), 336–341.

JOHN JORDAN CRITTENDEN
1787–1863

See Attorney General, 1841

CALEB CUSHING
1800–1879

Biographer Sister Mary Michael Catherine Hodgson wrote of Caleb Cushing, "None of the statesmen of the nineteenth century presents a more baffling personality to the student of history than does Caleb Cushing." The cousin of a Supreme Court Justice, Cushing served in Congress, as the U.S. minister to China and Spain, and as attorney general in a career that lasted more than half a century. Born in Salisbury, Massachusetts, on 17 January 1800, Cushing was the son of John Newmarch Cushing, a sailor and merchant, and Lydia (née Dow) Cushing.

His mother died when he was 10 years old, and he came under the care of a stepmother, Elizabeth Johnson, when his father remarried five years later. He attended a private school under the tutelage of an Irish teacher and, when only 13, matriculated at Harvard College, where he was a leader in his class with another future cabinet member, writer George Bancroft. After graduating in 1817, Cushing spent a year at Harvard Law School; he then studied the law in the office of Ebenezer Mosley in Newburyport and was admitted to the state bar in 1821. For the next twelve years he plied a successful law practice. Finally, in 1834, he ran for and was elected to a seat in the U.S. House of Representatives, serving for four terms until 1843. President Tyler saw in Caleb Cushing a man to include in his cabinet. He submitted his name to the Senate on 3 March 1843 as secretary of the treasury, but he was rejected, 27–19. Tyler, angered at the slight, resubmitted the nomination; this time, it was rejected, 27–10. Tyler, in a bit of comic opera, submitted the name a third time. This time, Cushing was rejected, 29–2. It was the first and only time in American history that one man was rejected for the same office by Congress three separate times.

Because of his service on the House Committee of Foreign Affairs, in 1843 President John Tyler selected Cushing as the U.S. commissioner to China, where he negotiated the Treaty of Wang-Hiya in 1845. Secretary of State Daniel Webster, pressured by Whigs to retire from the cabinet (he had remained when Tyler became president in 1841 because of his workload), issued ambassadorial instructions to Cushing, then resigned. When he returned from his ground-breaking mission to China, Cushing used some of his own money to raise an army to fight in the Mexican–American War (his state refused to send a contingent), while he rose to the rank of brigadier general.

In 1852, Senator Franklin Pierce of New Hampshire was elected president of the United States. There was much indecision as to the man the president-elect would select for the attorney general position; the *New York Herald* of 4 December 1852 reported that James Buchanan would be the secretary of state, with Henry A. Wise as attorney general. Yet the *New York Tribune* of 27 December reported that Cushing was the leading choice and explained, "Mr. Cushing is the foremost man, intellectually, in the Pierce ranks in New England. He has industry, force, clearness of thought, perspicacity [perception] of style . . . and polish of expression. Mr. Pierce needs such a man in the administration, in order to go easily and successfully to the close of his term." *The New York Herald* then reported in its 19 February 1853 edi-

tion that Cushing would be chosen for State, not attorney general. Six days later, after C. Edward Lester, an American correspondent for the London *Times,* went to Newburyport to interview Cushing, did the *Herald* finally report (on 25 February) that the cabinet selections were final, and that Cushing was to be attorney general.

Cushing as attorney general was in many ways overshadowed by several luminaries in Pierce's cabinet: among these men were Secretary of War Jefferson Davis, Secretary of State William Learned Marcy, and Secretary of the Interior Robert McClelland. Yet, biographer Henry Barrett Learned writes, "Certainly there was no more trusted man in the cabinet. Pierce held him in the highest regard. That he was of real assistance in keeping the cabinet together is a matter of authentic history." Under a congressional appropriation, the clerical staff in the office was improved to seven clerks, a general superintendent, and a messenger. Cushing delivered more opinions in his time as attorney general than any person up until 1909. Of the twenty-six volumes of the opinions of the attorneys general released between 1852 and 1909, encompassing all decisions from 1789 on, Cushing's filled three volumes (v, vi, and vii), covering more than two thousand pages of text. Cushing was the first attorney general to hold both his official and legal residence in Washington. Although he is historically considered one of the better attorneys general of the nineteenth century, he was not offered a spot in the new cabinet of President, and former Secretary of State, James Buchanan following the 1856 election, despite being of the same party. Instead, Cushing aided his successor, Jeremiah S. Black, to take over the office and returned to Newburyport. (An uncited article in the Cushing Papers relates that "even to this day Abolitionists remain to assert that Cushing would have been secretary of state [in Buchanan's cabinet] had not the South resented early speeches of his which condemned 'the peculiar institution' [of slavery].")

Nonetheless, three years later, as the winds of civil war began to envelop the nation, Cushing returned to politics when he served as permanent president of the National Democratic Convention, which met in Charleston, South Carolina, in April 1860 but broke up over the nomination of Stephen A. Douglas for president. By December of that year, with Southern states threatening to secede, President Buchanan, whose cabinet was coming apart over the slavery issue, sent Cushing to South Carolina to try to use his influence to head off a secession vote in that state. Cushing was unsuccessful, and within six months the country was at war.

During the Civil War, Cushing was sent by President Abraham Lincoln on several secret diplomatic missions. The construction of Southern ships in British ports during the war left bitter tensions between the United States and England after the war. To settle the growing dispute over American claims against the British, Cushing arranged a meeting between an old friend, Sir John Rose, and Secretary of State Hamilton Fish, to propose a conference on arbitration. A meeting was struck and, in 1871, Cushing appeared before the Geneva Tribunal of Arbitration acting as counsel for several interested parties. He was also counsel for the United States before a joint British–American council to settle a claim between the Hudson's Bay Company and the Puget Sound Company, from 1865–1870. Named by President Andrew Johnson as special minister to Colombia to try to negotiate a treaty allowing for the construction of a canal across the Panama isthmus, he also worked as counsel for the Mexican government.

As Cushing sailed for Geneva to appear before the arbitration commission, he learned that President Ulysses S. Grant had nominated him for chief justice of the U.S. Supreme Court. Grant's two earlier nominees, Senator Roscoe Conkling of New York and Attorney General George H. Williams, had either refused the nomination or had been turned down by the Senate. Cushing ran into immediate opposition. In a letter, General Benjamin F. Butler characterized the problem: "The sole ground of opposition was the fact that Mr. Cushing early in 1861

had written a harmless letter of introduction of a former clerk in his office, who belonged in the South and was going back there, to the President of the Confederate States. The letter, if it had been published when it was written, would never have caused a passing thought; but Mr. Cushing, sensitive to any ground for opposition, wrote to the President to withdraw his name, which was done." Grant then named Ohio attorney Morrison R. Waite, who was confirmed.

In his final years, Cushing served as the American minister to Spain. In 1877, he retired to Newburyport, where he died on 2 January 1879, fifteen days shy of his seventy-ninth birthday. Historian Henry Learned concludes, "Cushing left to posterity the most careful considerations on the historic development of the attorney-generalship up to his time. . . . They probably had something to help establish the attorney-general as the head of the department of justice in 1870. That Cushing perceived the need of some such organization is clear. Like [his predecessor, William] Wirt, Cushing determined to understand the structure and functions of his office, so far as the laws and practices of his predecessors could reveal them."

References: *The Attorney Generals of the United States, 1789–1985* (Washington, DC: Department of Justice, 1985), 46; Benetz, Margaret Diamond, ed., *The Cushing Reports: Ambassador Caleb Cushing's Confidential Diplomatic Reports to the United States Secretary of State, 1843–1844* (Salisbury, NC: Documentary Publications, 1976); Butler letter in Anson M. Lyman, "Caleb Cushing," *The Green Bag,* 24: 12 (December 1912), 555; Fuess, Claude Moore, *"Life of Caleb Cushing"* (New York: Harcourt, Brace; 2 vols., 1923), 1: 19, 2: 132–155, 392–393; Gara, Larry, *The Presidency of Franklin Pierce* (Lawrence: University Press of Kansas, 1991); Hodgson, Sister Mary Michael Catherine, "Caleb Cushing: Attorney General of the United States, 1853–1857" (Ph.D. dissertation, Catholic University of America, 1955), 5, 1–3, 66–117; Learned, Henry Barrett, *The Attorney General and the Cabinet* (Boston: Ginn & Company, 1909), 456; Lossing, Benson J., *Pictorial History of the Civil War in the United States of America* (Philadelphia: George W. Childs; 2 vols., 1866), 1: 19–20.

JEREMIAH SULLIVAN BLACK

1810–1883

Jeremiah Black may be better known among legal scholars for his two volumes of reports (called Black's Reports) written as the official reporter of the U.S. Supreme Court. Yet he was a learned lawyer who rose to become attorney general and secretary of state. Jeremiah S. Black, the son of Henry and Mary (née Sullivan) Black, was born near Stony Creek, Pennsylvania, on 10 January 1810. He attended irregularly opened schools in the area of Stony Creek, then finished his minuscule education at an academy near Bridgeport, Pennsylvania. He desired to study medicine, but under his father's urging instead turned to the law, studying under a local attorney, Chauncey Forward, and was admitted to the bar in 1830. (Black later married Forward's daughter.)

Shortly thereafter, Black was named as deputy attorney general for Somerset County and, in 1842, was appointed by Governor David R. Porter as presiding judge of the court of common pleas for the area including Somerset County. Nine years later, he was elected to the state Supreme Court, where he served from 1851 until 1857, three of those years as chief justice.

President James Buchanan, elected in 1856, desired not to include Attorney General Caleb Cushing in his cabinet; instead, he turned to Black, naming him as a compromise candidate to appease several Pennsylvania political factions. Black served as the chief law enforcement officer of the U.S. government from 4 March 1857 until 17 December 1860; during this tenure, he was forced to deal with the growing legal controversy over slavery, most notably the Fugitive Slave Act of 1850. As biographer Roy Nichols intones, "An incomplete picture of his life in Washington would be presented, however, if consideration were given only to his legal duties. As a member of Buchanan's cabinet he had to be politician and minister as well

as lawyer. As politician he aided Buchanan in keeping the Democratic Party solid. In this capacity his greatest task was his controversy with [Senator Stephen A.] Douglas when the latter attacked administration policy. . . . As cabinet minister, Black did his share in shaping the administration's Kansas policy, upholding the Lecompton Constitution as legally adopted, in the vain hope that statehood would bring an to an end the turmoil." With the election of Republican Abraham Lincoln to the presidency in November 1860, Black advised Buchanan to shore up government defenses in the Southern states in the event that the secession threatened by the Southern states came to pass. Objecting to this policy, Secretary of State Lewis Cass resigned. In a desperate move to have a legal adviser shape his foreign policy for the remainder of his term, Buchanan named Black to the vacant office. As secretary of state, serving only from 5 December 1860 until 4 March 1861, Black's main duty, according to historian John Findling, "was to instruct U.S. diplomatic representatives in Europe to do what they could to prevent European recognition of the Confederacy." On 30 June 1860, Supreme Court Justice Peter Vivian Daniel died. On 5 February 1861, a month before he was to leave office, Buchanan named Black to the vacant seat. The Senate, however, was not in the mood to confirm the nominee of a president whose term was almost over. On 21 February, the Senate refused to confirm his nomination, and it was left up to incoming President Abraham Lincoln to fill the seat.

Instead, in December 1861, broke and out of government, Black was named by the Court as the official court reporter. In those days, it was the duty of the official reporter to gather the opinions of the justices and publish them at their own cost, profiting from sales. He prepared two volumes, together known by legal scholars as Black's Reports, which are his most recognized works. During the war, he was an outspoken critic of Lincoln's policy to suspend the writ of *habeas corpus,* but he denounced the secession of the Southern states. In 1864, he went to Canada to meet with a cabinet colleague, former Secretary of the Interior Jacob Thompson, who was in Canada trying to raise awareness and funds for the Confederacy, to try and start peace talks, but Black was denounced. In 1868, he was set to be President Andrew Johnson's chief counsel in the president's impeachment trial before the U.S. Senate, but withdrew over a difference of opinion with the president. The following year, he was in a serious accident that deprived him of the use of his right arm.

In his last years, the former attorney general worked to revise the Pennsylvania state constitution, and represented Democrat Samuel J. Tilden before the Electoral Commission established to decide the 1876 election. Black died in York, Pennsylvania, on 19 August 1883, at the age of 73; he was buried in Prospect Hill Cemetery in York. Biographer Nichols writes of his legacy, "He defended Christianity, he defended Buchanan, he defended Tilden before the Electoral Commission . . . he lived and died a defender of the Constitution, the Union, and the Ten Commandments."

References: The Attorney Generals of the United States, 1789–1985 (Washington, DC: Department of Justice, 1985), 48; Black, Chauncey F., ed., *Jeremiah S. Black's Essays and Speeches* (New York: D. Appleton, 1885); Brigance, William N., *Jeremiah Sullivan Black* (Philadelphia: University of Pennsylvania Press, 1934); Clayton, Mary Black, *Reminiscences of Jeremiah Sullivan Black* (St. Louis: Christian Publishing, 1887); Findling, John E., *Dictionary of American Diplomatic History* (Westport, CT: Greenwood, 1989), 65; "Historical Notes on the last four months of Buchanan's Administration, Signed J. S. Black" (unpublished Black manuscript), Box 77, Jeremiah S. Black Papers, Library of Congress; Nichols, Roy F., "Black, Jeremiah Sullivan," in *DAB* 2: 310–312; Robb, Arthur, "Biographical Sketches of the Attorneys General" (Unpublished essay DOJ, Washington, DC, 1946), 31.

EDWIN MCMASTERS STANTON
1814–1869

Edwin Stanton is remembered best for his work as secretary of war for five years under President Abraham Lincoln and for two further years under Andrew Johnson. Yet Edwin McMasters Stanton served as attorney general in the last hectic, chaotic months of the James Buchanan administration, as Southern states seceded from the Union and the nation readied itself for a bloody civil war. Born on 19 December 1814 in Steubenville, Ohio, Stanton was the first of four children of David and Lucy (née Norman) Stanton, both religious Methodists. When he was ten, Edwin suffered from an attack of asthma and for the rest of his life his health was so precarious from the condition that he had to fight for each breath. David Stanton died less than two weeks after his son's thirteenth birthday, and the young Edwin was apprenticed to James Turnbell, a bookseller, who taught Stanton a love of books while allowing him to attend a prestigious Latin School.

It was there that Stanton studied the law and, after three years of intense study, was admitted to the Ohio bar in 1836. He began a practice in Cadiz, the seat of Harrison County. The following years he was elected prosecuting attorney of the county, serving until 1839. During this period he also assembled the official opinions of the Ohio Supreme Court, issuing them in volumes 11, 12 and 13 of the Court reports. He then returned to private practice, moving to Steubenville to become the law partner of U.S. Senator-elect Benjamin Tappan. He practiced there until 1847, when he moved to Pittsburgh, Pennsylvania. Two years later, he was named as official counsel for the state of Pennsylvania, serving until 1856. Two years later, he was named by President James Buchanan as special U.S. counsel on disputed California land grant cases. It was the success of his arguments in these cases, as well as the notice of resigning Attorney General Jeremiah Sullivan Black, which led Black to ask President Buchanan to name Stanton to succeed him as attorney general in the closing days of the Buchanan administration as Black moved over to serve as secretary of state. Buchanan named Stanton as attorney general on 20 December 1860, and he served until 3 March 1861, a term of seventy-two days. In this period, Stanton issued a mere ten opinions. When Lincoln came into office, Stanton left. Biographer Arthur Robb notes, Stanton mocked "the imbecility of this administration."

When Secretary of War Simon Cameron recommended at the end of 1861 that freed slaves be armed to fight for the Union, a proposal that Lincoln dismissed, Cameron left the cabinet and President Lincoln turned to Stanton to fill the position. His nomination was confirmed on 15 January 1862, and he took over the War Office five days later. In his six years in the post, according to department historian William Bell, Stanton "persuaded Congress that the government should assume selective control over the railroads and telegraph; prevailed upon the president to release political prisoners in military custody and transfer control over extraordinary arrests from the State to the War Department; and established a Bureau of Colored Troops." Stanton has been dubbed "the great War Secretary."

Following the assassination of Abraham Lincoln, President Andrew Johnson requested that Stanton stay on in the new administration. However, as time went on, the objectives of the president and his secretary seemed to diverge. At one point, Stanton confided to Congressman George S. Boutwell of Massachusetts that he felt Johnson was acting behind his back as far as military orders were concerned, and that he would work with Congress closely to circumvent these orders. Sometime in March 1866, the president met with Richard Taylor, son of former President Zachary Taylor and a general in the Confederate army during the war.

Taylor informed Johnson that Stanton "was in close alliance with his [the president's] enemies in Congress, and constantly betraying him." Taylor recommended that Stanton be removed, and he reported that Johnson agreed. Yet Johnson did not act immediately. Congress, however, got wind of the possible firing and passed the controversial Tenure of Office Act in response. The legislation banned the president from removing a government official who had received Senate approval, without further consent to dismiss. Ironically, Stanton advised Johnson that the enactment was unconstitutional and he should veto it; Johnson did, but was overridden in Congress.

Apparently, Johnson was waiting for Stanton to resign rather than being forced to fire him, "by every mode short of an expressed request that he resign." By refusing to remove Stanton himself, noted biographer Alexander Howard Meneely, the president "virtually gave his opponents a seat in the cabinet." By the beginning of August 1867, Johnson felt that Stanton was undermining his reconstruction policy. He then wrote to Stanton, "Sir: Public considerations of a high character constrain me to say that your resignation as Secretary of War will be accepted." Stanton replied, "Sir: Your note of this day has been received, stating that public considerations of a high character constrain you to say that my resignation as Secretary of War will be accepted. In reply, I have the honor to say that public considerations of a high character, which alone have induced me to continue at the head of this Department, constrain me not to resign the office of the Secretary of War before the next meeting of Congress." Johnson felt his power to fire one of his cabinet ministers was being challenged and fired off another letter one week later: "Sir: By virtue of the power and authority vested in me as President by the Constitution and laws of the United States, you are hereby suspended from office as Secretary of War, and will cease to exercise any and all functions pertaining to the same." General Ulysses S. Grant agreed to step in as secretary of war *ad interim* on that same date.

Stanton replied to Johnson, "Under a sense of duty I am compelled to deny your right, under the Constitution, and laws of the United States, without the advice and consent of the Senate, and without legal cause, to suspend me from office as Secretary of War, or the exercise of any or all functions pertaining to the same, or without such advice and consent to compel me to transfer to any person the records, books, papers, and public property in my custody as Secretary. But inasmuch as the General commanding the armies of the United States has been appointed *ad interim* and has notified me that he has accepted the appointment, I have no alternative but to submit, under protest, to superior force." During the next five months Grant served uncomfortably as a member of the cabinet, but when the Senate refused to concur in Stanton's removal Grant stepped aside. Johnson then dismissed Stanton outright, on 21 February 1868, but Stanton was determined to "continue in possession [of the office] until expelled by force." When Johnson named General Lorenzo Thomas as the secretary *ad interim,* Stanton ordered his arrest. He had guards placed outside of his office, where he remained day and night.

The fight over whether the president could remove Stanton led to a constitutional fight never before seen. The House established articles of impeachment, and the Senate held a trial in the first, and so far only, instance of its kind in American history. When the Republicans in Congress failed to impeach by one vote on 26 May 1868, Stanton relinquished the War Office. The entire ordeal had severely sapped his strength, and he spent much of the rest of the year resting.

In 1869, although ill, Stanton resumed the practice of law. He was gratified that his friend Ulysses S. Grant was elected president. On 31 January 1870, Supreme Court Justice Robert C. Grier resigned from the court. It was not until 20 December that President Grant nominated a replacement—the sickly Edwin Stanton. His nomination was confirmed that same day. On 24 December, just one day before he was to take the seat that he had fought all of his life to get, Stan-

ton succumbed, presumably to the asthma that had caused him such distress for much of his life. He was just five days past his fifty-fourth birthday; he was interred in Oak Hill Cemetery in Washington, D.C.

References: Bell, William Gardner, *Secretaries of War and Secretaries of the Army: Portraits and Biographical Sketches* (Washington, DC: U.S. Army Center of Military History, 1982), 72; Crenson, Gus Arthur, "Andrew Johnson and Edwin M. Stanton: A Study in Personalities, 1866–1868" (Ph.D. dissertation, Georgetown University, 1949); Flower, Frank A., *Edwin McMasters Stanton: The Autocrat of Rebellion, Emancipation and Reconstruction* (Akron, Ohio: Saalfied Publishing, 1905); Gorham, George C., *The Life and Public Services of Edwin M. Stanton* (Boston and New York: Houghton, Mifflin, 1899); Johnson-Stanton correspondence in Edward McPherson, *A Political Manual for 1868* (Washington, DC: Philp & Solomons, 1868), 261–264; Meneely, Alexander Howard, "Stanton, Edwin McMasters," in *DAB* 9: 520; Robb, Arthur, 'Biographical Sketches of the Attorneys General" (unpublished essay, DOJ, Washington, DC, 1946), 8; Taylor, Richard, *Destruction and Reconstruction* (New York: D. Appleton & Co., 1879), 252.

EDWARD BATES
1793–1869

Edward Bates served as the twenty-sixth attorney general, in the administration of Abraham Lincoln, the first of two men to hold the office during the Civil War. His tenure was marked by serious disagreement with administration policy over civil rights enforcement. Edward Bates was born on 4 September 1793 in Goochland County, west of Richmond, Virginia, the son and youngest of twelve children of Thomas Fleming Bates, a planter and merchant who died when Edward was a young boy, and Caroline Matilda (née Woodson) Bates. His older brothers aided much of his education, including time at the Charlotte Hall Academy in Maryland. A relative, James Pleasants, a member of Congress and former governor of Virginia, obtained for him an appointment as a midshipman in the Navy, but his mother's Quaker principles precluded him from attending. Edward Bates's brother, Frederick Bates, who later served as the territorial governor of the Louisiana Territory and Missouri Territory, invited his brother to join him in Missouri, and Bates moved to St. Louis in 1814. He studied law and was admitted to the bar in 1816.

In 1818, Bates was named as the circuit prosecuting attorney for Missouri, then served to help draft the state constitution in 1820. With the formation of the new state he was named attorney general, serving until 1824, then as U.S. attorney for Missouri, serving from 1824 to 1826. In 1823, he married Julia Coalter, who bore him seventeen children. Bates served a single term in the U.S. House of Representatives, 1827–1829, and then as a member of the State Senate, 1830. He then retired to his law practice. A leader in the state among Whigs, Bates was offered the secretaryship of war by President Millard Fillmore in 1850. He did serve for a short period as the judge of the Land Court in St. Louis from 1850 to 1853 and presided over the Whig National Convention in 1856.

Although he lived in Missouri, a slave state, Bates disliked the practice and, as civil war approached, became an outspoken opponent of secession. He joined the infant Republican Party, and in 1860 a Bates for President campaign was launched. His appeal seemed irresistible: a slave-state Whig who could be considered a moderate on the issue. At the Republican National Convention in Chicago, however, he received few votes against former Congressman Abraham Lincoln, who ultimately won the nomination and the election. Historian Thomas Marshall relates that Lincoln offered Bates a cabinet position *before* the election; Bates desired State, which ultimately went to William H. Seward. A member of Lincoln's administration, L. E. Chittenden, wrote in 1891, "It was quickly known [after the election] that Mr. Lincoln would call into his cabinet representative men like Senators Seward, Chase, and

Cameron, who would unite the country if they did not constitute a united cabinet, and that he would offer one or two places to true men from the disloyal states." Because he was considered a Virginian, Bates was probably one of these two men almost from the start of cabinet considerations. In his diary for 16 December 1860, Bates inscribed, "Last Thursday I recd. [received] a message from Mr. Lincoln to the effect that he would come down the next day to St. Louis, to see and consult me, about some points connected with the formation of his Cabinet. I thought I saw an unfitness in *his coming to see me* [Bates's emphasis], and that I *ought to go to him* [Bates's emphasis], as soon as his wish to see me was known. Accordingly, I had him telegraphed that I would wait on him Saturday. . . . I found him free in his communications and candid in his manner. He assured me that from the time of his nomination, his determination was, in case of success, to invite me into the Cabinet—and, in fact, was complimentary as to say that my participation in the administration, he considered necessary to its complete success." After Lincoln offered him State, Bates writes, "I told Mr. L[incoln] with all frankness, that if peace and order prevailed in the country, and the Government could now be carried on quietly, I would decline a place in the Cabinet, as I did in 1850—and for the same reasons. . . . He replied that he never intended to offer me either of the Departments deemed laborious, as involving a great many details of administrative business—That, in short, I must be either Sec.y. of State or Att.y. Gen.l." In the end, Bates took the latter position, and, on 5 March 1861, his nomination was confirmed by the Senate and he was sworn in that same day, making him the first cabinet officer in American history from west of the Missouri River.

In his three years and nearly nine months as attorney general, Bates argued constantly with the president, contending that many of Lincoln's war policies were infringing on the constitutional rights of the American people. He argued, through both his official opinions and his writings, that blacks could legally be considered citizens under the Constitution, even with the Supreme Court's *Dred Scott* decision. Constantly in the minority on the issue of constitutional rights inside the Lincoln cabinet, he finally gave up and resigned on 24 November 1864, returning home to St. Louis. He lived there only four and half years, dying on 25 March 1869 at the age of 75. He was buried in the Bellefontaine Cemetery in St. Louis.

References: The Attorney Generals of the United States, 1789–1985 (Washington, DC: Department of Justice, 1985), 52; Beale, Howard K., "The Diary of Edward Bates, 1859–1866," *Annual Report of the American Historical Association for the Year 1930* (Washington, DC: GPO; 4 vols., 1933), 6: xi–xiii, 164–179; Chittenden, L. E., *Recollections of President Lincoln and His Administration* (New York: Harper & Brothers, 1891), 79–83; Lehman, F. W., "Edward Bates and the Test Oath," *Missouri Historical Society Collections,* 4 (1923), 389–401.

JAMES SPEED
1812–1887

A personal adviser to President Abraham Lincoln about Kentucky during the early portion of the Civil War, James Speed was selected as Lincoln's attorney general in 1864 following the resignation of Edward Bates. The son of John Speed and his wife Lucy Gilmer (née Fry), James Speed was born on his father's farm, Farmington, in Jefferson County, Kentucky, about five miles from Louisville, on 11 March 1812. He attended St. Joseph's College in Bardstown and Transylvania University in Lexington, studying law at the latter, and was admitted to the bar in 1833. He then practiced at Louisville until 1847.

In 1847, Speed was elected to the state legislature, but left after only one term because he was strongly against slavery. He then wrote a series of letters to the *Louisville Courier* denouncing slavery, a position that seemed, in a slave state, to limit any political

advancement. From 1856 until 1858, Speed was a law professor at the University of Louisville. When the storm clouds of civil war began to appear, he stood tall in his denunciation of any secessionist moves by his state from the Union. Elected as a state senator in 1861 (serving until 1863), he remained an uncompromising Unionist and antislavery advocate.

When Speed left the State Senate in July 1863, he went to Washington. His older brother, Joshua Fry Speed, was a lifelong friend of President Abraham Lincoln, and within a few months James Speed was a close adviser to the president. On 24 November 1864, shortly after Lincoln was reelected, Attorney General Edward Bates resigned. Lincoln nominated Speed to the office, and he was quickly confirmed, serving from 2 December 1864 until 17 July 1866. He remained through a good portion of the term of President Andrew Johnson. In one of his opinions, he wrote simply to the president, "Sir: I am of the opinion that the persons charged with the murder of the President of the United States can be rightfully tried by a military court." Later in life, he refused to disclose whether or not he had delivered an appeal for the life of conspirator Mary Surratt to President Johnson. While Lincoln was alive, Speed adhered to the president's moderation toward the South; with Lincoln's death, however, Speed moved closer to the radicals. During the Johnson administration, Senator Charles Sumner of Massachusetts described him as "the best of the Cabinet." Nonetheless, Speed quickly became disenchanted with the new president's policy toward the Southern states. Favoring passage of the Fourteenth Amendment, Speed resigned as attorney general on 17 July 1866 when President Johnson vetoed the Freedmen's Bureau bill for the second time (the first had been that 19 February).

Speed lived twenty-one years after leaving the cabinet, and in that time he practiced law in Louisville and served as a law professor. He died in Louisville on 25 June 1887 at the age of 75 and was buried in Cave Hill Cemetery in Louisville. Abraham Lincoln once said of Speed, "[He is] an honest man and a gentleman, and one of those well-poised men, not too common here, who are not spoiled by big office."

References: Benson, Godfrey Rathbone, Baron Charnwood, *Abraham Lincoln* (New York: Henry Holt, 1917), 404; Cochran, Michael T., "Speed, James," in Patricia L. Faust, ed., *Historical Times Illustrated Encyclopedia of the Civil War* (New York: Harper & Row, 1986), 708; Coulter, E. Merton, "Speed, James," in *DAB* 9: 440–441; Hall, Benjamin F., et al., comps., *Official Opinions of the Attorneys General of the United States* (Washington, DC: Robert Farnham; 43 vols., plus annual updates, 1852–1996), 11: 215 (Speed opinion); Speed, James, *James Speed: A Personality* (Louisville, KY: J. P. Morton, 1914).

HENRY STANBERY
1803–1881

Henry Stanbery resigned as the twenty-eighth attorney general to defend President Andrew Johnson before the Senate during a historic impeachment trial. Successful in the effort, he was then denied reappointment as attorney general, as well as a seat on the U.S. Supreme Court. Henry Stanbery, the son of Dr. Jonas Stanbery, a New York physician, and Ann Lucy (née Seaman) Stanbery, was born in New York City on 20 February 1803. When he was eleven his family moved to Ohio and settled in the town of Zanesville. Henry Stanbery graduated from Washington College in Pennsylvania, then studied law and was admitted to the Ohio bar. He joined a law practice in Lancaster, Ohio, with Thomas Ewing, an Ohio attorney who later served as secretary of the treasury (1841) and secretary of the interior (1849–1850). In 1846, Stanbery was appointed as Ohio's first state attorney general, and during his five-year term he noted that the legal opinions he provided to state officials and county prosecutors "took more time than any of his responsibilities." During his term, the General Assembly made the office an elected one, and he left the post at the end of the term in April 1851. In 1853, he moved to Cincinnati and practiced there until 1866. He was counsel in a number of important Supreme Court decisions, including the landmark case *Ex parte Milligan*.

With the resignation of Attorney General James Speed on 17 July 1866, President Andrew Johnson offered the post to Stanbery, who accepted, serving from that date until 12 March 1868. During that period, little is reported on Stanbery's activities beyond the fact that he was a staunch supporter of President Johnson. Writes Chief Justice of the Supreme Court William H. Rehnquist, "In June [1867] Attorney General Henry Stanbery . . . presented to the cabinet for discussion opinions he had prepared as to the authority of the military commanders under the Reconstruction Acts. These opinions took a narrow view of the powers conferred on the commanders, limiting their authority to remove state officials, and holding that voter registrars could not look behind the statements made in the loyalty oath even if they believed the oath to be perjurious. [Secretary of War Edwin] Stanton expressed opposition to these views in Cabinet, but Johnson had them sent to the military commanders with the support of the rest of his Cabinet." Following the death of Supreme Court Justice John Catron on 30 May 1865, President Johnson nominated Stanbery for the vacant seat, but the Senate, angered at Johnson's response to the Republicans on Reconstruction, refused even to act on the nomination.

In March 1867, Congress, led by Radical Republicans, began to pass a series of measures to deal the heavy hand of Reconstruction on the defeated Southern states. These included instituting military rule and enacting a succession of edicts restricting presidential power—including the Tenure of Office Act, passed so that Secretary of War Stanton, a friend of the Republicans, could not be removed from office without Senate approval. When Johnson removed Stanton from office anyway, the House voted articles of impeachment and Johnson was tried in the Senate. Stanbery resigned as attorney general to become the president's chief counsel. Throughout the trial, which began on 30 March, Stanbery was ably assisted by former Supreme Court Justice Benjamin Robbins Curtis, who had dissented in the landmark *Dred Scott* decision; William Evarts (who would later replace Stanbery as attorney general and go on to serve as secretary of state); and attorney Thomas Nelson of Tennessee. Johnson was tried by the Senate in the spring of 1868, and Stanbery, who was so ill that by his doctors had ordered him to bed, rose in the Senate chamber to make his final arguments to the senators. The Senate failed to get the two-thirds vote required for conviction. The day after being cleared, Johnson then renominated Stanbery to be his attorney general for a second time, but the Senate voted down the nomination on 2 June of that same year, 11–29. Stanbery then retired to Cincinnati, where he resumed the practice of law until his eyesight began to fail about 1878. He died in New York City on 26 June 1881 at the age of 78 and was buried in Cincinnati.

References: *The Attorney Generals of the United States, 1789–1985* (Washington, DC: Department of Justice, 1985), 56; Meneely, Alexander Howard, "Stanbery, Henry," in *DAB* 9: 498–499; Rehnquist, William H., *Grand Inquests: The Historic Impeachments of Justice Samuel Chase and President Andrew Johnson* (New York: William Morrow, 1992), 211, 222, 225; Robb, Arthur, "Biographical Sketches of the Attorneys General" (Unpublished essay DOJ, Washington, DC, 1946), 36; *Trial of Andrew Johnson, President of the United States, Before the Senate of the United States, on Impeachment by the House of Representatives for High Crimes and Misdemeanors. Edited by Benjamin Perley Poore* (Washington, DC: GPO; 3 vols., 1868).

WILLIAM MAXWELL EVARTS
1818–1901

Historian William Henry Smith wrote of the man who served as the twenty-ninth attorney general a quarter century after his death, "William M. Evarts was one of the great lawyers of the country." A grandson of Roger Sherman, signer of the Declaration of Independence and the Articles of Confederation, and a member of the Constitutional Convention, Evarts was born in Boston, Massachusetts, on 6 February 1818. He was the son of Jeremiah Evarts, a noted religious writer, and Mehitabel (née Sherman) Evarts. William Evarts attended the prestigious Boston Latin School, then graduated from Yale College in 1833. (Some of his classmates of that graduating class include Chief Justice Morrison Remick Waite, Attorney General Edwards Pierrepont, and Samuel J. Tilden.) Evarts studied law in the office of Horace Everett in Windsor, Vermont, then attended Harvard Law School for one year, joining the law office of Daniel Lord in New York City in 1839. Two years later, he was formally admitted to the bar.

Starting in 1849, for a three year term, Evarts served as the assistant U.S. district attorney for the southern district of New York. Afterwards, he returned to the private practice of the law. A Whig and then a Republican in politics, he was strongly against slavery and spoke out against it on many occasions. Yet in 1868, when President Andrew Johnson was impeached on grounds of violating the law by firing Secretary of War Edwin Stanton, Evarts stepped forward to help the president who had vetoed the Freedmen's Bureau bill twice and had opposed passage of the Fourteenth Amendment. He was joined in his defense of the president before the Senate by former Attorney General Henry Stanbery, who had resigned his post just to aid the embattled executive.

In the period between Stanbery's resignation and the Senate confirmation of his successor, Orville Hickman Browning, the secretary of the interior, served as attorney general *ad interim* from 13 March 1868 until 20 June of that same year. His official opinions, of which their are a few, are contained in volume 12 of the *Official Opinions of the Attorneys General of the United States.*

It was the work of Evarts, Stanbery, and others who persuaded the Senate not to convict on the three articles of impeachment. With the end of the trial, it seemed that Evarts would return to his private practice, particularly when Johnson renominated Stanbery as his attorney general. However, Stanbery was defeated, and the president asked his other counsel, Benjamin Robbins Curtis, to take the position, but Curtis responded that "the first and most desirable of all places" for a attorney to be was "the front of the bar in a great city" and refused. Secretary of State William Seward then recommended Evarts. And although Evarts publicly did not approve of the president's policies (even though he defended him), Evarts was encouraged to take the appointment by some Republicans. He was nominated on 20 June 1868; but certain Republicans who desired to reject any Johnson appointee held out against confirmation. *The Sun* of New York related, "Mr. Evarts was defended by Messrs. [Roscoe] Conkling [of New York], [Lyman] Trumbull [of Illinois], and others. [John Milton] Thayer [of Maine] stated that had he known that Senators who were opposed to Mr. Stanbery would now favor Mr. Evarts, he and the others would have secured the nomination of Mr. Stanbery, for there was no argument made against one not equally good against the other." In the end, Evarts was confirmed by a vote of 29–5 on 16 July. Stanbery wrote to the president that Evarts had "put [Sen. George Sewell] Boutwell [of Maine] in the clouds, and Butler in the gutter." Evarts's cousin, Ebenezer Rockwood Hoar, however, wrote to him, "Your defense of the President could not be avoided, when he applied to you to undertake it; and with a little regret that you should be mixed up with it, it was very gratifying to see you fill so conspicuous a place with such masterly ability. Your position could be vindicated before angels and man. Every criminal has a right to the aid of counsel on his trial, and if defended at all, to be ably defended. It is the right even of the thief and the counterfeiter. But when, after the acquittal, the grateful client invites his counsel to go into partnership with him, some other considerations seem to apply. Well . . . prevent all the mischief you can. Depend on the judgment and sense of honor of yourself more than of your associates in the Cabinet, and God send you a good deliverance!" Serving from 23 July 1868 until the close of the Johnson administration on 4 March 1869, a period of eight months, Evarts merely coped with the position he had taken. Writes biographer Brainerd Dyer, "Evarts was busy for the most part with routine matters. He attended cabinet meetings, though not with great regularity; he gave official opinions advising the President and heads of departments in relation to their official duties, and expounding the Constitution, treaties, and laws of the country; he conducted in person many of the cases before the Supreme Court to which the United States was a party and directed the conduct of cases in which the government had an interest in every part of the country."

In 1876, Evarts served as chief counsel for the Republican Party during the election controversy between Republican Rutherford B. Hayes and Democrat Samuel Tilden, Evarts's classmate. Hayes's selection as president opened the door to Evarts being named as secretary of state in the new administration. In Hayes's diary, there are notes that show that Evarts was his selection for state from the start. However, he did write, "The chief disappointment among the influential men of the party was with Conkling, Blaine, Cameron, Logan, and their followers. They were very bitter. The opposition was chiefly to Evarts, [David McKendree] Key [selected as Postmaster General] and especially [Carl] Schurz [named as Secretary of the Interior]." Despite this opposition, Evarts was confirmed and served during the entire four years of Hayes's administration. Along with Secretary of the Treasury John Sherman and Schurz, he was considered one of the "big three" in the Hayes cabinet.

As secretary of state, Evarts received an office vastly different from that which had confronted his predecessor, Hamilton Fish. Writes Hayes biographer Kenneth Davison, "When he turned over his office to Evarts . . . the new Secretary inherited a smooth and efficiently run department based upon a major reorganization effected in 1870 and eight years of meticulous management by Fish." Historian Michael Devine adds, "In the position, Evarts opposed attempts by a French company to construct a canal across Panama but failed in his efforts to secure a new agreement to replace the Clayton-Bulwer Treaty of 1850. He took a strong stand to defend U.S. lives and property during a turbulent revolution in Mexico, although the administration eventually recognized and established friendly relations with the rebel government headed by Porfirio Diaz. His efforts led to the improvement of the consular reporting system and the negotiation of treaties with China to regulate commerce and immigration." After he left office in March 1881, Evarts served as delegate to the Paris Monetary Conference. In 1885, he was elected to the U.S. Senate and served a single term until leaving office in 1891.

In his final years, Evarts went blind and could no longer practice the law. He died on 28 February 1901, three weeks after his eighty-third birthday, and was buried in Ascutney Cemetery in Windsor, Vermont. Twice he had been considered to be named as Chief Justice of the U.S. Supreme Court—in 1864, upon the death of Roger B. Taney, and in 1874 when his friend and classmate, Morrison Waite, was selected instead. He is uniquely remembered for his work in the famed case of *Hepburn v. Griswold* `(1870) and in the Legal Tender Case and for his service on the Geneva Arbitration committee in 1871–1872. His great-grandson, Archibald Cox, became famous as the first of three special investigators looking into the Watergate burglary in 1972–1973.

See also Orville Hickman Browning

References: "Argument in the United States Supreme Court, on Behalf of the Government, in Sherman Evarts, ed. *Hepburn v. Griswold* (Legal Tender Case)," in *Arguments and Speeches of William, Maxwell Evarts* (New York: Macmillan; 3 vols., 1919), 1: 526–535; Barrows, Chester L., *William M. Evarts* (Chapel Hill: University of North Carolina Press, 1941); Davison, Kenneth E., *The Presidency of Rutherford B. Hayes* (Westport, CT: Greenwood, 1972), 194; Devine, Michael J., "Evarts, William Maxwell," in Bruce W. Jentleson and Thomas G. Paterson, senior eds., *Encyclopedia of U.S. Foreign Relations* (New York: Oxford University Press; 4 vols., 1997), 1: 123; Dyer, Brainerd, *The Public Career of William M. Evarts* (Berkeley: University of California Press, 1933), 102–103; Findling, John E., *Dictionary of American Diplomatic History* (Westport, CT: Greenwood, 1989), 179; Hicks, Frederick C., "Evarts, William Maxwell," in *DAB* 3: 215–218; Millington, Herbert, *American Diplomacy and the War of the Pacific* (New York: Columbia University Press, 1948); Smith, William Henry, *History of the Cabinet of the United States of America, From President Washington to President Coolidge* (Baltimore: Industrial Printing, 1925), 129.

EBENEZER ROCKWOOD HOAR
1816–1895

Scion of a famous nineteenth-century American family, Ebenezer Hoar was the last attorney general to serve in the Office of Attorney General and the first in the Department of Justice, as well as being the first of five attorneys general to serve during the two terms of President Ulysses S. Grant. Born in Concord, Massachusetts, on 21 February 1816, he was the son of Samuel Hoar and Sarah (née Sherman) Hoar, the daughter of American patriot Roger Sherman. His brother was politician George Frisbie Hoar, and his cousin, through his mother, was the man he would succeed as attorney general, William M. Evarts. Ebenezer Hoar graduated from

Harvard College in 1835, studied law in the office of his father and finished his legal education at Harvard Law School, receiving a law degree in 1839. The following year, he became interested in politics and served as a delegate to a Whig "young men's" convention in Massachusetts. In 1845, he signed, with Henry Wilson (later, ironically, to serve as vice-president in the Grant administration with Hoar), a petition calling for "the extinction of slavery on the American continent." Because of his views on slavery, Hoar left the Whig Party in 1848 and joined first the Free Soil Party, an abolitionist entity, and eventually the Republican Party. In 1849, Hoar was named as a judge of common pleas in Massachusetts, serving until 1855. In 1859 he began a ten-year tenure as an associate justice on the Supreme Court of Massachusetts.

Hoar's cousin, William Evarts, served as attorney general in the waning months of the administration of Andrew Johnson; after the election of General Ulysses S Grant as president in 1868, however, Evarts was thrown aside for a new man in the attorney general position. Hoar biographers Moorfield Storey and Edward Emerson intone, "In forming his Cabinet, the new President had offered the portfolio of the Interior to [Senator] George S. Boutwell [of Massachusetts], who declined it; but when he did so the President suggested that he might appoint an Attorney-General from Massachusetts. In reply to this suggestion Boutwell named Judge Hoar and advised his appointment. Senator [George] Hoar says that the same suggestion from another eminent Massachusetts man who was not in Congress had more weight. This gentleman suggested Judge [Nathan] Clifford, which did not interest General Grant, and then Judge Hoar. The President replied with great earnestness and emphasis, 'I know all about Judge Hoar!' He had met him, I think, on two occasions, and had sat next to him at dinner, and had a very hearty and cordial, though brief, acquaintance with him. The result was that Judge Hoar's name was sent in." Hoar was confirmed and served until 8 July 1870. During his tenure, he oversaw the congressional enactment that changed the Office

of the Attorney General to that of the Department of Justice, with the office officially opening just a week before Hoar left office. Department historian calls Hoar "one of the most effective department heads." Following the death of Associate Justice John Catron on 30 May 1865, Congress abolished his seat so as to deny President Andrew Johnson a chance to fill the vacancy. In 1869, however, after Johnson left office, they reestablished the seat, and President Ulysses S. Grant named Hoar to the seat on 15 December 1869. Hoar was popular, but he had angered many senators when he demanded as attorney general that candidates for judicial posts be chosen on the basis of merit and not patronage (some sources claim that the reason was that Hoar did not live in the area that his seat on the court would represent). For this insult against the right of senators to name patrons to judicial offices, the Senate refused to confirm Hoar, defeating his nomination on 3 February 1870 by a 24–33 vote. Senator Simon Cameron of Pennsylvania, a patronage king, said, "What could you expect from a man who had snubbed seventy senators!" Emboldened, some Southern senators approached the president and asked that Hoar be replaced with a "man from the south"; angered, Hoar resigned on 23 June 1870, to take effect 8 July. He remained friendly with Grant and accepted from the president a year after he left the Justice Department an appointment as a member of the commission that decided the Alabama Claims against Great Britain arising from the Civil War.

In the last quarter-century of his life, Hoar served a single term in Congress (1873–1875), alongside his brother, George. He ran an unsuccessful campaign for a House seat in 1876, then retired from politics altogether, retaining his law practice. Hoar died in Concord on 31 January 1895, three weeks shy of his seventy-ninth birthday.

References: *The Attorney Generals of the United States, 1789-1985* (Washington, DC: Department of Justice, 1985), 60; Hoar, George Frisbie, *Autobiography of Seventy Years* (New York: Scribner's;

2 vols., 1903); Hoar, William Stewart, *Branches of a Family Tree: The Hoar Ancestry* (Vancouver, Canada: Tangled Roots, 1986); Martin, Edward Winslow, *The New Administration; Containing Complete and Authentic Biographies of Grant and His Cabinet* (New York: George S. Wilcox, 1869), 150–155; Sparks, Bernice Ruth Hoare, *William and Mary Hoare: British-American Families* (Rockville, MD: Aquarius, 1974); Storey, Moorfield; and Edward W. Emerson, *Ebenezer Rockwood Hoar: A Memoir* (Boston: Houghton Mifflin, 1911), 163.

Amos Tappan Akerman
1821–1880

At a time when the freed slaves looked toward the United States government for a helping hand in combating the terror of the Ku Klux Klan, Attorney General Amos Akerman, almost alone, used the newly-enacted laws of Congress and amendments to the Constitution to aid them. Akerman, the son of Benjamin Akerman, a surveyor, and Olive (née Meloon) Akerman, was born in Portsmouth, New Hampshire, on 23 February 1821. He attended the prestigious Phillips Exeter Academy in New Hampshire, then graduated from Dartmouth College in 1842. Moving to Murphreesboro, North Carolina, he began work as a teacher, continuing in Richmond, Virginia, and Peoria, Illinois.

In 1845, Akerman moved to Savannah, Georgia, where be befriended attorney John McPherson Berrien, who had served in the Polk administration as attorney general. After working for a time as a tutor to Berrien's children and studying law under Berrien, Akerman opened a law practice in Clarksville, Georgia, and worked in it until 1860. Although at first he was an opponent of secession, he realized the futility of opposing it and joined the Confederate army, serving first under General Robert Toombs and later in the quartermaster's department, seeing action in several battles. An adoptive Southerner with Northern sympathies, following the war he changed his ideas, opposed slavery, and served as a member to the state constitutional convention in 1868. A year later, he was named as U.S. district attorney for the state of Georgia.

On 23 June 1870, Attorney General Ebenezer R. Hoar resigned after some disagreements with the Grant administration. Grant named Akerman, who was quickly confirmed and took office on 8 July, serving as the first appointee under the Department of Justice Act, enacted the previous month which had established the Justice department as a legal entity. A history of the department relates, "It was Akerman who organized the new department and launched it on its course. His task was made difficult by the fact that, while his official duties were defined and centralized, departmental facilities were not. The staff were scattered in various buildings in many parts of Washington. . . . Upon his appointment, Akerman was plunged into the Credit Mobilier controversy, a scandal of the Grant administration. His opinions supporting the government's position earned him the enmity of entrenched financial interests with powerful friends in Congress." Akerman spent much of his tenure, a total of eighteen months, cracking down on the railroad magnates (namely, Jay Gould and Henry Edwards Huntington). However, much of his time in office was dedicated to fighting the power of the Ku Klux Klan; in 1871, he persuaded the president to dispatch military troops to nine counties in South Carolina, suspend the writ of *habeas corpus,* and seize Klan members *en masse,* resulting in more than two thousand arrests. Akerman in fact toured Northern cities, denouncing the Klan in speeches. His outspokenness on the subject made him the most unpopular member of the cabinet among his colleagues. Secretary of State Hamilton Fish wrote that Akerman had the Klan "on the brain. It has got to be a bore to listen twice a week to this thing." Pressured by his friends to put a stop to Akerman's work, on 13 December 1871 Grant wrote to Akerman, in a letter marked "Confidential": "Circumstances convince me that a change in the office you now hold is desirable, considering the best interests of the government, and I there ask [for] your resignation. In doing so, however, I wish to express my appreciation of the zeal, integrity, and industry you have shown in the performance of all of your duties and the confidence I feel personally by tendering to you the Florida Judgeship, now vacant, or that of Texas. Should any foreign mission at my disposal without a removal for the purpose of making a vacancy, better suit your tastes, I would gladly testify my appreciation in that way. My personal regard for you is such that I could not bring myself to saying what I say here any other way than through the medium of a letter. Nothing but a consideration for public sentiment could induce me to indite this. With great respect, your obedient servant, U.S. Grant." Enraged at the slight, Akerman instead resigned on 10 January 1872, returning to his private law practice. He never held federal office again.

In the last decade of his life, Akerman practiced law in Cartersville, Georgia. He died there on 21 December 1880 of rheumatism at the age of 59.

References: *The Attorney Generals of the United States, 1789–1985* (Washington, DC: Department of Justice, 1985), 62; Grice, Warren, "Akerman, Amos Tappan," in *DAB* 1: 133–134; Parramore, Thomas C., "Akerman, Amos Tappan," in William S. Powell, ed., *Dictionary of North Carolina Biography* (Chapel Hill: University of North Carolina Press; 6 vols., 1879–1996), 1: 10–11; *Reconstruction: Extracts from the Speech of Hon. Amos T. Akerman Delivered at Atlanta, Georgia, September 1, 1870* (Washington, DC: Union Republican Congressional Committee, 1870[?]); Robb, Arthur, "Biographical Sketches of the Attorneys General" (Unpublished essay DOJ, Washington, DC, 1946), 41; *200th Anniversary of the Office of Attorney General, 1789–1989* (Washington, DC: Department of Justice, 1990), 43–44.

GEORGE HENRY WILLIAMS
1823–1910

If George Williams had been more politic as attorney general, or perhaps had married a different woman, there is every indication that he would have been confirmed as chief justice of the Supreme Court in 1874 instead of Morrison R. Waite. But since he had stepped on the toes of several senators, his nomination went down to a bitter defeat, and the Supreme Court seat he so desired was lost forever. He did, however, serve admirably as Ulysses S. Grant's third attorney general and as the thirty-second man to hold that position. Williams, the son of Taber Williams and Lydia (née Goodrich) Williams, was born in New Lebanon, New York, on 23 March 1823. When he was a small child, he parents moved to Onondaga County, also in New York, where he was educated in local schools and the Pompey Hill Academy. After studying law, he was admitted to the state bar in 1844 but moved to Iowa, where he opened a law practice in the town of Fort Madison.

After three years of private practice, Williams was elected as judge of the First Judicial Iowa District, serving until 1852; the following year he was named by President Franklin Pierce as chief justice of the Supreme Court of the Oregon Territory. During his tenure there, 1853–1857, he found for a freed slave who desired to retain custody of his children. Williams spoke out against slavery and its possible extension into Oregon Territory. He served as a member of the constitutional convention in 1858, helping the territory to become a state on 14 February 1859.

As an Unionist Democrat, Williams supported the election of Democrat Stephen A. Douglas for the presidency in 1860. He then joined the Union Party, which held a state convention in Eugene in 1862 and selected candidates. By 1864, Williams had joined the Republican Party, and that year he was elected to the U.S. Senate to represent Oregon. Serving until 1871, he supported the abolitionist Senator Thaddeus Stevens of Pennsylvania, introduced the Tenure of Office Act to stop President Andrew Johnson from firing Secretary of War Edwin M. Stanton, and voted to convict the president in an impeachment trial in 1868. Denied reelection in 1871, Williams served as a member of the Joint Commission that settled claims with Great Britain arising from shipping petitions during the Civil War, the Alabama Claims commission, which resulted in the Treaty of Washington (1871).

Following the resignation of Attorney General Amos Akerman on 10 January 1872, President Grant invited Williams to occupy the vacant post. During his tenure, which lasted for three years and three months, Williams was accused of covering up for massive election fraud in Oregon; later, he was accused of illegally removing from his post a government agent who was examining the frauds. This, as well as other actions involved in his handling of the Justice Department, earned him many enemies in Congress.

The death of Chief Justice Salmon Portland Chase on 7 May 1873 left the United States without a chief justice for only the second time since 1835. And for the first time in history, a president had to offer three separate nominations for chief justice. (Some earlier presidents had to go through several nominees to fill associate justice slots). According to a story in the *Toledo Sunday Commercial* in 1888, Grant first offered the chief justiceship to Senator Roscoe Conklin of New York, who turned it down flat, claiming that he "preferred some other way of being buried than by taking a seat upon the Supreme Court." The president then offered the spot to Williams. The reasons behind Williams's ultimate rejection by the Senate, prior to a vote, are shrouded in history. Grant biographer William McFeeley writes one story holds that Senator Simon Cameron of Pennsylvania demanded that someone from his state be named either to the cabinet or to the Court. Another story claims that the

extravagant lifestyle of Williams and his wife, a beauty who apparently aroused the envy of many women, led to his downfall. Williams was always seen moving about town in a fancy carriage, so much so that he was called "Landaulet" Williams. A third story holds that Williams had refused to rubber-stamp an unnamed senator's choice for a plum patronage post because he felt the man was not qualified and that the senator retaliated by getting his colleagues to turn down the Oregonian. Whatever the cause, Williams, seeing the handwriting on the wall, withdrew his name only a few weeks after he had been so gloriously nominated. Williams remained as attorney general until 15 May 1875, when he resigned; a friend of Treasury Secretary Benjamin Bristow wrote that Williams would "prefer to walk and talk Spanish rather than remain in the Attorney General's office." He was offered the ministership to Spain, but refused. In 1876, he was sent by Grant to Florida to work for the election of Republican Rutherford B. Hayes to the presidency.

After he returned to Oregon, Williams began a law practice in Portland, where he later served as mayor (1902–1905). He died there on 4 April 1910, just two weeks after his ninetieth birthday, and was buried in Riverview Cemetery in Portland. His published works include *Occasional Addresses* (1895).

References: *The Attorney Generals of the United States, 1789–1985* (Washington, DC: Department of Justice, 1985), 64; Clark, Robert C., "Williams, George Henry," in *DAB* 10: 262–263; McFeely, William S., *Grant: A Biography* (New York: W. W. Norton & Company, 1981), 392.

EDWARDS PIERREPONT
1817–1892

Edwards Pierrepont was the fourth of Ulysses S. Grant's five attorneys general and the shortest-serving of the five men.

Born Munson Edwards Pierpont in North Haven, Connecticut, on 4 March 1817, he was the son of Giles Pierpont and Eunice (née Munson) Pierpont. At some period when Edwards was in school, he dropped his first name and assumed a different spelling of his last name. He attended the local schools of New Haven and went on to Yale College, graduating from that institution in 1837. He studied the law at New Haven Law School and was admitted to the state bar in 1840.

Pierrepont served as a tutor at Yale, then moved to Columbus, Ohio, where he joined a law practice for five years. In 1846, he moved again, this time to New York City, where he established a practice on his own. A Democrat, he became active in politics, although it was not until 1857 that he ran for office and was elected as a judge of the superior court of New York City, serving until 1860. The following year, as tensions between North and South boiled over into civil war, he raised moneys as a member of the Union Defense Committee to send troops to the border slave states to keep them in the Union. In 1864, he parted with the Democratic Party when it nominated General George B. McClellan for president, forming a coalition of War Democrats who backed the reelection of Republican Abraham Lincoln. A supporter of moderation toward the defeated Southern states, Pierrepont defended the policies of President Andrew Johnson and excoriated those of the Radical Republicans. In 1868, with the nomination of New York Governor Horatio Seymour for president, Pierrepont left the Democratic Party for good and threw his backing behind the Republican, General Ulysses S. Grant. Named by Grant in 1869 as the U.S. attorney for the southern district of New York, he served for a year. He refused an offer by the president in 1873 to serve as U.S. minister to Russia.

The resignation on 15 May 1875 of Attorney General George Williams left the attorney general position vacant for the third time during the Grant administration. Williams had been nominated for chief justice of the U.S. Supreme Court, and, had he been confirmed, Secretary of the Treasury Benjamin Bristow would have succeeded him at Justice. After Williams's nomination for the Court was defeated and he resigned as attorney general, Bristow wrote to Grant declining the now vacant attorney generalship. Instead, the position was offered to Pierrepont, who accepted, and he served from 15 May 1875 until 22 May 1876, a period of a year and one week. Much of his tenure was spent prosecuting many of the frauds perpetrated in the Whiskey Ring scandal in which it was found that government agents in St. Louis were found to have stolen government revenues from the sale of whiskey. (For more information on the Whiskey Ring scandal, *see* Benjamin Helm Bristow, Secretary of the Treasury, 1874–1876.) Pierrepont resigned on 22 May 1876 to accept the office of minister to Great Britain, where he served until December 1877. He then returned to the United States and his law practice.

Edwards Pierrepont died in New York on 6 March 1892, two days after his seventy-fifth birthday. He was buried in St. Philip's Cemetery in Garrison, New York.

References: *The Attorney Generals of the United States, 1789–1985* (Washington, DC: Department of Justice, 1985), 66; McFeeley, William S., *Grant: A Biography* (New York: W. W. Norton, 1981); Robb, Arthur, "Biographical Sketches of the Attorneys General" (Unpublished essay DOJ, Washington, DC, 1946), 43; Smith, Edward Conrad, "Pierrepont, Edwards" in *DAB* 7: 585–587; Sobel, Robert, ed.-in-chief, *Biographical Directory of the United States Executive Branch, 1774–1971* (Westport, CT: Greenwood, 1971), 265; Starr, Harris Elwood, "Pierpont, James," in *DAB* 7: 585–587; Willson, Beckles, *America's Ambassadors to England (1785–1928): A Narrative of Anglo-American Diplomatic Relations* (London: J. Murray, 1929), 367–371.

ALPHONSO TAFT
1810–1891

See Secretary of War, 1876

CHARLES DEVENS

1820–1891

Charles Devens was known as the "beau of the [Hayes] cabinet" because he was a lifelong bachelor who became a social favorite of the administration. Charles Devens, the son of Charles Devens and Mary (née Lithgow) Devens was born in Charlestown, Massachusetts on 4 April 1820. He received his education at the Boston Latin School and Harvard College, from which he graduated in 1838. He attended Harvard Law School and was admitted to the bar in 1840. He established a private practice first in Northfield, and then in Greenfield, both in his home state.

Devens began his political career by serving two terms in the Massachusetts State Senate (1848–1849), after which he served, from 1849 until 1853, as the U.S. marshal for the district of Massachusetts. It was in this position that he was forced to escort an escaped slave back to his owner in the South under the Fugitive Slave Act of 1850. After leaving the marshal's office, he returned to the practice of law in Worcester with George Frisbie Hoar, a future U.S. congressman and senator. It was during this time that Devens served as Worcester city solicitor, from 1856–1858.

When the Civil War broke out, Devens left the law firm, volunteered for military service, and was commissioned a major in the Third Battalion of Massachusetts Rifles; he was promoted on 15 July 1861 to commander of the Fifteenth Regiment of the Massachusetts Volunteer Infantry. Devens saw major action during the war, including at the battles of Fredericksburg and Cold Harbor, and was wounded at the battles of Ball's Bluff, Fair Oaks, and Chancellorsville. He was at the head of the army that invaded Richmond at the end of the war and was promoted to major-general. After serving as second-in-command to General Dan Sickles in The Southeastern Department during the early days of Reconstruction, Devens left the military in June 1866. He returned to his law practice, but eventually served two judicial posts: in April 1867 he was named by Governor Alexander H. Bullock as justice of the superior court of Massachusetts; in 1873, he was elevated by Governor William B. Washburn as a justice on the state Supreme Court.

Following the Electoral Commission's certification of his election victory in the 1876 contest at the end of February 1877, Republican Rutherford B. Hayes was forced to assemble his cabinet quickly. To maintain sectional representation in the cabinet, Hayes asked Governor Alexander H. Rice of Massachusetts to serve as attorney general. When Rice turned down the offer, Hayes quickly turned to Devens to represent New England. Devens accepted and served as the thirty-fifth attorney general throughout the entire Hayes administration, from 12 March 1877 until 6 March 1881. Hayes historian Ari Hoogenboom reports that under Devens' Justice was "a small, stable department." In his annual report for 1880, Devens wrote, "The pressure upon the docket of the Supreme Court continues to increase." There were two landmark cases decided during that term: *Virginia v. Rives* (100 U.S. 313), in which the court held that no person could be kept off a jury because of his color, and *Strauder v. West Virginia* (100 U.S. 303), in which the conviction of a black man was set aside because other blacks were excluded from his jury. Devens was not retained in the new administration of James A. Garfield and upon returning to his home state was appointed by Massachusetts Governor John D. Long to his old position as judge of the superior court, a seat he held until his death.

Devens died in Boston on 7 January 1891 at the age of 70, and he was interred in the Trinity Church burial yard in Boston. Fort Devens, originally Camp Devens, in Ayer, Massachusetts, established in 1917 to train soldiers for World War I, was named in his honor.

References: *The Attorney Generals of the United States, 1789–1985* (Washington, DC: Department of Justice, 1985), 70; Davison, Kenneth E., *The*

Presidency of Rutherford B. Hayes (Westport, CT: Greenwood, 1972), 99; Fuess, Claude M., "Devens, Charles," in *DAB* 3: 260–262; Hoogenboom, Ari, *The Presidency of Rutherford B. Hayes* (Lawrence: University Press of Kansas, 1988), 122; Robb, Arthur, "Biographical Sketches of the Attorneys General" (Unpublished essay DOJ, Washington, DC, 1946), 45.

ISAAC WAYNE MACVEAGH
1833–1917

Issac MacVeagh served as attorney general for less than a year. His chief accomplishment during that tenure was the procurement of an indictment against Charles Guiteau, the assassin of President James A. Garfield. The brother of Franklin MacVeagh, secretary of the treasury (1909–1913), Isaac MacVeagh was born near the town of Phoenixville, Pennsylvania, on 19 April 1833, the son of Major John MacVeagh and Margaret (née Lincoln) MacVeagh. He attended local schools in nearby Pottstown, then received a law degree from Yale in 1853, finishing tenth in his class. After studying law in a private office, he was admitted to the Pennsylvania bar in 1856 and began his own practice. In 1859, he was elected as district attorney for Chester County, Pennsylvania, serving until 1864.

During the Civil War, MacVeagh served as a captain in an emergency infantry and by 1863 had reached the rank of major of cavalry. That same year he was named as chairman of the Republican State Committee, and was at Abraham Lincoln's side when the president delivered his immortal address at Gettysburg. With the end of the war, he moved his practice to the state capital, Harrisburg. His growing influence in the Republican Party led President Grant to name him U.S. minister in residence to Turkey (the Ottoman Empire) on 4 June 1870, where he served for a year. During a vacation back in the United States, he became so upset at the state of his party under the leadership of

Grant that he resigned his post and joined a number of Republicans opposed to the administration. MacVeagh served as a delegate to the Pennsylvania State Constitutional Convention in 1872, and within four years he had moved his practice to Philadelphia.

At the 1876 Republican National Convention, MacVeagh's leadership within the Pennsylvania delegation in opposition to a third term for Grant led to the nomination of Rutherford B. Hayes. When Hayes was elected with many votes in doubt, MacVeagh was sent by the new president to Louisiana to settle with Democrats to allow Hayes to become president without further opposition in exchange for the removal of U.S. troops enforcing Reconstruction. An independent and strong-willed lawyer, MacVeagh was a natural choice for attorney general when President James A. Garfield picked him for the post soon after the 1880 election. After taking office on 5 March 1881, writes historian William Henry Smith, "MacVeagh was Attorney General at the time the Star Route frauds were unearthed and began a vigorous prosecution of those accused of being concerned in the frauds." His official opinions are recorded in volume 17 of the *Official Opinions of the Attorneys General of the United States.*

On 2 July 1881, President Garfield was shot by a disappointed office seeker, Charles Guiteau, and died on 19 September. MacVeagh submitted his resignation to newly-installed President Chester A. Arthur, effective 24 October, but remained in office until 13 November, while he secured an indictment against Guiteau. He returned to private practice. Acting Attorney General S. F. Phillips signed the 1881 annual report.

MacVeagh served in the 1880s as state chairman of the Pennsylvania Civil Service Reform Commission. The Republican Party's stand against civil service reform finally led MacVeagh to desert to the Democratic Party; and he was then appointed by President Grover Cleveland (Democrat) as U.S. ambassador to Italy on 20 December 1893; he served for two years. In 1897 he joined a prestigious Washington law firm, and was counsel for the District of Columbia. Forgiven by Republicans for his switch in parties, he was appointed chief counsel for the United States during the Venezuelan arbitration hearings by President Theodore Roosevelt in 1903.

Isaac Wayne MacVeagh died in Washington, D.C., on 11 January 1917 at the age of 83.

References: The Attorney Generals of the United States, 1789–1985 (Washington, DC: Department of Justice, 1985), 72; Fuller, Joseph V., "MacVeagh, Isaac Wayne," in *DAB* 6: 170–171; Hall, Benjamin F., et al., comps., *Official Opinions of the Attorneys General of the United States* (Washington, DC: Robert Farnham; 43 vols., plus annual updates, 1852–1996); Robb, Arthur, "Biographical Sketches of the Attorneys General" (Unpublished essay DOJ, Washington, DC, 1946), 46; Smith, William Henry, *History of the Cabinet of the United States of America, From President Washington to President Coolidge* (Baltimore: Industrial Printing, 1925), 347; Sobel, Robert, ed.-in-chief, *Biographical Directory of the United States Executive Branch, 1774–1971* (Westport, CT: Greenwood, 1971), 229–230.

BENJAMIN HARRIS BREWSTER
1816–1888

Benjamin Brewster helped prosecute the Star Route frauds during the Chester Arthur administration. Born in Salem County, New Jersey, on 13 October 1816, Benjamin Brewster was the son of Francis Enoch Brewster and Maria (née Hampton) Brewster. He attended Princeton College and graduated in 1834. After studying law, he became a leading member of the Philadelphia bar.

In 1846, Brewster was named as a commissioner to settle claims of the Cherokee Indians. He switched from the Democratic Party to the Republican Party and saw his political fortunes rise. He became a close associate of the Simon Cameron machine and

was rewarded with an appointment as Pennsylvania state attorney general in 1867; he served for one year. In 1881, Attorney General Isaac Wayne MacVeagh hired him, along with attorney George Bliss of New York, to prosecute the Star Route frauds, a series of scandals involving mail routes and payoffs. When President James A. Garfield succumbed to the wounds inflicted by an assassin, Attorney General MacVeagh resigned and the new president, Chester A. Arthur, named Brewster as his replacement.

As attorney general from 19 December 1881 until 4 March 1885, Brewster was heavily involved in prosecuting the Star Route fraud trials. In his annual report for 1883, Brewster attempted to get appropriations for the proper preservation of the records of the attorney general's office prior to 1870, records that he felt were falling into disuse and were in threat of being destroyed. "[The records] are of a miscellaneous character, and are important, not only as a history of the Department during an interesting period, but they ought to be preserved because of the valuable information they contain concerning public affairs of the United States previous to the date mentioned," he wrote. "They are now without system or order, subject to loss and destruction. They should be collated in order of time, filed and labeled, so as to be of easy reference in investigations of any matters which happened in past years connected with the Department. " In his final report, filed on 1 December 1884, Brewster wrote, "I am pleased to report to Congress that the condition of the public service, so far as it relates to officials connected with this Department, is, I am satisfied, greatly improved. This, I think it is safe to say, is in a large measure due to the active efforts which have been taken by this Department during the present administration in checking irregularities, correcting abuses, and punishing frauds and exactions committed by district attorneys, marshals, and commissioners, which have existed in a number of districts. From the first I have exercised a strict supervision in this respect which is still [being] carried out."

Brewster left office in March 1885 and returned to the private practice of law. Only three years later at the age of 68, he died in Philadelphia on 4 April 1888.

References: *The Attorney Generals of the United States, 1789–1985* (Washington, DC: Department of Justice, 1985), 74; Paxon, Francis Logan, "Brewster, Benjamin Harris," in *DAB* 2: 26–27; Savidge, Eugene C., *Life of Benjamin Brewster, With Discourses and Addresses* (Philadelphia: J. B. Lippincott, 1891).

AUGUSTUS HILL GARLAND
1832–1899

Augustus Garland was involved in one of the most famous *ex post facto* cases ever heard by the U.S. Supreme Court, in which he won the right to be reinstated after the end of the Civil War to practice law before the Supreme Court. He was born in Covington, Tennessee, on 11 June 1832, the son of Rufus Garland and Barbara (née Hill) Garland. A year after his birth, Garland's parents moved to Arkansas, where he grew up and received much of his early education. His father died when he was young, and after his mother remarried, he was tutored at a private academy in Washington, Arkansas. He attended St. Mary's College in Lebanon, Kentucky, graduated from St. Joseph College in Bardstown, Kentucky, in 1849 and, after studying the law under his stepfather and being admitted to the Arkansas bar, opened an office in the capital, Little Rock, at the age of 18. In 1860, he was an elector for the Constitutional Union presidential ticket of John Bell and Edward Everett.

With the election of Abraham Lincoln to the presidency, Garland came out publicly against the secession of Arkansas from the Union, but in April 1861 changed his mind when the president called for the raising of troops to oppose the Confederacy. He was elected as one of five Arkansas delegates to the Confederate Provisional Congress; at 28, he was the youngest member of that transitional body. That November, he won a seat in the first Confederate Congress, representing the Third Arkansas district, and was reelected in 1863. The following year, he was named to fill the seat of deceased Senator Charles B. Mitchel, and, while he began his tenure when only 34, Garland continued to serve until the end of the war.

With the defeat of the South, he worked to have his state reintroduced into the Union as soon as possible. Almost immediately after the end of the conflict he received an unconditional pardon from President Andrew Johnson. When Congress passed an action that debarred from practice before the U.S. Supreme Court all persons who had sided with the Confederacy, Garland opposed it (with the assistance of former Attorney General Reverdy Johnson). His argument was that it represented an *ex post facto* law, which is forbidden by the Constitution. Taking his case to the U.S. Supreme Court, Garland won a landmark victory when the Court, in *Ex parte Garland* (1866), overturned the law, allowing him to practice again before the Court, as it were, a new man, and gives him a new credit and capacity.

In 1867 Garland was elected to the U.S. Senate, but to punish him for opposing the laws of the United States he was refused his seat by the other members of that body. On 13 October 1874, Garland was elected governor of Arkansas as a Democrat, serving until 1876. As governor, writes biographer David Thomas, "his chief problems were to finance the state, which he did partly by issuing bonds and by providing a sinking fund, and to put an end to the practice of guaranteeing railroad bonds." And although most of the state debt was incurred during the previous administration, set up after the end of the war, "Garland opposed repudiation and later stumped the state in opposition to . . . [an] amendment forbidding payment on all bonds."

In 1876, Garland was again elected by the state legislature to the U.S. Senate, to fill the seat of the retiring Clayton Powell, and this time was allowed to take his seat on 4 March 1877, where he worked for civil service and tariff reform. On 9 March 1885, he resigned to accept President Grover Cleveland's appointment as attorney general. In his four-year tenure, which ended on 4 March 1889, Garland attempted to get Congress to enact legislation creating more positions in the department to handle an increasing workload. In his annual report of 1887, Garland wrote, "There has been no reorganization of the Department of Justice since its establishment in 1870. Of course, additional officers have been provided for new districts when created, but the appropriations for United States courts have for years averaged very nearly the same amount, while the business of the Department has constantly grown, until its has assumed its present vast proportions; and the increase of its force has not kept pace with the increase of business . . . quite recent acts of Congress . . . have thrown an immense amount of business upon the Department, to which the determination of the Government to protect the public domain from plunder have added a large and increasing number of land-frauds and timber-trespass suits." In his final report, written in 1888, Garland simply added, "I respectfully submit the question of the desirability of a reorganization of the official force of the Department proper, to meets the needs of the increasing business."

After Grover Cleveland left office in 1889, Garland went into private practice in Washington, D.C. On 26 January 1899, while arguing a case before the U.S. Supreme Court, he fell ill and died in a matter of moments. Garland was 66 years old. He was buried in Mount Holly Cemetery in Little Rock. He was the author of *Experiences in the Supreme Court of the United States, with some Reflections and Suggestions as to that Tribunal* (1898).

References: *The Attorney Generals of the United States, 1789–1985* (Washington, DC: Department of Justice, 1985), 76; "Garland, Augustus Hill," in Robert Sobel and John Raimo, eds., *Biographical*

Directory of the Governors of the United States, 1789–1978 (Westport, CT: Meckler Books; 4 vols., 1978), 1: 73–74; Newberry, Farrar, "A Life of Mr. Garland of Arkansas" (Master's thesis, University of Arkansas at Arkadelphia, 1908), 22–36; Norton, Charles Benjamin, "The Department of Justice," in *The President and His Cabinet, Indicating the Progress of the Government of the United States under the Administration of Grover Cleveland* (Boston: Cupples and Hurd, 1888), 191–205; Thomas, David Y., "Garland, Augustus Hill," in *DAB* 4: 150–151; Thomas, David Y., *Arkansas in the War and Reconstruction, 1861–1874* (Little Rock, AR: United Daughters of the Confederacy, 1926); Warner, Ezra J.; and W. Buck Yearns, *Biographical Register of the Confederate Congress* (Baton Rouge: Louisiana State University Press, 1975), 95–96; Watkins, Beverly Nettles, "Augustus Hill Garland, 1832–1899: Arkansas Lawyer to United States Attorney-General" (Ph.D. dissertation, Auburn University, 1985).

WILLIAM HENRY HARRISON MILLER
1840–1917

William Miller was an unknown attorney when chosen by his good friend Benjamin Harrison to serve as the thirty-ninth attorney general. William H. H. Miller, the son of Curtis Miller, a farmer, and Lucy (née Duncan) Miller, was born in Augusta, New York, on 6 September 1840. He graduated from Hamilton College in Clinton, New York, then taught for a short period at Maumee, Ohio. In May 1862, he enlisted to fight in the Civil War with the Eighty-fourth Ohio Infantry, but never saw action and was mustered out that September with the rank of second lieutenant. He then studied law under Ohio attorney Morrison Remick Waite (who later served as chief justice of the Supreme Court, 1874–1888), finally finishing his legal studies in Peru, Indiana, while working as the superintendent of schools there. He was admitted to the Indiana bar in 1865 and the following year opened a practice in Fort Wayne.

It was at this time that Miller came to the attention of Benjamin Harrison, a former Civil War general and noted Indianapolis attorney. Miller was asked to join the law firm of Harrison and Hines. He remained there for the better part of the rest of his life, arguing cases involving Republicans numerous times, including a disputed lieutenant governor's contest in 1886. In 1888, Harrison was chosen as the Republican nominee for president, and was elected. In the time until inauguration, he stocked his cabinet with such men as James G. Blaine, William Windom, Jeremiah Rusk, and John Wanamaker, the latter a store-owner and millionaire. Harrison eventually added an important name to this list—William Henry Harrison Miller as attorney general.

There is evidence that while Harrison was partial to his law partner, he may have wanted Indiana Attorney General Louis Michener to fill that same slot in his cabinet. The issue was discussed, according to Harrison biographer Harry Sievers, but, "Michener . . . reluctantly refused, feeling bound to discharge the duties of his state office until the expiration of his term." Miller's name was submitted to the Senate on 5 March 1889, he was confirmed unanimously along with the rest of Harrison's nominees and took office on that same day. When he finally took his position in the cabinet, Miller, at 48, was the youngest man among his executive colleagues. Biographer Albert T. Volwiler wrote, "When Benjamin Harrison became president, Miller became his attorney general and one of his most trusted personal advisers. The appointment was a surprise to Republican leaders, for Miller was unknown outside of his state and had had practically no administrative experience. As Attorney General he endeavored to enforce the laws vigorously and impartially with a disregard of political influences that was often disconcerting to Republican leaders. His careful investigation into the records of men suggested for federal judicial appointments was responsible in part for the excellence of Harrison's judicial appointments."

Considered the first of the trust-busters,

Miller used the newly enacted Sherman Antitrust Act to sue the sugar interests. Among the cases he argued before the Supreme Court were *In re Neagle* (1890), in which the Court held that a federal marshal was subject, during his work, to federal and not state law, and *In re Cooper* (1893) the Bering Sea Seal case, which led to a British-American arbitration treaty on sealing in Alaska. Four vacancies on the Supreme Court almost led to Miller's elevation to that tribunal, but he was passed over.

Miller left office at the end of the Harrison administration in 1893 and returned to the practice of law in Indianapolis until 1910. He died in that city on 25 May 1917 at the age of 76, the last member of the Harrison cabinet to die. His great-nephew, Herbert Brownell, Jr., served as attorney general in the Eisenhower administration.

References: *The Attorney Generals of the United States, 1789–1985* (Washington, DC: Department of Justice, 1985), 78; Quinn, Maria Margaret, Sister, "William Henry Harrison Miller: Attorney General of the United States, 1889–1893" (Ph.D. dissertation, Catholic University, 1965); Sievers, Harry J., *Benjamin Harrison, Hoosier President: The White House and After* (Indianapolis: Bobbs-Merrill, 1968), 5; Socolofsky, Homer E., and Allan B. Spetter, *The Presidency of Benjamin Harrison* (Lawrence: University Press of Kansas, 1987), 29; Volwiler, Albert T., "Miller, William Henry Harrison," in *DAB* 6: 643.

RICHARD OLNEY
1835–1917

As attorney general, Richard Olney introduced the policy of "government by injunction" when he used the courts to force an end to a railway strike in Illinois based on the fact that it was interfering with interstate commerce. As secretary of state, he declared that under the Monroe Doctrine, the United States had the sovereign right of jurisdiction over strategic matters in the Western Hemisphere, encapsulating these principles in a treaty with Great Britain's Lord Pauncefote. Born in Oxford, Massachusetts, on 15 September 1835, Richard Olney was the son of Wilson Olney and Eliza (née Butler) Olney. He attended the Leicester Academy, Brown University in Rhode Island, and Harvard Law School, the latter institution awarding him a law degree in 1858. After being admitted to the bar the following year, he took over the law practice Boston attorney Benjamin F. Thomas.

Olney's only service in elective office came in 1873, when he was elected for a single term to the Massachusetts state legislature. Thus when he was under consideration for attorney general in the cabinet of President-elect Grover Cleveland in early 1893, he was little known outside of Boston legal circles. Olney biographer Gerald Eggert relates that Olney was considered for the position of secretary of the navy, with another Boston attorney, John Quincy Adams (grandson of the president and son of diplomat Charles Francis Adams), under scrutiny for attorney general. Olney rejected Navy, and Cleveland offered him the attorney general's spot if Adams then took Navy. Olney approached Adams with the offer, but he refused to serve. Cleveland then named Hilary Abner Herbert of Alabama to Navy and selected Olney as the fortieth attorney general.

In this post, he advised the president not to send American troops to end the insurrection against the Queen of Hawaii and handled the residual effects of the march of radical Jacob Coxey's "army" on Washington. Olney argued a landmark case before the Supreme Court, *In re Debs, Petitioner* (1895), in which the Court refused to release socialist agitator Eugene V. Debs from a contempt of court sentence. But the key issue that arose during his tenure was the Pullman rail strike. His 1894 report discussed the strike with clarity. He cleared up his role in the matter by explaining, "It is not germane to this report to consider the origin or the merits of the labor disturbance which has passed into history under the name of the 'Pullman strike.' The relation to it of the Department of

Justice was indirect and arose only when the railroads of the country became involved and the passage of the United States mails and the movements of interstate commerce were interfered with." Eggert writes, "Once in office, Olney complained of being 'driven very much by all sorts of work that I am not fitted for.' Although he spent some time in preparing legal opinions for the president and his cabinet colleagues, he was surprised at how much of his time went to managing the Justice Department. 'So far as strictly legal work is concerned,' he observed, 'the duties of the attorney general are not more exacting than those of a lawyer having a large general practice. But the truth is that the attorney generalship corresponds to what is known in European countries as the "Ministry of Justice"—that is, the duties are largely administrative.'" That 1894 annual report was Olney's last; on 10 June 1895 he resigned as attorney general and was named as secretary of state, to replace Walter Quintin Gresham, who had died. During his tenure as secretary of state, 10 June 1895 to 4 March 1897, Olney dealt with the Venezuelan boundary dispute in 1895. That same year, he published the Olney Corollary to the Monroe Doctrine. Cleveland wrote to Olney of his diplomatic message, "I read your deliverance on Venezuelan affairs the day you left it with me. It's the best thing of the kind I have ever read and it leads to a conclusion that one cannot escape if he tries—that is, if there is anything of the Monroe Doctrine at all. You show there us a great deal of that and place it, I think, on better and more defensible ground than any of your predecessors—*or mine* [italics, Cleveland]." In a letter to U.S. Ambassador to Great Britain Thomas F. Bayard (himself a former secretary of state) on 20 July 1895, Olney wrote that Britain was involving itself in South American affairs to the detriment of the United States and that "the United States is practically sovereign on this continent, and its fiat is law upon the subjects to which it confines its interposition." With Cleveland's permission, Bayard revealed the correspondence to the British government.

Secretary of the Navy Hilary A. Herbert, in an article in the *Century Magazine* in 1913, explained, "In 1895 the President and Secretary Olney were summering in Massachusetts when Mr. Olney's remarkable Venezuelan letter to Lord Salisbury was prepared. At Mr. Cleveland's request, Mr. Olney brought down and read this letter to the members of the cabinet, then in Washington. He also read the letter to Mr. Carlisle, Secretary of the Treasury, Judge Harmon, Attorney-General, Mr. Lamont, Secretary of War . . . and the writer. We all considered it carefully, and finally gave the document our warm approval, but not without at first some misgivings at its startling boldness. The letter thus agreed upon was the foundation of the famous Venezuelan message sent to Congress on December 17, 1895. The contents of the despatch to Lord Salisbury had been kept secret for four months, and when that message, in Mr. Cleveland's own nervous language, was published, it amazed the public and demoralized the stock-markets of the world. To many war seemed inevitable."

In his message to Great Britain of 17 December 1895, the president threatened American military intervention into the situation. The British, under Sir Julian Pauncefote, the British minister to the United States, then negotiated with Olney the Olney-Pauncefote Convention, signed 11 January 1897, which settled the dispute through arbitration. Historian Nelson M. Blake explains, "[The treaty] represented a victory for the American contention that a general arbitration agreement should cover all types of controversies and should provide a final decisions in most cases. Pecuniary claims not exceeding £100,000 were to be subject to the final decision of a tribunal composed of one arbitrator from each country and an umpire chosen by the two; all larger pecuniary claims and other controverted matters except territorial claims were to be submitted to a tribunal of three, but unless the decision of this tribunal were unanimous an appeal might be taken to a second tribunal of five, two from each country plus an umpire chosen by the four; territorial claims were reserved for a tribunal of

six members, three from each party with no umpire, and were not to be unless agreed to by at least five of the arbiters; in cases where there was disagreement over the choice of an umpire he was to be named by the king of Sweden." (Although the British Parliament ratified the treaty, the Senate rejected it, 43–26, in May 1897.)

Olney's term was nearing an end when the first signs of impending conflict with Spain over Cuba were appearing. In an article in the *Atlantic Monthly* in 1900, Olney explained, "The characteristic of the foreign relations of the United States at the outbreak of the late Spanish war was isolation. The policy was traditional, originating at the very birth of the Republic. It had received the sanction of its founders—of Washington preeminently—had been endorsed by most if not all of the leading statesmen of the country and had come to be regarded with almost as much respect as if incorporated in the text of the Constitution itself. What the policy enjoined in substance was aloofness from the political affairs of the civilized world in general and a strict limitation of the political activities of the United States to the concerns of the American continents. It had been distinguished by two salient features which, if not due to it as their sole or chief cause, had certainly been its natural accompaniments. One of them was the Monroe doctrine, so-called, directly affecting our relations with foreign powers. The other was a high protective tariff aimed at sequestering the home market for the benefit of home industries and, though legally speaking of merely domestic concern, in practical results operating as the most effectual of obstacles to intercourse with foreign peoples."

After leaving office in 1897, Olney returned to his law practice. He later rejected offers from President Woodrow Wilson to serve as U.S. ambassador to Great Britain and governor of the Federal Reserve Board. Olney died in Boston on 8 April 1917. He was 81 years old. He was interred in Mount Auburn Cemetery in Cambridge, Massachusetts.

References: *The Attorney Generals of the United States, 1789–1985* (Washington, DC: Department of Justice, 1985), 80; Blake, Nelson M., "The Olney-Pauncefote Treaty of 1897," *American Historical Review* 50: 2 (January 1945), 233–234; Doenecke, Justus D., "Olney, Richard," in Bruce W. Jentleson and Thomas G. Paterson, senior eds., *Encyclopedia of U.S. Foreign Relations* (New York: Oxford University Press; 4 vols., 1997), 3: 321–322; Eggert, Gerald G., *Richard Olney: Evolution of a Statesman* (University Park: Pennsylvania State University Press, 1974), 3–7, 47–61; Findling, John E., *Dictionary of American Diplomatic History* (Westport, CT: Greenwood, 1989), 390; *Foreign Relations of the United States: 1895* (Washington, DC: GPO; 2 vols., 1896), 1: 545–558 (Olney to Bayard); Fuller, Joseph V., "Olney, Richard," in *DAB* 7: 32–33; Herbert, Hillary A., "Grover Cleveland and His Cabinet at Work," *Century Magazine* 85: 5 (March 1913), 741–772; James, Henry, *Richard Olney and His Public Service. With Documents, including Unpublished Diplomatic Correspondence* (Boston and New York: Houghton Mifflin, 1923), 110–111 (Cleveland to Olney); Olney, Richard, "Growth of Our Foreign Policy," *Atlantic Monthly* 85: 509 (March 1900), 289–290.

JUDSON HARMON

1846–1927

Judson Harmon is one of the few men in American history to be elected to a governor's seat *after* serving in the cabinet. Judson Harmon went on to become one of Ohio's greatest governors and was a favorite-son candidate for the presidency in 1912. Born in the village of Newtown, Ohio, on 3 February 1846, Harmon was the eldest of eight children of Benjamin Franklin Harmon, a teacher and later a Baptist preacher, and Julia (née Bronson) Harmon. Judson Harmon received most of his education at home and in the local schools of Newtown. He graduated from Denison University in Granville, Ohio, in 1866. During the Civil War, he had joined the Ohio Home Guard to repel a possible invasion by Confederate General John Hunt Morgan.

After teaching for a year and serving as a principal in a small school in Columbia, Ohio, Harmon studied law in the Cincinnati office of George Hoadley (who was elected governor in 1884), received a law degree from the Cincinnati Law School in 1869 and was admitted to the state bar that same year. In 1876, he was elected as a judge of the common pleas court in Cincinnati, but his election was thrown out by the State Senate. In 1878, he was elected to a local superior court, where he served until 1887. Three years earlier, George Hoadley had been elected governor, and Harmon was selected to replace him in the firm of Hoadley, Johnston & Colson.

A Republican during the Civil War, Harmon switched to the Democratic Party after the conflict ended. He did work for the Liberal Republican Party in the election of 1872 but returned to the Democratic fold soon after. This support led President Grover Cleveland to consider Harmon and then formally name him as the forty-first attorney general to replace Richard Olney, who was resigning to become secretary of state. Harmon biographer Arthur C. Cole, writes, "He rendered distinguished services and acquired national fame as a lawyer. He directed the prosecution, under the Sherman [Anti-Trust] Act, of the Trans-Missouri Freight Association (166 U.S. 290) and the beginning of a suit against the Addystone Pipe & Steel Company (78 Federal Cases 712)." In his 1895 annual report, his first, Harmon discussed the new system of courts in the Indian Territory, which went into operation on 1 March 1895: "It should be remembered that the Federal courts are the only courts in Indian Territory. These, in addition to the work usually done by Federal courts, discharge all the duties which in the other States and Territories fall to police, probate, and general civil and criminal courts." Harmon's tenure, 8 June 1895 until 5 March 1897, is not considered noteworthy; Department histories barely mention his name.

After leaving office in 1897, Harmon returned to his law practice. Eight years later, he was named to investigate charges that the

Atchison, Topeka, & Santa Fe Railroad had "rebated" millions of dollars to supporters; Harmon found that one of these figures was Paul Morton, at that time secretary of the navy. To avoid any prosecutions, President Theodore Roosevelt stepped in and asked for, and received, Harmon's resignation as special counsel. Harmon then worked to restore the finances of the Cincinnati, Hamilton & Dayton railroad.

In May 1908, he was nominated by the Democrats for governor, and, that November, he narrowly defeated the incumbent, Andrew L. Harris, and became the first former cabinet official to be elected governor. During his two terms, 1909–1913, he helped push for the ratification of the Sixteenth Amendment (the income-tax amendment) to the U.S. Constitution, signed an action that attempted to clean up corrupt practices in voting in the state, endorsed a workmen's compensation act, and backed the creation of a Public Utility Commission. In 1910, he defeated an up-and-coming Ohio politician, newspaperman and future president Warren G. Harding, to win reelection. Harmon left office in 1913 and returned to his law practice. Even while governor, he had continued to operate his practice, appearing before the U.S. Supreme Court in two important cases, *Baltimore & Ohio Southwestern Rail Road Company v. United States* (1910) and *Wesley C. Richardson et al. v. Judson Harmon, Receiver of the Toledo Terminal & Railway Company* (1911). In his final years, he was also a professor of law at the Cincinnati Law School. Harmon died on 22 February 1927, three weeks after his eighty-first birthday. Harmon County, Oklahoma, is named in his honor.

References: *The Attorney Generals of the United States, 1789–1985* (Washington, DC: Department of Justice, 1985), 82; Cole, Arthur C., "Harmon, Judson," in *DAB* 4: 276–278; "Harmon, Judson," in Robert Sobel and John Raimo, eds., *Biographical Directory of the Governors of the United States, 1789–1978* (Westport, CT: Meckler Books; 4 vols., 1978), 3: 1225–1226.

JOSEPH MCKENNA
1843–1926

Joseph McKenna held office as attorney general for less than a year and made little impact on the office before being named to the U.S. Supreme Court. His twenty-six year tenure on the Court is one of the longest in the Court's history. Joseph McKenna, the son of John McKenna, an immigrant baker from Ireland, and Mary Ann Lucy (née Johnson) McKenna, an immigrant from England, was born in Philadelphia, Pennsylvania, on 10 August 1843. (There is some dispute as to this date; McKenna's baptismal certificate lists his date of birth as 14 August 1843.) The atmosphere against immigrants in Philadelphia was poisoned by ethnic hatred, and John McKenna was forced to move his bakery several times to avoid having it burned down. In 1854, when their son was 11, the family moved to Benicia, California, east of San Francisco. John McKenna died there four years later, but he had made enough money for his son to attend parochial school and, when he was old enough, study law at the Benicia Collegiate Institute, from which he graduated in 1864.

Joseph McKenna was admitted to the California state bar in 1865 and, after having a private practice for a few months, was elected as district attorney for Solano County, serving two terms until 1869. Entering politics as a Republican, he was elected to the California state assembly, serving a single term (1875–1876), and to the U.S. House of Representatives, where he sat for four terms (1885–1892). During his fourth term, a vacancy opened up on the Ninth Circuit Court of Appeals in San Francisco; California politicians, most notably Senator Leland Stanford (of Stanford University), recommended McKenna to President Benjamin Harrison, who nominated McKenna to the seat. McKenna sat on the court until 1897. Although he had been a friend of Stanford and the railroad interests, he was even-handed in his treatment of railroad cases.

When Congressman William McKinley of Ohio was elected president in 1896, he wanted to have a Californian in his cabinet. He approached his old friend McKenna, who had served with him in Congress, to be secretary of the interior. McKenna refused, holding that it would be an embarrassment for a Catholic to head a department that worked with Protestant missionaries on Indian reservations. Still seeking to have McKenna in his official family, McKinley offered the attorney general post, which McKenna agreed to take. He thus became the first Californian to serve in the cabinet. His tenure as attorney general lasted a mere nine months; although little business was conducted during the period, he had the opportunity to sign the attorney general's annual report for 1897, which was released on 30 November of that year.

On 16 December 1897 McKinley named him to U.S. Supreme Court to replace the retiring Stephen J. Field, thereby making him the first attorney general to be elevated to the Supreme Court since 1858 and the third in the history of the Court overall. McKenna's twenty-six years on the Court are little covered, mainly because he did not write opinions in most cases, merely concurrences or dissents, for a total of 659. Historian James O'Hara writes, "He· was a centrist, perhaps with a mild inclination toward the progressive liberalism of the day. His opinions tended to favor the growth of federal power, particularly in the regulation of business and industry. In anticipation of later positions of Holmes and Louis D. Brandeis, McKenna was very deferential to legislative decisions and tolerant of legislative experimentation." Historian Lewis J. Paper adds, "McKenna's brethren on the Court . . . noticed that their newest member lacked brilliance. Efforts were made to be careful in the assignment of opinions to him. More than once his work was so inferior that the chief justice had to assign it."

Suffering from the ravages of old age, McKenna resigned from the Court on 25 January 1925. He lived until Washington until his death less than two years later, on 21 November 1926, at the age of 77. He was interred in Mount Olivet Cemetery, Washington, D.C.

References: *The Attorney Generals of the United States, 1789–1985* (Washington, DC: Department of Justice, 1985), 84; McDevitt, Matthew, Brother, "Joseph McKenna: Associate Justice of the United States" (Washington, DC: Catholic University Press, 1946); O'Hara, James, "James McKenna," in Clare Cushman, ed., *The Supreme Court Justices: Illustrated Biographies, 1789–1995* (Washington, DC: Congressional Quarterly, 1995), 281, Paper, Lewis J., *Brandeis* (New York: Prentice-Hall, 1983), 284; Philbrick, Francis S., "McKenna, Joseph," in *DAB* 6: 87–88.

JOHN WILLIAM GRIGGS
1849–1927

John Griggs was nominated as the forty-third attorney general following the elevation of Joseph McKenna to the U.S. Supreme Court. John W. Griggs, the son of Daniel Griggs and Emeline (née Johnson), was born on his parent's farm near Newton, New Jersey, on 10 July 1849. Griggs attended the Collegiate Institute in Newton, then received his bachelor's degree from Lafayette College in Easton, Pennsylvania, in 1868. He then studied the law under former Congressman Robert Hamilton and Socrates Tuttle, the father-in-law of Griggs's friend Garret A. Hobart, who later served as vice-president of the United States (1897–1900). He was admitted to the bar in 1871 and immediately started a law practice with Tuttle.

In 1876, Griggs was elected to the New Jersey General Assembly, serving for two terms until he was defeated in 1878. That year, he was named as counsel for the Board of Chosen Freeholders of Passaic County, New Jersey, and later served as city counsel for the city of Paterson. In 1882, he was elected to the State Senate, serving at one point as senate president. A delegate to the Republican National Convention in 1888, he was asked by President Benjamin Harrison to accept an appointment to the U.S. Supreme

Court, but he refused that as well as a seat on the New Jersey Supreme Court. Instead, in 1895, he ran for governor, with his friend Hobart as his campaign manager. He was elected, serving a single term, in which he helped enact a constitutional amendment against gambling and passed a law to dam the Delaware River.

On 16 December 1897, Attorney General Joseph McKenna resigned to accept a seat on the U.S. Supreme Court. President William McKinley, most likely on a recommendation from his vice-president, Garret Hobart, asked Griggs to fill the vacancy. Griggs accepted and resigned the governorship on 25 January 1898. His tenure, until 30 March 1901, was marked by his work mainly in which he argued before the Supreme Court the case known as *Downes v. Bidwell* (1901), known as the first of the Insular Cases. Following McKinley's reelection in 1900, he asked that his entire cabinet resign except for one— John W. Griggs—intending to renominate all of them for another four years. Griggs told the president that he wanted to return to his law practice but intended to remain in office until 1 April 1901. He formally left the Justice Department on 29 March.

Later that year, shortly before he was assassinated, McKinley named Griggs as the first member of the American contingent to the Permanent Court of Arbitration at The Hague, where he served from 1901 until 1912. Near the end of his life, he served as president of the Marconi Wireless Telegraph Company and as general counsel and director of the Radio Corporation of America (RCA). Griggs died on 28 November 1927 at the age of 78.

References: The Attorney Generals of the United States, 1789–1985 (Washington, DC: Department of Justice, 1985), 86; "Griggs, John William," in Robert Sobel and John Raimo, eds., *Biographical Directory of the Governors of the United States, 1789–1978,* (Westport, CT: Meckler Books; 4 vols., 1978), 3: 1028; Robb, Arthur, "Biographical Sketches of the Attorneys General" (Unpublished essay DOJ, Washington, DC, 1946), 52; Vance, John T., "Griggs, John William," in *DAB* 4: 627–628.

PHILANDER CHASE KNOX
1853–1921

Philander Knox was known as the "trust-busting" attorney general—turned loose by President Theodore Roosevelt to "bust" the large-monied companies that ruled America at that time. As secretary of state, his service led to the term "dollar diplomacy." The son of David Smith Knox, a banker, and Rebekah (née Page) Knox, Philander Knox was born in Brownsville, Pennsylvania, on 6 May 1853. Knox attended the local schools of Brownsville, then the University of West Virginia at Morgantown and Mount Union College in Alliance, Ohio, receiving a bachelor's degree from the latter institution in 1872. While at Mount Union he became a close friend of William McKinley, then the district attorney of Stark County, Ohio. McKinley advised Knox to study the law, and he accomplished this in the office of H. B. Swope of Pittsburgh. Knox was admitted to the bar in 1875.

The following year, Knox served for a brief time as the assistant U.S. district attorney for the western district of Pennsylvania. He then opened a law practice in 1877 and remained a private attorney for the next two decades. In 1897, his friend William McKinley was inaugurated as president, and he asked Knox to serve as attorney general. Knox declined, apparently because he could not go from making $150,000 a year as a private attorney to the paltry $8,000 salary of the attorney general. In March 1901, after Attorney General John W. Griggs refused to serve in the second McKinley administration, the president asked Joseph H. Choate, the U.S. ambassador to Britain, to take the office, but he declined; Knox was then again offered the position, and he finally accepted. At first, his appointment was merely on an interim basis; however, after McKinley's assassination, in December 1901, President Theodore Roosevelt submitted Knox's name to the Senate for confirmation. The *World* of

New York editorialized, "In 251 days service as Attorney General what single thing has Philander C. Knox done to justify the Senate in believing that he is in sympathy with the Anti-Trust laws? And if he is not, then he is not fit for the position, and the Senate ought not to confirm his appointment." Nonetheless, Knox was confirmed on 16 December 1901, with his service lasting until 30 June 1904.

During that two-and-a-half-year period, Knox used the Sherman Antitrust Act, passed in 1890, and "initiated suit . . . against the Northern Securities Company to prevent a merger of the Great Northern, the Northern Pacific, and the Chicago, Burlington, and Quincy railroads." The Supreme Court ultimately upheld his argument in *Northern Securities Company v. United States* (1904). Knox also aided in the drafting of the legislation that created the Department of Commerce and Labor in 1903 and examined the papers of the French company that eventually transferred title of their interests in a potential Panama Canal to the United States. On 30 June 1904, Knox resigned when Pennsylvania Governor Samuel Whitaker Pennypacker named him to fill the U.S. Senate vacancy created when Senator Matthew Quay died.

Knox was subsequently elected to a full six-year term, but he resigned on 4 March 1909 when President William Howard Taft named him as secretary of state. During his tenure, which lasted for the entire four years of the Taft administration, he was deeply involved in many issues, including American interests in China and the Bering Sea fisheries question. Historian John Craig writes, "Knox managed the administration's policy of 'dollar diplomacy,' designed to expand U.S. economic penetration abroad while serving U.S. security needs. Knox used more explicit economic rhetoric than his predecessors at the Department of State, but his commitment to overseas expansion was generally consistent with the policies of previous administrations. His desire for stability in Latin America led to repeated threats of military intervention and to the invasion and occupa-

tion of Nicaragua beginning in 1912." State department historian Graham Stuart adds, "If an evaluation were to be made of the services of Philander C. Knox as Secretary of State from the sole standpoint of policy, he would not rate among the dozen most important Secretaries of State. If, however, we include his influence on the organization and work of the Department, he would surely rate among the top half dozen." Taft once said of Knox that while he was a good secretary of state, if "he were not so lazy he would make a great Secretary of State."

Knox returned to his law practice after leaving government, but three years later, he was elected a second time to the U.S. Senate, for a six-year term to end in 1923. He was one of the "Irreconcilables," a group of senators opposed to American entry into the League of Nations after World War I. On 12 October 1921, after delivering a speech, Knox left the Senate chamber, and was suddenly stricken with a stroke and died; he was 68 years old. He was interred in Washington Memorial Cemetery, Valley Forge, Pennsylvania.

References: *The Attorney Generals of the United States, 1789–1985* (Washington, DC: Department of Justice, 1985), 88; Beveridge, Albert J., "Philander Chase Knox, American Lawyer, Patriot, Statesman," *Pennsylvania Magazine of History and Biography* 47: 2 (1923), 89–114; Craig, John M., "Knox, Philander Chase," in Bruce W. Jentleson and Thomas G. Paterson, senior eds., *Encyclopedia of U.S. Foreign Relations* (New York: Oxford University Press; 4 vols., 1997), 3: 23; Eitler, Anita Torres, "Philander Chase Knox: First Attorney-General of Theodore Roosevelt, 1901–1904" (Ph.D. dissertation, Catholic University, 1959), 1–25, 33, 42; Leets, Juan, *United States and Latin America: Dollar Diplomacy* (New Orleans: L. Graham, 1912); Stuart, Graham H., *The Department of State: A History of Its Organization, Procedure, and Personnel* (New York: Macmillan, 1949), 223.

WILLIAM HENRY MOODY

1853–1917

See Secretary of the Navy, 1902–1904

CHARLES JOSEPH BONAPARTE

1851–1921

See Secretary of the Navy, 1905–1906

GEORGE WOODWARD WICKERSHAM

1858–1936

George Wickersham is remembered for his service as the head of the National Commission on Law Observance and Enforcement, referred to as the Wickersham Commission, which reported in 1931 on ways to enforce and reform the prohibition law. He also served as the attorney general for the entire period of the William Howard Taft administration. He was born Samuel George Woodward Wickersham in Pittsburgh, Pennsylvania, on 19 September 1858, the only son of Samuel Morris Wickersham, an inventor and a veteran of the Civil War, and Elizabeth Cox (née Woodward) Wickersham. His mother died soon after George Wickersham (who dropped the Samuel from his name at an early age) was born, and he was raised by his maternal grandparents. He attended local schools in Pennsylvania, then went to the Western University of Pennsylvania, Nazareth Hall, in Nazareth, Pennsylvania, and Lehigh University, where he studied civil engineering and received a degree in 1875. After serving in the office of attorney (and later U.S. Senator) Matthew Quay of Pennsylvania, he studied law in the office of Robert McGrath and then went to the University of Pennsylvania, from which he received a law degree in 1880.

Wickersham practiced law in Philadelphia, where he covered the local courts for a publication he edited, *Weekly Notes of Cases.* In 1882, he moved to New York, where he served as managing clerk of the prestigious law firm of Strong and Cadwalader until 1887, when he was made a full partner. He remained at the position for the next twenty-two years.

In 1908, shortly after winning the White House, President-elect William Howard Taft selected Wickersham as his attorney general. Little known outside of New York legal circles, Wickersham was nonetheless considered an ethical attorney whose expertise was respected. He was confirmed by the Senate and served for the entire four years of the Taft administration. As the forty-seventh attorney general, Wickersham aimed his sights at the hated trusts that several of his predecessors had been fighting since the drafting of the Sherman Antitrust Act in 1890. A history of the department relates, "Few Attorneys General have been more active than Wickersham. . . . An outstanding Wickersham accomplishment was the drafting, with Senator Elihu Root, of the income tax amendment to the Constitution, adopted in 1913, but enforcement of the antitrust laws also engaged much of his time and he made the closing arguments in the Supreme Court in the Standard Oil and American Tobacco cases and in the government suit for dissolution of the Union Pacific-Southern Pacific merger. The device of the consent decree, in which the defendants agree to negotiated settlements without resort to court trials, came into use in Wickersham's administration; nineteen of forty-seven suits begun by Wickersham ended in that way."

When Taft lost the White House in 1912 to Democrat Woodrow Wilson, Wickersham returned to his old law firm, only to be joined there by his boss William Howard Taft, establishing the new firm as Cadwalader, Wickersham, and Taft. He worked for the firm until his death. Wickersham remained involved in national affairs. He defended, in a little-known but important Supreme Court decision, the sergeant-in-arms of the U.S. Senate, John J. McGrain, against the brother of Attorney General Harry Daugherty when he was called before the Senate and refused to appear; the case, *McGrain v. Daugherty* (1927), established the right of the Senate to issue subpoenas to private citizens. At the end of World War I, he served as a special correspondent of the *New York Tribune* at the Paris Peace talks. In 1929, in his last public action, he was called by President Herbert Hoover to head the National Commission on Law Observance and Enforcement, better known as the Wickersham Commission, which examined ways to better enforce the prohibition laws.

Wickersham died on 26 January 1936 at the age of 77 and was buried in Rockside Cemetery in Englewood, New Jersey. He was the author of *The Changing Order,* a 1914 work that explained his thoughts in a series of essays, with a speech on the Sherman Anti-trust Act. The Wickersham Award is given out to attorneys for "their exceptional . . . dedication to the law profession."

References: The Attorney Generals of the United States, 1789–1985 (Washington, DC: Department of Justice, 1985), 94; *Enforcement of the Prohibition Laws* (Washington, DC: GPO; 14 vols., 1929–1931), 1: 3–4; German, James, "Taft's Attorney General: George W. Wickersham" (Ph.D. dissertation, New York University, 1969); Gordon, David, "Wickersham, George," in *Encyclopedia of the American Constitution,* Leonard W. Levy, ed.-in-chief, (New York: Macmillan; 4 vols. and 1 supp., 1986–1992), 4: 2062; Mowry, George E., "Wickersham, George Woodward," in *DAB* 2: 713–715; *200th Anniversary of the Office of Attorney General, 1789–1989* (Washington, DC: Department of Justice, 1990), 45–46.

JAMES CLARK MCREYNOLDS
1862–1946

James McReynolds was known for his irascible temper. Some say he was elevated to the U.S. Supreme Court because he angered so many politicians in his role as the forty-eighth attorney general, where he served for more than a quarter of a century, becoming one of the most influential justices of his time. Born on 3 February 1862 in Elkton, Kentucky, James McReynolds was the son of Dr. John Reynolds, a surgeon and physician, and Ellen (née Reeves) McReynolds. The family were members of the radical fundamentalist Campbellite sect of the Disciples of Christ church, and as such James McReynolds grew up in a strictly religious and highly structured household. A loner for most of his life (he never married), he attended Vanderbilt University in Nashville and graduated as the class valedictorian in 1882 with a degree in science. In fact, he began postgraduate work in biology when, suddenly in 1884, left for the University of Virginia to study law. Under the influence of Professor John B. Minor, McReynolds earned his law degree in only fourteen months. After graduating, he worked as an assistant to Senator Howell Edmunds Jackson of Tennessee, who later sat on the U.S. Supreme Court. He then returned to Nashville to open his own law practice.

In Nashville, McReynolds acquired a reputation as a meticulous attorney who served mostly corporate clients. In 1900, to supplement his income, he went to work part-time at Vanderbilt as a professor of commercial law. He ran unsuccessfully for Congress in 1896 (although he ran as a "Gold" standard Democrat, he received backing from the Republican Party). Noticed by officials in Washington, he was named, in 1903, by President Theodore Roosevelt as assistant attorney general under Philander C. Knox. Although he had been a corporate attorney, McReynolds viewed trusts, those industries controlled by just a few major interests, as "wicked," and he used his four years at Justice to aid Knox in taking many of these companies to court to break them up. In 1907, tired, he resigned his position and moved to New York City to open another law practice. Within two years, however, he was named by President William Howard Taft as special counsel to Attorney General George Wickersham to assist in the dissolution of the American Tobacco Company, which he publicly referred to as a group of "commercial wolves and highwaymen." Angered when he felt Wickersham had compromised over a tough decree, he resigned from the Justice Department for a second time and returned to Tennessee, joining the Democratic Party there.

McReynolds was in Nashville when he was called back to Washington to succeed Wickersham as attorney general in the new Woodrow Wilson administration. McReynolds was not Wilson's first choice for attorney general. Wilson biographer August Heckscher relates that "Wilson was strongly inclined to name Louis Brandeis as Attorney General." Brandeis, a labor lawyer in Boston who was later appointed to the U.S. Supreme Court, was considered very liberal, and the thought of a liberal Jew in the cabinet disturbed many Democratic Party leaders, particularly southerners. "From Boston, at the first rumor of such an appointment, came noisy protests," Heckscher adds. "The very mention of Brandeis' name, commented the Boston *Journal,* was enough to cause 'a general collapse' in banking and trust offices. Wilson personally reviewed the charges being circulated against the controversial lawyer. He was convinced they were groundless, yet to avoid a party split he gave in and nominated James C. McReynolds to the post." McReynolds's tenure as the forty-eighth attorney general was, as biographer David Pride relates, "brief and stormy." Tensions between McReynolds and Secretary of the Treasury William Gibbs McAdoo were so strong that correspondence between the two departments had to be handled by the White House. McReynolds angered congressmen

and senators on Capitol Hill with his temper, and he was accused of having federal judges spied on. However, relates a history of the Justice Department, "McReynolds . . . was also active in the antitrust field. Some achievements of his Attorney Generalship were the decree requiring the American Telephone and Telegraph Company to relinquish its monopoly of wire communications; the dissolution of the United States Thread Association; an injunction restraining the National Wholesale Jewelers' Association from a conspiracy to restrain trade; and the decree requiring the New Haven Railroad to relinquish a monopoly of transportation in New England."

The death on 12 July 1914 of Supreme Court Justice Horace H. Lurton allowed Wilson to name McReynolds to the Court. Nominated on 19 August 1914, he was confirmed ten days by a vote of 44–6, the fifth attorney general to be elevated to the high court. In his more than twenty-six years on the court, 1914 to 1941, McReynolds became one of the most important dissenters in the history of that tribunal. Although he wrote few majority opinions, those that he did author were libertarian: he struck down a Nebraska law that prohibited the teaching of a foreign language to students before the ninth grade (*Meyer v. Nebraska* [1923]) and a Hawaii statute that banned the teaching of Japanese in schools (*Farrington v. Tokushiga* [1927]). He formed, with Justices George Sutherland, Pierce Butler, and Willis Van Devanter, the group known as "The Four Horsemen" who helped strike down numerous New Deal decisions during the 1930s. However, as these justices died or left the court, McReynolds became more and more isolated, until, on 31 January 1941, he announced his retirement. He remained in Washington, where he died on 24 August 1946. He was buried in Glenwood Cemetery, Elkton, Kentucky.

References: *The Attorney Generals of the United States, 1789–1985* (Washington, DC: Department of Justice, 1985), 96; Biskupic, Joan; and Elder Witt, *Guide to the Supreme Court* (Washington, DC: Congressional Quarterly; 2 vols., 1997), 2:

920–921; Fletcher, R. V., "Mr. Justice McReynolds: An Appreciation," *Vanderbilt Law Review,* 2 (December 1948), 35–46; Heckscher, August, *Woodrow Wilson* (New York: Charles Scribner's Sons, 1991), 271; Jones, Calvin P., "Kentucky's Irascible Conservative: Supreme Court Justice James Clark McReynolds," *Filson Club History Quarterly* 57 (January 1983), 20–30; Pride, David T., "James C. McReynolds," in Clare Cushman, ed., *The Supreme Court Justices: Illustrated Biographies, 1789–1995* (Washington, DC: Congressional Quarterly, 1995), 326–330; *200th Anniversary of the Office of Attorney General, 1789–1989* (Washington, DC: Department of Justice, 1990), 46.

THOMAS WATT GREGORY
1861–1933

Thomas Gregory was the second of Woodrow Wilson's three attorneys general. Born in Crawfordsville, Mississippi, on 6 November 1861, he was the son of Capt. Francis Robert Gregory, a physician who died soon after his son's birth fighting for the Confederacy in the Civil War, and Mary Cornelia (née Watt) Gregory. He grew up in the home of his maternal grandfather. He attended local schools, then went to Southwestern Presbyterian University in Clarksville, Tennessee. In 1883 he went to the University of Virginia, where a classmate was James Clark McReynolds, whom he later succeeded as attorney general.

After graduating from the University of Texas in 1885 with a law degree, Gregory opened a law office in the capital, Austin. He served as assistant city attorney from 1891 to 1894, refusing appointments as assistant attorney general of Texas and a state judge. A lifelong Democrat, he was a delegate to the 1912 Democratic National Convention and threw his support behind Governor Woodrow Wilson of New Jersey. Afterwards, he worked in the Texas state campaign for Wilson when he became the party's nominee. After Wilson was elected, Gregory was named special assistant to the U.S. attorney general in New York trying to end the monopoly of the New York, New Haven & Hartford Railroad, a case that was settled before going to court. His work in this case, as well as his early and strong support of Wilson in 1912, led to his nomination on 29 August 1914 as attorney general.

In his nearly five years as the forty-ninth attorney general, Gregory dealt mainly with issues that arose out of World War I. A history of the Justice Department explains, "Gregory . . . wrote many opinions related to American participation in that struggle. The Clayton Act, the Federal Trade Commission Act, measures supplementing the Sherman Act, and other regulatory statutes were passed in Gregory's administration. Gregory himself opposed proposals to put aside for the duration of the war antitrust actions pending against several large corporations (but was overruled by President Wilson), and he presented in the Supreme Court motions to suspend suits against combinations in show machinery, farm machinery, steel, and other products." Gregory also supervised the arrests of more than 6,300 suspected spies and brought action against more than 220,000 men who did not comply with the Selective Service Act. In 1916, with the resignation of Justice Charles Evans Hughes from the Supreme Court, Wilson offered the vacancy to Gregory, who refused because his hearing was impaired and he did not like the "confining" atmosphere the court presented.

On 4 March 1919, as the Paris Peace Conference was ready to begin to draft the Versailles peace treaty ending World War I, Gregory resigned as attorney general. Wilson wrote to him, "I cannot tell you with what grief I think of your leaving the Cabinet. I have never been associated with a man whose gifts and character I have admired more. . . . I shall feel robbed of one of my chief supporters when you are gone." After serving for a short time as one of the president's advisers in Paris, Gregory returned to the United States and practiced law for a short time in Washington as a partner in the firm of Gregory and Todd. He then moved to Houston, where in his final years he served as a law professor at the University of Texas.

In 1921, he was counsel for the state of Texas in a boundary dispute that wound up before the U.S. Supreme Court (*State of Oklahoma v. State of Texas* 1921).

Prior to the inauguration of President Franklin D. Roosevelt in March 1933, Gregory went to Washington to confer with the new president on legal matters. While there, he contracted pneumonia and died on 26 February 1933 at the age of 71; his body was returned to Austin for burial. The Gregory gymnasium at the University of Texas at Austin is named in his honor, as is the Thomas Watt Gregory law professorship at the same institution.

References: The Attorney Generals of the United States, 1789–1985 (Washington, DC: Department of Justice, 1985), 98; Heckscher, August, *Woodrow Wilson* (New York: Charles Scribner's Sons, 1991), 528; Mallison, A. G., "Gregory, Thomas Watt," in *DAB* 1: 358–360; Robb, Arthur, "Biographical Sketches of the Attorneys General" (Unpublished essay DOJ, Washington, DC, 1946), 60; *200th Anniversary of the Office of Attorney General, 1789–1989* (Washington, DC: Department of Justice, 1990), 46–47.

ALEXANDER MITCHELL PALMER
1872–1936

A. Mitchell Palmer is remembered as the man who used all the power of the U.S. government to jail and deport suspected Bolshevik radicals in the years during and after World War I. A Quaker and a man of peace, his name has become synonymous with heavy-handed government power and the infringement of civil liberties. The son of Samuel Bernard Palmer and Caroline (née Albert) Palmer, Alexander Mitchell Palmer was born near White Haven, Pennsylvania, on 4 May 1872. Palmer attended schools in nearby Stroudsburg, then went to a Moravian parochial school in Bethlehem before graduating from Swarthmore College in 1891. He studied stenography in Scranton and was appointed as the official stenographer of the Forty-third Judicial District of Pennsylvania in 1892.

While working as a stenographer, Palmer studied the law and in 1893 was admitted to the state bar. He practiced law with a local judge, John B. Storm, until the latter's death in 1901. In the next decade, Palmer built up a strong legal base, becoming one of the more important attorneys in northeastern Pennsylvania. A member of the Democratic state executive committee, he was elected in 1908 to the Sixty-first Congress from Pennsylvania's Twenty-sixth Congressional District and was reelected in 1910 and 1912. It was in this final term, from 1913 until 1915, that he served as the House Democratic Caucus chairman.

A member of the Democratic National Committee from 1912 until 1920, Palmer worked to end the interstate shipping of products produced from child labor; he was considered an up-and-coming politician, and, in 1912, he threw his weight behind a little-known politician, New Jersey Governor Woodrow Wilson, for president. At the national convention, he managed affairs for Wilson and helped win for the governor the presidential nomination. During the campaign, he was one of Wilson's trusted advisers, and, when Wilson was elected president, Palmer was offered the spot of secretary of war, but he refused on the grounds of his Quaker religion. In 1914, he gave up his House seat to run for the U.S. Senate but was defeated by Gifford Pinchot. In April 1915, one month after leaving Congress, Palmer was named as a justice to the U.S. Court of Appeals but, because the salary was low, he declined and returned to his law practice.

During World War I Congress passed the Trading with the Enemy Act, which established an office to confiscate and administer the property of German citizens in the United States. On 22 October 1917, Wilson offered, and Palmer accepted, the post of Alien Property Custodian. It was in this office that he incurred many enemies, who swore revenge on him. Following the resignation of Attorney General Thomas Watt Gregory on 4 March 1919, Wilson turned the following day to Palmer, who was quickly confirmed. Wilson biographer August Heckscher writes that Wilson looked hard for anyone other than Palmer to replace Gregory. "He did not want Palmer," intones Heckscher. "He did not trust him, yet he came up with no name except a routine subordinate in the Justice Department."

Gregory had been denounced by some newspapers for his gentle treatment of radicals. The *World* of New York exclaimed, "The activities of the 'Reds' in New York, Philadelphia and other cities may cause an outbreak in Congress at any time. Congressmen are waiting to see what the Department of Justice will do." Palmer did not have to wait long. On the night of 2 June 1919, a huge explosion outside of his home shook him; later it was discovered that two men had tried to plant a bomb outside of his door, but it had exploded, killing both of them and leaving both unidentified forever. Undeterred and acting on information he obtained while alien property custodian, Palmer launched the Red Raids of suspected communist hideouts in January 1920, and some three thousand suspected Bolsheviks and communists were seized. Among those arrested and subsequently deported were anarchists Alexander Berkman and Emma Goldman. On 18 February 1920, Palmer wrote that he believed it was the job of the U.S. government "to rid the country of the Red agitators who are attempting to lay the foundation for such trouble."

He also used force to end a bituminous coal workers strike and got Congress to appropriate $500,000 to establish a Bureau of Investigation (later the Federal Bureau of Investigation) in the Justice Department, with former librarian J. Edgar Hoover as its head. Serving for a period of exactly two years, until the end of the Wilson administration on 4 March 1921, Palmer became one of the most controversial attorneys general to ever serve.

After leaving office, he returned to his law practice in Stroudsburg and practiced for a time in Washington, D.C.. Palmer was just a week past his seventy-fourth birthday when he died on 11 May 1936 and was buried in the Quaker Laurelwood Cemetery in Stroudsburg.

References: The Attorney Generals of the United States, 1789–1985 (Washington, DC: Department of Justice, 1985), 100; Clements, Kendrick A., *The Presidency of Woodrow Wilson* (Lawrence: University Press of Kansas, 1992); Coben, Stanley, *A. Mitchell Palmer: Politician* (New York: Columbia University Press, 1963), 1–7, 197–237; Dunn, Robert Williams, *The Palmer Raids* (New York: International, 1948); Heckscher, August, *Woodrow Wilson* (New York: Charles Scribner's Sons, 1991), 529; "Palmer, A[lexander] Mitchell," in *NCAB* A: 44–45; Preston, William, Jr., *Aliens & Dissenters: Federal Suppression of Radicals, 1903–1933* (Urbana: University of Illinois Press, 1994), 193–194 (Palmer to H. H. Hayhow).

HARRY MICAJAH DAUGHERTY
1860–1941

Harry Daugherty remains the only attorney general ever to resign facing serious criminal charges, although he was later acquitted of the allegations made against him in connection with the Teapot Dome scandal. Known as the "President Maker," Daugherty was responsible for the decision in the "smoke-filled room" when his mentor, Senator Warren G. Harding of Ohio, was nominated for president. Born in the village of Washington Court House, Ohio, on 26 January 1860, he was the son of John Harry Daugherty, a tailor, and Jane Amelia (née Draper) Daugherty. Daugherty studied at local schools and seemed to hover between the ministry, which his mother wanted, and a career as a physician, which a local doctor counseled him to follow. He studied medicine for a year, but, after working as a reporter for the *Cincinnati Enquirer* for a single year, he moved to the University of Michigan, where he studied law and received a degree in 1881, opening a practice in his hometown. Four years later he was admitted to the bar.

Almost immediately, Daugherty became involved in politics. He joined the Republican Party in 1881, served as a delegate to a state judicial convention, and was elected as township clerk. In 1890, he was elected to the Ohio state House of Representatives, serving until 1894; this would be the highest elective office he would ever attain. In 1895 he was an unsuccessful candidate for state attorney general, and, in 1897, he failed in an attempt to get the Republican nomination for governor. His final runs for office were two unsuccessful races for U.S. Senate in 1909 and 1916.

As a member of the prestigious law firm of Daugherty, Todd & Rarey, Daugherty represented many corporate clients, including American Tobacco, Armour & Co., the Western Union Telegraph Company, and others, all of which reportedly made him a wealthy man. During this time, however, he made many political enemies (he was accused of switching votes for bribes) with his calculating character and unsavory reputation. He was also a shrewd campaigner and party activist, and he made himself known in the campaigns of William McKinley in 1896 and William Howard Taft in 1908 and 1912. This natural leadership placed him to be in the back room of the 1920 Republican National Convention when the choice for president stalled, and he pushed for the compromise choice of Senator Warren G. Harding of Ohio. Although biographer James N. Giglio explains that Daugherty and Harding were never really as close as Daugherty later claimed, Harding was thankful for Daugherty's support at the convention and, when he was elected president, returned the favor with an offer to be attorney general. In his 1932 *mea culpa, The Inside Story of the Harding Tragedy,* Daugherty claimed that once he had gotten Harding elected, he had no real desire to serve in government. Nonetheless,

write Harding administration historians Eugene Trani and David Wilson, "Harding believed that it was the president's right to have one or two friends in the cabinet. Both Albert Fall [selected for Secretary of the Interior] and Harry Daugherty fell into this category. Daugherty was the president's closest political adviser, and Harding was deeply in debt for years of public service." Daugherty accepted the attorney general position and took office on 5 March 1921.

In his three short years as attorney general, culminating in his resignation in shame on 28 March 1924, he became swept up in more controversy than any man who had ever held the office. He was the subject of frequent attacks on Capitol Hill, particularly by Republicans, for his running of the Justice Department, where he was accused of inefficiency and criminal behavior. Daugherty was later accused of accepting a bribe from the American Metal Company to facilitate its return to the owners after it had been confiscated as alien property during World War I. Demands that he investigate individuals who had defrauded the government during the war were met with silence; Daugherty claimed he was moving in an "orderly way." This led Representative Oscar O. Keller, Republican of Minnesota, to try to impeach him, an effort that failed in the Senate. Daugherty then published *Facts of Record, from Official Congress Reports, and Editorials from the Press of the United States,* to demonstrate his innocence.

In 1924, a Senate committee began to investigate charges that government oil reserves at Teapot Dome, Wyoming, were being sold cheaply and that bribes were being paid to Secretary of the Interior Albert B. Fall for the sale of these lands. The committee found that these charges were true and, even worse, that Daugherty knew of the frauds, by Fall, Secretary of the Navy Edwin Denby, and oilmen Harry F. Sinclair and Edward L. Doheny, and yet had failed to prosecute them. Two special prosecutors, Deputy Attorney General Owen J. Roberts and former U.S. Senator Atlee Pomerene of Ohio, were hired to investigate; they concluded that Daugherty had not known about the frauds. Still, on 28 March 1924, President Calvin Coolidge asked for and received Daugherty's resignation.

Accused after leaving office of accepting a bribe in the American Metal Company matter, Daugherty was brought to court twice facing indictment, but the grand juries both times refused to indict. Daugherty spent his last years trying to vindicate himself in his role in Teapot Dome, for which Secretary Fall went to prison. In 1940, shortly before his death, Daugherty tried to exonerate himself in public. "What I did was done in the interest of the American people and my action was sustained by the courts," he wrote. "Notwithstanding the abuse I received, I can say now that given the same circumstances I would not change an official or personal act of mine while I was Attorney General. That's a clear conscience for you." He died in Columbus, Ohio, on 12 October 1941 at the age of 81 and was buried in his family's mausoleum in the Washington Court House Cemetery.

References: *The Attorney Generals of the United States, 1789–1985* (Washington, DC: Department of Justice, 1985), 102; Daugherty, Harry M., and Thomas Dixon, *The Inside Story of the Harding Tragedy* (New York: Churchill, 1932); Giglio, James M., "Daugherty, Harry Micajah," in *DAB* 3: 213–214; Giglio, James N., "The Political Career of Harry M. Daugherty" (Ph.D. dissertation, Ohio State University, 1968); ———, *H. M. Daugherty and the Politics of Expediency* (Kent, OH: Kent State University Press, 1978).

HARLAN FISKE STONE
1872–1946

Harlan Stone is only one of two former attorneys general to be elevated to Chief Justice of the U.S. Supreme Court and the only one to also serve as an associate justice. Named as attorney general during a period

in which he was also investigating rampant corruption in the wake of the Teapot Dome scandal, he served only a year before being named to the Court. The son of Frederick Lawson Stone, a farmer, and Ann Sophia (née Butler) Stone, Harlan Fiske Stone was born in the village of Chesterfield, New Hampshire, on 11 October 1872. When Harlan Stone was 2 years old, his parents moved to a farm near Amherst, Massachusetts. He attended the Massachusetts Agricultural College (now the University of Massachusetts) from 1888 to 1890 and then earned, in 1894, a bachelor of science degree from Amherst College. For the next two years, he taught at a high school in Newburyport, Massachusetts, and at an academy in New York City, work that paid for his legal education at Columbia University Law School. He graduated in 1898 and was admitted to the bar that same year, going to work for the Wall Street firm of Sullivan & Cromwell. He also taught at Columbia, rising to become adjunct professor of law in 1903.

Stone moved to another firm, which later became Wilmer, Canfield & Stone. He quit Columbia in 1905 to become a lawyer full time but, in 1910, was persuaded to return by Nicholas Murray Butler, president of Columbia, to serve as a professor of law and dean of the law school. His tenure, which lasted until 1923, saw a growth in the faculty and college curriculum. In 1923, Stone resigned a second time to once again join Sullivan & Cromwell as head of the firm's litigation department.

On 28 March 1924, President Calvin Coolidge, an Amherst classmate of Stone's, asked for the resignation of Attorney General Harry Daugherty, who had been caught up in the myriad of allegations relating to the massive Teapot Dome scandal. Coolidge approached Stone to fill the vacancy to "clean up" the Justice Department. He accepted and, on 7 April 1924, began work as the fifty-second attorney general. Assistant Attorney General Mabel Walker Willebrandt, the first woman to hold that position, wrote, "When Justice Stone was appointed Attorney General . . . the Department of Justice was in a turmoil . . . Senator [Burton K.] Wheeler [of Montana] was at that time demanding that the entire Department of Justice be 'cleaned out,' that all of it was tainted with 'Daughertyism.' " Stone directed to his subordinates that regardless of his feelings about the Eighteenth Amendment, Prohibition, the laws of the nation must be upheld, and he demanded that any Justice Department official who could not do this must go. His most significant mark in the short time he held the post was his appointment of J. Edgar Hoover to head the Federal Bureau of Investigation (FBI). A member of Coolidge's "medicine ball cabinet," he was with the president early each morning on the White House lawn exercising with a medicine ball.

On 5 January 1925, Supreme Court Justice Joseph McKenna, a former attorney general, announced his retirement from the court after almost twenty-seven years. After only eleven months as attorney general, Stone was tapped by Coolidge to take the open seat. Stone appeared before the Senate Judiciary Committee—the first Supreme Court nominee ever to do so—to deal with questions raised by his handling of what some considered political trials of Senator Wheeler in Montana. Stone was confirmed, 71–6, on 5 February 1925, and he took the oath on 2 March 1925. Stone thus became the first university professor ever named to the Court and, with Edward Douglass White, one of only two men named chief justice by a president of the opposite political party. His former assistant, Mabel Willebrandt, writes, "It had been suggested that because of his political 'naiveté' especially in the matter of contemplating [the] anti-trust prosecution of [former Secretary of the Treasury Andrew] Mellon's aluminum empire, and his politically inexpedient treading upon Senators' toes (particularly by disregarding their wishes with respect to appointments), Stone was 'kicked upstairs' to the Supreme Court. . . . I am sure Justice Stone *was* 'kicked upstairs' to the Supreme Court. I feel confident that he thought so too. When he told me of the offer, it was with a sense of regret, because as he said, 'I like doing this job. It

needs to be done and I've only just gotten started.' "

In his sixteen years as an associate justice, Stone "preached a philosophy of judicial restraint," reports biographer Catherine Barnes. His most significant achievement was the well-known "footnote 4" of the case *United States v. Carolene Products* (1938), in which he enumerated the doctrine that the First Amendment rights of the American people were fundamental and more important than any other right listed in the Constitution and that laws dealing with these special rights deserve special scrutiny. In 1940, he upheld this doctrine in a strong dissent in which the Court upheld a law demanding that all children, including those whose religion forbade it, salute the American flag; Stone's argument won the days in 1943 when the court overturned its earlier holding. At his death, the *New York Times* editorialized, "Appointed by a conservative president, he was an outspoken member of the liberal wing of the Court in a long series of decisions on the constitutionality of various New Deal measures."

On 12 June 1941, Stone was nominated by President Franklin Roosevelt, a Democrat, to succeed Chief Justice and former Secretary of State Charles Evans Hughes (with whom Stone had served in the Coolidge administration). Confirmed by a voice vote on 3 July 1941, Stone became the ninth chief justice and the second, and last, former attorney general to accept the top seat on the Court (the other was Roger B. Taney). In this role, he held that a military court sentencing a Japanese war crimes suspect to death was constitutional and that the curfew placed on Japanese Americans, as well as the internment by the government, was wholly constitutional under war powers. It was Chief Justice Stone who swore in Harry S Truman as president on the day of the death of President Roosevelt. His dislike of administrative duties, however, has led historians to conclude that Stone was not a good chief justice. Historian John P. Frank wrote, "As an individual justice, Stone was one of the great, dynamic contributors to American law. But as Chief Justice, he was strikingly unsuccessful."

During his tenure, which lasted less than five years, the court was usually divided among some of the more contentious issues of the day.

While reading a dissent in a naturalization case on 22 April 1946, Stone suffered a massive stroke and died later that day. He was 63 years old and was buried in Rock Creek Cemetery in Washington, D.C.

References: The Attorney Generals of the United States, 1789–1985 (Washington, DC: Department of Justice, 1985), 104; Barnes, Catherine A., *Men of the Supreme Court: Profiles of the Justices* (New York: Facts on File, 1978), 145–146; Irving Brant to Alpheus T. Mason, 22 July 1951, and Mabel Walker Willebrandt to Mason, 31 January 1951, in "Biographer's Papers," Box 83, Harlan Fiske Stone Papers, Library of Congress; Lusky, Louis, "Harlan Fiske Stone," in Clare Cushman, ed., *The Supreme Court Justices: Illustrated Biographies, 1789–1995* (Washington, DC: Congressional Quarterly, 1995), 361–365; Mason, Alpheus Thomas, *Harlan Fiske Stone: Pillar of the Law* (New York: Viking, 1956); Nash, A. E., Kier, "Stone, Harlan Fiske," in Kermit L. Hall, ed.-in-chief, *The Oxford Companion to the Supreme Court of the United States* (New York: Oxford University Press, 1992), 839–840; "Stone, Harlan Fiske," in Otis L. Graham, Jr., and Meghan Robinson Wander, eds., *Roosevelt: His Life and Times—An Encyclopedic View* (Boston: G. K. Hall, 1985), 408–409.

John Garibaldi Sargent
1860–1939

John Sargent served as the third of Calvin Coolidge's three attorneys general. Born in the village of Ludlow, Vermont, on 13 October 1860, John Garibaldi Sargent was the son of John Henmon (also spelled Henman) Sargent and Ann Eliza (née Harley) Sargent. One of his boyhood friends was Calvin Coolidge, who went on to become president of the United States. Sargent attended the Vermont Liberal Academy in Plymouth, Vermont, and the Black River Academy at Ludlow, graduating from the latter institution in

1883. He then entered Tufts College in Medford, Massachusetts, from which he received his law degree in 1887. He then studied law in the office of Ludlow attorney William W. Stickney (who was later elected governor of Vermont) and was admitted to the state bar in 1890. He served first as Stickney's law clerk for two years, then joined him in a law partnership in 1892.

In 1898, Sargent was elected as a Republican as state's attorney for Windsor County, Vermont, where he served for two years. In 1900, Sargent's law partner, Stickney, was elected governor, and Sargent was appointed as the state's secretary of civil and military affairs. After two years in this position, he returned to his law firm. In 1907, three years after the office of state attorney general was established, he was elected as Vermont's top law enforcement officer and served two full terms (1908–1912). He then returned to his law practice. During the next several years he became a wealthy man representing corporate interests.

On 1 March 1925, Attorney General Harlan Fiske Stone resigned to take a seat on the U.S. Supreme Court. Sargent's friend Calvin Coolidge, who had become president in 1923 upon the death of Warren G. Harding, first chose Charles Beecher Warren, a noted attorney and a former ambassador to Mexico and Japan, to succeed Stone. However, Warren ran into opposition on Capitol Hill regarding his close association with the sugar trusts, and his nomination was turned down, 39–41, on 10 March 1925. Two days later, Coolidge named him a second time, but, within four days, Warren was again defeated, 39–46. Coolidge admitted defeat and requested of Sargent to come to Washington to assume the attorney general's office. Sargent was confirmed and served from 18 March 1925 until the end of the Coolidge administration, 4 March 1929.

Much of his time was spent enforcing prohibition laws. Two of the key cases that he argued before the Supreme Court and won were *Myers v. United States* (1926), in which the Court upheld the right of the president to dismiss an executive branch officer who had received the "advice and consent" of the U.S. Senate, and *Olmstead et al. v. United States* (1928), in which evidence gathered through a wiretap was found to be constitutional. When fellow cabinet member Herbert Hoover, the secretary of commerce, was elected president in 1928, there is no evidence that he asked Sargent to remain in the Justice Department. Sargent left Washington and rejoined his old law firm in Ludlow.

In the final decade of his life, Sargent served as a referee to reorganize the state's railroads and argued a case before the U.S. Supreme Court regarding the border between Vermont and New Hampshire. He was corporate counsel to the Boston & Maine Railroad, Traveler's Insurance, and the Rutland Railway Light & Power Company. In 1935, two years after the death of former President Coolidge, he was the head of a committee that raised funds to restore and establish as a landmark Coolidge's birthplace in Plymouth. Sargent died in Ludlow on 5 March 1939 at the age of 78.

References: *The Attorney Generals of the United States, 1789–1985* (Washington, DC: Department of Justice, 1985), 106; Fuess, Claude M., *Calvin Coolidge: The Man from Vermont* (Boston: Little, Brown, 1940); "John Garibaldi Sargent," in *NCAB* 32: 370–371 and A: 12–13; Robb, Arthur, "Biographical Sketches of the Attorneys General" (Unpublished essay DOJ, Washington, DC, 1946), 64.

WILLIAM DeWITT MITCHELL
1874–1955

But for politics, William Mitchell would have been named to a seat on the U.S. Supreme Court. A solicitor general in the Coolidge administration and attorney general in the Hoover administration, he was passed over on at least two, and possibly three, occasions. Mitchell, the son of William Mitchell, an attorney who later served as a Minnesota

state Supreme Court justice for some twenty years, and Frances (née Merritt) Mitchell, was born in the village of Winona, Minnesota, on 9 September 1874. He received his early education in the public schools of Winona and in Lawrenceville, New Jersey, after which he entered the Sheffield Scientific School at Yale University to study electrical engineering in 1891. Within two years, however, his interest had shifted from engineering to law, and he left Sheffield to attend the University of Minnesota, which awarded him a bachelor's degree in 1895 and, after work at that institution's law school, an LL.B. degree the following year. Mitchell studied law under his father and was admitted to the state bar that same year. He opened a law office in St. Paul.

Mitchell served in several firms, including a partnership with his father until the latter's death in 1900. In 1898, with the onset of the Spanish-American War, he served in the army and was promoted to second lieutenant in the Fifteenth Minnesota Infantry; he also worked as the judge advocate for the Second U.S. Army Corps. From 1899 to 1901 he advanced to engineer officer of the Third Brigade, First Division of that corps and captain and adjutant of the Fourth Regiment of the Minnesota National Guard. After his war service, he returned to St. Paul, where he joined the prestigious firm of How, Butler & Mitchell, one of his partners being the distinguished lawyer Pierce Butler, who would later sit on the U.S. Supreme Court. Mitchell was apolitical and was not involved in the Minnesota or national political scene.

After seeing service during World War I as a colonel in the Sixth Minnesota Infantry, Mitchell in 1919 became regional counsel for the U.S. Railroad Commission. Over the next several years, he refused several judicial appointments. On 4 June 1925, when Solicitor General James M. Beck resigned, Supreme Court Justice Butler asked President Coolidge to appoint Mitchell to the vacant post. Serving until the end of the Coolidge administration, he argued numerous cases, especially those dealing with law enforcement issues in the prohibition fight, before the Supreme

Court. Mitchell was so highly regarded, particularly by the justices of the Supreme Court, that they all wrote to President-elect Hoover in 1928 to name the solicitor general as his attorney general.

Mitchell, however, was not on Hoover's list when the commerce secretary and president-elect sat down to build his cabinet. According to Hoover administration historian Martin Fausold, Hoover's first choice was Col. William J. Donovan, head of the antitrust division in the Justice Department during the Coolidge administration. However, Donovan was against prohibition and was a Catholic—two lightning rods over which Hoover did not want a fight. Senator William Borah of Idaho and labor leader William N. Doak warned Hoover that the Senate would revolt if Donovan was named. After passing over the World War I veteran, Hoover set his sights on former attorney general and Supreme Court Justice Harlan Fiske Stone, who refused to leave the bench. William R. Castle, whom Hoover had asked for a report on Mitchell, wrote to the president-elect that the solicitor general was "a man of the finest intellectual caliber and in any position there could never be [a] question of his integrity." Mitchell was nominated and confirmed. He served the entire four years of the Hoover administration.

The *New York Times* wrote upon Mitchell's death in 1955, "Throughout his term [he] firmly upheld the antitrust laws. He took this position in relation to the big oil interests, the big film companies, the radio industry and all others." A Justice Department history relates, "Mitchell . . . followed [Attorney General William] Wirt's historic precept by refusing to give the Senate an opinion regarding proposed railroad mergers, but he advised the President that proposed legislation authorizing Congress to make final decisions on tax refunds of more than $20,000 would be an unconstitutional transfer to the legislative branch of a function of the execution branch. Enforcement of prohibition was a burdensome duty of Mitchell's term, and reorganization of the federal prison system [was] one of his accomplishments." In one of his last reports as attorney general, he defended the use of government troops against World War I veterans, called "Bonus Marchers," who marched on Washington demanding a bonus for their service in the war, calling the protesters communists and criminals. With the act of 3 July 1930, Congress appropriated first $10 million (later increased to $12 million) for the construction of a permanent structure for the department. Mitchell oversaw initial construction; the building was not completed until the tenure of his successor, Homer Cummings. He was considered for vacant seats on the Supreme Court in 1930 and 1932, but was passed over for Owen Josephus Roberts and Benjamin Cardozo, respectively.

With the election of Franklin D. Roosevelt in 1932, Mitchell left government to work at a Wall Street firm. In the next several years, he was deeply involved in revising the federal rules of civil procedure, considered one his most important contributions to American law. In 1945, he advised, as chief counsel, a congressional investigation into the Pearl Harbor attack. In his final years, he denounced Roosevelt and a Supreme Court that he saw as straying too far from the Constitution. On 24 August 1955, two weeks short of his eighty-first birthday, Mitchell died after a prolonged illness.

References: *The Attorney Generals of the United States, 1789–1985* (Washington, DC: Department of Justice, 1985), 108; Danelski, David J., *A Supreme Court Justice Is Appointed* (New York: Random House, 1964); Fausold, Martin L., *The Presidency of Herbert C. Hoover* (Lawrence: University Press of Kansas, 1985), 34–35; Kreuter, Kent, "Mitchell, William DeWitt," in *DAB* 5: 501–503; *200th Anniversary of the Office of Attorney General, 1789–1989* (Washington, DC: Department of Justice, 1990), 48.

HOMER STILLÉ CUMMINGS

1870–1956

Homer Cummings was the first of the four men who served as attorney general during the three full terms of President Franklin D. Roosevelt, and during this term he helped draft the controversial court-packing scheme, which aroused vehement oppostion in Congress and was ultimately abandoned. Homer Cummings, the son of Uriah C. Cummings, whom biographer Carl Swisher called "a distinguished inventor, manufacturer, and writer on technical subjects," and Audie Schuyler (née Stillé) Cummings, was born on 30 April 1870 in Chicago, Illinois. He attended the Heathcote School in Buffalo, New York, Yale College, and Yale Law School, graduating from the latter institution in 1893. That same year he was admitted to the Connecticut bar.

Cummings formed a law partnership with two attorneys, Samuel Fessenden and Galen A. Carter, and established a firm in Stamford, Connecticut. In 1900, the firm was dissolved, by which time, Cummings had made his name as a lawyer of some note. In 1909, he established a firm with Charles D. Lockwood, whom he remained a partner with until joining the cabinet in 1933. A Democrat who had supported William Jennings Bryan for the presidency in 1896, Cummings was elected mayor of Stamford in 1900, 1901, and 1904, for three single two-year terms; he was known as a progressive whose municipal program helped build new streets and sewers. He also served as president of the Stamford Board of Trade from 1903 until 1909, as corporation counsel from 1908 to 1912, and as the state's attorney for Fairfield County from 1912 to 1924. It was in this latter office that he cleared a man of murder despite a confession that Cummings felt was forced (*State v. Harold Israel,* 1924), a case that was later made into the 1947 motion picture *Boomerang.*

A member of the Democratic National Committee from 1900 to 1925, Cummings was a speaker on behalf of Woodrow Wilson in the 1912 campaign, where he met and befriended another supporter, Franklin D. Roosevelt, who later served in the Wilson administration as assistant secretary of the navy. At the 1920 Democratic National Convention, he delivered the keynote address and worked to end political divisions at the 1920, 1924, and 1928 conventions. He was the man selected to deliver the official notification of nomination to the 1920 vice-presidential candidate, Franklin Roosevelt. In 1919, Cummings was named by President Wilson as chairman of the Democratic National Committee, serving until 1920.

In 1932, New York Governor Franklin Roosevelt ran for the Democratic presidential nomination; Cummings, a delegate-at-large from Connecticut, was one of his leading supporters, acting as floor manager for the Roosevelt campaign to round up convention delegates. With Roosevelt's election, Cummings was suggested for various cabinet positions. For his attorney general, Roosevelt chose Senator Thomas J. Walsh of Montana, whose investigations of the Harding administration in the 1920s led to the Teapot Dome scandal, but two days before the inauguration, Walsh suffered a massive heart attack and died. Roosevelt had selected Cummings to succeed Theodore Roosevelt, Jr., as governor-general of the Philippines. With Walsh's death, however, Roosevelt asked Cummings to come to Washington to serve as attorney general *ad interim* until a replacement for Walsh could be found. A month later, the president startled Cummings when, during a cabinet meeting, he announced that the appointment would be permanent.

As attorney general, Cummings served for six years as Roosevelt's legal adviser on everything from the constitutionality of New Deal measures to law enforcement by the Federal Bureau of Investigation (FBI). This tenure was the longest in the history of the department in a century, since that of William Wirt (1817–1829). The Supreme Court's striking down of key New Deal legislation, which Cummings had argued was constitutional, during Roosevelt's first term led the president to ask Cummings to draft a reorganization of the Supreme Court to allow Roosevelt to name a new justice to the court for everyone over the age of 70 who did not retire. This Supreme Court Reorganization Bill was so badly received on Capitol Hill, particularly by Democrats, that it nearly destroyed the Roosevelt presidency. After 168 days, senators from both parties killed the bill by returning it to committee.

Cummings was also noted for arguing the Gold Clause cases before the Court and for overseeing completion of the Department of Justice building in Washington, the first permanent home of the department. His biographer, Carl Swisher, writes, "As 1938 drew to a close, the reforms to which Attorney General Cummings had committed himself had largely been achieved. In the fields of crime control, of procedural reform, and, to some extent, of judicial reform his work was done." On 2 January 1939, Cummings resigned to resume the practice of law. On 10 September 1956, he died at his home in Washington, D.C. He was 86 years old.

References: *The Attorney Generals of the United States, 1789–1985* (Washington, DC: Department of Justice, 1985), 110; "Cummings, Homer Stillé," in *Roosevelt: His Life and Times—An Encyclopedic View,* Otis L. Graham, Jr., and Meghan Robinson Wander, eds., (Boston: G. K. Hall & Co., 1985), 87–88; Feinstein, Estelle F., "Cummings, Homer Stillé," in *DAB* 6: 136–138; Swisher, Carl Brent, *Selected Papers of Homer Cummings, Attorney General of the United States, 1933–1939* (New York: Charles Scribner's Sons, 1939), xi–xvi.

FRANCIS WILLIAM MURPHY

1890–1949

Francis Murphy served as Franklin D. Roosevelt's second attorney general for only a year, and he is better known for his nine years on the U.S. Supreme Court. A popular governor of Michigan, Frank Murphy was also a mayor of Detroit and governor-general of the Philippines. Born in Sand Beach (now Harbor Beach), Michigan, on 13 April 1890, he was the son of John Murphy, an attorney, and Mary (née Brennan) Murphy. He attended local schools, then the University of Michigan Law School, from which he received his law degree in 1914. He was admitted to the bar that same year and became a law clerk in the Detroit office of the firm of Monaghan and Monaghan. He taught night school for the three years he worked at the firm. He then started his own private practice, which lasted from 1916 to 1917.

When the United States entered World War I, Murphy enlisted in the U.S. Army and was commissioned a first lieutenant, rising to the rank of captain of infantry of an officer's training school. Later, he was sent to Europe and saw limited action in France and Germany before the end of the war. He then served in the army of occupation in Germany until 1919, when he took additional law studies at Lincoln's Inn in London and Trinity College in Dublin. Back in Detroit, he was named assistant U.S. attorney for the eastern District of Michigan, where he served from August 1919 until February 1922. He helped prosecute fraud cases arising from the war and was noted for not losing a single decision. After leaving the office, he served as an instructor in law at the University of Detroit.

In 1923, Murphy was elected as judge of the Recorders Court In Detroit. When the incumbent mayor of Detroit was removed in June 1930 on charges of corruption, Murphy was nominated to succeed him. Elected that November, he served for two years, dealing with the Depression and creating the U.S. Conference of Mayors. In 1932, he backed New York Governor Franklin D. Roosevelt for president; with Roosevelt's election, Murphy was named as governor-general of the Philippine Islands, a post he held until 1935. That year, when the Philippines were granted commonwealth status, Murphy took the position as high commissioner. During his tenure, he enacted New Deal–style reforms and supported eventual Philippine independence. In 1936, he returned to Michigan when he was nominated by the Democrats for governor and was elected that November. In his two years in that office (1937–1939), Murphy used his state as an experimental "little New Deal" forum for innovative government programs to end the Depression. He faced the massive General Motors strike in 1937, when workers, sitting down to protest wage cuts, invented the "sit-down" strike. Murphy injected himself into the negotiations; it was he who left a Detroit hotel conference room at 3:00 A.M. on 11 February 1937 to announce, "Gentlemen, an agreement has been reached."

With the resignation of Attorney General Homer S. Cummings on 2 January 1939, Roosevelt offered the position to Murphy, who accepted, although he had wanted the secretary of war portfolio. His tenure as the fifty-sixth attorney general, which lasted from 2 January 1939 until 18 January 1940, was marked by an increased crackdown on political corruption and trusts, as well as the establishment of the Civil Rights Division in the Department of Justice. The *New York Times* later commented, "As Attorney General he encouraged the prosecution of both business and labor for alleged violations of the antitrust laws. He sponsored the investigation of official and judicial corruption, a campaign that led to the ousting of the Pendergast machine in Kansas City, the reopening of investigations of corruption in Louisiana, and the removal of Martin T. Manton, tenth ranking justice of the United States, from the bench of the Circuit Court of Appeals in New York. Mr. Manton was jailed, as was 'Boss' Pendergast." On 16 November 1939, Supreme Court Justice Pierce Butler died; on 4 January 1940, Roosevelt nominated Murphy for the vacancy. Confirmed by a voice vote in the Senate on 16 January 1940, he was sworn in on 5 February.

In his nine years on the Court, Murphy was one of the most liberal justices in the nation's history. His opinions on civil rights, freedom of religion, and labor are landmark. In *Thornhill v. Alabama* (1940), he upheld the right of workers to peacefully picket a labor dispute; in a dissent in *Korematsu v. United States* (1944), he condemned the Court for allowing the internment of Japanese Americans on the West Coast merely because of their ethnicity. After the Japanese attack on Pearl Harbor on 7 December 1941, Murphy wanted to join the army, but he was told he was too old. He asked the president to assign him as a commander in or near the Philippines, but he was refused. Instead, he spent the war as a chairman of Philippine War Relief and as chairman of the National Committee against Nazi Persecution and Extermination of the Jews.

While still sitting on the court, Murphy died in Detroit on 19 July 1949 at the age of 59, and he was buried in Our Lady of Lake Huron Cemetery, Harbor Beach.

References: *The Attorney Generals of the United States, 1789–1985* (Washington, DC: Department of Justice, 1985), 112; Biskupic, Joan, and Elder Witt, *Guide to the Supreme Court* (Washington, DC: Congressional Quarterly; 2 vols., 1997), 2: 943–935; Howard, J. Woodford, Jr., "Frank Murphy and the Sit-Down Strikes of 1937," *Labor History* 1: 2 (Spring 1960), 103–140; Howard, J. Woodford, *Mr. Justice Murphy: A Political Biography* (Princeton, NJ: Princeton University Press, 1968); Lunt, Richard D., *The High Ministry of Government: The Political Career of Frank Murphy* (Detroit: Wayne State University Press, 1965); "Murphy, Frank," in *Biographical Directory of the Governors of the United States, 1789–1978,* Robert Sobel and John Raimo, eds. (Westport, CT: Meckler Books; 4 vols., 1978), 2: 763; Roche, John P., "The Utopian Pilgrimage of Mr. Justice Murphy," *Vanderbilt Law Review* 10: 2 (February 1957), 369–394.

ROBERT HOUGHWOUT JACKSON
1892–1954

Robert Jackson served as solicitor general, attorney general, associate justice on the U.S. Supreme Court, and chief prosecutor at the Nuremberg war crimes trials. The son of

William Eldred Jackson, a farmer, and Angelina (née Houghwout) Jackson, Jackson was born in the small town of Spring Creek, Pennsylvania, on 13 February 1892 and was raised in Frewsburg, New York. He attended Jamestown schools and, after declining to follow his father's wishes to become a doctor, studied law with a local attorney, completed a two-year course in law at the Albany Law School in a single year, and was admitted to the New York bar in 1913. Although he was a Democrat, Jackson was such a nonpartisan that the Republican-dominated town council of Jamestown named him as corporation counsel. He also served as counsel for many businesses and soon established a reputation as a careful and honest attorney.

Jackson first became acquainted with Franklin Roosevelt when, in 1930, Governor Roosevelt named Jackson to serve as a member of the New York State Commission to Investigate the Administration of Justice; in that capacity Jackson recommended needed legal reform in the state. After Roosevelt was elected president in 1932, he brought Jackson to Washington to serve as general counsel to the Bureau of Internal Revenue. After finishing his work there, he was moved to the Justice Department, where he was named assistant attorney general, first in charge of the Tax Division, then the Antitrust Division. In 1937, Jackson told Roosevelt that he wanted to quit government and return to New York; instead, the president named Jackson as solicitor general, the right-hand of the attorney general in charge of arguing cases for the government before the U.S. Supreme Court. Jackson served in this office for nearly two years.

With the resignation of Attorney General Homer S. Cummings on 2 January 1939, Solicitor General Jackson might have been expected to get the job. Instead, Governor Frank Murphy of Michigan was selected. Roosevelt wrote to Jackson, "I want you for my attorney general, Bob, but I want to name Murphy immediately to something and since I can't name him to what he himself wants [Murphy asked to become the Secretary of War], it is desirable to use the attorney generalship temporarily for that purpose." A year later, however, Murphy was elevated to the U.S. Supreme Court, and, on 18 January 1940, Jackson was nominated as the fifty-seventh attorney general. During his tenure of eighteen months, ending in 10 July 1941, Jackson advised the president that allowing the United States to lease battleships and bases to Great Britain when this country was still neutral in the early years of World War II was constitutional without the authority of Congress. He also oversaw early civil liberties cases arising from the Depression and Prohibition.

When he became attorney general, Jackson was apparently promised by Roosevelt that when Chief Justice Charles Evans Hughes retired, Jackson would get the vacant seat. When Hughes did announce his retirement on 12 June 1941, Roosevelt, Hughes and Jackson decided to elevate Associate Justice Harlan Fiske Stone, a former attorney general, and place Jackson in Stone's seat. Jackson was confirmed on 7 July 1941 by a voice vote in the Senate and on 11 July was sworn in as the eighth attorney general elevated to the Supreme Court.

In his thirteen years on the court, Jackson was considered more moderate than he had been previously. In 1945, he argued with Justice Hugo Black over the *Jewell Ridge Coal* case; later, when Chief Justice Stone died, there were reports that when Jackson was considered as Chief Justice, Black threatened to resign from the court. Jackson released a statement displaying his arguments with Black, a first in the Court's history. In 1945, he was instrumental in helping to formulate in London the principles that established guidelines for the trial of Nazi war criminals. Starting that May, Jackson recused himself from the court for eighteen months to become the chief American prosecutor at the Nuremberg war crimes trials in Germany. His son, William Eldred Jackson, also an attorney, served as his father's aide during the trials. Jackson was able to get nineteen guilty verdicts, all handed down on 1 October 1946. On his return to the court, he became more conservative, upholding with the majority in *Dennis v. United States* (1951) the convictions of Communist Party members under the Smith Act, holding that the Fourth Amendment applied to the states (*Wolf v. Colorado,* [1949]), and finding with a unanimous Court that President Truman's seizure of steel mills in 1952 was invalid (*Youngstown Sheet & Tube Co. v. Sawyer* [1952]).

On 9 October 1954, Jackson had a heart attack and died. Jackson was 62. He was buried in the Maple Grove Cemetery in Frewsburg, New York.

References: *The Attorney Generals of the United States, 1789–1985* (Washington, DC: Department of Justice, 1985), 116; Barnes, Catherine A., *Men of the Supreme Court: Profiles of the Justices* (New York: Facts on File, 1978), 101–103; Biskupic, Joan, and Elder Witt, *Guide to the Supreme Court* (Washington, DC: Congressional Quarterly; 2 vols., 1997), 2: 937–938; Marsh, James M., "Robert H. Jackson," in Clare Cushman, ed., *The Supreme Court Justices: Illustrated Biographies, 1789–1995* (Washington, DC: Congressional Quarterly, 1995), 406–410; *200th Anniversary of the Office of Attorney General, 1789–1989* (Washington, DC: Department of Justice, 1990), 51.

FRANCIS BEVERLEY BIDDLE
1886–1968

Francis Biddle is only one of two attorneys general to have been born overseas (the other was Henry D. Gilpin, born in England). He served at the head of the Justice Department for four years as the last of Franklin Roosevelt's four attorneys general. Born in Paris, France, on 9 May 1886, he was the son of Algernon Sydney Biddle and Frances (née Robinson) Biddle. Algernon Biddle was a professor of law at the University of Pennsylvania (the Biddle Law Library at the university is named in his honor) and was touring Europe with his wife when his son was born. Francis Biddle was a direct descendent of Edmund Randolph, the first attorney gen-

eral. Biddle attended Haverford School in Pennsylvania, then Groton School and Harvard University, both in Massachusetts, finishing his education by graduating from the Harvard Law School with honors in 1911.

Biddle was then chosen by Supreme Court Justice Oliver Wendell Holmes as his private secretary, serving from 1911 until 1912. Admitted to the bar in that latter year, he began a practice of law in Philadelphia that lasted more than a quarter of a century, first with the firm of Biddle, Paul & Jayne, then from 1917 to 1939 with Barnes, Biddle & Myers. During that period, he served as a special assistant U.S. attorney for the eastern district of Pennsylvania from 1922 to 1926, chairman of the National Labor Relations Board (NLRB) from 1934 to 1935, and chief counsel of the Special Joint Congressional Committee to Investigate the Tennessee Valley Authority, 1938–1939.

Biddle was a registered Republican during the early part of his life; it was not until the Depression that he changed to the Democratic Party. In 1939, he was named by President Franklin Roosevelt as a judge on the U.S. Court of Appeals for the Third Circuit, where he served for a year. Biddle felt "bored" in this position, and he asked Roosevelt to name him as solicitor general as had been earlier promised. Roosevelt ignored the request until Biddle came to the White House to ask for the post. Finally, with the vacancy created by the elevation of Attorney General Frank Murphy to the Supreme Court, and the movement of Solicitor General Robert H. Jackson to Murphy's job, the office did open and Biddle was named. Appearing before the Supreme Court in some twenty cases, he saw success in a landmark case: *United States v. Darby* ([1941]), the Darby Lumber case, in which the government's wages and hours law was upheld as constitutional.

On 10 July 1941, Attorney General Jackson was named to the Supreme Court, and on 5 September, Roosevelt named Biddle to succeed him as the fifty-eighth attorney general. During his tenure, which ended on 30 June 1945, Biddle was burdened with work connected to World War II. Biographer Peter

Irons writes, "His most difficult decision in this post, and one he intensely regretted, was to abandon his objections to the mass evacuation and internment of 120,000 Americans of Japanese ancestry living on the West Coast. Biddle later attributed his capitulation to his status as the 'new boy' in Roosevelt's cabinet and his deference to Secretary of War Henry L. Stimson, the elder statesman 'whose wisdom and integrity I greatly respected.' " A history of the Department of Justice adds, "When eight Nazi saboteurs were captured and tried before a military commission in 1942, Biddle directed the prosecution and argued successfully in the Supreme Court in opposition to their petitions for habeas corpus. Six of the eight were executed, one sentenced to life imprisonment, and the other to thirty years." (Their case was decided in *Ex parte Quirin* [1942]). Upon the death of Roosevelt on 12 April 1945, Vice-president Harry S Truman succeeded to the presidency; he requested a cabinet of his own choosing, and Biddle handed in his resignation upon the selection of his successor.

In September 1945, Truman rewarded him by naming the former attorney general as a member of the Nuremberg war crimes tribunal. Beginning in November 1945, Biddle, along with judges from Britain, France, and the Soviet Union, sat in judgment of twenty-two Nazi war leaders. Biddle drafted much of the justices' final rendering, delivered on 1 October 1946, which found nineteen of the twenty-two defendants guilty and offered various sentences from death to some prison time. Biographer Catherine Barnes intones, "[His judgment] affirmed that a nation lacked authority to resort to war except in necessary self-defense or as permitted by appropriate international procedure. It also held that the individual was responsible for actions considered illegal under international law." After returning to the United States, he presented a report to President Truman on his actions at Nuremberg.

Biddle found his war crimes experience tiring and felt no desire to return to the legal practice. "I had lost touch with the law," he later wrote. He then spent the rest of his life in retirement in Cape Cod and Washington, D.C. In his final years, he wrote *The Fear of Freedom* (1951), in which many of his writings are collected; *A Casual Past* (1961), on his early years; and *In Brief Authority* (1962), which dealt with his New Deal service. Biddle died in Cape Cod on 4 October 1968 from a heart attack at the age of 82.

References: The Attorney Generals of the United States, 1789–1985 (Washington, DC: Department of Justice, 1985), 118; Barnes, Catherine A., "Biddle, Francis (Beverly)," in Eleanora W. Schoenebaum, ed., *Political Profiles: The Truman Years* (New York: Facts on File, 1978), 35; Irons, Peter, "Biddle, Francis Beverley," in Otis L. Graham, Jr., and Meghan Robinson Wander, eds., *Roosevelt: His Life and Times—An Encyclopedic View,* (Boston: G. K. Hall & Co., 1985), 26–27; Robb, Arthur, "Biographical Sketches of the Attorneys General" (Unpublished essay DOJ, Washington, DC, 1946), 74–76.

THOMAS CAMPBELL CLARK
1899–1977

The first of Harry Truman's three attorneys general, Thomas Clark went on to become a Supreme Court justice. Born in Dallas, Texas, on 28 September 1899, the son of William Clark and Virginia (née Falls) Clark, he received a bachelor's degree in 1921 and a law degree in 1922, both from the University of Texas. Prior to graduating, he had enlisted in the Texas National Guard and served in the 153rd Infantry in Texas. After receiving his law degree, he began a practice in the Dallas law firm of his father and brother, Clark & Clark.

A strong Democrat, in 1927 he left the firm after being named as assistant district attorney for Dallas County. A close friend of District Attorney William McCraw, Clark joined the district attorney in 1932 when Mc-Craw opened a private law practice. Two years later, McCraw ran a successful race for state attorney general, with Clark serving as his campaign manager. In 1937, he was named by President Franklin D. Roosevelt to the Justice Department as a special assistant of the War Risk Insurance Office, where he decided claims by servicemen from World War I. A year later, he was transferred to the Antitrust Divisions and investigated companies connected to the late Senator Huey Long of Louisiana.

In 1940, Clark was sent to the West Coast, first as head of the antitrust office there and, after the Japanese attack on Pearl Harbor, as head of the Alien Enemy Control Office of the Western Defense Command. In this office, he supervised the evacuation and internment of more than 60,000 Japanese Americans. Although at the time he supported the order and carried out it to the fullest, Clark later said that the episode "was the biggest mistake of my life." Impressed by his handling of his duties, Attorney General Francis Biddle assigned Clark to prosecute two German spies who had landed on the coast of Maine with sabotage in mind. Clark was able to secure both convictions and death sentences (later commuted by President Truman). In Washington Clark became a friend of Truman, then U.S. senator from Missouri with whom he worked on the Senate War Investigating Committee. In his duties in the Justice Department to prosecute frauds against the government during the war, Clark frequently turned to Truman for assistance.

At the 1944 Democratic National Convention, Vice-president Henry Wallace was pushed from the national ticket, to be replaced by Speaker of the House Sam Rayburn. When Rayburn refused the honor, Clark interceded to get Truman on the ticket. Less than six months after being reelected president for the fourth time, Franklin D. Roosevelt died and was replaced by Truman. The new president asked for the resignations of the entire cabinet and Clark was appointed to succeed Biddle as the fifty-ninth attorney general. In his four years in the position, a tenure that lasted until 18 August 1949, Clark was noted for numerous antitrust

cases and for appearing three times to argue before the Supreme Court, a task usually left to the solicitor general. Biographer Robert Langran adds, "Clark initiated programs reflecting his personal concerns. He continued to be a strong advocate for antitrust laws, and he began a campaign against juvenile delinquency. To promote knowledge of American history, he organized the Freedom Train, which traveled around the country carrying the nation's major historic documents." Of the 414 antitrust cases prosecuted before the Supreme Court while he was attorney general, he won 314 of them.

The death of Supreme Court Justice Frank Murphy, himself a former attorney general, on 19 July 1949 gave President Truman an opportunity to fill a vacancy on the high Court. On 2 August of that year he nominated Clark, who was confirmed by the Senate on 18 August by a vote of 73–8 and sworn in on 24 August, the last of nine attorneys general to be elevated to the high Court. Clark's tenure on the court lasted for eighteen years. Many of his decisions were conservative: in *Garner v. Board of Public Works* (1951), he upheld the right of the city of Los Angeles to require city employees to swear that they were not members of the Communist Party; in *Adler v. Board of Education* (1952), he sustained a New York law that forbade the hiring of "subversives" to teach in the public school system; and in *Carlson v. Landon* (1952), he allowed the attorney general to hold suspected alien Communists in detention if he believed they were a threat to national security. However, he also held that a ban on the Italian film *The Miracle* was unconstitutional (*Burstyn v. Wilson*[1952]) and struck down segregation at the University of Texas Law School and the University of Oklahoma graduate school (*Sweatt v. Painter* [1950] and *McLaurin v. Oklahoma State Regents* [1950]).

In 1966, President Lyndon Johnson named Justice Clark's son Ramsey as attorney general. To avoid even the appearance of a conflict of interest (because he would have to rule on cases the Department of Justice would bring before the Court), Clark resigned from the court on 12 June 1967. In the final decade of his life, he served as a sitting judge in circuit courts of appeals across the nation; at his death, he was believed to have been the only man ever to have sat on all eleven circuits. Clark died in New York City on 13 June 1977 at the age of 76 and was buried in Restland Memorial Park, Dallas.

References: Barnes, Catherine A., "Clark, Thomas C(ampbell)," in Eleanora W. Schoenebaum, ed., *Political Profiles: The Truman Years* (New York: Facts on File, 1978), 93–95; Langran, Robert M., "Tom C. Clark," in Clare Cushman, ed., *The Supreme Court Justices: Illustrated Biographies, 1789–1995* (Washington, DC: Congressional Quarterly, 1995), 426–430; Temple, Larry, "Mr. Justice Clark: A Tribute," *American Journal of Criminal Law* 5 (October 1977), 271–274.

JAMES HOWARD MCGRATH
1903–1966

James Howard McGrath resigned as attorney general under a cloud that dealt with political corruption and the firing of a special prosecutor. Yet he was a popular governor and U.S. senator from Rhode Island and, in 1948, ran Harry Truman's astonishing reelection campaign. Born in Woonsocket, Rhode Island, on 28 November 1903, McGrath was the son of James J. McGrath, an Irish immigrant who owned his own insurance and real estate business, and Ida Eleanor (née May) McGrath. McGrath, attended local schools before graduating from the La Salle Academy in Providence in 1922; four years later, he was awarded a Ph.B. degree from Providence College. He then studied law and, in 1929, was awarded his law degree from the Boston University Law School. He was admitted to the Rhode Island bar that same year and began a private practice that specialized in labor law. He had become the state Democratic Party chairman in 1928.

As one obituary summed up years later, "It was the New Deal that made him." In 1934,

McGrath was appointed U.S. district attorney for Rhode Island. Six years later, he resigned to run for governor of the small state. Elected, he served three two-year terms. It was while governor that he seconded Harry S Truman's nomination for vice-president at the 1944 Democratic National Convention. A year later, President Franklin Roosevelt was dead, Truman was president, and Attorney General Francis Biddle had been replaced by Tom C. Clark. Truman called McGrath to Washington to offer him the position of solicitor general, the second highest office in the Department of Justice. He accepted the offer, was confirmed on 28 September, and served until October 1946, when he resigned to run for the U.S. Senate from his home state. During his tenure, he had argued the constitutionality of a death sentence given to a Japanese war criminal by an American military tribunal (*In the Application of Yamashita* [1946]).

Elected to the Senate despite a Republican sweep of the New England states in the off-year elections, McGrath voted for administration policies, opposing the Taft-Hartley Act, supporting an expansion of Social Security and desegregation, and advocating bills that would have established a national health insurance system. In October 1947, McGrath was elected as chairman of the Democratic National Committee; he played a key role in helping President Truman win reelection in 1948. McGrath's work in getting out the vote for the embattled president and mobilizing party machines won him high marks from his fellow Democrats. His book, *The Power of the People,* was published that same year.

With the death of Supreme Court Justice Frank Murphy on 19 July 1949, President Truman elevated Attorney General Clark to the empty seat. He asked McGrath to replace Clark, and on 18 August 1949, he was confirmed as the sixtieth attorney general. McGrath's tenure at Justice is not considered to be one of the high points of the Department's history. Biographer Catherine Barnes writes, "He reportedly did not keep adequate control over the Justice Department and left much of its administration to subordinates."

Truman historian Andrew Dunar adds, "He was more politician than administrator, and critics considered him ineffective."

In 1951, a scandal in the Bureau of Internal Revenue (BIR) broke, and McGrath was chastised for not responding quickly enough to it. When Truman asked for the resignation of Assistant Attorney General T. Lamar Caudle for his part in covering up the scandal, he considered firing McGrath as well. But the attorney general asked to remain, and Truman gave him new impetus to root out the corruption. McGrath hired a Republican attorney from New York, Newbold Morris, to head up the investigation. Morris, sensing a cover-up in the Justice Department, made it public that that agency would be the first target in his probe. The House Judiciary Committee, on 29 January 1952, voted unanimously to initiate an inquiry into McGrath's conduct. On 3 April 1952, when it seemed that Morris's investigation would reach right into McGrath's office, the attorney general fired the investigator. Truman immediately demanded McGrath's resignation, which was quickly tendered. Truman immediately named Federal judge James P. McGranery, an old friend, as the new attorney general.

McGrath was known for his wry wit. After being fired by Truman, he allegedly wired his successor, McGranery, "My heartiest congratulations, and I suggest you bring a pair of asbestos trousers with you." McGrath returned to his law practice, becoming wealthy from numerous corporate clients. In 1960, he sought his old Senate seat, but he was defeated in the Democratic primary by Claiborne Pell.

James McGrath died in his sleep of a heart attack on 2 September 1966 at the age of 62. He was buried in the St. Francis Cemetery, Pawtucket.

References: *The Attorney Generals of the United States, 1789–1985* (Washington, DC: Department of Justice, 1985), 120; Barnes, Catherine A., "McGrath, J(ames) Howard," in Eleanora W. Schoenebaum, ed., *Political Profiles: The Truman Years,* (New York: Facts on File, 1978), 351–353; Donovan, Robert J., *Tumultuous Years: The Presidency of Harry S Truman, 1949–1953* (New York: W. W. Norton, 1982); Dunar, Andrew J., "McGrath, J. Howard," in Richard S. Kirkendall, ed., *The Harry S Truman Encyclopedia* (Boston: G. K. Hall, 1989), 228–229; ———, *The Truman Scandals and the Politics of Morality* (Columbia: University of Missouri Press, 1984); Perry, Anna B., "McGrath, James Howard," in *DAB* 8: 405–406.

JAMES PATRICK MCGRANERY
1895–1962

James McGranery became attorney general in the midst of a scandal over the firing of an investigator hired to expose government corruption. A former federal judge, James McGranery served a short tenure until the end of the Truman administration. The son of Patrick McGranery and Bridget (née Gallagher) McGranery, both Irish immigrants, James P. McGranery was born in Philadelphia, Pennsylvania, on 8 July 1895. He received his primary education in the schools of Philadelphia, then attended the Temple University School of Law, where he received a law degree in 1928. He established a practice in Philadelphia and became active in local Democratic politics.

An unsuccessful candidate for several local offices, in 1936 McGranery was elected to the U.S. House of Representatives, representing the Second Pennsylvania District. In the House, he was a resolute New Deal advocate, giving his complete support to the administration of Franklin D. Roosevelt. In 1943, while serving in his fourth term, he was named as an assistant to the attorney general, working under Francis Biddle and, for a time, Tom C. Clark, as the chief administrative officer of the Department. In 1946, he was named as a U.S. district court judge for the eastern district of Pennsylvania. McGranery served for more than five years on the bench.

In the midst of a major scandal involving the Department of Justice, Attorney General James McGrath was fired on 3 April 1952.

President Harry Truman quickly replaced the disgraced attorney general with McGranery, who was still sitting in Philadelphia. Although he was a close friend of Truman's, many in Congress were hesitant to confirm him. Yet McGranery promised a vigorous campaign against government corruption. After being confirmed in May, he went on a rapid campaign to root out the corruption that had consumed his predecessor.

Biographer Alonzo Hamby writes, "During his brief term as Attorney General, Mc-Granery was active in several other areas. He either initiated, or laid the groundwork for, major antitrust cases in oil, steel, detergent manufacturing, the diamond trade, and magazine wholesaling. A militant anticommunist, he approved Smith Act prosecutions against several important leaders of the American Communist Party. He began denaturalization and deportation proceedings against notorious underworld figures. Perhaps Mc-Granery's most important decisions was to sanction the presentation of a strong integrationist *amicus curiae* brief to the Supreme Court in the initial hearing of the school desegregation case *Brown v. Board of Education of Topeka, Kansas* in December 1952." McGranery, the sixty-first attorney general and the third man to serve under Harry S Truman, left office when the Truman administration ended in January 1953.

In the last decade of his life, McGranery practiced law in Washington and Philadelphia. In 1955, Congress established the Commission on Government Security, with former President of the American Bar Association Loyd Wright named as chairman and Senator John C. Stennis of Mississippi as vice-chairman. One of the distinguished men named to the commission, which reported its findings in June 1957, was McGranery.

James McGranery was in Palm Beach, Florida, when he suffered a fatal heart on 23 December 1962. He was 67 years old. He was buried in Arlington National Cemetery.

References: *The Attorney Generals of the United States, 1789–1985* (Washington, DC: Department of Justice, 1985), 122; Barnes, Catherine A., "Mc-Granery, J(ames) P(atrick)," in Eleanora W. Schoenebaum, ed., *Political Profiles: The Truman Years* (New York: Facts on File, 1978), 350–351; Donovan, Robert J., *Tumultuous Years: The Presidency of Harry S Truman, 1949–1953* (New York: W. W. Norton, 1982), 381; Hamby, Alonzo L., "Mc-Granery, James Patrick," in *DAB* 7: 500–501.

HERBERT BROWNELL, JR.
1904–1996

Herbert Brownell was a little-known New York lawyer when he advised Dwight D. Eisenhower in the 1952 presidential campaign and was rewarded with the post of attorney general. His term, lasting almost five years, was one of the longest at the Justice Department in nearly a century. Herbert Brownell, the son of Herbert Brownell, Sr., a university professor, and May Adeline (née Miller) Brownell, was born in the village of Peru, Nebraska, on 20 February 1904. He attended local schools, then the University of Nebraska, where he served on the college newspaper. He received a bachelor's degree from Nebraska in 1924. Three years later, he earned a law degree from the Yale University Law School.

Soon after graduating from Yale, Brownell joined the New York law firm of Root, Clark, Buckner & Ballantine, where he served for two years. He then moved to the more prestigious firm of Lord, Day & Lord, with which he would be associated for the rest of his life except for his periods of government service. In 1932, in the midst of a Democratic landslide in American politics, Brownell was elected to the New York Assembly, where he served from 1933 until 1937. Spotted as an up-and-coming Republican politician, he was picked by District Attorney Thomas E. Dewey, first to manage his unsuccessful campaign for the governorship of New York in 1938 and, four years later, to manage his second campaign, which turned out to be successful. In 1944, Brownell was selected because of the victory to become chairman of the Republican National Committee, and he ran Dewey's unsuccessful presidential campaign that year. Although he stepped down in 1946 as Republican National Committee chair, Brownell managed Dewey's second unsuccessful run for the presidency in 1948.

Considered a moderate Republican, Brownell used his influence at the 1952 Republican National Convention to shift support among some delegates from Senator Robert Taft of Ohio, considered more conservative, to General Dwight D. Eisenhower, who ultimately won the nomination and the election. A close adviser to the general during the campaign, Brownell was set to be named to a cabinet post after the election. On 21 November 1952, Eisenhower designated Brownell as attorney general in the new administration. Confirmed quickly and sworn in as the sixty-second attorney general, serving from January 1953 until 23 October 1957, Brownell helped Eisenhower select several cabinet members, advised the president on matters of civil rights, and counseled him to deny a pardon to atomic bomb spies Julius and Ethel Rosenberg. (One of his assistants, in charge of the civil division, was Minnesota attorney Warren Earl Burger, who later served as chief justice of the U.S. Supreme Court. Ironically, when Chief Justice Earl Warren resigned in 1968, Eisenhower wrote to President-elect Nixon to name Brownell to the post, which instead went to Burger.)

Brownell informed Eisenhower that he intended to leave the Department of Justice after the 1956 election. However, the government was soon faced with a crisis over the desegregation of the Little Rock, Arkansas, school system. Brownell delayed his departure to advise the president to order Arkansas Governor Orval Faubus to admit black students to a formerly all-white school or government intervention would follow, and, when Faubus refused, Brownell counseled Eisenhower to send in the National Guard to keep the peace. On 23 October 1957, after serving as attorney general for almost five years, Brownell wrote to President

Eisenhower that he intended to resign. Brownell returned to the private practice of law at his old firm, where he served until 1977 as a senior partner and from 1977 to 1989 as counsel.

Herbert Brownell survived longer than any member of the Eisenhower administration, dying of cancer on 1 May 1996 at the age of 92.

References: *The Attorney Generals of the United States, 1789–1985* (Washington, DC: Department of Justice, 1985), 124; Brownell, Herbert, Jr., with John P. Burke, *Advising Ike: The Memoirs of Attorney General Herbert Brownell* (Lawrence: University Press of Kansas, 1993); "Brownell, Herbert, Jr.," in *NCAB* 1: 350–351; Denton, Thomas D., "Brownell, Herbert, Jr.," in Eleanora W. Schoenebaum, ed., *Political Profiles: The Eisenhower Years* (New York: Facts on File, 1980), 70–73; Pach, Chester J., Jr., and Elmo Richardson, *The Presidency of Dwight D. Eisenhower* (Lawrence: University Press of Kansas, 1991).

WILLIAM PIERCE ROGERS
1913–

William Rogers served as attorney general in the Eisenhower administration and secretary of state in the Nixon administration, yet he is probably better remembered for his work as chairman of the Presidential Commission on the Challenger Space Shuttle Accident, known better as the Rogers Commission, which investigated the 1986 disaster. William Rogers, the only child of Harrison Alexander Rogers, an insurance agent, and Myra (née Beswick) Rogers, was born in Norfolk, New York, on 23 June 1913. After attending local schools, he received a bachelor's degree from Colgate University in 1934 and his law degree from Cornell University three years later. A year later, he was named as an assistant to Thomas E. Dewey, the "racket-buster" district attorney of New York, who brought to trial many noted criminals, and Rogers became involved in more than one thousand criminal trials.

In 1942, Rogers resigned to volunteer in the U.S. Naval Reserve with the rank of lieutenant junior grade. After training at Quonset Point, Rhode Island, he served on the aircraft carrier U.S.S. *Intrepid,* seeing action during the battle of Okinawa and the raids on Japan. When the war ended, he was commissioned as lieutenant commander. At the end of the war, he returned to New York, where the new district attorney, Frank Hogan, named Rogers as chief of the Bureau of Special Sessions. In April 1947, although he was a Republican, Rogers was selected as chief counsel for the Senate Special Committee to Investigate President Truman's National Defense Program. A year later, when the Senate Executive Expenditures Committee took over the investigation, Democratic Senator Clyde R. Hoey of North Carolina retained Rogers as committee counsel. It was Rogers who uncovered the scheme that allowed government officials to profit by awarding contracts to private firms and then getting kickbacks—five-percenters. While working for the committee, Rogers met and befriended a young California congressman, Richard M. Nixon, who was advised by Rogers to get a perjury charge leveled against Alger Hiss, a State Department employee accused of passing secret documents to the Soviet Union.

In March 1950, Rogers resigned from the committee and joined the Washington office of the New York law firm of Dwight, Royall, Harris, Koegel & Caskey. Two years later, as a delegate to the Republican National Convention, he used his influence to help seat the delegates of four southern states who favored General Dwight D. Eisenhower and not Senator Robert A. Taft of Ohio, thereby ensuring Eisenhower's nomination for the presidency. When Eisenhower chose Senator Nixon as his running mate, Rogers was established as a close personal adviser. When charges of financial improprieties arose against Nixon, Rogers advised him to make an impromptu television address—dubbed the Checkers speech—that saved Nixon's place on the ticket. With Eisenhower's vic-

tory, Rogers was named as deputy attorney general under Eisenhower adviser Herbert Brownell. In his four and a half years in this position, Rogers became an intimate adviser, not only to Brownell, but to President Eisenhower and Vice-president Nixon. When Eisenhower was felled by a near-fatal heart attack, Rogers counseled Nixon on possibly taking control of the government if the need arose. For his work during this period, Nixon later wrote of Rogers in his book *Six Crises* that Rogers was a "cool man under pressure, had excellent judgment, a good sense of press relations, and was one to whom I could speak with complete freedom."

On 23 October 1957, following the resolution of a bitter crisis over the desegregation of the Little Rock, Arkansas, school system, Attorney General Brownell submitted his resignation. Rogers stepped right into the situation; he had been the behind-the-scenes planner during the Little Rock crisis. Sworn in as attorney general on 7 November, he was later confirmed by the Senate as the sixty-third attorney general. During his tenure, which lasted until the end of the Eisenhower administration on 20 January 1961, Rogers worked closely with the courts to end segregation in the schools, arguing that the 1954 Supreme Court decision of *Brown v. Board of Education* was a mandate that could not be ignored.

Although it was his predecessor, Herbert Brownell, who championed the passage of the Civil Rights Act of 1957, it was Rogers who was there when it was signed into law. Under the provisions of the act, Rogers established within the department the Civil Rights Division, making integration and pursuit of the law in this area a chief concern. He also fought for voting rights reform and called for criminal action against threats by officials to block court implementation of integrationist measures.

After leaving office in 1961, Rogers went back to work for his old law firm, which was now known as Royall, Koegel, Rogers & Wells. During the period 1961–1964 he served as general counsel for the *Washington Post* and defended the *New York Times* in a lawsuit before the U.S. Supreme Court. In 1965, he was chosen by President Lyndon Johnson as a member of the American delegation to the United Nations, served in 1967 as a member of a UN committee on Southeast Asia, and sat on the President's Commission on Law Enforcement and Administration.

On 10 December 1968, after talks with president-elect Nixon on the formation of a cabinet, Rogers was offered the position of secretary of state. He accepted, and, in a press conference that day announcing his selection, Nixon called him "a superb negotiator." Much of Roger's tenure as secretary of state dealt with the Vietnam conflict, the Middle East tensions between Israel and its Arab neighbors, and the structure of the North Atlantic Treaty Organization (NATO). On 19 March 1971, Rogers initiated the Rogers Plan to end the conflict in the Middle East by calling for the Israeli withdrawal from disputed lands, occupied since the Six Day War in 1967, in exchange for Arab recognition of Israel's right to exist. On 24 January 1973, he signed the cease-fire ending American participation in the Vietnam War.

Rogers spent much of his tenure in conflict with National Security Adviser Henry Kissinger over policy and connections to the president. On 23 September 1973, Rogers was asked to resign by Nixon so that Kissinger could become secretary of state. Rogers returned to the private practice of law.

Thirty years after first coming on the national scene, Rogers was selected for government service again. The horrific explosion of the space shuttle *Challenger* on 28 January 1986, in which seven astronauts died, led to a massive investigation into the disaster. The following month, President Ronald Reagan asked Rogers to chair the Presidential Commission on the Challenger Accident, better known as the Rogers Commission. After numerous televised hearings, the commission report released that June blamed the National Aeronautics and Space Administration (NASA) for lax measures that led to a faulty piece of equipment failing to work during flight. Rogers was widely praised for the commission's work.

References: *The Attorney Generals of the United States, 1789–1985* (Washington, DC: Department of Justice, 1985), 126; David, Glenn B., "Rogers, William P(ierce)," in Eleanora W. Schoenebaum, ed., *Political Profiles: The Eisenhower Years* (New York: Facts on File, 1980), 519–520; Maddock, Shane J., "Rogers, William Pierce," in Bruce W. Jentleson and Thomas G. Paterson, senior eds., *Encyclopedia of U.S. Foreign Relations* (New York: Oxford University Press; 4 vols., 1997), 4: 13; "Rogers, William P(ierce)," in Charles Moritz, ed., *Current Biography 1969* (New York: H. W. Wilson, 1969), 372–374.

ROBERT FRANCIS KENNEDY
1925–1968

Robert Kennedy is the only person to serve in the cabinet of an immediate family member; he was attorney general in the cabinets of his brother, John F. Kennedy, and his successor, Lyndon B. Johnson, from 1961 to 1964. The son of Joseph Patrick Kennedy, who later served as ambassador to Britain, and Rose (née Fitzgerald) Kennedy, in Brookline, Massachusetts, on 20 November 1925, Robert F. Kennedy was born into a privileged family. After attending local schools, he went to the Milton Academy in Massachusetts; he later earned a bachelor's degree from Harvard University in 1948 and a law degree from the University of Virginia in 1951. He had enlisted in the U.S. Navy in 1944 and served, ironically, on a ship named *Joseph P. Kennedy, Jr.* after his older brother, who was killed in Europe during World War II. After returning home and graduating from Harvard, he served for a short period as a correspondent for the *Boston Post* covering the crisis between the Israelis and Palestinians. In 1951, he was admitted to the Massachusetts bar.

He started his legal career as an attorney with the criminal division of the Department of Justice in Washington, where he worked on political corruption cases. The following year, 1952, he resigned to manage his older brother John's campaign for the U.S. Senate from Massachusetts. With John's election, Robert was selected as assistant counsel on the Permanent Subcommittee on Investigations. He fought with the committee's chairman, Senator Joseph McCarthy, Republican of Wisconsin, and in July 1953 resigned. He rejoined in February 1954 as chief counsel for the Democratic minority and, when the Democrats took over the Senate that November, he was named chief counsel. From 1957 to 1959, Kennedy also served as chief counsel for the Senate Rackets Committee, headed by Senator John L. McClellan of Arkansas. He left in 1959 when his older brother John began campaigning for the presidency.

During the 1960 election, Robert Kennedy was his brother's chief counsel and adviser. John Kennedy's election made him the youngest man ever elected president. Historian James N. Giglio writes, "His first choices for attorney general were Abraham Ribicoff, the governor of Connecticut, and Adlai Stevenson, the former governor of Illinois and Democratic presidential candidate [1952 and 1956]; neither of whom wanted the position." Ribicoff remembered: "The first person Kennedy sent for after the election was me. I came to Palm Beach. He offered me attorney general, and I turned it down. He was shocked and surprised, and he said, 'Who should I take?' and I said, 'Take Bobby.' He said, 'You're crazy; the country wouldn't stand for it.' I said, 'Look, Mr. President, I've known you two people intimately for so long, and whenever you have been faced with a crisis, as to a decision, you automatically turn to Bobby. . . . The first and most important person to you is Bobby. You're not going to able run the presidency without Bobby's help. The worst thing you could do is, when you need Bobby, he has to come through the front door. In front of the public, so they know it, so the press knows it.' I also said to him, 'Civil rights is going to be a big issue, and there's going to be hell to pay. But the worst thing that could happen is that you have a Catholic president use a Jew as attorney general, to push the blacks down the throats of white Protestants. It would hurt the presidency; it would hurt you; and it would hurt the civil rights cause.' " In the end, Kennedy took Ribicoff's advice and named his brother as the sixty-fourth attorney general.

Robert Kennedy's tenure as attorney general lasted through the administration of his brother and into that of Lyndon Johnson. It was marked by stormy fights over civil rights and battles against organized crime. These efforts were marred by illegal wiretapping on individuals such the Rev. Dr. Martin Luther King, Jr., in which Kennedy secretly worked hand in hand with FBI director J. Edgar Hoover. Robert Kennedy advocated the passage of the Criminal Justice Act, passed in 1964, which aided indigent defendants accused of crimes who could not afford an attorney; faced down southern governors to aid in the ending of segregation in the public schools and colleges; and investigated the Bay of Pigs fiasco in 1961. He assembled a staff of aides that included Byron White, later named to the U.S. Supreme Court, and Nicholas de B. Katzenbach, who was later to serve as attorney general when Kennedy resigned. Historian Joseph C. Holub writes, "As the brother of the president, Robert Kennedy had influence and power not available to other high administration officials. He had the full confidence of President Kennedy and the strong rapport, friendship, and loyalty between the two made the Attorney General the President's alter ego and aide." During the Cuban Missile Crisis in October 1962, President Kennedy established a group of nineteen advisers known as the Executive Committee of the U.S. National Security Council (EX-COMM), to aid him in the crisis. Robert Kennedy was one of those advisers. According to tape recordings made public three decades later, Robert Kennedy was in on all the Oval Office briefings in which the fate of the world hung in the balance for nearly two weeks. In 1969, his book on the crisis, *Thirteen Days: A Memoir of the Cuban Missile Crisis,* was published posthumously.

President Kennedy's assassination in Dallas, Texas, on 22 November 1963 left his brother remaining as attorney general in the new administration of President Lyndon Johnson. Historian Jeff Shesol highlights the animosity between the two men. Less than a year after the assassination, on 3 September 1964, Kennedy resigned as attorney general to run for a U.S. Senate seat in New York State. Elected in what was ironically a landslide for Johnson, who was running for a term of his own that same year, Kennedy became a leading liberal voice in the Senate, where he concentrated on problems relating to poverty and the poor and civil rights. Starting in 1967, he began to speak out against American participation in the Vietnam War. By 1968, the war between the two men had become open, with Kennedy threatening to challenge Johnson for the Democratic nomination for the presidency. Kennedy initially stayed out of the race while Senator Eugene McCarthy of Minnesota beat the president in the New Hampshire primary. On 31 March 1968, Johnson announced that he was not running, and the next day Kennedy announced that he was getting in the race.

On 4 April 1968, as Kennedy was campaigning, he was told that the Rev. Martin Luther King, Jr., had been assassinated. Kennedy stepped in front of the crowd and, in a few moments, delivered unprepared remarks that many have called his greatest. After telling the crowd the sad news, he challenged them, "In this difficult day, in this difficult time for the United States, it is perhaps well to ask what kind of a nation we are and what direction we want to move in. For those of you who are black—considering the evidence there evidently is that there were white people who were responsible—you can be filled with bitterness, with hatred, and a desire for revenge. We can move in that direction as a country, in great polarization— black people amongst black, white people amongst white, filled with hatred toward one another. Or we can make an effort, as Martin Luther King did, to understand and to comprehend, and to replace that violence, that stain of bloodshed that has spread across our land, with an effort to understand with compassion and love." He added, "For those of you who are black and are tempted to be filled with hatred and distrust at the injustice of such an act, against all white people, I can only say that I feel in my own heart the same kind of feeling. I had a member of my family killed, but he was killed by a white man. But we have to make an effort in the United States, we have to make an effort to understand, to go beyond these rather difficult times."

Two months later, on 5 June 1968, Kennedy won the California Democratic primary, and after a victory celebration he was shot. More than twenty-three hours later, Kennedy succumbed to his wounds at the age of 42, and, after a grand funeral, was laid to rest in Arlington National Cemetery next to his slain brother. He was the first cabinet officer assassinated in the nation's history.

References: *The Attorney Generals of the United States, 1789–1985* (Washington, DC: Department of Justice, 1985), 128; Giglio, James N., *The Presidency of John F. Kennedy* (Lawrence: University Press of Kansas, 1991), 21; Holub, Joseph C., "Kennedy, Robert F(rancis)," in Nelson Lichtenstein, ed., *Political Profiles: The Kennedy Years* (New York: Facts on File, 1978), 275–278; "Kennedy, Robert Francis," in *NCAB* J: 28–34; Shesol, Jeff, *Mutual Contempt: Lyndon Johnson, Robert Kennedy, and the Feud That Defined a Decade* (New York: W. W. Norton, 1997); Strober, Gerald S., and Deborah H. Strober, *Let Us Begin Anew: An Oral History of the Kennedy Presidency* (New York: HarperCollins, 1993), 110–116.

NICHOLAS DE BELLEVILLE KATZENBACH
1922–

In one of the most famous moments of the twentieth century, Deputy Attorney General Nicholas de Katzenbach, stood on the steps of the University of Alabama and faced down Governor George Wallace with a demand that black students James Hood and Vivian Malone be allowed to register at the university. He then escorted the two students past Wallace and integrated the school without violence. It was this cool-headed demeanor that led to his selection as attorney general upon the resignation of Robert Kennedy. Nicholas Katzenbach, the son of Edward Lawrence Katzenbach, an attorney, and Marie Louise (née Hilson) Katzenbach, was born in Philadelphia, Pennsylvania, on 17 January 1922. Katzenbach attended schools in Trenton and Princeton; he later went to Phillips Exeter Academy in New Hampshire before entering Princeton University in 1939, where he majored in international relations.

His studies were cut short when after the Japanese bombed Pearl Harbor he volunteered for the U.S. Army Air Corps as a navigator. In October 1943, his plane was shot down and taken prisoner by the Italians. He attempted to escape twice. The second time, he was transferred to German control served the rest of the war in a German prisoner of war camp, spending his hours reading books donated by the Red Cross. When he was liberated in April 1945, he was awarded the Air Medal with three clusters and was released from service with the rank of first lieutenant. Katzenbach returned to Princeton, graduating with a bachelor's degree cum laude in 1945, and entered Yale Law School, where he served as editor of the *Yale Law Review*. After getting his law degree in 1947, Katzenbach was selected as a Rhodes scholar and studied at Balliol College in Oxford, England. He was admitted to the New Jersey bar in 1950 and joined the law firm of Katzenbach, Gildea & Rudner in Trenton.

Katzenbach divided much of the next ten years between private law practice and teaching law at the University of Chicago. After the election of John F. Kennedy to the presidency in 1960, Katzenbach was asked to join the Justice Department. His old friend from Yale Law School, Byron White, was named as deputy attorney general, and he recommended Katzenbach for a position in

the agency. At first, Katzenbach served as the assistant attorney general in charge of the Office of Legal Counsel until May 1962; thereafter, he was promoted to deputy attorney general when White was named to the U.S. Supreme Court. On 22 August 1964, Attorney General Robert Kennedy announced his intention to resign to run for a U.S. Senate seat in New York; he formally stepped down on 3 September. That same day, President Lyndon Johnson named Katzenbach as acting attorney general. Historians Richard Schott and Dagmar Hamilton write, "Johnson's decision was cautious; by making Katzenbach 'acting' the president committed himself to keeping Katzenbach through the [1964] election, but not necessarily longer." It was not until 28 January 1965 that Katzenbach was officially nominated for attorney general. Presidential adviser Clark Clifford, who later served as secretary of defense, said that because Johnson mistrusted Katzenbach as a "Kennedy man," he wanted to give him a testing period to see if he was loyal to the new administration.

During Katzenbach's tenure, which lasted from 3 September 1964 (he was sworn in as the attorney general on 11 February 1965 after Senate approval) until 3 October 1966, the Department filed lawsuits against segregated school districts under the Civil Rights Act of 1964. In this same period, the department supervised the first-time voting by some 500,000 blacks under the Voting Rights Act of 1965. In a speech he gave at a symposium marking the two hundredth anniversary of the office of the attorney general, he said, "One of the conclusions that we came to within the department after the '64–'65 Civil Rights Act was a rather simple conclusion: That enforcement of the laws, enforcement of the Constitution, was an absolutely necessary ingredient in establishing formal equality in this country which had not heretofore been enjoyed; was a necessary condition, but it wasn't a sufficient condition." During his tenure, three important civil rights cases bearing his name were decided by the U.S. Supreme Court: *Katzenbach v. McClung* (1964), in which the interstate commerce portion of the Civil Rights Act of 1964 was upheld; *South Carolina v. Katzenbach* (1966), which upheld the Voting Rights Act of 1965 as "a valid effectuation of the Fifteenth Amendment"; and *Katzenbach v. Morgan* (1966), which held that the Voting Rights Act prohibited states from erecting barriers to voting based on language.

On 21 September 1966, Katzenbach resigned as attorney general to become undersecretary of state. He was replaced by Ramsey Clark. Soon after assuming his new position, Katzenbach traveled with Secretary of Defense Robert McNamara on an inspection tour of South Vietnam. He was deeply involved in the policy over Vietnam, but by the time Clark Clifford was brought in as secretary of defense in 1968 he had concluded the war would be lost.

Katzenbach left the State Department in 1969, and today he is a writer and adviser on political subjects. He is the author of *U.S. Arms for the Developing World: Dilemmas of Foreign Policy* (GPO, 1967), and a coauthor, with Morton A. Kaplan, of *The Political Foundations of International Law* (New York: Wiley, 1961). The Nicholas de B. Katzenbach Professorship of Law has been established in his name at the Yale Law School.

References: The Attorney Generals of the United States, 1789–1985 (Washington, DC: Department of Justice, 1985), 130; "Katzenbach, Nicholas deB(elleville)," in Charles Moritz, ed., *Current Biography 1965* (New York: H. W. Wilson, 1965), 212–215; Schott, Richard L., and Dagmar S. Hamilton, *People, Positions, and Power: The Political Appointments of Lyndon Johnson* (Chicago: University of Chicago Press, 1983), 43–44; *200th Anniversary of the Office of Attorney General, 1789–1989* (Washington, DC: Department of Justice, 1990), 71.

WILLIAM RAMSEY CLARK
1927–

Ramsey Clark was the first son of a former attorney general to serve in that same position; his advancement to the post, however, forced his father, a justice on the U.S. Supreme Court, to resign to avoid the appearance of a conflict of interest. After leaving the job he became a noted activist against American foreign policy. Ramsey Clark, the son of Thomas C. Clark, attorney general from 1945 to 1949, and Mary Jane (née Ramsey) Clark, attended local schools in Dallas, Los Angeles, and Washington, D.C. He earned a bachelor's degree from the University of Texas in 1949 and a master's degree in history and a law degree from the University of Chicago the following year. In 1951, he was admitted to the Texas bar.

Clark joined the Dallas law firm of Clark, Coon, Holt & Fisher (originally founded by his grandfather, William H. Clark), first as an associate, and later as a partner, representing corporate clients. A Democrat in the style of his father, who had served in the Franklin Roosevelt and Harry Truman administrations, Ramsey Clark campaigned for Democrat Adlai Stevenson for president in 1956 and worked in the John F. Kennedy campaign in 1960. Kennedy named Clark as assistant attorney general in charge of the Lands Division of the Department of Justice. He earned the trust of Attorney General Robert Kennedy, and his responsibilities were expanded to include civil rights, including work involving the 1962 riots at the University of Mississippi over integration and the 1963 crisis in Birmingham, Alabama. This work made his advice valuable in discussions leading to the passage of the 1964 Civil Rights Act. With the Robert Kennedy's resignation, Deputy Attorney General Nicholas Katzenbach became acting attorney general, and Clark was advanced into the deputy's post on 13 February 1965. He served in that position for almost two years. He was put in charge of handling department intervention in the Selma-to-Montgomery civil rights march, the Watts riots, and the drafting of the Voting Rights Act of 1965.

On 21 September 1966, Attorney General Katzenbach resigned to become assistant secretary of state. President Johnson, then unsure whether Clark had the necessary skills to serve as the top law enforcement officer of the nation, named Clark as the acting attorney general, a trial period that ultimately lasted for 148 days. Clark believed that he was not under consideration, especially after Johnson sought his advice on possible candidates. These included Clark Clifford, a close Johnson adviser who eventually became secretary of defense; Leon Jaworski, a Houston lawyer who later became Watergate special prosecutor); Orville Freeman, secretary of agriculture; Thurgood Marshall, the solicitor general;, and Burke Marshall, former assistant attorney general for civil rights. However, Katzenbach advised Johnson to name Clark, and the president took the recommendation seriously. On 28 February 1967, Johnson nominated Clark, and he was confirmed on 2 March as the sixty-sixth attorney general. Clark found out about the illegal wiretapping activities conducted by his two predecessors, and condemned them, claiming that no such authority would be granted during his tenure. On the president's command, Clark flew to Memphis, Tennessee, on 5 April 1968 to coordinate the investigation of the assassination of the Rev. Dr. Martin Luther King, Jr.

Clark left office when the Johnson administration ended in 1969. In 1971, he defended Frank Serpico, a New York City policeman who called public attention to police corruption. Since then, however, he has become an outspoken opponent of U.S. foreign policy: in June 1980, against travel restrictions placed by the government, he traveled to a peace conference in Iran, which was then holding forty-four U.S. Embassy workers hostage. Although prosecution by the Justice Department was threatened, charges were never brought. During the time leading up to, and after, the war against Iraq in 1991,

Clark condemned the United States and asked for war crimes trials against American leaders. In 1997 and 1998, he further denounced the continued U.S. sanctions against Iraq. In 1999, he briefly appeared on American television to protest American bombing in Serbia and Kosovo. He is the author of *Crime in America: Observations on its Nature, Causes, Prevention, and Control* (1970) and *War Crimes: a Report on United States War Crimes against Iraq* (1992).

References: *The Attorney Generals of the United States, 1789–1985* (Washington, DC: Department of Justice, 1985), 132; "Clark, (William) Ramsey," in Charles Moritz, ed., *Current Biography 1967* (New York: H. W. Wilson, 1967), 72–74; Schott, Richard L., and Dagmar S. Hamilton, *People, Positions, and Power: The Political Appointments of Lyndon Johnson* (Chicago: University of Chicago Press, 1983), 90–91.

JOHN NEWTON MITCHELL
1913–1988

John Mitchell is the only attorney general to go to prison for crimes committed while in office, eventually serving nineteen months for conspiracy, obstruction of justice, and lying under oath. John Mitchell, the son of Joseph C. Mitchell and Margaret (née McMahon) Mitchell, was born in Detroit, Michigan, on 15 September 1913, although he grew up on Long Island and Queens, New York. He attended local schools, then went to Fordham Law School, from which he received a law degree in 1936. He sold sporting goods for a while before going to work in 1936 for the New York law firm of Caldwell & Raymond as a clerk. After receiving his law degree and passing the New York bar, he became a staff attorney at Caldwell & Raymond.

Working on public housing issues and the financing of bonds to pay for such housing, Mitchell was soon made a full partner in the firm. In 1943, he joined the U.S. Navy and was made the commander of several squadrons of torpedo boats, including PT-109, piloted by a young John F. Kennedy. After the war, he returned to the firm, which had become Caldwell, Trimble & Mitchell. He continued to work on the public financing of public housing and became one of the leading attorneys in the nation on the subject. Starting in 1960, he worked closely with New York Governor Nelson Rockefeller to formulate state policies in housing.

On 1 January 1967, Mitchell's firm merged with another in California that included former Vice-president Richard Nixon, to become Nixon, Mudge, Rose, Guthrie, Alexander & Mitchell. Although Mitchell and Nixon had not known each other, they soon became close friends, and, when Nixon decided to run in 1968 for the presidency for the second time (he had lost a close race to Senator John Kennedy in 1960), he chose Mitchell as his campaign manager. It was Mitchell's message of "law and order" against Vietnam War protesters and black radicals that made Nixon's message so appealing to millions of Americans and won the election for the Republicans.

In a press conference on 11 December 1968, President-elect Nixon announced much of his cabinet, including his selection of Mitchell as the attorney general. He was easily confirmed by the Senate on 20 January 1969 and took office as the sixty-seventh attorney general. In his first year in office, Mitchell launched Operation Intercept, intended to end the flow of drugs from Mexico, and asked Congress to enact new crime measures, which it refused to do. In 1971, Mitchell advocated congressional action in the area of judicial reform, a system that he described as "an astonishing tale of neglect." On 14 July 1971, he ordered the *New York Times* and the *Washington Post* not to publish a classified Pentagon report on the history of American policy in Vietnam; when the papers refused, Mitchell took them to court to stop publication on the grounds of national security. Two weeks later, on 30 June, the U.S. Supreme Court, in *New York Times Co. v. United States,* held that the pa-

pers had the right to publish under the First Amendment. Mitchell announced on 1 July 1971 that he had ordered the Justice Department to prosecute "all those who have violated Federal criminal law" in leaking the report to the newspapers. Mitchell also came under fire in the area of wiretapping. In 1971, Mitchell had said in a press conference, "Since I believe so fully and wholeheartedly in the protection of the privacy of the individual, I will make sure that nothing is done in this area of electronic surveillance that will invade the privacy of individuals." However, in September 1971, he admitted that the government had wiretapped conversations by the radical group the Weathermen without court orders.

Nevertheless, Mitchell soon became embroiled in activities that undermined his tenure and eventually sent him and many Nixon administration officials to prison. It was sometime in 1971 that G. Gordon Liddy met with Mitchell in his office in the Justice Department and laid out a grand scheme, called Operation Gemstone. Liddy was the head of "the Plumbers," a secret White House unit assigned to plug security and press leaks. His plan entailed a multitude of illegal acts designed to instigate surveillance against Nixon's political enemies. Although Mitchell turned down this initial plan, he did later get involved. As Watergate testimony revealed, he approved of giving Liddy and the other "plumbers" some $250,000 straight from the coffers of Nixon's 1972 reelection campaign for bugging and break-in activities, including those at the Democratic headquarters at the Watergate building in Washington, D.C.

On 15 February 1972, Mitchell resigned as attorney general to head up Nixon's reelection effort. However, his wife, Martha, a flamboyant Washington socialite, became distraught at having her husband run the campaign, and, on 1 July of that same year, he resigned to return to his New York law firm. Soon after, Watergate exploded on the national scene, and the following year, hearings were held by the Senate and House on the matter. During the proceedings, Mitchell, with his dour look and signature pipe constantly in hand, soon became a familiar face to audiences across America as he denied for three days being involved in the Watergate operation. He called fellow conspirator Jeb Stuart Magruder's testimony that Mitchell was deeply involved in Watergate "a palpable, damnable lie."

Mitchell's undoing came in September 1972, when the *Washington Post* quoted sources close to the investigation as saying that Mitchell, while serving as attorney general, had "personally controlled a secret Republican fund used to gather information about the Democrats." When *Post* reporter Carl Bernstein, one of two principal reporters on the story, called Mitchell to get a response to the allegation, Mitchell reportedly said, "All that crap, you're putting it in the paper? It's all been denied. [*Washington Post* publisher] Katie Graham's gonna get her tit caught in a big fat wringer if that's ever published. Good Christ! That's the most sickening thing I ever heard." Later, however, under oath, Mitchell admitted that he at least knew about the cover-up of the break-in, but did not inform the president of his knowledge, "so he could go on through the campaign without being involved." In May 1973, however, Mitchell and former Commerce Secretary Maurice Stans were indicted on federal charges of obstructing an investigation into an illegal contribution made by financier Robert Vesco to the Nixon campaign. In April 1974, both men were acquitted.

Mitchell, however, was not through. A month before his acquittal in the Vesco matter, he was indicted by a grand jury in Washington on charges of conspiracy, perjury, and obstruction of justice in the Watergate matter. He went on trial at the end of 1974 (after Nixon had resigned in disgrace), along with four codefendants—former White House Chief of Staff H. R. (Bob) Haldeman, former White House Chief Domestic Adviser John D. Ehrlichman, former Assistant Attorney General Robert C. Mardian, and Kenneth W. Parkinson, a lawyer who had represented the Nixon campaign after Watergate. On 1 January 1975, all but Parkinson were found guilty. In the end, Mitchell admitted to his crimes and took his punishment with stoic courage. He was sentenced to two-and-one-half to eight years, although Judge John Sirica later reduced this to one to four years. He ultimately served nineteen months in a federal facility at Maxwell Air Force Base in Alabama.

After being paroled on 20 January 1979, Mitchell returned to his Washington and, having been disbarred, worked as a private consultant. In 1981, publishing house Simon and Schuster sued the former attorney general after he failed to deliver a promised Watergate memoir. In the 1985 Supreme Court decision *Mitchell v. Forsyth* (1985), the Court held that Mitchell, even though a cabinet officer, was not immune from lawsuits dealing with actions taken while in office. In the opinion, Justice Byron White wrote, "His [Mitchell's] status as a Cabinet officer is not in itself sufficient to invest him with absolute immunity. The considerations of separation of powers that call for absolute immunity for state and federal legislators and for the President do not demand a similar immunity for Cabinet officers or other high executive officials. Nor does the nature of the Attorney General's national security functions—as opposed to his prosecutorial functions—warrant absolute immunity."

Mitchell suffered a fatal heart attack and died on 9 November 1988 at the age of 75. He was interred in Arlington National Cemetery.

References: *The Attorney Generals of the United States, 1789–1985* (Washington, DC: Department of Justice, 1985), 134; "Mitchell, John N(ewton)," in Charles Moritz, ed., *Current Biography 1969* (New York: H. W. Wilson, 1969), 291–293.

RICHARD GORDON KLEINDIENST
1923–2000

Although never implicated directly in the Watergate scandal that consumed the administration of Richard Nixon, Richard Kleindienst was forced to resign and later pleaded guilty to perjury for lying to Congress about a portion of the Watergate case. The son of Alfred Kleindienst, a railroad brakeman on the Santa Fe Railroad, and Gladys (née Love) Kleindienst, Richard Kleindienst was born near the town of Winslow, in northern Arizona, on 5 August 1923. Kleindienst attended local schools in Winslow. Raised by a Navajo woman after the death of his mother, he became fluent in the Navajo language. He also developed a concern for the rights of American Indians, who constituted a majority in the Winslow area. He attended the University of Arizona in Tucson, where he joined the Reserve Officer Training Corps (ROTC).

During World War II, Kleindienst's ROTC unit was activated, and at the tail end of the war he served as a navigator with the Fifteenth Air Force. He was promoted to first lieutenant before being discharged in 1946. He then attended Harvard University on the G.I. Bill, established to fund the college studies of needy former soldiers, and he graduated magna cum laude with a bachelor's degree in 1947. While working as a law clerk in the offices of the Boston firm of Ropes, Grey, Best, Coolidge & Rugg, Kleindienst studied at the Harvard Law School and, in 1950, was awarded a law degree. Returning to Arizona, he became a partner in the Phoenix firm of Jennings, Strouss, Salmon & Trask. Specializing in cases dealing with industrial disputes, he soon moved to another firm, Shimmel, Hill, Kleindienst & Bishop, which made him a senior partner; he worked here until 1969.

An associate of Arizona Senator Barry Goldwater, Kleindienst began a career in politics in 1952 in which he served as a delegate to the Republican National Convention. A year later, he was elected to a single term in the Arizona state House of Representatives. He later served as chairman of the Arizona Young Republican League and the Republican State Central Committee and as a member of the Republican National Committee. In 1964, he ran unsuccessfully for governor of Arizona. That same year, he ran state operations for Goldwater's unsuccessful presidential campaign. Two years later, he managed the campaign of Republican John R. Williams, who won the governorship of Arizona.

These skills came to the attention of former Vice-president Richard Nixon, who was mounting a presidential run in 1968. Nixon selected Kleindienst as national director of field operations for his campaign and, after he won the presidential nomination, as general counsel for the Republican National Committee. During the campaign, he also served as deputy to Nixon's campaign manager, John N. Mitchell. With Nixon's election, Kleindienst accepted the position as deputy attorney general, directly under Mitchell, who got the top spot at the Justice Department. The *New York Times* wrote of his stint, "Mr. Kleindienst has been in the thick of a series of sensitive Justice Department situations—ranging from the Supreme Court nominations to the Mayday antiwar protests to Representative Hale Boggs's attack on the Federal Bureau of Investigation." On 15 February 1972, Attorney General Mitchell resigned, effective 1 March, to head up Nixon's 1972 reelection effort. Kleindienst was named as his successor that same day.

Hearings were held on Kleindienst's nomination, and it appeared that he had passed senatorial muster. However, before a full Senate vote could be held, explosive accusations became public. Jack Anderson of the *Washington Post* alleged that Kleindienst, as deputy attorney general, had been involved in the I.T.T. (International Telegraph & Telephone) investigation. I.T.T. was accused of making an illegal $400,000 payoff to the Nixon campaign in 1968 in order that a government antitrust suit against the company might be dropped. New hearings into these allegations were then held in the midst of Kleindienst's confirmation hearing; this new investigation entailed the longest confirmation hearings for a cabinet nominee who was later confirmed. Senator Birch Bayh of Indiana asked Kleindienst whether he had ever talked with anyone at the White House about the I.T.T. investigation. Even though, as he stated at a later time, he had spoken at length to President Nixon on the case and how to handle it, in the hearing he denied under oath that such a conversation had taken place. The committee voted to confirm and Kleindienst was confirmed by the Senate, 64–19. He took office as the sixty-eighth attorney general on 12 June 1972.

In his eleven months in the position, Kleindienst became bogged down in the Watergate investigation that exploded just weeks after he took office. Burglars working for Nixon's reelection campaign were caught trying to bug Democratic Party headquarters in the Watergate Building in Washington, D.C., and officials inside the Nixon White House were soon accused of covering the affair up. Kleindienst has never been accused of being in on the cover-up; in fact, when conspirator G. Gordon Liddy went to the attorney general and asked him to release the Watergate burglars from custody before their identities could be known, Kleindienst refused. However, rumors began to circulate soon after that Kleindienst would be axed following the 1972 election because of the "public airing" of the I.T.T. matter. However, reports one source, his old friend Senator Goldwater apparently talked to Nixon and spared Kleindienst, at least for a period of time.

That time, however, ended soon after the election. On 15 April 1973, former reelection official Jeb Stuart Magruder told a grand jury that White House counsel John Dean and former Attorney General Mitchell were implicated in the planning of the Watergate break-in. Four days later, when the news became public, Kleindienst announced that he was recusing himself of any further involvement in the Watergate matter and turning over jurisdiction to Assistant Attorney General

Henry Peterson. For the next week and a half, as Kleindienst writes, he wrestled with the idea of resigning, because he could not serve as "half an Attorney General." On 20 April 1973, only eleven days after recusing himself, Kleindienst's resignation was announced on television by President Nixon. In his letter of resignation, he wrote, "Even though, as you know, I had previously indicated a desire to leave the government this year for family and financial reasons, the circumstances surrounding the disclosures made to me on Sunday, April 15, 1973 by Assistant Attorney General Peterson, United States Attorney [Harold H.] Titus [Jr.], and Assistant United States Attorney [Earl] Silbert, dictate this decision at this time." Kleindienst was quickly replaced by Secretary of Defense Elliot Richardson, but stayed on the job until Richardson was confirmed on 22 June 1973.

On 31 October 1973, Kleindienst, now in private practice, told Watergate special prosecutor Archibald Cox that he had had conversations with President Nixon on the I.T.T. matter and had lied during his Senate confirmation. He was charged with lying to Congress and, on 7 June 1974, a year after leaving Justice, he pleaded guilty in a Washington, D.C., court, to one count of perjury. His sentence of a month in prison and a $100 fine was suspended to one month's probation. Kleindienst did not escape Watergate altogether, however; he was even mentioned in the second article of impeachment drafted against Nixon by the House Judiciary Committee. He then settled in Arizona. Kleindienst died of cancer at his home in Prescott, Arizona, on 3 February 2000 at the age of 76.

References: *The Attorney Generals of the United States, 1789–1985* (Washington, DC: Department of Justice, 1985), 136; Kleindienst, Richard G., *Justice: The Memoirs of Attorney General Richard Kleindienst* (Ottawa, IL: Jameson Books, 1985); "Kleindienst, Richard G(ordon)," in Charles Moritz, ed., *Current Biography 1972* (New York: H. W. Wilson, 1972), 258–260.

ELLIOT LEE RICHARDSON

1920–

See Secretary of Health, Education, and Welfare, 1970–1973

WILLIAM BART SAXBE

1916–

William Saxbe stepped in to serve as attorney general during the turmoil of Watergate. A U.S. senator from Ohio, he was generally considered an honest man put in a job in which two of his predecessors had been implicated in the Watergate cover-up or related activities. Born in Mechanicsburg, Ohio, on 24 June 1916, he was the son of Bart Rockwell Saxbe, and Faye Henry (née Carey) Saxbe. Saxbe attended the public schools of Mechanicsburg before receiving a bachelor's degree from Ohio State University in 1940. In 1937, he enlisted in the Ohio National Guard, serving in the 105th Division. During World War II and the Korean War, he served in the Guard in two stateside tours. Following the Korean conflict, he was discharged with the rank of colonel. He contemplated becoming an Episcopal minister, but instead began the study of law. While studying at Ohio State, he was elected to the Ohio state House of Representatives, where he served four terms (1947–1954), serving as majority leader in his third term and as speaker in his fourth. He graduated with a law degree from Ohio State in 1948 and was admitted to the bar that same year. He then opened a private practice in the city of Columbus.

In 1957, Saxbe was elected as Ohio state attorney general, where he served until 1958; he was elected a second time in 1963, serving until 1968. In the intervening years he practiced the law. In 1968, while serving for a second time as state attorney general, he

was elected as a Republican to the U.S. Senate, defeating law professor and Vietnam War opponent John J. Gilligan by more than 116,000 votes. In the Senate, he was known for his independence from the Nixon administration, although he was loyal on most votes. He decried the resumption of the bombing of North Vietnam, saying that the president "appears to have lost his senses." On 11 October 1973, he was asked whether the Nixon administration was the most corrupt in history. "I don't know whether it's one of the most corrupt, but it's one of the most inept. They just couldn't plan a scenario as ridiculous as what's been going on, and if it keeps on, they're going to have to get 'em clown suits." Three weeks later, however, Saxbe agreed to serve as Richard Nixon's attorney general.

On 4 January 1974, Saxbe was sworn in as the seventieth attorney general, filling a gap that had existed since Elliot Richardson's resignation in October 1973. (Solicitor General Robert H. Bork served as acting attorney general in the interim.) In his single year as attorney general, Saxbe served mainly as a caretaker—recusing himself in the Kent State shooting investigation (he did not want to become involved because his old National Guard unit was embroiled in the incident) and refusing to interfere with any investigation into Watergate. (In 1975, Saxbe related that advisers close to the president had demanded he back the president in his claim of executive privilege of the Oval Office tapes, but he had refused.) In late 1974, he advised President Gerald Ford that he intended to resign, and he left office on 2 February 1975.

Saxbe was named as U.S. ambassador to India, where he served until the end of the Ford administration in January 1977. He then returned to Ohio, where he practiced law until his retirement. He settled in his hometown of Mechanicsburg. He is the author of *Seems Like Yesterday* (1975).

References: *The Attorney Generals of the United States, 1789–1985* (Washington, DC: Department of Justice, 1985), 140; Pollitt, Daniel H., "Senator/Attorney-General Saxbe and the 'Ineligibility

Clause' of the Constitution: An Encroachment Upon Separation of Powers," *North Carolina Law Review* 53 (1974–1975), 111–133; Saxbe, William B., *Seems Like Yesterday* (private printed, 1975); "Saxbe, William B(art)," in Charles Moritz, ed., *Current Biography 1974* (New York: H. W. Wilson, 1974), 345–347.

EDWARD HIRSCH LEVI

1911–

Edward Levi was a highly respected professor of law and president of the University of Chicago when chosen as Gerald Ford's second attorney general. His tenure, which lasted for a little more than a year, saw the establishment of a new set of guidelines for FBI surveillance. Edward Levi, the son of Gerson Levi and Elsa (née Hirsch) Levi, was born in Chicago, on 26 June 1911. Edward Levi attended local schools in Chicago before going to the University of Chicago and earning a Ph.B. degree in 1932 and a law degree there three years later. In 1938, after a year at Yale University, he was awarded a Doctor of Juristic Science degree. In 1936, he was named as an assistant professor of law at the University of Chicago.

After four years of teaching at Chicago, in 1940 Levi was granted a leave of absence to serve as a special assistant on antitrust matters to Attorneys General Robert H. Jackson and Francis Biddle, serving until 1945. He then returned to the University of Chicago, where he served until 1975 as a professor of law. In 1950, he signed an *amicus curiae* brief in the landmark education segregation case *Sweatt v. Painter* (1950). From 1950 until 1962, he also served as dean of the University of Chicago Law School and, from 1962 to 1968, as provost of the university. In 1968, he was named president of the university.

The resignation of Attorney General William B. Saxbe in late December 1974, effective as soon as his successor could be sworn in, left the Department of Justice with a vacancy for the fifth time since 1968. Levi was then asked to assume the office, despite his lack of political experience and connections. Levi was formally nominated on 14 January 1975 and confirmed on 5 February, taking office as the seventy-first attorney general. During his tenure, which lasted until the end of the Ford administration on 20 January 1977, Levi issued a series of rules, known as the Levi Guidelines, which established FBI procedure on wiretaps, rules that have been updated by Levi's successors, William French Smith and Richard Thornburgh. Levi also was a key adviser when President Ford chose jurist John Paul Stevens to replace Supreme Court Justice William O. Douglas. His tenure, for the most part, is seen as a stabilizing influence on a department shaken to its roots by the resignations of two of its leaders during the Watergate scandal and the imprisonment of a third.

Leaving office in January 1977, Levi returned to the University of Chicago, first as professor of law until 1985 and then as professor emeritus. He is the author of *An Introduction to Legal Reasoning* (University of Chicago Press, 1949) and *Points of View: Talks on Education* (University of Chicago Press, 1969) and contributed an essay to *The Real War on Crime: The Report of the National Criminal Justice Commission* (1996).

References: *The Attorney Generals of the United States, 1789–1985* (Washington, DC: Department of Justice, 1985), 142; Greene, John Robert, *The Presidency of Gerald R. Ford* (Lawrence: University Press of Kansas, 1995), 98–99; "Levi, Edward H(irsch)," in Charles Moritz, ed., *Current Biography 1969* (New York: H. W. Wilson, 1969), 255–258; Navasky, Victor, "The Attorney General as Scholar, Not Enforcer," *New York Times Magazine,* 7 September 1975, 86.

GRIFFIN BOYETTE BELL

1918–

Griffin Bell was the most controversial of Jimmy Carter's nominations for cabinet positions; a longtime friend of the president, he had compiled a record on civil rights as a judge on the Court of Appeals for the Fifth Circuit that many considered too conservative. Griffin Bell was born in Americus, Georgia, on 31 October 1918, the son of A. C. Bell and Thelma (née Pilcher) Bell. Bell in fact knew Carter as a child, and Bell was a close friend of Carter's cousin Don Earl Carter, who ran a newspaper. After attending local schools in Americus, Bell worked his way through Georgia Southwestern College by working part time as a clerk in his father's gas station and in a kitchen appliance store. During World War II, he served in the army stateside, rising from the rank of private to that of major. In 1948, he graduated with honors from Mercer University School of Law, having been admitted to the Georgia bar the previous year.

Bell began his legal career in the Savannah firm of Lawton & Cunningham, moving to another firm in Rome as a senior partner in 1952 and finally joining the firm of King & Spaulding in 1953, with which he would be identified most for the remainder of his life. Slowly getting involved in Democratic Party politics, he supported gubernatorial candidate Ernest Vandiver, who was elected governor in 1958; Bell then served as his chief of staff from 1959 to 1961. Vandiver's opposition to the federal government's attempt to end segregation in the public schools came back to haunt Bell years later when he was criticized by civil rights advocates. In 1960, Bell worked on John F. Kennedy's Georgia campaign for president; with Kennedy's election, the Georgian was named to a seat on the U.S. Court of Appeals for the Fifth Circuit, headquartered in Atlanta, in 1961. In his fifteen years on the court, Bell was known for his conservative opinions, particularly in the area of civil rights and desegregation, handing down decisions that moderated the drive to desegregate southern society in an attempt to head off controversy. Bell returned to King & Spaulding in early 1976 after leaving the Fifth Circuit seat.

During Jimmy Carter's presidential campaign Bell had raised needed funds and had been an adviser. President-elect Carter appointed his old friend to the top law enforcement post in the nation. Announcing Bell's selection on 20 December 1976, Carter said, "I think Judge Bell has a superb civil rights record"; the nominee promised to make the Justice Department "a hallowed place" that would stand for "equal justice under law." However, writes historian Burton Kaufman, "For a politician who had been remarkably successful in defying the odds by winning the White House, Carter also displayed lapses in political judgment. His appointment of Griffin Bell as attorney general stirred up a hornet's nest because of Bell's decisions in earlier segregation cases and his membership in two segregated social clubs. The transition team at the Department of Justice had warned the president-elect of the outcry that would follow Bell's nomination and had recommended that he choose someone who was more 'respected by responsible minority leaders.' But Carter refused even to meet with civil rights leaders to discuss the appointment." Although many Democrats opposed Bell's nomination, he was ultimately confirmed as the seventy-second attorney general on 25 January 1977 by a vote of 75–21.

In his two years at Justice, Bell was embroiled in numerous controversies. In the summer of 1977, two Pennsylvania Democratic congressmen, Joshua Eilberg and Daniel Flood, asked Bell to dismiss U.S. Attorney David Marston, for reasons unknown. After Bell fired Marston, it was learned that he had been investigating allegations of political corruption against the two. An outcry arose that Bell was trying to obstruct the Marston probes; Bell later admitted that the dismissal was "politically motivated," but Marston was not reinstated. Flood ultimately resigned from the House and later pleaded guilty to conspiracy involving a bribery charge. In *Briscoe, Governor of Texas, et al. v. Bell, Attorney General, et al.* (1977), the Supreme Court held that the Voting Rights Act of 1965 did not allow a judicial review of an attorney general's decision in census cases. In March 1979 Bell announced that the Justice Department was revising the rules for admitting students into the United States on student visas, a slap at Iranians, who numbered between 50,000 and 100,000 in the United States. (The United States at that time was involved in an international squabble with Iran, which later that year burst into the hostage crisis.) Although immediately ruled unconstitutional by a federal judge, the revision was upheld by a court of appeals later that year.

On 19 July 1979, President Carter initiated the largest cabinet shakeup since the Eaton affair of 1836 when he accepted the resignations of Secretary of Health, Education and Welfare Joseph Califano, Secretary of the Treasury W. Michael Blumenthal, and Bell. While Califano's and Blumenthal's ousters were unexpected, Bell had been quietly saying for months that he wanted to return to Atlanta and the private practice of law. His resignation was accepted on the day that Califano and Blumenthal were purposely axed. Bell returned to the law firm of King & Spaulding.

Bell's conservative credentials were confirmed when in 1986 he appeared before the Senate Judiciary Committee to support Justice William H. Rehnquist's elevation to Chief Justice. In his testimony, he remarked, "Justice Rehnquist is a leader on the Court, because of his towering intellect, his well-known and recognized capacity as a constitutional law scholar, and because he is, beyond doubt, greatly respected by the other members of the Court." Rehnquist, after difficult hearings, was ultimately confirmed. In 1999, Bell, considered a leading authority on constitutional law, was one of the key witnesses before a Senate panel investigating whether to renew the independent counsel statute.

References: *The Attorney Generals of the United States, 1789–1985* (Washington, DC: Department of Justice, 1985), 144; "Bell, Griffin B(oyette)," in Charles Moritz, ed., *Current Biography 1977* (New York: H. W. Wilson, 1977), 45–48; Kaufman, Burton I., *The Presidency of James Earl Carter, Jr.* (Lawrence: University Press of Kansas, 1993), 27–28; Testimony of Bell in United States Senate, Committee on the Judiciary, *Nomination of Justice William Hubbs Rehnquist: Hearings Before the Committee on the Judiciary, United States Senate, Ninety-ninth Congress, Second Session, on the Nomination of Justice William Hubbs Rehnquist to be Chief Justice of the United States, July 29, 30, 31, and August 1, 1986* (Washington, DC: GPO, 1986), 73–75.

BENJAMIN RICHARD CIVILETTI

1935–

Benjamin Civiletti was named attorney general in the midst of the most massive "purge" of cabinet officials in American history: with the resignations in two days of five department heads, including Attorney General Griffin Bell, Benjamin Civiletti, the deputy attorney general, became the chief of the Justice Department. He was born in Peekskill, New York, on 17 July 1935. He attended the local schools of Baltimore, Maryland, where he grew up, and earned a bachelor's degree in 1957 from Johns Hopkins University. Legal studies at the University of Maryland Law School ended with his being awarded a law degree in 1961, and he was admitted to the Maryland bar that same year.

Civiletti's first job after law school was service as a clerk for U.S. District Court Judge William Calvin Chesnut in Baltimore. He then was named as assistant U.S. attorney in Baltimore, where he served from 1962 until 1964 prosecuting fraud cases. In the latter year he joined the prestigious Baltimore law firm of Venable, Baejter & Howard (later Venable, Baejter, Howard & Civiletti), where he served until 1977 first as a partner, then as head of the firm's litigation division. During this period he also served on various state commissions, including a stint from 1975 to 1976 as a member of the Maryland state legislature's Task Force on Crime.

During his years at Venable, Baejter & Howard, Civiletti worked with Charles H. Kirbo, a former law partner of Judge Griffin Bell, at that time recently retired from his seat on the U.S. Circuit Court of Appeals for the Fifth Circuit. Kirbo was serving as an adviser to Georgia Governor Jimmy Carter, running for president. With Carter's election, Kirbo recommended to the president-elect that Civiletti be named to the Justice Department as an assistant attorney general. Carter then nominated Civiletti to the department's Criminal Division on 16 February 1977, and he took the oath on 10 March. In his one year in this position, Civiletti worked closely with Attorney General Griffin Bell on fraud cases, including an indictment of Carter confidant Bert Lance, and payments made to congressmen in the Koreagate corruption scandal. Carter historian Burton Kaufman calls Civiletti "Bell's trusted lieutenant." In late 1977, Deputy Attorney General Peter F. Flaherty resigned, and President Carter named Civiletti to the post, first in an acting capacity and, on 26 January 1978, in a permanent fashion. After protracted hearings involving his handling of a scandal over the firing of a U.S. attorney in Pennsylvania who was investigating two Democratic congressmen, Civiletti was confirmed.

On 19 July 1979, Attorney General Bell, having privately announced to the president months earlier that he wanted to return to Atlanta, resigned. Bell asked that Civiletti be named to replace him; Carter formally nominated him on that same day. After three days of committee hearings, Civiletti was confirmed by the Senate on 1 August by a vote of 94–1. Serving until the end of the Carter administration on 20 January 1981, he reacted to recent department controversies by establishing a set of regulations, known officially as the "Attorney General's Guidelines on General Crimes, Racketeering Enterprise and Domestic Security/Terrorism Investiga-

tions," but better known as the Civiletti Rules. These were instituted to "encourage agents of the FBI to perform their duties with greater certainty, confidence and effectiveness," as well as to "give the public firm assurance that the FBI is acting properly under the law." Civiletti also established the Office of Special Investigations (OSI) to research and institute legal proceedings, including denaturalization and deportation, against suspected Nazi war criminals in the United States.

After leaving office, Civiletti returned to his old firm, becoming chairman of the Baltimore office and working on issues involving banking, white collar crime, and government regulation.

References: "Civiletti, Benjamin R(ichard)," in Charles Moritz, ed., *Current Biography 1980* (New York: H. W. Wilson, 1980), 45–48; Kaufman, Burton I., *The Presidency of James Earl Carter, Jr.* (Lawrence: University Press of Kansas, 1993), 147.

WILLIAM FRENCH SMITH
1917–1990

William French Smith was perhaps Ronald Reagan's closest adviser, a man who had suggested that the former actor run for governor of California in 1966. As Reagan's personal attorney and friend since 1965, he was a clear choice for attorney general in Reagan's first cabinet. The son of William French Smith and Margaret (née Dawson) Smith, Smith was born in Wilton, New Hampshire, on 26 August 1917. His father was president of the Mexican Telegraph & Telephone Company, and he took his family to live in Boston where the company was headquartered. After his father died when he was six, Smith traveled with his mother, particularly to California. He entered the University of California at Berkeley, graduating summa cum laude in 1939, and received his law degree from Harvard in 1942. After a period in the naval reserve during the war, he joined the Los Angeles law firm of Gibson, Dunn & Crutcher, remaining with them for the next thirty-four years.

In 1964, Smith heard Ronald Reagan, whom he already knew slightly, speak on behalf of Republican presidential candidate Barry Goldwater and was deeply impressed by the talk. After the speech Smith joined several wealthy California Republicans to urge Reagan to run for governor. Two years later, Reagan ran a successful campaign against Governor Edmund "Pat" Brown; Smith was one of his leading backers. Governor Reagan named Smith as a member of the University of California Board of Regents; he also served, in the 1970s, as a member of the board of the Legal Aid Foundation, which offered legal assistance to economically disadvantaged people. In 1976, Reagan made his first run for the presidency, an abortive attempt to deprive President Gerald Ford of the Republican nomination; Smith served as vice-chairman of the California delegation. Four years later, Reagan had gathered enough support in the party to win the nomination and subsequently the election. Smith worked closely with him during the campaign, becoming a member of Reagan's "kitchen cabinet." On 11 December 1980, President-elect Reagan named, Smith as his attorney general. On 22 January 1981 Smith was confirmed by the Senate, and he took over at the Department of Justice the next day as the seventy-fourth attorney general.

In his four years as the top enforcement officer in the nation, Smith revised the Levi Guidelines, a series of guidelines issued by Smith's predecessor, Edward Levi, in 1976. This revision clarified the authority of the Federal Bureau of Investigation to use the "recruitment or placement of informants in groups, 'mail covers,' or electronic surveillance," in order to investigate whether a certain group "is engaged in an enterprise for furthering political or social goals wholly or in part through activities that involve force or violence." In his autobiography, Reagan mentions that Smith was his chief adviser in the push to place a woman on the U.S. Supreme Court as soon as a vacancy opened; Arizona state Senator Sandra Day O'Connor eventually became the first woman ever named to the high court. On 8 January 1982, the Justice Department dropped its antitrust suit against American Telephone and Telegraph Co. (AT&T) after the company agreed to divest itself of the twenty-two Bell operations that operated most of the nation's phone business, establishing a system of baby Bells. Robert Pear of the *New York Times* wrote in 1984, "In three years as Attorney General, William French Smith [has] supervised profound changes in Federal policy on civil rights, antitrust enforcement and criminal justice." Legal writer Stuart Taylor, Jr., added that Smith changed federal laws to conform with his and Reagan's conservative philosophy, sometimes conflicting with court precedents. Smith later said that the best part of his tenure was the passage of the Comprehensive Crime Act of 1984, which changed the federal bail and sentencing guideline systems.

Smith announced his intention to resign on 22 January 1984; he did not leave officially until February 1985, when his successor, Edwin Meese III, was finally confirmed and sworn in.

In his final years, Smith continued to practice law. On 29 October 1990, he died of cancer in Los Angeles; he was 73 years old. He was buried in Forest Lawn Memorial Park in Glendale, California.

References: *The Attorney Generals of the United States, 1789–1985* (Washington, DC: Department of Justice, 1985), 148; Reagan, Ronald, *An American Life: The Autobiography of Ronald Reagan* (New York: Simon & Schuster, 1990), 279–280; "Smith, William French," in Charles Moritz, ed., *Current Biography 1982* (New York: H. W. Wilson, 1982), 402–405.

EDWIN MEESE III

1931–

Edwin Meese's tenure was marred by charges of scandal and the first investigation of a sitting attorney general by an independent prosecutor in American history. Yet although he resigned under a cloud, he was never formally charged with any crime. Edwin Meese III, the son of Edwin Meese, Jr., and Leone Meese, was born in Oakland, California, on 2 December 1931. Meese went to school in Oakland and attended Yale University on a scholarship, graduating in 1953. He worked for a short time in an iron foundry, then entered the Boalt Law School at the University of California at Berkeley. His law studies were interrupted by two years in the U.S. Army, and he received his law degree in 1958.

After leaving law school, Meese worked as the deputy district attorney in Alameda County, service that came during the rise of protests against the Vietnam War. The atmosphere around him, as well as his strict Republican upbringing, made Meese more and more a conservative "law and order" man. These views brought him to the attention of California Governor Ronald Reagan, who named Meese his secretary on clemency and crime issues. When antiwar riots broke out on the Berkeley campus in 1969, Meese advised the governor to declare a state of emergency. During Reagan's second term (1971–1975), Meese served as his executive assistant and chief of staff. After Reagan left office, Meese served briefly in the public sector before taking a position as a professor of criminal justice at the University of San Diego Law School as well as director of the Center for Criminal Justice Policy and Management.

After Reagan announced in late 1979 that he was seeking the Republican presidential nomination, he named Meese as his "advisor on key issues in the campaign." After Reagan's election in 1980, Meese was named as the president's counselor. Close aides called him "President Meese" because he handled many of Reagan's day-to-day activities. He served as one of Reagan's three major aides (along with James A. Baker III, the chief of staff, and Michael K. Deaver, the deputy chief of staff) from January 1981 until 1985. He also served as chairman of the Domestic Policy Council, a White House advisory board, and the National Drug Policy Board. As a member of the National Security Council, he was able to advise the president on many foreign policy initiatives.

The announcement on 22 January 1984 that Attorney General William French Smith was resigning allowed Reagan to name Meese as Smith's successor the next day. Questions over Meese's financial dealings clouded the nomination, and for a time it seemed that it would be withdrawn. Finally, an independent counsel, noted Washington attorney Jacob Stein, was appointed to look into the matter. His report, which finally cleared Meese after a year of inquiries, led to Meese's confirmation on 23 February 1985 as the seventy-fifth attorney general by a vote of 63–31; this was the highest number of dissenting votes cast against an attorney general nominee since the defeat of nominee Charles B. Warren in 1925. Meese served from March 1985 until July 1988. During his tenure Meese was deeply involved in shaping federal drug policy, backed the unsuccessful nominations of Robert Bork as a justice on the U.S. Supreme Court and of William Bradford Reynolds as assistant attorney general, and launched the investigation that culminated in the Iran-Contra scandal. Meese himself writes, "I soon discovered that taking charge of the Department of Justice, with some 72,000 employees, a budget of $3.6 billion, and an array of responsibilities that ranged from drug enforcement to civil rights to judicial selection was a colossal responsibility."

Meese, however, soon became embroiled in his own scandal: he was implicated, but eventually cleared, of connections with a New York defense contractor, Wedtech Corp. (this scandal also ruined the career of Secretary of Labor Raymond Donovan; see Raymond James Donovan, secretary of labor

1981–1985, for more information on the Wedtech scandal). An independent counsel, James McKay, after a lengthy inquiry, found that while Meese might have acted improperly regarding Wedtech as well as a proposal by a friend to gain access to building an oil pipeline across Jordan, he was not criminally responsible. To avoid further embarrassment to the administration in its waning days, Meese resigned on 5 July 1988, and he stepped down later that month.

Today, Meese is a writer and analyst for several conservative Washington think tanks, including the Heritage Foundation, and serves as president of the Council for National Policy, a conservative advocacy group. He is the author of *With Reagan: The Inside Story* (1992).

References: "Meese, Edwin, 3d," in Charles Moritz, ed., *Current Biography 1981* (New York: H. W. Wilson, 1981), 285–289; Meese, Edwin, III, *With Reagan: The Inside Story* (Washington, DC: Regnery Gateway, 1992), 304.

RICHARD LEWIS THORNBURGH
1932–

A former governor of Pennsylvania and the head of the Pittsburgh chapter of the American Civil Liberties Union (ACLU), Richard Thornburgh was chosen by a Ronald Reagan, a Republican, to serve as his third attorney general; Thornburgh also served in the administration of President George Bush. Born in Rosslyn Farms, a prosperous suburb of Pittsburgh, on 16 July 1932, Thornburgh was the son of Charles Garland Thornburgh and Alice (née Sanborn) Thornburgh. He grew up in a Republican home, attending local schools in Rosslyn Farms. At first he wanted to be a sportswriter, but he soon fell back on the profession of his grandfather and great-grandfather: engineering. He earned a bachelor of engineering degree

from Yale in 1954, but he soon changed his mind as to a career and entered the University of Pittsburgh School of Law, from which he received a law degree in 1957. He was admitted to the Pennsylvania bar the following year.

Thornburgh first worked as counsel for the Aluminum Company of America until 1960, then joined the Pittsburgh law firm of Kirkpatrick, Lockhart, Johnson & Hutchinson. A moderate Republican, he ran unsuccessfully for a seat in the U.S. House of Representatives in 1966 on a platform opposing the Vietnam War and supporting recent civil rights legislation. After the loss, Thornburgh joined the National Association for the Advancement of Colored People (NAACP) and became the director of the Pittsburgh chapter of the ACLU. In 1969, President Richard Nixon named Thornburgh as the U.S. attorney for the Western District of Pennsylvania. Under the Organized Crime Control Act of 1970, Thornburgh became the first attorney to impanel a grand jury to investigate charges of racketeering. In 1975, President Gerald Ford named Thornburgh as assistant attorney general in charge of the Department of Justice's Criminal Law Division, where he served until the end of the Ford administration in January 1977, after which he returned to his old law firm.

In 1978, Thornburgh ran for the governorship of Pennsylvania, defeating six other candidates (including Philadelphia district attorney Arlen Specter, later a U.S. senator) in the Republican primary and former Pittsburgh mayor Joe Flaherty in the general election. Serving two terms as governor from 1979 to 1987, Thornburgh is best remembered for signing into law the Pennsylvania Abortion Control Act of 1982, which required doctors to inform women of the risks of having an abortion and that the options to carry the pregnancy to term and adoption were available. He was then sued to the U.S. Supreme Court, which held in *Thornburgh v. American College of Obstetricians & Gynecologists* (1986) that the law impeded a woman's right to an abortion. He also dealt with the aftereffects of the Three Mile Island fiasco, in which a nuclear power plant near Harrisburg nearly melted down in March 1979. Barred from seeking a third term, Thornburgh turned down offers to become the head of the Federal Bureau of Investigation and instead was named as director of the Institute of Politics at the John F. Kennedy School of Government at Harvard University.

On 5 July 1988, Attorney General Edwin Meese announced his resignation. President Ronald Reagan, in the last months of his second term, considered for the vacancy Transportation Secretary Elizabeth Dole, which would have made her the first female attorney general. Instead, Reagan reached out to Thornburgh, who accepted the nod on 12 July 1988. Asked at the press conference announcing his selection whether he would be in the "tradition of Ed Meese," Thornburgh replied, "I'll be an Attorney General in the tradition of Dick Thornburgh." He was confirmed unanimously by the Senate on 11 August, and he took office several days later. During his tenure as the seventy-sixth attorney general, which lasted through the remainder of the Reagan administration and two years of the Bush administration, Thornburgh was, wrote *New York Times* reporter David Johnston on Thornburgh's resignation, "best known as the unbending point man" for many of his boss's policies. He twice took cases to the U.S. Supreme Court: in *Thornburgh v. Abbott* (1989), the Court held that the U.S. Bureau of Prisons could properly exclude certain publications from inmates if they were deemed to be "detrimental to the security, good order, or discipline of the institution or if it might facilitate criminal activity"; another case involved a Detroit newspaper strike.

On 9 August 1991, Thornburgh resigned his position to run for the U.S. Senate seat from Pennsylvania that had been held by Senator John Heinz, who had been killed in a helicopter accident. That November, Thornburgh was upset by Harris Wofford, who had been temporarily named to the seat until the election. Today, Thornburgh practices law and appears on numerous television programs as a legal commentator.

References: "Thornburgh, Richard Lewis," in John W. Raimo, ed., *Biographical Directory of the Governors of the United States, 1978–1983* (Westport, CT: Meckler, 1985), 265–266; "Thornburgh, Richard L(ewis)," in Charles Moritz, ed., *Current Biography 1988* (New York: H. W. Wilson, 1988), 560–563.

WILLIAM PELHAM BARR
1950–

William Barr was, at 41, the third-youngest man installed as attorney general, after Robert Kennedy and Ramsey Clark; and in his two short years as the seventy-seventh attorney general, William Barr was forced to deal with a major international bank scandal and the legal implications of the American invasion of Panama. Barr, the son of Donald Barr and Mary (née Ahern) Barr, both New York–based educators, was born in New York City on 23 May 1950. His father taught English for ten years at Columbia University in New York before being appointed as headmaster in 1964 of the private Dalton School in the same city. William Barr attended schools in Manhattan, slowly becoming a conservative Republican, refusing to protest the Vietnam War, and dreaming of becoming the director of the Central Intelligence Agency (CIA). He earned bachelor's degrees (1971) and master's degrees (1973) in Chinese studies from Columbia. After the latter degree was awarded, he was hired by the CIA as an analyst of Chinese affairs and, later, as a legislative assistant to aid the director in preparing to testify before Congress. That director was George Bush.

At the same time that he worked for the CIA, Barr was attended the George Washington University Law School, from which he earned a law degree in 1977. Admitted to the bar that same year, he left the CIA to take a position as a clerk for Judge Malcolm Wilkey of the U.S. District Court of Appeals for the District of Columbia Circuit. Impressed by the young attorney's drive, Wilkey recommended after a year that Barr join the Washington law firm of Shaw, Pittman, Potts & Trowbridge, mainly, as David Johnston later wrote, "in civil law and Federal administrative matters." In 1980, a friend got him a job on the team handling Ronald Reagan's transition to the presidency; two years later, Barr was named to the Domestic Policy Council in the White House itself. One of the men he impressed was C. Boyden Gray, who was then serving as Vice-president George Bush's chief counsel. Barr returned to his law firm in 1983 and was soon made a full partner.

In 1988, Barr left the law temporarily to work on Bush's presidential campaign. After the election, Bush named him as assistant attorney general in charge of the Office of Legal Counsel, which advises the White House, as well as other cabinet-level departments, on legal matters; it was in this capacity that he drafted the legal opinion, handed down by Attorney General Richard Thornburgh, that justified the United States invasion of Panama to capture strongman Manuel Noriega. In 1990, Barr was promoted to deputy attorney general after one potential deputy had withdrawn his name and another had resigned after just six months. Barr stepped in and cleaned up the office.

On 9 August 1991, Attorney General Thornburgh resigned to run for a U.S. Senate seat in his native Pennsylvania. For two months, Barr served as acting attorney general because it seemed that his conservative leanings would preclude President Bush from officially nominating him to the post. Names mentioned for the position included former California Governor George Deukmejian, Governor (and later U.S. Senator) John Ashcroft of Missouri, and Secretary of Transportation Samuel Skinner. Instead, on 16 October 1991, Bush announced that Barr would be named permanently to the post. Biographer David Johnston said of him, "His affable, unpretentious style at the Department of Justice has been an antidote to the aloof and sometimes imperious approach of Mr. Thornburgh." During his confirmation hearings, Barr stated unequivocally that he opposed the Supreme Court abortion decision, *Roe v. Wade,* saying, "I don't believe a right to privacy extends to abortion." Nonetheless, he was confirmed by a voice vote on 20 November, and sworn in six days later. In his year and four months as the top law enforcement officer in the nation, Barr was faced with the residual effects of the Persian Gulf War. When the FBI announced that vital records dealing with the Banca Nazionale del Lavoro (BNL), an Italian bank that had been making loans to Iraq, had been withheld from investigators in Atlanta, Barr refused to appoint an independent counsel to investigate the matter; later, however, after much criticism, he named former federal judge Frederick Lacey, who reported directly to Barr. Historian Peter Levy writes, "His focus was on crime. This included a reorganization of the Federal Bureau of Investigation in order to devote more of its manpower to domestic crime and less to counterintelligence." He transferred three hundred counterintelligence agents to domestic street crime, the largest shake-up in the bureau's history. When President Bush argued that he had the power to line-item veto congressional bills, Barr warned him in a legal opinion that only Congress could enact a line-item veto law.

Barr left office in January 1993 at the end of the Bush administration and went to work in the private sector, including service as vice-president and general counsel of GTE Telecommunications in New York.

References: "Barr, William P.," in Judith Graham, ed., *Current Biography 1992,* (New York: H. W. Wilson, 1992), 51–55; Levy, Peter, *Encyclopedia of the Reagan-Bush Years* (Westport, CT: Greenwood, 1996), 32–33; Mervin, David, *George Bush and the Guardianship Presidency* (New York: St. Martin's, 1996).

JANET RENO

1938–

Janet Reno was President Bill Clinton's third choice for attorney general. Her ultimate ascension as the first female attorney general made history; yet her tenure was marred by charges that she covered for the president in several scandals, including those involving campaign finance irregularities and spying by Chinese operatives in American nuclear laboratories. Janet Reno was born on 21 July 1938 in Miami, Florida, the daughter of Henry Reno, a Danish immigrant and police reporter for the *Miami Herald*, and Jane (née Wood) Reno, an investigative reporter for the now-defunct *Miami News*. Reno attended schools in Dade County, Florida, then earned a bachelor's degree in chemistry from Cornell University in 1960. She then enrolled in the Harvard University Law School at a time when women law students were still a novelty. After receiving her law degree and being admitted to the Florida bar, Reno soon found work at a small Miami law firm, Brigham & Brigham. In 1967, she became a junior partner in the firm of Lewis & Reno.

After serving from 1971 to 1972 as staff director of the Judiciary Committee of the Florida House of Representatives, and from 1972 to 1973 as counsel for the Criminal Justice Committee for the Revision of Florida's Criminal Code of the Florida State Senate, Reno took a position as assistant state attorney for Florida's Eleventh Judicial Circuit. Named as head of the juvenile division, she reorganized the juvenile system in just a few months. In 1976, she left the Dade state attorney's office to join the Miami law firm of Steel, Hector & Davis; however, in 1978, when her former boss State Attorney Richard Gerstein stepped down, he advised Governor Ruben Askew that Reno be named in his place. She thus became the first woman ever to serve as head of a county prosecutor's office in Florida. Editors Jeffrey Trammell and Gary Osifchin said in 1994, "Reno earned her

battle scars—and a reputation as a tough but judicious prosecutor—during a fourteen-year tour of duty as state attorney in Miami. She won reelection five times in a Republican county and survived a number of controversial court cases that threatened to derail her career. J. J. Plummer, a Miami Beach commissioner, remarked, "As state attorney, people aren't going to love you always, but she is definitely respected and seen as fair.' " Reno was Dade state attorney from 1978 until 1993.

However, when Bill Clinton, a Democrat, was elected president in 1992, he turned to a corporate attorney for the Aetna Life and Casualty insurance company, Zoë Baird, as his first choice for attorney general. Baird, however, had what soon became known as a "nanny problem"—she had employed undocumented workers as household help and had not paid Social Security taxes for them. Criticized for breaking the law when she herself would be carrying out the laws, she withdrew her name. Clinton then turned to federal district judge Kimba Wood on 5 February 1993. A day later, however, Wood, too, was gone: she too had a "nanny problem." The situation was getting impossible when, on 11 February 1993, Clinton finally named Reno. Ignoring criticism that he was out to name a woman regardless of her qualifications, Clinton explained that he had called eight other candidates, both men and women. Reno was quickly confirmed and took office on 12 March 1993 as the seventy-eighth attorney general and the first woman to hold the position.

Reno's tenure has been marked by serious wrangling with Congress and numerous charges of covering for Clinton in various scandals. Soon after taking office, she ordered FBI agents to raid the compound of a religious group, the Branch Davidians, in Waco, Texas. The Davidians resisted, leaving several agents dead. A standoff then ensued for several weeks, culminating in a horrendous conflagration that consumed the compound and left eighty-six people, including seventeen children, dead. Reno took responsibility for the incident, and in a report on the incident she was widely criticized. Exercising her powers under the Independent Counsel Act of 1978, she named several investigators to look into charges against the president and several members of the cabinet, including allegations related to a twenty-year-old land deal called Whitewater. Yet in 1997, Reno came under extensive criticism when she failed to name an investigator to look into charges of massive political campaign fundraising fraud by the Democrats. It was in the case of *Reno, Attorney General of the United States, et al. v. The American Civil Liberties Union et al.* (1997) that the U.S. Supreme Court struck down the Communications Decency Act of 1996, enacted to regulate the Internet, as unconstitutional. In 1999, when allegations of spying by Chinese operatives in American nuclear laboratories was disclosed, it was discovered that Reno, as attorney general, had refused to allow the FBI to wiretap a Chinese physicist under suspicion for spying, prompting additional calls for her resignation. In 2000, her handling of the Elian Gonzales case, which involved a young Cuban boy whose mother drowned while the two fled Cuba, provoked both criticism and praise.

Reno is considered a hard-bitten but determined prosecutor. Her service since 1993 makes her one of the longer serving attorneys general in recent times.

References: Drew, Elizabeth, *On the Edge: The Clinton Presidency* (New York: Simon & Schuster, 1994), 36–41, 53–54; "Reno, Janet," in Judith Graham, ed., *Current Biography 1993* (New York: H. W. Wilson, 1993), 485–489; Trammell, Jeffrey B., and Gary P. Osifchin, eds., *The Clinton 500: The New Team Running America, 1994* (Washington, DC: Almanac, 1994), 293.

COMMERCE

In his first address as president, George Washington stated, "The advance of agriculture, commerce and manufactures by all proper means will not, I trust, need recommendation." An executive department to handle these matters, however, was not initially created; instead, a congressional committee of commerce and manufactures was established in 1795, with the Senate adding a commerce committee in 1816. The first American industry to receive cabinet rank status was agriculture in 1889. Two years earlier, President Grover Cleveland had signed into law the Interstate Commerce Law. The 1893 financial panic and the weakness of the government response to it became the rationale, led by the National Association of Manufacturers, behind the demand for the establishment of a federal department of commerce and industry, and as a subagency, the Bureau of Labor, which had been created in 1884 by Congress. However, no action was taken on the establishment of a federal department.

In 1898 Congress formulated the U.S. Industrial Commission to examine the economic and social structure of the nation. It was not until Theodore Roosevelt became president, in 1901, that the initiative was taken. In his first message to Congress, 3 December 1901, Roosevelt asked that a "Department of Commerce and Industries" be instituted. Those in Congress who backed such a proposal compromised with those demanding a similar department for labor interests and formed the Department of Commerce and Labor. Roosevelt signed the bill into law on 14 February 1903. For more than ten years, the agency operated with four different men serving as secretary. However, labor advocates in the nation were angered that business and labor shared the same offices. A movement began to reorganize the agency into two entities. This was accomplished with the act of 4 March 1913, signed into law by President William Howard Taft on his final day in office. The next day, President Woodrow Wilson chose Congressman William Cox Redfield as the first secretary of the new Department of Commerce. Redfield, who served until 31 October 1919, saw the agency through World War I and a consoli-

145

dation of those activities that had not been transferred to the separate Department of Labor. The second secretary, Joshua W. Alexander, stayed to the end of Wilson's term. He was succeeded by Herbert Hoover, a mining engineer who had served under Wilson to bring needed food and supplies to famine victims in Russia after the war. Hoover served from 1921 until 1929, when he left to become president of the United States. Hoover organized the department and made it the main government office involved in national commerce matters.

During the Depression, the department, under Roy D. Chapin, Daniel C. Roper, Harry L. Hopkins, and Jesse H. Jones, attempted to alleviate the conditions of the economic downturn. For the first years of the New Deal, the department was mainly in charge of the administration of the National Recovery Act (NRA), which was struck down as unconstitutional by the Supreme Court in 1937. Roper left after he disagreed with a department reorganization in 1938; after he left, the department was stripped of the Bureau of Air Commerce, the Bureau of Lighthouses, and the Foreign Commerce Bureau. During World War II, the department strove to maintain American exports. After the war, Secretary Henry Wallace, the only former vice-president to hold a cabinet position, served for a little more than a year and a half. Truman's final two secretaries were W. Averill Harriman and Charles Sawyer, both former ambassadors.

In the 1950s, the department was run by Charles Sinclair Weeks, Lewis L. Strauss, and Frederick H. Mueller. These men saw the nation through the Korean War, with wartime allocation becoming an important model of government efficiency; the beginning of the construction of the federal highway system; and the renegotiation of the General Agreement on Tariffs and Trade (GATT). In the 1960s, Luther Hodges, John T. Connor, Alexander Trowbridge, and Cyrus Smith ran the department. By 1969, Commerce constituted sixteen agencies with 25,400 employees. Under Maurice Stans, the Office of Telecommunications was established, and the National Oceanic and Atmospheric Administration was created from other older bureaus. This expansion increased the size of the department to 35,000 employees by 1972. The tenures of Secretaries Peter Peterson and Frederick Dent saw restrictions on trade with the Soviet Union relaxed in the era of détente. Juanita Kreps, the first of two women to serve as secretary, led the department in the 1970s.

Under Secretary Malcolm Baldrige, the Commerce Department got special cabinet treatment with the creation of a trade strike force to correct unfair trading practices abroad. Following Baldrige's death on 25 July 1987, the post was held by C. William Verity, Robert Mosbacher, and Barbara Franklin.

In 1993, Ronald Brown, a former head of the Democratic National Committee, became the first African American to be named to Commerce. Brown turned the department into a strong advocate for American trade worldwide, but one that was criticized for possibly selling secret American technology to China. While on a trade mission to Bosnia, Brown and his entourage were killed in a plane crash on 3 April 1996. Brown was succeeded by the U.S. trade representative, Mickey Kantor and, in 1997, by William Daley. In July 2000 Daley resigned to become the chairman of Vice-president Al Gore's presidential campaign, and former Congressman Norman Y. Mineta became the first Asian American to serve in the Cabinet.

The Commerce Department, as a separate agency, has been in existence for eighty-five years, in which thirty-three men and women have served as secretary, an average tenure of two years seven months. Herbert Hoover served the longest (eight years), Roy D. Chapin the shortest (less than seven months). *The United States Government Manual*

1996/1997 reports, "The Department . . . encourages, serves, and promotes the Nation's international trade, economic growth, and technological advancement. [It] provides a wide variety of programs through the competitive free enterprise system. It offers assistance and information to increase America's competitiveness in the world economy; administers programs to prevent unfair foreign trade competition; provides social and economic statistics and analyses for business and government planners; provides research and support for the increased use of scientific, engineering, and technological development; works to improve our understanding and benefits of the Earth's physical environment and oceanic resources; grants patents and registers trademarks; develops policies and conducts research on telecommunications; provides assistance to promote domestic economic development; and assists in the growth of minority businesses."

The department oversees such operations as the Bureau of the Census, the National Oceanic and Atmospheric Administration (NOAA), the International Trade Administration, the Bureau of Export Administration, the Patent and Trademark Office, and the National Telecommunications and Information Administration. The Commerce Department is housed in the Herbert Hoover Building, named in honor of the third secretary. The Malcolm Baldrige Auditorium in that building is named in honor of the twenty-seventh secretary, one of two commerce secretaries to die in office. The headquarters of the department, located at Fifteenth Street and Pennsylvania Avenue, encompasses three complete city blocks. When it was constructed, it was one of the largest office buildings in the world. The department did not always have such auspicious offices, however. "From the time of its creation, and even after it was split from the Department of Labor into a separate agency, Commerce was housed in numerous offices around the nation's capital. In the 1920s, an area near the Post Office Building at Twelfth and Pennsylvania, where the Department of the Navy headquarters was located, was selected for the new home of Commerce. The land was purchased in 1910 for $2.46 million, but for the next decade and a half it remained a swampland. Pierre L'Enfant, the designer of the original District of Columbia, had envisioned a great canal at this site, where water from the district would be drained. This plan was eventually shelved. Construction of the new Department of Commerce Building began in 1927, with President Herbert Hoover, who once headed the department, laying the cornerstone on 10 June 1929. The structure, made of limestone, was completed in 1932 at a cost of $17.5 million. In 1982, on the building's fiftieth anniversary, it was dedicated as the Herbert Hoover Commerce Building.

References: Department of Commerce, Office of the Secretary, *From Lighthouses to Laserbeams: A History of U.S. Department of Commerce* (Washington, DC: GPO, 1995); *United States Government Manual 1996/1997* (Washington, DC: GPO, 1996), 150.

WILLIAM COX REDFIELD
1858–1932

William Redfield was a leading American manufacturer and congressman when President Woodrow Wilson chose him to be-

come the first secretary of the newly designed Department of Commerce. He served as the head of the department through World War I, until 1919. Born in Albany, New York, on 18 June 1858, Redfield was the son of Charles Bailey Redfield and Mary Ann (née Wallace) Redfield. In 1867, William C. Redfield moved with his parents to Pittsfield, Massachusetts—there he attended public schools and received home instruction. However, he left school at age fifteen when adverse business conditions led to setbacks for his father, and Redfield helped to support the family. He initially went to work in the Pittsfield Post Office; then he worked as a salesman for a local paper company, a position that led to his move to New York City in 1877.

Redfield worked for R. Hoe & Company, which manufactured newspaper printing presses, but he moved, in 1883, to work for J. H. Williams & Company of Brooklyn, which produced steel and iron drop forgings. He eventually entered the world of banking and life insurance. By the 1890s, he was a wealthy man, with investments in numerous companies.

A staunch Democrat, in the early 1890s Redfield sided with the "Gold" wing of the Democratic Party, led by President Grover Cleveland, which believed the nation's economy should be on the gold standard. When the party nominated William Jennings Bryan, a "Silver" Democrat, for president, Redfield and others left and formed the "Gold Democrat" Party; Redfield served as a delegate to 'their only national convention, held in Indianapolis in 1896. He was nominated by the party for a seat in Congress, but was defeated. In 1902 and 1903, he served as commissioner of Public Works for the borough of Brooklyn.

In 1910, Redfield was nominated for a seat in Congress by the regular Democrats for the Fifth New York District, normally a strong Republican district, but Redfield won a decisive victory. Redfield served in the Sixty-second Congress, from 4 March 1911 until 3 March 1913, and stood for tariff reduction, and authored *The New Industrial Day*. In 1912, Redfield wanted the nomination for vice-president; when the Democrats selected Indiana Governor Thomas Marshall instead, Redfield chose not to run for reelection to Congress and instead devote his time to getting presidential candidate Woodrow Wilson elected. On 26 January 1913, shortly before taking the oath, President-elect Wilson wrote to Redfield, "I write to ask if you will not accept the post of Secretary of Commerce and Labor. . . . It would be a real pleasure to me to be associated with you—and, what is better, a great advantage to the Department of Commerce to have you take charge of it." Redfield later wrote in his autobiography, *With Congress and Cabinet:* "With such a problem before me I wanted the counsel of an old friend in whose character and wisdom long years had taught me confidence. I went over to the Senate and had a long talk with such a man whom I had known almost from boyhood—Senator [Winthrop Murray] Crane of Massachusetts. He was then about to retire from the Senate and we spoke together very frankly concerning his plans and my own. It was quite in accord with his judgment that I accepted President Wilson's unexpected invitation and four days later entered his cabinet." Wilson confidante Ray Stannard Baker wrote about how Wilson chose Redfield, "Many names had been suggested but Wilson thought that Redfield came nearest to what was demanded in a department dealing so largely with the industrial and commercial affairs of the nation. Redfield had been a manufacturer who had maintained, while a member of Congress, a strong belief in low tariffs. Wilson had been impressed by several of Redfield's tariff speeches, and attracted, as he often was, by his facility in expression. Redfield had recently been around the world and visited the Philippine Islands, which seemed to Wilson an added qualification. Redfield promptly accepted."

Redfield's tenure as the first secretary of commerce lasted until 31 October 1919. Redfield was a frequent and invited adviser to Wilson. Redfield wrote in his autobiography, "Several important events were related closely to my own personal work. With most, not all, of the others I was familiar as an adviser. Sometimes my advice was taken, sometimes not. As I see results today they seem to justify my counsels whether for or against."

In September 1913, writer Burton J. Hendrick wrote, in a lengthy article on Redfield that appeared in the journal *World's Work,* "The Wilson administration has a traveling salesman in the Cabinet. Quite appropriately, this traveling salesman occupies the post of Secretary of Commerce. Perhaps it would be more respectful and dignified to describe Mr. William C. Redfield as a 'successful business man.' However, the fact is that, although Mr. Redfield has filled nearly every position in several large manufacturing plants from shipping clerk to president, his most striking qualities are those usually possessed by the resourceful, energetic getter of business. He is the man who has transformed his factory from a domestic concern into one with trade ramifications in all parts of the world, whose business imagination has reached from Brooklyn to Germany, Egypt, India, and Japan. As Secretary of Commerce Mr. Redfield is also a kind of sublimated commercial traveler for the Nation. His chief ambition is to widen the horizon of American industry; to lift the American business man out of the slough of parochialism into which he has fallen—largely as a result of a coddling protective tariff and to make him, what his natural advantages and his own industry and genius entitle him to be, the most aggressive and successful competitor in the world."

When Redfield began his tenure at the Department of Commerce he had to separate the former Commerce and Labor Department and start with new offices. In his first annual report, he wrote, the inner workings of the "new" department: "The Department consists of nine bureaus and the Office of the Secretary, the latter being divided into five divisions—Office of the Chief Clerk (including the Division of Supplies), Disbursing Office, Appointment Division, Division of Publications, and Office of the Solicitor. The nine bureaus are respectively those of Foreign and Domestic Commerce, Corporations, Standards, Census, Fisheries, Lighthouses, Coast and Geodetic Survey, Steamboat-Inspection Service, and Navigation. . . . The Office of the Secretary and five bureaus have been concentrated since October 1 in the Commerce Building, Pennsylvania Avenue and Nineteenth Street NW. The Bureau of Standards, Bureau of the Census, Bureau of Fisheries, and the Coast and Geodetic Survey

are in separate buildings in various parts of Washington, all of which, save that occupied by the Census, are owned by the Government." On 12 August 1913, the president wrote to Secretary Redfield, "I hate to burden you with extra tasks, but we have a most important and interesting Congressional election pending in Maine and nobody could be more serviceable in the speaking campaign which is about to begin up there than you, yourself. The issue is to be the tariff. We are to be challenged to justify the pending action of Congress about the import duties. Nobody can expound that matter better than you can, and it is the unanimous opinion of the executive committee of the [Democratic] national committee . . . that it is indispensable that you should devote several days to speaking in the district."

Redfield was involved in drafting a shipping bill that helped establish the Merchant Marine. Redfield wrote, on 28 October 1915, to Secretary of the Navy Josephus Daniels, "I hand you [the] draft of [the] proposed shipping bill. The matter was left in my hands by Mr. McAdoo when he went west and the bill has been drawn in careful compliance with his Indianapolis address and following two sketches prepared by Mr. B. N. Baker." Redfield was most responsible as the first secretary in expanding the Bureau of Standards, writing that "on the whole American manufacturers failed to apply science to industry." He saw the department through the war, during which time he helped launch a campaign to recycle paper, the first such crusade of its kind, and reorganized the Bureau of Foreign and Domestic Commerce, which assisted the amazing growth of the American economy in the 1920s.

Tired of government service, Redfield shocked Wilson when he resigned on 31 October 1919, a year before the 1920 presidential election. He remained close to Wilson and his wife. Following Wilson's death on 3 February 1924, Redfield sent his private correspondence to Mrs. Wilson to be used in a collection of Wilson's letters. He authored three other books, including his memoirs, *With Congress and Cabinet, Dependent*

America, and *We and the World.* He was engaged in numerous banking enterprises and also was active in civil and philanthropic affairs. Redfield died in New York City on 13 June 1932, five days before his seventy-fourth birthday. He was buried in the Albany Rural Cemetery.

References: *Annual Report of the Secretary of Commerce 1913* (Washington: GPO, 1913), 7–8; Baker, Ray Stannard, *Woodrow Wilson: Life and Letters* (Garden City, NY: Doubleday, Doran; 3 vols., 1940), 3: 456; *From Lighthouses to Laser-beams: A History of the U.S. Department of Commerce* (Washington: Office of the Secretary, Department of Commerce, 1995), 11–13; Hendrick, Burton J., "A Commercial Traveler in the Cabinet: Secretary William C. Redfield, of the Department of Commerce," *World's Work* 26: 5 (September 1913), 564; Kline, Omer Urban, "William Cox Redfield, Secretary of Commerce for Woodrow Wilson, 1913–1919" (Master's thesis, Catholic University of America, 1955); Meneely, Alexander Howard, "Redfield, William Cox," in *DAB* 8: 442–443; Redfield to Daniels, 28 October 1915, Josephus Daniels Papers, Reel 28, Library of Congress; Redfield, William Cox, *With Congress and Cabinet* (New York: Doubleday, Page, 1924), 19–20.

JOSHUA WILLIS ALEXANDER
1852–1936

Joshua Alexander was selected as the second secretary of commerce, not by President Woodrow Wilson, but by his wife, Edith Bolling Galt Wilson. Born in Cincinnati, Ohio, on 22 January 1852, Alexander was the son of Thomas Wilson Alexander and Jane (née Robinson) Alexander. Joshua Alexander's father apparently died when he was young; in 1863, when he was 11, he and his mother moved to Canton, in Daviess County, Missouri. There, he attended public and private schools and graduated from Christian University (now Culver-Stockton College) in Canton, in 1872. Alexander moved to Gallatin, Missouri, the following year, where he studied the law in the offices of Judge Samuel Richardson. In 1875, Alexander was admitted to the Missouri state bar and opened a practice in Gallatin.

In 1876, Alexander was elected the public administrator for Daviess County, serving from 1877 until 1881. In 1882, he was elected to a seat in the Missouri House of Representatives, as a Democrat, where he served from 1883 until 1901. During this tenure, he served as the chairman of the Committee on Appropriations in 1886 and as Speaker in 1887. Alexander was the mayor of Gallatin in 1891 and 1892, and was a member of the Gallatin Board of Education for many years. In 1900, he was named as a judge on the Seventh Judicial Circuit of Missouri, where he served until 1907. He resigned this seat in 1906, when he was nominated by the Democrats for a seat in the U.S. House of Representatives; he was elected and served from 4 March 1907 until 15 December 1919. Alexander was a member, and later served as chairman, of the Committee on Merchant Marines and Fisheries. Following the sinking of the R.M.S. *Titanic* in April 1912, Alexander submitted a resolution calling for President Taft to send an American delegation to the International Conference on Safety of Life at Sea. After Woodrow Wilson became president, in 1913, he rewarded Alexander for his support for the conference by naming the Missouri congressman chairman of the American delegation to the conference, which met in London from 12 November 1913 to 20 January 1914.

Wilson historian Arthur Link wrote of Alexander's service as chairman of the House Committee on Merchant Marines and Fisheries: "By late October 1915, [Secretary of the Treasury William Gibbs] McAdoo had drafted a new shipping bill, which furnished the basis for administration discussions during the following weeks. Then, on January 31, 1916, Chairman Alexander of the Merchant Marine Committee introduced the administration's measure in the House. Carefully phrased to meet the objections of the Democratic Senators who had helped to defeat ship purchase bill a year before, the Alexander bill authorized the appointment of a United States Shipping Board, which might spend up to $50 million in the construction or purchase of merchant ships suitable for use as naval auxiliaries. The Board was empowered to operate shipping lines but might also lease or charter its vessels to private corporations. Finally, the agency was endowed with full power to regulate the rates and services of all vessels engaged in the interstate, coastwise, and foreign trade of the United States." The bill passed both houses of Congress, and Wilson signed it into law on 7 September 1916.

On 31 October 1919, Secretary of Commerce William Redfield resigned. Wilson, after suffering a stroke during a western train trip in support of the Senate ratification of the League of Nations treaty, apparently had no role in the selection of Redfield's successor. According to the *Seattle Post-Intelligencer* of 11 September 1919, President Wilson wanted Edward N. Hurley, former chairman of the U.S. Shipping Board, to succeed Redfield. Years later it was discovered that Wilson's wife, who in many respects was serving as a "shadow president," selected Alexander because of his loyalty. Wilson biographer August Heckscher supports this claim, writing of Wilson's first cabinet meeting on 14 April 1920, "Joshua W. Alexander had been picked more or less at random—after being interviewed by Mrs. Wilson—to replace Redfield at Commerce." Nominated on 4 December 1919, he was confirmed a week later as the second commerce secretary.

Because he took office at the beginning of an election year, Alexander's chances for getting anything done were remote from the start. In his sole annual report, delivered in October 1920, Alexander spent more time asking for funds to construct a permanent home for the department than on potential policy matters. He wrote, "I have the honor to submit herewith . . . the eighth annual report of the Secretary of Commerce. Having assumed office December 16, 1919, this report covers a portion of the administration of my predecessor. . . . One of the greatest

needs of the Department is a permanent home for the proper housing of its several bureaus and divisions. This matter has been repeatedly mentioned by my predecessor, who has covered the subject so thoroughly that I can only emphasize what has already been said. The Commerce building, a rented structure, houses the divisions of the Office of the Secretary, three of the Department's bureaus, and portions of two others. The building is inadequate to the growing needs of the Department, and it is obvious that, with the overcrowding and scattering of activities, results so highly desirable cannot be obtained. It is earnestly recommended that steps be taken at an early date looking to the erection of a building suitably adapted to the efficient administration of the Department." Alexander served throughout the remainder of the Wilson administration, leaving office on 4 March 1921.

Alexander returned to Gallatin, Missouri, and the practice of law. In May 1922, in his last political act, he served as a delegate to the state's constitutional convention. Alexander died in Gallatin on 27 February 1936, a month past his eighty-fourth birthday. He was buried in the Brown Cemetery in Gallatin.

References: "Alexander, Joshua Willis," in *The National Cyclopædia of American Biography* (New York: James T. White; 57 vols., suppls. A-J, 1897–1974), 27: 429–430; Heckscher, August, *Woodrow Wilson* (New York: Charles Scribner's Sons, 1991), 631; Link, Arthur S., *Woodrow Wilson and the Progressive Era, 1910–1917* (New York: Harper & Brothers, 1954), 191; *Reports of the Department of Commerce, 1920: Report of the Secretary of Commerce and Reports of Bureaus* (Washington, DC: GPO, 1921), 9; Sponaugle, Gail Ann Kohlenberg, "The Congressional Career of Joshua W. Alexander" (Master's thesis, Northeast Missouri State University, 1979).

HERBERT CLARK HOOVER
1874–1964

Herbert Hoover was called "the Secretary of Commerce and undersecretary of everything else." He served for seven and one-half years as the secretary of commerce—a record tenure in Commerce—under two different presidents; Hoover was elected president in 1928—the last cabinet member to be elected as the chief executive of the United States. Hoover, a Quaker, was born in West Branch, Iowa, on 10 August 1874, the son of Jesse Clark Hoover and Huldah (née Minthorn) Hoover. Jesse Hoover died in 1880 at age 34, and his wife, who supported the family by working as a seamstress, died from pneumonia three years later, leaving $2,000 for the education of her children. Hoover went to live with his paternal uncle Alan Hoover in West Branch. A year later, however, he was sent to live with his maternal relatives in Oregon, spending much of his time with his uncle Henry John Minthorn. In 1889, at age 17, he moved to Salem, Oregon, and went to work as an office boy and attended night school, where he learned math and Latin. In 1891, desiring an engineering degree, he went to California and entered Stanford University. At day he attended classes, and at night he worked odd jobs. Hoover received his bachelor of arts degree in geology in 1895 and started working as a mine laborer, then as an assistant mining engineer, and finally, in 1896, as an aide to the manager of mines at Landsburg, New Mexico.

In 1897, Hoover joined the British mining firm of Bewick, Moreing and Company, and was named to inspect and examine the firm's mines in western Australia. The head of the firm, Charles Moreing, was so impressed by Hoover's work that he offered him a chance to oversee the firm's mines in China with a rise in pay. He worked in the coal and iron mines of Manchuria, Mongolia, and the city of Tientsin. He was in the city when the Society of Righteous Harmonious Fists, or the Boxers, rebelled against foreign rule in China, the so-called Boxer Rebellion. He became a leader in the fight against the Boxers, and after the insurrection had been put down, several nations, including the Belgians and the Germans, asked Hoover to remain in China to oversee their mining interests. He became the general manager of several mining concerns. However, later that year, he was offered, and accepted, a position as Bewick Moreing's junior partner.

He moved to London, and became the firm's world traveler. He was a promoter and financier for the company, raising funds to finance mine takeovers. In 1907, Hoover left Bewick Moreing and started his own mine engineering business, opening offices in New York, London, San Francisco, and Moscow. He also consulted on various mining and metallurgical projects. He spent much of his time arranging for the concerns of the governments of England, France, and Germany for the Panama-Pacific International Exposition, to be held in San Francisco in 1915.

In 1914, World War I broke out, and Hoover found himself stranded in Europe, along with countless other Americans. Because he had such good relations with nations on both sides of the conflict, the U.S. ambassador to the Court of St. James, Walter Hines Page, asked Hoover to assist in getting Americans off the continent to safety; Hoover organized the American Committee for Repatriation of American Citizens from Europe. Using his personal funds, as well as the donations of other wealthy Americans, Hoover was able to assist some 120,000 Americans. While working on this project, Hoover saw the need to assist innocent European civilians who were affected by the war. Again, using his own money, he was able to purchase foodstuffs for the city of Brussels after the German Army occupied Belgium. Establishing a system that handed out food to refugees and other starving people, Hoover formed the American Commission for Relief of Belgium (CRB), which was able to lobby governments around the world to assist. The budget for the relief mission reached $25 million a month, and Hoover was able to employ 200 ships to bring food and other supplies to approximately 10 million civilians a day. Hoover worked tirelessly for the CRB, at no salary. When the war ended, an audit of the organization found that less than one-half of 1 percent of all the money raised went for administrative costs and other expenses, an amazing figure considering that the work was being done in the midst of a war. Ambassador Page wrote to President Woodrow Wilson that Hoover was a "simple, modest, energetic little man who began his career in California and will end it in Heaven, and he doesn't want anybody's thanks." Numerous governments offered him awards and commendations, but he did not accept any of them.

When the United States entered the war in 1917, Hoover was forced to leave Europe because his neutrality was now in question. President Wilson named him as U.S. Food Administrator, to oversee the American operation of distributing food nationally under the Food Control Bill, as well as try to end profiteering and control prices. He called for the conservation of food and instituted meatless Mondays and wheatless Wednesdays. The measures came to be known as "Hooverizing." Hoover formed the U.S. Grain Corporation, which, with a loan of $500 million, purchased excess American grain and sent it to Allied countries with food shortages from the war. He also established the Sugar Equalization Board, which, with a budget of $5 million, purchased Cuba's entire sugar crop to be sold to the American and allied governments at a low cost. In all, during his less than two-year tenure at the Food Administration, he purchased $9 billion in food and other materials and made the agency one of the most successful during the war.

When the war ended in November 1918, Wilson asked Hoover to return to Europe to confer with European governments to assist them in supplying food to areas devastated by the war. Hoover immediately formed the Supreme Economic Council and, with an appropriation of $100 million from Congress,

organized the American Relief Administration (ARA) to send needed food supplies into devastated areas; at the same time, the ARA helped to rebuild shipping fleets, railways, farms, and delivered trucks and trains to furnish the continent with supplies. In 1921, the Russian writer Maxim Gorky wrote to Hoover that Russia, which had closed its borders after the Communist revolution, was suffering from massive famine. Hoover, acting apolitical, said, "Twenty million people are starving, and whatever their politics they should be fed." He lobbied Congress for $20 million and, with an additional $8 million of medical supplies, delivered one million tons of food and medicine to Russia in just sixty days. Feeding stations were established; he employed a staff of over 120,000 Russian workers. In 1922 alone, 18 million starving people were fed, and more than 7 million were given life-saving inoculations and other drugs. Even after the ARA officially ended on 30 June 1919, Hoover remained in Europe, forming the ARA European Children's Fund as a private entity to continue his work in raising money and delivering "food packs" to needy children. It can be said with some certainty that Herbert Hoover saved more lives than any person in the twentieth century, through his generosity and kindness.

Hoover returned to California. Politically, he was a Democrat, and in 1916, he had supported the reelection of President Wilson. But in 1920 he remained neutral. After Senator Warren G. Harding of Ohio was elected, Harding considered him for a seat in the cabinet, most likely as secretary of the Interior. Republicans who disliked Hoover's politics resisted, but Harding, who liked Hoover, said that the conservative Republicans' candidate for a cabinet post, Andrew Mellon, would only be accepted if Hoover was. Thus, Mellon was named as secretary of the Treasury, and Hoover was appointed as secretary of commerce. *The Independent* wrote in a 12 March 1921 editorial, "Probably the most discussed appointment, and certainly the most popular, was that of Herbert Hoover as Secretary of Commerce. Mr. Hoover was reluctant to accept, in spite of his friendliness to the new administration, because of the duties he had already undertaken with respect to European relief. But President Harding pressed him hard and he finally agreed to assume office on two conditions: the first was that he be permitted to continue for a time his connection with relief work. 'I have no right,' he said, 'to ask the public to give money and then shed all responsibility of administering it at once.' The second condition was that the Department of Commerce be reorganized and made a much more vital factor in developing our foreign trade than it is at the present."

Nominated officially on 4 March 1921, Hoover was unanimously confirmed by the Senate, and he was sworn in as the third secretary of commerce. In taking over the department, Hoover later wrote, "Very little had been done by the Democratic administration [Wilson] in reconstruction from the war, and development had been suspended during that time. Even important reconversion matters had been neglected because of President Wilson's illness. Many of the problems required fundamental solutions which would take time. But we soon had to face an emergency in the shape of the postwar depression of 1921–22 and general economic demoralization with rising unemployment." Historian Joseph Brandes wrote, "Hoover's term as Secretary of Commerce began in the midst of the primary post-war depression, when agriculture and the export trade were particularly hard-hit. Even then, he did not hesitate to make his opposition to government stimulation of the economy by deficit financing in such forms as unemployment and relief payments. Hoover felt that an essential answer to the crisis, and one more consonant with American tradition, lay in assisting agriculture and industry to compete with foreign producers. In calling the Economic Conference of September 1921, Hoover asked for measures 'to promote business recovery, for the only real and lasting remedy for unemployment is employment. . . . It is not consonant with the spirit of institutions of the American people that a demand should be made upon the public

treasury for the solution of every difficulty.'" Hoover changed the way the Department of Commerce worked.

When he took over the office, he called in the leaders of over 100 different industries and outlined plans to standardize sizes for all types of items, from hardware and tools to building materials and automotive supplies, and he established a Division of Simplified Practices in the Bureau of Standards to oversee this plan. He expanded the Bureau of Foreign and Domestic Commerce to develop markets at home and abroad for American goods and, because of the growing use of air travel, he held a conference to develop a new code of regulations for that industry. Starting with the President's Conference on Unemployment, held in 1921, Hoover called 250 conferences on national industrial and commercial problems. Hoover demanded that industry pay workers well and give them good working conditions; at the same time, he frowned on unions and denounced collective bargaining agreements. He formed the Business Cycles Committee in 1923; chaired by banker and economist Owen D. Young; it reported that year that unemployment insurance and wage stabilization measures be instituted for the private, but not public, sector. He also held a series of conferences in 1922, 1923, 1924, and 1925 in an effort to oversee regulation of the blossoming radio industry.

Hoover remained at Commerce through the Harding administration and, following Harding's death in August 1923, the administration of Calvin Coolidge. In 1928, when Coolidge announced that he would not run for reelection, Hoover became the frontrunner for the Republican presidential nomination. When the party convened in national convention in Kansas City on 12 June 1928, Hoover was the only candidate the party wanted to nominate, and they did so unanimously on the first ballot. Hoover then chose Senator Charles Curtis of Kansas, a Native American, as his running mate. On 10 July 1928, after formally being nominated for president, Hoover resigned as commerce secretary. The *New York Times* explained in an editorial (22 August 1928), "President Coolidge has held on to Mr. Hoover as long as he could. It was obvious that the duties of the Secretary of Commerce and the pleasure of a candidate for President could not long be attended to by the same man. Mr. Hoover's resignation has been in the President's hands for some time."

The issues involved in the election were the continuance of the prosperity of the 1920s and Prohibition. Running against him were New York Governor Alfred E. Smith and Senator Joseph T. Robinson of Arkansas; Hoover campaigned infrequently, calling for "rugged individualism" and denouncing the Democratic platform as "state socialism." On election day, 6 November 1928, Hoover won a decisive victory: he took 444 electoral votes in 40 states, with Smith getting 87 electoral votes in 8 states. Further, the former commerce secretary won 21.4 million votes to Smith's 15 million. He became the last cabinet member to be sworn in as president of the United States.

Less than a year after Hoover took office, the Depression struck. Immediately, Hoover tried to make the crisis seem as just another economic problem that he could deal with, and he asked for moderate measures—a lowering of income taxes, asking businessmen to keep wages at their normal levels, and calling on private groups to give assistance to the needy. Unfortunately, these measures did little to help, and with a Democratic Congress refusing to assist him in any way, he was unable to change the direction of the economy. In his heart, Hoover believed the Depression was just a mild economic downturn that would soon end. Then a drought hit the farmers in the Midwest, and Hoover agreed to supply indirect aid to assist them. In 1932, when the Depression deepened, Hoover agreed to federal assistance and established the Reconstruction Finance Corporation, which loaned federal dollars to banks and businesses hard hit by the crisis. By that summer, when the Republican Party had no choice but to renominate him and Curtis, there were 12 million people unemployed in the nation, with another 18 million

on some sort of assistance. The Democrats chose New York Governor Franklin D. Roosevelt. Roosevelt promised the people "a New Deal," and with this pledge he won the election in a landslide. Hoover left the White House in March 1933, blamed for the Depression and the government's lack of assistance to end it.

Hoover returned to California and, he continued his previous work as a lecturer at Stanford University and a mine consultant. In 1939, when World War II broke out, he formed the Polish Relief Commission to send aid and food to starving children in Poland, an effort that was halted by the Germans in 1941. Hoover, however, continued to send aid to Western European nations, such as Holland and Belgium. He also spent his time at the Hoover Institution on War, Revolution, and Peace at Stanford, which was established 1919. He spent his postpresidential years collecting papers for the institute on issues ranging from war and peace to the rise of Communist, Nazi, and Fascist regimes in Europe.

Following the end of the war, President Harry S Truman called on Hoover to head the Famine Emergency Commission, which studied the patterns of famine and came up with a program to deal with the problem. After a year of work, he submitted his report to the president. In 1947, Congress asked Hoover to head up a commission to reorganize the Executive branch and make it more efficient. The Commission on the Organization of the Executive Branch of Government, more commonly called the Hoover Commission, worked from 1947 to 1949, and again from 1953 to 1955; many of the 280 recommendations from the two reports were accepted by Congress and implemented.

After serving government this final time, Hoover retired, writing articles and several books. On 20 October 1964, at the age of 90, Hoover died in New York City, having lived longer than any former president other than John Adams. His birthplace, in West Branch, Iowa, is a national historic site and is the location of the Hoover Presidential Library, where he was laid to rest next to his wife. The building housing the Department of

Commerce, located at Fourteenth and Constitution Avenues in Washington, D.C., is named the Herbert Clark Hoover Building in his honor.

References: Brandes, Joseph, *Herbert Hoover and Economic Diplomacy: Department of Commerce Policy, 1921–1928* (Pittsburgh: University of Pittsburgh Press, 1962), 11; Hoover, Herbert, *The Memoirs of Herbert Hoover: The Cabinet and the Presidency, 1920–1933* (New York: Macmillan, 1952), 41; Hoover, Herbert, *The Memoirs of Herbert Hoover: Years of Adventure, 1874–1920* (New York: Macmillan, 1951), 1–3; "Hoover, Herbert Clark," in John N. Ingham, *Biographical Dictionary of American Business Leaders* (Westport, CT: Greenwood, 5 vols., 1983), 2: 607–615; "Hoover, Herbert Clark," in *The National Cyclopædia of American Biography* (New York: James T. White; 57 vols., suppls. A-J, 1897–1974), C: 1–7.

WILLIAM FAIRFIELD WHITING

1864–1936

William Whiting served as the fourth secretary of commerce for less than a year, following Herbert Hoover's resignation; after Hoover was elected, he was replaced. Whiting was born in Holyoke, Massachusetts, on 20 July 1864, the son of William Whiting, a prosperous businessman and Massachusetts politician, and Anna Maria (née Fairfield) Whiting. Whiting attended local schools at Holyoke and the Williston Academy in Easthampton, Massachusetts and received his bachelor's degree from Amherst College in 1886. He then joined his father's paper company, working his way up until he took over as president in 1911. By the time he resigned to become secretary of commerce in 1928, Whiting had built the company into one of the largest paper firms in the United States.

A longtime Republican, Whiting was a delegate to the Republican National Conven-

tions in 1920, 1924, 1928, and 1932. In August 1928, when Secretary of Commerce Herbert Hoover resigned, President Calvin Coolidge, a former governor of Massachusetts, named Whiting as Hoover's successor. Many expected Julius Klein, chief of the Bureau of Domestic and Foreign Commerce in the Commerce Department and a close friend of Hoover's, to be named to the vacancy. Because Congress was in recess, Whiting's nomination was not made official until 6 December 1928, after Hoover had been elected. The Senate confirmed Whiting's nomination five days later, and he completed Coolidge's term as the fourth secretary of commerce. Little in the way of policy initiatives can be traced to him. What is known is that after Hoover's election, the president-elect chose to have his own man run Commerce, and he passed over Whiting for Robert P. Lamont. Little else is known of Whiting's life. He died in Holyoke, Massachusetts, on 31 August 1936 at the age of 72.

Reference: "Whiting, William Fairfield," in *The National Cyclopædia of American Biography* (New York: James T. White; 57 vols., suppls. A-J, 1897–1974), C: 380–381.

ROBERT PATTERSON LAMONT

1867–1948

Robert Lamont was a professional businessman when asked by President Herbert Hoover, in 1928, to serve as his secretary of commerce. His tenure was marked by the onset of the Great Depression, which forced him from office in 1932. Lamont was born in Detroit, Michigan, on 1 December 1867, the son of Robert Lamont, and Isabel (née Patterson) Lamont. Lamont attended local schools in Detroit, then entered the University of Michigan, from which he earned a bachelor of science degree in civil engineering in 1891. Two years later, he assisted in the engineering work to help build the World's Fair in Chicago. He then joined the contracting firm of Shailer & Schinglan as a secretary and engineer, working for that firm for four years. In 1897, he left to become the vice-president of the Simplex Railway Appliance Company, where he served until 1905.

Starting in 1905, Lamont went to work as the first vice-president of the American Steel Foundries of Chicago, and, in 1912, he became the company's president. Lamont served in this capacity until March 1929, when he resigned to enter the cabinet. During these years, Lamont helped build American Steel Foundries into one of the nation's largest steelworks. During World War I, Lamont served the U.S. government as chief of the Procurement Division of the Ordnance Department of the War Department, assisting in the purchase of ordnance. After the war, he was awarded the Distinguished Serve Medal. On 30 August 1928, Secretary of Commerce Herbert Hoover resigned after he was nominated for President by the Republicans and was replaced by William Whiting. Once elected president, Hoover chose Robert Lamont as his secretary of commerce. Lamont was nominated, officially, on 5 March 1929, and confirmed by the Senate that same day as the fifth secretary of commerce. His tenure lasted until 3 August 1932.

Unfortunately for Lamont and for Hoover, the nation's economy took a tumble in October 1929, and this economic crisis turned into the Great Depression. A history of the department noted, "Between 1929 and 1932, the national income declined monetarily by more than 50 percent, from $87.4 billion to $41.7 billion, and more than 40 percent in terms of goods and services. Exports fell 34 percent and imports 37 percent. U.S. foreign trade was at its lowest level point since the 1913 creation of the Department." No matter what the administration tried, the nation sank deeper and deeper into depression. Historian Martin Fausold summed up the efforts of Hoover and Lamont: "The administration's antidepression efforts made little news during the first half of 1930. . . . On the third day

of 1930 Secretary of Commerce Lamont had told the president that twenty-nine governors had planned, cumulatively, $1.3 billion worth of public-works construction, far more than during the previous year, and that public utilities, railroads, and the American Telephone and Telegraph Company planned, respectively, to spend on public employment $14 billion, $1 billion, and $700 million. The federal government itself expedited and increased its public works construction on federal highways, veterans' hospitals, federal buildings, waterway improvements, and military facilities by $19 million, although such expenditures were minuscule in comparison to the outlays made by state and local governments and industry." Lamont oversaw the laying of the cornerstone of the building that eventually became the main building of the Commerce Department, which was renamed after Herbert Hoover in 1982.

Faced with mounting pressure over his attempts to combat the Depression, and exhausted from his efforts, Lamont resigned on 3 August 1932. Lamont served as president of the American Iron and Steel Institute for a year after leaving the cabinet. He died at his daughter's home in New York City on 20 February 1948 at the age of 80.

References: Department of Commerce, Office of the Secretary, *From Lighthouses to Laserbeams: A History of U.S. Department of Commerce* (Washington, DC: GPO, 1995), 17; Fausold, Martin L., *The Presidency of Herbert C. Hoover* (Lawrence: University Press of Kansas, 1985), 97; Lamont, Robert Patterson," in *The National Cyclopædia of American Biography* (New York: James T. White; 57 vols., suppls. A-J, 1897–1974), C: 13–14.

ROY DIKEMAN CHAPIN
1880–1936

Roy Chapin was a successful car manufacturer who was selected by Herbert Hoover to serve as secretary of commerce in the waning days of his administration. He was born in Lansing, Michigan, on 23 February 1880, the son of Edward Cornelius Chapin and Ella Rose (née King) Chapin. Chapin attended the University of Michigan but left in 1901 without graduating, to take a position at the Olds Motor Works in Detroit. By 1904, Chapin became the company's general sales manager; Olds had become the world's largest manufacturer of automobiles. In 1906, Chapin left Olds and, with E. R. Thomas, Howard E. Coffin, Frederick O. Bezner, and James J. Brady, formed the E. R. Thomas–Detroit Company. Chapin served as treasurer and general manager of this company until 1908.

In 1908, Chapin sold his share of E. R. Thomas-Detroit and organized, with Howard Coffin and Hugh Chalmers, the Chalmers-Detroit Motor Company, which marketed the Chalmers-Detroit. A year later, however, Chapin and the group formed a partnership with Joseph L. Hudson and Roscoe B. Jackson to make the Hudson Motor Car Company, in February 1909, with Hudson as president, Chalmers as vice-president, and Chapin as secretary. In 1910, Chapin succeeded Hudson as president, and he held that position until 1923, when he became chairman of the Hudson board of directors. Chapin helped make Hudson one of the most successful cars in America. During World War I, Chapin served as chairman of the Highways Transport Committee of the Council of National Defense, which was established to develop a plan for a national highway system to be utilized in times of war. From 1927 to 1928, he served as president of the National Automobile Chamber of Commerce.

On 3 August 1932, Secretary of Commerce Robert P. Lamont resigned. President Herbert Hoover named Chapin to serve in the vacant cabinet post. Chapin was confirmed by the Senate in December 1932, but by that time Hoover had lost to Democrat Franklin D. Roosevelt, and Chapin's service only lasted until the end of the Hoover administration on 4 March 1933. A history of the Commerce Department states of his tenure that "he was instrumental in getting the automobile industry to provide data for the expansion of the Department of Commerce 'Survey of Current Business.' "

After leaving office, Chapin returned to Hudson, and served as president of the company from 1934 until his death. Chapin died suddenly on 16 February 1936, seven days before his fifty-sixth birthday.

Reference: "Chapin, Roy Dikeman," in *The National Cyclopædia of American Biography* (New York: James T. White; 57 vols., suppls. A-J, 1897–1974), C: 400.

DANIEL CALHOUN ROPER
1867–1943

Daniel Roper served as the first of Franklin D. Roosevelt's three secretaries of commerce, and he helped establish the Business Advisory Council to advise the administration on the perspectives and opinions of American business leaders. Roper was born in Marlboro County, South Carolina, on 1 April 1867, the son of John Wesley Roper, a farmer and merchant, and Henrietta Virginia (née McLaurin) Roper, Daniel C. Roper was born in Marlboro County, South Carolina, on 1 April 1867, Roper attended local schools and graduated from Trinity College (now Duke University), in 1888. He then taught school for four years before he was elected, as a Democrat, to the South Carolina House of Representatives, serving until 1894. He was a strong advocate of the prohibition of alcohol and, while in the state House, introduced a measure to prohibit the sale of distilled liquors. In 1893, during a break in the legislative term, Roper went to Washington, D.C., where he was hired as a clerk for the U.S. Senate Committee on Interstate Commerce, where he served until 1897. He then attended law classes at the National University and received his bachelor of laws degree in 1901.

In 1900, Roper went to work as an expert in census work at the U.S. Census Bureau.

He stayed until 1910, working as a authority on cotton farming, counting bales of cotton nationally and submitting reports to the government. In 1911, he took a position as the clerk of the U.S. House of Representatives Ways and Means Committee. Two years later, he left the post to serve in the administration of President Woodrow Wilson as first assistant postmaster general under Postmaster General Albert Burleson. During his tenure, which lasted until 1916, he was placed in charge of administering the parcel post service. In 1916, Wilson named Roper as chairman of his 1916 reelection campaign. In March 1917 Wilson named Roper as vice-chairman of the U.S. Tariff Commission. That September, however, he moved Roper over to become commissioner of the Internal Revenue, which had recently been established under the Sixteenth Amendment to collect income taxes from the American people. Considered a more than efficient administrator, Roper served in this office until 31 March 1920. After leaving office, Roper for the first time practiced the law, joining the Washington, D.C., firm of Roper, Hagerman, Hurrey & Parks as a partner. Remaining active in Democratic Party circles, he helped run former Secretary of the Treasury William Gibbs McAdoo's unsuccessful attempt to gain the 1924 Democratic presidential nomination.

In 1932, Roper became an early supporter of New York Governor Franklin D. Roosevelt for the Democratic presidential nomination. Following his election, Roosevelt asked Roper to serve in his administration in an attempt to get the McAdoo wing of the party to accept Roosevelt's economic program, called "the New Deal." Nominated along with the rest of Roosevelt's cabinet selections on 4 March 1933, Roper was confirmed the same day, and he took office as the seventh secretary of commerce. Saying that he believed the principal function of the department he now led was "to promote the legitimate interests of business large and small."

Roper set out to prove the department's value, even as it was coming under attack, particularly from congressional budget-cutters in a time of depression. Senator Sam G. Bratton of New Mexico proposed a joint Senate-House committee "to consider the advisability of abolishing the Department of Commerce and the transfer of its indispensable services to other agencies." Roper countered that the department was "important under normal conditions . . . [but] was at this time suffering from the fact that business was in the dog-house." Under Roper, the department oversaw the chief functions of the National Industrial Recovery Act, which regulated the marketplace for the first time in American history and established minimum price scales. In 1935, the U.S. Supreme Court struck down the act as unconstitutional; Roper, instead, established the Business Advisory Council, in order to have 'the attitudes of American business transmitted to the government so as to shape policymaking.

Roper was a close adviser to Roosevelt during the first years of the New Deal, but because he was not a close friend of the president's, he was not in the inner circle. By 1938, Roper was tired of his position and after Roosevelt ordered a reorganization of Commerce that Roper felt was not needed, he resigned, on 23 December 1938, after less than six years in office. Roosevelt named Roper as U.S. chief of mission to Canada, to succeed Norman Armour. Roper served in Ottawa only from 19 May 1939 until 20 August 1939, when, tired of this position, he resigned. He retired to Washington, D.C., where he lived less than four years. Roper died in Washington on 11 April 1943, ten days after his seventy-sixth birthday. He was buried in Rock Creek Cemetery in Washington, D.C.

References: Department of Commerce, Office of the Secretary, *From Lighthouses to Laserbeams: A History of U.S. Department of Commerce* (Washington, DC: GPO, 1995), 17–19; Roper, Daniel C., *Fifty Years of Public Life* (Durham, NC: Duke University Press, 1941); "Roper, Daniel Calhoun," *in The National Cyclopædia of American Biography* (New York: James T. White; 57 vols., suppls. A-J, 1897–1974), D: 18–19; "Roper, Daniel Calhoun," in Otis L. Graham, Jr., and Meghan Robinson Wander, eds., *Roosevelt: His Life and Times: An Encyclopedic View* (Boston: G. K. Hall, 1985), 376–377.

HARRY LLOYD HOPKINS
1890–1946

Harry Hopkins is remembered for his zest in service to President Franklin Delano Roosevelt, from 1933 until he died in 1946, literally working himself to death. Roosevelt told Wendell Willkie, his 1940 opponent for President, "As president . . . You'll learn what a lonely job this is, and you'll discover the need for somebody like Harry Hopkins who asks nothing except to serve you." An influential administrator, Hopkins served from 1938 to 1940 as secretary of commerce. Born in Sioux City, Iowa, on 17 August 1890, he was the son of David Aldona Hopkins, a harness shop owner, and Anna (née Pickett) Hopkins. Just after Hopkins was born, the family moved to Council Bluffs, Iowa, and then to Kearney and Hastings, Nebraska, before spending two years in Chicago. They finally settled down in Grinnell, Iowa, about 1901. Hopkins attended local schools in Grinnell and then entered Grinnell College, from which he graduated cum laude in 1912. At college he was a founder of a Woodrow Wilson Club for the 1912 election.

Hopkins then entered the field of social work, moving to New York City and joining the Association for Improving the Condition of the Poor (AICP), founded by Dr. John A. Kingsbury, as well as working for the American Red Cross, and the New York Tuberculosis Association. Jacob A. Goldberg, the secretary of the Tuberculosis Association, later called the chain-smoking and always nervous Hopkins "the ulcerous type." Goldberg said that Hopkins came to work "looking as though he had spent the previous night sleeping in a hayloft. He would wear the same shirt three or four days at a time. He managed to shave almost every day—usually at the office." In 1914, Kingsbury assisted in getting Hopkins named as executive secretary of the Board of Child Welfare by New York City mayor John P. Mitchel. During World War I, Hopkins did not serve because of a detached retina—instead, he served as head of the Gulf Division of the American Red Cross, headquartered in New Orleans, where he helped serve relief to soldiers' families. In 1920, he was made the head of the Department of Civilian Relief's Red Cross mission to assist Mexico.

In 1922, Kingsbury named Hopkins as chief of the AICP's division on health conditions. Two years later, he became executive director of the New York Tuberculosis Association, and he soon helped the group merge with the New York Heart Committee to become the New York Tuberculosis and Public Health Association. Hopkins assisted in numerous reform movements in the area of health, helping to combat tuberculosis, silicosis, and other diseases among the poor, and he helped form a special committee on social hygiene. During the Depression, these programs were inadequate; in response to the needs of the communities he oversaw, Hopkins established a Red Cross relief program that became the model of the nation. Governor Franklin D. Roosevelt of New York, impressed by the work, established a statewide program based on Hopkins's program, called the New York State Temporary Emergency Relief Administration, in 1931, which emphasized the use of government-backed work rather than welfare payments to the unemployed. Roosevelt named Hopkins the executive director, and then the program's chairman. Over one million New Yorkers were supplied with relief from 1931 to 1933.

In 1932, Roosevelt was elected president on a platform of using government programs to end the Depression nationally. On 22 May 1933, he named Hopkins as the director of the Federal Emergency Relief Agency (FERA), one of the New Deal "alphabet agencies." Modeled on the New York program, FERA handed out millions of dollars to the unemployed through grants to the states. When Roosevelt felt that the Public Works Administration (PWA), under the command of Secretary of the Interior Harold Ickes, was not moving fast enough to alleviate conditions, he took Hopkins's recommendation to expand the power of the Civil Works Authority (CWA) to provide work relief for unskilled and semiskilled people. By January 1934, more than 20 million people were getting work through the expanded CWA program; when its mandate ended in May 1934, it was folded into FERA rather than PWA. By 1938, Hopkins was in control of spending more than $8.5 billion in unemployment relief, assisting some 15 million people, covering his service as a member of the President's Drought Committee, the National Resources Planning Board, and the National Emergency Council, as well as heading up the Federal Surplus Relief Corporation. He was known as "the chief apostle of the New Deal." In 1938, one political observer wrote of him, "Quick, alert, shrewd, bold, and carrying it off with a bright Hell's bells air, Hopkins is in all respects the inevitable Roosevelt favorite."

Following the resignation of Secretary of Commerce Daniel C. Roper, Roosevelt named Hopkins to the vacancy, on 23 December 1938, more with an eye to having Hopkins replace him as president in 1940. Hopkins was interested in the presidency since 1935, and the selection seemed to bolster those chances. However, Hopkins was in ill health. In 1937, suffering from stomach ailments, he had half of his stomach removed when cancer was discovered. He was described as being "slim, wan, and frequently wracked by illness." Thus his year and a half as the eighth commerce secretary was marked by only a few weeks at work, with long absences caused by a stomach and digestive disorder that sapped his strength. On 24 August 1940, he resigned and was replaced by Jesse H. Jones. Roosevelt wrote to him, "In giving me this letter of resignation it is possible only for you to break the official ties that exist between us—not the ties of friendship that have endured so happily through the years. I am accepting your resignation, therefore, to take effect at a date to be determined later and, I repeat, that this resignation is accepted only in its official sense. In other words, you may resign this office—only the office—and nothing else. Our friendship will and must go on as always."

Hopkins continued to work for Roosevelt. Starting in July 1940, shortly before he left the cabinet, he served as Roosevelt's personal manager at the 1940 Democratic National Convention, when Roosevelt had to convince Democrats to support him for an unprecedented third term. In 1941, before the United States entered World War II, Hopkins made several visits to Europe to head off American involvement in the conflict in Europe, including a trip to England, in January 1941, to ascertain what supplies and materiel that nation might need if war did come. Reporters asked Roosevelt if Hopkins was to become the next U.S. ambassador to England, but the president responded that "Harry isn't strong enough for that job." Because of the recent resignation of Ambassador Joseph F. Kennedy, and the death of British ambassador to the United States, Lord Lothian, there were no high-level officials except Hopkins who could be sent on such a mission. Following the meeting with Prime Minister Winston Churchill and other British leaders, Lord Beaverbrook wrote that Hopkins's talks "left us feeling that although America was not yet in the war, she was marching beside us, and that should we stumble she would see that the President and the men about him blazed with faith in the future of Democracy." When Roosevelt delivered a fireside chat to the nation and said that the United States needed to be "the great arsenal of democracy" in supporting Britain against Germany, it was Hopkins who came up with the phrase. Hopkins became known as Roosevelt's "deputy president."

Hopkins was a loyal and trusting confidant and adviser, who was one of only a handful of people who had the nerve to disagree with Roosevelt to 'his face. In May 1940, the president allowed Hopkins to move into the White House's Lincoln study, where he remained until December 1943, when he moved to a home in Georgetown. In 1941, Roosevelt named him to head the Lend-Lease program of shipping war materials to the British, and later as a member of the War Production Board and the Pacific War Council.

Hopkins was a delegate to the Cairo, Tehran, Casablanca, and Yalta conferences with Roosevelt. Following Yalta, however, he returned to the United States near death. After a period of recuperation, he went on a trip for Harry Truman, who had become president on Roosevelt's death, to Moscow to meet with Soviet Premier Josef Stalin and arrange the Potsdam meeting in Germany between Truman, Stalin, and British Prime Minister Winston Churchill. Upon returning to the United States, Hopkins resigned his posts in the government, in July 1945. He returned to New York and took a job with the cloak and suit industry in New York, spending most of time planning a book on the war and Roosevelt that was never written. In September, Truman awarded him the Distinguished Service Medal. On 29 January 1946 Hopkins died at the age of 55.

References: Adams, Henry H., *Harry Hopkins* (New York: G. P. Putnam's Sons, 1977); Charles, Searle F., "Harry L. Hopkins," in Otis L. Graham, Jr., and Meghan Robinson Wander, eds., *Roosevelt: His Life and Times: An Encyclopedic View* (Boston: G. K. Hall, 1985), 183–186; Rollins, Alfred B., Jr., "Hopkins, Harry Lloyd," in *DAB* 4: 391–394.

JESSE HOLMAN JONES
1874–1956

Jesse Jones served as director of the Reconstruction Finance Corporation, a New Deal agency, from 1933 to 1939, and as secretary of commerce from 1940 to 1945. Born on his father's tobacco farm in Robertson County, Tennessee, on 5 April 1874, he was the son of William Hasque Jones, a tobacco farmer, and Anne (née Holman) Jones. Jones received his education in the small community schools of Robertson County. After completing his primary education, he worked on his father's farm, but when his father died, he gave his inheritance of $2,000 to his sisters and moved to Dallas, Texas, where he went to work as a clerk in his uncle's lumber business. Jones never received any additional schooling.

Jones became the general manager of his uncle's business in 1898. However, he wanted to own his own business, so, in 1902, he left and established the South Texas Lumber Company in Houston. The company soon expanded into real estate, banking, publishing, and building construction, making Jones a wealthy man. In politics, he was a Democrat and supported that party in Texas. His first stand on the national scene came when he backed the candidacy of New Jersey Governor Woodrow Wilson for president in 1912. Wilson rewarded Jones by naming him, in 1917, as director of general military relief in Europe during World War I, a position Jones held until 1918. During the 1920s, when the Democrats were out of power, Jones was the leading Democrat in the party in Texas. In an effort to attract Texans back to the party, he got the Democrats to hold their 1928 convention in Houston. Democrats lost that presidential election as well, but the victor, Republican Herbert Hoover, named Jones as director of the Reconstruction Finance Corporation (RFC). From 1929 until 1932, more than 5,000 banks failed, leaving millions of people destitute because the government did not back up their savings. The RFC was an agency established by Hoover to loan emergency funds to crippled banks during the Depression. Hoover had hoped that his naming of Jones would lead some southern conservative Democrats to side with Hoover over the Democratic presidential candidate, Franklin Delano Roosevelt, in the 1932 election, but Hoover lost the election.

Roosevelt continued Jones in office, and named him chairman of the RFC. Roosevelt saw Jones as a powerful and effective administrator and, later in 1933, named him as a member of the National Emergency Board, a New Deal agency. In 1936, he became chairman of the executive committee of the Export-Import Bank of Washington. Jones devoted these years to public service, overseeing large-scale government spending to help people survive the Depression. In 1934, the RFC moved from lending to banks to helping individual businesses. In essence, Jones was running the government's assistance programs, so much so that he was called, by some, "the fourth branch of government." In his years in the government, he lent some $50 billion. Senator Robert Taft of Ohio said that Jones "had more power than any other man in the history of this Government."

Jones had ambitions for high political office. As the 1940 election approached, it appeared that Roosevelt would stand aside for his vice-president, John Nance Garner of Texas, a former Speaker of the U.S. House, and Jones, a close friend of Garner's, hoped to be named as the Democrats' vice-presidential candidate. But Roosevelt broke historical precedent and sought a third term; Garner quit the ticket in anger, and Roosevelt ran with Secretary of Agriculture Henry Wallace. Still Jones remained committed to Roosevelt. In 1939, Jones was named as administrator of the Federal Loan Agency, which was the oversight board for the RFC and the Export-Import Bank, and he became one of the most powerful men in Washington.

On 24 August 1940, Secretary of Commerce Harry L. Hopkins resigned. On that same day, Roosevelt offered the position to Jones, who accepted. Officially nominated on 13 September 1940 and confirmed by the Senate the following day, Jones took office as the ninth secretary of commerce. His tenure lasted until 1 March 1945. A history of the Commerce Department states, "Pearl Harbor brought the full forces of the Department into the World War II effort. Uniform standards to ensure absolute interchangeability of parts for airplanes, tanks and guns came from the Bureau of Standards working with the Bureau of Domestic and Foreign Commerce to increase war production. Pilot training programs by the Civil Aeronautics Administration were greatly expanded to provide Army and Navy flying cadet recruits. Commerce oversaw the National Inventors Council to expedite the screening of inven-

tions and suggestions with national defense potential. From the scientists at the Bureau of Standards came the proximity fuze and an early version of the guided missile. Commerce became an essential source of maps, meteorological projections and other data."

Even though he was serving as secretary, Jones continued, through a special congressional exemption, to run the RFC. However, he soon became a bitter enemy of Vice-president Wallace, who was also the head of the Board of Economic Warfare, which purchased arms abroad for the U.S. military with funds lent by the RFC. Wallace publicly accused Jones of not lending enough money fast enough for arms purchases and putting the nation into danger militarily. Jones denied the accusation, saying that "squandering the people's money even in wartime is no proof of patriotism." Roosevelt initially ended the feud by abolishing the Board of Economic Warfare and diminishing some of the power of the RFC to purchase arms abroad. But the Jones-Wallace hostility continued, and, after Roosevelt won a fourth term in 1944, rumors began to fly that Jones, ill with pneumonia, would be replaced. On 1 March 1945, Roosevelt asked for and received his resignation, replacing him with Wallace. Jones told reporters that the former vice-president was "inexperienced in business and finance." Jones at first remained in Washington, but he left when Wallace accused him of continuing to run the RFC "from his hotel room."

Jones returned to Houston, where, for the remainder of his life, he served as the publisher of the *Houston Chronicle*. He had made Houston a major American city. In 1951, he published *Fifty Billion Dollars,* his account of his service as head of the RFC. Jones died at his home outside Houston on 1 June 1956 at the age of 82. He was buried in the Forest Park Cemetery in Houston.

References: Block, Maxine, ed., *Current Biography: Who's News and Why, 1940* (New York: H. W. Wilson, 1940), 440–442; Department of Commerce, Office of the Secretary, *From Light-*

houses to Laserbeams: A History of U.S. Department of Commerce (Washington, DC: GPO, 1995), 19–21; "Jones, Jesse Holman," in John N. Ingham, *Biographical Dictionary of American Business Leaders* (Westport, CT: Greenwood; 5 vols., 1983), 2: 680–682; Kimball, Warren F., "Jones, Jesse Holman," *DAB* 6: 324–326; Timmons, Bascom N., *Jesse H. Jones: The Man and the Statesman* (New York: Henry Holt, 1956).

HENRY AGARD WALLACE
1888–1965

See Secretary of Agriculture,
1933–1940

WILLIAM AVERELL HARRIMAN
1891–1986

A verell Harriman served as U.S. ambassador to Great Britain, secretary of commerce, and governor of New York; his public career lasted more than half a century. Born in New York City on 15 November 1891, he was the son of Edward Henry Harriman, a noted financier and one of the most powerful railroad owners in the United States, and Mary (née Averell) Harriman. Harriman attended Groton School in Massachusetts and graduated from Yale University with a bachelor of arts degree in 1913. He began his employment with the Union Pacific Railroad (which his father had bought in 1898) in 1915, working as a clerk in the railroad's offices in Omaha, Nebraska. In late 1913, he was named as director of purchases and, in 1915, was promoted to vice-president of purchases and supplies for the entire company. In 1917, he formed the Merchant Shipbuilding Corporation, which eventually controlled the largest merchant shipping fleet ever to fly under the American flag. In 1920, he formed W. A. Harriman and Company, an investment banking concern in New York, and he soon turned it into one of the largest banking firms in the world. In 1931, it merged with Brown Brothers to become Brown Brothers Harriman.

Harriman served as chairman of the Union Pacific from 1932 to 1946. He then entered the world of politics; as a Democrat, he formed a close relationship with New York Governor Franklin D. Roosevelt, and when Roosevelt was elected president in 1932, Harriman was brought into his administration as a member of the National Recovery Administration (NRA). In 1934, following the resignation of Hugh S. Johnson, Harriman was named as administrative officer of the NRA. In June 1940, Harriman served as a member of the National Defense Advisory Commission (NDAC), which coordinated the build up of American defense materials in the event of American participation in World War II. Harriman also served in NDAC's successor agency, the Office of Production Management. In March 1941, Roosevelt named Harriman as the U.S. minister to London to expedite aid to Britain under the Lend-Lease Act.

Harriman was a key participant at the summit between Roosevelt and British Prime Minister Winston Churchill, in 1941, where the Atlantic Charter was signed. In September 1941, Roosevelt sent Harriman to Moscow, with the special rank of ambassador, to assist the Soviet Union with war aid in its fight against Nazi Germany. Two years later, on 1 October 1943, Roosevelt named Harriman as the U.S. ambassador to the Soviet Union to succeed William H. Standley. During his time there, he worked closely to aid the Soviet government and was a participant at the Tehran and Yalta conferences attended by Roosevelt, Churchill, and Soviet leader Joseph Stalin.

After the war, Harriman was one of the earliest voices warning that the Soviets were a threat to the free world and that they would use Communist treachery to bore into nations and destabilize them. He warned Roosevelt of probable Soviet intentions, but Roosevelt died just days after he received the message. Harry S Truman, who succeeded Roosevelt as president, was impressed by Harriman's analysis of the situation and was briefed by the ambassador days before Truman met with Soviet Foreign Minister Vyacheslav Molotov and, based on Harriman's advice, took a hard stand with the Soviet diplomat. Harriman also convinced Truman to end Lend-Lease aid to the Soviets with the end of the war. He asked to be relieved of his post, and in March 1946, Truman named Harriman as U.S. ambassador to Great Britain. He was there only seven months. Harriman biographer Rudy Abramson wrote, "[Harriman] was called home, Truman needing him to help to quell an eight-day uproar that made headlines in Europe as well as across the United States. [Secretary of Commerce] Henry Wallace, whose sympathetic view of the Soviet Union had been tolerated although it was egregiously out of step with the view of the rest of the administration, had finally made the mistake of venting it at the very moment the United States was stiffening its posture toward Moscow, announcing to his Madison Square Garden audience that his remarks had the endorsement of the President. . . . Angry and embarrassed, [Secretary of State James] Byrnes demanded that Truman either accept Wallace's resignation or put an end to the free-lance family criticism. Truman at first tried to explain it all away, but he couldn't because the truth was that he had scanned Wallace's text and offered no objection. So, to quell the political storm, he asked for Wallace's resignation and turned to Harriman to take over the Commerce Department."

Historian Jason Berger explained Harriman's two years at Commerce, "While at the Commerce Department foreign affairs continued to take up most of his time. Following Secretary of State George C. Marshall's call for a massive recovery program in Europe in June 1947, Truman appointed Harriman as chairman of the President's Committee on Foreign Aid to translate Marshall's proposal into a program and lobby for its passage in Congress. The Committee report on 'European Recovery and American Aid,' released

in November, claimed that if Congress refused to provide aid, all of Europe, the Middle East and North Africa would fall to the Communists. The panel stressed the importance of Germany in the success of the aid program and recommended special emphasis be put on assistance to that nation to redevelop its purchasing and producing power and prevent it from falling into the hands of the Soviet Union." On 21 April 1948, Harriman resigned from Commerce and was named by Truman as the special representative in Europe for the European Cooperation Administration, which doled out Marshall Aid assistance. Harriman also worked to unify Western European nations against the Communist threat. He also served as the U.S. ambassador extraordinary and plenipotentiary.

In 1950, Truman recalled Harriman home a second time, this time to serve as a special assistant to the president. He assisted Truman in dealing with domestic difficulties during the president's last two years in office. He played a key role in helping Truman send troops to South Korea to defend that Asian nation against an invasion by North Korea. From 1951 to 1953, Harriman served as the director of the Mutual Security Agency, which distributed foreign aid.

After the end of the Truman administration, Harriman returned to New York, where he resumed a life in politics. In 1952, he had run, unsuccessfully, for the Democratic presidential nomination, and, in 1956, he ran a second unsuccessful, race for that position. However, in 1954, the Democrats nominated him for governor of New York, and, in November of that year, he was elected over Republican Irving Ives by about 11,000 votes out of some 5 million cast. Historians Robert Sobel and John Raimo write, "During his administration, a Two Track Racing Bill was passed; bingo was legalized; and the state's Jobless Pay Plan was ruled legal by the courts." In November 1958, running for a second four-year term, Harriman was defeated by Republican Nelson A. Rockefeller.

In 1961, President John F. Kennedy named him as U.S. ambassador-at-large, as well as assistant secretary of state for Far Eastern affairs, serving Kennedy and President Lyndon B. Johnson. Harriman helped negotiate the Nuclear Test Ban Treaty of 1963. In 1968, Johnson utilized his talents by naming him head of the U.S. delegation to peace talks in Paris with the Viet Cong, the South Vietnamese Communists. In 1978, President Jimmy Carter named him as the senior member of the U.S. delegation to the United Nations General Assembly's Special Session on Disarmament. The elder statesman of his party, he continued to visit the Soviet Union, his last trip there occurring in 1982, at age 91.

Averell Harriman died at his home in Yorktown Heights, New York, on 26 July 1986, at the age of 94. The Harriman Institute at Columbia University in New York City was named in his honor in 1982.

References: Abramson, Rudy, *Spanning the Century: The Life of W. Averell Harriman, 1891–1986* (New York: William Morrow,1992), 409–410; Berger, Jason, "Harriman, W(illiam) Averell," in Eleanora W. Schoenebaum, ed., *Political Profiles: The Truman Years* (New York: Facts on File, 1978), 213; "Harriman, W(illiam) Averell," in Anne Rothe, ed., *Current Biography 1948* (New York: H. W. Wilson, 1948), 243–244; "Harriman, William Averill," in Robert Sobel and John Raimo, eds., *Biographical Directory of the Governors of the United States, 1789–1978* (Westport, CT: Meckler Books, 4 vols., 1978), 3: 1104–1105; Twing, Stephen W., *Myths, Models and U.S. Foreign Policy: The Cultural Shaping of Three Cold Warriors* (Boulder, CO: Lynne Reiner, 1998), 93–144.

CHARLES SAWYER
1887–1979

Charles Sawyer's name is connected with one of the most important cases decided by the Supreme Court this century. He served for five years as Harry S Truman's second secretary of commerce. A respected politician who served his party as lieutenant governor of Ohio, he also served as ambassador to Belgium and ambassador to Luxembourg. Born in Cincinnati, Ohio, on 10 February 1887, he was the son of Edward Milton

Sawyer and Caroline (née Butler) Sawyer, both teachers. Charles Sawyer attended local schools in Cincinnati, then entered Oberlin College in Ohio, which awarded him a bachelor's degree in 1908, after just three years of work. He then entered the Law School of the University of Cincinnati and, in 1911, received his bachelor of laws degree. That same year he was admitted to the Ohio bar.

Sawyer did not immediately practice the law. Instead, he entered politics, as a Democrat, and, in 1911, was elected to a seat on the Cincinnati City Council, serving until 1915. In April 1917, after the United States entered World War I, Sawyer volunteered for service in the U.S. Army; assigned to the American Expeditionary Force, he spent eight months serving in the European theater and was promoted to captain of infantry and, just prior to his discharge in 1919, promoted again to major of infantry. When he returned to the United States, he opened a law practice in Cincinnati, but, within two years, he had joined the law firm of Dinsmore, Shohl, Sawyer, and Dinsmore as a senior partner. In 1932, he left the firm to run, as a Democrat, for governor of Ohio. Sawyer served until 1934, when he left office and joined the Democratic National Committee, remaining with the party in this capacity until 1944.

That year, President Franklin Roosevelt named him one of five ambassadors to the Western European nations that had been liberated from the Nazis. Sawyer was named as the ambassador to Belgium and minister to Luxembourg. In his year in these posts, he earned the respect of his hosts, assisting with postwar difficulties by helping with a request for some $200 million in U.S. aid, as well as trying to secure art treasures stolen by the Germans during the war. When he resigned on 20 November 1945, he did so claiming that the "first phase" of Belgian relief had ended and the immediacy of his mission as well. When he returned to Ohio, there were rumors that he intended to run for the U.S. Senate, but instead he went to Washington, D.C., to advise President Truman on postwar matters such as Marshall aid relief and the containment of communism.

On 21 April 1948, Secretary of Commerce W. Averill Harriman resigned. At the same time, Truman named Sawyer to replace Harriman. Nominated, officially, on 22 April, he was confirmed by the Senate on 5 May and sworn in as the twelfth secretary of commerce. Sawyer is most remembered for the steel strike episode that led to a showdown between the executive and judicial branches of the federal government. Historian William Wagnon wrote, "As a cabinet member, Sawyer attempted to reverse antibusiness attitudes within the administration. He emphasized cooperation between business and government and reinvigorated the Business Council as a network for channeling business ideas into the Fair Deal [the name for Truman's national economic policy]. During the 1949 recession, Sawyer undertook a nationwide tour, soliciting suggestions from businessman about federal economic policy."

Sawyer's annual reports reflect this increasing anxiety toward the burgeoning postwar economic lag. In his first report, released on 3 December 1948, Sawyer explained, "The fiscal year 1948 was a period of continuing inflation at home and of renewed and expanding responsibilities abroad. The impact of these developments on the Government was felt with particular force in the Department of Commerce, which was a major participant both in the formation of policies and in the execution of programs. . . . Owing to the sustained demand for goods and services by both consumers and business, production and employment were maintained at peak peacetime levels throughout the period. On the industrial front, production inched up about 3 percent during the course of the fiscal year, while employment increased by 1 percent. Unemployment meantime continued to approximate 2 million as new additions to the labor force promptly found employment. Plainly, the industrial economy was operating at a ceiling that could be raised only gradually. As a result, most any excess demand was necessarily translated into higher prices rather than greater output."

His concern grew, as expressed in his 1949 report: "The marked downturn of industrial production was a major feature of the first general decline to be experienced since the end of hostilities in 1945. During 1945–46 there had been a sharp contraction of production, as reconversion to the economy from war to peace was begun. Both business and consumer expenditures expanded steeply, however, reflecting the backlogs of investment and consumption needs backed up by unprecedented amounts of corporate reserves and liquid personal savings. The decline in output which had resulted from the slashing of Government expenditures to about one-third of their wartime peace was thus moderated very significantly in its impact on total economic activity, and unemployment was prevented from rising to serious levels." Sawyer's three subsequent reports reflect his concern at the growing economic crisis that would ultimately cost the Democrats the White House in 1952.

In 1952, however, Sawyer's mind turned to matters of strikes. In April 1952, the steelworkers in the United States threatened to strike nationwide. To avert this potential crisis, which he believed threatened the national security, Truman issued an executive order, based on Sawyer's advice and counsel, that directed Sawyer to seize the steel mills and direct their owners to run them as if they were officers of the U.S. government. As it was later stated, Truman was not acting on either presidential, legislative, or statutory authority—instead, he believed that as commander-in-chief, he had the sole power to act based on his powers enumerated under the Constitution. Truman asked Congress for congressional authority to act, but Congress, finding the action to be beyond the president's powers, did not act. Instead, the steel mill owners sued Sawyer and asked for relief from Truman's order. A federal appeals court stayed the order, and the mill owners appealed to the U.S. Supreme Court.

The Court heard arguments and issued their judgment that same year. In *Youngstown Sheet & Tube Company v. Sawyer* (1952), the Court held unanimously that Truman's order was unconstitutional. Justice Hugo Black, writing for the Court, stated, "The Executive Order was not authorized by the Constitution or laws of the United States, and it cannot stand. . . . Even if it be true that other Presidents have taken possession of private business enterprises without congressional authority in order to settle labor disputes, Congress has not thereby lost its exclusive constitutional authority to make the laws necessary and proper to carry out all powers vested by the Constitution "in the Government of the United States, or any Department or Officer thereof."

After leaving office, Sawyer returned to Cincinnati, where he joined the law firm of Taft, Stettinius, and Hollister as a partner. He also belonged to a number of civic, business, legal, and philanthropic concerns. He served on a number of boards of directors of corporations, including the Cincinnati Reds baseball team. Sawyer was in Palm Beach, Florida, when he died on 7 April 1979 at the age of 92. He was the author of *Concerns of a Conservative Democrat*.

References: Marcus, Maeva, *Truman and the Steel Seizure Case: The Limits of Presidential Power* (New York: Columbia University Press, 1977); "Sawyer, Charles," in Anne Rothe, ed., *Current Biography 1948* (New York: H. W. Wilson, 1948), 549–551; *The Steel Seizure Case: Briefs for the Government and the Companies and the Record Filed in the Supreme Court of the United States in the Steel Seizure Case* (Washington, DC: GPO, 1952); *Thirty-seventh Annual Report of the Secretary of Commerce, 1949* (Washington, DC: GPO, 1949), 1–2; *Thirty-sixth Annual Report of the Secretary of Commerce, 1948* (Washington, DC: GPO, 1948), 6; Wagnon, William O., Jr., "Sawyer, Charles," in Richard S. Kirkendall, ed., *The Harry S Truman Encyclopedia* (Boston: G. K. Hall, 1989), 320.

CHARLES SINCLAIR WEEKS
1893–1972

Sinclair Weeks became only the third man (after James Donald Cameron and William Howard Taft) to have served with his father in a cabinet position. A longtime Massachusetts politician, he headed the state's Republican Party and served for a short time in the U.S. Senate. The son of John Wingate Weeks, secretary of war under Presidents Warren G. Harding and Calvin Coolidge, and Martha (née Sinclair) Weeks, Charles Sinclair Weeks was born in West Newton, in Middlesex County, Massachusetts, on 15 June 1893. He went to public schools in Middlesex County, then attended Harvard University. After graduating in 1914, he entered the banking business in Boston. Two years later, in 1916, he joined the Massachusetts National Guard and, initially, was sent to the Mexican border, where he served with General John J. "Black Jack" Pershing to subdue the Mexican revolutionary Pancho Villa. Weeks then joined the U.S. Army and, as a lieutenant with the 101st Field Artillery of the 26th Division, he fought in Europe during World War I. When he was discharged in 1919, he held the rank of captain.

After returning to the United States, Weeks continued in the banking business, even after his father, a former U.S. senator, joined the cabinet of President Warren G. Harding as secretary of war. Sinclair Weeks changed businesses in 1923, moving from banking to the manufacturer of metals at a silver works, which he continued until he was named to a cabinet position in 1953. He served as an alderman for the town of Newton from 1923 to 1930 and, from 1930 to 1935, as its mayor.

Weeks served as a member of the Republican National Committee from 1941 until 1953, during that time acting as treasurer of the party from 1941 to 1944. In 1936, he had run for a seat in the U.S. Senate, but lost the Republican nomination to Henry Cabot Lodge, Jr. On 3 February 1944, Senator Lodge resigned his seat to volunteer for active duty in World War II; five days later, Massachusetts Governor Leverett Saltonstall appointed Weeks to fill the remaining year in Lodge's term. Weeks served from 8 February 1944 until 19 December 1944, when Governor Saltonstall, who had been elected to the seat, took over.

In 1952, Weeks became the head of General Dwight D. Eisenhower's drive for votes in the Republican primaries. Later, at the 1952 Republican National Convention in Chicago, Weeks led the effort to gain delegates for Eisenhower. Weeks himself even asked the leading candidate for the presidential nomination, Senator Robert Taft of Ohio, to step aside in the name of party unity, but Taft refused. After Eisenhower received the presidential nomination and was elected, Eisenhower asked Weeks to serve as the chairman of the Republican National Committee. Instead, Weeks asked for the Commerce portfolio as a place to use his business ideals. Historians Chester Pach and Elmo Richardson wrote, "Sinclair Weeks, the former finance chair of the Republican National Committee, held economic views that were even more conservative than [Secretary of the Treasury-designate George M.] Humphrey's. Although Eisenhower did not think of him as an advocate for special interests, Weeks perpetuated the Commerce Department's traditional role as [the] defender of the nation's business."

After Eisenhower's election, the president-elect named Weeks to a panel to investigate dropping the wage and price controls instituted by the outgoing Truman administration. As head of the group, Weeks advised Eisenhower to drop all such controls after he took office. In February 1953, a month after taking office, Eisenhower followed Weeks's advice and ordered all wage and price controls dropped. After he was sworn in as the thirteenth secretary of commerce, Weeks clashed with Secretary of Labor Martin Durkin. Durkin, a union man, wanted to undo certain provisions of the Taft-Hartley Act, which organized labor opposed. Neither Durkin nor Weeks, the latter resisting any changes to the law, was able to get a presidential promise for change or for the status quo. Instead, two presidential advisers drew up a nineteen-point memo that gave Durkin many concessions, and Durkin was able to convince Eisenhower to send a message to Congress asking for repeal of these measures, including one that forced union leaders to sign anticommunist oaths. However, on the day that the message was to be sent to Congress, 31 July 1953, Senator Taft, the coauthor of the legislation, died, and Eisenhower postponed it. Weeks, joined by Vice-president Richard Nixon, then lobbied Eisenhower to kill the message, which he finally agreed to do. On 9 September, Eisenhower informed Durkin that the changes would not be asked for, and Durkin, feeling betrayed, resigned.

Weeks's tenure as commerce secretary, which lasted until 22 October 1958, was marked by the renegotiation of the General Agreement on Tariffs and Trade (GATT), the worldwide agreement that oversaw world trade, and the establishment of the Office of International Trade Fairs in 1955. He remained a strong and conservative business voice inside the Eisenhower administration until his retirement.

Weeks left office and returned to the private business world. He was elected director of the First National Bank of Boston. In 1964, he joined the investment firm of Hornblower & Weeks, Hemphill, Noyes, as a partial partner. He remained active right up until his death, although he retired from business in 1970. Weeks died in Concord, New Hampshire, on 7 February 1972 at the age of 78. He was buried in the Summer Street Cemetery in Lancaster.

See also John Wingate Weeks

References: Davis, Glenn B., "Weeks, Sinclair," in Eleanora W. Schoenebaum, ed., *Political Profiles: The Eisenhower Years* (New York: Facts on File, 1980), 636–637; Pach, Chester J., Jr., and Elmo Richardson, *The Presidency of Dwight D. Eisenhower* (Lawrence: University Press of Kansas, 1991), 36.

LEWIS LICHTENSTEIN STRAUSS

1896–1974

Lewis Strauss was the first cabinet nominee refused confirmation by the U.S. Senate in over a quarter of a century, and only one of nine in the history of the U.S. government. Strauss was a longtime government official, who served as an aide to Herbert Hoover during the latter's mission to help relieve hunger in Europe after World War I, as well as head of the Atomic Energy Commission; Strauss served for just eight months as secretary of commerce before his rejection. He was born in Charleston, West Virginia, on 31 January 1896, the son of Lewis S. Strauss, the president of a wholesale shoe company, and Rosa (née Lichtenstein) Strauss. The family moved to Richmond, Virginia, where Lewis attended public school. He was the valedictorian in his class in high school and would have attended the University of Virginia after graduation, but he was stricken with typhoid fever and did not graduate with the rest of his class. Instead, after he recovered, he found his father's shoe business in dire shape from the 1913 recession, so he joined the company as a salesman and never attended college.

Strauss became the leading salesman for his father's company. By 1917, he had saved enough money to go to college. That same year, however, he read of Herbert Hoover, the engineer who was trying to save the lives of Belgian refugees starving in Europe because of the war. Strauss wrote to Hoover to volunteer his services, without pay, as an assistant. Hoover accepted Strauss's assistance and, after a few months, found Strauss to be an excellent coordinator. (In later years, Strauss assisted Hoover when Hoover served as secretary of commerce, as well as in his presidential campaigns in 1928 and 1932.) Hoover asked Strauss to help coordinate food programs in Europe with the Jewish Joint Distribution Committee (JJDC), which sent food packages to Jews in European nations affected by war.

The head of the JJDC, Felix Warburg, also saw Strauss's potential. Warburg, who was also a partner in the international banking firm of Kuhn, Loeb, and Company, recruited Strauss away from Hoover and food assistance and made him a member of the firm. In March 1919, Strauss served as one of four American delegates at a conference in Brussels to speak with German representatives about an armistice to end the war. He then returned to the United States and joined Kuhn, Loeb. In 1928, Strauss was named as a full partner in the firm. Ever interested in physics, the field he intended to study in college, he became friends with numerous eminent physicists, including Robert Millikan and Niels Bohr. He made suggestions to the men; one of the ideas involved using radioactive isotopes in medicine, and Millikan conducted studies based on these suggestions. In January 1926, Strauss accepted a commission in the U.S. Naval Reserve as an intelligence officer, with the rank of lieutenant commander. He held this rank until called into active duty to serve in the Navy's Bureau of Ordnance in February 1941, serving as assistance to the chief of the office, a post he held until December 1943. Here, he assisted in improving the Navy's system for purchasing war materials and in development programs. Strauss also served in the Army-Navy Munitions Board and the Naval Reserve Policy Board. Most reserve officers did not have a future in the postwar Navy, and Strauss, a Jew, had even less of a chance. However, 'in May 1944, Secretary of the Navy James Forrestal named Strauss as his special assistant. Strauss's work on the two boards earned him several citations, including the Oak Leaf Cluster from the army. In July 1945, he was promoted to commodore, and, in November of that same year, President Harry S Truman personally promoted him to rear admiral—a rare distinction for a naval reservist. A few months later, in July 1946, Truman named Strauss to the Atomic Energy Commission.

The United States had initiated the atomic age with its development and use of the atomic bomb, and a governmental body was needed to oversee U.S. atomic work; the Atomic Energy Commission (AEC) was established by the McMahon Atomic Energy Act of 1946. The commission was initially headed by David Lilienthal, the former head of the Tennessee Valley Authority, and included Strauss, Professor Robert F. Bacher, former Securities and Exchange Commissioner Sumner Pike, and W. W. Waymack, a newspaper editor and writer on peace issues. Strauss soon disagreed with the four others on the commission regarding numerous issues, including atomic laboratory and base security and the construction of the hydrogen bomb, in which Strauss was joined by physicist Edward Teller's report on the hydrogen bomb, its need and uses, and potential Russian construction of the bomb, led President Truman to order an American hydrogen bomb on 31 January 1950. That same day, Strauss resigned, having accomplished the main goal of his service on the AEC. However, he continued to advise Truman on atomic issues.

He took a position as a financial adviser to the Rockefeller brothers, but he desired to return to public life. In May 1953, President Dwight D. Eisenhower named Strauss as chairman of the AEC. It was here, during this second tenure on the commission that Strauss became involved in politics. During his research into the feasibility of a hydrogen bomb, he was opposed by the commission's General Advisory Committee, headed by J. Robert Oppenheimer, who had been part of the Manhattan Project, which constructed the atomic bomb. Oppenheimer argued, unsuccessfully, that the construction of a hydrogen bomb would set off an unlimited arms race between the United States and the Soviet Union. In late 1953, Oppenheimer's security clearance was taken away because of his prewar association with left-wing groups. A loyalty board found Oppenheimer to be without fault, but hearings before the AEC, led by Strauss, led to a commission vote of 4 to 1 to uphold the denial of the security

clearance. Strauss was also against a test ban treaty, which earned him enmity from numerous peace groups.

In 1958, with Secretary of State John Foster Dulles ill, Eisenhower asked Strauss to succeed him. However, Strauss felt that the undersecretary of state, Christian Herter, a good friend of Strauss's, should have the position. In October 1958, Secretary of Commerce Sinclair Weeks advised President Eisenhower that he wanted to resign. On 24 October, Eisenhower named Strauss as Weeks's successor. The appointment was a recess one, coming just prior to the 1958 elections. Nonetheless, Strauss was sworn in as the fourteenth secretary of commerce on 13 November. During the elections, the Democrats won twelve seats in the Senate, and Alaska was added as the forty-ninth state, sending two more Democrats to the Senate for a majority of 64 to 34. Initially, it appeared as if Strauss would win confirmation. However, certain Democrats, among them Clinton P. Anderson of New Mexico and Majority Leader Lyndon B. Johnson of Texas, opposed the nomination, and Johnson made opposition to Strauss a must as a sign of party loyalty. On 19 June 1959, forty-seven Democrats and two Republicans voted to send Strauss's nomination down to defeat, only the eighth time in history a president's nominee for a cabinet office was not confirmed, and the first time since 1925. President Eisenhower denounced the Senate vote and called it "the second most shameful day in Senate history" next to the impeachment of President Andrew Johnson in 1868. The press, sympathetic with Strauss, condemned the Democratic-led Senate for what *Time* magazine called "a stinging personal slap." Strauss was replaced at Commerce by Frederick H. Mueller, who served for the remainder of Eisenhower's term.

Strauss retired to private life, remaining active in numerous causes and charities for the remainder of his life. On 21 January 1974, ten days before his seventy-eighth birthday, he died. He was laid to rest in the Salem Fields Cemetery in New York.

References: Baker, Richard A., "A Slap at the 'Hidden-Hand Presidency': The Senate and the Lewis Strauss Affair," *Congress and the Presidency* 14 (Spring 1987), 1–15; Bluestone, Miriam B., "Strauss, Lewis L(ichtenstein)," in Eleanora Schoenebaum, ed., *Political Profiles: The Eisenhower Years* (New York: Facts on File, 1980), 586–588; Pfau, Richard, *No Sacrifice Too Great: The Life of Lewis L. Strauss* (Charlottesville: University Press of Virginia, 1984), 1–3; "Strauss, Lewis L(ichtenstein)," in Anne Rothe, ed., *Current Biography 1947* (New York: H. W. Wilson, 1947), 614–617.

FREDERICK HENRY MUELLER

1893–1976

Frederick Mueller was promoted to secretary of commerce after Lewis Strauss was refused confirmation by the Senate. Mueller, a furniture manufacturer from Grand Rapids, Michigan, then served as secretary of commerce for the final two years of the Eisenhower administration. He was born in Grand Rapids on 22 November 1893, the son of John Frederick Mueller, a German immigrant who was a skilled cabinetmaker, and Emma (née Oesterle) Mueller. Mueller learned his father's trade while still in school. He earned a bachelor's degree in mechanical engineering from Michigan State University in 1914. His father made him a partner in his business that same year, and by 1923 he had been made general manager in charge of operations. When his father retired, he was named president of the company, a position he held until his retirement in 1955.

Mueller became an important businessman in Grand Rapids serving during World War II as president and general manager of Grand Rapids Industries, a consortium of Grand Rapids woodworking businesses that pooled their labor and facilities to assist in building airplanes for the military.

In politics, Mueller was a staunch Republican. Following the resignation of Assistant Secretary of Commerce for Domestic Affairs Lothair Teetor, President Dwight D. Eisenhower named Mueller to the vacancy on 22 November 1955. In his four years in this position, Mueller was a proponent of a revised tax system and became an expert in the area of oil imports.

When Lewis L. Strauss was named as secretary of commerce in November 1958, Mueller was promoted to Strauss's old position of undersecretary of commerce. Mueller was confirmed for this office by the Senate, but on 18 June 1959 the Senate denied Strauss confirmation. Three days later, Eisenhower nominated Mueller for the empty position, and, following hearings, Mueller was confirmed by the Senate on 6 August 1959, making him the fifteenth secretary of commerce, the last of three men to hold that position under Eisenhower.

During his tenure, which lasted until the end of the Eisenhower administration on 20 January 1961, Mueller served mainly in a caretaker function. After leaving the government he served as a member of the boards of directors of two companies, the Fruehauf Trailer Company, and the Detroit Edison Company. Mueller died in Sarasota, Florida, on 31 August 1976, at the age of 82. His remains were interred in the Graceland Mausoleum in Grand Rapids.

References: "Mueller, Frederick H(enry)," in Charles Moritz, ed., *Current Biography 1959* (New York: H. W. Wilson, 1959), 312–314; Pach, Chester J., Jr., and Elmo Richardson, *The Presidency of Dwight D. Eisenhower* (Lawrence: University Press of Kansas, 1991).

LUTHER HARTWELL HODGES

1898–1974

Luther Hodges was the governor of North Carolina when selected by President-elect John Kennedy to serve as his secretary of commerce. Hodges was born on a tenant farm in Cascade, Virginia, on 9 March 1898, the son of John James Hodges, a tenant farmer, and Lovicia (née Gammon) Hodges. Soon after Luther's birth, the family moved to Leaksville (now Eden), North Carolina, and it was here that Hodges grew up. At age 12, he left school to work as an office boy in a textile mill in Spray, North Carolina. He later attended the University of North Carolina at Chapel Hill while working, and, when the United States entered World War I, Hodges was commissioned a second lieutenant in the U.S. Army and served for a short time at Camp Grant, Illinois. He then returned to North Carolina, where he received his bachelor's degree in 1919. He then got a position as assistant to the general manager of Marshall Field's eight textile mills in the Leaksville area. In 1927, he was promoted to manager of the Marshall Field blanket mill in Spray and, by 1939, was serving as general manager of all twenty-nine of Marshall Field's mills in the United States and abroad. In 1943, he was named as vice-president in charge of mills and sales, a post he held until he left the company in 1950.

In 1944, Hodges went to work for the U.S. government, purchasing some $4 billion in textiles for the Office of Price Administration. The following year, he went to work as a special consultant to Secretary of Agriculture Clinton P. Anderson. After leaving Marshall Field in 1950, Hodges was named as chief of the Industry Division of the Economic Cooperation Administration (the government entity that carried out the mandate of the Marshall Plan aid program in western Europe), serving in West Germany. In 1951, he served as a consultant to the State Department in managing the affairs of an International Management Conference, which provided European businesses with technical assistance.

Hodges was active in North Carolina civic and educational affairs and, in 1952, was nominated for lieutenant governor. He ran with former U.S. Senator William B. Umstead, who received the Democrats' gubernatorial nomination. The two men were elected and took office in January 1953. However, Umstead soon became ill, and Hodges served as the governor ad interim. As president of the state Senate, he dealt with problems such as the U.S. Supreme Court's order to desegregate North Carolina schools. On 7 November 1954, Governor Umstead died, and, two days later, Hodges was sworn in as governor to serve the remaining twenty-six months of Umstead's term. In 1956, he was elected to a full four-year term, and he served until January 1961. His tenure was marked by his ability to attract business to the state, utilizing trade missions and establishing the Research Triangle, which combined educational and employment centers at Duke University in Durham, the University of North Carolina at Chapel Hill, and North Carolina State College at Raleigh. He also backed the state's first minimum wage law and dealt with the desegregation of the state's schools. In 1959, he called out the National Guard to manage a strike at the textile mills at Henderson.

In 1960, Hodges supported Senator John F. Kennedy's presidential campaign and was named as Kennedy's secretary of commerce. Historians Deane and David Heller wrote in 1961, "Mr. Hodges' selection as Secretary of Commerce came as a considerable surprise to many observers—including himself, he declares. At the Democratic National Convention of 1960, Governor Hodges supported [Senate Majority Leader] Lyndon Johnson of Texas. But when Senator Kennedy was nominated, he vigorously supported the Massachusetts lawmaker. As an influential businessman, he was named to lead the National Businessmen for Kennedy Committee. . . . But nothing was ever said at any time during the campaign about an office in the new administration, Mr. Hodges said, 'and I planned to retire after leaving the Governor's office'. . . . But, on December [3] . . . the soft-spoken North Carolinian was introduced to a crowd of eager reporters as the second member of the Kennedy cabinet." Nominated on 20 January 1961, he was confirmed by the Senate the following day, and he took office as the sixteenth secretary of commerce.

His tenure, which lasted until 18 January 1965, was marked by deteriorating relations with business. Hodges dealt with the Business Advisory Council (BAC), a business group that met with Commerce Department officials to keep informed on government policy while at the same time stressing business ideas. However, Hodges tried to replace the chairman of the BAC, Ralph Cordiner, chairman of General Electric, who had recently been indicted in a price-fixing scheme. The BAC members chose Roger Blough of U.S. Steel, but refused to allow small businessmen in the council or to conform to some of Hodges's other suggestions. In July 1961, the BAC voted to stop meeting with the Commerce Department, and Kennedy vetoed Hodges's plan to form a new BAC. Historian Thomas O'Brien adds, "Congress' decision in the spring of 1961 to place the newly created Area Redevelopment Administration (ARA) in the Commerce Department was a victory for Hodges. The ARA was authorized to spend $400 million in loans and grants in regions beset by chronic unemployment. . . . Hodges also convinced Congress in May to create the U.S. Travel Service in an effort to attract more foreign tourists. . . . He joined the Administration's offensive against the steel price rise in April 1962, calling it 'a disservice to the country and to the business community as a whole.' The Secretary also testified before the Congress in support of Kennedy's proposed $11 billion tax reduction plan in February 1963. Hodges was one of the less influential members of the Kennedy cabinet, serving more as an enthusiastic defender of Administration programs than an architect of its policies."

In his 1961 annual report, Hodges stressed the outreach program to business that he initiated: "To realize more fully the Department's potentialities as a source of vital production and marketing information, an intensive campaign was undertaken to familiarize businessmen with Department services and resources. This effort included the preparation of an Advertising Council campaign to tell businessmen through national publications and radio how they can expand their export and domestic business through the use of Commerce Department services. . . . The Department began to overhaul its own publications to make them more useful to businessmen, and speeded up all reporting functions of the Department to provide more timely economic information. In many cases the time-lag between the close of the reporting period and the publication of the data was reduced by as much as one-half." In his 1963 report he outlined his accomplishments, including the establishment of the Offices of Assistant Secretary of Commerce for Economic Affairs and of Assistant Secretary of Commerce for Domestic and International Business; he oversaw enactment of the Federal-Aid Highway Act of 1962 and the Trade Expansion Act of 1962.

Following President Kennedy's assassination in November 1963, Hodges and the rest of the cabinet stayed on to show a sense of continuity with the new administration of Lyndon B. Johnson. Even though Hodges had initially endorsed Johnson for the presidency in 1960, the two men were not close, and, four days before Johnson won a full four-year term in November 1964, Hodges handed in his resignation, which took effect when his successor, John T. Connor, took office on 18 January 1965. Hodges returned to North Carolina, where he went to work for the Research Triangle Foundation, at a salary of one dollar a year, as an economic advocate, at the same time lecturing at the School of Business Administration at the University of North Carolina at Chapel Hill. On 6 October 1974, Hodges died of a heart attack at his home in Chapel Hill, at the age of 76, and was buried in Overlook Cemetery in Eden.

References: 1961 annual report in *Commerce in 1961* (Washington, DC: GPO, 1961), 5; 1962 annual report in *Annual Report of the Secretary of Commerce, the Fiscal Year Ended June 30, 1962* (Washington, DC: GPO, 1962), 1; 1963 annual report in *Annual Report of the Secretary of Commerce, the Fiscal Year Ended June 30, 1963* (Washington, DC: GPO, 1963), 2; "Hodges, Luther H(artwell)," in Marjorie Kent Candee, ed., *Current Biography 1956* (New York: H. W. Wilson, 1956), 276–278; "Hodges, Luther Hartwell," in Robert Sobel and John Raimo, eds., *Biographical Directory of the Governors of the United States, 1789–1978* (Westport, CT: Meckler Books, 4 vols., 1978), 3: 1162–1163; Heller, Deane, and David

Heller, *The Kennedy Cabinet: America's Men of Destiny* (Derby, CT: Monarch Books, 1961), 85–86; O'Brien, Thomas, "Hodges, Luther H(artwell)," in Nelson Lichtenstein, ed., *Political Profiles: The Kennedy Years* (New York: Facts on File, 1976), 227–228.

JOHN THOMAS CONNOR

1914–

John Connor only served as secretary of commerce for two years (1965–1967); he is better known as a drug and chemical industries leader than as a government official. Connor was born in Syracuse, New York, on 3 November 1914, the son of Michael J. Connor and Mary (née Sullivan) Connor. He attended Syracuse University and graduated summa cum laude in 1936; three years later he received a bachelor of laws degree from Harvard University's School of Law. He was then admitted to the New York bar and joined the New York law firm of Cravath, de Gersdorff, Swaine, & Wood.

During World War II, Connor served in Washington, D.C., as general counsel for the Office of Scientific Research and Development under Director Vannevar Bush, working on a program to get private pharmaceutical companies involved in the production of penicillin. For his wartime work, Connor was awarded a Presidential Certificate of Merit by President Franklin D. Roosevelt. In 1944, he volunteered for service in the Marines and was stationed, with the rank of second lieutenant, in the Pacific as an air combat intelligence officer. He was promoted to first lieutenant and stationed in Japan after the end of the war. Connor was recalled to Washington in late 1945 to finish up the penicillin program and assist the U.S. Navy in taking over functions of the Office of Scientific Research and Development. During 1946, he served as council in the new agency, the Office of Naval Research, before he was appointed as a special assistant to Secretary of the Navy James V. Forrestal.

In 1947, Connor left government service to join Merck & Company, a pharmaceutical firm, as their general attorney. Later that year, he was promoted to secretary and, in 1950, to vice-president of the company. In September 1955, he was elevated to president. Connor immediately increased, by 7 percent, monies invested in research; by 1957, with the introduction of several new medicines, Merck became one of the leading drug companies in the world.

During the 1964 campaign, Connor, although a registered Republican, supported the election of President Lyndon Johnson, a Democrat, to a full term. Connor served as cochairman of the National Independent Committee for Johnson-Humphrey and helped energize business support for Johnson's candidacy. Connor began to pay a price for his support. Johnson's opponent, Arizona Senator Barry Goldwater, opposed Johnson's initiative to have a national health care system, and many doctors supported Goldwater's stand. To punish Connor for his support of Johnson, doctors refused to prescribe Merck products for several months during the campaign. Johnson later wrote Connor that his support for the president was "a real personal sacrifice" and that the president understood "the burdens that are being put upon you, and I want to let you know how appreciative I am."

Four days before the 1964 election, Secretary of Commerce Luther Hodges submitted his resignation to Johnson. Johnson sought Thomas Watson, chairman of IBM and a prominent member of the Business Advisory Council, to succeed Hodges, but Watson did not want to become involved in the politics of the Commerce Department. Johnson also considered Franklin D. Roosevelt, Jr., son of the former president and, at that time, the undersecretary of commerce. Jack Valenti, an aide to Johnson and later head of the Motion Picture Association of America, endorsed Connor. The Merck executive was offered the position by Johnson, and, on 20 December 1964, his nomination was announced to the press. Historians Richard Schott and Dagmar Hamilton wrote, "The [Connor] appointment was a clear effort to reach outside the Kennedy circle and to end the antagonism between the Department of Commerce and big business that had festered during the Kennedy administration. . . . While the Connor appointment appeared, on the surface, as one of the smoothest in the Johnson administration, trouble between President Johnson and his new appointee began almost immediately from the moment the president announced his nomination. Only eighteen months after Connor was sworn in, Johnson began to search for a successor." In fact, even before Connor was confirmed there was a breach between the two men that never fully healed. Within a week of the announcement of his nomination, Johnson learned that steel executives were going to raise the price of steel, which could cause harm to the U.S. economy. Johnson called Connor and asked him to "call up your friends in the steel industry" and ask them to avoid raising prices. Connor refused, saying that he was still only a private citizen and could not ask such a thing; he further angered Johnson when he said that Secretary Hodges, still on the job, should make the call. The second incident came when it was learned that Connor had purchased Merck stock cheaply after word of his nomination had leaked. Johnson demanded that he sell the stock, to avoid all appearances of impropriety; Connor offered to put the stock in a blind trust, which Johnson refused. Connor told the president that he would withdraw his name from nomination if forced to sell the stock. Connor was further intimidated by stories in the *New York Times* and the *Washington Post,* that gave details of the exchange on the stocks, details that could only have come from inside the White House.

Connor was officially nominated on 6 January 1965 and confirmed nine days later as the seventeenth secretary of commerce. His tenure lasted exactly two years. Historian Thomas O'Brien wrote, "Connor's chief preoccupation was the balance of payments deficit, which had averaged $3 billion annually from 1958 through 1964. A 15% tax on American investments abroad was seriously

discussed within the Administration as a possible antidote. Connor argued against this measure, and his success in substituting a program of voluntary business cooperation in reversing the dollar outflow was the major achievement in his two tenure in office." *Fortune* magazine said in a February 1966 editorial, "No Commerce Secretary in recent years has stood higher with the business community than Connor. . . . No Secretary has done a better first-year job of administration, either." Connor's tenure was marked by his stepping in to help settle a dock strike along the eastern coast of the United States in February 1965 and a General Electric employees' strike in October 1966.

On 18 January 1967, Connor resigned as commerce secretary to take the position of president of the Allied Chemical Company. He had long been in conflict with Johnson, and that antagonism reached a head when Johnson did not push hard enough to merge the Departments of Commerce and Labor. After leaving office, Connor worked in private business until his retirement in the 1980s. On 4 January 1975, reacting to various reports about covert Central Intelligence Agency (CIA) actions, President Gerald R. Ford created the Commission on CIA Activities within the United States. To head up the commission, he named Vice-president Nelson A. Rockefeller (the commission is sometimes called the Rockefeller Commission). He also named, among others, former Secretary of the Treasury C. Douglas Dillon, former California Governor Ronald Reagan, and Connor.

References: O'Brien, Thomas, "Connor, John T(homas)," in Nelson Lichtenstein, ed., *Political Profiles: The Johnson Years* (New York: Facts on File, 1976), 127–128; Schott, Richard L., and Dagmar S. Hamilton, *People, Positions, and Power: The Political Appointments of Lyndon Johnson* (Chicago: University of Chicago Press, 1983), 60–64.

ALEXANDER BUEL TROWBRIDGE, JR.

1929–

Alexander Trowbridge was named by President Lyndon B. Johnson as secretary of commerce in 1967, to serve the final year and a half of his administration. The youngest secretary in the department's history at age 38, Trowbridge's appointment, to many, signaled a "reduction" in the influence of the department. Born in Englewood, New Jersey, on 12 December 1929, he was the son of Alexander Buel Trowbridge Sr., and Julie (née Chamberlain) Trowbridge. 'When he was a child, the family moved to Winter Park, Florida, where his father was a professor at Rollins College, and it was here that Trowbridge grew up. He prepared for college at the Philips Academy (now the Philips Andover Academy) in Andover, Rhode Island, then entered Princeton University and studied at that school's Woodrow Wilson School of Public and International Affairs. He received his bachelor degree cum laude in 1951.

For six months after graduating, Trowbridge worked at the Central Intelligence Agency. In late 1951, he left to join the Marines, serving as a platoon leader with the rank of second lieutenant in the First Marine Division in Korea; he was awarded the Bronze Star with a combat V for valor. He returned to the United States, and upon the recommendation of George F. Kennan, under whom he had studied at Princeton, Trowbridge entered the international oil business, going to work for the California Texas Oil Company, a subsidiary of Texaco and Standard Oil of California. After a year with that firm's New York office, he was transferred to Manila, where he worked for another subsidiary, Caltex Philippines. In 1958, he resigned to work for Standard Oil in New Jersey and, a year later, went to work for Esso (now Exxon), then a subsidiary of Standard. For a time he was involved in marketing in the Caribbean and Central America, as well as Cuba, where he worked until Esso's properties were seized by Cuban dictator Fidel Castro. He remained with Esso until 1965.

In early 1965, Trowbridge was named by President Lyndon Johnson as assistant secretary of commerce; Trowbridge was confirmed on 6 May 1965. For the next two years, he served as the close adviser to Secretary of Commerce John Connor in all aspects of industry and trade, both domestic and international. He also oversaw a program of allowing more foreign businessmen to visit the United States and invest in American industries. On 18 January 1967, Secretary of Commerce Connor resigned, and, on the same day, Johnson named Trowbridge as acting secretary, with the eventual goal of having Congress accept his recommendation to reunite the departments of Commerce and Labor, as it had been originally established in 1903. However, labor unions and Congress resisted the effort, and on 22 May 1967, after four months as acting secretary, Trowbridge was named as secretary when Johnson gave up trying to have the two departments merge. During his time as acting secretary, Trowbridge worked to get Johnson's idea through Congress; afterwards, when it was resisted, he desired to leave when he felt that the department needed a full-time secretary, only accepting the secretaryship when Johnson seemed unable to find another candidate. After confirmation hearings, Trowbridge was sworn into office on 14 June 1967 as the eighteenth secretary of commerce.

His tenure was marked by declining health. Trowbridge, who had suffered a heart attack before joining the Commerce Department, had gotten a clearance from his doctor before accepting the secretaryship, but he had a recurrence of heart trouble soon after taking control of Commerce. In declining health, he tendered his resignation on 16 February 1968 and returned to private business.

After leaving government, Trowbridge served as chairman of the Allied Chemical Corporation and, from 1980 to 1990, as president of the National Association of Manu-facturers. In the latter year, he became the president of Trowbridge Partners, Inc., a public relations firm in Washington, D.C.

References: Schott, Richard L., and Dagmar S. Hamilton, *People, Positions, and Power: The Polit-ical Appointments of Lyndon Johnson* (Chicago: University of Chicago Press, 1983), 93–95; "Trow-bridge, Alexander B(uel)," in Charles Moritz, ed., *Current Biography 1968* (New York: H. W. Wil-son, 1968), 402–404.

CYRUS ROWLETT SMITH
1899–1990

Cyrus Smith, known as "Mr. C. R.," became the president of American Airlines when just 35 years of age. He left the industry, in 1968, to serve as secretary of commerce in the final year of the administration of his friend, President Lyndon B. Johnson. Smith was born on 9 September 1899 in Minerva, Texas, the son of Roy Edgerton Smith and Marion (née Burck) Smith. When Cyrus was seven, his father abandoned the family; his mother taught school and took in boarders; Cyrus left school at age 9 and took a job as an office boy for a local cattleman in Amar-illo. He then worked at odd jobs to support his family, including as a store clerk, a book-keeper, a cotton picker, and a bank teller. His schooling was sporadic, yet he entered the University of Texas School of Business Ad-ministration and Law at Austin, where he studied economics and business. He also worked as a bank examiner at a Federal Re-serve bank in Austin. In 1924, Smith gradu-ated, and he took a job as a clerk in the ac-counting firm of Peat, Marwick, Mitchell, and Company in Dallas. One of the firm's clients, a utilities magnate named A. P. Barrett, took a notice of Smith and hired him as an assis-tant treasurer for the Texas-Louisiana Power Company.

In 1928, Barrett bought Texas Air Trans-port and appointed Smith as secretary and treasurer of the company. The following year, Barrett founded Southern Air Transport, folded Texas Air Transport into the new cor-poration, and named Smith as vice-president. When Southern Air Transport was changed to the Aviation Company, in 1930, the direc-tors of the company established American Airways and appointed Smith as vice-presi-dent of the company's southern divisions. In April 1934, American Airways became Amer-ican Airlines. On 25 October 1934, Cyrus Smith was elected as the president of Ameri-can Airlines. Smith took a struggling airline and built American into one of the aviation industry's leaders, changing from a patch-work of airplanes to a fleet of brand-new DC-3 aircraft, which he had helped to de-sign. In April 1942, after the United States en-tered World War II, Smith volunteered with the Army Air Corps Ferrying Command, with the rank of colonel, and he helped establish the Air Transport Command (ATC), with two divisions: the Ferrying Command, and the Air Transportation Command. The ATC was charged by the War Department to help ferry cargo, personnel, and mail to troops in the European and Pacific theaters of operations. As chief of staff, and later as deputy com-mander of the ATC, Smith helped map routes for supplies to be sent; by 1943, this number was over 95,000 outside the United States and more than 35,000 inside the United States. In October 1942, Smith was made a brigadier general and, in September 1944, a major general. After the war ended in Europe in July 1945, Smith retired from the army. On 12 July, the board of directors of American Airlines elected Smith as chairman of the board. Smith then led American Airlines into the jet age, including introducing the first transcontinental American jet service on 25 January 1959.

In early February 1968, Secretary of Com-merce Alexander B. Trowbridge announced his intention to resign. President Lyndon Johnson, like Smith, a Texan, and a close friend of the airline executive, asked Smith to serve at Commerce for the last year remain-ing in Johnson's administration. Smith agreed and, after being nominated on 19 February

1968, was confirmed on 1 March and took office five days later as the nineteenth secretary of commerce. His tenure lasted until 20 January 1969, a term of office of a little more than ten months. Smith's work was mainly in a position of caretaker, overseeing the department during the heightened years of the Vietnam War, when the Department of Commerce was little recognized in the government.

After he left Commerce in January 1969, Smith, who had resigned as chairman of American Airlines to avoid a conflict of interest, took a position as a partner in the investment banking firm of Lazard Freres and Company. However, in 1973, when he was 74 years old, Smith was called back into service for American Airlines, which, since his departure, had suffered several years of economic decline. Smith agreed to take over again as chairman until a full-time replacement could be found. Five months later, he resigned when Albert V. Casey was elected as chairman.

After his retirement, Smith remained active in civic and other affairs in Washington, D.C. On 4 April 1990, at the age of 90, he died in Annapolis, Maryland. He was buried in Arlington National Cemetery. The American Airlines C. R. Smith Museum in Fort Worth, Texas, is named in his honor.

References: Department of Commerce, Office of the Secretary, *From Lighthouses to Laserbeams: A History of U.S. Department of Commerce* (Washington, DC: GPO, 1995), 85; "Smith, C(yrus) R(owlett)," in Anne Rothe, ed., *Current Biography 1945* (New York: H. W. Wilson, 1945), 554–556.

MAURICE HUBERT STANS
1908–1998

Maurice Stans served as the director of the Bureau of the Budget in the Eisenhower administration before his service as secretary of commerce in the Nixon adminis-

tration from 1969 to 1972. He was caught up in the Watergate affair and, with former Attorney General John Mitchell, tried on charges of influence peddling; both men were acquitted. Stans, the son of J. Hubert Stans, a house painter and musician, and his wife Mathilda (née Nyssen) Stans, was born in Shakopee, Minnesota, on 22 March 1908. In 1925, he started work at the firm of Harry Levi & Co. as a clerk. In 1928, he moved over to work at Alexander Grant & Company as an office boy, working his way up to become a junior accountant. He became a partner in the certified public accounting firm in 1931 and, seven years later, became the company's managing and executive partner. He also became the chairman of the board of the Moore Corporation, a manufacturer of stoves in Joliet, Illinois, as well as the director of several other major companies, so that by 1940 Stans was a wealthy man. In 1940, he established the Stans Foundation, "to assist organized charitable, religious, scientific, and educational institutions." The foundation gave money to research a cure for cancer, a disease that had claimed the lives of both of Stans's parents.

In 1953, Stans, along with other businessmen, were called to Washington, D.C., by the Republicans on the House of Representatives Appropriations Committee to study ways to cut the budget. *Business Week* magazine stated, "By chance, [Stans] was assigned to look at Post Office operations and produced a 100-page memorandum that recommended an increase in spending for research, along with an overhaul of business practices." The report so impressed Postmaster General Arthur E. Summerfield that he hired Stans as a financial consultant for the Post Office Department. In September 1955, President Dwight D. Eisenhower named Stans as deputy postmaster general; he served in this position until March 1958. At that time, Eisenhower named him as director of the Bureau of the Budget (now called the Office of Management and Budget, or OMB). Stans was able to get Eisenhower to agree, in September 1959, to cut each agency's employment by 2 percent and, with Eisenhower, threatened the Democrats in the Congress that if their budget exceeded his, he would veto it. The scheme worked, and Eisenhower, with Stans's assistance, was able to achieve a budget surplus of approximately $1 billion in 1960. Stans said that a budget was "a seat of calculations that confirm your worst suspicions." Stans's budget was one of the last with a surplus until the 1990s.

After the Eisenhower administration ended in 1961, Stans left government and entered private business as an investment banker, but he remained close to politics, writing a syndicated column, from 1961 to 1962, and working with former Vice-president Richard Nixon to raise campaign funds for a Nixon run for the governorship of California in 1962, which Nixon lost. However, six years later, when Nixon ran for the presidency, Stans served as chairman of the Nixon Finance Committee, and that same year in a similar position for the Republican National Committee, raising $34 million to help elect Nixon as the thirty-seventh president. The president-elect returned the favor and named Stans as his secretary of commerce. The *New York Times* said at the time of Stans's selection, "He throws things—pencils and rulers—not at anybody, but across the room or against the wall to indicate impatience with bureaucratic slowness or somebody's mistake . . . the temper, which some old acquaintances suggest may be calculated, rather than ungovernable, has the effect . . . Stans, the new Secretary of Commerce, is well-remembered throughout official Washington as a man who demands results, and demands them fast."

Stans was nominated on 20 January 1969 and confirmed by the Senate the same day as the twentieth secretary of commerce. Historian Joseph C. Holub summarized his tenure: "Despite Stans' predictions of a 'business-oriented' administration, he could not reverse the trend which had put Commerce's old functions into the hands of the State Department and the Council of Economic Advisers. . . . The Secretary traveled widely in an effort to improve the nation's trade deficit. His November 1971 trip to Moscow was a

notable success and an important ingredient in Nixon's pursuit of détente. However, Stans' diplomatic gaffes elsewhere irritated the State Department and damaged his goal of securing trade concessions for American business. In May 1969 his table-pounding demands for voluntary restrictions on Japanese textile exports to the U.S. only alienated his Tokyo hosts. His effusive praise of the Greek government for its 'attitude toward American investment' on a May 1971 visit to Athens went beyond the bounds of protocol and irritated the State Department, which had pointedly refrained from warm endorsements of the Greek regime." Stans was a conservative, but he worked to assist minorities when he established the Office of Minority Business Enterprise inside the Commerce Department.

On 27 January 1972, Stans resigned to serve as campaign finance chairman for the Committee to Reelect the President—dubbed "CREEP" by its critics. In the 1972 election, he went on to raise $60 million to facilitate Nixon's reelection. However, Stans got caught up in the Watergate scandal. In June 1972, burglars from CREEP entered Democratic headquarters at the Watergate building in Washington and were caught trying to leave listening devices. Money found on the men and checks in their accounts were traced directly to CREEP, and to Stans, who was the organization's finance chairman. In May 1973, Stans, along with former Attorney General John Mitchell, was indicted by a New York grand jury on ten counts of perjury and conspiracy involving a $200,000 contribution to CREEP by financial Robert Vesco. Stans and Mitchell became the first cabinet officers indicted in over fifty years, but on 28 April 1974 both men were acquitted. However, Stans later pleaded guilty to five counts of campaign financing violations and paid a $5,000 fine. He later told the *Washington Post,* "They were two charges of non-willful receipt of illegal campaign contributions . . . and three minor counts of late reporting of contributions. Out of nearly a million transactions that year! . . . They had nothing to do with Watergate," he added.

Stans stood by Nixon, even after the president was implicated in covering up Watergate crimes and was forced to resign the presidency on 9 August 1974—he later raised $27 million for the Nixon presidential library in California.

In his final years, Stans spoke out on Watergate and authored two works on his experiences in government: *The Terrors of Justice: The Untold Side of Watergate* and *One of the Presidents' Men: Twenty Years with Eisenhower and Nixon.* Stans died in Pasadena, California, of a heart attack on 14 April 1998 at the age of 90. He was writing a novel called *Agenda for a Dictator* when he died.

References: *Annual Report of the Secretary of Commerce, Fiscal Year Ended June 30, 1971* (Washington, DC: U.S. Department of Commerce, 1971); Holub, Joseph C., "Stans, Maurice H(ubert)," in Eleanora W. Schoenebaum, ed., *Political Profiles: The Nixon/Ford Years* (New York: Facts on File, 1982), 615–616; Sloan, John W., *Eisenhower and the Management of Prosperity* (Lawrence: University Press of Kansas, 1991), 84, 90; "Stans, Maurice H(ubert)," in Marjorie Kent Candee, *Current Biography 1958* (New York: H. W. Wilson, 1958), 410–411.

PETER GEORGE PETERSON
1926–

Peter Peterson served as the chairman of the board of the Bell & Howell Company prior to going to work as the special assistant to President Richard M. Nixon. Named as secretary of commerce in February 1972, he served until December 1973. Peterson was born on 5 June 1926 in Kearney, Nebraska, the son of George Peterson and Vent Peterson. He attended local schools in Kearney, then completed a two-year course at the State Teacher's College in Kearney before studying at Massachusetts Institute of Technology, and earned his bachelor of science at Northwestern University and his 'master of business administration from the University of Chicago in 1951. He then entered private

business, beginning at the advertising firm of McCann-Erickson in 1953. Five years later, he moved over to work at Bell & Howell, moving up to serve as chairman of the board and CEO from 1968 to 1971.

In 1971, President Richard Nixon named Peterson as his special assistant to the president for foreign economic policy, working with Secretary of the Treasury John Connally as head of the newly created Council on International Economic Policy. The *New York Times* said at the time, "In his new job, Mr. Peterson faces probably the biggest challenge of his career. As executive director of a new Cabinet-level Council on Foreign Economic Policy, he will have responsibility for bringing unity of purpose to 20 different departments, agencies and committees dealing mainly with trade, international monetary affairs and foreign aid." In this capacity, he worked with administration officials to devise Nixon's "New Economic Policy," backed by Connally's policy of stabilizing the dollar internationally.

On 27 January 1972, Secretary of Commerce Maurice Stans resigned. On that same day, Nixon named Peterson as Stans's successor. On 21 February, the Senate confirmed the nomination, and Peterson was sworn in as the twenty-first secretary of commerce. During his tenure, which lasted until January 1973, he was key in helping to foster détente in U.S.-Soviet trade matters. On 18 October 1972, he signed a three-year trade agreement with the Soviets, clearing up their Lend-Lease debt, which had been a issue since the end of World War II, and requesting from Congress the right to have the Soviet Union named as a "most favored trading nation." A month after signing a similar trade deal with Poland, Peterson resigned. A burgeoning scandal over the Nixon administration's involvement in delaying antitrust suits against International Telegraph & Telephone, a major Nixon campaign donor, touched Peterson when he was accused by the Securities and Exchange Commission of being "actively involved" in the delay. Peterson denied the allegation and was never criminally charged. After leaving office, he became the chairman of the board of Lehman Brothers, a major New York investment bank.

References: Goldner, Loren, "Peterson, Peter," in Eleanora W. Schoenebaum, ed., *Political Profiles: The Nixon/Ford Years* (New York: Facts on File, 1982), 495–496; "Peterson, Peter G(eorge)," in Charles Moritz, ed., *Current Biography 1972* (New York: H. W. Wilson, 1972), 349–351.

FREDERICK BAILY DENT
1922–

Frederick Dent was called a "soft spoken" nominee when selected by Richard Nixon, in 1972, as his third secretary of commerce. He was the head of the American Textile Manufacturers Institute in South Carolina. Dent went on to serve for the remainder of Nixon's term and a year of President Gerald Ford's. Dent was born in Cape May, New Jersey, on 17 August 1922, the son of Magruder Dent, Jr., and Edith (née Baily) Dent. Dent received his preparatory education at St. Paul's, an Episcopal school in Concord, New Hampshire, and his secondary education at Yale University, where he earned a bachelor's degree in 1943. He then entered the U.S. Naval Reserve, and saw service in the Pacific Theater of Operations during World War II, including the American landing at Okinawa; he left the service with the rank of lieutenant, junior grade.

Dent then joined his family's business in New York City, Joshua Baily & Co. a textile manufacturer founded by Dent's maternal great-grandfather in 1876. At the same time, he went to work for his family's textile mill, Mayfair Mills, in Acadia, South Carolina. In 1958, Dent became the president of Mayfair and gradually built it up into a major textiles and factoring firm. Dent was also well known for fair and balanced treatment in the hiring of blacks. He served, first, as the president of the Carolina Textile Manufacturers

Association, then was elected as president of the American Textile Manufacturers Association in 1967. During the Vietnam War, when textile sales from the United States to the rest of the world shrank, Dent made numerous trips overseas to sell American products and to arrange agreements with nations to lower imports to the United States. Generally, Dent was regarded as a "protectionist" rather than a "free trader." This apparent disagreement with fellow Republicans came in stark contrast when Secretary of Commerce Pete Peterson denounced the Burke-Hartke Bill pending in Congress in 1972 as protectionist and "a national disaster for the United States." Following his election in 1972, President Nixon decided to replace Secretary of Commerce Peterson with Dent. Although the change displayed a firm about-face in policy in the administration on the issue of foreign trade, Dent played down the differences after his name was announced for secretary of commerce on 6 December 1972. As historian Loren Goldner wrote, "Dent's appointment to the post of Secretary of Commerce . . . represented a concession to domestic producers eager for tariff protection against foreign competition. After assuming office in January, 1973, however, Dent was plunged immediately into the growing raw material and agricultural shortages that surfaced in the hyperinflationary boom conditions of that year. In June 1873, with Secretary of Agriculture Earl Butz, Dent placed export controls on soybeans and cottonseed to prevent a domestic livestock feed shortage. In July, Dent extended the controls to forty-one other farm commodities. Several weeks later he was one of two cabinet-level officials to attend the annual conference of the Joint Japan-United States Committee on Foreign Affairs, at which the American delegation attempted to assure Japan of a 'stable supply' of key commodities." Dent oversaw, the continuation of a relaxation of trade barriers against the Soviet Union and overtures to China following President Nixon's historic visit there in 1972.

Following President Nixon's resignation in August 1974, new president, Gerald Ford, retained Dent and in the fall of 1974 named him to the Council on Wage and Price Stability. In February 1975, Ford named him as the president's special representative for trade negotiations, more commonly known as the U.S. trade negotiator. This allowed the president to replace Dent at Commerce with his own appointee. On 26 March 1975, acceding to Ford's wishes, Dent resigned, to be replaced by Secretary of the Interior Rogers C. B. Morton. Dent· spent his tenure of twenty-three months in this new position working for agreements with foreign governments on issues surrounding steel and non-rubber shoe imports. When Ford was defeated for reelection to a full term in 1976 and left office the following March, Dent left government and returned to his old position as president of Mayfair Mills. In 1988, Dent was named as chairman of the Mayfair Mills board of directors. In 1994, he was inducted into the South Carolina Business Hall of Fame.

References: "Dent, Frederick B(aily)," in Charles Moritz, ed., *Current Biography 1974* (New York: H. W. Wilson, 1974), 105–107; Goldner, Loren, "Dent, Frederick B(aily)," in Eleanora W. Schoenebaum, ed., *Political Profiles: The Nixon/ Ford Years* (New York: Facts on File, 1982), 166–168.

ROGERS CLARK BALLARD MORTON
1914–1979

See Secretary of the Interior, 1970–1975

ELLIOT LEE RICHARDSON
1920–1999

See Secretary of Health, Education and Welfare, 1970–1973

JUANITA MORRIS KREPS
1921–

Juanita Kreps was the vice-president and professor of economics at Duke University in North Carolina when she was selected by President-elect Jimmy Carter as his secretary of commerce, the fourth woman to be named to the cabinet. She was born Juanita Morris on 11 January 1921 in Lynch, a coal mining town in Harlan County, Kentucky, the daughter of Elmer Morris, a mine operator, and Larcenia (née Blair) Morris. When her parents divorced in 1925, Juanita went to live with her mother and was educated at a Presbyterian boarding school. In 1938, she entered Berea College in Kentucky. As she said in interview in 1977, "I was always interested in social problems. If you read the newspapers and had a sense of where the world was, you couldn't help being concerned. I thought economics would give me more insight into what was going on." She earned a bachelor of arts degree in economics from Berea in 1942, then did graduate work in that field at Duke University, which awarded her a master's degree in 1944 and a Ph.D. degree in 1948.

While a student at Duke, Kreps taught there part-time beginning in 1942, and after earning her Ph.D., she taught full-time until 1964. In 1943 and 1944, Kreps worked as an economist with the National War Labor Board, first in Atlanta and then in Washington, D.C. In 1945, before she earned her doctorate, she worked as an instructor and then assistant professor in economics at Denison University in Granville, Ohio. She also lectured at Hofstra College (now Hofstra University) and Queens College, both in New York, before returning to Duke in 1955 as a visiting professor in economics. She was named a full professor at Duke in 1968 and, four years later, was awarded the James B. Duke professorship in economics. She specialized in labor demographics; in 1971, she wrote *Sex in the Marketplace: American Women at Work.*

In 1976, Governor James E. "Jimmy" Carter was elected president. Carter, who had committed himself to appointing at least one woman to this cabinet, initially selected Jane Cahill Pfeiffer, a former vice-president of IBM, for secretary of commerce. Pfeiffer, however, turned down the offer, and the president-elect then asked Professor Kreps. Kreps had briefed Carter on labor issues soon after his election, but did not expect a cabinet position. However, after she left Carter at his headquarters in Plains, Georgia, rumors circulated that she was in the running either for a seat on the Council of Economic Advisers, or as secretary of labor. On 20 December 1976, Carter announced her appointment; she became one of two women in his original cabinet (the other was Patricia Roberts Harris, chosen for secretary of housing and urban development). At that press conference, Kreps told the reporters, "My enthusiasm is only slightly dampened by the fact that, as you members of the press know, I was not Mr. Carter's first choice." Carter responded, "You are now." Nominated on 20 January 1977, she was confirmed the same day, unanimously, and took office as the twenty-fifth secretary of commerce and the first economist to head that department.

Kreps's tenure, which lasted until 31 October 1979, was marked by her becoming the first commerce secretary to travel to China. She reorganized some of the department's bureaus, namely the Domestic and International Business Administration, into the new Industry and Trade Administration. The act that established the Department of Energy transferred the Office of Energy Programs from Commerce to that new department.

In her 1978 report, she outlined one of her major initiatives of that year: "Throughout Fiscal Year 1978 we conducted a special 'Footwear Industry Revitalization Program' to deal with the problems posed by the effects of increased exports. Three Commerce agencies worked together to strengthen the domestic footwear industry by providing financial and technical assistance, by facilitating development and application of new technologies, and by stimulating export performance. The assistance provided by this program helps to create jobs and minimize economic dislocation in areas where individual firms are located." In her final report, in 1979, she explained, "In every instance, the aim [of the Department] is to strengthen the social and economic fabric of the Nation. In the years ahead, worldwide industrial development and the potential for increased East-West trade post competitive challenges of an unprecedented scope for the United States. We can meet those challenges and retain our global economic leadership only by realizing the full synergistic potential of our strengths, not only within the government, but also among all segments of the public and private sectors. The Department of Commerce, through improved management of its extraordinary diverse resources in economics, trade, industry and technology, will continue to play a major role in this undertaking."

On 31 October 1979, Kreps resigned, Since then, the Juanita Kreps Award, named in her honor, has been presented each year by J. C. Penney to American women for notable achievements. Past winners include Congresswoman Barbara Jordan and astronaut Sally Ride; Kreps herself was the first recipient. She is the author, coauthor, or editor of thirteen books, as well as hundreds of articles and papers.

References: "Kreps, Juanita M(orris)," in Charles Moritz, ed., *Current Biography 1977* (New York: H. W. Wilson, 1977), 259–262; *Managing the Nation's Commerce: The Annual Report of the Secretary of Commerce for the Fiscal Year Ended September 30, 1978* (Washington, DC: GPO, 1978), 2; *New Directions in Commerce: The Annual Report of the Secretary of Commerce for the Fiscal Year Ended September 30, 1977* (Washington, DC: GPO, 1977), 3; *U.S. Department of Commerce Annual Report, Fiscal Year 1979* (Washington, DC: GPO, 1979), 2.

PHILIP MORRIS KLUTZNICK
1907–1999

Philip Klutznick's name is attached to one of the most important affirmative action cases ever heard by the Supreme Court—the 1980 decision in *Fullilove v. Klutznick* (1980), in which the Court struck down minority set-aside programs as discriminatory. Because of his long scholarship in Jewish history, Klutznick is better known for his scholarly work in Jewish history than for his short service as the twenty-fifth secretary of commerce. Born in Kansas City, Missouri, on 9 July 1907, the son of a shoemaker, Klutznick graduated from the University of Nebraska and Creighton University Law School. He began his career as a municipal attorney in Omaha, Nebraska. He was appointed by President Franklin Roosevelt as the commissioner of federal housing, a position equal to the status of the current secretary of housing and urban development. He became involved in numerous philanthropic measures, including trying to build housing for the poor, and was president of B'nai B'rith. He developed the model suburb called Park Forest outside of Chicago, Illinois, in 1946.

Klutznick served as the U.S. representative to the United Nations Economic and Social Council from 1961 to 1962, acting as the chief economic adviser to U.S. Ambassador to the United Nations Adlai Stevenson, under whom he had served when Stevenson was governor of Illinois. Klutznick was a longtime Democratic fund-raiser. He was a partner in the New York investment firm of Salomon Brothers and chairman of the board of the Continental Foreign Trade Bank in Geneva, Switzerland. From 1977 to 1979, he served as president of the World Jewish Congress.

Following the resignation of Secretary of Commerce Juanita Morris Kreps, President Carter considered replacing her with such candidates as Sol Linowitz, who was eventually named as Carter's special envoy to the Middle East, Robert S. Strauss, chairman of the Democratic National Committee, or J. Irwin Miller, the former chairman of the Cummins Engine Company of Columbus, Indiana. Instead, on 16 November 1979, he named Klutznick to the vacancy. Although he served more than a year as the twenty-sixth secretary of commerce, barely anything has been written about his tenure.

After leaving government on 20 January 1981, Klutznick returned to his work as a philanthropist. The B'nai B'rith Klutznick National Jewish Museum, located in Washington, D.C., was named in his honor, as was Creighton University's Klutznick Chair in Jewish Civilization and Center for the Study of Religion and Society, which holds an annual Klutznick Symposium on Jewish language and culture. Klutznick died on 14 August 1999 at the age of 92. He was buried in the Shalom Memorial Cemetery in Arlington Heights, Illinois.

References: Haas, Garland A., *Jimmy Carter and the Politics of Frustration* (Jefferson, NC: McFarland, 1996), 85; Klutznick, Philip M., and Sidney Hyman, *Angles of Vision: A Memoir of My Lives* (Chicago: I. R. Dee, 1991).

HOWARD MALCOLM BALDRIGE
1922–1987

The *New York Times* said of Ronald Reagan's first secretary of commerce, Malcolm Baldrige, "Some people think that [he] is really two people. . . . There is the Malcolm Baldrige who is a member of the Business Council, director of several large corporations such as AMF, Bendix and Uniroyal, and chairman of the board of Scovill Inc., a diversified manufacturing company with sales of about $1 billion a year and a sleek new corporate headquarters. . . . Then there is the

Malcolm Baldrige, known as 'Mac,' a steer roper on the professional rodeo circuit, a 'heeler' in a two-man roping team who lassos the hind legs and flips the steer while his partner ropes the head. The lanky, soft-spoken industrialist . . . moves easily between the seemingly contradictory worlds of a corporate executive and a cowboy."

Born in Omaha, Nebraska, on 4 October 1922, he was the son of Howard Malcolm Baldrige Sr., an attorney, and Regina (née Connell) Baldrige. Baldrige attended local schools and Hotchkiss School in Connecticut, where he graduated in 1940, and then went to Yale, where he received his bachelor's degree in English in 1944. After graduating, Baldrige volunteered for service in the U.S. Army. Assigned as a private, he was stationed in the Pacific in the field artillery brigade of the Twenty-seventh Infantry Division; when he was released, in 1946, he held the rank of captain.

Once back in the United States, Baldrige got a job as a mill hand and, later, a foundry foreman at the Eastern Malleable Iron Company in Naugatuck, Connecticut. By 1960, Baldrige was president of the company. Two years later, the Scovill Corporation, an international manufacturing firm, hired him. When Baldrige joined Scovill as an executive vice-president in 1962, he led the way for the company to acquire other concerns and expand their sales base to consumer items, highlighted by the takeover of Westinghouse's small appliance division in 1972. By that time, Baldrige was president of the company, and he had quadrupled sales. In 1980, the year before he left the company, sales were up to $1 billion annually.

Baldrige became active in Republican Party politics in the early 1960s. Even though he was a westerner, he sided with the so-called "eastern," or moderate, wing of the party in its battles with the farther right of the party, particularly during the 1964 election, when he backed Governor William Scranton of Pennsylvania for the party's presidential nomination against Senator Barry Goldwater of Arizona. He was a delegate to the party's convention that year in San Francisco; four

years later, he served as the head of former Vice-president Richard Nixon's campaign in Connecticut. During these years, he was also serving as the head of other companies and fashioning Scovill into a giant conglomerate. A member of the National Association for the Advancement of Colored People (NAACP), Baldrige was an early exponent of giving blacks equal opportunities in business.

Baldrige became close friends with George Bush, and when Bush ran for president in 1980, he asked Baldrige to serve as his campaign manager in Connecticut. Baldrige helped Bush win in the state's primary against former California Governor Ronald Reagan. Reagan won the party's presidential nomination, and when he chose Bush as his running mate, Baldrige served as a fund-raiser for Businessmen for Reagan-Bush. Following Reagan's election that November, Reagan looked for a businessman to run the Commerce Department. Baldrige was Reagan's choice for the position. Ron Brownstein and Nina Easton wrote, "When Reagan called the Baldrige household to offer him the Commerce job, so the story goes, his wife told the President-elect that Malcolm couldn't come to the phone; he was out riding. 'That,' said the President, 'is my kind of guy.'" On 11 December 1980, Reagan announced his selection of Baldrige. The Senate confirmed his nomination on 22 January 1981 by a vote of 97 to 1, and he was sworn in the following day as the twenty-seventh secretary of commerce.

During his tenure, which ended on 25 July 1987, Baldrige was a staunch advocate of free trade and deregulation, but he also believed that trade restrictions against American products, particularly by the Japanese, needed to be answered forcefully to end the massive trade deficit. A 1995 history of the department relates, "In the 1980s, under the leadership of Secretary Malcolm Baldrige, the Department of Commerce again became a major force in national policy making. The International Trade Administration was strengthened with new trade promotion and policing powers. The Commerce Secretary was named by the President to chair a Cabinet-level Trade Strike Force to search out unfair trading practices and recommend corrective measures.... Commerce took a lead role in supporting passage of the Export Trading Company Act of 1982 to provide new export-related jobs by allowing small- and medium-sized businesses to enter exporting.... In one six-day stretch in June 1985, Secretary Baldrige held trade conferences with General Secretary Gorbachev of the Soviet Union, Prime Minister Gandhi of India, and Premier Zhao Ziyang of the People's Republic of China."

In his 1983 report, Baldrige discussed budget-cutting measures: "During the past three years, we have cut our budget by 36 percent and reduced administrative personnel by the same percentage. Our new Review Board is saving millions by ensuring that no federal funds go to organizations that owe the government money or submit proposals that are unworthy of funding. I am please also that our Plain English program has boosted productivity. More than 3,000 persons have undergone training. The result: better comprehension and better performance." In his 1985 report, he expanded on the accomplishments of his tenure: "We improved service to exporters by speeding up the processing of export license applications. Less than 5 percent of all applications received were still pending at year's end. Eighty percent of all license requests, with a total dollar value of more than $53 billion, were approved. The Department's Office of Export Administration returned another 16 percent of applications for additional information and denied less than 1 percent of them.... At the same time, we improved our efforts to ensure that sensitive goods and technology do not fall into the wrong hands. The number of checks on potentially illegal shipments was up 80 percent. As a result, we kept more than $1 billion in strategically controlled technology from being diverted to adversary nations." In 1987, when Vice-president Bush began his campaign for president in 1988, many assumed that if elected he would name Baldrige as his secretary of the Treasury.

Baldrige's greatest love was rodeos: in the 1960s, he had become a professional steer roper, and in March 1981, two months after he became commerce secretary, he participated in a rodeo in Phoenix, Arizona, where he was named as the Professional Rodeo Cowboy's Association Man of the Year. In 1984, he was elected to the National Cowboy Hall of Fame. On 25 July 1987, while in Walnut Creek, California, practicing for an upcoming rodeo, the horse he was on fell on top of him, crushing him. Malcolm Baldrige was dead at the age of 64. The Japanese minister of international trade and industry, Hajime Tamura, called Baldrige's death "an immeasurable loss" to U.S.-Japanese trade relations. His body was flown back to Connecticut and buried in the cemetery in Woodbury.

The Department of Commerce sponsors the Baldrige Award, given annually to companies or individuals cited for their attempts to improve the quality of their product or the way of making their product. Award winners include AT&T and Motorola. In honor of the secretary, a research ship operated by the National Oceanic and Atmospheric Administration was renamed the *Malcolm Baldrige*.

References: "Baldrige, Malcolm," in Charles Moritz, ed., *Current Biography 1982* (New York: H. W. Wilson, 1982), 20–23; Brownstein, Ronald, and Nina Easton, *Reagan's Ruling Class: Portraits of the President's Top 100 Officials* (Washington, DC: Presidential Accountability Group, 1982), 30; Department of Commerce, *Annual Report of the Secretary of Commerce, Fiscal Year 1983* (Washington, DC: Dept. of Commerce, 1984), 2; Department of Commerce, *Annual Report of the Secretary of Commerce, Fiscal Year 1985* (Washington, DC: Dept. of Commerce, 1986), 2; Department of Commerce, Office of the Secretary, *From Lighthouses to Laserbeams: A History of U.S. Department of Commerce* (Washington, DC: GPO, 1995), 25; Levy, Peter B., *Encyclopedia of the Reagan-Bush Years* (Westport, CT: Greenwood, 1996), 30–31.

CALVIN WILLIAM VERITY, JR.

1917–

Calvin William Verity, Jr., known as C. William Verity, replaced Secretary of Commerce Malcolm Baldrige following Baldrige's death. Verity, who served for the final two years of the Reagan administration, helped expand trade with the Soviet Union at the same time that he advocated trade sanctions against Japan. He was born in Middletown, Ohio, on 26 January 1917, the son of Calvin William Verity, Sr., chairman of the American Rolling Mill Company, a steel manufacturer in Middletown founded by his father, and Elizabeth (née O'Brien) Verity. Verity attended Choate School in Wallingford, Connecticut, and Phillips Exeter Academy in Exeter, New Hampshire, from which he graduated in 1935. He received a bachelor's degree in economics from Yale University in 1939.

Verity then began a trip around the world that was interrupted by World War II. He moved to New York City, where he went to work for the advertising firm of Young & Rubicam, later serving as the manager of a restaurant owned by the president of the firm. After a year in New York, however, Verity returned to Ohio to work for his family's company, starting as a laborer in the company's plant in Hamilton, Ohio. This work was interrupted by Verity's volunteering for the U.S. Navy in 1942 and serving in the Pacific. He was discharged, in 1946, with the rank of lieutenant. Returning to the American Roll Milling Company, which in 1948 became ARMCO, he took care of labor relations at the Middletown, Ohio plant, then moved, in 1950, to the company's plant in Ashland, Kentucky. In 1953, he became assistant to the works manager in charge of staff operations. Four years later, he was moved back to Middletown to serve as director of ARMCO's organizational planning and company development. In 1965, he was elected as president

and chief executive officer of ARMCO and, in 1971, chairman of the board. It was during these years that ARMCO grew to become the fourth largest steel manufacturer in the world, with revenues, in 1971, of $1.3 billion. Verity made ARMCO the first steel company to offer the eight-hour working day and the first group insurance program; because of this attitude, the steelworkers' union has never struck ARMCO.

An influential industrialist who was widely praised in the business community as a leader on international trade issues, Verity was named by President Richard M. Nixon in 1973 as a member of the President's Export Council and by President Gerald R. Ford as a member of the Advisory Committee on Trade Negotiations in 1975; he served on the latter council until 1981. In 1981, President Ronald Reagan named him chairman of the President's Task Force on Private Sector Initiatives, and he later served as a member of the task force's advisory council and its chairman in 1985. From 1979 to 1984, Verity served as cochairman of the U.S.-U.S.S.R. Trade and Economic Council, established in 1973 to urge détente between the two nations in the area of trade. Verity believed, at this time, that trade barriers should be lowered between the United States and the Soviet Union, while deterrents to lower-priced goods coming from Japan and other Asian nations should have been raised.

Following the death of Secretary of Commerce Malcolm Baldrige, Clarence J. Brown, a former Republican congressman from Ohio who had served as deputy secretary of commerce since 1983, became secretary ad interim. Many industry presidents urged President Ronald Reagan to name S. Bruce Smart, the undersecretary of commerce in charge of the International Trade Administration, to permanently succeed Baldrige. Instead, on 9 August 1987, Reagan named the 70-year-old Verity to the vacancy. Verity, who had stepped down as ARMCO chairman in 1982, was praised for his leadership. Richard Lesher, president of the U.S. Chamber of Commerce, remarked, "[Verity] is a good friend of the business community who really understands that the trade deficit is partly of our own making and partly the result of how our trading partners play the game." At the announcement of his nomination, he told Reagan, "I'm just happy at this opportunity at what I think is a historic time in international trade. . . . I look forward to trying to help you in the job of making this country more competitive." Despite his record, Verity was questioned during confirmation hearings—not by Democrats, but by Republicans who felt he had been too friendly toward potential Soviet trade. Nonetheless, he was confirmed on 13 October 1987 by an 84 to 11 vote.

On the day he was sworn in as the twenty-eighth secretary of commerce, the Dow Jones Industrial Average suffered one of the worst losses in American history at that time, a record 508 points. Verity spent the first months of his tenure trying to calm fears of an economic slowdown such as the one that proceeded the Great Depression in 1929. He was part of a delegation to Moscow in April 1988 to investigate ways to broaden trade, while he criticized the Japanese for refusing to abide on international restraints on fishing practices that killed whales, and to this end he threatened Japan with an embargo of that country's fish products into the United States. When the Office of Management and Budget recommended placing a tax on export licenses, Verity denounced the measure and fought it. Despite being attacked by conservative Republicans who did not like his trade policies vis-à-vis the Soviet Union, Verity remained a free trader.

Verity left office at the end of the Reagan administration in January 1989 and returned to private life. In 1993, he coauthored *Unlocking Japan's Markets: Seizing Marketing and Distribution Opportunities in Today's Japan*.

References: Brandes, Stuart D., "Verity, George Matthew," in John A. Garraty and Mark C. Carnes, gen. eds., *American National Biography* (New York: Oxford University Press; 24 vols., 1999), 22: 329–330; Verity, C(alvin) William, Jr.," in Charles Moritz, ed., *Current Biography 1988* (New York: H. W. Wilson, 1988), 588–591.

ROBERT ADAM MOSBACHER
1927–

Robert Mosbacher was a key strategist and fundraiser for Vice-president George Bush in the 1988 election and was named to his cabinet post in reward for his service. His tenure at Commerce was marked by his attempts, particularly with Japan and the European Economic Community, at ending trade restrictions against American goods. Born on 11 March 1927 in Mt. Vernon, New York, he was the son of Emil Mosbacher, a stock trader, and Gertrude (née Schwartz) Mosbacher. Mosbacher, was educated at Choate School in Wallingford, Connecticut, then Washington and Lee University in Lexington, Virginia, where he graduated in 1947 with a bachelor's degree in business administration. He then went to work for his father for a year, after which he moved to Texas, beginning a thirty-year career in the oil business. Mosbacher opened a business with capital of about $500,000, all of his own money, but it was two years before he drilled his first well.

In 1954, after several years of hard work, Mosbacher's company drilled a well of natural gas that made him a millionaire. Over the years, he expanded the Mosbacher Energy Company into one of the largest energy businesses in the United States, with holdings in numerous states. In the 1960s, Mosbacher became acquainted with another oil man, George H. W. Bush. The two had many things in common: both were eastern moderate Republicans, both were the sons of wealthy men, and both had moved to Texas to enter the oil business. In 1964 and 1970, when Bush ran, unsuccessfully, for the U.S. Senate, Mosbacher raised money to finance his campaigns, as well as Bush's successful campaigns for a U.S. House seat in 1966 and 1968. He also served as Texas finance chairman for former Vice-president Richard Nixon's 1968 presidential campaign and as the Republican finance chairman for Texas in 1971 and 1972. In 1975, he was named the chief fund-raiser for President Gerald Ford's campaign and, in 1976, was named finance cochairman of the Republican Party. In 1980, he served as finance chairman along with another Bush friend, James A. Baker III, during Bush's unsuccessful run for the Republican presidential nomination. Mosbacher, in fact, was the man who told Bush to pull out of the race when his chances for capturing the nomination were slim, and to back the eventual nominee, former California Governor Ronald Reagan, in the hopes of being named as Reagan's running mate. Mosbacher proved correct, for Reagan did select Bush, and both men were elected. After the campaign, Mosbacher returned to Texas to continue his service as chairman and CEO of the Mosbacher Energy Company. From 1984 to 1985, he served as chairman of the National Petroleum Council.

In 1988, Vice-president Bush ran and won the Republican presidential nomination, with Mosbacher serving as his finance chairman, assisting in raising $75 million for the campaign effort. On 6 December 1988, Bush named Mosbacher as secretary of commerce. His nomination was widely praised in the business community. Arthur Levitt, Jr., the chairman of the American Business Conference, as well as the American Stock Exchange, said, "He's a great believer in our markets, a frontiersman in the best sense of the word in having built his own business." Mosbacher, an experienced sailor, announced that he intended to use the National Oceanic and Atmospheric Administration in the Commerce Department to expand its commitment to fighting pollution on the world's oceans. Although his nomination was opposed by Public Citizen, a public interest group that decried his fund-raising, Mosbacher was confirmed unanimously, on 31 January 1989, and took office as the twenty-ninth secretary of commerce.

His tenure, which lasted until 15 January 1992, was marked by threats to impose trade restrictions on Japan, South Korea, and European nations, which had either refused to lower tariffs against American goods or had heavily subsidized homemade items, making American products prohibitively expensive. He worked with the U.S. trade representative, Carla A. Hills, in trying to open Japanese markets and was key in placing economic sanctions on China after the Tiananmen Massacre in 1989.

Mosbacher resigned in December 1991 and became the finance chairman for President Bush's reelection campaign, returning to private business after Bush's defeat. On 3 September 1997, he was named as general finance chairman of the Republican Party.

References: Alexander, Herbert E., and Monica Bauer, *Financing the 1988 Election* (Boulder, CO: Westview Press, 1991), 77; Department of Commerce, Office of the Secretary, *From Lighthouses to Laserbeams: A History of U.S. Department of Commerce* (Washington, DC: GPO, 1995), 75; "Mosbacher, Robert Adam" in Charles Moritz, ed., *Current Biography 1989* (New York: H. W. Wilson, 1989), 416–420.

BARBARA HACKMAN FRANKLIN
1940–

Barbara Franklin served as the twenty-ninth secretary of commerce during the last year of the Bush administration, becoming the highest-ranking woman to serve under Bush. Born Barbara Hackman on 19 March 1940 in Lancaster County, Pennsylvania, she was the daughter of Arthur A. Hackman, the principal at the school his daughter later attended, and Mayme (née Haller) Hackman. In a letter to the author, Franklin wrote, "My father was always my biggest supporter. His philosophy was: 'You can do whatever you want to do. But, what ever it is, do it well.' This was not a common view at that time for a father to have, and I appreciate his being ahead of his time." Hackman received her bachelor's degree in political science with distinction in 1962 from Pennsylvania State University, and her Master's of Business Administration degree (MBA) in 1964 from Harvard Business School, where she was one of 12 women in a class of 632. In 1966, Hackman went to work for the Singer Company in New York City as a market analyst, moving up to corporate planning and environmental analysis, studying Singer's competition in business around the world. In 1969, Citibank hired her as a financial analyst, and, when Congress enacted a law against the company's interests, Hackman recommended that a government relations department be established. For this work, she was asked to head up the new department and was named as an assistant vice president of the company.

In 1971, Hackman left Citibank to go to work in the White House for President Richard M. Nixon, helping the administration to recruit talented women for jobs in the administration. She wrote that she intended to stay in Washington for only six months, but actually remained for two years. Upon her recommendations, the number of women in high positions in the government tripled in her first year. In 1973, Nixon named her as commissioner of the newly established U.S. Consumer Product Safety Commission. Confirmed by the Senate for a seven-year term, she ultimately served until 1979. As Franklin writes, "It was a new agency without processes for getting things done or organization. So, it fell to me as the first vice chairman to begin to organize Commission meetings, create a budget process, and the like. I stayed for nearly 6 years, concentrating on safety for children, pioneering the use of cost/benefit analysis (then a new concept), and pushing for a better managed governmental approach to the control of carcinogens."

Franklin then joined the faculty of the Wharton School of Business at the University of Pennsylvania as a senior fellow and later as director of the school's government and business program, where she worked to help bring MBA candidates to Washington, D.C., to study. At the same time, she was offered seats on various corporations, including Dow Chemical, Aetna Insurance, and Westing-

house; she was the first woman to hold directorships in some of these companies. In the late 1980s, she was called by the American Management Association one of the fifty most influential corporate directors in the United States. Because she was considered an expert on corporate auditing and financial reporting practices, in 1982 she was appointed by President Ronald Reagan as a member of the President's Advisory Committee for Trade Policy and Negotiations,; she served until 1986. In 1984, she established Franklin Associates, an international trade consulting firm.

A longtime Republican who had attended every Republican National Convention since 1972, Franklin was a good friend of George Bush. On his election in 1988, Bush offered Franklin the positions of head of the Small Business Administration and governor of the Federal Reserve System, but she refused. She did, however, serve for a second time as a member of President's Advisory Committee for Trade Policy and Negotiations (1989 to 1992) and as a delegate to the United Nations General Assembly.

On 26 December 1991, Bush announced that Franklin would succeed Secretary of Commerce Robert A. Mosbacher, who was resigning to become the finance chairman of Bush's 1992 reelection effort. Franklin ultimately served until the end of the Bush administration on 20 January 1993. Perhaps her biggest accomplishment in office was her trip to China, of which she wrote, "In December 1992, I undertook a difficult mission to China, the purpose of which was to normalize business relations with that country and remove one of the sanctions the US had placed on China after the incidents at Tiananmen Square in June, 1989. The mission was important and successful. . . . I left for China . . . with the express purpose of reconvening with my counterpart the Joint Commission on Commerce and Trade. The mission was historic for these reasons: I was the first Cabinet minister to visit China officially after the events of June 1989. That act removed the sanction on ministerial contact, signaling to US businesses that it was now appropriate to go to China. They did, and two-way trade and investment in China mushroomed during the ensuing years. Had this mission not been made, US businesses would have lost a year or two to other global competitors . . . I met with Premier Li Peng, my counterpart Li Lanqing, and numerous other officials. And, I was pleased to bring back $1 billion in signed contracts for US companies, including that large Boeing order. A great deal of the other business flowed from this trip."

After leaving office, Franklin established Barbara Franklin Enterprises, a private consulting and investment firm of which she is the president and chief executive officer.

References: The author wishes to thank Mrs. Franklin for her letter to him, 1 May 2000, on her life and cabinet service, without which this entry could not have been completed. *Who's Who in America: 2000 Millennium Edition* (New Providence, NJ: Marquis Who's Who; two volumes, 2000), 1: 1595.

RONALD HARMON BROWN
1941–1996

Ronald Brown was the first African American named as secretary of commerce. The son of William Brown and Gloria Brown-Carter, Brown was born in Washington, D.C., on 1 August 1941. He attended Hunter College Elementary School in New York City, and preparatory schools, Rhodes School, and the Walden School. In 1958, he enrolled in Middlebury College in Vermont, and he became the first black to enter the Sigma Phi Epsilon fraternity. In 1962, he graduated from Middlebury with a bachelor of arts degree in political science, and he immediately joined the U.S. Army. He was trained at Fort Eustis, Virginia; afterward, he was sent to West Germany to learn logistics. Promoted to the rank of captain, Brown was sent to South Korea, where he assisted in the training of Korean soldiers to interact with American troops.

When he returned to the United States, in 1966, Brown went to work as a welfare caseworker for the National Urban League in New York City. He attended night classes at St. John's University School of Law and was awarded a law degree in 1970. In 1971, he was elected as the district leader for the Democratic Party in Mount Vernon, New York. Two years later, he moved to Washington, D.C., and once again joined the National Urban League as their spokesman. By 1978, he had risen to vice-president of the Washington office of the Urban League. In an interview, Brown said of this period, "Coming to Washington was a way for me to establish my own identity, my own base, my own group of contacts and relationships, putting me into a spokesman role at a . . . time when the Urban League was a very important organization."

Brown soon attracted the attention of Senator Ted Kennedy, Democrat of Massachusetts, who was, at the time, contemplating a challenge to President Jimmy Carter for the 1980 Democratic presidential nomination. Kennedy asked Brown to serve as his deputy manager; he assisted Kennedy in winning the California primary, although the senator failed in winning his party's nomination. Nonetheless, the work Brown did for Kennedy earned him respect inside the party, and in 1980 Kennedy, the chairman of the Senate Judiciary Committee, named Brown as the committee's chief counsel. In 1981, Kennedy named Brown as his own general counsel and staff director. Later in the year, Brown became the chief counsel to the Democratic National Committee, then he was named as the party's deputy chairman in 1982. In 1981, Brown joined the Washington lobbying firm of Patton, Boggs & Blow as a partner. Brown soon became one of Washington's top lobbyists, representing the Duvalier government of Haiti in Washington, as well as corporate clients like Toshiba, Sony, and American Express. In 1988, Brown joined the presidential campaign of the Rev. Jesse Jackson as his strategist. Although Jackson had no chance of winning his party's presidential nomination, he hoped for either a vice-presidential nomination or some impact on the party platform. At the Democratic National Convention in Atlanta, Brown served as an intermediary to the campaign of Massachusetts Governor Michael Dukakis, who won the presidential nomination. Five months after the convention was held, Paul G. Kirk, Jr., the chairman of the Democratic National Committee, announced he would not seek a second four-year term as chairman. With the backing of Senator Kennedy, Brown was elected to the position, the first time an African American was named as a major party chairman. He then spent the next three years coordinating with the party to identify states that the party had lost in the last three presidential elections and to change party turnout.

In 1992, Brown helped heal party rifts, which allowed Arkansas Governor Bill Clinton to win the White House for the Democrats for the first time in twelve years. Almost immediately, Brown was considered for a cabinet position. Journalist Elizabeth Drew wrote, "The job of ambassador to the United Nations was first offered to Ronald Brown, to whom the Clintons were very grateful for the way he played his role as Democratic Party chairman in 1992, but Brown wanted to be Secretary of State. He felt that the UN job would be just another in a line of blacks who had filled the post, and he turned it down. After it was made clear that the State Department wasn't to be his, he accepted Secretary of Commerce." He was confirmed by the Senate, on 21 January 1993, and sworn in as the thirty-first secretary of commerce.

Writers Jeffrey Trammell and Gary Osifchin described his first year in office: "Having worked toward passage of the North American Free Trade Agreement during most of his first year in office, Brown is expected to focus his attention in the coming year on increasing U.S. exports. This will be done through two means: one, the Clinton Administration's National Export Strategy with the aim of total exports exceeding $1 trillion and the creation of 6 million new jobs by the year 2000; two, a new Administration initiative designed to improve American industry's inter-national technological competitiveness. Brown has also been and will continue to be active in promoting the Administration's health care and 'reinventing government' plans."

Almost immediately after he took office, Brown ran into questions of corruption. In August 1993, allegations arose that Brown had accepted, or discussed accepting, a $700,000 bribe by a Vietnamese businessman to assist in lifting the U.S. trade embargo on Vietnam. After telling his story to the FBI, the businessman, Ly Thanh Binh, went before a grand jury. The matter was still being investigated in 1995. Another allegation was that a woman paid Brown $400,000 for his part in a business in which he had done little or no work. But perhaps the most damaging allegation against Brown dealt with his numerous trips abroad with American businessman. Called "Brown junkets," or "junkets for cash," Brown was accused of getting these businessmen seats on trade flights, which resulted in lucrative deals for them and their companies, in exchange for donations to the Democratic National Committee. Attorney General Janet Reno initially refused to appoint an independent prosecutor to investigate the validity of these allegations, but, on 16 May 1995, she asked for just such a special counsel.

All of these allegations were made moot with Brown's death on 3 April 1996, and the investigations of the special counsel came to a halt. Brown had accompanied a number of American industry leaders on a mission to investigate ways to assist the rebuilding of the Balkan area following a number of conflicts there. Brown and thirty-four others, including fourteen executives, died in a plane crash near Dubrovnik, Croatia. He was just 54 years old. Brown was the second commerce secretary to die in office. *Time* magazine called him "a master politician and a super salesman of American industry."

References: "Brown, Ron(ald Harmon)," in Charles Moritz, ed., *Current Biography 1989* (New York: H. W. Wilson, 1989), 73–76; Drew, Elizabeth, *On the Edge: The Clinton Presidency*

(New York: Simon & Schuster, 1994), 28; Fedarko, Kevin, "The Joyful Power Broker: Washington Mourns Ron Brown, the Secretary of Commerce Who Conquered Barriers and the World," *Time,* 15 April 1996, 68–70; Trammell, Jeffrey B., and Gary P. Osifchin, eds., *The Clinton 500: The New Team Running America, 1994* (Washington, DC: Almanac Publishing, 1994), 111.

MICHAEL "MICKEY" KANTOR

1939–

Michael Kantor served as the U.S. trade representative from 1993 to 1995, during which time he helped to conclude the final act of the Uruguay round of the General Agreement on Tariffs and Trade. Michael Kantor was born on 7 August 1939 in Nashville, Tennessee, the son of Henry Kantor, the owner of a furniture store. Kantor was brought up under the influence of his grandfather, Isadore Kantor, a bookbinder from Brooklyn who was a member of the Socialist Party. Mickey Kantor attended Vanderbilt University in Nashville and graduated with a bachelor's degree in business and economics in 1961. He then entered the U.S. Navy, serving until 1965, with the rank of lieutenant. After he was discharged, he studied law at the Georgetown University Law Center, which awarded him a doctor of law degree in 1968. He worked for a time at the Office of Legal Services in Florida, representing migrant workers.

In 1972, Kantor entered the political field when he went to work as a staff coordinator for the vice-presidential campaign of R. Sargent Shriver, who was running with Senator George McGovern of South Dakota. The Democratic ticket lost that year to the Republicans, and, in 1973, Kantor moved to California, where he established the Los Angeles Conservation Corps to help underprivileged youth. In 1974, he served as the manager for the successful reelection campaign of Senator Alan Cranston, and, in 1976, Kantor ran

the unsuccessful presidential campaign of former California Governor Edmund G. "Jerry" Brown. In 1980, Kantor served as the California chairman of President Jimmy Carter's unsuccessful reelection effort, and, in 1982, he again served as Brown's campaign manager, this time in an unsuccessful run for a U.S. Senate seat. In 1984, Kantor was the California chairman for the unsuccessful presidential campaign of former Vice-president Walter Mondale. In 1988, Kantor, after this string of defeats, stayed out of presidential politics. In 1991, he served on the Christopher Commission, headed by former Assistant Secretary of State Warren M. Christopher, which investigated allegations of police misconduct in Los Angeles.

In 1992, Kantor decided to reenter presidential campaigning. Although his former client Jerry Brown was trying to capture the Democratic presidential nomination, Kantor instead backed Arkansas Governor William Jefferson "Bill" Clinton, and Kantor was named as Clinton's campaign manager. Kantor helped steer Clinton through the early primaries and, after the nomination was wrapped up, recommended Senator Albert Gore, Jr., of Tennessee, as his running mate. Following Clinton's election, Kantor was a member of the transition team and was in line for a position in the administration. He was considered along with Ron Brown, chairman of the Democratic National Committee, former Arizona Governor Bruce Babbitt, and former Reagan administration official Clyde Prestowitz, Jr., to serve as U.S. trade representatives. On 24 December 1992 Clinton named Kantor to the position. Established in 1962, the Office of the U.S. Trade Representatives coordinates all foreign and domestic trade matters among all government departments, as well as negotiating trade deals with foreign countries; the office reports directly to the president. Kantor spent three years in this position, threatening Japan with trade sanctions if that nation continued to "dump" cheap steel on the American market, intimating similar penalties on goods from the European Community (EC; now the European Union [EU]) because of subsidies from European governments, and helping to negotiate the North American Free Trade Agreement (NAFTA), which dropped trade restrictions between the United States, Mexico, and Canada.

On 3 April 1996, Secretary of Commerce Ron Brown was killed. Nine days later, Clinton named Kantor as Brown's successor, and Kantor was confirmed and sworn in as the thirty-second secretary. His tenure lasted until 30 January 1997. Kantor served in a caretaker role, making sure that business was conducted properly through the 1996 election. Kantor had hoped to be named as White House chief of staff, but was passed over in favor of Erskine Bowles.

Kantor went to work for the lobbying firm of Mayer, Brown & Platt. In 1998, he was hired by Clinton to serve as legal counsel during Clinton's impeachment proceedings before the U.S. Senate. The following year, he was retained by the Washington Wheat Commission to represent the wheat industry before the World Trade Organization.

Reference: "Kantor, Mickey," in Judith Graham, ed., *Current Biography Yearbook 1994* (New York: H. W. Wilson, 1994), 289–293.

WILLIAM MICHAEL DALEY
1948–

William Daley served as chairman of the White House Task Force to help enact the North American Free Trade Agreement (NAFTA) in 1994 and as secretary of commerce in the second term of the Clinton administration. Born in Chicago, Illinois, on 9 August 1945, Daley was the son of Richard J. Daley, a powerful Chicago mayor (1955–1976), and Eleanor (née Guilfoyle) Daley. Daley attended local schools, then earned a bachelor's degree in political science from Loyola University in Chicago in 1970 and a law degree from the John Marshall Law School in Chicago in 1975. Admitted to the state bar that same year, he joined the law firm of Daley & George. In 1985, he joined

the Chicago law firm of Mayer, Brown & Platt. He then worked as vice-chairman of Amalgamated Bank of Chicago, from 1989 to 1990, then president and CEO from 1990 to 1993. He returned to Mayer, Brown & Platt from 1993 until 1997.

An adviser to his brother when Richard Daley was elected mayor in 1989, Daley was also a key Democratic adviser in the presidential campaigns of Walter Mondale in 1984 and Michael Dukakis in 1988 and the Senate campaign of Senator Joseph R. Biden of Delaware. In 1992, he was the Illinois chairman for the presidential campaign of Arkansas Governor William Jefferson Clinton and expected to be named either secretary of transportation or secretary of commerce. He was passed over for both positions, but in mid-1993 Clinton named Daley as special counsel to the president for the passage of NAFTA. The trade agreement, a landmark treaty between the United States, Mexico, and Canada, promised, in effect, to make the borders between the three countries invisible to trade. Traditional Democratic constituencies, such as labor unions and environmentalists, argued against passage, but Daley persevered, gaining enough votes for its passage in November 1993. Clinton then named Daley as a member of the board of the Federal National Mortgage Association, known as "Fannie Mae."

During the 1996 campaign, Daley helped to bring the Democratic National Convention back to Chicago for the first time since the riots of 1968. Daley served as cochairman of the host committee; he raised millions of dollars to host the convention. The success of the convention led many to believe that Clinton would name Daley to a cabinet vacancy.

The resignation of Secretary of Commerce Mickey Kantor after the election made this possible, although Clinton also considered Representative Bill Richardson of New Mexico, former Texas Governor Ann Richards, and West Virginia Governor W. Gaston Caperton. On 13 December 1996, Clinton named Daley to the position. Confirmed by the Senate on 30 January 1997 after a heated debate over his support of NAFTA, Daley was sworn in as the thirty-third secretary.

His tenure was marked by a sort of "rebuilding program," forced by the death of Secretary Ron Brown in 1995, at a time when allegations that Brown sold junkets to foreign businessmen for campaign contributions to the Democratic Party, as well as that he allowed computers and other sensitive technology to go to China without adequate controls, were under investigation. Daley immediately initiated an expanded ethics program, advising people at the Commerce Department that "they must live up to the spirit as well as the letter of ethics laws." Daley used several trade missions in his first year to expand American trade. He also configured the department to deal with the rapidly expanding field of e-commerce, and helped launch Census 2000. In July 2000 Daley resigned to head up Al Gore's presidential campaign.

References: "Daley Plans Extended DOC Ethics Program," *Commerce People,* March/April 1997, 2; "Daley, William M." in Elizabeth A. Schick, ed., *Current Biography 1998* (New York: H. W. Wilson, 1998), 145–147.

NORMAN YOSHIO MINETA
(1931–)

In 2000 Norman Mineta became the first Asian American to be named to a cabinet position. Born in San Jose, California, on 12 November 1931, the son of Kay Kunisaku Mineta and Kane (née Watanabe) Mineta, he grew up in San Jose's "Japantown." During World War II he and his family were incarcerated in a government internment camp for Japanese Americans in Wyoming. The experience changed Mineta. As he later said in an interview, "Some say the internment was for our own good. . . . But even as a boy of 10, I could see that the machine guns and the barbed wire faced inward." After the war, the Mineta family returned to San Jose. Mineta received his B.S. degree from the University of California at Berkeley in 1953 and served in the army from 1953 to 1956.

From 1962 to 1964, Mineta served on the San Jose Human Relations Commission. In 1966, he was elected as a member of the board of directors of the San Jose Housing Authority. Elected to the San Jose city council in 1967, the following year he was elected vice mayor and in 1971, mayor. A longtime Democrat, Mineta was elected to a seat in the U.S. House of Representatives in 1974 and served from 3 January 1975 until 10 October 1995. Perhaps his greatest accomplishment was the passage of legislation compensating Japanese Americans for internment during World War II. Mineta was also a leader in transportation issues; he rose to become, shortly before he left the House, the chairman of the House Committee on Public Works and Transportation (1993–1995). In 1992, President-elect Bill Clinton wanted to name Mineta as his secretary of transportation, but Mineta wanted to remain in the House. During his two years as chairman, the first Asian American to hold the chairmanship of a House committee, he worked closely with the administration to formulate transportation policy and appropriations. In 1995 Mineta resigned his seat to become vice-president of Lockheed Martin's Transportation System and Services Division. In 1997, Secretary of Transportation Rodney Slater appointed him chairman of the Federal Aviation Administration's National Civil Aviation Review Commission.

Mineta was named as William Daley's replacement on 29 June 2000 and sworn in on 21 July 2000. Deputy Secretary of Commerce Robert L. Mallett had been considered the leading candidate for the position. A factor in Mineta's selection was probably the Clinton administration's desire to improve relations with Asian Americans in the wake of charges of anti-Asian prejudice in the Wen Ho Lee case. The appointment was widely praised.

References: Who's Who in America: 2000 Millennium Edition (New Providence, NJ: Marquis Who's Who; 2 vols., 2000), 2: 3384; Lacey, Marc, "First Asian-American Picked for Cabinet," *New York Times,* 30 June 2000, A15.

COMMERCE AND LABOR

The Department of Commerce and Labor, the first federal agency established in the twentieth century, brought the number of cabinet departments to nine. It survived for ten years, with four men having served as the head of the department.

In his message to Congress of 3 December 1901, two months after he assumed the presidency, Theodore Roosevelt asked Congress to establish a new department to handle national commercial matters. "There should be created a Cabinet officer, to be known as Secretary of Commerce and Industries, as provided in the bill introduced at the last session of Congress," he wrote. "It should be his province to deal with commerce in its broadest sense; including among other things whatever concerns labor and all matters affecting the great business corporations and our merchant marine." After several hearings, a bill was drafted creating the department. In support, Congressman Charles F. Cochran remarked, "What do we expect to accomplish by creating a Department of Commerce? The name of the new Department answers the question. We hope to develop new ideas of profitable trade and foster old ones. We hope to facilitate industrial development and promote commerce at home and abroad. . . . We will look to the Department to give direction to the energetic campaign that had for its object the conquest of the markets of the world by American merchants and manufacturers." On 14 February 1903, an act of Congress established the Department of Commerce and Labor, and Roosevelt named George B. Cortelyou to the post as the agency's first director. According to the first annual report, released in 1903, "The Department was established in the executive offices of the White House, where the first steps toward organization were taken. On March 17 temporary quarters were obtained for the personal staff of the Secretary at No. 719 Thirteenth Street N.W. On June 16 the present office at No. 513 Fourteenth Street N.W. [the Willard Building] was formally opened." In its first year, the department had 1,289 employees and a budget of $9.8 million.

On 1 July 1904, Cortelyou resigned to become the chairman of the Republican National Committee and run Roosevelt's reelection campaign, and the president asked

Republican Rep. Victor Howard Metcalf to be the second secretary. According to biographer Paul Heffron, Metcalf was "acknowledged as an efficient and economical administrator."

On 12 December 1906, Secretary of the Navy Charles J. Bonaparte resigned to become Roosevelt's attorney general; Metcalf was subsequently shifted to the Navy Department. Roosevelt selected Oscar Solomon Straus to succeed Metcalf. Solomon, a member of the prestigious Straus family of New York and a former minister to Turkey, became the first Jewish American to hold a cabinet position. During his term, which lasted slightly more than two years, Straus spent much of his time dealing with issues relating to Japanese immigration, particularly to the state of California. Straus later wrote of Commerce and Labor, "The scope of the department as constituted then was probably the largest of the nine branches of the Government. It was charged with promoting the commerce, mining, manufacturing, shipping, and fishery industries of the country, as well as its transportation facilities and its labor interests; in addition it had jurisdiction over the entire subject of immigration. It had twelve bureaus: corporations; manufactures; labor; lighthouses; census; coast and geodetic survey; statistics, including foreign commerce; steamboat inspection; immigration and naturalization; and standards."

When William Howard Taft became president in 1909, Straus accepted another term as U.S. ambassador to Turkey, and was replaced by the fourth and final man to hold the post of secretary of commerce and labor: Charles Nagel. Nagel, a former member of the Missouri legislature and a noted St. Louis jurist and corporate attorney, also became the first man to serve in the post for an entire four-year term. During his tenure, the first treaty between the United States, Russia, Great Britain, and Japan to ban pelagic seal hunting in Alaska was signed. He complained, in each of his four reports, of the rents paid by the government to lease space in ten buildings across Washington to house the department, showing that in 1909 alone the department paid $66,000 for rent, including $1,500 for a "department stable." In his 1912 report, the last for Nagel and the department, the secretary wrote that appropriations for the fiscal year ran to $15.9 million, a decrease of $236,135 from the previous year. He ended by writing, "This year I have given a very extensive account of the Department's work in the hope that some impression of the extent of that work may be given."

From its inception in 1903, labor leaders were opposed to the new department because it combined business with labor in one agency, and they worked diligently in Congress to have a separate department established. After ten years and opposition from President Theodore Roosevelt and then from President William Howard Taft, a new law was drafted and, although Taft wanted to veto it, on 4 March 1913, his final day in office, he signed it into law. The cabinet now had ten posts. Woodrow Wilson, on his first day as president, named William C. Redfield as the secretary of commerce and William Bauchop Wilson as the secretary of labor.

See also Department of Commerce; Department of Labor

References: Department of Commerce and Labor, *First Annual Report of the Secretary of Commerce and Labor, 1903* (Washington, DC: GPO, 1903), 5, 50; Department of Commerce, Office of the Secretary, *From Lighthouses to Laserbeams: A History of U.S. Department of Commerce* (Washington, DC: GPO, 1995), 4; Richardson, James D., ed. *A Compilation of the Messages and Papers of the Presidents, 1789–1902* (Washington, DC: GPO; 9 vols., 1 app., 1897–1907), 15: 6647.

GEORGE BRUCE CORTELYOU
1862–1940

A close friend of Theodore Roosevelt, George Cortelyou served as the first secretary of commerce and labor, as postmaster general, and as secretary of the Treasury, all within a six-year span. Born on 26 July 1862 in New York City, the son of Peter Crolius Cortelyou and Rose (née Seary) Cortelyou, George Cortelyou was educated at the Hempstead Institute, in Hempstead on Long Island, and at the State Normal School in Westfield, Massachusetts, from which he graduated in 1882. Although he studied music for a short time, he turned to the art of stenography, and became an expert in shorthand. From 1883 until 1885, he worked for the New York firm of James E. Munson as a verbatim law reporter.

After working as the principal in New York's preparatory school system until 1889, Cortelyou joined the U.S. Customs service as a stenographer. Two years later, he was transferred to Washington, D.C., to work as a clerk in the postmaster general's office. In 1895, Postmaster General Wilson S. Bissell recommended him to President Cleveland because of his stenographic ability, and Cortelyou became the president's executive clerk. When Cleveland left office, he suggested to his successor, William McKinley, to keep Cortelyou on, and he was named as assistant secretary to the president. Cortelyou served in this capacity for three years; in the final year, he assisted the president when his own secretary, John Addison Porter, became ill, and Cortelyou officially took over as secretary in April 1900.

In September 1900, President McKinley was shot while attending a fair in Buffalo, New York. Cortelyou was at his side at the time of the shooting and remained by the president until he died less than a week later. Under McKinley's successor, Theodore Roosevelt, Cortelyou served as more than a secretary—he was the president's intimate and closest advisor.

On 14 February 1903, Congress established the ninth cabinet department, the Department of Commerce and Labor. Two days later, Roosevelt named Cortelyou as the first secretary of the new cabinet department. Senator Chauncey Depew of New York reported the nomination favorably to the Senate and asked for immediate consideration and, with a voice vote showing no opposition, Cortelyou was confirmed. One biography of him states, "In this new office he demonstrated his capacity for organization. He had to create the executive force of his department out of entirely new materials, except where bureaus were transferred to him from other departments." In his first and only annual report as secretary, Cortelyou wrote, "The Department deals with the great concerns of commercial and industrial life. To be of service to these interests it must have their hearty cooperation and support. It must be a Department of business. It must be progressive, but at the same time conservative. It must not deviate from its course from the pathway of justice, strict and impartial. It must be nonpartisan in the highest and broadest sense. It must recognize no distinction as between large and small interests, as between the affluent or powerful and the humblest citizen. If it attempts to occupy a field that properly belongs to private endeavor, it will inevitably fail to realize the high hopes of its present wellwishers."

Cortelyou served until 30 June 1904, when he resigned to become chairman of the Republican National Committee and run Roosevelt's 1904 reelection campaign. When Cortelyou was accused, during the campaign, of accepting contributions for political favors, Roosevelt's political opponents called for an end to "Cortelyouism." In the end, the charges came to nothing, and the president was reelected.

On 4 March 1905, Cortelyou was nominated by Roosevelt as postmaster general, considered the most political of the cabinet offices. Dorothy Fowler, in a history of the Post Office Department, wrote, "When George Cortelyou became head of the Post Office Department in March 1905, the precedent was established for a practice which by now has become generally recognized—that is, the rewarding of the chairman of the national committee with the Cabinet position of Postmaster General." Cortelyou was familiar with the inner workings of the department, having worked there as a clerk ten years earlier. He spent much of his time on party activities, holding both positions until he left the Post Office on 3 March 1907. Much of his work dealt with extending patronage for the Republican Party. When Secretary of the Treasury Leslie Shaw asked to leave the administration, Cortelyou resigned from the Post Office to take over as secretary of the Treasury, a post he assumed on 4 March 1907, the third cabinet post he held under Roosevelt. During his tenure, which lasted for the rest of the Roosevelt administration, Cortelyou battled to contain the financial panic of 1907. His work to prepay government bonds led to a lessening of the crisis and earned him high praise for his leadership. Biographer Paul J. Kubik writes, "Aware of the difficulties caused by the inflexible, population-based structure of the National Banking System, Cortelyou, anticipating the later Federal Reserve arrangement, proposed that the banking facilities of the country be divided up along regional lines. A reserve framework would then be established in each individual zone, with the reserves of that area held within the zone." Although Secretary of War William Howard Taft was considered Roosevelt's hand-picked successor, many in the Republican Party sought to nominate Cortelyou for the presidency instead. Roosevelt, although a close friend of Cortelyou, issued a statement from the White House that he supported Taft.

Cortelyou left government on 4 March 1909 and went to work in New York City for the Consolidated Gas Company. He died there on 23 October 1940 at the age of 78.

References: "Cortelyou, George Bruce," in *The National Cyclopædia of American Biography* (New York: James T. White; 57 vols., suppls. A-J, 1897–1974), 14: 18–20; Department of Commerce and Labor, *First Annual Report of the Secretary of*

Commerce and Labor, 1903 (Washington, DC: GPO, 1903), 51; Ford, Benjamin Temple, "A Duty to Serve: The Governmental Career of George Bruce Cortelyou" (Ph.D. dissertation, Columbia University, 1963); Fowler, Dorothy Ganfield, *The Cabinet Politician: The Postmasters General, 1829–1909* (New York: Columbia University Press, 1943), 287; Kubik, Paul J., "George B. Cortelyou," in Bernard S. Katz and C. Daniel Vencill, eds., *Biographical Dictionary of the United States Secretaries of the Treasury, 1789–1995* (Westport, CT: Greenwood, 1996), 87–90.

VICTOR HOWARD METCALF
1853–1936

Victor Metcalf was the second man to serve as the secretary of commerce and labor, and he later served as secretary of the navy, both during the administration of Theodore Roosevelt. Victor Metcalf, the son of William Metcalf and Sarah (née Howard) Metcalf, was born in Utica, New York, on 10 October 1853. He attended public schools in Utica, as well as the Utica Free Academy and Russell's Military Institute in New Haven, Connecticut, before attending Yale College in 1872. He left Yale after his junior year, but entered the Yale Law School, from which he graduated with a law degree in 1876. He began a private practice in Utica but, two years after graduating, left New York for Oakland, California.

Metcalf became a leading attorney in Oakland and, in the late 1890s, was an important figure in local Republican politics. In 1898, he was elected to the U.S. House of Representatives, serving from 1899 until 1904. A member of the House Committee on Naval Affairs, he pushed to have more battleships built in government shipyards. During his time in the House, he remained in close contact with President Theodore Roosevelt. On 1 July 1904, Secretary of Commerce and Labor George B. Cortelyou resigned from his position, and Roosevelt asked Metcalf to accept the secretary of commerce and labor position. Metcalf served from 1 July 1904 until 12 December 1906 and, in that time, according to the *New York Herald-Tribune,* "One of his most important reports was on the probable effect of the enactment of a bill to restrict a day's labor to eight hours on all government work and all work let by the government to private contractors." Metcalf joined his predecessor, Cortelyou, in asking for new office space for the department. In his annual report for 1905, Metcalf wrote, "it seems to me imperative that Congress should at once authorize the leasing, for a term of years, of a building large enough to accommodate the various bureaus and offices of the Department now occupying rented buildings [spread across the city]. . . . The delay, inconvenience, and expense incident to the transaction of daily business by so scattered an organization are self-evident."

On 12 December 1906, Secretary of the Navy Charles J. Bonaparte resigned to succeed Attorney General William H. Moody, who was appointed to the Supreme Court. Roosevelt then moved Metcalf to Navy. During his tenure, which lasted until 13 November 1908, "sixteen battleships and their auxiliaries made a cruise which was considered one of the most remarkable in naval history until that time," the Great White Fleet tour, in which these ships steamed around in the world in a demonstration of American naval power.

By the end of 1908, Metcalf was ill, and he resigned from the Navy secretaryship. Metcalf went to work as an attorney and banking executive. He died in Oakland, California, on 20 February 1936, at the age of 82. Metcalf was buried in Mountain View Cemetery in Oakland.

References: Department of Commerce and Labor, *Reports of the Department of Commerce and Labor, 1904: Report of the Secretary of Commerce and Labor and Reports of Bureaus* (Washington, DC: GPO, 1905), 48; Department of Commerce and Labor, *Reports of the Department of Commerce and Labor, 1905: Report of the Secretary of Commerce and Labor and Reports of Bureaus* (Washington, DC: GPO, 1906), 56; Heffron,

Paul T., "Victor H. Metcalf," in Paolo E. Coletta, ed., *American Secretaries of the Navy* (Annapolis, MD: Naval Institute Press; 2 vols., 1980), 1: 482–487; O'Gara, Gordon C., *Theodore Roosevelt and the Rise of the Modern Navy* (Princeton, NJ: Princeton University Press, 1943); Smith, William Henry, *History of the Cabinet of the United States of America, from President Washington to President Coolidge* (Baltimore, MD: Industrial Printing Co., 1925), 441.

OSCAR SOLOMON STRAUS
1850–1926

Oscar Straus was the first Jew to sit in the cabinet. A noted diplomat who had served as an ambassador in both Republican and Democratic administrations, Oscar Straus was also the third man to serve as the secretary of commerce and labor. Straus was born in the village of Otterberg, Bavaria, on 23 December 1850, the son of Lazarus Straus and Sara (née Straus) Straus, who were first cousins. Oscar's father left for America in 1852, arriving in Philadelphia and then moving to Talbottom, Georgia; he sent for his family, and they arrived when Oscar was four. They moved to Columbus, Georgia, in 1863, then to New York City in 1867. During these years, Oscar attended the Collinsworth Institute and private schools in Columbus. In 1867, Oscar entered Columbia College and, four years later, Columbia's Law School, from which he graduated in 1873.

After studying law in the offices of the New York City firm of William Jones and Whitehead, Straus opened his own firm of Hudson & Straus with New York attorney James A. Hudson. After eight years, Straus retired to join his father and brothers, who had established the firm of L. Straus & Sons, manufacturers and importers of china and glassware.

In 1882, Straus entered politics, serving as secretary to a group that favored the reelection of William R. Grace as mayor of New York. Two years later, he was a leading New

York supporter of Governor Grover Cleveland's bid for the White House. In 1887, the Rev. Henry Ward Beecher recommended Straus's name to Cleveland to be minister to Turkey. Confirmed by the U.S. Senate on 21 December of that year, Straus left the United States and visited Egypt, the Jewish quarter in Palestine (now Israel), and Syria. During his two-year tenure in Constantinople, Straus spent much of his time protecting American missionary schools there. Admired by the Turkish government, Straus was asked by the sultan to arbitrate a matter between the Turkish government and railroad magnate, Baron Maurice de Hirsch, on the construction of a rail line. With the 1888 election of Benjamin Harrison, a Republican, Straus resigned his ambassadorship and returned home. Straus met with the new president and asked for help to aid the condition of Jews in Russia, which Harrison mentioned in his State of the Union message in 1889.

Straus returned to private business. In 1896, when the Democrats, advocated the free coinage of silver, Straus, a Democrat, came out for William McKinley, the Republican candidate for president. On 27 May 1898, Straus was again offered the ministership to Constantinople, which he accepted. He was confirmed on 3 June and served until 1900. In 1899, during a meeting with Zionist Theodor Herzl, Straus recommended that a national Jewish homeland in the area of Mesopotamia (now Iraq) be considered by European and American Jews. After McKinley's assassination, Straus became a trusted and close adviser of the new president, Theodore Roosevelt. In 1902, Roosevelt named Straus to the Permanent Court of Arbitration in The Hague, the Netherlands, where he served until 1906. On 12 December 1906, Secretary of the Navy Charles Bonaparte resigned to become attorney general; to replace him, Roosevelt shifted Secretary of Commerce and Labor Victor Metcalf to Navy and asked Straus to replace Metcalf. In a meeting that had been held the previous January, he had said to Straus, "I don't know whether you know it or not, but I want you to become a member of my Cabinet. I have

a very high estimate of your judgment and your ability, and I want you for personal reasons. There is still a further reason: I want to show Russia and some other countries what we think of Jews in this country." Straus reported he told the president that he was interested in a cabinet position, but would not ask about it until Roosevelt broached the subject, and that he found the position to be "of the highest honor." On 17 December, after being confirmed by the Senate, Straus took his place among the cabinet as the third secretary of commerce and labor. He wrote in his autobiography, "In order to coordinate the work of the various bureaus I instituted the simple method employed by large business administrators of having the several bureau chiefs come together with me twice a month to discuss and confer regarding the more important administrative subjects. This enabled me to keep better informed and served to make the various heads of bureaus conversant with the whole scope of the Department, preventing overlapping and duplication of functions. I learned that this simple administrative method had never been made use of before in federal departments, but thereafter it was adopted by several of the other department heads."

In his three years as secretary, ending on 4 March 1909, Straus spent much of his time dealing with the issue of Japanese immigration to the United States and attitudes toward the new immigrants, particularly in California, traveling to California and Hawaii to assess the situation. In 1907, he oversaw the first public release of records relating to the first census, taken in 1790. He wrote in his annual report for 1908, "Our age has been very properly called an era of commercial development and expansion, and the United States, by reason of its many exceptional advantages, its boundless natural resources, and possessing a growing, intelligent, energetic, enterprising, and self-reliant population, is reaping a greater share of industrial and commercial prosperity than any of the other nations of the world. . . . As the head of the Department, it has been my constant aim to so administer its various branches as to afford the greatest amount of assistance, information, and guidance to the various industrial and commercial activities that come under its administrative scope."

Straus left office in March 1909, but the following month, with a recommendation by Secretary of State Philander C. Knox, President William Howard Taft offered Straus the ambassadorship to Turkey, the third time he would hold this post. Straus accepted and served until December 1910, when he resigned to run for governor of New York on the Progressive ticket in 1912. Although he was badly defeated, Straus did not leave politics. He joined with former President Taft in the League to Enforce Peace, an American group that advocated the establishment of a league of nations to end war. In 1925, Straus served as the chairman of the welcoming committee at the Sesquicentennial Exposition in Philadelphia, but he was already ill and died on 3 May 1926 in New York City.

References: Adler, Cyrus, "Oscar S. Straus: A Biographical Sketch," in George S. Hellman, ed., *Record of the Oscar S. Straus Memorial Association* (New York: Columbia University Press, 1949), 9; Department of Commerce and Labor, *Reports of the Department of Commerce and Labor, 1908: Report of the Secretary of Commerce and Labor and Reports of Bureaus* (Washington, DC: GPO, 1909), 7; Elkus, Abram I., "Straus, Oscar Solomon," in *DAB* 9: 130–132; "Straus Family: Oscar Solomon Straus," in John N. Ingham, *Biographical Dictionary of American Business Leaders* (Westport, CT: Greenwood; 5 vols., 1983), 4: 1379–1385; Straus, Oscar S., *Under Four Administrations: From Cleveland to Taft—Recollections of Oscar S. Straus* (Boston: Houghton Mifflin, 1922), 213.

CHARLES NAGEL
1849–1940

Charles Nagel was a little-known St. Louis jurist and corporate attorney for Adolphus Busch when selected by William Howard Taft to be secretary of commerce and labor, the fourth man to hold that position. Nagel was the last man to occupy that position, as well as the only one to hold it for a full four years. Charles Nagel, the son of German immigrants Hermann Nagel and Friedericke (née Litzmann) Nagel, was born on his family's farm in Colorado County, Texas, on 9 August 1849. Hermann Nagel took his family from Texas soon after the start of the Civil War and moved first to Mexico and then New York before finally settling in St. Louis, Missouri. It was there that Charles Nagel was placed in a boarding school for his elementary education; he later went to high school in that city. After receiving a year of private tutoring, he studied law at Washington University in St. Louis, while reading the law in the firm of Glover & Shepley.

In 1872, Nagel graduated from Washington University and then spent a year studying Roman law and political economy at the University of Berlin. He returned to St. Louis in 1873, and soon after he began a private law practice he joined the firm of Finkelnburg, Nagel & Kirby, which became one of the most important law firms in the southern part of the United States. Elected to the Missouri state legislature in 1881, Nagel also ran, unsuccessfully, for seats on the St. Louis City Council and on the state supreme court. In 1893, he was elected, as a Republican, as president of the St. Louis City Council, where he served until 1897.

Soon after his election as president of the United States, William Howard Taft tapped the completely unknown Nagel to head the Department of Commerce and Labor. Historian Paolo Coletta writes that Nagel was chosen "most likely as a reward to a Taft patron and to like-minded businessmen." In his four years as head of the agency, Nagel helped to establish the Chamber of Commerce of the United States, oversaw the 1910 census, and expanded the Bureau of Immigration and Naturalization. In his annual report for 1909, he wrote, "During the last four years the appropriations for the entire Department have been increased only 3.2 percent. It may be assumed that the activities of none of the older bureaus can be reduced, with proper regard to the needs to be served, and that some of the more modern bureaus, whose activities have been more or less experimental, must necessarily be extended. If appropriations are to be held at the present figures, it will therefore become necessary to make a dollar go farther than it has." Nagel was only able to maintain appropriations, avoiding budget cuts in the final fiscal year, when he decreased spending by more than $236,000 from the previous year. Nagel did about as well as could be expected of someone with so little governmental experience. Historian William Henry Smith writes, "His administration of the department was one of marked success. He brought it up to a high degree of efficiency." However, historian Coletta adds, "If Charles Nagel, at the Department of Commerce and Labor, did anything remarkable, it was to place his agency more than ever before the disposal of America's businessmen."

Nagel left office on 4 March 1913 when the department was split into separate Departments of Commerce and Labor. Returning to his law practice in St. Louis, Nagel appeared before the U.S. Supreme Court at least three times. Nagel died in St. Louis on 6 June 1940, two months before his ninety-first birthday.

References: Coletta, Paolo E., *The Presidency of William Howard Taft* (Lawrence: University Press of Kansas, 1973), 50, 256; Department of Commerce and Labor, *Reports of the Department of Commerce and Labor, 1911: Report of the Secretary of Commerce and Labor and Reports of Bureaus* (Washington, DC: GPO, 1912), 9; Department of Commerce and Labor, *Tenth Annual Report of the Secretary of Commerce and Labor, 1912* (Washington, DC: GPO, 1912), 7; Hinsdale, Mary Louise, *A History of the President's Cabinet* (Ann Arbor, MI: George Ware, 1911), 280; "Nagel, Charles," in *The National Cyclopædia of American Biography* (New York: James T. White; 57 vols., suppls. A-J, 1897–1974), 16: 356–357, D: 266; Smith, William Henry, *History of the Cabinet of the United States of America, From President Washington to President Coolidge* (Baltimore: Industrial Printing Co., 1925), 497.

DEFENSE

———⟫●⟪———

H oused in the world's largest office complex, the Pentagon, located in Virginia across the river from Washington, D.C., the Department of Defense is responsible for providing the armed forces needed to deter war and protect national security. From 1921 until 1945, about fifty proposals came before Congress to merge the Departments of War and Navy into a Department of National Defense in an effort to increase efficiency and cut costs. During this period, however, the secretaries of both departments opposed the move. With the end of World War II, however, the heads of the two departments, Robert Patterson (War) and James V. Forrestal (Navy), admitted that consolidation was gaining strength in Congress and agreed to a unification plan. After Congress held hearings regarding the move and drafted appropriate legislation, the National Security Act was enacted on 26 July 1947 and sent to President Truman for his signature. Under the act the offices of the secretary of navy and the secretary of war were merged, and a new office, the secretary of defense, was established with sole responsibility over the U.S. military. Four new offices—chiefs of staff of the army, navy, air force, and marines—were created and, with a separate chairman, constituted the Joint Chiefs of Staff. The act's purpose was "to provide a comprehensive program for the future security of the United States; to provide for the establishment of integrated policies and procedures for the departments, agencies, and functions of the Government relating to the national security; to provide three military departments for the operation and administration of the Army, the Navy . . . and the Air Force . . . to provide for their authoritative coordination and unified direction under civilian control but not to merge them; to provide for the effective strategic direction of the armed forces and for their operation under unified control and for their integration into an efficient team of land, naval, and air forces."

Almost immediately, as James Forrestal was being sworn in as the first secretary of defense, the department was faced with fighting the cold war against the Soviet Union. Yet, while Forrestal was the first secretary of defense, there was no Defense Department per se. In place of the War and the Navy Departments, Congress had created the National Military Establishment, which consisted of the Departments of the Army (originally the Department of War), the Navy, the Air Force, and several other agencies. It allowed the secretary of defense to retain control, but not complete authority, over the military branches, an inherent weakness that Congress sought to correct with the 1949 amendments to the National Security Act, on 10 August 1949. Forrestal, who had differences with President Truman over the new department's budget, had quit in early January 1949 and was replaced by Louis A. Johnson, a former assistant secretary of war who had been Truman's chief fundraiser in the 1948 presidential campaign. Johnson oversaw an explosion in the defense budget, from $14 billion in 1950 to $24 billion in 1951, due in large part to the Korean War. Johnson's motto was "a dollar's worth of defense for every dollar spent." His tenure was also marked by the Berlin blockade and the establishment of the North Atlantic Treaty Organization (NATO). However, because he was considered a political appointee, he was not well received by the rest of the government, and he resigned on 20 September 1950, replaced by General and former Secretary of State George C. Marshall.

Marshall, the first and last military man to run the Defense Department, served just fifty-one weeks. He is nonetheless considered the best secretary of defense in the nation's history. Under his leadership, American troop strength in Korea rose from 1.46 million in July 1950 to 3.25 million by June 1951; the number of American soldiers in Europe was increased; and several important treaties, including the ANZUS (Australia–New Zealand–United States) Pact, were signed to aid in western mutual defense. Finally, the department budget increased to $57 billion in 1952. Marshall had warned Truman upon taking the job that he would serve only a year, particularly to stabilize the Korean situation. His replacement was his deputy secretary, Robert A. Lovett. The son of a judge from Texas, Lovett was a lawyer and longtime military man who had risen to the rank of lieutenant commander. Lovett's chief goal was to end the Korean War, but at the same time to ask for budgets that would allow for continued military training and effectiveness in times of peace. In 1953 spending was down to $44 billion, less than in 1952, but Lovett oversaw continued troop and materiel mobilization to fight the Korean War. He left office on 20 January 1953, six months before the conclusion of the conflict. He was the last of Truman's four secretaries of defense.

The first of Dwight D. Eisenhower's three secretaries, Charles E. Wilson, was the president of General Motors when picked for cabinet duty, and he supervised the end of the Korean War as well as a massive reorganization of the department. The recommendations of the Rockefeller Commission, also called the Committee on Department of Defense Reorganization, concluded that Congress had given the secretary of defense more power than any other cabinet officer. In effect, the secretary was "the principal assistant to the President in all matters relating to the Department of Defense." Eisenhower sent several recommendations to Congress in his Reorganization Plan No. 6 of 20 April 1953. In it, he called for strict civilian control over the Office of the Secretary of Defense (OSD) and the decentralization of control to the Joint Chiefs of Staff. In his "New Look" plan, Eisenhower, backed by Wilson, called for more reliance on nuclear arms and strategic air power and less dependence on conventional weaponry. Under Wilson, budget figures ran from $30 billion in 1954 to $41 billion in 1958. Under Wilson's successors, Neil McElroy and Thomas S. Gates, budgets were (1959: $42 billion; 1960: $40 billion) similar.

Although John F. Kennedy's first choice for his defense secretary was former Secretary Robert A. Lovett, Lovett instead recommended the new president of Ford Motor Company, Robert S. McNamara. Taking office in January 1961, McNamara served until February 1968, the longest tenure in Defense Department history. McNamara, serving through the Kennedy and Johnson administrations, oversaw the Bay of Pigs incident, the Cuban Missile Crisis and the prosecution of the Vietnam War. The number of Americans in Vietnam grew from just a few hundred advisers in January 1961, to more than 535,000 troops by June 1968. When he submitted his resignation to go to work for the World Bank in 1968, McNamara had become one of the most controversial government figures in American history. He was replaced by attorney and defense expert Clark Clifford, who also spent most of his time concerned with Vietnam. The Vietnam issue dogged his successors who served in the Nixon administration: former Congressman Melvin Laird, former Secretary of Health, Education, and Welfare Elliot Richardson, and Central Intelligence Agency (CIA) Director James R. Schlesinger. It was Schlesinger who oversaw the end of American involvement in Vietnam. The department had seen four secretaries in eight years. Secretary Harold Brown directed department affairs during the Soviet invasion of Afghanistan, the passage of the SALT II treaty, and the taking of American hostages in Iran and the military response to the crisis. Budgets went from $116 billion in 1978 to $176 billion in 1981.

During the 1980s and early 1990s, the Defense Department became the largest, in expenditure, in the federal government. Under Secretaries Caspar Weinberger, Frank Carlucci, and Dick Cheney, budgets rose from $211 billion in 1982 to $291 billion in 1990. A massive building program, from increased troops, to the construction of new missiles, planes, tanks, and guns, highlighted the increase. The military buildup under Presidents Ronald Reagan and George Bush enabled the country to fight and win the Persian Gulf War in 1991; many consider that it also led to the "winning" of the cold war, which ended with the breakup of the Soviet Union in 1991.

The tenures of Les Aspin, William J. Perry, and former Senator William J. Cohen, all during the Clinton administration, faced problems of decreasing budgets and several military controversies, including the massacre of American troops in Somalia, the stationing of troops in Haiti and Bosnia, and the issue of homosexuals in the military. The budget rose to more than $250 billion for 1998.

Former secretaries remained active in the security area. On 4 February 1995, seven former secretaries, representing every administration, since Nixon, wrote an open letter to President Bill Clinton asking that the B-2 bomber program not be abolished under budgetary cutbacks.

The department is the only one not headquartered in Washington, D.C. Looking across the Potomac River, from Washington, D.C., one can see the Pentagon, the result of a master plan to house all the operations of the American military infrastructure under one roof. In 1941, the War Department was housed in seventeen buildings across the District of Columbia and, soon after a new building was opened that same year, it became filled and obsolete all at the same time. In 1941, however, Brigadier General Brehon B. Somervell, of the construction division of the U.S. Army Quartermaster General, proposed that a massive headquarters for the War Department be built on Arlington Farms, an extensive 67-acre plot in Virginia, where the Department of Agriculture kept an experiment station. A three story building with pentagonal sides and 5 million feet of office space was considered. Congress debated the proposal: Should the government expand outside of Washington, D.C.? Should land once set aside for the extension of Arlington National Cemetery be used? In the end, Congress approved the appropriation, which was signed into law by President Franklin D. Roosevelt on 25 August 1941.

Under contractor George E. Bergstrom, with the actual building being done by the

John T. McShain Company of Philadelphia, construction began in September 1941; two months later, with the Japanese attack on Pearl Harbor, the number of floors was expanded from four to five because of the need for additional space during the war. The first section of the building was completed on 30 April 1942, eight months after groundbreaking, and War Department staff began to move in. The entire building was completed on 15 January 1943, at a cost of about $80 million, $5 million more than the original estimate. It is the largest office building in the world and a major tourist attraction. Department historian Roger Trask writes, "The 5-story Pentagon building has 5 concentric rings connected by 10 spoke-like corridors ranging out from the inner, or A, ring. The combined length of the corridors and rings is 17 ½ miles, and the total gross floor area is more than 6.5 million square feet."

In the more than half a century since the department was established, twenty men have held the office of secretary of defense. The longest term of office to date is that of Robert McNamara, who served for eighty-five months, while the shortest is Elliot Richardson's four months. Of these twenty secretaries, ten had national security experience—having held an office where they gained knowledge or experience relating to national security matters. Seven of them worked prior to their service as secretary in the department of its predecessor agencies, the War and Navy Departments, while two others worked in related agencies (the Atomic Energy Commission, the CIA, or the State Department).

References: Cole, Alice C., Alfred Goldberg, Samuel A. Tucker, and Rudolph A, Winnacker, eds., *The Department of Defense: Documents on Establishment and Organization, 1944–1978* (Washington, DC: Secretary of Defense Historical Office, 1979); Trask, Roger R., *The Secretaries of Defense: A Brief History, 1947–1985* (Washington, DC: Office of the Secretary of Defense Historical Office, 1985), 3–8.

JAMES VINCENT FORRESTAL
1892–1949

See Secretary of the Navy,
1944–1947

LOUIS ARTHUR JOHNSON
1891–1966

Louis Johnson was a former assistant secretary of war before his service as the second secretary of defense. Johnson was born in Roanoke, Virginia, on 10 January 1891, the son of Marcellus Johnson and Katherine Leftwich (née Arthur) Johnson. Johnson attended schools in the Roanoke area before going to the University of Virginia and

earned a law degree in 1912. He then opened a private law practice in Clarksburg, West Virginia, joining a local lawyer in the firm of Rixey & Johnson. In one of his cases, he was named as a prosecutor for Harrison County and took the case all the way to the U.S. Supreme Court. There he met Philip Pendleton Steptoe, a leading attorney, and with him formed the firm of Steptoe & Johnson in 1913, which later became one of the largest firms in the state.

In 1917, Johnson, a Democrat, was elected to the West Virginia House of Representatives, where he served as the chairman of the judiciary committee and as majority floor leader. He had barely begun his service when he was inducted into the American Expeditionary Force sent into France to assist the Allied cause soon after the United States entered World War I. He served as head of his infantry unit at the battles of St. Mihiel and Meuse-Argonne. Discharged with the rank of major, he returned home in 1919 to continue his service in the state legislature, which ended in 1924. That year, he was a delegate to the Democratic National Convention in New York City.

Louis Johnson was an original organizer of the American Foreign Legion, founded in Paris in 1919; he later served as its national commander from 1932 to 1933. In 1936, he was named by President Franklin D. Roosevelt as assistant secretary of war, serving as the chief assistant to Secretary Harry H. Woodring. In that capacity, writes biographer Paolo Coletta, "[He helped] hasten . . . industrial preparedness and shortened World War II." During this period, he also served as chairman of the Finance Committee of the Democratic National Committee, first from 1936 until 1940 and again in 1948 during President Harry Truman's campaign for the presidency. In 1940, when Secretary Woodring stepped down, Johnson expected to be named as his successor; instead, President Roosevelt named a former secretary, Henry Stimson. Johnson resigned, returning to the practice of law. He later served as Roosevelt's personal representative to oversee Allied operations in India from 16 March until 17 December 1942. Journalist Drew Pearson reported that Johnson became a close friend of Indian independence activists Mohandas K. Gandhi and Jawaharlal Nehru.

In 1948, when President Truman ran for election, he selected Johnson as his personal campaign finance chairman. Johnson raised the funds to help Truman win against Republican Thomas E. Dewey. Truman then named Johnson the secretary of defense on 4 March 1949. There was an immediate uproar that Johnson's appointment was a political payoff, but his service as assistant secretary of war quieted his critics, and he was unanimously confirmed on 23 March. Johnson took the oath of office five days later. Officially, he was considered the secretary of the National Military Establishment, which did not become the Department of Defense until Congress amended the original National Security Act later in 1949.

Historian Bernard Weisberger calls Johnson "the polar opposite" of his predecessor,

Forrestal. His motto was that the American taxpayer "was going to get a dollar's worth of defense for every dollar spent" in defense of the nation. He canceled the construction of the aircraft carrier U.S.S. *United States,* because its deck held B-29 bombers, which Johnson felt duplicated the Air Force's B-36 bombers. With this announcement, Secretary of the Navy John L. Sullivan resigned, the start of what was called "The Revolt of the Admirals." Johnson quickly replaced Sullivan with a lawyer from Omaha, Francis P. Matthews, and the revolt died down.

Later, after Johnson ordered numerous cuts in the defense budget, his reasoning was questioned before a House Armed Services Committee hearing by Admiral Louis Denfield, chief of Naval Operations. Johnson then had Secretary of the Navy Matthews fire Denfield, which attracted political opposition to the department. Johnson's cuts in the budget came back to haunt him when the Korean War broke out, and it seemed for a time that the United States would suffer a quick and decisive defeat in Korea. When Johnson and Secretary of State Dean Acheson were blamed for mishandling American participation to save South Korea, Truman needed to use one of the two men as a scapegoat. In early September, word was leaked that Johnson was on the way out. He stormed into the White House to demand that the president publicly back him; if not, he could not carry out the orders of the department properly. Truman responded, "Well, Louis, if you feel that way about it, in your resignation, mention George Marshall as your successor." Crushed, Johnson resigned that day, 12 September 1950. In his letter to the president, he wrote, "When I undertook to serve as Secretary of Defense, at your request and that of Secretary Forrestal, I remarked to you privately and also remarked publicly that it was inevitable, in the conscientious performance of my duties as Secretary of Defense, that I would make more enemies than friends. Somewhat ruefully, I now admit, I was right." Historian Roger Trask writes, "In his last speech as secretary of defense the day before he left office, Johnson observed, 'When the hurly burly's done and the battle is won I trust the historian will find my record of performance creditable, my services honest and faithful commensurate with the trust that was placed in me and in the best interests of peace and our national honor.'"

Johnson returned to the law firm of Steptoe & Johnson, where he served until his death on 24 April 1966 at the age of 75. The Louis A. Johnson Veteran's Administration Medical Center in Clarksburg, West Virginia, is named in his honor.

References: Borklund, Carl W., *Men of the Pentagon: From Forrestal to McNamara* (New York: Frederick A. Praeger, 1966), 65–88; Coletta, Paolo E., "Johnson, Louis Arthur," in Richard S. Kirkendall, ed., *The Harry S Truman Encyclopedia* (Boston: G. K. Hall, 1989), 189–190; Coletta, Paolo E., "The U.S. Navy and Defense Unification, 1947–1953 (Newark: University of Delaware Press, 1981); "Johnson, Louis A(rthur)" in Charles Moritz, ed., *Current Biography 1949* (New York: H. W. Wilson, 1949), 298–300; Reardon, Steven L., *The Formative Years: 1947–1950* (Washington, DC: Historical Office, Office of the Secretary of Defense, 1984); Swanstrom, Todd, "Johnson, Louis A(rthur)," in Eleanora W. Schoenebaum, ed., *Political Profiles: The Truman Years* (New York: Facts on File, 1978), 258–260; "Texts of Johnson's Resignation and President's Reply," *New York Times,* 13 September 1950, 10; Trask, Roger R., *The Secretaries of Defense: A Brief History, 1947–1985* (Washington, DC: Office of the Secretary of Defense Historical Office, 1985), 12–14; Weisberger, Bernard A., *Cold War, Cold Peace* (New York: American Heritage, 1985), 96–97.

GEORGE CATLETT MARSHALL, JR.
1880–1959

See Secretary of State, 1947–1949

ROBERT ABERCROMBIE LOVETT
1895–1986

Robert Lovett, an expert in defense and national security matters, served as the secretary of defense during most of the Korean War, when he led the American military through the biggest buildup of manpower since the end of World War II. Born in Huntsville, Texas, on 14 September 1895, Robert Lovett was the son of Robert Scott Lovett, a Texas lawyer and Livinia Chilton (née Abercrombie) Lovett. At the age of 15, he moved with his parents to New York City when his father became the president of the Union Pacific and Southern Pacific Railroads, and he attended Yale University; however, in his junior year, his studies were interrupted by World War I. Lovett, who was enamored with flying and airplanes, organized a unit of fliers at Yale. He entered the U.S. Navy as an ensign, flying for a time with the British Naval Air Force until the United States entered the war in 1917, and he commanded a naval air squadron. Before being discharged from the navy he had risen to the rank of lieutenant commander. Lovett returned to Yale, which awarded him a bachelor's degree in 1918. He took postgraduate courses in business administration at Harvard University and a course in law at Harvard's law school, but left after a year. He then entered private business, beginning his career as a clerk at the National Bank of Commerce in New York City.

In 1921, Lovett moved to his father's firm, Brown Brothers, first as a clerk, then becoming a partner within five years. Because of his father's influence, Lovett was elected as a director of the Union Pacific Railroad in 1926. In 1931, he helped direct a merger of his old firm, Brown Brothers, and the Harriman banking concern that his father had become the head of, to form Brown Brothers Harriman & Co. In the 1930s, Lovett made several trips to Europe to consolidate his investments and, while in Germany, saw that Adolf Hitler was building up the German military, which had been destroyed after World War I. He made a report to Undersecretary of the Navy James Forrestal. Forrestal shared Lovett's findings with Secretary of War Henry Stimson, who was so impressed by Lovett's advice that he invited Lovett to come to Washington and serve as his assistant. Lovett accepted and, starting in December 1940, worked closely with the War Department on increasing American air power. In April 1941, Lovett was named as assistant secretary of war for Air. During World War II, he was in charge of the evaluation, oversight, and procurement of newer and better aircraft to fight the German and Japanese air forces. In September 1945, President Harry S Truman awarded Lovett the Distinguished Service Medal, calling him "the eyes, ears and hands of the Secretary of War in respect to the growth of that enormous American air power which has astonished the world and played such a large part in bringing the war to a speedy and successful conclusion." Secretary of War Robert Patterson added, "The fact that our air forces achieved their huge expansion in time was due more to Bob Lovett than to any other man." On 22 October 1945, Secretary Patterson established the Lovett Committee with the duty to advise the U.S. government on postwar intelligence activities. The existence of this council was unknown to outsiders until 1989, when an official Central Intelligence Agency history disclosed it, and its records have never been found. Lovett left government in November 1945.

Lovett returned to Brown Brothers Harriman, but a year later he was called back to Washington. General George C. Marshall was named secretary of state and, having worked closely with Lovett during the war, insisted on having him as undersecretary of state during his tenure. Lovett received high praise for his work on the Marshall Aid Plan to help Western Europe rebuild after World War II, as well as his labors to formulate the North Atlantic Treaty Organization (NATO). Lovett returned to private business in January 1949;

however, a year later, when Marshall was named as secretary of defense, he again insisted on having Lovett as deputy secretary. This position was one in which future secretaries were groomed.

As deputy secretary, Lovett handled the day-to-day administration of the Pentagon, gaining expertise in the formulation of the budget and materiel procurement. On 12 September 1951, after a year as secretary, Marshall announced his resignation and recommended Lovett as his successor. President Truman named Lovett as the fourth secretary of defense on 12 September 1951. During his tenure, which lasted until 20 January 1953, Lovett was faced with a Congress that did not want radical changes because of the feeling that Republican Dwight Eisenhower would be elected president in 1952. Department historians Roger Trask and Alfred Rosenberg write, "Lovett strongly supported universal military training, regarding it as the only viable long-term approach to building a reserve force, and thus making possible a small regular military establishment. A firm proponent of NATO, he played an important role when the NATO Council in February 1952 adopted force goals totaling 50 divisions and 4,000 aircraft to be achieved at the end of 1952." Nearing the end of his administration, Lovett detailed numerous recommendations in a long letter to President Truman, which Lovett wanted to have read by the incoming president, Dwight Eisenhower. These initiatives were met with such enthusiasm by the new president that he passed them on to Lovett's successor, Charles Wilson, who implemented many of them.

Lovett returned to Brown Brothers Harriman after leaving office in 1953. When Senator John F. Kennedy of Massachusetts was elected president in 1960, he initially approached Lovett to serve in his administration as either the secretary of state, secretary of defense, or the secretary of the treasury, which ever he wanted. Lovett declined the offers, telling Kennedy that after four separate tenures in government, he was tired. "It seemed every time I left, I had to go to have some of my insides taken out," he explained.

"I just can't afford to lose any more of my insides." Because of his health, he said, "It would be a disservice to the nation for me to accept a position calling for an eighteen-hour day." However, during the Cuban Missile Crisis in October 1962, he joined a select number of national security experts summoned by President Kennedy—the Executive Committee, including Vice-president Lyndon Johnson, Secretary of State Dean Rusk, Secretary of Defense Robert McNamara, and Lovett, all of whom provided the president with advice during the crisis. On 6 December 1963, President Lyndon Johnson awarded Lovett the Presidential Medal of Freedom, the highest award given to a civilian in the United States. Robert Lovett was involved in private business almost until his death. He retired from the board of the Union Pacific Railroad in 1978 but continued to serve as a partner with Brown Brothers Harriman. Suffering from cancer and liver failure, he died at his home in Locust Valley, New York, on 7 May 1986 at the age of 90.

References: Bernstine, Mel, "Lovett, Robert A(bercrombie)," in Eleanora W. Schoenebaum, ed., *Political Profiles: The Truman Years* (New York: Facts on File, 1978), 324–325; Borklund, Carl W., *Men of the Pentagon: From Forrestal to McNamara* (New York: Frederick A. Praeger, 1966), 114–137; "Lovett, Robert A(bercrombie)," in Anna Rothke, ed., *Current Biography: Who's News and Why, 1951* (New York: H. W. Wilson, 1951), 378–380; Trask, Roger R., and Alfred Goldberg, *The Department Of Defense, 1947–1997: Organization and Leaders* (Washington, DC: Historical Office, Office of the Secretary of Defense, 1997), 67–68; Watson, George M., Jr., "Lovett, Robert Abercrombie," in Richard S. Kirkendall, ed., *The Harry S Truman Encyclopedia* (Boston: G. K. Hall, 1989), 219–220; Wetterau, Bruce, *The Presidential Medal of Freedom: Winners and Their Achievements* (Washington, DC: Congressional Quarterly, 1996), 64.

CHARLES ERWIN WILSON
1890–1961

Charles Wilson may be best known for the famous statement "I thought what was good for the country was good for General Motors and vice versa." A respected businessman who headed one of the nation's largest automobile manufacturers, Charles Wilson served as the first of Dwight D. Eisenhower's three secretaries of defense. Wilson was born in Minerva, Ohio, on 18 July 1890, the son of Thomas Erwin Wilson, a principal in a Minerva school, and Rosalind (née Unkefer) Wilson, a teacher. He earned a bachelor's degree in electrical engineering from Carnegie Institute of Technology in Pittsburgh in 1909, then joined the Westinghouse Electric Company as an engineering apprentice. He began working on automobile electrical systems.

During World War I, Wilson worked on Westinghouse's program to build radio generators and auto generators for the U.S. Navy and U.S. Army. In 1919, Wilson moved to Remy Electric, a subsidiary of General Motors, as their chief engineer. Over the years, he moved up the ladder of General Motors corporate leadership and, by 1941, he was president of the company. During World War II, he spurred General Motors's effort to provide the U.S. military with cars and other automobiles, an endeavor that earned Wilson the U.S. Medal of Merit in 1946.

In 1952, General Dwight D. Eisenhower was elected president, and he put his campaign manager, Herbert Brownell, Jr., in charge of selecting cabinet officials. Brownell recommended Wilson as secretary of defense. Historians Chester Pach and Elmo Richardson write, "Eisenhower wanted Wilson to apply his administrative skills so that the Pentagon would operate smoothly and efficiently." During his confirmation hearings, he was asked whether he would make any decision that was adverse to the bottom line of General Motors because of his holdings in General Motors stock. He answered that he could not believe such a situation would happen, "because for years I thought what was good for the country was good for General Motors and vice versa." The quote was jumbled by reporters to read "What's good for General Motors is good for the country," and Wilson was seen by many as an insensitive executive. Nonetheless, he was confirmed by a vote of 77 to 6, although many believe that his relations with Congress were strained from that point.

Wilson had told Eisenhower that he would serve for only one four-year term. During that period, which was extended by six months, Wilson applied his managerial skills to the running of the nation's military. At the beginning of his administration, Wilson was hesitant to act on his own and usually conferred with Eisenhower on policy. Annoyed, the president reportedly said to him, "Charlie, you run defense. We both can't do it, and I won't do it. I was elected to worry about a lot of other things than the day-to-day operations of a department." Historian E. Bruce Geelhoed writes, "Wilson presided over a significant programmatic shift in defense operations between 1953 and 1957. He reduced the size of the standing army, encouraged the development of newer and more modern weapons systems, gave a special emphasis to upgrading nuclear technology, and instituted a cost-conscious approach to Pentagon management." Wilson was initially saddled with Truman's final 1953 budget of $44 billion, which had included Korean War expenditures. During his tenure, budgets went from $30 billion in 1954, to $34 billion in 1956, $33 billion in 1957, and $41 billion in 1958. Wilson's public pronouncements, which embarrassed him and the administration, eventually made him a liability. Once Eisenhower had won reelection in 1956 and Wilson asked to be replaced, the president searched for a replacement. He selected Neil H. McElroy, the chairman of Proctor and Gamble. Wilson's 4 years at the Pentagon ranked as the longest tenure until that of Robert McNamara.

Charles Wilson returned to private busi-

ness, eventually settling in Michigan and, a few years later, on an estate in Norwood, Louisiana. Wilson died there in his sleep on 26 September 1961 at the age of 71.

References: Borklund, Carl W., *Men of the Pentagon: From Forrestal to McNamara* (New York: Frederick A. Praeger, 1966), 138–160; Geelhoed, E. Bruce, *Charles E. Wilson and Controversy at the Pentagon* (Detroit: Wayne State University Press, 1979); Geelhoed, E. Bruce, "Executive at the Pentagon: Re-examining the Role of Charles E. Wilson in the Eisenhower Administration," *Military Affairs* 44: 1 (February 1980), 1–7; Pach, Chester J., Jr., and Elmo Richardson, *The Presidency of Dwight D. Eisenhower* (Lawrence: University Press of Kansas, 1991); "Wilson, Charles Erwin," in John N. Ingham, *Biographical Dictionary of American Business Leaders* (Westport, CT: Greenwood; 5 vols., 1983), 4: 1642–1647.

NEIL HOSLER MCELROY
1904–1972

Neil McElroy was the second of Dwight D. Eisenhower's three secretaries of defense. The son of Malcolm Ross McElroy and Susan Harriet (née Hosler) McElroy, both schoolteachers, Neil McElroy was born in Berea, Ohio, on 30 October 1904. He attended local schools in the Cincinnati area, then earned a bachelor's degree in economics from Harvard University in 1925. Upon returning to Cincinnati, McElroy went to work in the advertising department of Proctor and Gamble. Over the next twenty years, he advanced in the company, becoming the director of advertising in 1943, and advancing to president of Proctor and Gamble in 1948. In October of 1957, Eisenhower selected McElroy to replace Charles Wilson. McElroy was a political neophyte whose only prior political experience had been as chairman of a White House conference on education in 1955. As an executive, McElroy was earning $285,000 a year; at Defense, he would make $25,000 a year. "I guess you can say it isn't for profit," he told one interviewer. "It falls in the area of being a good citizen." After being confirmed by the Senate, McElroy was sworn in as the sixth secretary of defense on 9 October 1957. Almost immediately, he was forced to deal with the so-called Sputnik problem. Five days earlier, the Soviet Union had launched Sputnik, the first earth-orbiting satellite, which could open up a whole new area in intelligence and spying. A second Sputnik launch a month later made the situation all the more serious. However, while he did not see Sputnik as a major military threat, Secretary McElroy did realize the impact the launch would have on world opinion about American military leadership. Under his command, the American rocket *Vanguard* was rushed to the launch pad; its accidental explosion delayed, but did not end, America's race to space. Defense expenditures for space research within the Pentagon went from $20 million in 1956 to $110 million in 1958. The money spent led to the launch of *Explorer I* on 31 January 1959 and the formation, after he left office, of the National Aeronautics and Space Administration. McElroy spent much of his time allaying public and congressional fears over a supposed missile gap that was growing between the United States and the Soviet Union. Historians Chester Pach and Elmo Richardson write, "Like his predecessor, Charles E. Wilson, McElroy had headed one of the country's largest corporations. Unlike Wilson, who could not control bickering among the services or his own propensity toward embarrassing public statements, McElroy used his background in advertising to build support within the Pentagon and among the public for the president's policies."

On 12 March 1959, after less than two years at Defense, McElroy announced that he would retire. On 1 December he formally resigned; in his letter to President Eisenhower, he said that he was resigning "for reasons of an urgent nature." He did not formally leave office until his successor, Thomas S. Gates, had been confirmed by the Senate on 26 January 1960. Although his tenure was short, he

is considered to have been a major influence on cold war military and strategic thinking. In an interview before he left, he said, "It is our belief that we are prepared for either nuclear or non-atomic limited war."

Neil McElroy returned to Proctor and Gamble, where he worked as chairman of the board until October 1972, shortly before his death. McElroy died of cancer at his home in Cincinnati on 30 November 1972 at the age of 68.

References: Borklund, Carl W., *Men of the Pentagon: From Forrestal to McNamara"*(New York: Frederick A. Praeger, 1966), 161–183; "McElroy, Neil H(osler)," in Anna Rothke, ed., *Current Biography: Who's News and Why, 1951* (New York: H. W. Wilson, 1951), 387–388; Pach, Chester J., Jr., and Elmo Richardson, *The Presidency of Dwight D. Eisenhower* (Lawrence: University Press of Kansas, 1991), 183; Trask, Roger R., and Alfred Goldberg, *The Department Of Defense, 1947–1997: Organization and Leaders* (Washington, DC: Historical Office, Office of the Secretary of Defense, 1997), 73–74.

THOMAS SOVEREIGN GATES, JR.
1906–1983

The *Washington Post* wrote of Thomas Gates upon his death, "In the course of his federal service, which included some of the worst years of the Cold War, Thomas Gates was credited with modernizing the Navy by mothballing obsolete ships and concentrating on nuclear powered submarines and aircraft carriers; drawing attention to the necessity of being able to fight limited as well as global wars, and establishing clear administrative guidelines for the Navy and the Marine Corps and otherwise mitigating interservice rivalries." Gates, the son of Thomas Sovereign Gates, Sr., a lawyer and investment banker, and Marie (née Rogers) Gates, was born in Germantown, in Philadelphia, Pennsylvania, on 10 April 1906. Gates attended the Chestnut Hill Academy in Philadelphia before going to the University of Pennsylvania, where he earned a B.A. degree in 1928. Soon after, he entered his father's investment firm, Drexel & Co., where he worked until 1942, becoming a partner in 1940.

Gates, who had been a member of the U.S. Naval Reserve since 1935, was called into active duty in April 1942. After training in Rhode Island, he was assigned to the staff of the commander in chief of the Atlantic Theater of Operations to assist in the organization of the Naval Intelligence Center. Initially joining the crew of the aircraft carrier U.S.S. *Ranger,* Gates saw action during the landings of American troops at Casablanca in North Africa. In 1943, he was transferred to the U.S.S. *Monterey,* and was at the landings at Tarawa and Kwajalein Island and assorted strikes against New Guinea, New Britain, and the island of Truk. In 1944 and 1945, he assisted in the drafting of a planned American invasion of France called Operation Dragoon. After being awarded a bronze star and gold star and rising to the rank of lieutenant commander, he was discharged from active duty in October 1945. He then returned to the United States and resumed work at Drexel.

On 2 October 1953, President Dwight D. Eisenhower named Gates to succeed Charles S. Thomas as undersecretary of the navy. Gates later said that when Navy Secretary Robert B. Anderson called him to encourage him to accept the position that he was flabbergasted. Although he said he would serve only a year, he remained for three years, until Anderson was promoted to Treasury secretary. On 1 April 1957, Eisenhower named Gates to succeed Anderson. During this period, writes historian Roger Trask, "Gates strove to build up the Navy's fleet and strengthen its organization." In May 1959, Eisenhower named Gates as assistant secretary of defense. As the chief assistant to Defense Secretary Neil H. McElroy, he was considered McElroy's likely replacement should the secretary step down. Gates had replaced

Deputy Secretary Donald A. Quarles, who had died. McElroy had announced his intention to step down at the end of 1959,which he did on 1 December, and Gates was announced as his successor. Gates was sworn in, on an interim basis, the following day; Senate confirmation came on 26 January 1960.

In his nearly fourteen months as defense chief, Gates dealt with the growing peception of a "missile gap" between the United States and the Soviet Union. He argued that American defense policy was "to deter the outbreak of general war by maintaining and improving our present capability to retaliate with devastating effectiveness in case of a major attack upon us or our allies." The defense budget that he had the most impact on, for 1961, reached $45 billion. Considered a caretaker in his short tenure, he impressed defense observers. "It's a terribly difficult job," he said after leaving government. "I went to work at it. I didn't really think about the lame duck business." Much of his tenure was dedicated toward the defense establishment's transition from World War II and Korean-era weaponry to more modern weapons, such as the Triad, intercontinental ballistic missiles (ICBMs), submarine-launched ballistic missiles (SLBMs), and manned bombers. On 20 January 1961, Gates left the Pentagon. He was so highly regarded by both sides of the political spectrum that for a time after his election as president, John F. Kennedy considered naming him as his secretary of defense. Instead, Kennedy selected a Democrat, Robert McNamara.

Gates went to work as president of Morgan Guaranty Trust, eventually advancing to chairman of the board and chief executive officer in 1966. In 1976, his old shipmate from his Navy days, President Gerald Ford, asked him to replace George Bush as U.S. liaison, with the rank of ambassador, to the People's Republic of China.

In May 1977, at the age of 71, Gates retired from public life. He died in Philadelphia on 25 March 1983 at the age of 76. The Ticonderoga class cruiser the U.S.S. *Thomas S. Gates* (CG 51) was named in his honor.

References: Borklund, Carl W., *Men of the Pentagon: From Forrestal to McNamara* (New York: Frederick A. Praeger, 1966), 184–205; "Gates, Thomas S(overeign), Jr.," in Charles Moritz, ed., *Current Biography 1957* (New York: H. W. Wilson, 1957), 201–203; Smith, J. Y., "Thomas Gates Dies; Defense Secretary Under Ike," *Washington Post*, 26 March 1983, B4; Trask, Roger R., *The Secretaries of Defense: A Brief History, 1947–1985* (Washington, DC: Office of the Secretary of Defense Historical Office, 1985), 26; Trask, Roger R., and Alfred Goldberg, *The Department Of Defense, 1947–1997: Organization and Leaders* (Washington, DC: Historical Office, Office of the Secretary of Defense, 1997), 75–77.

ROBERT STRANGE McNAMARA

1916–

More than two decades after the end of the Vietnam War, the name of Robert McNamara, more than any other, is inextricably linked to the disastrous policies of the American government during the war. McNamara, the son of Robert James McNamara, a sales manager, and Clara Nell (née Strange) McNamara, was born in San Francisco, California, on 9 June 1916. Robert McNamara attended local schools before graduating from the University of California at Berkeley with a bachelor of arts degree in economics and philosophy in 1937. He then studied at the Harvard Graduate School of Business Administration and earned his M.B.A. degree in 1939.

After leaving Harvard, McNamara worked for a year for the accounting firm of Price, Waterhouse, but returned to Harvard in August 1940, to teach at the business school. In 1943, he, along with other instructors at Harvard, were commissioned by the U.S. Army to transfer some of the lessons in business to the air war. This use of "stat control," basing bombing runs on statistics, became highly successful. Initially inducted as a captain, McNamara advanced to the rank of lieutenant colonel by the time he was discharged from active duty in 1946.

That same year, along with nine other stat control officers, McNamara went to work for the Ford Motor Company. He worked as a manager of planning and financial analysis. This group of economic analysts became known industry-wide as "the whiz kids." McNamara's skill and talent helped him advance rapidly, and by 1960, he was prepared to become the president, the first person outside the Ford family to hold that position. At the same time, Senator John F. Kennedy of Massachusetts was contemplating a run for the U.S. presidency. Through his contacts at Harvard he became aware of McNamara and his talent for running successful ventures. On 9 November 1960, McNamara was named as the president of Ford to succeed Henry Ford II. Five weeks later, although he was a registered Republican, McNamara was offered the defense post by President-elect Kennedy's brother-in-law, Sargent Shriver.

McNamara accepted the offer and was confirmed by the Senate. He was sworn in as the eighth secretary of defense on 21 January 1961. Historians Roger Trask and Alfred Goldberg write, "Although not especially knowledgeable about defense matters, McNamara immersed himself in the subject, learned quickly, and soon began to apply an 'active role' management philosophy, in his own words, 'providing aggressive leadership —questioning, suggesting alternatives, proposing objectives and stimulating progress.'"

During his tenure at the Pentagon, which lasted seven years, the longest such service at the Department of Defense to date, McNamara saw the department through the disastrous Bay of Pigs invasion of Cuba in April 1961 and the Cuban Missile Crisis in October 1962, in which he advocated a naval quarantine, not a nuclear strike, on Soviet missiles on Cuba), and he promoted the idea of "flexible response"—the idea that U.S. forces could respond to any threat in the world with a varying stockpile of weaponry. It was during his administration that the idea of mutually assured destruction (MAD), allowing that the threat of mutual destruction of the

Soviet Union and the United States by nuclear weapons precluded the use of such weapons, was first put forward. In his annual report for 1962, McNamara wrote, "The most significant aspect of Defense policy in fiscal year 1962 was the emphasis given to the creation of a more flexible deterrent for the United States . . . military policies and programs were adjusted in line with this objective during the past year."

The assassination of President Kennedy on 22 November 1963 did not end McNamara's work. He served closely with President Lyndon Johnson, especially in the area of increasing the number of American advisers to Vietnam from a few hundred, when he first took office in 1961, to more than half a million troops fighting a ground war by the time he left. McNamara was so involved in the planning and execution of the war that the conflict has been called by some McNamara's War. In 1967, in order to understand how the conflict had taken shape, McNamara ordered the in-house collection of all papers dealing with the policy in Vietnam, from the Truman administration up until the present time.

In 1971, after McNamara was out of office, the papers were leaked to the press and became known as the Pentagon Papers, detailing the top-secret policy making that went into making the war possible. The report, consisting of some 3,000 pages of narrative and more than 4,000 additional pages of added exhibits that clearly indicated that the government had acted covertly to get the United States involved in Vietnam from the late 1940s, shocked many. On 29 November 1967, just two months short of seven years in office, McNamara was appointed by Johnson as head of the International Bank for Reconstruction and Development, also known as the World Bank. Many believe that McNamara's failure to win the Vietnam War led to his reassignment. In his letter of resignation to Johnson, McNamara explained that George Woods, the man McNamara was succeeding, came to him in 1967 and told the defense secretary that he wanted McNamara to be his successor. Telling Woods that he felt obligated to remain as long as Johnson needed him, His successor at the Pentagon, Clark Clifford, was not sworn in until March 1968, making McNamara the longest-serving secretary of defense in the nation's history.

On 28 February 1968, his last day in office, McNamara was awarded the Presidential Medal of Freedom by President Johnson. McNamara then served as president of the World Bank from 1968 until 1981.

By the mid-1980s, questions over McNamara's handling of the Cuban Missile Crisis and Vietnam still lingered. Starting in 1987, and lasting until 1992, he was involved in five historic meetings with Soviet and Cuban officials, talking over how the crisis was managed and what steps could be taken in the future to avoid such a dilemma. The meetings also showed that had McNamara's advice during the missile crisis been ignored, the Soviets most likely would have started a nuclear war. In 1995, to understand where he and his advisers had gone wrong over Vietnam, McNamara visited Vietnam, speaking with former government officials. In a rare and historic meeting, he talked with General Vo Nguyen Giap, who had masterminded the final assault on South Vietnam in 1975.

In the preface of his 1995 work, *Retrospect: The Tragedy and Lessons of Vietnam,* McNamara wrote, "We in the Kennedy and Johnson administration who participated in the decisions on Vietnam, acted according to what we thought to be the principles and traditions of this nation, yet we were wrong, terribly wrong. We owe it to future generations to explain why." He asserts in the book that he was having second thoughts about administration policy in Vietnam in the later 1960s and became an opponent of the war when he finally left the Pentagon in 1968; this fact, however, was not known until the book was published. Many blame McNamara for the indelible scar the Vietnam War left on the American psyche.

References: Barrett, David M., "The Mythology Surrounding Lyndon Johnson, His Advisers, and the 1965 Decision to Escalate the Vietnam War," *Political Science Quarterly* 103: 4 (1988–1989),

637–663; Borklund, Carl W., *Men of the Pentagon: From Forrestal to McNamara* (New York: Frederick A. Praeger, 1966), 206–236; Department of Defense, *Department of Defense Annual Report for Fiscal Year 1962, Including the Reports of the Secretary of Defense* (Washington, DC: GPO, 1963), 3; Hendrickson, Paul, *The Living and the Dead: Robert McNamara and Five Lives of a Lost War* (New York: Alfred A. Knopf, 1996); McNamara, Robert, *Retrospect: The Tragedy and Lessons of Vietnam* (New York: Times Books, 1995), 4; "McNamara, Robert S(trange)," in Charles Moritz, ed., *Current Biography 1960* (New York: H. W. Wilson, 1961), 291–293; "McNamara, Robert Strange," in John N. Ingham, *Biographical Dictionary of American Business Leaders* (Westport, CT: Greenwood; 5 vols., 1983), 2: 911–912; Shapley, Deborah, "McNamara, Robert Strange," in Bruce W. Jentleson and Thomas G. Paterson, senior eds., *Encyclopedia of U.S. Foreign Relations* (New York: Oxford University Press; 4 vols., 1997), 3: 128–129.

CLARK MCADAMS CLIFFORD

1906–1998

A highly respected attorney who had counseled Democratic presidents from Truman to Carter, Clark Clifford may be best remembered for his short service as secretary of defense in the last year of the Lyndon Johnson administration. Clifford, the son of Frank Andrew Clifford, an official with the Missouri Pacific Railroad, and Georgia (née McAdams) Clifford, was born in Fort Scott, Kansas, on 25 December 1906. The Clifford family moved, soon after Clark's birth, to St. Louis, where Clifford attended local schools. He then went to Washington University in St. Louis, where he received a bachelor's degree and, in 1928, a law degree. He practiced law in St. Louis from 1928 until 1943.

In 1944, Clifford was commissioned a lieutenant, junior grade, in the U.S. Naval Reserve. Assigned to the staff of the Pacific Naval Supply office in San Francisco, he later served as assistant to James K. Vardaman,

naval aide to President Harry S Truman; later, he succeeded Vardaman and until 1946 served the president directly. In February 1946, when Samuel Rosenman, the president's special counsel, resigned, Clifford was named first as his initial replacement and, on 27 June of that year, as his permanent replacement. During this period, Clifford worked to draft portions of the National Security Act of 1947, which established the Department of Defense; the National Intelligence Authority Act, which later became the Central Intelligence Agency; aided President Truman in his Middle East policy, recognizing the formation of the Jewish state of Israel; and supported Marshall Plan aid to Western Europe. Although he was persuaded to run for a U.S. senate seat from Missouri, he instead wanted to return to the practice of law. On 1 February 1950, he resigned and joined the Washington, D.C. firm of Clifford & Miller as a senior partner.

Although he was out of the politics during the Eisenhower years, he was an adviser for the presidential campaign of Senator John F. Kennedy in 1960, and he served on the Committee on the Defense Establishment after Kennedy had been elected. In May 1961, Kennedy named Clifford to the Foreign Intelligence Advisory Board, and in April 1963, he became chairman. Later, he served President Lyndon Johnson as a frequent adviser on the Vietnam War, traveling to southeast Asia in 1967 with General Maxwell Taylor. Unknown to most people, he was telling the president that further troop advances in Vietnam were a mistake. In a letter to Johnson on 17 May 1965, Clifford wrote, "I wish to make one major point. . . . I believe our ground forces in South Vietnam should be kept to a minimum, consistent with the protection of our installations and property in that country. My concern is that a substantial buildup of U.S. ground troops would be construed by the Communists, and the world, as a determination on our part to win the war on the ground. . . . This could be a quagmire. It could turn into an open end commitment on our part that would take more and more ground troops, without a realistic hope of ultimate victory. . . . I do not think the situation is comparable to Korea. The political posture of the parties involved, and the physical conditions, including terrain, are entirely different. . . . I continue to believe that the constant probing of every avenue leading to a possible settlement will ultimately be fruitful. It won't be what we want, but we can learn to live with it."

On 29 November 1967, Secretary of Defense Robert McNamara was named as president of the World Bank. For two months there was no announcement of a successor. Clifford, in his autobiography, writes that the day after he helped Johnson draft his 1968 State of the Union speech, the president called to see him. "'In the past,' he said, 'you've said your interest was foreign policy and national security. Now I've got exactly the right place for you—Secretary of Defense. It will suit you and you cannot possibly have any objection to it.' I knew at this time I could not refuse his request, nor did I wish to do so. I thanked him, and we shook hands."

After asking for McNamara's consideration on the nomination, Johnson publicly announced his choice on 19 January 1968. Four days after his nomination, the U.S.S. *Pueblo,* an intelligence ship monitoring North Korea, was captured by North Korean forces along with eighty-two of its crew. Dealing with this problem and the growing issue of Vietnam were on Clifford's plate after he was unanimously confirmed by the Senate on 30 January. This period coincided with the Tet Offensive in Vietnam, and a request, in the midst of massive American protests over the war, for an additional 205,000 American troops to be sent to fight. Clifford was not sworn in until 1 March, eventually serving a little more than eleven months as secretary.

Clifford's tenure has been considered by many historians to have been a caretaker position, and he spent much of his time letting Deputy Secretary Paul Nitze handle much of the day-to-day administration. When Clifford became secretary, the 1969 budget had already been completed, giving his department $78 billion, an increase of $3 billion from the 1968 budget. He worked closely on the 1970 budget, which eventually was $76 billion. He formed the Clifford Task Force, which was composed of former Secretary McNamara, Treasury Secretary Henry Fowler, CIA Director Richard Helms, Deputy Secretary Nitze, and several others, including himself, to discuss the increase in troop movements to Vietnam, and if so, how to meet that demand with more defense dollars and a cut in Johnson's Great Society programs. The task force eventually asked the questions: Should American policy in Vietnam be changed? Was there a chance to end the war sooner if the additional 205,000 troops were sent? On the day he took office, Clifford recommended that only 22,000 men be sent and that pressure be put on the South Vietnamese army to win the war. As historians Irwin and Debi Unger write, "Taken as a whole, it was more a proposal for slowing escalation than reversing it, though it did hold out the possibility of a more thorough reassessment following another major study." When Clifford became secretary, total U.S. troop strength in Vietnam was 525,000; although he was authorized to raise the number with an additional 24,500, he never did. Negotiations to end the war opened in Paris in May 1968, culminating in an end to a halt of the U.S. bombing of North Vietnam ordered by President Johnson on 31 October 1968. On his last day in office, 20 January 1969, Clifford was awarded the Presidential Medal of Freedom, the highest civilian award in the United States, by President Johnson.

The defeat of Democrat Hubert Humphrey, running for the presidency in 1968, left Clifford out of the government. Clifford returned to the practice of law. In 1991, he published his memoirs, looking back at a grand and influential life. Unfortunately for Clifford, in that same year, he and his law firm agreed to represent the Bank of Credit and Commerce International (BCCI), and Clifford and his law partner, Robert Altman, were later implicated in several illegalities. Altman was tried and acquitted, and Clifford was never tried because of his age and health. However, in 1992, a congressional committee investigating the bank found that Clifford and Altman "withheld from regulators critical information that they possessed to secret BCCI's ownership" of an American bank and that they "deceived regulators and the Congress concerning their own knowledge of and personal involvement in BCCI's illegalities in the United States." A long and distinguished career of government and private service thus ended under a cloud.

Clifford died at his home in Bethesda, Maryland, on 10 October 1998 at the age of 91.

References: "Clifford, Clark (McAdams)," in Charles Moritz, ed., *Current Biography 1968* (New York: H. W. Wilson, 1968), 90–93; Clifford, Clark; with Richard Holbrooke, *Counsel to the President: A Memoir* (New York: Random House, 1991); Frantz, Douglas, and McKean, David, *Friends In High Places: The Rise and Fall of Clark Clifford* (Little, Brown, 1995); Lytle, Mark H., "Clifford, Clark McAdams," in Bruce W. Jentleson and Thomas G. Paterson, senior eds., *Encyclopedia of U.S. Foreign Relations* (New York: Oxford University Press; 4 vols., 1997), 1: 267–268; U.S. Senate, Committee on Foreign Relations, "The BCCI Affair: A Report to the Committee on Foreign Relations, United States Senate, by Senator John Kerry and Senator Hank Brown" (Senate Print 102–140, 102d Congress, 2d Session, December 1992); Unger, Irwin, and Debi Unger, *Turning Point: 1968* (New York: Charles Scribner's Sons, 1988), 117.

MELVIN ROBERT LAIRD

1922–

Melvin Laird, Richard Nixon's selection for secretary of defense, was the first congressman to occupy that office. Laird was born in Omaha, Nebraska, on 1 September 1922, the son of Melvin Robert Laird, Sr., a Presbyterian minister, and Helen (née Connor) Laird. Melvin Laird, moved with his parents to Wisconsin when he was an infant, and he attended local schools in the village of Marshfield, in Wood County. He graduated

from Carleton College in Northfield, Minnesota, with a bachelor's degree in political science in 1942.

Laird enlisted in the U.S. Navy in 1942, receiving a commission to ensign two years later and was on board the U.S.S. *Maddox* in the Pacific fighting against the Japanese. While stationed in Cleveland in 1946, his father, then sitting in the Wisconsin State Senate, died, and Laird returned home and successfully ran, at age 23, as a Republican to occupy his father's vacant seat. He served until November 1952, when he was elected to the U.S. House of Representatives, representing the Seventh Congressional District. In his eight terms in the House (1953–1969), he became a noted expert in defense matters, serving as a member of the Defense Subcommittee of the House Appropriations Committee, continually criticizing the Pentagon for what he saw as wasteful spending. He authored *A House Divided: America's Security Gap* (1962) to discuss his views on foreign policy. Although he was a strong conservative, Laird voted for civil rights legislation in 1954 and 1964.

The election of Richard Nixon in 1968 allowed the Republicans to occupy the White House for the first time in eight years. Nixon asked Laird, a leading member of Congress, to take the Defense Department post, the first time the position was offered to a sitting member of Congress. The outgoing Johnson administration had left Nixon and his secretary of defense to deal with the Vietnam War. Laird, accepted the challenge; however, when he resigned from Congress to be sworn in as the tenth secretary, he said that intended to serve no more than four years. Laird spent much of that time implementing the Nixon formula of massive bombing of North Vietnam to force the country's leaders to the bargaining table; executing an invasion of Cambodia to close off the Ho Chi Minh Trail, used by the North Vietnamese and Vietcong to supply their troops in the south; and carrying out a planned gradual turning over of the war to the South Vietnamese army, a process called Vietnamization.

During his tenure, the Defense Mapping Agency and the Defense Security Assistance Agency were established. Laird was able to keep all four of his budgets relatively similar: $75.5 billion in 1970, $72.8 billion for 1971, $76.4 billion for 1972, and $78.9 billion in 1973. Troop levels in Vietnam went from 549,500 when he entered office to 69,000 on 1 May 1972; as well, combat deaths during the period declined more than 95 percent from 1968 levels. In his annual report for 1973, Laird wrote, "As a consequence of the success of the military aspects of Vietnamization, the South Vietnamese people today, in my view, are fully capable of providing for their own in-country security against the North Vietnamese." Privately, however, Laird disagreed with the 1972 Christmas bombings of Hanoi and Haiphong in North Vietnam, which did force the North Vietnamese to the bargaining table to end the war. This occurred, however, after he had announced that he was resigning. On 28 November 1972, Nixon named Elliot Richardson as Laird's successor. On 27 January 1973, two days before Laird left office, a settlement in the Vietnam War was signed in Paris.

Laird was in private business for a short time when Nixon called him back to the White House in June 1973 in the midst of the Watergate crisis to serve as counselor to the president for domestic affairs. On 26 March 1974, President Nixon awarded Laird the Presidential Medal of Freedom.

After leaving the White House in February 1974, Laird joined *Reader's Digest* as a counselor for national and international affairs, a post he still holds and, in 1992, he became the board chairman of COMSAT, a communications satellite concern. He is the author of *Energy, A Crisis in Public Policy* (American Enterprise Institute for Public Policy Research, 1977).

References: "Laird, Melvin R(obert)," in Charles Moritz, ed., *Current Biography 1964* (New York: H. W. Wilson, 1964), 241–243; Trask, Roger R., and Alfred Goldberg, *The Department Of Defense, 1947–1997: Organization and Leaders* (Washington, DC: Historical Office, Office of the Secretary of Defense, 1997), 86–89.

ELLIOT LEE RICHARDSON
1920–

See Secretary of Health, Education, and Welfare, 1970–1973

JAMES RODNEY SCHLESINGER
1929–

James Schlesinger served as the chairman of the Atomic Energy Commission (AEC) and as director of the Central Intelligence Agency (CIA) before serving as secretary of defense in the Nixon administration and then as secretary of energy in the Carter administration, the first man to hold this position in the new department. Born in New York City on 15 January 1929, James Schlesinger is the son of Julius Schlesinger and Rhea (née Rogan) Schlesinger. James Schlesinger received a bachelor's degree in 1950, a master's degree in 1952, and a Ph.D. degree in 1956 in economics from Harvard University. From 1955 until 1963, he taught economics at the University of Virginia and, for a time, lectured at the Naval War College (NWC). In 1960, his lectures at the NWC were published as *The Political Economy of National Security: A Study of the Economic Aspects of the Contemporary Power Struggle*. In 1963, Schlesinger began to work for the Rand Corporation as a staff analyst.

In 1969, Schlesinger joined the Nixon administration as assistant director of the Bureau of the Budget, where he worked on defense matters, particularly those dealing with the Defense Department; he was able to aid in the trimming $6 billion from the 1970 budget. In 1971, Nixon named him as chairman of the AEC, where he initiated several reforms to help in the group's regulatory oversight. For this work, Secretary of State Henry Kissinger recommended that Schlesinger be named to replace Richard M. Helms as director of central intelligence; the nomination came on 21 December 1972, and Schlesinger was confirmed unanimously on 23 January 1973. During his tenure, which lasted from 2 February until 2 July 1973, Schlesinger was noted for his reorganization of the Office of National Estimates, which gave the president and his national security team secret reports and analyses on current world crises.

The political scandal of Watergate thrust Schlesinger into the national spotlight. On 20 April 1973, Attorney General Richard Kleindienst, implicated in the Watergate affair, resigned and was replaced by Secretary of Defense Elliot Richardson, who had been on the job for only four months. On 10 May 1973, President Nixon nominated Schlesinger to replace Richardson. He was confirmed unanimously by the Senate on 28 June and sworn in as the twelfth secretary of defense on 2 July. During his tenure, he dealt with the end of the American involvement in Vietnam, the Yom Kippur War between Israel and its Arab neighbors, the Turkish-Greek conflict over the island of Cyprus, and the strengthening of the conventional capabilities of the North Atlantic Treaty Organization (NATO).

Department historians Roger Trask and Alfred Goldberg write, "In spite of the controversy surrounding both his tenure and dismissal, Schlesinger was by most accounts an able secretary of defense. A serious and perceptive thinker on nuclear strategy, he was determined that the United States not fall seriously behind the Soviet Union in conventional and nuclear forces and devoted himself to the modernization of defense policies and programs." On 2 November 1975, after disagreements between Secretary of State Henry Kissinger and Schlesinger, President Gerald Ford asked for and received Schlesinger's resignation. When he left office officially on 19 November, he claimed that his problems with the president were caused by differences over the defense budget. Schlesinger spent the next two years writing about national security matters.

During the 1976 presidential campaign, Democrat Jimmy Carter called for the establishment of a federal department of energy. On 24 December 1976, the president-elect named Schlesinger, a liberal Republican, as a presidential adviser on energy matters. Three months after he was inaugurated, on 18 April 1977, Carter announced in a national speech on energy his National Energy Plan, which included the proposal for a new federal agency. Congress passed his proposal, and on 4 August 1977 he signed into law the Department of Energy Organization Act. Carter named Schlesinger as the first secretary of energy; confirmed by the Senate, he was sworn in on 5 August 1977. He spent many months in charge of a department that had no office, no staff, and little chance to enact policy initiatives. During his term, which ended on 20 July 1979, Schlesinger dealt with the growing energy needs of the nation, as well as the accident at the Three Mile Island nuclear power plant in Pennsylvania on 28 March 1979. Carter's signing of the National Energy Act, as well as the Natural Gas Policy Act and other pieces of similar legislation, allowed Schlesinger to initially establish policy for the entire nation, including the use of solar energy and conservation measures. On 20 July 1979, five days after Carter's address to the nation on energy matters, Schlesinger resigned, citing the "onerous and miscellaneous responsibilities falling to the lot of the 'energy czar.'" Today, James Schlesinger is a noted writer and lecturer on national security issues.

References: "Schlesinger, James R(odney)," in Charles Moritz, ed., *Current Biography 1973* (New York: H. W. Wilson, 1973), 379–381; Trask, Roger R., and Alfred Goldberg, *The Department Of Defense, 1947–1997: Organization and Leaders* (Washington, DC: Historical Office, Office of the Secretary of Defense, 1997), 91–94.

DONALD HENRY RUMSFELD

1932–

At 43, Donald Rumsfeld became the youngest man to ever serve as secretary of defense. An investment banker and former congressman, he also served as director of the Office of Economic Opportunity (OEO) under Richard Nixon and chief of staff under Gerald Ford. Donald Rumsfeld, the son of George Rumsfeld, a real estate developer, and Jeannette (née Husted) Rumsfeld, was born in Evanston, Illinois, on 9 July 1932. When he was five, the Rumsfelds moved to the nearby town of Winnetka, where he grew up. After attending local schools, he went to Princeton University, where he earned a bachelor's degree in political science in 1954. He then entered the U.S. Navy with the rank of ensign, serving for three years as a jet pilot and instructor.

After leaving the navy in 1957, Rumsfeld joined the staff of Rep. David Dennison of Ohio as an administrative assistant. Two years later, he became the administrative assistant in the office of Rep. Robert Griffin of Michigan. In 1960, Rumsfeld returned to Illinois, where he went to work for the firm of A. G. Becker & Company as an investment broker. Bitten by the political bug, in 1962 he ran for a seat in the U.S. House of Representatives to represent the Thirteenth Congressional District. Elected, Rumsfeld served for three terms, during which time he was considered a conservative.

Shortly after starting his fourth term, Rumsfeld resigned his House seat to accept an offer, on 21 April 1969, from President Richard Nixon to become the director of the OEO, a Great Society program started during the Johnson administration. Because federal law prohibited a member of Congress from serving in a federal post if he had voted for a pay increase for that office, Rumsfeld was sworn in as the head of OEO but was named as an assistant to the president, with cabinet status, and was paid as a member of the President's Urban Affairs Council. Rumsfeld served until February 1973, when Nixon named him as U.S. ambassador to the North Atlantic Treaty Organization (NATO). He served in this position until August 1974, when, in the midst of Nixon's resignation over Watergate, Rumsfeld was recalled by Vice-president Gerald Ford to serve on Ford's presidential transition team and, after Ford was sworn in as the thirty-eighth president, as the new president's chief of staff. Over the next fifteen months, Rumsfeld became one of President Ford's closest and most trusted advisers.

On 2 November 1975, President Ford fired Secretary of Defense James Schlesinger and the following day, named Rumsfeld as Schlesinger's replacement. Quickly confirmed, Rumsfeld was sworn in as the thirteenth secretary of defense on 20 November 1975. His tenure, which lasted until 20 January 1977, a term of fourteen months, saw him work extensively on the 1977 and 1978 budgets, which saw total the budget reach $108 billion in 1977 and $116 billion in 1978. Department historians Roger Trask and Alfred Goldberg write that "while Rumsfeld maintained the momentum begun by Schlesinger to halt the decline in defense spending, his brief term and the change in administration limited his success." On his second to last day in office, 19 January 1977, Rumsfeld was awarded the Presidential Medal of Freedom by President Ford.

After leaving office, Rumsfeld briefly taught at Northwestern University, served as president and chief executive officer of G. D. Searle & Company, and returned to government from November 1983 to May 1984 when President Ronald Reagan named him special U.S. ambassador to the Middle East. In 1996, he served as the campaign manager for Senator Bob Dole, the unsuccessful Republican candidate for president.

References: "Rumsfeld, Donald," in Charles Moritz, ed., *"Current Biography 1970* (New York: H. W. Wilson, 1970), 365–367; Trask, Roger R., *The Secretaries of Defense: A Brief History, 1947–1985* (Washington, DC: Office of the Secretary of

Defense Historical Office, 1985), 43–45; Trask, Roger R., and Alfred Goldberg, *The Department Of Defense, 1947–1997: Organization and Leaders* (Washington, DC: Historical Office, Office of the Secretary of Defense, 1997), 94–95.

HAROLD BROWN
1927–

Harold Brown was the first scientist to serve as secretary of defense. A former secretary of the air force, he saw the department through the final years of the 1970s. Harold Brown, the son of Abraham Harold Brown, a lawyer in New York City, and Gertrude (née Cohen) Brown, was born in New York City on 19 September 1927. He attended New York City schools. and received a bachelor's degree, with honors, in physics and mathematics from Columbia University in 1945, as well as his master's in 1946 and Ph.D. from the same institution in 1949. From 1947 to 1950, he lectured at Columbia on physics.

In 1950, Brown left Columbia when he was appointed to the research and development team at the University of California's E. O. Lawrence Radiation Laboratory at Berkeley. He was an expert in the development of atomic weapons. In 1952, he moved to the Lawrence Radiation Laboratory at Livermore, California, becoming director in 1960, succeeding Dr. Edward Teller. During this period, Brown was an important member of Project Plowshare, which researched the possible peaceful uses of nuclear power. He also advised the U.S. Air Force on nuclear issues and, during the tenure of Robert Mc-Namara as secretary of defense, worked with the Pentagon as the director of defense research and engineering.

On 1 October 1965, President Lyndon Johnson nominated Brown as secretary of the Air Force to succeed Secretary Eugene M. Zuckert. During his tenure, Brown advocated the limited use of air power to fight North Vietnam. One historian called Brown the architect of the American bombing campaign during the Vietnam War. His thoughts on the bombing campaign were subsequently published as part of the Pentagon Papers. The election of Richard Nixon, a Republican, in 1968, left Brown out of the Pentagon for the first time in nearly five years. He was soon hired as the president of the California Institute of Technology (Caltech). As president of Caltech, Brown instituted an equal opportunity program for minorities and allowed women to be admitted for the first time as undergraduates. He also was forced to deal with antiwar protests on the campus.

Democrat Jimmy Carter was elected to the presidency in 1976 and Brown became a leading choice for secretary of defense. On 21 December 1976, he was officially nominated. As Brown was being named, Carter was pledging to reduce defense spending by $5 to $7 billion dollars. Brown was confirmed by the Senate on 20 January 1977 and took office the following day. During his four years at Defense, he dealt with such situations as the Soviet war in Afghanistan, the U.S. hostage crisis in Iran, and Senate approval of the Strategic Arms Limitation Treaty (SALT II) in 1979. Budgets during his tenure, went from $116 billion in 1978, to $125 billion in 1979, to $142 billion in 1980, and finally to $176 billion in 1981. Historians Roger Trask and Alfred Goldberg write, "Brown involved himself in practically all areas of departmental activity. Consistent with the Carter administration's objective to reorganize the federal government, Brown launched a comprehensive review of defense organization that eventually brought significant change . . . with regard to strategic planning, Brown shared much the same concerns as his Republican predecessors—the need to upgrade U.S. military forces and improve collective security arrangements—but with a stronger commitment to arms control." To this end, Brown was instrumental in the signing of SALT II between the United States and the Soviet Union. (The treaty was never ratified by the U.S. Senate because of the Soviet invasion of Afghanistan, although the United

States continued to abide by its obligations for another decade.)

Brown left office on 20 January 1981 and joined the Johns Hopkins School of Advanced International Studies as a visiting professor; later he became chairman of the university's Foreign Policy Institute. In 1992, he joined the Center for Strategic and International Studies as a counselor. A consultant to various companies on several foreign policy issues, Brown is also a writer and lecturer. He is the author of *Thinking about National Security: Defense and Foreign Policy in a Dangerous World* and *Is S.D.I. Feasible?*), and is the coauthor, with Lynn E. Davis, of *Nuclear Arms Control Choices*.

References: "Brown, Harold," in Charles Moritz, ed., *Current Biography 1977* (New York: H. W. Wilson, 1977), 86–89; Trask, Roger R., and Alfred Goldberg, *The Department Of Defense, 1947–1997: Organization and Leaders* (Washington, DC: Historical Office, Office of the Secretary of Defense, 1997), 96–99.

CASPAR WILLARD WEINBERGER
1917–

See Secretary of Health, Education and Welfare, 1973–1975

FRANK CHARLES CARLUCCI III
1930–

The *New York Times* called Frank Carlucci "a tough pragmatist in Pentagon's corner" when he was selected to replace Caspar Weinberger as the secretary of defense in 1987. A longtime government bureaucrat who had served as Weinberger's deputy when the latter was director of the Office of Management and Budget (OMB), secretary of health, education and welfare, and in the Defense Department, he had also worked in Democratic administrations. The son of Frank Charles Carlucci, Jr., an insurance broker, and Roxanne (née Bacon) Carlucci, Frank Carlucci was born in Scranton, Pennsylvania, on 18 October 1930. Carlucci attended the Wyoming Seminary College Preparatory School in Kingston, Pennsylvania, before enrolling in Princeton University and graduating with a bachelor of arts degree in 1952. He then served two years in the U.S. Navy as a gunnery officer on the U.S.S. *Rombach*. After being discharged with the rank of lieutenant junior grade, he spent a year in the Harvard Graduate School of Business Administration but left before getting his degree. He then spent several years in private business, first as a rental agent and then as a salesman.

In July 1956, Carlucci joined the State Department as a foreign service officer. His work took him overseas, to assignments in South Africa, the Congo, Zanzibar, and Brazil, before he left the service in 1969. It was at that time that President Richard Nixon named him to the Office of Economic Opportunity as an assistant director; he became director the following year. In 1971, he became the associate director of OMB, working under Caspar Weinberger, was promoted to director in 1972. When Weinberger was made the secretary of health, education and welfare in 1973, Carlucci was made undersecretary. In 1975, Carlucci was named as U.S. ambassador to Portugal, serving until 1978. That year, President Jimmy Carter named Carlucci as deputy director of the Central Intelligence Agency, where he served until Ronald Reagan became president in 1981.

At that time, Reagan nominated Weinberger as secretary of defense and named Carlucci as deputy secretary. Carlucci was viewed with suspicion by some Republicans because he had worked for the Carter administration, but he was confirmed and served until 1983. During the first years of the massive military build-up that marked Weinberger's tenure, Carlucci instituted a number of reforms, called the Carlucci initiatives, which attempted to bring order and stability to defense procurement procedures. Carlucci left the Pentagon in 1983 to serve as president and chief executive officer of Sears World Trade. From 1985 to 1986, he served on the President's Commission on Defense Management (chaired by executive David Packard, it became known as the Packard Commission), delivering a report on budgeting in the Pentagon. In 1986, President Reagan named him as assistant to the president for national security affairs (or national security adviser).

On 2 November 1987, Defense Secretary Weinberger announced to President Reagan that he would be resigning that week. It was soon known that Carlucci would replace Weinberger. Weinberger's resignation became official on 5 November, and Carlucci was nominated. Hailed as a brilliant successor to the man known as Cap the Knife for his ability to chop budgets, Carlucci was confirmed by the Senate by a 91–1 vote on 20 November and sworn in three days later as the sixteenth secretary of Defense. His tenure, which lasted until 20 January 1989, was marked by his attempts at streamlining defense procurement. Historians Roger Trask and Alfred Goldberg write, "[Carlucci] was in no sense a caretaker. His initiatives on management, his relationships with Congress, his views on major defense issues, such as the budget, procurement, weapons systems, and the downsizing of the military—all contained his own stamp." In his final annual report, he wrote, "As the 1980s opened, our nation's armed forces were suffering from severe neglect. . . . the President and the Congress together enacted a major rebuilding program to restore American strength. That effort has had a clear effect. Our nation will enter the 1990s far stronger than it did the present decade. . . . While our forces are now stronger, we continue to face a host of threats. Foremost among them is Soviet military power, the single most significant factor we consider in determining the forces required to guarantee our national security. Neither glasnost not the stirrings of economic reform within the Soviet Union have resulted in any redirection of resources away from the Soviet military machine. Deterring Soviet or Soviet-inspired aggression will remain the prime aim of our national security strategy, and the benchmark against which we must measure our strength."

After leaving the Pentagon on 20 January 1989, Carlucci joined the Carlyle Group, a Washington, D.C. investment firm. In 1993 he joined several former secretaries of defense in denouncing the Clinton administration plan to send American troops to the former Soviet Union and to Bosnia to calm potential conflicts there.

References: "Carlucci, Frank (Charles, 3d)," in Charles Moritz, ed., *Current Biography 1981* (New York: H. W. Wilson, 1981), 49–52; Department of Defense, *Report of the Secretary of Defense, Frank C. Carlucci, to the Congress, on the Amended FY 1988/FY 1989 Biennial Budget* (Washington, DC: GPO, 1989), 3; Trask, Roger R., and Alfred Goldberg, *The Department Of Defense, 1947–1997: Organization and Leaders* (Washington, DC: Historical Office, Office of the Secretary of Defense, 1997), 106–109.

RICHARD BRUCE CHENEY
1941–

As secretary of defense during the last years of the cold war, Richard Cheney oversaw the American buildup in the Persian Gulf prior to, and during, the Persian Gulf War. The son of Richard Herbert Cheney, a soil conservation agent, and Marjorie Lauraine (née Dickey) Cheney, Richard Cheney was born in Lincoln, Nebraska, on 30 January 1941. When he was young, Cheney's parents moved to Caspar, Wyoming, where he grew up, attending local schools. He went to Yale University for three semesters, but dropped out, returning to the western United States and worked on power lines. He then returned to school, receiving his bachelor's and master's degrees in political science from the University of Wyoming in 1965 and 1966, respectively. He then entered an internship for the National Center for Education in Politics, which allowed him to work on the staff of Governor Warren Knowles of Wisconsin.

Cheney served as a congressional fellow from 1968 to 1969. In 1969, he was named as a special assistant to the director of the Office of Economic Opportunity, Donald Rumsfeld. When Rumsfeld went to the White House in 1970 to serve as a counselor to President Richard Nixon, Cheney went with him. In February 1973, Rumsfeld was named as U.S. ambassador to the North Atlantic Treaty Organization (NATO), and Cheney left government service.

After serving as a financial consultant for Bradley, Woods & Company, a Washington, D.C. investment firm, Cheney was again back in the White House. When Gerald Ford became president upon Nixon's resignation, he named Rumsfeld as his chief of staff. Rumsfeld, in turn, appointed Cheney as his deputy. On 3 November 1975, Ford named Rumsfeld as secretary of defense to succeed James Schlesinger. Cheney immediately became Ford's chief of staff. When Ford lost the presidential election in 1976, Cheney left Washington and returned to Wyoming, where he began a business in banking. In 1978, Cheney decided to run for the at-large seat in Congress for Wyoming. His successful campaign started him on a career in the House, where he eventually became minority whip. During his ten years in Congress, throughout five full terms, he became widely respected, particularly in matters involving national security matters.

After being elected president in 1988, George Bush's first choice for secretary of defense, was Senator John Tower of Texas, widely praised and highly thought of expert on foreign and defense-related issues. Tower was rejected on 9 March 1989 by a 53–47 vote, the first time a potential cabinet officer was denied confirmation since Lewis Strauss was defeated for commerce secretary in 1959. After considering former Rep. Jack Ed-wards of Alabama, former Defense Secretary Donald Rumsfeld, Norman Augustine of the Martin Marietta Corporation, Senator William S. Cohen of Maine, and Brent Scowcroft, his national security adviser, Bush selected Cheney the day after Tower's defeat. On 17 March, a week after being nominated, Cheney was confirmed without dissent by the Senate, and he was sworn in that same day. Starting off his tenure by selecting General Colin Powell as chairman of the Joint Chiefs of Staff, the first black man to hold that position, Cheney met and conferred with Secretary of State Baker, National Security Adviser Scowcroft, General Powell, and President Bush to formulate policy. An expert in congressional matters, he consulted numerous times with his colleagues on Capitol Hill. The defense budget for 1990 was more than $300 billion; immediately, Bush ordered Cheney to cut more than $6 billion from this total. Cheney eventually was able to save nearly $10 billion. Military strength was cut from 2.2 million troops when he entered office to 1.6 million by early 1991, shortly before the Persian Gulf War.

Cheney's biggest challenge during his tenure was the Persian Gulf War. Starting with the Iraqi invasion on 2 August 1990, and culminating in the air war that began on 15 January 1991, Cheney worked closely with the president and his national security team to formulate policy and help the American troop and materiel deployment in the desert. In his annual report for 1991, released in February 1992, he wrote, "In the Gulf, more than half a million servicemen and women, both active-duty and reserve, carried out an historic campaign to liberate Kuwait and stop a ruthless aggressor from dominating this region and its global energy lifelines. The high quality of our forces and their superb training, advanced weapons technologies, well-organized logistics and support, and outstanding military leadership and planning contributed to a swift victory with unprecedentedly low casualties. More than 30 nations provided forces for the Gulf coalition, and many others gave financial and diplomatic support." He added, "The changes we have made in U.S. force structure allow sharply reduced defense spending. Just five years ago, defense spending was 27 percent of the federal budget. Next year, it will be 18 percent—less than one in every five federal dollars—and this percentage is decreasing. By 1997, national defense will account for just 16 percent of the federal budget, compared to 61 percent of federal spending which will then be devoted to payments to individuals."

After the presidential election of Bill Clinton in 1992, Cheney left the Pentagon. He was widely praised and considered one of the best secretaries of defense in the agency's history. Cheney was considered as a leading candidate for the 1996 Republican presidential nomination. However, because he had had several heart operations, his health was questioned, and he did not run. Instead, he became the president and chief executive officer of the Halliburton Company, headquartered in Dallas, Texas. On 25 July 2000, Republican presidential candidate George W. Bush named Cheney as his running mate.

References: "Cheney, Richard B(ruce)," in Charles Moritz, ed., *Current Biography 1989* (New York: H. W. Wilson, 1989), 102–106; Department of Defense, *Annual Report to the President and Congress, Dick Cheney, Secretary of Defense* (Washington, DC: GPO, 1992), 5, 8; Kuniholm, Bruce R., "Cheney, Richard Bruce," in Bruce W. Jentleson and Thomas G. Paterson, senior eds., *Encyclopedia of U.S. Foreign Relations* (New York: Oxford University Press; 4 vols., 1997), 1: 237–238; Levy, Peter, *Encyclopedia of the Reagan-Bush Years* (Westport, CT: Greenwood, 1996), 76–77; Trask, Roger R., and Alfred Goldberg, *The Department Of Defense, 1947–1997: Organization and Leaders* (Washington, DC: Historical Office, Office of the Secretary of Defense, 1997), 111–116.

LESLIE ASPIN, JR.
1938–1995

Congressman Les Aspin was considered one of the leading experts on foreign and military policy. His tenure as secretary of defense was marked by a clash over a policy regarding homosexuals and an American military failure in Somalia. Aspin, the son of Les Aspin, Sr., and Marie (née Orth) Aspin, was born in Milwaukee, Wisconsin, on 21 July 1938. Aspin attended local schools before earning a bachelor's degree summa cum laude from Yale in 1960, a master's degree in economics from Oxford University in 1962, and a Ph.D. degree in economics from Massachusetts Institute of Technology in 1965. Starting just after he graduated from Yale in 1960, Aspin worked as an aide for Senator William Proxmire of Wisconsin; three years later, he served as a staff assistant to Walter W. Heller, chief of the Council of Economic Advisers under President John F. Kennedy. After earning his doctorate degree, Aspin worked in the office of Secretary of Defense Robert McNamara as an economics analyst in the Office of Systems Analysis from 1966 to 1968.

In 1968, Aspin resigned from the Pentagon to return to Wisconsin to help manage the statewide campaign for the reelection of President Lyndon Johnson. When Johnson pulled out of the race at the end of March, Aspin ran for the state treasurer's position. He lost in the primary, but the campaign gave him valuable electoral experience. Two years later, he ran a successful campaign for the U.S. house of representatives seat held by Republican Henry Shadeberg, representing Wisconsin's First Congressional District. Aspin would hold this seat until 1993, a total of twelve terms. His major committee assignment was as a member of the House Armed Services Committee where, in 1985, he was named chairman. As a member of the committee, Aspin became a leading defense issues expert. He spent much of his time castigating the military establishment for their handling of appropriations. As chairman, he worked closely with the Reagan and Bush administrations to formulate congressional policy on defense matters. Prior to the beginning of the Persian Gulf War, Aspin was quick to explain that while he supported sanctions to remove Iraqi troops from Kuwait, he did not believe a ground war would be bloodless. Nonetheless, once the war was voted on in the House, he gave his support, and, with a series of white papers, showed a detailed blueprint of strategy.

Many in the Congress and defense establishment knew that Aspin wanted to serve some day as secretary of defense. However, with Republican administrations in the 1980s and early 1990s, his chances remained slim. When Democrat Bill Clinton was elected in 1992, the situation changed. Journalist Elizabeth Drew writes, "Aspin, the chairman of the House Armed Services Committee, had been a big help in the campaign and was a bona fide defense intellectual. There was some discussion as to whether Aspin was too abrasive to be Secretary of Defense and whether the military, with whom he had tangled, would accept him. Serious consideration was given to naming Colin Powell, the Chairman of the Joint Chiefs of Staff, to the Defense job, but this would have required a change in the law that bars a former military official from taking the job for ten years. There was also the question of whether it was a good idea to name someone who had served two Republican Presidents. Once it was determined that letting the House Armed Services Committee fall into the hands of Ron Dellums, a leading California product of the radical politics of the sixties and a leading defense critic, wasn't dangerous—Dellums had played a responsible role as a member of the House Intelligence Committee—the Defense job went to Aspin." On 22 December 1992, Aspin was named at the same press conference in which Warren Christopher was named as secretary of state. The *New York Times* called him a "pathfinder . . . of the middle ground."

During his tenure as secretary of defense, January to December 1993, Aspin became bogged down in political and military maneuvers inside the Pentagon. Faced with the controversy over Clinton's decision to lift the ban on homosexuals serving in the military, as well as the question of whether women should serve in front-line units, Aspin's effectiveness was blunted. He did not support the dispatch of American troops to Haiti, and the changing of the mission goals in Somalia, both of which ended in disappointment. Aspin said in an interview in November 1993, "I am the secretary of defense, not the secretary of state, and not to be too aggressive of foreign policy issues is a deliberate decision. And as we get to know each other better, and as we get to be more comfortable working with each other, I feel more comfortable in asserting a point of view and pushing for my point of view."

However on 15 December 1993, less than a year after being named to the position, Aspin resigned, although many believe he reacted to a dismissal that was long in coming. The *New York Times* editorialized, "Many who welcomed Mr. Aspin's appointment were disappointed with his slowness to master the Pentagon bureaucracy and his failure to project a convincing new vision for the nation's defense. He leaves behind a defense establishment that still respects him as a thinker but feels he lacked the managerial skills of his immediate predecessors. The promised 'bottom-up' review of defense spending, a natural showcase for the analytical and budgeting skills Mr. Aspin honed in Congress, emerged as little more than a place-holder, deferring structural reductions to a later date."

After leaving Defense, Aspin worked for a think tank based in Washington, D.C., writing numerous papers on defense-related issues. He also worked, for a short time, on a commission established by the president that tried to make the espionage agencies of the U.S. work better. On 20 May 1995, Aspin, who had suffered from heart trouble for years, suffered an attack and died the next day in Washington, D.C. He was 56 years old. He was the author of *Challenges to Values-Based Military Intervention.*

References: "Aspin, Les(lie), Jr.," in Charles Moritz, ed., *Current Biography 1986* (New York: H. W. Wilson, 1986), 24–27; "Aspin, Leslie (Les) Jr.," in Bruce W. Jentleson and Thomas G. Paterson, senior eds., *"Encyclopedia of U.S. Foreign Relations* (New York: Oxford University Press; 4 vols., 1997), 1: 111; Drew, Elizabeth, *On the Edge: The Clinton Presidency* (New York: Simon & Schuster, 1994), 29.

WILLIAM JAMES PERRY

1927–

When William Perry was sworn into office on 3 February 1994 as the nineteenth secretary of defense, he was considered a technocrat. A former deputy secretary of defense who had served in two administrations, he became widely regarded for his slow and methodical decision-making capability during his three-year tenure. Perry was born in Vandergrift, Pennsylvania, a small village north of Pittsburgh, on 11 October 1927, the son of Edward Martin Perry, a grocer, and Mabelle Estelle (née Dunlap) Perry. William Perry grew up in the nearby town of Butler, where he attended local schools. After graduating from high school in 1945, he had joined the U.S. Army as a noncommissioned officer; he saw limited service as part of the American occupation forces in Japan and Okinawa as a surveyor from 1945 until 1948. In 1948, he joined the Reserve Officer Training Corps (ROTC), and was commissioned a lieutenant two years later. He left the ROTC in 1955. Perry earned bachelor's and master's degrees from Stanford University in 1949 and 1950, respectively and, in 1957, a Ph.D. degree from Pennsylvania State University, all in mathematics.

Starting in 1954, Perry became involved with a series of companies in the field of defense industries. He began work as a director of defense laboratories for GTE Sylvania; ten years later, he left that company to found ESL Inc., a military electronics defense firm, where he worked from 1964 until 1977. In 1977, he was named by President Jimmy Carter as undersecretary of defense for research and engineering, where he served until 1981. As undersecretary, Perry was in charge of weapons research, development, and procurement, and served as Secretary Harold Brown's chief advisor on weapons technology and communications. One of his investigations was into stealth technology and whether it could work; its success years later was attributed to Perry himself.

After leaving government, Perry worked in the private sector, first as executive vice president of a California banking company that researched high technology, then as founder of a company that helped small companies develop defense-related materials. Following the election of Bill Clinton to the presidency in 1992, Perry was named as deputy secretary of defense under Les Aspin. As deputy secretary, a term that lasted a year, he was widely praised for his managerial skills. On 15 December 1993, after less than a year on the job, Aspin resigned. President Bill Clinton's first choice to succeed Aspin, Admiral Bobby Ray Inman, the former deputy director of the Central Intelligence Agency (CIA), was widely considered to be an easily confirmable candidate. However, after columnist William Safire wrote a column critical of Inman, the candidate demanded that his nomination be withdrawn, during a press conference in which he intimated that critics in Congress were out to get him. Perry was passed over again when President Clinton considered Senator Sam Nunn, Democrat of Georgia, and former Secretary Warren Rudman, Republican of New Hampshire, for the post. After both men declined, Clinton then named Perry for the position on 24 January 1994. On 3 February, he was confirmed unanimously by the Senate and was sworn in the same day.

During his tenure, which lasted until 24 January 1997, Perry was involved in few controversies, as opposed to his predecessor, Aspin. He was able to negotiate with Congress the deployment of American ground troops to Bosnia-Herzegovina, arrange with North Korea for the trading of food for the end of its nuclear weapons program, and advocate a "new strategy for a new era" in which economic implications would become a leading concern of national security. In his 1995 annual report, Perry wrote, "American security is now increasingly tied to the security and stability of other regions. Imagine, for example, the impact on the U.S. economy of any major disruption in trade as a result of instability in Asia or Europe." In his 1996 report, he discussed how the end of the cold war had affected American security concerns. "The new post–Cold War dangers make the task of protecting America's national security different and in some ways more complex than it was during the Cold War. Our task of planning force structure is more complex than when we had a single, overriding threat. Previously, our force structure was planned to deter a global war with the Soviet Union, which we considered a threat to our very survival as a nation. All other threats, including regional threats, were considered less-but-included cases. The forces we maintained to counter the Soviet threat were assumed to be capable of dealing with any of the lesser challenges. Today, the threat of global conflict is greatly diminished, but the danger of regional conflicts is neither lesser nor included and had therefore required us to take this danger explicitly into account in structuring our forces." Budgets during Perry's tenure went from $254 billion in 1995 to $243 billion in the 1997 budget.

Following President Clinton's reelection in November 1996, Perry stated that he wished to return to private life. His resignation was formally announced on 6 November and, after the confirmation of his successor, Senator William Cohen of Maine, he returned to private business. In 1998, Perry was named by President Clinton as the first U.S. coordinator for policy in North Korea. On 12 October 1999, he released a declassified version of his report to the Senate Foreign Relations Committee, in which he stated his recommendation that the United States ease economic sanctions on North Korea in exchange for a promise for a cessation to the North Korean nuclear weapons program. Perry is the

author of *Defense Strategy in the Post Cold-War Era,* and *Preventive Defense: A New Security Strategy for America,* written with Ashton B. Carter.

References: Department of Defense, *Annual Report to the President and the Congress: William J. Perry, Secretary of Defense, February 1995* (Washington, DC: GPO, 1995), 1; Department of Defense, *Annual Report to the President and the Congress: William J. Perry, Secretary of Defense, March 1996* (Washington, DC: U.S. Government Printing Office, 1996), 7–8; "Perry, William J.," in Judith Graham, ed., *Current Biography 1995* (New York: H. W. Wilson, 1995), 474–477; Trask, Roger R., and Alfred Goldberg, *The Department Of Defense, 1947–1997: Organization and Leaders* (Washington, DC: Historical Office, Office of the Secretary of Defense, 1997), 121–126.

WILLIAM SEBASTIAN COHEN
1940–

William Cohen was the first Republican to serve as secretary of defense in a Democratic administration; a former U.S. senator who was considered an experienced foreign policy expert, Cohen became involved in American military action in Bosnia. Born in Bangor, Maine, on 28 August 1940, he is the son of Reuben Cohen, and Clara (née Hartley) Cohen. His early schooling was at a Hebrew school; later he attended local public schools, and earned a bachelor's degree in Latin from Bowdoin College in Maine in 1962 and a law degree from the Boston University Law School three years later. Admitted to the Maine bar in 1965, he became a partner in the Bangor law firm of Paine, Cohen, Lynch, Weatherbee, & Kobritz.

After working for several years both as an attorney and teacher in Bangor schools, Cohen served as a member of the Bangor board of appeals from 1967 to 1969, and he was the mayor of Bangor from 1971 until 1972. In 1972, Rep. William Dodd Hathaway, a Democrat, ran for a vacant seat in the U.S.

Senate; Cohen ran for Hathaway's open seat and was elected. During three terms in the U.S. House of Representatives, Cohen became known as one of the Republicans on the House Judiciary Committee who voted for articles of impeachment against President Richard Nixon. In 1978, he challenged Hathaway for the U.S. Senate seat; Cohen was elected and began to serve what became three six-year terms. In the Senate, he was considered a moderate Republican. Doing service on the Senate Armed Services and Senate Governmental Affairs Committees, and later on the Senate Intelligence Committee, Cohen was regarded as an expert on national security and defense issues.

He challenged Republican and Democratic presidents alike for their policies; he believed that Congress was ultimately responsible for matters dealing with war and the deployment of American troops overseas. Adam Clymer, writing in the *New York Times*, said of Cohen, "In the Senate, he had argued for many years that Presidents are obliged to get Congressional consent before committing United States troops abroad. In 1991, before voting to support an invasion of Iraq, he told the Senate: 'There is no doubt in my mind that Congress has the sole power to declare, and the President has the sole power to execute, wars.'" He was instrumental in drafting several major pieces of legislation in the national defense and security area, including the Competition in Contracting Act (1984), the 1984 GI Bill amendments, the Goldwater-Nichols Defense Reorganization Act (1986), and the Intelligence Oversight Reform Act (1991). He has written eight books, teaming with former Senator Gary Hart on a novel about international espionage, with former Senate Democratic leader George Mitchell on an account of the Iran-Contra affair, and with Thomas B. Allen on a murder mystery and composing three books of poetry.

In 1996, instead of running for a fourth term, Cohen announced his resignation from the Senate so that he could continue to write books and establish a defense and intelligence consulting business. The secretary of defense, William Perry, indicated that he would not serve in a second Clinton administration. On 5 December 1997, a month after being reelected, the president named Cohen to succeed Perry. The president said that Cohen was "the right person . . . to secure the bipartisan support of America's armed forces must have and clearly deserve." Cohen's nomination came before the Senate Armed Services Committee, where he directly said that he would not refuse to criticize the Clinton administration publicly when he thought it was wrong. He also chastised the president for the policy on Bosnia, saying that it did not have clear goals and lacked a proper strategy. Two hours after the hearing ended, the Senate voted 92–0 to confirm him. He was sworn in as the twentieth secretary of defense on 24 January 1997. He was forced to deal immediately with the situation in Bosnia and with a possible confrontation with Iraq in February 1998. In his 1997 annual report, Cohen wrote, "The world today is one that is constantly evolving with new security challenges. The threat of a nuclear holocaust has been greatly diminished, but the proliferation of weapons of mass destruction threatens our interests, our forces, and even our homeland. Hostile regimes, instability, and ethnic tensions threaten American interests in key regions. Terrorism, international organized crime, and drug trafficking remain threats to our national interests and to peace and stability. Finally, as recent history clearly reminds us, new dangers can arise suddenly and unpredictably. Even as our security picture evolves, the world is undergoing unprecedented economic, political, and technological change—at a pace that is sometimes breathtaking. These changes are binding our destiny ever more closely to that of our allies and economic partners around the world. This works to our advantage as we seek to promote free markets and principles of democracy, but it also increases the degree to which we are affected by developments overseas. We should not—and cannot—insulate ourselves from the forces that are sweeping the globe."

In his 1998 report, he explained, "Having

inherited the defense structure that won the Cold War and Desert Storm, the Clinton Administration intends to leave as its legacy a defense strategy, a military, and a Defense Department that have been transformed to meet the new challenges of a new century. . . . Our strategy will ensure that America continues to lead a world of accelerating change by shaping the emerging security environment to reduce threats and to promote our interests and by responding to crises that threaten our interests. We will execute the strategy with superior military forces that fully exploit advances in technology by employing new operational concepts and organizational structures. And we will support our forces with a Department that is as lean, agile, and focused as our warfighters. Toward this end, the Department of Defense last year conducted perhaps the most fundamental and comprehensive review ever conducted of defense posture, policy, and programs. The Quadrennial Defense Review (QDR) examined the national security threats, risks, and opportunities facing the United States today and out to 2015. Based on this analysis, we designed a defense strategy to implement the defense requirements of the President's National Security Strategy for a New Century. Our defense strategy has three central elements: 1) Shape the international security environment in ways favorable to U.S. interests by promoting regional stability, reducing threats, preventing conflicts, and deterring aggression and coercion on a day-to-day basis; 2) Respond to the full spectrum of crises that threaten U.S. interests by deterring aggression and coercion in a crisis, conducting smaller-scale contingency operations, and fighting and winning major theater wars; and 3) Prepare now for an uncertain future through a focused modernization effort, development of new operational concepts and organizations to fully exploit new technologies, programs to ensure high quality personnel at all levels, and efforts to hedge against threats that are unlikely but which would have disproportionate security implications such as the emergence of a regional great power before 2015. . . . This is not mere rhetoric. It is the basis for what our defense planners and military forces do every day." Cohen also oversaw an increase of $2.8 billion in the 1997 budget, which rose to $251 billion.

Journalists Barbara Starr and Stacey Evers reported that to Cohen "the daily, non-military-unique ability to collect, analyze and distribute information will be the 'equivalent of . . . Stealth technology,' . . . Preventing the enemy from denying the USA access to the Global Positioning System or hacking into Pentagon computer systems 'are the kinds of things we have to contend with in the future.'"

References: *Annual Report to the President and Congress: William S. Cohen, Secretary of Defense. March 1997* (Washington, DC: GPO, 1997); *Annual Report to the President and Congress: William S. Cohen, Secretary of Defense, February 1998* (Washington, DC: GPO, 1998); "Cohen, William S(ebastian)," in Charles Moritz, ed., *Current Biography 1982* (New York: H. W. Wilson, 1982), 71–74; Starr, Barbara, and Stacey Evers, "Interview," in *Jane's Defence Weekly* 29: 6 (10 August 1997); Trask, Roger R., and Alfred Goldberg, *The Department Of Defense, 1947–1997: Organization and Leaders* (Washington, DC: Historical Office, Office of the Secretary of Defense, 1997), 127.

EDUCATION

⇒⊷⊷⇐

The work to establish a federal department to oversee the management of education began after the end of the Civil War and had to do with educating freed slaves. Representative Ignatius Donnelly of Minnesota introduced a measure in Congress in 1865 that called for the establishment of and education office in the newly created Freedmen's Bureau. His legislation called for an agency "to enforce education, without regard to race or color," specifically in the Southern states where former slaves still had few, if any, rights. The proposal died in committee.

National education leaders, however, were interested in the idea, and when they met in Washington, D.C., at a convention in February 1866, the president of the National Association of School Superintendents, Emerson E. White of Ohio, approached his friend, Representative James A. Garfield of Ohio, with the idea of a federal department of education. Garfield asked for a bill to be drafted, and White drew one up based on the legislation that created the Department of Agriculture. But when Garfield introduced the bill, Congress resisted. Whereas it had created a bureau relating to agriculture as a concession to farmers, it was feared that if the new agency were created, any group with an agenda would ask for a government agency for their concerns. Democrats were particularly against it, fearing a government takeover of local and religious schools. Garfield was able to convince his fellow legislators of its promise, and it was enacted on 3 December 1866.

The department was established "for the purpose of collecting such statistics and facts as shall show the condition and progress of education in the several States and territories, and of diffusing such information respecting the organization and management of schools and school systems and methods of teaching as shall aid the people of the United States in the establishment and maintenance of efficient school systems, and otherwise promote the cause of education throughout the United States."

President Andrew Johnson signed it into law on 2 March 1867, stating that "without federal intervention, there is no such thing as equitable education. The State base is controlled more by wealth than by word." Henry Barnard, an educator in New England and the editor of the *American Journal of Education,* was named as the first commissioner of education. The office consisted of the commissioner, four supporting staff, and a budget of $15,400.

Within a year, many in Congress wanted to end the agency, mainly because Barnard had used the office to sell subscriptions to his journal. In 1868, the budget was cut to $600 and two clerks were dismissed. Congressman Thaddeus Stevens called Barnard "a worn out man" and said he regretted his vote to establish the department "more than almost any vote" he had ever cast.

By an act of Congress of 28 July 1868, effective 30 June 1869, the Education Department became the Office of Education within the Department of the Interior. Garfield wrote to Emerson White, who had drafted the initial legislation, that Barnard was wholly to blame that he was "utterly destitute of administrative ability" and that "it was a great misfortune that he should have been appointed." In his 1869 annual report, Secretary of the Interior Orville Browning asked Congress to do away, altogether, with the agency, saying that responsibility for education belonged to the states. He wrote, "At the federal level, there is no necessity of anyone knowing anything about education." In March 1870, frustrated by his work, Barnard resigned.

The second commissioner, John Eaton, desired to be named as minister to Constantinople, but was offered Education instead. In his first report, Eaton wrote that "I found that the entire working force of this bureau . . . consisted of two clerks, at a salary of $1,200 each, and that the rooms assigned to its use were so crowded with books, pamphlets, and desks as to be wholly unfit for successful clerical work." Eaton remained in office until 1886, and he was followed by a number of educators who continued to serve with the title of commissioner of education.

In 1953, the office was consolidated within the new cabinet-level Department of Health, Education, and Welfare (HEW), with the new head of the office serving as undersecretary of education. Lee Thurston was the first to hold this office; one of his successors was Terrel H. Bell (served 1974–1976), who later became the second secretary of education. During the 1976 campaign, Democratic presidential candidate Jimmy Carter pledged that if elected, he would separate the education matters from HEW and establish a new cabinet-level department. However, even after he was elected, there was opposition to federal control over education, and it was not until 1979 that Carter could gain support in Congress. On 17 October 1979, he signed the Department of Education Organization Act.

Opening for business on 4 May 1980, the agency consolidated all of the functions that had been part of HEW's education offices, including the National Institute for Education and the National Center for Education Statistics. It also inherited several other offices from HEW, including the Rehabilitation Services Administration, the National Institute for Handicapped Research (now the National Institute on Disability and Rehabilitation Research), and the education-related functions of HEW's Office for Civil Rights. Carter selected Judge Shirley M. Hufstedler of the U.S. Circuit Court of Appeals for the Ninth Circuit as the first secretary of the new department.

In her annual report for 1980, Hufstedler wrote, "On October 17, 1979, when President Carter signed the enabling legislation, the Department of Education took its place at the President's Cabinet table. At long last, there was a national voice for education at the highest level of government—a voice made necessary by the many issues in education today which extend beyond the reach of state and local resources, and beyond their territorial jurisdictions as well." Hufstedler served until January 1981. She was replaced by

Terrel H. Bell, who had served as commissioner of education from 1974 to 1976. Bell was charged with eliminating the department by President Ronald Reagan. Bell, who wrote that he was horrified of the demise of an agency he himself supported, worked to increase its influence and is best remembered for the department's 1983 report, *A Nation at Risk,* which called attention to America's failing schools.

Bell's successor, William J. Bennett, was a respected conservative activist who decried political correctness in the United States, particularly in the education system, and attacked affirmative action programs based on race, which he felt discriminated against white students. In 1988, Bennett was replaced by Lauro Cavazos, who became the first Hispanic to serve in the cabinet.

Cavazos, who, like Bell, supported the department's mandate, clashed with two Republican presidents, Reagan and Bush, over spending and appropriations; he resigned in late 1990. Former Tennessee Governor Lamar Alexander, a leader in national education standards, served as secretary from 1991 to 1993. Secretary Richard W. Riley is currently the head of the department, with an appointment from 1993 to 2001. Riley reversed the policies of his predecessors and made available scholarships to minority students to undo past discrimination.

The department's official mission policy states, "The Department of Education establishes policy for, administers, and coordinates most Federal assistance to education. Its mission is to ensure equal access to education and to promote educational excellence throughout the Nation." Its official seal is made up of a tree, the leaves, and the sun. Secretary Hufstedler, who invented the seal, wrote, "With its sturdy trunk set in solid earth, the tree expresses the confidence and strength imparted to the individual through the development of the mind and the assimilation of knowledge. The glory and satisfaction of achievement are exhibited in its leaves. The background of sun and rays suggests the role of the Department in the promotion, nurturing, and encouragement of the best in all aspects of the nation's educational system."

References: Horiuchi, Ellen Nobuko, "The United States Department of Education, 1981–1985: Agenda for Abolishment" (Ph.D. dissertation, Arizona State University, 1990); King, Joan Hutchon, "Establishing the U.S. Department of Education during the Carter Administration, 1978–1979" (Ph.D. dissertation, Claremont Graduate School, 1980); Kursch, Harry, *The United States Office of Education: A Century of Service* (Philadelphia: Chilton Books, 1965), 12–13; Miles, Rufus E., Jr., "A Cabinet Department of Education: An Unwise Campaign Promise or a Sound Idea?" *Public Administration Review* 39: 2 (March/April 1979), 103–110; Peskin, Allan, "The Short, Unhappy Life of the Federal Department of Education," *Public Administration Review* 33: 6 (November/December 1973), 572–575; Smith, Darrell H., *The Bureau of Education: Its History, Activities, and Organization* (Baltimore: Johns Hopkins University Press, 1923).

SHIRLEY ANN MOUNT HUFSTEDLER
1925–

Shirley Hufstedler, a judge on the U.S. Court of Appeals of the Ninth Circuit, was named by President Jimmy Carter as the first secretary of education after the education area of administration was removed from the Department of Health, Education, and Welfare (HEW), and became the Department of Education. She was born in Denver, Colorado, on 24 August 1925, the daughter of Earl Stanley Mount, a construction contractor, and Eva (née von Behren) Mount.

Hufstedler received a bachelor's degree from the University of New Mexico in 1945 and a law degree from the Stanford Law School, where she served as editor of the law review. After her graduation in 1949, she moved to Los Angeles, where she practiced law until 1961, when she was appointed to the Los Angeles Superior Court. Five years later, she was named to the California Court of Appeal, and, in 1968, President Lyndon B. Johnson nominated her for a seat on the U.S. Court of Appeals for the Ninth Circuit. For many years, Hufstedler was considered a likely candidate to be the first woman named to the U.S. Supreme Court, but there was no opportunity for her appointment.

Carter had run, in 1976, calling for the separation of the education administration from the Department of Health, Education, and Welfare, into its own department. Congress resisted for a time, but the Department of Education was established with the passage of the Department of Education Organization Act on 27 September 1979. Carter waited a month before naming a secretary to head the new department. Possible candidates included Jerry Apodaca, the former Democratic governor of New Mexico; Wilson Riles, the superintendent of instruction for the state of California; Alan Campbell, the head of the Office of Personnel Management; and Mary Berry, the assistant secretary of education in the Department of Health, Education, and Welfare.

When Carter chose Hufstedler on 30 October 1979, it was a complete surprise to almost all observers, but Carter was under pressure from women's and minority groups to choose someone from their ranks. Despite the initial skepticism on her nomination, Hufstedler was praised at her confirmation hearing by Senator Alan Cranston, Democrat of California, who called her a "skilled and brilliant generalist."

Confirmed on 30 November 1979, by a vote of 81–2, Hufstedler was installed as the first secretary of education. Her tenure, which lasted until the end of the Carter administration on 20 January 1981, was marked by putting together the offices that had once existed as a subcabinet agency in HEW into a cohesive cabinet department. The initial

budget for the department was $14.2 billion, with some 17,200 employees, making it larger than five previously existing agencies. In her annual report for 1980 she wrote, "In 1980, the Department of Education had a significant legislative agenda. In addition to complicated and continual work on appropriations, the Department assumed responsibility for the reauthorization of the Higher Education Act, as part of the Education Amendments of 1980. Working closely with the President, key members of Congress, and affected interest groups, it helped bring the Amendments to passage. . . . The Department also assumed the responsibility for developing and presenting the President's major domestic initiative of 1980: The Youth Act. Besides taking the lead in drafting the legislation, the Department worked aggressively on its behalf in the Congress. With strong bipartisan support, the Act passed the House, as well as the Committee on Labor and Human Resources of the Senate. Unfortunately, a crowded Senate calendar foreclosed enactment of the Youth Act. . . . In 1980, the Department's agenda for executive action was also extensive. . . . High priority concerns included efforts to improve civil rights enforcement, to carry out presidential initiatives, and to respond to emergency problems"

Hufstedler left office in January 1981. In 1996, President Bill Clinton named her as chairman of the President's Commission on Immigration Reform, created by the Immigration Act of 1990 to review and evaluate the impact of immigration on domestic affairs and foreign policy.

References: *1980 Annual Report: U.S. Department of Education* (Washington, DC: GPO, 1980), 4–5; Haas, Garland A., *Jimmy Carter and the Politics of Frustration* (Jefferson, NC: McFarland, 1992), 88; "Hufstedler, Shirley (Ann) M(ount)," in Charles Moritz, *Current Biography 1980* (New York: H. W. Wilson, 1980), 139–161; King, Joan Hutchon, "Establishing the U.S. Department of Education during the Carter Administration, 1978–1979" (Ph.D. dissertation, Claremont Graduate School, 1980).

TERREL HOWARD BELL
1921–1996

Terrel Bell served as the U.S. commissioner of education, the subcabinet-level agency within the Department of Health, Education, and Welfare (HEW), from 1974 to 1976. His service as the second secretary of education (1981–1985) was marked by the establishment of the National Commission on Excellence in Education and the release of the 1983 report *A Nation at Risk,* which launched the school reform movement among conservatives in the United States.

Bell was born in the small farming community of Lava Hot Springs, Idaho, on 11 November 1921, the son of Willard Dewain Bell and Alta (née Martin) Bell. Bell's father died when Bell was small, and his mother sold the family farm; Bell attended several rural schools in Idaho. He enlisted in the Marine Corps when World War II started, serving with the rank of sergeant and working as a machine gun instructor. After his return to the United States, he earned a bachelor's degree from the Southern Idaho College of Education at Albion in 1946; he then went on to receive a master's degree from the University of Idaho in 1954 and a doctorate in education from the University of Utah in 1961.

Bell was involved in education for most of his life. After earning his bachelor's degree, he taught science at Eden Rural High School in Eden, Idaho, from 1946 to 1947. Afterward, he received a Ford Foundation fellowship in school administration from the University of Utah. He served as professor and chairman of the department of educational administration at Utah State University from 1962 to 1963. In 1963, he was named as superintendent of public instruction for all of the public schools in Utah, a post he held until 1970.

Bell, a Republican, was named by President Richard M. Nixon as deputy commissioner for school systems in the U.S. Office

of Education, a subcabinet agency of HEW and served, from 1970 to 1972, under Commissioner Sidney P. Marland, Jr. When Marland left office in November 1972, Bell was named as the acting commissioner until John Ottina took over in August 1973.

When Ottina left, in May 1974, after just nine months in office, Nixon named Bell as the permanent head of the office. During his tenure, which lasted until July 1976, Bell oversaw congressional passage of the Education Amendments of 1974, which established the National Center for Education Statistics in the Office of the Assistant Secretary for Education, and the Education for All Handicapped Children Act, which called for full educational advantages for handicapped children. In 1976, Bell resigned to become commissioner and chief executive officer of the Utah System of Higher Education, where he worked until 1981.

After the election of former California Governor Ronald Reagan as president in 1980, he sent one of his chief aides, Edwin Meese, to meet with Bell to convince him to take the post of secretary of education in the new administration. As Bell wrote later, he was horrified by what he heard. Meese told him that despite Bell's support for the establishment of Education as a cabinet department, Reagan had promised to abolish it if elected.

However, when Bell had served as commissioner of education, his boss was Caspar Weinberger, who had served as secretary of HEW and was Reagan's choice to serve as Secretary of Defense. Bell speculated that Weinberger had "put in a good word for him." Notwithstanding the fact that Bell would head a department he supported and Reagan wanted to do away with, Bell wanted the position. Convinced he could persuade Reagan to keep the department, he accepted, and his selection was announced on 7 January 1981, the last of Reagan's cabinet choices. Confirmed by the Senate on 22 January by a vote of 90 to 2, Bell took office as the second secretary of education.

In his memoirs, *The Thirteenth Man: A Reagan Cabinet Memoir,* Bell recalled, "In

January 1981 the department had a budget in excess of $14.7 billion and a staff of over 7,000 employees. Yet the department did not have a home. Its units were scatted all over the city in sixteen different locations. . . . Our mission was primarily one of advocating, monitoring, and supporting equal educational opportunity. For example, we allocated over $3.5 billion each year to schools to provide help to enhance learning for disadvantaged children. This financial assistance had to be allocated to school districts on the basis of the number of low-income children as defined by law. . . . They were to supplement what the states and local schools districts provided. The law was complex and required a staff of education specialists and auditors to prevent fraud and [the] misuse of funds. We also tried to keep schools informed of new and improved ways to teach the disadvantaged."

Despite Bell's insistence on fully funding the department, Reagan and his administration saw its creation as a concession to the National Education Association, a liberal teachers' union. Despite this plan to cut the department's budget, however, Reagan was only able to keep the Democrats from spending more than he wanted—starting with his Omnibus Reconciliation Act of 1981, Education saw an increase in appropriations from $13.9 billion in 1980 to $15.3 billion in 1984—a 10 percent increase, but a 14 percent cut in real dollar expenditures.

Bell's enduring legacy at Education may well be the establishment of the National Commission on Excellence in Education on 26 August 1981, and its 1983 report, *A Nation at Risk: The Imperative for Educational Reform*. In the report, the commission members wrote: "Our Nation is at risk. Our once unchallenged preeminence in commerce, industry, science, and technological innovation is being overtaken by competitors throughout the world . . . the educational foundations of our society are presently being eroded by a rising tide of mediocrity that threatens our very future as a Nation and a people. What was unimaginable a generation ago has begun to occur—others are match-ing and surpassing our educational attainments. . . . If an unfriendly foreign power had attempted to impose on America the mediocre educational performance that exists today, we might well have viewed it as an act of war. As it stands, we have allowed this to happen to ourselves. . . . We have, in effect, been committing an act of unthinking, unilateral educational disarmament. . . . Our society and its educational institutions seem to have lost sight of the basic purposes of schooling, and of the high expectations and disciplined effort needed to attain them. This report . . . seeks to generate reform of our educational system in fundamental ways and to renew the Nation's commitment to schools and colleges of high quality throughout the length and breadth of our land. . . . That we have compromised this commitment is . . . hardly surprising, given the multitude of often conflicting demands we have placed on our Nation's schools and colleges. They are routinely called on to provide solutions to personal, social, and political problems that the home and other institutions either will not or cannot resolve . . . these demands on our schools and colleges often exact an educational cost as well as a financial one."

Bell felt constrained in his role at the Department of Education because Reagan continued to work to cut the department's budget. Bell resigned on 8 November, effective 31 December 1984. Bell returned to private life in Utah, serving as a professor at the University of Utah. Bell died on 22 June 1996 at the age of 74. Bell had authored such works as *Effective Teaching: How to Recognize and Reward Competence, A Philosophy of Education for the Space Age, Your Child's Intellect: A Guide to Home-Based Preschool Education* (1962), and *A Performance Accountability System for School Administrators* (1974). In 1997, a year after his death, he was inducted into the Idaho Hall of Fame.

References: Bell, Terrel H., *The Thirteenth Man: A Reagan Cabinet Memoir* (New York: Free Press, 1988), 32–33; Verstegen, Deborah A., "Educational Fiscal Policy in the Reagan Administration," *Educational Evaluation and Policy Analysis* 12: 4 (Winter 1990), 367.

WILLIAM JOHN BENNETT
1943–

William Bennett has been called "the conscience of America" for his numerous books on ethics, including *The Death of Outrage* (1998). A strong voice in the conservative movement as the founder of Empower America with former Secretary of Housing and Urban Development Jack F. Kemp, William Bennett also served as the drug czar and secretary of education during the Reagan administration. Born in Brooklyn, New York, on 31 July 1943, Bennett attended local schools, then received his bachelor's degree from Williams College in 1965, his Ph.D. degree in philosophy from the University of Texas in 1967, and a law degree from Harvard Law School in 1971.

In 1972, Bennett went to work as an assistant to the president of Harvard University, until 1976. He then became the director and president of the National Humanities Center in Chapel Hill, North Carolina, where he became a spokesman for cultural and moral issues. In 1981, President Ronald Reagan named Bennett, at that time a registered Democrat, as the chairman of the National Endowment for the Humanities (NEH), a federal agency that distributes monies to the arts and culture nationally. As director of the NEH, Bennett moved the agency in a more conservative direction, He issued a report, *To Reclaim a Legacy: A Report on the Humanities in Higher Education,* in which he criticized the decline of the teaching of the humanities. He also attacked so-called multiculturalism and affirmative action.

On 8 November 1984, Secretary of Education Terrel Bell announced his resignation; possible successors included John R. Silber, president of Boston University, Gary L. Jones, the undersecretary of education, and Bennett. On 10 January 1985, Reagan announced Bennett's selection. Confirmed on 6 February 1985 by a vote of 93 to 0, he served until 20 September 1988.

Bennett's tenure at Education was a rocky one. He urged the passage of a constitutional amendment that would allow prayer in schools and asked for congressional enactment of a school voucher program, which would allow children in failing schools to take their tax dollars to go to another school, either public, private, or religious. *New York Times* journalist Edward B. Fiske wrote (18 September 1988), "Bennett noted with pride new regulations that Congress approved at his urging, allowing schools to spend federal funds on a wider variety of teaching methods used in bilingual education programs rather than one prescribed method. 'That was a huge victory,' he said, adding that he would be 'glad to compare our legislative accomplishments with those of any other Reagan administration officers.'"

Bennett resigned on 9 August 1988, and left on 20 September after his successor, Lauro Cavazos, was confirmed by the Senate. Bennett became the president of the Madison Center, a public policy forum, in Washington, D.C. However, soon after Vice-president George Bush was elected president in 1988, he named Bennett as head of the Office of National Drug Control Policy. Confirmed as the director, known as the drug czar, on 9 March 1989 by a vote of 97 to 2, he spent his tenure of a year on increased spending on drug control and law enforcement, although some critics contended that little was spent on education.

Bennett left office in 1990 and wrote several books, including *The Book of Virtues* (1993), *The Index of Leading Cultural Indicators* (1994), and *The Death of Outrage* (1998). He cofounded, with former Secretary of Housing and Urban Development Jack F. Kemp, the organization known as Empower America, which speaks on conservative social issues and policies. He also helped to establish the National Commission on Civic Renewal in 1997.

References: "Bennett, William John," in Robert Sobel, ed.-in-chief, *Biographical Directory of the United States Executive Branch, 1774–1989* (Westport, CT: Greenwood, 1990), 24–25; "Bennett,

William John," in Peter B. Levy, *Encyclopedia of the Reagan-Bush Years* (Westport, CT: Greenwood, 1996), 35–37.

LAURO FRED CAVAZOS
1927–

Lauro Cavazos was the first Hispanic named to a cabinet position; he served under two presidents—Reagan and Bush—as secretary of education. Born in Kingsville, Texas, on 1 April 1927, Cavazos is the son of Lauro Fred Cavazos, Sr., and Tomes (née Quintanilla) Cavazos. Cavazos entered the U.S. Army at the end of World War II, in 1945; after returning to the United States, he intended to become a commercial fisherman, but his father convinced him to get an education, and he studied for a time at Texas Agricultural and Industrial College in Kingsville, before he transferred to the Texas Technological College (now Texas Tech University) in Lubbock, where he earned a bachelor's degree in zoology in 1949 and a master's degree in zoological cytology in 1951. He then went to Iowa State University and received his doctorate in physiology in 1954.

Cavazos became an associate professor of anatomy at the Medical College of Virginia. In 1964, he became a full professor of anatomy at the Tufts University School of Medicine in Massachusetts, where he remained until 1980. During those years, he also served as a professor of anatomy and a professor of biological sciences at the Texas Tech University Health Sciences Center and then at Texas Tech University. From 1975 to 1980, Cavazos served as dean of the Tufts School of Medicine and, after leaving Tufts, as president of the Texas Tech University Health Sciences Center and Texas Tech University.

Cavazos, a Democrat, had criticized the Reagan administration for its cutbacks in the Department of Education. Still, when Secretary of Education William J. Bennett resigned on 9 August 1988, Reagan named Cavazos as his successor. Reagan's choice was hailed by Hispanics, but also decried as an attempt to gain Hispanic voters. Cavazos was confirmed on 20 September 1988 by a vote of 94 to 0. During his tenure, which lasted until 12 December 1990, Cavazos was criticized by Hispanic leaders for calling attention to the failure of Hispanic children in schools because of their poor English skills.

In an interview, Cavazos said, "Parental involvement and language competency are basic." He later said, "I have been criticized because I have continued to insist that additional funding is not the answer" to ending the problem of failing schools. He wrote that in the 1980s federal spending on education rose by $42 billion, but that test scores had failed to go up at all. He was a supporter of allowing parents vouchers to choose the schools their children attended, but he did not use the office as a bully pulpit as did his predecessor, William Bennett. Because of this, many criticized his leadership. On 12 December 1990, President Bush, looking for another, more effective, voice in education, asked for and received Cavazos's resignation. The former secretary then went to work as an adjunct professor of community health at Tufts University.

References: "Cavazos, Lauro Fred," in Robert Sobel, ed.-in-chief, *Biographical Directory of the United States Executive Branch, 1774–1989* (Westport, CT: Greenwood, 1990), 63–64; Conti, Kathe A., "Lauro F. Cavazos," in Joseph C. Tardiff and L. Mpho Mabunda, eds., *Dictionary of Hispanic Biography* (Detroit: Gale Research, 1996), 204–205.

ANDREW LAMAR ALEXANDER, JR.
1940–

Lamar Alexander may be better remembered for his two terms as governor of Tennessee (1979–1987) and his two unsuccessful campaigns for president (1996, 2000) than for his two years as the fifth secretary of education. Born in Knoxville, in Blount County, Tennessee, on 3 July 1940, he is the son of Andrew Alexander and Floreine (née Rankin) Alexander, both teachers. Alexander grew up in Maryville, Tennessee, and attended local schools. He graduated Phi Beta Kappa from Vanderbilt University in 1962; he was nominated twice for a Rhodes Scholarship. He earned his law degree from the New York University Law School in 1965. At that time, he became a law clerk for Judge John Minor Wisdom of the U.S. Court of Appeals for the Fifth Circuit in New Orleans. Wisdom was noted as one of the judges who used the law to desegregate much of the South in the 1960s. Alexander supplemented his pay by working in a jazz band in a bar in New Orleans.

In 1966, Alexander served as an campaign aide for Republican Howard Baker, who was running for the U.S. Senate. When Baker was elected, Alexander went to Washington to serve as Baker's legislative assistant. In 1969, based on his work for Baker, President Richard M. Nixon named Alexander as an executive assistant to Bruce Harlow, the president's congressional relations director.

Alexander worked in the White House until 1970, when he left to work for the Tennessee gubernatorial campaign of Republican Winfield Dunn. He then went to work as an attorney with the law firm of Dearborn & Ewing in Nashville. In 1974, Alexander captured the Republican gubernatorial nomination on his own, but was defeated by Democrat Ray Blanton. He then became a commentator for Nashville television station WSM and, in 1977, when Senator Baker became the Senate minority leader, returned to Washington as his special counsel.

In 1978, Alexander once again sought the governorship in Tennessee. Having run a campaign four years earlier that many considered aloof, this time he walked 1,000 miles across the state. He won the Republican nomination and, using the issue of payoff scandals that had rocked the Blanton administration, defeated Democrat Jake

Butcher by more than 140,000 votes out of some 1.2 million cast. Blanton, who had been implicated in selling pardons to cronies, began to pardon numerous felons days before he was to leave office. Alexander took the oath of office on 17 January 1979, three days before he was constitutionally able, and had police bar Blanton from his office until his term had officially ended. Alexander was reelected overwhelmingly in 1982. He served as chairman of the National Governors Association from 1985 to 1986.

After he left office, Alexander moved to Australia, where he wrote *Six Months Off* and established a company called Common Arms Outdoors. In 1988, he was named as president of the University of Tennessee, where he served until 1991. On 12 December 1990, Secretary of Education Lauro Cavazos resigned; five days later, President George Bush named Alexander as Cavazos's successor. His work on education issues as governor of Tennessee, as well as his national attention to education as the chairman of the National Governors Conference, made him a leading candidate to head up the Department of Education.

Confirmed on 14 March 1991, Alexander served for two years, until the end of the Bush administration on 20 January 1993. In an interview with journalist Edward Klein in *Parade* magazine in August 1991, Alexander stated, "Our country is facing a dual crisis in education. On the one hand, most American students aren't being taught what they need to know and ought to be able to do in order to live a happy and productive life. At the same time their parents have been caught in the middle of their lives undereducated and underskilled." Klein wrote, "Along with many others, Alexander says that the U.S. faces a clear and present danger to its existence because of . . . the failure of our schools. He is aware, of course, that generations of reformers going back to the philosopher-educator John Dewey have tried, and often failed, to fix the country's educational system. Nonetheless, Alexander, a man of boundless energy and enthusiasm, has stepped forward to propose both a clear-cut strategy and a timetable for achieving what many people think will be the impossible." Many consider him to have been a successful administrator, even though no major congressional legislation was enacted during his service.

After leaving office in 1993, Alexander went to work for the Knoxville law firm of Fowler, Roundree and Robertson. In 1995 and 1999, he ran unsuccessfully for the Republican presidential nomination, remembered for his plaid woolen shirt that he wore to numerous campaign appearances and his stands on educational improvement. His 1994 trek across America, to gain insight on the thinking of average Americans, was chronicled in his book, *We Know What to Do.*

References: "Alexander, Lamar," in John W. Raimo, ed., *Biographical Directory of the Governors of the United States, 1978–1983* (Westport, CT: Meckler Publishing, 1985), 295–296; "Alexander, Lamar," in Marie Marmo Mullaney, ed., *Biographical Directory of the Governors of the United States, 1983–1988* (Westport, CT: Meckler Publishing, 1989), 319; Klein, Edward, "'We're Talking About a Revolution': Secretary of Education Lamar Alexander Says He Means to Spark a Transformation in America's Schools," *Parade,* 25 August 1991, 4.

RICHARD WILSON RILEY
1933–

Richard Riley, a former governor of South Carolina, is the longest-serving secretary of education and will have served eight full years in the office if he remains until the end of Bill Clinton's term in 2001. Riley was hailed during his gubernatorial terms for his reforms in education and nuclear waste disposal. He was selected in 1992 by President-elect Bill Clinton, for secretary of education. Riley, born on 2 January 1933 in Greenville County, South Carolina, is the son of Edward Patterson Riley, an attorney, and Martha Elizabeth (née Dixon) Riley. He attended local schools and earned his bachelor's degree with honors from Furman University in Greenville in 1954.

Riley then joined the U.S. Navy and served on a minesweeper patrol ship from 1954 to 1956. After leaving the service, he entered the University of South Carolina Law School and received his law degree in 1959. He was admitted to the state bar that same year and joined his father in the law firm of Riley & Riley. In 1960, his father, a Democrat, went to work for the presidential campaign of Senator John F. Kennedy, and Riley went to Washington, D.C., and became legal counsel for the Senate Judiciary Committee. Riley returned to South Carolina in 1963 and ran for a seat in the state House of Representatives won, and served until 1967. Riley supported racial desegregation in the state; he weathered bitter criticism and was elected to the state Senate in 1967. In 1974, he ran for the Democratic gubernatorial nomination, but lost to Congressman William Jennings Bryan Dorn.

In 1975, he resigned his seat in the state Senate to assist in the presidential campaign of Georgia Governor Jimmy Carter. Returning to South Carolina, he again ran for governor in 1978, defeating Lieutenant Governor W. Brantley Harvey in the primary, and defeating Republican Congressman Edward Young in the general election by 150,000 votes out of some 650,000 cast; he took office on 10 January 1979. Historian Marie Marmo Mullaney wrote, "As chief executive, Riley was prominent particularly as an environmentalist. He refused to permit the dumping of nuclear waste from the Three Mile Island nuclear generator in his state after the accident at that plant. Riley urged a federal solution to the difficulty. In 1980 President Carter named him to the Nuclear Waste Disposal Council."

Riley's enduring legacy in South Carolina was his work to reform the state school system. After he convinced the state legislature to change the constitution allowing for a governor to serve two terms, he was easily reelected in 1982. In 1983, he sent an education reform package to the state legislature, but before submitting it, he spent time canvassing voters and other constituencies to build support for another package proposal. In 1984, his Education Improvement Act was passed with support from both business and teachers' unions. By the time he left office in 1987, Riley's program was getting results in South Carolina schools, including a rise in Scholastic Aptitude Test (SAT) scores.

After leaving office, Riley went to work as the partner of the Greenville and Columbia law firm of Nelson, Mullins, Riley, and Scarborough. In 1992, after Arkansas Governor Bill Clinton was elected president, Riley was asked to serve as personnel director of the transition team, assisting in selecting hundreds of applicants to fill government positions. On 21 December 1992, Clinton named Riley to serve as his secretary of education, a selection that drew bipartisan praise. Confirmed on 21 January 1993, he was sworn in the next day as the sixth secretary of education.

During his eight years, Riley has sought to save his department from being merged with another cabinet agency. Under attack from Republicans for years of failing school grades nationwide despite massive federal spending, he worked with Secretary of Labor Robert Reich to mold a reform package that would streamline the agency, but at the same time assist in its mandate. He also reversed a ruling enunciated under his predecessor, Lamar Alexander, that setting aside scholarships for black students only was a form of reverse discrimination against whites. In a 3 July 1995 article in the *Washington Post,* he denounced a proposed congressional enactment that would merge the Department of Education into another cabinet department: "In an era in which education is more than ever the key to a strong and prosperous America, maintaining a separate, efficient Department of Education with a secretary who has the ear of the president is essential to manage federal education programs effectively and to bring critical education issues to the attention of the nation. . . . While critics point to the education department's "bureaucracy" as a primary reason for its elimination, in truth, this administration is the first since the department's creation 15 years ago to eliminate or consolidate unnecessary programs, reduce regulations and cut staff. . . . The Department of Education . . . administers more dollars per employee—about $6 million annually—than any other Cabinet agency. . . . As a result of significant staff reductions, the department's administrative costs account for just 2 percent of its budget, much of which goes to accountability and quality control. Administrative costs will fall even further as the department trims its staff by an additional 9 percent by the year 2000."

In 1996, Riley announced in his State of Education address that the most urgent task facing American schools was to teach children to read. "Our national reading scores are flat and have been flat far too long," he said. "America does reasonably well on international comparisons when it comes to literacy. But too many of our young people are groping through school without having mastered the most essential and basic skill." In 1997, Riley attacked school vouchers, saying that they were "a very simplistic world view, a silver-bullet solution, and it is just dead wrong." He believed vouchers diverted money from public schools to private schools and benefited primarily wealthy students.

References: "Riley, Richard W.," in Judith Graham, ed., *Current Biography 1993* (New York: H. W. Wilson, 1993), 490–493; "Riley, Richard Wilson," in John W. Raimo, ed., *Biographical Directory of the Governors of the United States, 1978–1983* (Westport, CT: Meckler Publishing, 1985), 277; "Riley, Richard Wilson," in Marie Marmo Mullaney, ed., *Biographical Directory of the Governors of the United States, 1983–1988* (Westport, CT: Meckler Publishing, 1989), 299–300.

ENERGY

———⊰●⊱———

The Department of Energy was added as the twelfth department to the cabinet in 1977 from the remnants of the Federal Energy Administration and the Energy Research and Development Administration, after years of American concern for the country's sources of energy, particularly oil from the Middle East. Unlike other agencies that became cabinet departments over long periods of time, Energy became a department just four years after the importance of energy as a national issue was first voiced.

On 29 June 1973, President Richard M. Nixon established the Energy Policy Office. Prior to this time, energy concerns in the U.S. government were focused in three areas: the Atomic Energy Commission, the Federal Power Commission, and the Department of the Interior, which had jurisdiction over national oil reserves and the oil and coal industries. The Atomic Energy Commission, until it was abolished by Congress in 1974, had full control over the development and use of atomic, and then nuclear, power and experimentation in the United States after the end of World War II.

Founded in 1920, the Federal Power Commission was established to regulate the growing electric power industry after the end of World War I. The Interior Department's involvement in the oversight of national oil reserves led to the Teapot Dome scandal in the early 1920s, but it continued its supervision of the coal and oil industries through the Bureau of Mines (established in 1910), oversaw the leasing of public lands for exploration for these resources through the U.S. Geological Survey, and managed their use through the Bureau of Land Management. This patchwork of agencies did not overlap in their responsibilities, but they did not coordinate them, either.

In 1974, Congress abolished the Atomic Energy Commission and established two new offices, the Energy Research and Development Administration having responsibility over nuclear development and the Nuclear Regulatory Commission overseeing regulation of the nuclear industry and the uses of nuclear power. This development, along with Nixon's creation of the Energy Policy Office, signaled the growing issue of energy in the daily lives of Americans.

In October 1973, when the Yom Kippur War broke out in the Middle East, the Organization of Petroleum Exporting Countries (OPEC) initiated a boycott of oil against the United States for supporting Israel. Nixon proposed a cabinet restructuring in which all energy-related offices would be grouped into a new Department of Energy and National Resources, which would include the Department of the Interior. When this plan died, he instead created the Federal Energy Office to replace the Energy Policy Office and then created the Federal Energy Administration. However, Nixon soon became preoccupied with the Watergate scandal, and the idea never came to fruition before the president resigned from office in August 1974. President Gerald R. Ford, in his short time in office, did not have a chance either to expound on Nixon's idea or to establish his own. He did sign, on 22 December, the Energy Policy and Conservation Act, which mandated fuel efficiency standards in automobiles.

The administration of President Jimmy Carter made energy its top domestic issue when it came into office in January 1977. Carter was determined to abolish several sub-cabinet-level agencies that overlapped in their jurisdiction over national energy matters and create one encompassing federal agency. On 2 February 1977, he signed into law the Emergency Gas Act of 1977; five days later he named John F. O'Leary as the administrator of the Federal Energy Administration. On 1 March 1977, President Carter submitted to Congress a plan to establish a Department of Energy, incorporating the Federal Energy Commission, the Federal Power Commission, and the Energy Research and Development Administration into one cabinet-level agency.

On 18 April 1977, he gave a national address in which he said that any delay in coping with the energy situation in the United States would result in a national catastrophe. Two days later, he submitted to Congress a 103-page report called the *National Energy Plan,* which laid out his blueprint to correct the growing energy crisis. In the plan, he called for several goals that he said could be met by 1985—a reduction in the nation's annual growth of needed energy to less than 2 percent, reduction of imported oil amounts to half of 1977 levels, a cut in the use of gasoline by 10 percent, the creation of a national oil reserve of some 1 billion barrels, an increase in coal production by at least two-thirds, and the use of solar energy by 2.5 million homes by that date.

The plan was ambitious; it included a five-cent per gallon standby tax on gasoline. After congressional hearings, throughout which numerous critics of the plan denounced it, the House passed the Carter bill intact but without the gasoline tax; the Senate soon broke the bill into separate bills and passed these with some major differences. A House-Senate conference ironed out distinctions between the two pieces of legislation, renamed the new bill the Department of Energy Organization Act, and passed it in both houses, and Carter signed it into law on 4 August 1977.

In its statement of findings, the Congress, in the department organic act, found that:

1. the United States faces an increasing shortage of nonrenewable energy resources;

2. this energy shortage and our increasing dependence on foreign energy supplies present a serious threat to the national security of the United States and to the health, safety and welfare of its citizens;

3. a strong national energy program is needed to meet the present and future energy needs of the Nation consistent with overall national economic, environmental and social goals;

4. responsibility for energy policy, regulation, and research, development and demonstration is fragmented in many departments and agencies and thus does not allow for the com-

prehensive, centralized focus necessary for effective coordination of energy supply and conservation programs; and

5. formulation and implementation of a national energy program require the integration of major Federal energy functions into a single department in the executive branch.

Congress also formulated the objectives of the department: "To achieve, through the Department, [the] effective management of energy functions of the Federal Government, including consultation with the heads of other Federal departments and agencies in order to encourage them to establish and observe policies consistent with a coordinated energy policy, and to promote maximum possible energy conservation measures in connection with the activities within their respective jurisdictions. . . . To provide for a mechanism through which a coordinated national energy policy can be formulated and implemented to deal with the short-, mid- and long-term energy problems of the Nation; and to develop plans and programs for dealing with domestic energy production and import shortages. . . . To create and implement a comprehensive energy conservation strategy that will receive the highest priority in the national energy program. . . . To carry out the planning, coordination, support, and management of a balanced and comprehensive energy research and development program. . . . To place major emphasis on the development and commercial use of solar, geothermal, recycling and other technologies utilizing renewable energy resources."

The day after signing the law, President Carter named former Secretary of Defense James Schlesinger as the first secretary of energy. The department was activated on 1 October 1977, per an executive order signed by President Carter. On 9 November, he signed the National Energy Act, which included the National Energy Conservation Policy Act, the Powerplant and Industrial Fuel Use Act, the Public Utilities Regulatory Policy Act, the Energy Tax Act, and the Natural Gas Policy Act. These measures established favorable tax rates and research grants to develop and expand the use of fuel ethanol as an alternative to oil.

In his first annual report for the new department, Schlesinger wrote of the new directives of the new agency: "The nation's demand for energy is increasing, while its supplies of oil and natural gas are diminishing. As these powerful trends have collided in recent years, imports have risen rapidly to fill the gap. Recent events have underscored the cost and vulnerability of such imports. And, unless strong action is taken now and steadfastly sustained, imports—and their costs—will rise rapidly in the future, implying disastrous consequences for the nation's economy and political security." Schlesinger oversaw the creation of the department, including Carter's early program to increase the use of solar energy and the decontrol of oil prices in response to continued energy shortages.

The firing of Schlesinger led to the appointment of Charles Duncan, Jr., deputy secretary of defense and a former president of Coca-Cola, in July 1979. Duncan spent the one and a half years of his tenure establishing new assistant secretaries for fossil fuels and for nuclear energy. On 30 June 1980, Carter signed the Energy Security Act, which consisted of six individual pieces of legislation: the Biomass Energy and Alcohol Fuels Act, the Renewable Energy Resources Act, the Solar Energy and Energy Conservation Act and Solar Energy and Energy Conservation Bank Act, the Geothermal Energy Act, the Ocean Thermal Energy Conversion Act, and the United States Synthetic Fuels Corporation Act. These acts, the first major congressional legislation to deal with the effects of the Arab oil embargo, established favorable tax rates and research grants to develop and expand the use of fuel ethanol, an alternative to oil.

The presidency of Ronald Reagan saw the installation of former South Carolina Governor James B. Edwards as the department's third secretary. Edwards knew when he accepted the nomination that President Reagan was intending to abolish the agency. Edwards claimed that he looked forward to "working myself out of a job." Almost immediately, Reagan and Edwards began to work to do just that—make Energy the first department to leave the cabinet since the Post Office Department in 1971.

On 28 January, Reagan signed Executive Order 12287, which ordered immediate government decontrol over crude oil and other refined petroleum products. Further, in his 1982 budget, Reagan got the Democratic-controlled Congress to cut $2.3 billion of the department's $6.8 billion budget. In September, Edwards announced that he recommended to Reagan that an additional $2.3 billion be cut from the 1983 budget. In addition, in October 1981 Edwards laid off 2,000 department workers—10 percent of the agency's workforce—in a move that showed how quickly Reagan was planning to be rid of Energy.

Edwards, in the meantime, was working to improve the department he was preparing to eliminate. He announced a major reorganization of the department on 25 February 1981, with the aim of improving management and increasing the emphasis on research, development, and production. On 17 July 1981 he released the department's third national energy plan, *Securing America's Future*. But Reagan continued with his plan to dismantle the department. On 24 September 1981 he announced, "We do not need an Energy Department to solve our basic energy problems." The following May, he recommended to Congress that all of its functions be transferred to the Department of Commerce. However, under Secretaries Donald P. Hodel (1982–1985) and John Herrington (1985–1989), the department continued its responsibilities, including new obligations under the Nuclear Waste Policy Act of 1982 and the establishment of the Office of Civilian Radioactive Waste Management.

Reagan never got congressional authority to abolish the agency, because Democrats on Capitol Hill refused to bring such an enactment to the floor for a vote even though 1,200 federal positions would have been eliminated and savings of some $100–250 million annually would be immediately realized. Senator Thomas Eagleton of Missouri stated in 1982, "This is not simply a reorganization. For all its flaws, the Department of Energy symbolizes our recognition of the problem which hangs over our prosperity and our national security like Damocles' sword. We should be doubling our efforts to free ourselves from our dependence on foreign oil."

Under President George Bush, the plan to eliminate the department was dropped. His secretary, Admiral James D. Watkins, emphasized more environmental protection, especially with the establishment of the Office of Environmental Restoration and Waste Management, initiated new waste management programs, and oversaw the initial fight over the use of Yucca Mountain in Nevada to store radioactive waste. Watkins's biggest accomplishment during his four-year tenure (1989–1993) was his National Energy Strategy in December 1990.

Under President Bill Clinton, three secretaries have served: Hazel O'Leary (1993–1997), the first black and the first woman to head the department; Federico Peña (1997–1998), the first Hispanic; and Bill Richardson (1998–present), also a Hispanic and a former U.S. congressman. Under O'Leary the department solidified its hold as a permanent cabinet agency. Her key accomplishment was the "openness" campaign she launched, opening and revealing the files on old nuclear tests from the 1940s through the 1990s—films of early nuclear tests and information on plutonium left behind by the United States in Vietnam at the end of the war.

Her successor, Federico Peña, served only a year in a mainly transitional tenure, but he pushed administration policy on arms testing, nuclear weapons proliferation, and oversight of the U.S. nuclear stockpile. Peña was replaced by Bill Richardson, a seven-term congressman from New Mexico who had served a year as U.S. ambassador to the United Nations. During his tenure with the Energy Department, allegations of spying by Chinese scientists in the United States arose and gas prices exploded to their highest levels since the oil boycott of the early 1970s. In 2000, two computer hard drives were misplaced at the Los Alamos National Laboratory, leading to harsh criticism from Capitol Hill of lax security at nuclear laboratories, as well as Richardson's handling of the matter.

Budgets for the department have continued to grow since its inception. The budget request for 1980 was $8.4 billion; this increased to $12.8 billion in 1985, $15 billion in 1990, and $18.5 billion in 1995.

The department, although housed in thirteen buildings across the District of Columbia, has its main headquarters in the James Forrestal Building, located at 1000 Independence Avenue.

References: Fehner, Terrence R., and Jack M. Holl, *Department of Energy, 1977–1994: A Summary History* (Washington, DC: Department of Energy, 1994); Pratt, Joseph, "Department of Energy," in Donald R. Whitnah, ed.-in-chief, *Government Agencies* (Westport, CT: Greenwood, 1983), 110–116; Schlesinger report in *U.S. Department of Commerce: Annual Report to Congress, 1978* (Washington, DC: GPO, 1979), 5.

JAMES RODNEY SCHLESINGER
1929–

See Secretary of Defense, 1973–1976

CHARLES WILLIAM DUNCAN, JR.
1926–

Charles Duncan was serving as the deputy secretary of defense when President Jimmy Carter initiated a major restructuring of his cabinet that included replacing Secretary of Energy James R. Schlesinger. Carter named Charles Duncan as the second secretary of the Energy Department, from August 1979 until the end of the Carter administration in January 1981. Born in Houston, Texas, on 9 September 1926, Duncan is the son of Charles William Duncan, Sr., a Houston businessman, and Mary Lillian (née House) Duncan.

Duncan attended Houston schools, then was sent to the Sewanee Military Academy in Sewanee, Tennessee. From 1944 until 1946, he served in the U.S. Army; when discharged, he entered Rice University in Houston, which awarded him a bachelor of science degree in chemical engineering in 1947. He worked, for a short time, as a roustabout and chemical engineer for the Humble Oil and Refining Company in Houston, then went to the University of Texas to take do additional study in management.

Duncan went to work for his family's business, the Duncan Coffee Company, run by his uncle. However, when the uncle died in 1957 and the company was merged with a larger company, Duncan disagreed with the new owners in his new role as administrative vice-president. In 1958, Duncan and his brother John helped buy back the business, and they formed the Duncan Foods Company. In 1966, Duncan merged this new company with Coca-Cola.

Duncan was president of the Coca-Cola Food Division in Houston from 1964 to 1967. In 1967, Coca-Cola named Duncan as the chairman of Coca-Cola Europe, in charge of all of their interests on that continent. In 1970, they recalled him to the United States, impressed with his administrative skills, and named him as executive vice-president of the corporation. In November 1971, he was named as president and appeared to be headed to become chairman. However, on 7 May 1974, he resigned from Coca-Cola to become the chairman of the board of the Rotan Mosie Financial Corporation, an investment banking firm in Houston.

While he was working in Atlanta, Duncan met and became a friend of Georgia's governor, Jimmy Carter, as well as Carter's attorney and friend, Charles H. Kirbo. When Carter was elected president in 1976, he named Duncan as deputy secretary of defense under Harold Brown. Duncan put his holding in Coca-Cola and other companies into a blind trust, and he easily won Senate confirmation. In his two and a half years at the Pentagon, Duncan oversaw the day-to-day operations of the department, pushed for the building of the F-16 fighter plane, and advanced the cause on Capitol Hill for the right of women to serve in combat positions in the armed forces. He vigorously defended Carter's position to return the Panama Canal to Panama before Congress.

In 1979, Carter offered Duncan the post of administrator of the General Services Administration, but he declined. Instead, following the resignation of Secretary of Energy James Schlesinger, Carter named Duncan to the vacancy on 20 July 1979. The *Washington Post* was disdainful of the new appointee: "Mr. Duncan has a strong reputation as an administrator and technician. He appears to score well on the new standard of loyalty, and, according to advance reports, will do as he is told. But who is going to tell him? . . . the choice of Mr. Duncan indicates that the president wants a secretary who will devote himself to the questionable administrative chaos within the department. . . . The implication of Mr. Duncan's appointment is that Mr. Carter intends to direct energy policy from the White House. But how? He cannot do it all himself and his staff cannot do it, yet his recent speeches have set in motion programs requiring the most skillful and forceful political guidance."

Even though some senators considered Duncan a mere figurehead, believing that energy policy would be run from the White House, Duncan was easily confirmed on 31 July 1979 by a 95 to 1 vote. He took office on 24 August as the second energy secretary. During his tenure, which lasted until the end of the Carter administration on 20 January 1981, Duncan was involved in a restructuring of the department, categorizing the bureaus by technology or by fuel, and adding assistant secretaries for fossil fuels and for nuclear energy.

In his 1980 annual report, Duncan wrote, "The Department of Energy sees its mission as assuring the Nation's orderly transition from an economy dependent upon oil to an economy relying upon diversified energy resources. . . . From 1985 to 2000, the world will begin to make a significant move away from oil dependence. During this period, the world has several attractive options for reducing demand for oil and diversifying its energy supply. These include more coal and coal-derived synthetic fuels, solar technologies, oil shale, unconventional gas supplies and nuclear power, as well as continued improvements in the efficiency of energy use." Duncan oversaw the enactment of the Energy Security Act of 1980.

When the Carter administration ended, Duncan returned to private business.

References: Department of Energy, "Secretary's Annual Report to Congress: January 1980" (Washington, DC: GPO, 1980), 1; "Duncan, Charles W(illiam, Jr.)," in Charles Moritz, ed., *Current Biography 1980* (New York: H. W. Wilson, 1980), 81–84.

JAMES BURROWS EDWARDS

1927–

James Edwards, an oral surgeon and former governor of South Carolina, was Ronald Reagan's choice as the third secretary of energy. Edwards was born on 24 June 1927 in Hawthorne, Florida, the son of O. Morton Edwards and Bertie (née Hieronymus) Edwards. When he was young, his parents, both schoolteachers, moved to Mount Pleasant, South Carolina. During World War II, Edwards served in the U.S. Maritime Service. After the war, he attended the College of Charleston, from which he earned a bachelor of science degree in 1950. Five years later, he earned a D.M.D. degree from the University of Louisville School of Dentistry in Kentucky. From 1955 until 1957, Edwards served in the U.S. Navy; after being discharged with the rank of lieutenant commander, he completed his training to become an oral surgeon with an internship at the University of Pennsylvania Graduate Medical School from 1957 to 1958, and as a resident of oral surgery at the Henry Ford Hospital in Detroit, Michigan, from 1958 to 1960. Soon after, he established a dental practice in Charleston. In addition to his practice, Edwards served as a consultant to the U.S. Public Health Service.

In 1964 he was elected chairman of the Charleston County Republican Party and, in 1968, was a delegate to the Republican National Convention in Miami Beach, Florida. In 1971, he ran for a seat in the U.S. House of Representatives, but lost to Democrat L. Mendel Rivers. The following year, Edwards was elected to a seat in the South Carolina State Senate.

In 1974, he was unopposed for the Republican nomination for governor and defeated Democrat William Jennings Bryan Dorn with 51 percent of the vote. Edwards thus became the first Republican governor of South Carolina since Reconstruction. Serving a single four-year term, from 1975 to 1979, Edwards established the South Carolina Energy Research Institute, chaired the Nuclear Energy Subcommittee of the National Governors Association, and was chairman of an energy committee for the Republican Governors Association. He angered blacks by arguing for cuts in welfare waste, but earned credit for cracking down on police corruption. Edwards was highly popular and could have run for a second term in 1978, or for a U.S. Senate seat, but he decided to retire to his dental practice.

However, Edwards remained politically active. In 1976, he was a major backer of former California Governor Ronald Reagan, who lost the presidential nomination that year to President Gerald R. Ford; in fact, Edwards delivered South Carolina's delegates for Reagan at the 1976 convention. In 1980, when Reagan ran again and won the presidency, Edwards was a driving force in his state. Reagan then named Edwards as his secretary of energy. Despite the fact that Edwards's only experience in energy matters had come when he had clashed with the Carter administration over the reopening of a nuclear reprocessing plant in Barnwell, South Carolina, and that the department he was to head was targeted by Reagan for elimination, Edwards accepted. He told reporters that "I'd like to go to Washington and close the Energy Department down and work myself out of a job."

Confirmed by the Senate on 22 January 1981, by a vote of 93 to 3, Edwards took office as the third secretary of energy. During his tenure, which lasted until 5 November 1982, Edwards worked studiously to have Congress abolish the department and transfer its responsibilities to the Department of Commerce. In the meantime, he worked to end price controls on crude oil and gasoline and streamlined the department with massive cuts in employees—more than 2,000, or 10 percent of the total, let go in October 1981. Under Edwards, the department saw a slashing of its budget, from $6.8 billion to $4.5 billion in 1982, and Edwards, before leaving office, asked that an additional $2.3 billion be cut from the 1983 budget. Edwards's biggest accomplishment was his release of the department's third national energy plan, *Securing America's Future.*

Edwards resigned on 5 November 1982 to become president of the Medical University of South Carolina (MUSC). In 1990, President George Bush nominated Edwards to serve as a member of the board of directors of the Communications Satellite Corporation (COMSAT). In December 1999 Edwards retired from the Medical University of South Carolina. The Dr. James B. Edwards College of Dental Medicine at MUSC is named in his honor.

References: "A Dentist for Energy," *Newsweek,* 5 January 1981, 18; "Edwards, James B(urrows)," in Charles Moritz, ed., *Current Biography 1982* (New York: H. W. Wilson, 1982), 106–109; "Edwards, James Burrows," in John W. Raimo, ed., *Biographical Directory of the Governors of the United States, 1978–1983* (Westport, CT: Meckler Publishing, 1985), 273–275.

DONALD PAUL HODEL
1935–

On 5 November 1982, President Ronald Reagan named Donald P. Hodel as the fourth secretary of energy, replacing James B. Edwards. Hodel, who had given up his post as undersecretary of the Interior, had vast experience in the field of energy, serving as deputy administrator and administrator of the Bonneville (Washington State) Power Administration (BPA). He later served, from 1985 until 1989, as secretary of the Interior.

Hodel was born on 23 May 1935 in Portland, Oregon, on 23 May 1935, the son of Philip E. Hodel and Theresia Rose (née Brodt) Hodel. He became interested in politics at a young age and studied government at Harvard University. While there, he became a member of the Young Republicans Club and served as treasurer and president. He graduated with a bachelor of arts degree in 1957, then earned a law degree from the University of Oregon Law School in 1960. He then joined the Portland firm of Davies,

Biggs, Strayer, Stoel, & Boley.

In 1963, Hodel left the firm to join the Georgia-Pacific Corporation, a major American lumber and paper products company, as a corporate attorney. In 1969, he left Georgia-Pacific to become the deputy administrator of BPA, a federal agency that sells cheap power to the northwest United States. Hodel served as deputy administrator until 1972, when he was named as administrator. He held this position until 1977 and, during these years, played an active role in energy planning for the Northwest. Part of his plan was the construction of five nuclear power plants in Washington State, a project called the Washington Public Power Supply System, or WPPSS. However, due to cost overruns, the project became nicknamed "Whoops" and was eventually dropped. After leaving the BPA, Hodel established Hodel Associates, an energy consulting firm and remained its head until 1981.

In 1981, Hodel was named by President Ronald Reagan as undersecretary of the Interior, serving under Secretary James Watt. Watt was a controversial figure because he fought environmentalists on opening up public lands for the exploration of oil and other natural resources, as well as for grazing by cattle. Hodel, as his deputy, helped formulate departmental policy, but was also more moderate in his ideas than Watt. Journalist Philip Shabacoff said that Hodel exhibited "political shrewdness, pragmatism, an efficient management style, and plain hard work." These qualities made Hodel a leading figure for a cabinet position, and when Secretary of Energy James B. Edwards resigned in November 1982, Reagan named Hodel, with his vast experience in energy-related matters, as his successor.

Confirmed by the Senate on 8 December 1982, by a vote of 86 to 8, Hodel took office as the fourth secretary of energy, the first head of that department with real energy experience. Hodel strove to improve department morale after the major job and budget cuts Reagan and Edwards had initiated and set in motion the biennial department energy policy plan in 1983.

In his 1983 report, Hodel explained, "The U.S. energy situation today is significantly better than it was in 1981 . . . total energy efficiency has increased; domestic energy resources are being developed more effectively; prices have declined; U.S. dependence on foreign energy sources have diminished; and the Nation's vulnerability to energy supply disruptions has been markedly reduced, especially through additions to our strategic petroleum reserves and through lower levels of oil imports." Assistant Secretary Robert C. Odle said of Hodel, "Six months after he got to the Energy Department he knew more about the jobs of all the assistant secretaries than the assistant secretaries themselves."

On 10 January 1985, Reagan named Hodel as secretary of the interior, to replace William P. Clark. Ruth Norris wrote in 1985, "Hodel accepted the Interior Department nomination along with a five point mission: 'Preserving the nation's national park, wilderness, and wildlife resources, enhancing America's ability to meet our energy and mineral needs with domestic resources; increasing the supply of quality water resources; improving the federal government's relationship with state and local governments; and developing the economic and social resources of native Americans and people of the U.S. territories.'"

Confirmed on 6 February 1985, by a vote of 93 to 1, Hodel became the forty-seventh secretary of the Interior. During his service, which lasted until the end of the Reagan administration in January 1989, Hodel tried unsuccessfully to get Congress to approve development of oil resources in the Arctic National Wildlife Refuge in Alaska and the opening of the outer continental shelf to oil drilling, stands that earned him enmity from his critics.

After leaving government, Hodel returned to the private sector. From 1997 to 1999, he served as head of the Christian Coalition, a group of conservative religious groups.

References: Department of Energy, "Secretary's Annual Report to Congress, September 1983" (Washington, DC: GPO, 1983), 1; "Hodel, Donald P(aul)," in Charles Moritz, ed., *Current Biography 1987* (New York: H. W. Wilson, 1987), 234–238; Norris, Ruth, "Words and Deeds," *Audubon* 87 (September 1985), 28–31.

JOHN STEWART HERRINGTON
1939–

John Herrington was a California attorney with close ties to Ronald Reagan when selected to serve as the fifth secretary of energy; he had served with distinction as the deputy assistant to the president, the director of the Office of White House Personnel, and assistant secretary of the Navy for Manpower and Reserve Affairs. Born on 31 May 1939 in Los Angeles, California, John Herrington is the son of James Herrington and Mary Herrington. He graduated from Stanford University, with a bachelor's degree in economics in 1961, and he earned his LL.B. and J.D. degrees at the University of California's Hastings College of Law in 1964. He was admitted to the California bar and opened a private practice, in 1965, dealing with corporate, real estate, taxation, and business law until 1981.

In 1966 Herrington, a Republican, volunteered to work for the California gubernatorial campaign of Ronald Reagan; because of his loyalty to Reagan, he was labeled a Reaganite. In 1980, Herrington served as the director of advance for the western region for Reagan's 1980 presidential campaign. After Reagan was elected, Herrington was named assistant secretary of the navy for manpower and reserve affairs in September 1981. In 1983 he moved to the White House to serve as special assistant to James A. Baker, the White House Chief of Staff. He also served as an assistant to the president for personnel.

On 10 January 1985, in a cabinet shake-up, Reagan named Secretary of Energy Donald Hodel as secretary of the Interior and named Herrington to replace Hodel at Energy. Nominated on 18 January, Herrington was confirmed by the Senate on 6 February, by a vote of 93 to 1, and he took office as the fifth secretary of energy.

Herrington spent his tenure, which ended on 20 January 1989, trying to reform the department. He streamlined the federal government's uranium enrichment program into a more efficient policy and closed enrichment facilities in Ohio and Tennessee to cut the budget. He gave priority to cleaning up abandoned nuclear waste sites and studied the idea of merging the department into the Department of the Interior. A history of the department recounts, "One of Herrington's first actions was to order a special report assessing the environmental, health, and safety activities within the Department. The report . . . termed these departmental activities 'a disgrace.' . . . Morale is low, and as successive reports recommending action are followed by no action, it sinks further. Herrington moved quickly to resolve the problem. On 18 September 1985, he announced the restructuring of the Department's environmental, safety and health program. Previously scattered responsibilities within the Department were consolidated under the direction of a newly-created assistant secretary for environment, safety and health. Herrington observed that the 'environmental problems we are finding now at DOE facilities are, for the most part, legacies from the past, from activities conducted in a different atmosphere and under different standards than today's. What was acceptable in 1945 is not acceptable in 1985.' Herrington also ordered a thorough environmental survey of all departmental facilities to identify problem areas and technical safety appraisals of the Department's nuclear facilities."

After leaving office, Herrington served, in the 1990s, as chairman of the California state Republican Party.

References: Fehner, Terrence R., and Jack M. Holl, *Department of Energy, 1977–1994: A Summary History* (Washington, DC: Department of Energy, 1994), 41; "Herrington, John," in Robert Sobel, ed.-in-chief, *Biographical Directory of the United States Executive Branch, 1774–1989* (Westport, CT: Greenwood, 1990), 174.

JAMES DAVID WATKINS
1927–

James Watkins became the first military man to head a nondefense cabinet-level agency when selected as President George Bush's secretary of energy. A career naval officer with experience in nuclear technology, Watkins was born in Alhambra, California, on 7 March 1927, the son of Edward Francis Watkins, an executive with the Southern California Edison Company, and Louise Whipple (née Ward) Watkins. In 1938, Louise Watkins became the first woman in California history to run for a seat in the U.S. Senate. After finishing high school, James Watkins enrolled in the U.S. Naval Academy at Annapolis and graduated with a bachelor of science degree in naval science, after which he went on active duty as an ensign.

He rose through the ranks of the navy and, in 1958, was a lieutenant commander when he was awarded a master's degree in mechanical engineering at the Naval Postgraduate School in Monterey, California. He was invited to join the navy's new nuclear submarine program, and he served directly under Admiral Hyman G. Rickover, the father of America's nuclear navy. He later served as Rickover's administrative assistant. In 1964, Watkins was placed in charge of the U.S.S. *Snook,* a nuclear submarine. During his command, the ship became the first nuclear-powered vessel to visit Japan, spawning protests.

Watkins served as the executive officer of the U.S.S. *Long Beach,* the Navy's first nuclear-powered cruiser then held a series of administrative offices, including as the commander of the Sixth Fleet, as vice-chief of naval operations and commander-in-chief of the Pacific Fleet. From 1975 to 1978 he served as chief of naval personnel. On 18 March 1982, President Ronald Reagan named Watkins as chief of Naval Operations, the highest-ranking naval officer in the Pentagon, one of five positions on the Joint Chiefs of Staff, to succeed the retiring Admiral Thomas B. Hayward. During his four years of service, he helped to modernize the navy as part of Reagan's massive defense build-up. He was considered the leading candidate to replace General John W. Vessey, Jr., as chairman of the Joint Chiefs, but he was passed over for Admiral William Crowe in 1985. On 30 June 1986, Watkins retired from the navy with the rank of admiral.

On 23 July 1987, Reagan named Watkins as one of thirteen presidential appointees to the Presidential Commission on the Human Immunodeficiency Virus (HIV) Epidemic, to study the effects of acquired immune deficiency syndrome (AIDS), which was spreading across the United States. Watkins was selected for the panel because he had instituted the first AIDS testing program in the military in 1985. When the selected chairman, Dr. W. Eugene Mayberry, resigned just a few weeks later, Reagan offered the chairmanship to Watkins. The committee's final report in June 1988 urged the president to declared AIDS a national health emergency and recommended steps to implement safeguards to protect the rights of those with AIDS. Watkins expressed satisfaction that his work was over; he told one interviewer that "I'm not a health expert, I'm a manager. . . . So if you've got a difficult task, like national energy policy, I'd love it."

Following the 1988 presidential election, President-elect George Bush named Watkins as his choice for secretary of energy. Confirmed by the Senate on 1 March 1989, by a vote of 99 to 0, Watkins became the sixth secretary of energy, serving until the end of the Bush administration on 20 January 1993. During his tenure, he announced a ten-point plan to strengthen environmental protection policies at department facilities, established a Modernization Review Committee to review an Energy 2010 report that the White House had had prepared in 1992, instituted the Office of Environmental Restoration and Waste Management in the department, and ordered an increase in national oil production to offset losses incurred during the Iraqi invasion of Kuwait. Watkins helped formulate Bush's National Energy Strategy, which was presented to Congress in February 1991, and oversaw passage of the Energy Policy Act of 1992, which implemented the strategy.

Watkins left office in 1993 and retired to Washington, D.C. In 1999, his name was mentioned when allegations arose of spying by Chinese operatives of nuclear secrets due to lax security measures in department facilities; Watkins was faulted for making restructuring the department and, not security, a key point in his administration.

References: "James D. Watkins," in Dean R. Heaton, *Four Stars: The Super Stars of United States Military History* (Baltimore: Gateway Press, 1995), 302; "Watkins, James (David)," in Charles Moritz, ed., *Current Biography 1989* (New York: H. W. Wilson, 1989), 613–617.

HAZEL REID ROLLINS O'LEARY
1937–

President-elect Bill Clinton considered a number of people for his energy secretary, among them—Representative Philip Sharp of Indiana, Jessica Matthews of the World Resources Institute, and Senator Tim Wirth of Colorado, chairman of the Senate Energy and Natural Resources Subcommittee on Energy Regulation and Conservation. Yet Clinton had not made up his mind by the time Hazel Rollins O'Leary, who had had previous experience in the area of energy, was interviewed in Little Rock, Arkansas, on 18 December. Three days later, O'Leary was named as the seventh secretary of energy. Born as Hazel Reid on 17 May 1937, in Newport News, Virginia, she was the daughter of

Russel E. Reid and Hazel (née Palleman) Reid, both physicians. However, the couple divorced when Hazel was 18 months old, and she was raised by her father and stepmother.

O'Leary was educated in Newport News and in Newark, New Jersey, when sent to live with an aunt. She graduated from Fisk University in Nashville, Tennessee, with a bachelor's degree cum laude in history and earned a law degree at Rutgers University School of Law 1966. She worked for a time as an assistant prosecutor in Essex County, New Jersey, and then as the assistant attorney for the state of New Jersey. She then went to work as a partner at Coopers & Lybrand, an accounting and consulting firm in Washington, D.C.

In 1977, when Jimmy Carter became president, he named O'Leary as his director of the Office of Consumer Affairs at the Federal Energy Administration, the major executive branch office dealing with energy matters at that time. After Carter lost his reelection bid in 1980, O'Leary and her husband, John F. O'Leary, a former deputy energy secretary, opened O'Leary Associates, an energy consulting firm that worked around the world. One of their clients was the General Public Utilities Company, which ran the Three Mile Island nuclear power plant in Pennsylvania. When John O'Leary died in 1987, Hazel O'Leary closed the firm down. In 1989, she became the vice-president of corporate affairs for the Northern States Power Company in Minneapolis, Minnesota, where she worked until 1993.

On 21 December 1992, President-elect Bill Clinton selected O'Leary to serve as his secretary of energy. Despite Clinton's endorsement of O'Leary as "an energy expert with hands-on experience in both business and government," many thought of O'Leary's appointment as a concession to women's and minority groups that had assisted in Clinton's election in 1992. O'Leary, in fact, had worked to raise funds for Clinton's campaign. Nonetheless, O'Leary won easy approval from the Senate Committee on Energy and Natural Resources and was confirmed by the Senate on 21 January 1993 as the seventh secretary of energy. Her tenure lasted until 12 March 1997.

During her four years in office, O'Leary was credited with declassifying and releasing once-secret files on nuclear testing done in the earliest years of the cold war, including the annual megatonnage of the blasts from 1945 to 1994, the number of weapons retired, and tests that heretofore had been unannounced. O'Leary later released films of some atomic and nuclear tests that had never before been seen. She was criticized for numerous junkets she took overseas, leading to congressional inquiries into her travel, but there was no formal investigation of the matter.

At the end of the first Clinton term, O'Leary decided to leave government for private business.

References: *Drawing Back the Curtain of Secrecy: Restricted Data Declassification Policy, 1946 to the Present (RDD-1), June 1, 1994* (Washington, DC: Department of Energy, 1994); *Expanded Test Information for Nuclear Tests with Unannounced Simultaneous Detonations* (Washington, DC: Department of Energy, 1994); "O'Leary, Hazel R.," in Charles Moritz, ed., *Current Biography 1994* (New York: H. W. Wilson, 1994), 410–414.

FEDERICO PEÑA
1947–

See Department of Transportation, 1993–1997

WILLIAM BLAINE RICHARDSON
1947–

William Richardson became the fifth Hispanic to serve in the cabinet, named by President Bill Clinton on 18 June 1998 to replace Federico Peña as secretary of energy. Born in Pasadena, California, on 15 November 1947, Richardson is the son of William Richardson, a banker, and Maria Luisa (née Zubiran) Richardson. Bill Richardson grew up in Mexico City, where his father served as an executive with Citibank. Richardson returned to the United States and attended the Middlesex Preparatory School in Concord, Massachusetts. A pitcher for his school, he was drafted by the Kansas City Athletics (now the Oakland A's) baseball team when he graduated in 1967, but was persuaded by his father to attend college. He entered Tufts University in Medford, Massachusetts, graduated with a bachelor of arts degree in international relations in 1970 and earned a master's degree in the same field, in 1971, from Tufts's Fletcher School of Law and Diplomacy.

After leaving college, Richardson was hired by the State Department's Office of Congressional Relations. He worked there for four years. In 1975, he became a member of the staff of the Senate Foreign Relations Committee. In 1978, Richardson returned to New Mexico and became the head of the state's Democratic Party. In 1980, he ran for a U.S. House seat from New Mexico's Second Congressional District, against Representative Manuel Lujan; Richardson lost by 5,000 votes out of some 250,000 cast. In 1981, based on the 1980 census, New Mexico received an additional congressional seat with a large American Indian and Hispanic population, and Richardson ran for this seat. Richardson was easily elected in 1982 from the Third Congressional District and served from 3 January 1983 until 13 February 1997.

Richardson was a member of the Energy Committee and Commerce Committee and later chairman of the Indian Affairs Subcommittee; he worked on immigration issues and opposed the building of a nuclear waste storage site in Carlsbad, New Mexico. He supported aid to the Contras, the anticommunist rebels fighting the Nicaraguan government, and worked to modify the Simpson-Mazzoli Immigration Bill, which imposed sanctions on employers who hired illegal aliens. He was also a leader in the passage of the North American Free Trade Agreement (NAFTA), which opened trade borders with Mexico and Canada.

Richardson became known for his diplomatic exploits. Starting when he became a member of the House Select Committee on Intelligence, he helped monitor elections in the former East Germany and Nicaragua and traveled to Myanmar (Burma) to deliver a message to Aung San Suu Kyi, a Nobel Peace laureate who was under house arrest there for her opposition to the military government. In 1994, he went to North Korea to help get a nuclear disarmament agreement ratified. Just before his visit, a U.S. helicopter was shot down over North Korea, and one of the two pilot was captured. Richardson used his visit to negotiate the release of the pilot. In 1995, he helped negotiate the release of two American engineers who had unwittingly crossed the Iraqi-Kuwait border.

He earned the respect of diplomats worldwide for his forthright approach. In 1996, President Bill Clinton named Richardson as the U.S. ambassador to the United Nations to replace Madeleine K. Albright, who was named as secretary of state. Richardson won easy Senate confirmation and served until 10 September 1998. He was a proponent of paying American dues to the United Nations, which were in arrears, and spoke on such issues as the continuing crisis in Iraq.

On 6 April 1998, Secretary of Energy Federico Peña resigned. Although Deputy Secretary Elizabeth Moler was considered a leading candidate, on 18 June 1998 Richardson was named to the vacancy. In his testimony before the Senate Energy and Natural Resources Committee, Richardson said, "My home state of New Mexico is home to much of the history of the Department of Energy. America developed the world's first nuclear device at Los Alamos National Laboratory and tested it in the desert at Alamogordo, New Mexico. The world's fastest supercomputer is exploring a universe of knowledge at Sandia National Laboratory near Albuquerque, New Mexico. And the world's first geologic repository for transuranic waste is in Carlsbad, New Mexico, marking a major milestone in our nation's efforts to clean up the environmental legacy of the Cold War. . . . While representing New Mexico and serving on the House Energy and Commerce and Interior committees, and during my subsequent experience as America's ambassador to the United Nations, I became well aware of the importance and complexity of the Department's diverse missions and the many issues it confronts both at home and abroad. Its responsibilities extend from helping secure world peace to helping develop energy-efficient appliances for the American consumer."

He won easy Senate confirmation, and, on 18 August, he was sworn in as the ninth secretary. During his tenure, Richardson has become caught up in the scandal over massive security breaches at several nuclear labs, allegations of spying by Chinese agents on nuclear secrets, and the Wen Ho Lee case, in which a U.S. scientist of Chinese descent was accused of stealing vital information. As a result, he instituted sweeping new security reforms in all nuclear laboratories, as well as signing a series of nonproliferation agreements with Russia to safeguard their nuclear stockpile from theft and pushing environmental cleanups of areas contaminated by uranium drilling and processing.

References: "Richardson, Bill," in Judith Graham, ed., *Current Biography 1996* (New York: H. W. Wilson, 1996), 458–462; *Testimony of Secretary-Designate Bill Richardson before the Senate of the United States, Committee on Energy and Natural Resources, July 22, 1998* (Washington, DC: GPO, 1998).

HEALTH, EDUCATION, AND WELFARE

⎯⎯⟫◉⟪⎯⎯

The Department of Health, Education, and Welfare (HEW) became the largest executive agency in the federal government in terms of expenditures. HEW oversaw the vast areas of human health, education, civil rights enforcement, and Social Security. But the 1953 beginning of HEW was just one step in a long trail of establishing a federal agency to handle the issues relating to the health, education, and welfare of the American people. Even from the earliest days of the Republic, health matters were of the utmost importance. On 16 July 1798, President John Adams signed An Act for the Relief of Sick and Disabled Seamen, which established the Marine Hospital Service as a recuperative station for men who served the nation's new U.S. Navy, established that same year from an arm of the Department of War. This hospital service, which deducted twenty cents a month from the sailors' pay as the first medical care plan in America, was the forerunner of the today's Public Health Service, now part of the Department of Health and Human Services.

While most histories of HEW trace its inception back to the days of the New Deal program to assist Americans in the Great Depression, actually the move to create an agency to deal with these matters started during the nineteenth century. Besides hospitals for veterans of the nation's military, a mechanism was needed to investigate drugs and chemicals in the public marketplace. In 1862, President Abraham Lincoln named Charles M. Wetherill, a chemist, as the head of the Bureau of Chemistry in the new Department of Agriculture (until 1889 a subagency without cabinet rank). The Bureau of Chemistry was the precursor of the Food and Drug Administration (FDA). Forty years later, in August 1887, the Laboratory of Hygiene, a bacteriological laboratory, was established at the Marine Hospital on New York's Staten Island under the administration of Dr. Joseph J. Kinyoun to study cholera and other infectious diseases. The Laboratory of Hygiene would become the National Institutes of Health. The passage by Congress in 1906 of the Pure Food and Drug Act authorized the government to directly oversee the purity of foods and the safety of medicine.

The Department of the Interior's Indian Medical Services worked hand in hand with the Public Health Service to deliver health care to American Indians. This service would be transferred to the HEW in 1954 and is today the Indian Health Service. In 1928, Congress established the Food and Drug Administration as separate independent agency. (See Department of Education for the history of the Office of Education, which was later folded into the Department of Health, Education, and Welfare.) The New Deal economic program of President Franklin D. Roosevelt expanded the government's authority. Passage of the Social Security Act in 1935, to offer old-age security, was the first of these measures; four years later, all related agencies in the fields of health, education, social insurance, and all other human services were placed under one administration with the enactment of Reorganization Plan No. 1 of 1939, which created the Federal Security Agency (FSA), with Paul V. McNutt as administrator. Over the next fourteen years, despite little support from Congress to make the FSA into a cabinet-level agency, its budget grew. The agency was presided over by Watson B. Miller (1945–1947), Oscar R. Ewing (1947–1953), and Oveta Culp Hobby (January–April 1953).

In 1950, the Presidential Commission on Organization of the Executive Branch of Government, better known as the Hoover Commission after its chairman, former Secretary of Commerce and former President Herbert Hoover, recommended in a second round of reports that a department of social welfare be established with cabinet-level rank. In 1953, when General Dwight D. Eisenhower became president, he nominated Oveta Culp Hobby, who had served as head of the Women's Army Corps during World War II and had worked closely with Eisenhower, as the administrator of the FSA. Eisenhower charged Hobby with making the FSA into a cabinet department. The first step was a name for the department: suggestions ranged from the Department of Welfare to the Department of General Welfare to the Department of Human Resources. One possibility, the Department of Health, Education, and Social Security, was rejected when someone noticed that its acronym—HESS—was the last name of Rudolf Hess, Adolph Hitler's deputy. Finally the name Health, Education, and Welfare was adopted. On 1 April 1953, Eisenhower signed Reorganization Plan No. 1, establishing the new department, the tenth in the cabinet, with operations to begin effective 11 April 1953.

On that date, the FSA was abolished, and all of its functions were transferred to Health, Education, and Welfare. Hobby was named as the new department's first secretary, making her the second woman (after Secretary of Labor Frances Perkins) to serve in the cabinet. Historian John W. Sloan wrote, "As its name suggests, HEW was engaged in the widest array of programs of any department—everything from medical research on cancer, to testing food and drugs, to financial assistance for schools in federally-affected areas, to social security. Its bureaucrats had no problem justifying more money for, first, studies and then programs to benefit children, the sick, and the needy. The multitude of worthy causes served by HEW meant that it was politically painful to constrain its expenditures. No other department presented a greater challenge to policymakers to forge a politically acceptable balance between compassion and fiscal prudence." At its inception, HEW had 34,000 employees and total expenditures of $5.4 billion, which included $3.4 billion in Social Security trust funds.

Hobby served until 31 July 1955 and was replaced by Marion B. Folsom, the undersecretary of the treasury and one of the early leaders for a national plan of social insurance. Folsom served for three years; he oversaw a White House Conference on Education and, despite Eisenhower's disagreement, pushed for the first federal aid for education.

Eisenhower's third and final HEW Secretary, Arthur S. Flemming, was the president of the Ohio Wesleyan University and had served in both Republican and Democratic administrations. Serving until the end of the Eisenhower administration on 20 January 1961, Flemming was involved in the so-called cranberry scare in 1959, in which he prevented the sale of that year's cranberry crop because it had been sprayed with a pesticide. Flemming was praised for showing, for the first time, the regulatory strength of the new department.

Under Presidents John F. Kennedy and Lyndon B. Johnson (1961–1969), HEW expanded into a department with a budget larger than any other in the U.S. government. The four men who held the office of secretary of HEW during this period—Abraham Ribicoff (1961–1962), Anthony Celebrezze (1962–1965), John W. Gardner (1965–1968), and Wilbur J. Cohen (1968–1969)—expanded welfare payments, undertook investigations of schools to end segregation, and oversaw the establishment of the Medicare and Medicaid programs.

Ribicoff left after just a year because he found the department so broad and expansive as to be unmanageable, and his warnings that it needed to be broken up, despite a firm commitment or plan as to how that could be done, were a portent of things to come. Celebrezze, who had been the mayor of Cleveland, Ohio, before entering the cabinet, immediately was swamped by the Social Security and welfare systems, and ordered a reorganization, separated the two check-writing agencies into the Social Security and Welfare Administrations. It was under Celebrezze that Congress added more responsibilities to the department's already overburdened workload—passing, as part of President Lyndon Johnson's Great Society, such acts as the Clean Air Act, the Mental Retardation Facilities and Community Mental Health Construction Act of 1963, the Vocational Education Act of 1963, the Maternal and Child Health and Mental Retardation Planning Amendments of 1963, the Civil Rights Act of 1964, the Elementary and Secondary Education Act of 1965, and the Medicare and Medicaid 1965 amendments to the Social Security Act. Celebrezze was never able to handle the rigors of the job, and when Johnson offered him a circuit court of appeals judgeship in Ohio, he accepted.

Celebrezze was replaced by John W. Gardner, a respected educator who was serving as the president of the Carnegie Corporation. Although both of his predecessors recommended splitting HEW up into two or even three new departments, Gardner saw HEW as a complete instrument for serving American citizens. In fact, he recommended that the agency be made into a super department consisting of three subdepartments—a Department of Health, a Department of Education, and a Department of Individual and Family Services. This proposal came about because of growing pressure to remove Education from HEW and make it into a separate department. Nonetheless, Gardner's proposition died, mainly because many feared that each subcabinet agency would become a fiefdom within a kingdom, answerable to no one except the secretary of the entire department. Gardner instead focused on civil rights, establishing the special assistant to the secretary for civil rights and, in his first budget, asked for appropriations to create 348 positions in civil rights enforcement. Gardner resigned in December 1967, to take effect a month later.

For the last year of Johnson's administration, Wilbur J. Cohen, who had served Ribicoff, Celebrezze, and Gardner as undersecretary, served as acting secretary, and then as secretary, until 20 January 1969. Cohen, the nation's chief expert on social security policymaking, had spent his time in office, since 1961, as the chief legislative aide of HEW in enacting all of its landmark legislation in Congress. But when Cohen became secretary, Johnson had announced that he would not be a candidate for president in 1968 and Cohen's tenure was as a caretaker. The four men who served under Presidents Richard M. Nixon and Gerald R. Ford were not activists, although important legislation, such as the establishment of the National Health Service Corps in 1970, the signing of the National

Cancer Act in 1971, and the creation of the Child Support Enforcement program did mark the tenures of Robert H. Finch (1969–1970), Elliot Richardson (1970–1973), Caspar Weinberger (1973–1975), and F. David Mathews (1975–1977).

Finch drastically restricted the uses of DDT and cyclamates, and Richardson attempted to establish a national health insurance plan from tax surcharges. The naming of Caspar Weinberger, who had headed the Federal Trade Commission and had served in the Office of Management and Budget, initiated an era of change in that new agencies were added to HEW's roster, including the Indian Health Service and other health functions from the Department of Labor, and the establishment of the Office of Equal Opportunity. After Weinberger left, F. David Mathews, president of the University of Alabama, was named by President Ford. Mathews oversaw the department in an era when calls for its disbanding grew louder, and Congress initiated a series of investigations on fraud and abuse inside the department.

The final two secretaries, Joseph A. Califano Jr., and Patricia Roberts Harris, serving under President Jimmy Carter, served in the last days of HEW as a department. The undoing of HEW was its drastically growing budget. When it was established in 1953, its total outlays had been 7.5 percent of the entire federal budget; by 1973, this number had reached 33 percent, and Nixon's 1974 budget increased it to 35 percent. The 1973 expenditures were a staggering $83 billion—more than the Department of Defense received. Under Califano, it was estimated by Congress that a full 5 percent of the yearly budget was being wasted on fraud; in 1978, fifteen present and former HEW employees were indicted on fraud charges. Califano was charged with getting Congress to pass a national health care initiative and welfare reform, but when he could do neither, he was replaced. When Patricia Roberts Harris took over, HEW was being eliminated. President Carter sent a proposal to Congress in 1978 to create a separate Department of Education, but it failed. In 1979, however, this legislation passed and, on 17 October 1979, HEW was abolished with the passage of the Department of Education Organization Act. All of its education offices were transferred to this new department, and the remainder were transferred to the new Department of Health and Human Services.

See also Department of Education; Department of Health and Human Services

References: Greenberg, George D., "Governing HEW: Problems of Management and Control at the Department of Health, Education, and Welfare" (Ph.D. dissertation, Harvard University, 1972); Miles, Rufus E., Jr., *The Department of Health, Education, and Welfare* (New York: Praeger, 1974); Mixdorf, Gordon F., "Origins and Development of the Department of Health, Education, and Welfare" (Master's thesis, University of Northern Iowa at Cedar Rapids, 1959); Sloan, John W., *Eisenhower and the Management of Prosperity* (Lawrence: University Press of Kansas, 1991), 91; Terrell, John Upton, *The United States Department of Health, Education and Welfare: A Story of Protecting and Preserving Human Resources* (New York: Duell, Sloan, and Pearce, 1965).

OVETA CULP HOBBY
1905–1995

Oveta Hobby was the second woman to hold a cabinet-level post, and the first secretary of the new Department of Health, Education, and Welfare (HEW). Born Oveta Culp on 19 January 1905 in Killeen, Texas, she was the daughter of Isaac William Culp, a lawyer and Texas state legislator, and Emma Elizabeth (née Hoover) Culp. She attended the public schools of Austin, where she went when her father was elected to the state legislature in 1919, and also had private tutors.

She studied at Mary Hardin Baylor College in Belton and the University of Texas Law School and became a cub reporter for the Austin *Statesman*. In 1925, at the age of 20, she was named as the parliamentarian for the Texas state House of Representatives. During her service, which lasted until 1931 (and, later, from 1939 to 1941), she also served as a clerk of the State Banking Commission and helped codify the banking laws of the state for the first time. In 1928, when the Democratic National Convention was held in Houston, she was a worker for the convention authority. After the convention nominated Governor Al Smith of New York for president, she went to work for the U.S. Senate campaign of Democrat Thomas Connally. In 1929, she worked on a Houston mayoral campaign and was invited to become city attorney. In 1930, she ran, unsuccessfully, for a seat in the state legislature.

Oveta Culp Hobby, after marrying William Hobby, publisher of the *Houston Post-Dispatch* (later the *Post*) and former Texas governor, started working in newspaper publishing—writing editorials, editing copy, and reviewing books for the *Post;* she served as book editor from 1933 to 1936, assistant editor from 1936 to 1938, and executive vice-president after 1938. She also authored *Mr. Chairman,* a work on parliamentary law. In 1940 Hobby and her husband purchased a Houston radio station, KPRC, and she went to Washington to get a license from the Federal Communications Commission for the station. At that time, she met with General David Searles, who asked her to organize a women's activities section in the U.S. Army. Initially she refused, but later, as her husband said, Hobby "was a patriot in the real sense of the word . . . she thought you must do whatever your country asks you to do. . . . Any thoughtful person knows that we are in this war, and that every one of us is going to have to do whatever we are called on to do."

She became the head of the Women's Interest Section of the War Department Bureau of Public Relations, serving until early 1942.

After the Japanese attacked Pearl Harbor in Hawaii and the United States entered the war, Hobby was made the director of the Women's Army Corps (WACs); she was given the rank of colonel (the first American woman to hold that rank), and helped recruit, organize, and train women across the country. By war's end in 1945, Hobby had commanded some 100,000 women and had worked with General Dwight D. Eisenhower, the supreme commander of Allied forces in Europe. She called her service "a debt to democracy and a date with destiny." She was awarded the Distinguished Service Medal. After the war, Hobby returned to Houston to assist her husband in running the *Post*.

In 1952, when Eisenhower ran for president as a Republican, Hobby, a Democrat, came out on his behalf, heading up the Democrats for Eisenhower movement. Eisenhower, after being elected, named Hobby as chairman of the Federal Security Agency (FSA), which at that time ran all health and education programs in the U.S. government. Eisenhower wanted to make the FSA a cabinet-level department, and to this end he ordered Hobby to prepare the agency for department status.

For the second time, Hobby took a skeleton staff and assembled a cabinet department—the first to be established since the Department of Commerce and Labor was split in 1913. On 11 April 1953, Reorganization Plan No. 1 went into effect, and Hobby became the first secretary of the Department of Health, Education, and Welfare (HEW) and the second woman to hold a post in the cabinet. Hobby, who served until 1955, was the first of three people in this position under Eisenhower. Historian John Sloan wrote, "Eisenhower had the least conflict with Hobby. She was a southern Democrat from Texas who shared many of the conservative fiscal views of the president. Even so, Hobby submitted a memo to the president in November 1954 proposing an ambitious set of programs that would fulfill 'your Administration's concern for the individual American.' Hobby's memo congratulated Eisenhower for establishing HEW and for proposing legislation that extended social security benefits to an additional ten million citizens. She suggested that in 1955 the administration concentrate on the health problems of the American people and in 1956 on educational issues. Proposed health programs included providing medical care for public assistance recipients, stimulating construction of more medical facilities, encouraging the training of more medical personnel, granting federal money to the states for mental health programs, and providing federal assistance for state and local programs in water and pollution control." Bureau of the Budget Director Rowland Hughes opposed Hobby's recommendations because they would drastically inflate the budget of HEW, already at $5.4 billion in 1953.

In July 1955, Hobby's husband became ill, and on 31 July 1955 she resigned from the cabinet. Of her tenure, Health and Human Services Secretary Donna Shalala wrote at the time of her death in 1995, "In her first year as Secretary, the NIH [National Institutes of Health] Clinical Center was dedicated. During her tenure, a nationwide program for hospital construction was begun. The FDA undertook action to protect consumers from pesticide residue on agricultural products. Social Security was amended to extend to farm and domestic workers and the self-employed. And in a crowning event, the Salk polio vaccine was successfully developed, tested, licensed and distributed nationwide."

She returned to Houston and resumed her role as president and editor of the *Post*. Despite numerous calls for her to return to public service, she remained by her husband's side until his death in 1964. Hobby then dedicated her time to numerous causes; the library at Central Texas College in Killeen was named in her honor. On 16 August 1995, she died in Houston at the age of 90. In 1988, Hobby was named to the National Women's Hall of Fame.

References: "Hobby, Oveta Culp," in Charles Moritz, ed., *Current Biography 1953* (New York: H. W. Wilson, 1953), 267–269; Pach, Chester J., Jr., and Elmo Richardson, *The Presidency of Dwight D. Eisenhower* (Lawrence: University Press of Kansas, 1991); Sloan, John W., *Eisenhower and the Management of Prosperity* (Lawrence: University Press of Kansas, 1991), 91; "Statement by HHS Secretary Donna E. Shalala, Remembering Oveta Culp Hobby, First HEW Secretary," Press Release of the HHS Press Office, 16 August 1995.

MARION BAYARD FOLSOM
1893–1976

Marion Folsom was the assistant to George Eastman, the founder of Eastman Kodak, for many years, rising to become director of the company before he joined the Eisenhower administration as undersecretary of the Treasury in 1953. Two years later, Marion Folsom succeeded Oveta Culp Hobby as the second secretary of health, education, and welfare. The son of William Bryant Folsom and Margaret Jane (née McRae) Folsom, Folsom was born in the town of McRae, Georgia, on 23 November 1893. Folsom graduated from the University of Georgia at Athens with a bachelor's degree with honors in 1912. He went on to receive his master of business administration degree from the Harvard University Business School two years later.

In 1914, Folsom went to work for the Eastman Kodak Company. Folsom was assigned to the office of Frank Lovejoy, the vice-president of manufacturing, and he also served in the accounting department. During World War I, Folsom took a leave of absence from the company to serve in the U.S. Army, first as part of the First Officers Training Camp and then as a captain with the Twenty-sixth Division; seeing limited action in France. In 1919, Folsom returned to Eastman Kodak, and a year later became the company's statistical secretary and organized the statistical department. He became an assistant to Eastman in 1921 and, four years later, when Eastman was named chairman of the board, became an assistant to that position. He rose to become treasurer in 1935 and director of the company in 1947.

Folsom was also actively involved in a national movement to establish a government social security system. In 1934, he served on the President's Advisory Council to the Committee on Economic Security and was a key member in drafting the enactment that became the Social Security Act of 1935. He continued to remain at the forefront of the social insurance movement, testifying before congressional committees, and, from 1935 to 1950, served on the New York State Advisory Council on Unemployment Insurance. He also served as staff director, from 1944 to 1946, of the U.S. House Special Committee on Postwar Economic Policy and Planning, known as the Colmer Committee after its chairman, Representative William Meyers Colmer of Mississippi.

In 1953, following the election of President Dwight D. Eisenhower, Folsom was named as undersecretary of the Treasury under Secretary George M. Humphrey. He worked on the first complete federal tax law revision since Secretary Benjamin H. Bristow's revision in 1874. Folsom also worked closely with Secretary of Health, Education, and Welfare Oveta Culp Hobby on all legislation from 1953 to 1955 dealing with Social Security.

On 13 July 1955, Secretary Hobby announced her resignation, effective 31 July, and President Eisenhower named Folsom to succeed her. Following Senate confirmation on 20 July 1955, Folsom took office as the second secretary of health, education, and welfare. Department historian Rufus Miles wrote, "Marion Folsom brought to the Department a carefully worked out philosophy against which he could test most issues as they came to him for consideration. The core of that philosophy was that the primary roles of government in the social field should be, first, to provide a framework of social insurance protection from the hazards of an industrial society against which most people could not be expected to fully protect themselves, second, to find and apply methods of preventing people from becoming dependent or so ill as to minimize the trauma and cost of cures, and, third, to provide early and

total rehabilitation service to disabled people who had prospects of regaining the capacity for self-support. The second of these components caused him to stress programs of medical research and education. His philosophy was later picked up, amplified, and further articulated by his assistant secretary, Elliot Richardson (HEW secretary from 1970 to 1973)." Secretary Folsom oversaw the White House Conference on Education, which had been planned by Hobby, and sent seventy-two recommendations to President Eisenhower to improve elementary and secondary education in the United States. He also requested more budget appropriations, which earned him enmity from people in the Bureau of the Budget. Folsom said, "When I was in Treasury, I was on one side of these things; now I'm with HEW on the other side, the liberal side." He argued, "I felt the need for many of these programs. Especially when they trying to hold expenditures down, I was arguing with the Budget people all the time . . . in a growing country and expanding economy, it was natural that programs would cost more, not to mention the new needs developing."

Folsom tried to get Congress to appropriate monies for the federal construction of classrooms, but failed; he did, however, get enacted the National Defense Education Act of 1958, which gave grants to students who desired to get an education and become college or university professors, as well as money to states to shore up instruction in the sciences, mathematics, and modern foreign languages.

When he took over at HEW, Folsom had agreed to serve only two years, but he was persuaded by President Eisenhower to remain for a third year. On 31 July 1958, exactly three years after his predecessor had left, Folsom resigned and was replaced by Arthur S. Flemming. Renamed to the board of directors of Eastman Kodak, he served in that capacity until his retirement in 1964. Folsom died on 27 September 1976, two months before his eighty-third birthday. He was interred in Arlington National Cemetery.

References: "Folsom, Marion B(ayard)," in Charles Moritz, ed., *Current Biography 1950* (New York: H. W. Wilson, 1950), 146–148; Miles, Rufus E., Jr., *The Department of Health, Education, and Welfare* (New York: Praeger, 1974), 33; Sloan, John W., *Eisenhower and the Management of Prosperity* (Lawrence: University Press of Kansas, 1991), 91–93; Witte, Edwin E., *The Development of the Social Security Act* (Madison: University of Wisconsin Press, 1963).

ARTHUR SHERWOOD FLEMMING

1905–1996

Arthur Flemming was a longtime government servant whose service included work on the U.S. Civil Service Commission, the Hoover Commission, and the White House Conference on Aging (1971). Flemming is better known for his service, from 1958 to 1961, as the third secretary of health, education, and welfare. Born in Kingston, New York, on 12 June 1905, he was the son of Harry Hardwicke Flemming, a lawyer who became a judge on New York's surrogate court, and Harriet (née Sherwood) Flemming.

After graduating from high school in 1922, Arthur Flemming worked for a year as a reporter before entering Ohio Wesleyan University, where he served as president of the college's Republican Club. He received his bachelor's degree in 1927. For the next three years, Flemming worked as an instructor in government and as a debate coach at American University in Washington, D.C., where he earned a master's degree in political science in 1928. In 1930, Flemming went to work as a reporter for the *United States Daily* (now the *U.S. News & World Report*), remaining there for four years. At the same time, he studied the law at George Washington University in Washington, D.C., and was awarded a law degree in 1933. The following year, after leaving journalism, he became the director of American University's School of Public Affairs, serving until he was named as

executive officer of that university in October 1938.

In 1939, President Franklin D. Roosevelt named Flemming, a moderate Republican, as the one Republican member of the three-member U.S. Civil Service Commission. He remained in this position until 1948, also serving, during this period, as a member of the chief of labor supply in the Office of Production Management from 1941 to 1942 and as a member of the War Manpower Commission from 1942 to 1945, in which he recruited workers to fill empty labor positions during World War II. For his work on the U.S. Navy's Manpower Survey Board, Flemming was awarded the Navy's Distinguished Civilian Service Award.

On 17 July 1947, Flemming was named as a member of the twelve-member Presidential Commission on Organization of the Executive Branch of Government, better known as the Hoover Commission after its chairman, former Secretary of Commerce and former President Herbert Hoover. This commission was established to recommend changes in the executive branch, including budget-cutting measures and ways to streamline the bureaucracy. However, after just a short time on this commission, in June 1948 the trustees of Ohio Wesleyan University elected Flemming as president of that university. Resigning from his government positions on 31 August 1948, he became the ninth president, and the first former alumnus to serve in that capacity, of the Methodist-affiliated college since its founding in 1841.

Flemming continued to advise government offices. In September 1948, he was named as the chairman of the personnel advisory board of the Atomic Energy Commission. In February 1951, he took a leave of absence from Ohio Wesleyan to serve as an assistant to Charles E. Wilson, the director of the Office of Defense Mobilization (ODM). When President Dwight D. Eisenhower promoted Wilson to secretary of defense in 1953, he named Flemming as Wilson's replacement at ODM. He remained in this position until 1957, when he returned to Ohio Wesleyan.

Flemming was committed to staying as president of the university, but he accepted a government position again. In July, 1958, Secretary of Health, Education, and Welfare Marion B. Folsom resigned, and Eisenhower approached Flemming as Folsom's replacement. Flemming initially turned down the offer, but it was made several times—Eisenhower wanted Flemming for the position. It was a difficult decision for Flemming; his wife wrote in 1991, "Arthur was deeply sensitive to the fact that it is no small honor to invited to serve in the president's cabinet. Besides, the department he had been asked to head covered all of the areas of his special interest. . . . In addition, Arthur felt a particular closeness to the department since he had had a hand in the creation and naming of that newest executive department. As a member of President Eisenhower's Advisory Committee on Government Organization, along with Nelson Rockefeller and Milton Eisenhower, he had helped work out the organizational details to merge the Federal Security Administration, the Public Health Service, and the Office of Education into a cabinet-level department."

Finally, he agreed and was nominated on 7 May 1958. Confirmed on 9 July 1958, Flemming took office as the third secretary of health, education, and welfare. His tenure lasted two and a half years, until the end of the Eisenhower administration on 20 January 1961. Department historian Rufus Miles wrote, "Flemming's 30-month service as Secretary . . . was marked less by spectacular legislative developments than by steady growth of the Department and increasing complexities of administration. The National Defense Education Act was being carried out; the National Institutes of Health continued to have its appropriations greatly increased by Congress each year; the Social Security program expanded inexorably; and preparations were made for the sixth decennial White House Conference on Children and Youth. These typified the scores of developments that preoccupied the Secretary."

Flemming's tenure was marked by two major issues: one dealing with cranberries and the other with segregation. The first came in late 1959, when the department found out that that year's cranberry crop had been sprayed with a lethal pesticide that was banned from being applied to food. When word leaked out, just before the Thanksgiving holiday, there was a cranberry scare. Flemming was forced to ban all sales of cranberries and ordered the remaining stores of that year's harvest to be destroyed. Despite the huge loss incurred by the cranberry industry, Flemming was praised for moving quickly to contain the crisis and at the same time showed the management capacity HEW had over food and its safety for the public.

Flemming was a staunch advocate of desegregating schools across the nation, and he also launched investigations into air and water pollution. Eisenhower historian John Sloan noted that Flemming took notice of the rapid growth in spending for medical research conducted by HEW since its inception. Sloan explained, "Recent legislative history demonstrated that the administration had lost control in determining the costs of these programs to a network of officials in the medical field, federal bureaucracies, and congressional committees. To regain executive control, Flemming advocated that the administration develop a plan on how much the nation should be spending on medical research over the next twelve years and then hammer out an agreement on what share should be carried by the federal government, the states, the universities, and the private sector. Flemming concluded that this formula could serve as a model for other policy areas: 'I think that this is the approach we should consider very carefully in other areas. If we as an administration can reach agreement on a national goal, and then if we talk to the nation about these goals and about the proportionate load that should be assumed by private groups, the state governments and the Federal government, we might be able to get on the offensive in dealing with these problems instead of being put in a defensive position.'"

In January 1961, shortly before his tenure ended, Flemming hosted the first White

House Conference on Aging. At that meeting, he said, "We have not yet adjusted our sense of values, our social and cultural ways of life, our public and private programs, to accommodate the concerns of [the] vast legion of old and aging people. For far too many people, old age means inadequate income, poor or marginal health, improper housing, isolation from family and friends, the discouragement of being shunted aside from the mainstream of life. . . . Not only must we give a higher priority to solving some of the more immediate problems of concern to older people, but we must be developing more effective long-range plans in this area."

Flemming left office in January 1961 and served as president of the University of Oregon 1968; he then served for three years as president of Macalester College in St. Paul, Minnesota, from 1968 to 1971. During that period, he was also president of the Oregon Council of Churches and served under Presidents John F. Kennedy and Lyndon B. Johnson as a member of the National Advisory Committee on the Peace Corps (1961–1968).

In 1971, HEW Secretary Elliot Richardson, who had worked as Flemming's assistant when Flemming was secretary of HEW, named Flemming as chairman of the U.S. Commission on Aging. He continued in this position through the Nixon and Ford administrations and into the Carter administration until 1978. In 1973, President Nixon named Flemming as the third U.S. commissioner on aging, a post that was established under the Older Americans Act of 1965. In his years of service during the 1970s, Flemming brought new attention to the role older Americans play in American society. In 1972, Flemming was named as chairman of the U.S. Commission on Civil Rights, serving until 1981, and worked to ensure that the elderly, as well as others, were not discriminated against based on their age, race, or national origin.

Flemming was the recipient of two Presidential Medals of Freedom—one bestowed by President Eisenhower in 1957, and a second by President Bill Clinton in 1994. From 1982 until his death Flemming served as chairman of the Citizens' Commission on Civil Rights, a nonprofit advocacy group.

Flemming died in Alexandria, Virginia, on 7 September 1996 at the age of 91.

References: "Flemming, Arthur S(herwood)," in Charles Moritz, ed., *Current Biography 1960* (New York: H. W. Wilson, 1960), 140–142; Flemming, Bernice, *Arthur Flemming: Crusader at Large: A Memoir* (Washington, DC: Caring Publishing, 1991), 1–5, 185–197; Miles, Rufus E., Jr., *The Department of Health, Education, and Welfare* (New York: Praeger Publishers, 1974), 36–37; Sloan, John W., *Eisenhower and the Management of Prosperity* (Lawrence: University Press of Kansas, 1991), 93.

ABRAHAM ALEXANDER RIBICOFF
1910–1998

Abraham Ribicoff was a longtime Connecticut politician who served his state in the U.S. Congress, the U.S. Senate, and as governor. Born in New Britain, Connecticut, on 9 April 1910, he was the son of Samuel Ribicoff, a factory worker, and Rose (née Sable) Ribicoff. Ribicoff attended local schools and, after graduating from high school, spent a year working in a factory in New Britain to earn enough to pay for college. He went to New York University for a year; in 1929, he left school to go to work as the head of the office at the G. E. Prentice Company, of Chicago, which manufactured buckles and zippers. At the same time, he took afternoon classes at the University of Chicago Law School and graduated with a law degree in 1933. He had also served as editor of the university's law review.

Ribicoff returned to Connecticut, where he practiced law in Kensington and later in the capital, Hartford. He was offered a job with the Tennessee Valley Authority, but declined. In 1938, he ran for and was elected to a seat in the Connecticut General Assembly and was reelected in 1940. In 1941, he became a judge in the Hartford Police Court, serving until 1943; he served in the same post from 1947 to 1947. In 1941, he was also elected as chairman of the Connecticut Assembly of Municipal Court Judges.

In 1947 and 1948, Ribicoff served as a hearing examiner under the Connecticut Fair Employment Practices Act, which helped to uncover racial discrimination in hiring practices in the state. In 1948, he ran for and won a seat in the U.S. Congress, defeating the Republican incumbent, Representative Ellsworth Bishop Foote, and, at the same time, assisting in the election of Democrat Chester Bowles to the governor's mansion. While in the House, he was a supporter of the policies of President Harry S Truman, including the Marshall Plan aid to Europe.

In 1952, Ribicoff gave up his seat to run against Republican Prescott S. Bush to fill the Senate seat of the deceased Senator Brien McMahon, but Ribicoff was unsuccessful. In 1954, he was nominated, by the Democrats, for governor and was elected over Republican John Davis Lodge by 240,000 votes out of some one million cast. He was the only Democrat elected that year. Historians Robert Sobel and John Raimo wrote, "After his inauguration on January 5, 1955, Ribicoff faced an early crisis. Devastating floods struck Connecticut in August and October of 1955, and caused wide destruction. The governor personally led recovery efforts and pushed a rehabilitation program through the legislature, an action that gained bipartisan support. The leader of a reform administration, Ribicoff supported education and welfare program. In 1957, at his urging, the legislature approved a $52 million budget for expanding the state's educational system and for other welfare and humane programs. The governor also supported a state constitutional amendment which provided broader home rule powers to municipalities."

In 1960, Ribicoff supported Senator John F. Kennedy of Massachusetts for the presidency. The two men had been close friends since Ribicoff served in Congress. In 1956, when the Democrats considered putting Kennedy on the ticket as vice-president, Ribicoff nominated him before the party's convention, but Kennedy lost to Senator Estes Kefauver of Tennessee. Four years later, Ribicoff served as the convention floor manager for the Kennedy campaign at the party's convention in Los Angeles and campaigned for him in the general election.

After Kennedy won a close race against Vice-president Richard M. Nixon, Kennedy asked Ribicoff to serve in his cabinet as attorney general. Ribicoff declined, feeling that it would be impolitic for a Jewish attorney general to enforce civil rights laws on the South. He instead recommended the president-elect's own brother, Robert F. Kennedy, for the post. When Kennedy said he wanted Ribicoff to serve in the cabinet, Ribicoff selected the Department of Health, Education, and Welfare (HEW).

Ribicoff became the first person officially named to the cabinet. Nominated on 20 January 1961, he was confirmed the following day and, after resigning as governor of Connecticut, was sworn in as the fourth secretary of HEW. However, Ribicoff was unhappy as secretary of HEW. In fact, as he said later, "I'm used to being my own man. I was Governor, I was a Member of Congress. I'm used to being my own man, instead of having to support positions that are someone else's that I really didn't support or having to oppose other positions that I really did support."

It was his lack of enthusiasm that caused him to begin to try to get out of the cabinet almost as soon as he entered it. He described, in a humorous manner, the job of HEW secretary: "[He] wears 20 different hats a day, runs 110 programs and is responsible for 75 separate budget items. And the list is growing all the time." In fact, his assistant secretary, Wilbur J. Cohen, who worked closely with Ribicoff and his successors Anthony Celebrezze and John W. Gardner, added more than 200 additional programs to HEW's responsibility over the next decade. Ribicoff's most important accomplishment in the sixteen months he spent in office was his work with Senator Clinton Anderson of New Mexico, a former secretary of agriculture, on the landmark Medicaid Bill, which failed until President Lyndon Johnson got it passed in 1965.

On 13 July 1962, Ribicoff resigned to run for a U.S. Senate seat from Connecticut that had opened when Senator Prescott Bush decided not to seek reelection. Ribicoff defeated Republican Representative Horace Seely-Brown Jr. and took his seat in January 1963. He served eighteen years, winning reelection in 1968 and 1974; he served as chairman of the Committee on Government Operations and the Committee on Governmental Affairs.

Ribicoff was an initial supporter of the war in Vietnam, but broke with President Johnson near the end of the 1960s. During this period, Ribicoff is best known for standing up during the 1968 Democratic National Convention in Chicago and protesting the "Gestapo tactics" of the Chicago police, who were using force against antiwar protesters. As chairman of the Senate Committee on Government Operations' Subcommittee on Executive Reorganization, Ribicoff held hearings on urban problems known as the Ribicoff Hearings. He was a staunch advocate for the speedy integration of schools and opposed farm price supports.

In 1980, Ribicoff, at the age of 70, decided not to seek a fourth term. He resumed the practice of law in New York City with the firm of Kaye, Scholer, Fierman, Hayes, & Handler and resided in Cornwall Bridge, Connecticut. Ribicoff died in New York City on 22 February 1998 at the age of 87. He was buried in the Cornwall Cemetery in Cornwall, Connecticut. In 1980, the building in Hartford, Connecticut, where he had once worked as a young lawyer was renamed the Abraham A. Ribicoff Federal Building and U.S. Courthouse in his honor.

References: "Abraham Ribicoff and the Department of Health, Education, and Welfare," in Deane Heller and David Heller, *The Kennedy Cabinet: America's Men of Destiny* (Derby, CT: Monarch Books, 1961), 114–126; Davidson, Roger H. "Campaigns and Elections: Two Cases: Abraham Ribicoff of Connecticut," in John Bibby and Roger H. Davidson, eds., *On Capitol Hill: Studies in the Legislative Process* (New York: Holt, Rinehart & Winston, 1967), 30–52; Jones, Charles O., and Layne D. Hoppe, eds., *Urban Crisis in America: The Remarkable Ribicoff Hearings* (Washington, DC: Washington National Press, 1969); Miles, Rufus E., Jr., *The Department of Health, Education, and Welfare* (New York: Praeger, 1974), 41–43; Ribicoff, Abraham A., and Jon O. Newman, *Politics: The American Way* (Boston: Allyn & Bacon, 1967); "Ribicoff, Abraham Alexander," in Robert Sobel and John Raimo, eds., *Biographical Directory of the Governors of the United States, 1789–1978* (Westport, CT: Meckler Books, 4 vols., 1978), 1: 205; Wunsch, James L., "Ribicoff, Abraham A(lexander)," in Nelson Lichtenstein, ed., *Political Profiles: The Kennedy Years* (New York: Facts on File, 1976), 429–431.

ANTHONY JOSEPH CELEBREZZE
1910–1998

Anthony Celebrezze was a highly popular mayor of Cleveland, Ohio, when President John F. Kennedy selected him to replace Abraham Ribicoff as head of the Department of Health, Education, and Welfare (HEW). His short tenure there was marked by the passage of landmark legislation, including the establishment of Medicare, the Clean Air Act, the Civil Rights Act of 1964, and the creation of the Head Start educational program for children. Celebrezze was the son of Rocco Celebrezze, a railroad track worker, and Dorothy (née Marcoguiseppe) Celebrezze. Celebrezze was born while his parents were in Anzi, a village in southern Italy, looking for work, on 4 September 1910. Celebrezze began to work at the age of six selling newspapers at a stand in the Cleveland; the stand became known as Celebrezze Corner. He attended local schools, then went to John Carroll University in Cleveland for year before transferring to Ohio Northern University in Ada, where he received his law degree in 1936 and was admitted to the Ohio state bar.

Celebrezze's first job out of law school was as an attorney on the staff of the Ohio Bureau of Unemployment Compensation, working cases during the Depression. Three years later, however, he left the state position to open his own law office in Cleveland. He would remain an independent attorney until 1952, except for four years during World War II, when he served as a seaman in the U.S. Navy. A Democrat, Celebrezze entered the political arena in 1950, when he ran for a seat in the Ohio state Senate and was elected. Reelected in 1952, he served on the judiciary, taxation, and veterans affairs committees. In 1953, Mayor Thomas B. Burke of Cleveland decided against running for reelection after nine years as mayor, and the Democrats nominated Albert S. Porter. Celebrezze entered the race as an independent against the Democratic Party machine, and defeated Porter, and the Republican, Judge William J. McDermott, to become mayor. Celebrezze would go on to serve an unprecedented five terms as mayor. His time as mayor was marked by the rise of urban blight and flight from the cities, but Celebrezze tried to combat this by cutting the budget and reducing the number of city employees while spending more to improve roads, a new airport, and other parts of the infrastructure. He remained popular; in his last election, in 1961, Celebrezze received a record 73.8 percent of the vote. On 12 July 1962, HEW Secretary Abraham Ribicoff resigned, and President John F. Kennedy asked Celebrezze to accept the nomination to replace Ribicoff. Nominated on 16 July, Celebrezze was confirmed four days later, and took office as the fifth secretary of health, education, and welfare. His tenure, however, was an unhappy one for him, despite getting more congressional legislation passed than any other secretary in the history of the department. Historian James L. Baughman wrote, "Kennedy . . . respected the Cleveland politician's skills as an urban administrator. With the aid of Undersecretary Wilbur J. Cohen and Education Commissioner Francis Keppel, Celebrezze reorganized his 112-program department, once called 'unmanage-

able' by Abraham Ribicoff. In January 1963 Celebrezze separated the public assistance and child health and welfare functions from the Social Security Administration and transferred these programs to the new Welfare Administration . . . the HEW chief worked for the passage of the Administration's Medicare and aid-to-education measures in 1962 and 1963. He told the House Education and Labor Committee in February 1963 that 'dependence on traditional sources of financial support to education will no longer suffice in every community.' Private and public universities, he added, required the 'substantial and immediate aid' included in the White House education package to accommodate the needs of a rapidly increasing college age population."

During his tenure, from 31 July 1962 until 17 August 1965, Celebrezze oversaw the congressional passage of some of the most important legislation in the history of the country—including the Clean Air Act, the Manpower Act of 1965, the Civil Rights Act of 1964 and the Voting Rights Act of 1965, the Elementary and Secondary Education Act of 1965, and, the Medicare and Medicaid Amendments to the Social Security Act of 1935, which gave health insurance and other assistance to the elderly and the disabled. In all, 60 new programs were added to the 112 he headed when taking over HEW.

The three years he spent at HEW were difficult for Celebrezze, and when President Johnson offered him a judgeship on the U.S. Court of Appeals for the Sixth Circuit in Ohio, Celebrezze accepted and left office in August 1965. He served on the Court of Appeals for fifteen years, stepping down in 1980; he continued to hear cases as a senior judge until his retirement in 1995. Celebrezze died in Cleveland on 30 October 1998 at the age of 88.

References: Baughman, James L., "Celebrezze, Anthony J(oseph)," in Nelson Lichtenstein, ed., *Political Profiles: The Kennedy Years* (New York: Facts on File, 1976), 79–80; "Celebrezze, Anthony Joseph," in Charles Moritz, ed., *Current Biography 1962* (New York: H. W. Wilson, 1963), 62–64;

Miles, Rufus E., Jr., *The Department of Health, Education, and Welfare* (New York: Praeger, 1974), 44–46.

JOHN WILLIAM GARDNER

1912–

John Gardner was president of the Carnegie Corporation when selected for the cabinet. Born in Los Angeles, California, on 8 October 1912, he is the son of William Frederick Gardner and Marie (née Flora) Gardner. Gardner received his bachelor's degree, in 1935, and a master's degree, in 1936, from Stanford University. He then earned his Ph.D. degree from the University of California at Berkeley in 1938. Gardner became an instructor at the Connecticut College for Women from 1938 to 1940. He then served as an assistant professor at Mt. Holyoke College from 1940 to 1942.

During World War II, Gardner served as the head of the Latin American Section of the Foreign Broadcast Intelligence Service, an arm of the Federal Communications Division. From 1943 to 1946, he served with the Office of Strategic Services, the forerunner of the modern Central Intelligence Agency, and as a captain in the U.S. Marine Corps.

After being discharged from the Marines, he went to work as vice-president of the Carnegie Corporation, one of the nation's leading research foundations. He became president in 1955 and oversaw the corporation's funding of James B. Conant's study of American high schools in the 1950s, as well as other studies on ways to improve American education. In 1965, President Lyndon B. Johnson named Gardner as the chairman of the President's Advisory Committee on Aid to Primary and Secondary Education, which recommended a formula that federal monies disbursed by HEW be distributed to areas based on the economic condition of that area.

In late July 1965, Johnson informed Gardner, a liberal Republican, that HEW Secretary Anthony Celebrezze was going to resign to take a seat on the U.S. Court of Appeals for the Sixth Circuit in Ohio and that Gardner would be nominated as his replacement. Named on 27 July 1965, he was confirmed by the Senate on 11 August as the sixth secretary of HEW. Historian James Wunsch wrote, "Shortly after he assumed office, Gardner faced charges from liberal congressmen, the NAACP Legal Defense Fund and other civil rights groups that HEW lagged in its efforts to integrate schools and hospitals. The Southern Regional Council pointed out that only 5.2% of Negro students in 11 Southern states were attending integrated schools in 1965. In February 1966 the Civil Rights Commission criticized HEW for law enforcement of Title VI of the 1964 Civil Rights Act, which barred racial discrimination in any federally assisted program or activity . . . Gardner issued a new set of guidelines for all federally assisted schools and hospitals in March 1966. The guidelines stipulated percentage rates of desegregation expected in the South for the 1966–67 school years and mandated the closing of small, inadequate schools maintained for Negro and other minority groups. They also called for an end to discrimination in the hiring of teachers and to segregation in hospital facilities. The guidelines did not apply to de facto segregation in cities outside the South."

Whereas his two predecessors, Abraham Ribicoff and Anthony Celebrezze, had at some point advocated splitting the huge and unwieldy department up, Gardner proposed turning the department into a "super-department." His recommendation to Johnson was that three separate subcabinet agencies be instituted in the department—a Department of Health, a Department of Education, and a Department of Individual and Family Services, each with its own undersecretary answerable to the secretary of the entire department. This plan was based primarily on the Department of Defense model, which had grouped the former Departments of War and Navy under one department with secretaries of these individual bureaus now accountable to the secretary of defense. But the Bureau of the Budget had not been consulted before Gardner had announced his proposal and it was immediately denounced as a potential creation of a huge kingdom with small fiefdoms on each of these issues. The idea quickly died. For his work in government Gardner was awarded the Presidential Medal of Freedom by President Johnson on 14 September 1964.

Gardner resigned on 25 January 1968, effective immediately, without any explanation to President Johnson. Many historians speculate that he quit because of his opposition to Johnson's prosecution of the Vietnam War, but Gardner has never spoken or written on the matter. After leaving office, Gardner served as the chairman of the National Urban Coalition from 1968 to 1970. On 18 August 1970, he founded Common Cause, a nonprofit, nonpartisan citizens' lobbying organization. The group remains active on such issues as campaign finance reform. Gardner served as chairman until 1977. In the 1980s, Gardner served as the cofounder and chairman of Independent Sector, an independent organization that encourages "philanthropy, volunteering, not-for-profit initiative and citizen action that help us better serve people and communities," and in the early 1990s served as chairman of the National Civic League. In 1989 he joined the faculty of Stanford University, and he currently holds the Miriam and Peter Hass Centennial Chair of Public Service at that school. He is the author of *Recovery of Confidence* (1970), *In Common Cause* (1972), *Self-Renewal* (1981), *Excellence* (1984), and *On Leadership* (1990).

References: "Gardner, John W(illiam)," in Charles Moritz, ed., *Current Biography 1976* (New York: H. W. Wilson, 1976), 153–156; Miles, Rufus E., Jr., *The Department of Health, Education, and Welfare* (New York: Praeger, 1974), 44–46; Wetterau, Bruce, *The Presidential Medal of Freedom: Winners and Their Achievements* (Washington, DC: Congressional Quarterly, 1996), 103; Wunsch, James L., "Gardner, John W(illiam)," in Nelson Lichtenstein, ed., *Political Profiles: The Johnson Years* (New York: Facts on File, 1976), 201–202.

WILBUR JOSEPH COHEN
1913–1987

Wilbur Cohen's service as assistant secretary of Health, Education, and Welfare (HEW) from 1961 to 1968 saw an explosion in legislation in all fields of human resources, welfare, civil rights, and education, but when he finally became secretary of the department in 1968, the administration he worked for was crushed by Vietnam, and he in effect became a caretaker. Cohen was born in Milwaukee, Wisconsin, on 20 June 1913, the son of Aaron Cohen, a store owner, and Bessie (née Rubenstein) Cohen. Cohen attended local schools, then entered the University of Wisconsin, from which he received a Ph.B. degree in economics in 1934.

Cohen studied economics under Professor Edwin E. Witte, and following his graduation Cohen followed Witte to Washington, D.C., where the professor had been named by President Franklin D. Roosevelt to the President's Cabinet Committee on Economic Security, a commission to study the feasibility of establishing a system of national social insurance. Cohen worked with Secretary of Labor Frances Perkins and others, drafting the enactment that became the Social Security Act of 1935, a landmark piece of legislation.

In 1935 one of his coworkers, Arthur Altmeyer, was named as chairman of the Social Security Board, and Cohen was named as his technical assistant. In 1946, when the board was renamed the Social Security Administration, Altmeyer was named its administrator. Except for a short period in 1938 when Cohen went to Europe to study European social insurance programs, he remained a part of the social security bureaucracy as technical adviser until 1952. He later served as a consultant to both the U.S. House of Representatives Committee on Ways and Means and the U.S. Senate Committee on Finance.

From 1953 to 1956, he served as the director of the bureau of research in the Social Security Administration. During his years with the social security bureaucracy in its varied forms, Cohen was responsible for the drafting and congressional passage, of numerous amendments to the original Social Security Act, including provisions to pay benefits to survivors of original Social Security recipients, to farm workers and the self-employed, and those who were blind, permanently disabled, and for dependent children.

In 1956, Cohen left government to serve as professor of public welfare administration at the University of Michigan at Ann Arbor. He was a consultant to the Senate Committee on Labor and Public Welfare and, in 1959, to the White House Conference on Aging. Although he was a Democrat, in 1959 Cohen was invited by Secretary of HEW Arthur S. Flemming to serve as a member of the department's Public Assistance Advisory Council.

During the 1960 election, Cohen served as a consultant to the campaign of Senator John F. Kennedy, the Democratic presidential nominee. Following Kennedy's election, he named Cohen as the head of a task force on health and Social Security. In 1961, after Kennedy took office, he nominated Cohen as assistant secretary of HEW; however, because Cohen was considered out of the mainstream on many health-related issues, his confirmation became a contentious one; he was confirmed by a margin of only one vote.

During his tenure as assistant secretary, under Secretary Abraham Ribicoff and then Secretary Anthony Celebrezze, Cohen helped draft and push through Congress some of the most wide-ranging legislation ever enacted in the areas of human health, education, welfare and medical reform, and civil rights. Perhaps his crowning achievement was the passage in 1965 of the so-called Social Security Amendments, which established the Medicare and Medicaid programs, giving federal medical assistance to the elderly, poor, and disabled.

In April 1965, Cohen succeeded Ivan A. Nestingen as undersecretary of HEW. In this capacity, he had full administrative control over the Medicare and Medicaid programs, and he continued to design new legislation, including the Elementary and Secondary Education Act of 1965, the Heart Disease, Cancer, and Stroke Amendments of 1965, and the Child Health Care Act of 1967. Thus from 1961 to 1968, Wilbur Cohen placed his personal imprint on every major and minor piece of federal legislation dealing with health, education, and human services.

On 25 January 1968, Secretary of HEW John W. Gardner resigned, and President Lyndon B. Johnson named Cohen as acting secretary. Because of the pressures of the Vietnam War abroad and urban strife at home, Cohen remained in an acting capacity until 23 March, when Johnson nominated him to fill the vacancy. A week later, however, Johnson announced he would not run for election to a second term. Thus, Cohen, who was confirmed by the Senate on 9 May 1968 and sworn in seven days later as the seventh secretary of HEW, would serve only a limited time, until 20 January 1969. As assistant secretary and as undersecretary Cohen had had tremendous power over legislation and department affairs; as the secretary in an administration that was rapidly coming to an end, Cohen could not do much more than serve as a caretaker.

After leaving government, Cohen returned to the University of Michigan as a professor and dean of that university's School of Education. He also campaigned across the country to defend Social Security, and, in the early 1970s, became the president of the American Public Welfare Association. When President Jimmy Carter sought to scale back, for budgetary reasons, many of Cohen's programs, he denounced the plans as "tragic, unsound, immoral, [and] unjustified." Cohen founded Save Our Security (SOS) as a lobbying group, which helped to stave off or reduce many of these proposed cutbacks. Cohen remained a leading voice in SOS after leaving the University of Michigan in 1980 to become a professor of public affairs at the University of Texas at Austin. He later served as cochairman of the group with former HEW Secretary Arthur Flemming.

On 18 May 1987, Cohen was attending a symposium in Seoul, South Korea, on Aging and Welfare for the Aged when he died. He was 73. In 1987, the building for HHS, the department from which HEW was established after its education functions were transferred to the Department of Education, was renamed the Wilbur J. Cohen Federal Building.

References: Berkowitz, Edward D., *Mr. Social Security: The Life of Wilbur J. Cohen* (Lawrence: University Press of Kansas, 1995), 1–5, 266; "Cohen, Wilbur J(oseph)," in Charles Moritz, ed., *Current Biography 1968* (New York: H. W. Wilson, 1968), 96–99; Shearon, Marjorie O'Connell, *Wilbur J. Cohen: The Pursuit of Power—A Bureaucratic Biography* (Chevy Chase, MD: Shearon Legislative Service, 1967).

ROBERT HUTCHINSON FINCH
1925–1995

Robert Finch served as lieutenant governor of California (1967–1969) until he was selected by President-elect Richard M. Nixon to serve as secretary of Health, Education, and Welfare (HEW). His service in that position lasted almost a year and a half, until he moved to the White House to serve as counselor to the president. Finch was born in Tempe, a suburb of Phoenix, Arizona, on 9 October 1925. The family moved to California, and Finch attended local schools there before he joined the Marines, serving during World War II. After he returned to the United States, Finch entered Occidental College in Los Angeles. Finch was active in politics at Occidental; he was one of the founders of a local Young Republicans Club. He earned his bachelor's degree in 1947. Thereafter, he went to Washington, D.C., to serve as an administrative aide to Representative Norris Paulson from California. While working for Paulson, Finch became good friends with Congressman Richard M. Nixon of California.

Finch then studied at the University of Southern California, where he earned a law degree in 1951. After he was admitted to the California bar, Finch practiced law while making two unsuccessful runs for a U.S. House seat, in 1954 and 1956. In 1958, he served as an assistant to Vice-president Richard Nixon.

In 1960, Finch was the manager for Nixon's presidential run. He disapproved of Nixon's run for governor of California in 1962 and did not participate in the campaign.

Finch remained in politics, helping to engineer George Murphy's election victory to the U.S. Senate over Kennedy spokesman Pierre Salinger in 1964. Despite being a moderate Republican, Finch was nominated in 1966 by the Republicans for lieutenant governor, to run with the more conservative Ronald Reagan. The two men were elected, and Finch spent the next two years moderating Reagan's program to get it passed in the state legislature.

In 1968, Nixon ran for a second time for president, and Finch served as one of his close advisers. Once Nixon had the presidential nomination, he offered Finch the vice-presidential position, but Finch refused, citing the closeness of the two men over the years. After Nixon's close election victory in November 1968, Nixon offered Finch the attorney general portfolio, but Finch asked for HEW, mainly because he felt he could do some good with the department's wide range of programs.

Confirmed on 20 January 1969, the same day he was officially nominated, Finch took office as the eighth secretary of HEW. He served seventeen months, until 23 June 1970. During his tenure Finch restricted the use of the pesticide DDT when it was found to be damaging to the environment. On 18 October 1969, Finch issued an order that required a reduction in the usage of cyclamate, the artificial sweetener, because it was found to cause cancer.

Finch also became involved in administration policy on the desegregation of schools.

During the 1968 campaign, Nixon intimated that as president he would ease strict court and government desegregation orders that were highly unpopular among white southerners. However, Finch, more moderate, aimed to enforce these orders, bring his department into conflict with both the White House and southern congressmen and senators. Finally, in March 1970, Finch convinced Nixon that the law had to be followed, and the administration announced that the desegregation orders would be carried out.

Department historian Rufus Miles wrote in 1974, "Finch found HEW a most difficult and disconcerting Department to administer. He could well understand why its manageability was widely questioned. The press, however, which had started out with an unusually favorable attitude, had little understanding of, or sympathy for, his difficulties, and within a year began to show its disappointment. To compound Finch's problems, HEW seemed to be a haven for activist employees who were constantly protesting, demanding, and demonstrating. He had the misfortune to be Secretary during the period when organized dissatisfaction with the Establishment was at its height. He was without experience in handing internal backfires." Faced with a secretary who could not handle this burden, on 6 June 1970, Nixon announced to his cabinet that Finch was stepping down as secretary of HEW to become a counselor to the president with cabinet rank, to be replaced by Elliot L. Richardson.

The move to the White House did not satisfy Finch, and he resigned in December 1972 to return to his law practice in California. In September 1974, President Gerald R. Ford named him to a clemency committee to study the cases of Vietnam draft dodgers and deserters. In 1976, he challenged Senator S. I. Hayakawa for the Republican nomination, but lost. Finch resumed his law practice in California. On 10 October 1995, one day after his seventieth birthday, he died at his home in Pasadena.

References: "Finch, Robert H(utchinson)," in Charles Moritz, ed., *Current Biography 1969*

(New York: H. W. Wilson, 1970), 143–146; Miles, Rufus E., Jr., *The Department of Health, Education, and Welfare* (New York: Praeger, 1974).

ELLIOT LEE RICHARDSON
1920–1999

Elliot Richardson is the only man to have served in four separate cabinet posts—secretary of health, education and welfare (HEW), secretary of defense, attorney general, and secretary of commerce. Elliot Richardson was born in Boston, Massachusetts, on 20 July 1920, the son of Edward P. Richardson, a physician and professor at the Harvard Medical school, and Clara (née Shattuck) Richardson.

After earning a bachelor's degree cum laude from Harvard University in 1941, he volunteered for service in the U.S. Army in 1942, enlisting as private, and receiving a commission as a first lieutenant in the Fourth Infantry Division of the Army, he was a participant in the Allied landings at Normandy on D-Day, 6 June 1944, and was wounded, receiving a Bronze Star for heroism. After the war, he returned to Harvard, where he entered the Harvard Law School and served as editor of the *Harvard Law Review*. He earned his law degree in 1947. That same year, he became a law clerk of Judge Learned Hand of the U.S. Court of Appeals, serving for one year and, in 1948, went to work as a law clerk for Supreme Court Justice Felix Frankfurter.

In 1949, Richardson entered private law practice when he joined the Boston law firm of Ropes, Gray, Best, Collidge, and Rugg, but tired of the work after four years and left the firm to become an aide to Massachusetts Governor Leverett Saltonstall in 1953. After leaving the governor's office in 1954, Richardson returned to his old law firm, but left again in 1957 when President Dwight D. Eisenhower appointed him as assistant secretary for legislation in HEW, serving under Secretary Marion B. Folsom.

Two years later, Richardson left Washington when he was named by Eisenhower as U.S. attorney for Massachusetts, a post he held until 1961. That year, despite being a Republican, Richardson was named by President John F. Kennedy as a special assistant to Attorney General Robert F. Kennedy. A year later, he resigned to run in the Massachusetts Republican primary for state attorney general, but lost. Two years later, however, he was nominated for lieutenant governor, and was elected, serving under Governor John Volpe. He took an active role in pushing Volpe's social welfare program.

In 1966, Richardson ran for and was elected as state attorney general, serving until 1969. In that latter year, following the election of former Vice-president Nixon as president, Richardson was named as undersecretary of state in the new administration, serving under Secretary of State William Rogers. Many credit him with serving as a bridge between the department and foreign policy adviser Henry Kissinger, who in many ways ignored Secretary Rogers.

Following the announcement on 6 June 1970 that Secretary of HEW Robert H. Finch would leave office, President Nixon named Richardson to the vacancy. The choice was a surprise, even though Richardson had served at HEW in the Eisenhower administration. After Senate confirmation, Richardson was sworn in on 24 June 1970 as the ninth secretary of HEW. His tenure lasted until 29 January 1973, during which time he attempted to formulate Nixon's policy on cutting back the department's ever-growing appropriations. As historian Margaret Wyzomirski wrote, "As a progressive Republican with a reputation and a service record as a strong administrator and a loyal team member, Richardson was suited to both the President's and the Department's needs. In addition, he had experience in HEW during the Eisenhower administration. The combination of these assets led Richardson to declare that he was 're-turning to an old love,' while the President commented that he was 'the best qualified man in the country' to head HEW."

During his tenure, Richardson sought to decentralize department funding to the states, and streamline programs. He desired to fully implement forced busing to integrate schools, but tempered his approach to be consistent with administration policy, which wanted minimal busing as required then by law. After Nixon was reelected in 1972, Richardson moved to the Defense Department when Secretary of Defense Melvin Laird resigned. As the eleventh secretary of defense, Richardson served only for four months, the shortest tenure in that department's history, from 30 January to 24 May 1973. Since this period of service was so short, he barely made any impact on department policy. His biggest role at Defense was his testifying before Congress on the department's fiscal year 1974 budget requirements.

What necessitated Richardson's move from the Defense Department was the Watergate scandal. Arising from a break-in at Democratic Party headquarters in the Watergate building in June 1972 that was traced to operatives working for Nixon's 1972 reelection committee, the affair was, by early 1973, threatening the Nixon presidency. Attorney General Richard Kleindienst was forced to resign amid allegations he had lied to Congress. Thus, on 30 April 1973, Nixon announced that Richardson would be nominated as attorney general. He continued as secretary of defense until 23 May, when he was confirmed by the Senate and took office as the sixty-ninth attorney general.

Richardson had been selected because as a liberal Republican he was acceptable to Democrats who were leading investigations into Watergate on Capitol Hill; he was also well known for his crackdowns on corruption while in Massachusetts. But Richardson's tenure at the Justice Department was short and bitter. At his confirmation hearings, which lasted for three weeks, Richardson was forced to agree that he would allow a special prosecutor unfettered complete access to all papers and documents dealing with Watergate and would not interfere in any way with the investigation. As he took office, he quickly became caught in the middle between the White House and Special

Prosecutor Archibald Cox. Cox officially worked under Richardson; only Richardson could fire him, and only then for "extraordinary improprieties."

On 23 July 1973, Cox issued a subpoena for tapes recorded in the Oval Office that allegedly contained statements on Watergate. The White House resisted the subpoena, offering instead edited transcripts of the conversations. When Cox refused to accept these, Nixon ordered Richardson to dismiss Cox on Saturday, 20 October 1973. Richardson refused, and immediately submitted his resignation. Nixon then ordered the deputy attorney general, William D. Ruckelshaus, to fire Cox—he, too, refused and resigned. It was left up to Solicitor General Robert H. Bork to carry out the command. The entire episode has come to be known as the Saturday Night Massacre. The outrage over the resignations and firing of Cox led to more problems for Nixon, and he eventually resigned on 8 August 1974. For a time, Richardson was considered a hero for standing his ground in the face of adversity, and he toured the lecture circuit for a year. On 20 February 1975, President Gerald R. Ford named him as U.S. ambassador to Great Britain, to replace Walter H. Annenberg. Richardson remained in London until his resignation on 16 January 1976, which came about because of conflicts with Secretary of State Henry Kissinger. On 3 November 1975, when Secretary of Commerce Rogers C. B. Morton resigned, President Ford named Richardson as his successor and, following Senate confirmation on 11 December 1975, he became the twenty-fourth secretary of commerce. Richardson was the only man in American history to have held four separate cabinet positions. His tenure in office lasted until the end of the Ford administration on 20 January 1977; he served mainly in a caretaker capacity and brought stability to the Commerce Department.

After leaving office, Richardson continued to serve government. In 1977, President Jimmy Carter named Richardson as U.S. ambassador-at-large and as the U.S. representative to the Law of the Sea Conference (1977–

1980). He then practiced the law with the Washington, D.C., office of the New York firm Milbank, Tweed, Hadley, & McCloy until his retirement in October 1992. In 1998, President Bill Clinton bestowed on him the Presidential Medal of Freedom, the highest award given to an American citizen. Richardson died on 31 December 1999 at the age of 79.

References: The Attorney Generals of the United States, 1789–1985 (Washington, DC: U.S. Department of Justice, 1985), 138; Miles, Rufus E., Jr., *The Department of Health, Education, and Welfare* (New York: Praeger, 1974), 59–61; "Richardson, Elliot L(ee)," in Charles Moritz, ed., *Current Biography 1971* (New York: H. W. Wilson, 1971), 343–345; Wyzomirski, Margaret J., "Richardson, Elliot Lee," in Eleanora Schoenebaum, ed., *Political Profiles: The Nixon/Ford Years* (New York: Facts on File, 1982), 524–528.

CASPAR WILLARD WEINBERGER

1917–

Casper Weinberger helped lead the United States to ultimate victory in the cold war as secretary of defense under President Ronald Reagan, from 1981 to 1987; he also served as secretary of Health, Education, and Welfare (HEW), from 1972 to 1975. Weinberger was born in San Francisco, California, on 18 August 1917, the son of Herman Weinberger, an attorney, and Cerise (née Carpenter) Weinberger. Weinberger attended local schools and then received a bachelor's degree magna cum laude in 1938 from Harvard University; three years later, he received a law degree from the Harvard Law School. He had served as president of the newspaper, *Harvard Crimson*. When the United States entered World War II, he enlisted as a private in the U.S. Army, was commissioned as a lieutenant, and served in the Pacific. At the end of the war, he had risen to the rank of captain and was serving on the intelligence staff of General Douglas McArthur. When he returned home from the war, he served as a law clerk for a federal judge and then joined a law firm in San Francisco.

In 1952, Weinberger was elected to a seat in the California state Assembly and won re-election in 1954 and 1956. He left his seat in 1958 to run a campaign for California state attorney general; he was unsuccessful. He remained active in politics, however, becoming chairman of the California state Republican Party in 1962. Three years later he met Ronald Reagan, who was elected governor of the state. In 1967, Reagan named Weinberger as chairman of the Commission on California State Government Organization and Economy and, in early 1968, named him as state director of finance, a position he held until 1970. He left Sacramento when President Richard M. Nixon appointed him chairman of the Federal Trade Commission, although later that same year Nixon moved him over to become deputy director, and then in 1972, director of the Office of Management and Budget.

On 28 November 1972, following Nixon's reelection, Secretary of HEW Elliot L. Richardson moved from HEW to the Department of Defense to replace Secretary Melvin Laird, and Weinberger was named as Richardson's replacement. Following Senate confirmation on 8 February 1973 by a vote of 61 to 10, Weinberger became the tenth secretary of HEW. His tenure, which lasted until 8 August 1975, was marked by a continuation of his tough budget-cutting practices. Known since his earliest days in state offices as "Cap the Knife," he kept the total expenditures for the department from rising drastically—from 1973, when the budget minus Social Security funds was $25.46 billion, it rose only to $29.55 billion by 1975.

Department historian Rufus Miles wrote in 1974, when Weinberger was still in office, "Secretary Weinberger . . . made his new under secretary, Frank Carlucci, the internal manager of the Department with the understanding that he is to accelerate the movement toward regional decentralization of intergovernmental programs begun under

[Secretary Robert H.] Finch and additional developed by [Secretary] Richardson. He has created a new assistant secretary for Human Development, bringing together the Office of Child Development, the Administration on Aging, and miscellaneous other functions previously scattered. And he has reorganized HEW's health programs, abolishing the unsuccessful Health Services and Mental Health Administration, and putting in its place four organizations: a Health Services Administration, a Health Resources Administration, a Center for Disease Control, and an Alcohol, Drug Abuse, and Mental Health Administration." In March 1973, Weinberger spoke of the huge bureaucracy that had been created in the government around social programs—he called this bureaucracy the education-health-poverty complex. He departed from HEW on 8 August 1975 for private business as the vice-president and general counsel of the Bechtel Group in California.

Following the election of Weinberger's former boss, Ronald Reagan, as president, in 1980, Weinberger was invited to become secretary of defense in the new administration. Weinberger accepted the position and was confirmed on 20 January 1981, by a vote of 97 to 2, to become the fifteenth secretary of defense. His tenure, which lasted until 23 November 1987, was a period of massive growth of military expenditures—in his first weeks in office, he asked for a supplemental appropriation of nearly $7 billion for the 1981 budget that had been passed by the Congress in the Carter administration; thus, Congress granted $176 billion in 1981 and $211 billion for 1982. By 1985, spending at the Pentagon was up to $285 billion, an increase of 100 percent over the 1980 numbers of $142 billion.

Roger Trask, a Defense department historian, wrote, "Although Weinberger obtained large increases between 1981 and 1985, Congress consistently provided less than requested and became less willing to go along with those requests. Weinberger resisted congressional reductions, contending that he prepared budget submissions carefully according to real needs. In a book on his years in the Pentagon, he wrote of having 'acquired a reputation of being stubborn, uncompromising, immoderate and unpragmatic.' The new secretary quickly established a good working relationship with the leaders of the military services, making manifest in words and actions his respect for them and his firm intention to get for them the funds needed for the buildup that the administration thought necessary. The military reciprocated this attitude, which was no doubt furthered by Weinberger's success in securing large appropriations for Defense. Indeed, Weinberger gave the services their head to a greater extent than they had enjoyed for a long time."

With this massive infusion of money, Weinberger started and purchased major weapons systems, changed operational plans to meet new challenges in the world regarding the deployment of American troops, and played the major administration role in confronting the challenge of the Soviet Union. Toward this latter end, Weinberger oversaw the development of a stealth aircraft, the development of the Trident missile, the production of 100 MX (Peacekeeper) missiles and their deployment in Western Europe, and advocated the creation of an antimissile defense system, the Strategic Defense Initiative, derided by critics as Star Wars. Weinberger was a slow but later staunch defender of Reagan's attempts to secure arms control agreements with the Soviets, including the Strategic Reduction Talks and the Intermediate Nuclear Forces talks. Weinberger was also key in the use of force in Grenada and Lebanon in 1983 and Libya in 1986.

Near the end of his tenure, Weinberger was accused of being involved in the Iran-Contra Affair, in which monies from arms sold to Iran were used to buy weapons and materiel for the anticommunist Nicaraguan rebels known as the Contras. This military aid to the Contra rebels was illegal under the Boland Amendment. In fact, Weinberger and Secretary of State George Shultz opposed illegal aid to the Contras. After he resigned in November 1987, questions continued to follow him regarding his role. Although there was evidence that Weinberger had nothing to do with the Iran-Contra funding, a special prosecutor indicted him. Before Weinberger's trial began President George Bush pardoned him in December 1992. Caspar Weinberger served as secretary of defense for six years and ten months, the second longest tenure in that office after Robert S. McNamara (1961–1968). After leaving office, he became the publisher and editor of *Forbes* magazine, and he authored several works, including *Fighting for Peace* (1990), and coauthored *The Next War* (1996), in which he called for a new military policy after the end of the cold war.

References: Miles, Rufus E., Jr., *The Department of Health, Education, and Welfare* (New York: Praeger, 1974), 61–62; Trask, Roger R., *The Secretaries of Defense: A Brief History, 1947–1985* (Washington, DC: Office of the Secretary of Defense, 1985), 49–51; Weinberger, Caspar W., *Fighting for Peace: Seven Critical Years in the Pentagon* (New York: Warner Books, 1990), 14.

FORREST DAVID MATHEWS
1935–

The president of the University of Alabama when selected as the eleventh secretary of Health, Education, and Welfare (HEW), F. David Mathews was the youngest man, at only 39, to hold the position. At age 33, Mathews was the head of the University of Alabama—the youngest man to head a major American university as well. Born in Grove Hill, Alabama, on 6 December 1935, he is the son of Forrest Lee Mathews, a teacher and school superintendent, and Doris (née Pearson) Mathews. Mathews attended local schools, then entered the University of Alabama at Tuscaloosa and studied American history and classical Greek, earning a bachelor's degree in history in 1958. He was awarded a master's degree the following year and a Ph.D. degree from Columbia University in New York in 1965. From 1959 to 1960 he served in the U.S. Army.

After finishing his military service, Mathews returned to the University of Alabama as assistant dean of men (1960–1965), and then interim dean of men (1965–1966). He then became executive assistant in the office of the university president, Frank Rose. After serving as executive vice-president from 1968 to 1969, Mathews replaced Rose in the latter year as president of the university.

In early 1975, President Gerald R. Ford named Mathews as a member of the Advisory Council for the American Revolution Bicentennial Commission. On 26 June 1975, Ford named Mathews to succeed Caspar Weinberger as secretary of HEW. Following Senate confirmation on 22 July 1975 by a voice vote, Mathews was sworn in on 8 August 1975 as the eleventh secretary of HEW.

His service continued until the end of the Ford administration on 20 January 1977. He was the head of a department with over 330 different programs and more than 129,000 employees. Historian Joseph N. Reilly wrote, "A major task facing Mathews was to curtail the steady rise in HEW's health care budget, much of which was attributed to fraud and mismanagement particularly in the Medicaid program. . . . At the end of 1975 Mathews reported the formation of a new criminal investigation unit to identify Medicaid fraud and abuse, which was resulting in the loss of an estimated $750 million a year. Criticism of the program mounted in January 1976 when a report by the House Government Operations subcommittee charged that HEW's fraud detection resources were 'ridiculously inadequate.' Two months later, Mathews outlined a new campaign that would combine an expanded force of HEW investigators with state officials focusing on criminal violations by nursing homes, clinical laboratories, pharmacists, and doctors receiving Medicaid funds." Mathews also established a program that allowed people to comment and give advice on new regulations from the department before they were published, a radical change. Mathews, who had no government experience before he joined the cabinet, did

an adequate job containing the explosion of a department that was far too big for any one secretary.

After leaving office, Mathews returned to the presidency of the University of Alabama, which had been held for him by Acting President Richard Thigpen during his absence. Mathews remained as president of the university until 1980. He then served as a professor of American history at the university until 1995. He is currently serving as president and chief executive officer of the Charles F. Kettering Foundation in Dayton, Ohio, a research foundation that focuses on international affairs and government problem solving. Mathews is the author of several books, including *Politics for People: Finding a Responsible Public Voice* (1994), as well as more than eighty articles on such subjects as southern history and federal social policy. He also serves on the board of directors of the Southern Institute on Children and Families, a lobbying group involved in children's health issues.

References: "Mathews (Forrest) David," in Charles Moritz, ed., *Current Biography 1976* (New York: H. W. Wilson, 1976), 260–262; Reilly, Joseph N., "Mathews (Forrest) David," in Eleanora Schoenebaum, ed., *Political Profiles: The Nixon/Ford Years* (New York: Facts on File, 1982), 428–430.

JOSEPH ANTHONY CALIFANO, JR.

1931–

Joseph Califano was known as the "deputy President of the Great Society" for assisting, while serving as President Lyndon Johnson's assistant for domestic affairs, in formulating many of Johnson's economic and social programs. He got a chance to manage those programs as secretary of Health, Education, and Welfare (HEW) in the Carter administration, but his tenure ended with a purge of the cabinet, and the department that he ran was abolished just months later. Califano was born in Brooklyn, New York, on 15 May 1931, the son of Joseph A. Califano, Sr., an administrative assistant at IBM, and Katherine (née Gill) Califano. Califano was educated in Roman Catholic schools in New York City, then attended the Brooklyn Preparatory School and entered Holy Cross College in Worcester, Massachusetts, from which he received a bachelor's degree in 1952. Three years later, he earned his law degree from the Harvard Law School.

After he graduated from law school, Califano joined the U.S. Navy as a legal officer in the Office of the Judge Advocate General and was discharged in 1958 with the rank of lieutenant. After leaving the service, he joined the New York law firm of Dewey, Ballatine, Bushby, Palmer, and Wood, a firm that once boasted former New York Governor Thomas E. Dewey as a senior partner.

Although he had not been interested in politics, following the election of Democrat John F. Kennedy as president in 1960, Califano decided to try for a job in the new administration. He wrote to Cyrus R. Vance, newly named as the general counsel for the Department of Defense, with his qualifications for office, and he was hired as Vance's assistant. In 1962, when Vance was named secretary of the Army, he made Califano as his assistant to that office as well.

In July 1963, Califano was named as general counsel for the Department of the Army. In early 1964, Secretary of Defense Robert S. McNamara appointed Califano as special assistant to the secretary and the deputy secretary of the department. Called one of McNamara's "Whiz Kids," a number of aides he surrounded himself with known for the intensity of their work. As such, Califano oversaw McNamara's ideas for cost cutting and supervising the use of federal troops in civil rights protests in the American South.

As a liaison to the White House for the department, Califano became close to President Lyndon B. Johnson. Prior to the 1964 election, Johnson asked to have Califano transferred to the White House; McNamara initially resisted, but he acquiesced in early 1965. Over the next four years, as the assistant to the president for legislative coordination and domestic troubleshooting, coordinating Johnson's Great Society of economic and social programs on Capitol Hill. Califano helped to draft legislation that created the Office of Economic Opportunity, the Model Cities Program, and the organic act of the Department of Transportation. He was also involved in policymaking in HEW.

After President Johnson decided not to run for reelection, and his term ended on 20 January 1969, Califano went to work for the Washington law firm of Arnold & Porter, where he remained for two years, until he joined the Washington firm of attorney Edward Bennett Williams, making the firm Williams, Connolly, and Califano. He also served as general counsel to the Democratic National Committee from 1970 to 1972.

In 1976, Governor Jimmy Carter of Georgia was elected president, and he selected Califano as his choice for secretary of HEW. Califano, in his memoirs, *Governing America,* wrote, "By Tuesday morning, December 21 [1976], Carter had named all his Cabinet except Secretary of HEW. . . . Just as I was leaving my home for the office, the phone rang . . . 'This is Jimmy Carter. I'd like you to be my Secretary of Health, Education, and Welfare.' 'I thought you'd never ask, Mr. President,' I quipped, and promptly added, 'It would be an honor and a privilege.'" Nominated on 20 January 1977, Califano was confirmed four days later, by a vote in the U.S. Senate of 95 to 1, and took office as the twelfth secretary of HEW. His tenure lasted until 19 July 1979.

In an interview in 1995, Califano recalled why he took the position in the cabinet, and the tremendous problems he had in his first days in office: "I wanted to prove that the Great Society programs could be managed. That was number one. Number two, I wanted to get across to the liberals that you had to have competence and efficiency as well as compassion. There was no sense of efficiency among the liberal establishment, no sense of what that meant. For example, the Child Support Enforcement program. I went after fathers in the Welfare program with Russell Long. The liberals were all aghast in those days at doing that. I found out there were a billion dollars in college loans unpaid, and we hadn't sent anybody any bills. Nobody pays bills they haven't gotten. . . . Leo Kornfeld was running ADP, the check writing company, Automatic Data Processing. I went to him and said, 'I want you to take over this college loan program and get these damn things paid.' HEW kept records on shoeboxes, index cards. I couldn't get Leo and seven or eight people on the payroll fast enough, so I had them create a non-profit corporation so we could get started on the thing, gave the corporation the job, and then ultimately we worked through Civil Service and brought them into HEW. It was crazy to have Medicare and Medicaid separated. We lost all the leverage. And that's what it was about. The overall reorganization of HEW was to make it so I could *run it,* or anybody could run it. Sure, Carter wanted the government to be more efficient. . . . Indeed, if we had more of that, we'd have less of what we have today in terms of the tremendous reaction to waste in the social programs."

Historian Donald Whitnah wrote of Califano's tenure, which followed years of allegations of fraud and abuse under the Nixon and Ford administrations: "The Jimmy Carter White House years until HEW's demise proved to be no less controversial. . . . Califano remained until his removal until 1979, supposedly because he opposed Carter over a new Department of Education, moved relentlessly with his anti-smoking bias, was too favorable towards Carter's arch-rival [Senator] Edward Kennedy, and had failed to gain from Congress national health care insurance, a check on rising hospital costs, and the overhaul of the welfare system. Califano originally vigorously upheld the controversial quota system for minorities in job hiring, and ordered a probe of cancer patients who had been exposed to earlier atomic testing."

On 19 July 1979, Califano was summarily removed during a shake-up in the cabinet that saw the resignation or firing of Secretary of the Treasury W. Michael Blumenthal, Secretary of Energy James Schlesinger, Secretary of Transportation Brock Adams, Attorney General Griffin Bell, and Califano, who was allowed to offer a letter of resignation. Califano's ineffectiveness, and Carter's wish to sever the education functions of the department, was HEW's ultimate undoing. Under the next secretary, Patricia Roberts Harris, who had served as secretary of Housing and Urban Development, HEW was abolished in October 1979, just months after Califano departed.

Since leaving office, Califano has remained a staunch advocate for the rights of people to access to improved health care, and he has authored several books. In 1992, Califano founded the National Center on Addiction and Substance Abuse at Columbia University, a national renowned organization that strives to educate parents and children of the harmful side effects of smoking and using drugs.

References: Califano Health Care Financing Administration oral history interview, 31 August 1995, courtesy of the Social Security Administration, Baltimore, MD; Califano, Joseph A., Jr., *Governing America: An Insider's Report from the White House and the Cabinet* (New York: Simon and Schuster, 1981), 17, 430–437; "Califano, Joseph A(nthony), Jr.," in Charles Moritz, ed., *Current Biography 1977* (New York: H. W. Wilson, 1977), 93–95; Karst, Kenneth L., "Califano v. Goldfarb," "Califano v. Webster," and "Califano v. Westcott" in Leonard W. Levy, ed.-in-chief, *Encyclopedia of the American Constitution* (New York: Macmillan; 4 vols., 1986), 1: 197–198; Whitnah, Donald R., "Department of Health and Human Services," in Donald R. Whitnah, ed.-in-chief, *Government Agencies* (Westport, CT: Greenwood, 1983), 121.

PATRICIA ROBERTS HARRIS
1924–1985

See Secretary of Housing and Urban Development, 1977–1979

HEALTH AND HUMAN SERVICES

———⟫●⟪———

Following passage of the Department of Education Organization Act of 1979, which established a separate Department of Education from what had once been the Department of Health, Education, and Welfare (HEW), the Department of Health and Human Services (HHS) was created on 4 May 1980. At the time of its establishment, HHS received 140,000 employees of the 157,000 who had formerly worked at HEW, and its initial budget was $226 billion. President Jimmy Carter had tried to establish a separate Department of Education in 1978, but he failed; in 1979, he was successful, and he named Secretary of Health, Education, and Welfare Patricia Roberts Harris as the first secretary of health and human services. Critics of the new addition to the cabinet charged that it reached too far into American life, dealing with issues HEW had not addressed such as sex education and abortion.

In 1980, former California Governor Ronald Reagan was elected president, and he named retiring U.S. Senator Richard Schweiker of Pennsylvania as the second secretary of HHS; Schweiker spent the two years of his tenure trying to cut back on the bureaucracy of the department, but he was unsuccessful in working with the Democratic-controlled Congress. His successor, former Representative Margaret M. Heckler, did not have good relations with Reagan during her two years in office (1983–1985) and was considered ineffective, even though she oversaw the initial investigations into the causes of AIDS and saw the National Organ Transplantation Act signed into law.

Her successor, Otis Bowen, was a folksy physician who had served as governor of Indiana for two terms; he was seen as an capable and efficient administrator, using his office to push for congressional passage of the McKinney Act, which provided health care to the homeless. The fifth secretary, Louis W. Sullivan, of the Morehouse School of Medicine in Atlanta, saw the establishment of the Agency for Health Care Policy and Research, the Human Genome Project, and the Ryan White Comprehensive Resource Emergency (CARE) Act, supporting AIDS victims. The sixth secretary, Donna Shalala, a former university administrator, saw the enactment of welfare reform under the Personal Responsibility and Work Opportunity Reconciliation Act of 1996, as well as having the Food and Drug Administration promulgate new rules on tobacco sale to minors.

According to the *United States Government Manual 1999/2000,* "The Secretary of Health and Human Services advises the President on health, welfare, and income security plans, policies, and programs of the Federal Government. The Secretary directs Department staff in carrying out the approved programs and activities of the Department and promotes general public understanding of the Department's goals, programs, and objectives. The Secretary administers these functions through the Office of the Secretary and the Department's 12 operating divisions."

The Department oversees the Social Security Administration, the Food and Drug Administration, Medicare and Medicaid, Head Start, aid for low-income families, immunization and other disease-eradicating programs, child support enforcement, and programs to prevent domestic violence.

References: Department of Health and Human Services, *This is HHS* (Washington, DC: Department of Health and Human Services, 1980); *United States Government Manual 1999/2000* (Washington, DC: GPO, 2000), 273; Whitnah, Donald R., "Department of Health and Human Services," in Donald R. Whitnah, ed.-in-chief, *Government Agencies* (Westport, CT: Greenwood, 1983), 121–122.

PATRICIA ROBERTS HARRIS
1924–1985

See Secretary Housing and Urban Development, 1977–1979

RICHARD SCHULTZ SCHWEIKER
1926–

Richard Schweiker is best remembered as the man Ronald Reagan chose as his "running mate" during Reagan's attempt to win the 1976 Republican presidential nomination. Reagan lost to President Gerald R. Ford, but four years later, when Reagan was elected president, he selected Schweiker as his secretary of health and human services. Born in Norristown, in Montgomery County, Pennsylvania, on 1 June 1926, Schweiker is the son of Malcolm A. Schweiker and

Blanche (née Schultz) Schweiker. Schweiker grew up on the family's farm near Worcester, Pennsylvania, where he attended local schools. During World War II, he enlisted in the U.S. Navy and served aboard the aircraft carrier *Tarawa* from 1944 until 1946. After he left the military, he returned to Pennsylvania, where he entered Slippery Rock State College; two years later, he transferred to Pennsylvania State University, from which he earned a bachelor's degree in psychology in 1950. He then joined his family's tile business and worked as a sales executive and then as vice-president in charge of sales until 1960.

A moderate Republican, Schweiker served as a Republican committeeman for Montgomery County. In 1960, he ran for a U.S. House seat against conservative Republican Representative John A. Lafore, Jr., and beat him, as well as his Democratic challenger in November. Schweiker served in Congress from 3 January 1961 until 3 January 1969, during which time he supported civil rights and Medicare legislation; he was an early supporter of American policy in Vietnam, but eventually became an opponent of the war.

In 1968, Schweiker gave up his House seat to run for the Senate against Senator

Joseph S. Clark, a liberal Democrat who, like Schweiker, opposed the Vietnam War. Clark was also a supporter of gun control legislation, which made him unpopular in his state. With gun rights groups backing him, Schweiker easily beat Clark and entered the U.S. Senate on 3 January, serving until 3 January 1981. During this period, Schweiker repeatedly clashed with President Richard M. Nixon over policy issues, including Supreme Court appointments, and, when Nixon was implicated in the Watergate affair, Schweiker was the third Republican in the Congress to demand his resignation. Despite being considered a liberal Republican, Schweiker was opposed to government financing of abortion and was against using busing to achieve racial integration in schools.

Schweiker was chosen by Reagan as the second Secretary of Health and Human Services for his long commitment to health issues and also because of the need to have a liberal Republican voice in a cabinet dominated by conservatives. He was confirmed by his Senate colleagues for this new post on 21 January 1981 by a vote of 99–0. During his tenure, which lasted until 11 January 1983, Schweiker exerted little influence in his own department, deferring to Reagan administration proposals to cut inspections of nursing homes that had a proven track record of quality care and to put a cap on Medicare payments to the states to encourage ending administrative mistakes. Overseeing a department of more than 132,000 employees with a budget of $253 billion (which Schweiker called "awe-inspiring . . . [the department] spends more money than any country in the world except for the Soviet Union and the United States"), Schweiker advocated eliminating many programs and folding them into block grants to states, allowing them to spend the monies as they saw fit. Schweiker also oversaw a Reagan proposal to "buy out" state responsibilities for health and safety in exchange for each state assuming responsibility for such programs as Aid to Families with Dependent Children (AFDC) and food stamps. Although pro-choice on abortion, Schweiker was

strongly against government funding of abortions and stated unequivocally that "the government should not be in the business of sex education." He also imposed rules forcing family planning organizations that received federal funds to inform parents when their minor children requested contraceptives. Schweiker said, "We've built a Berlin Wall between the kid and the parents. . . . We think that is wrong."

Schweiker resigned on 11 January 1983 to take a post with the American Council on Life Insurance, an industry trade group.

References: Landes, Burton, *Making of a Senator, 1974: A Biography of Richard S. Schweiker* (Trappes, PA: Landes, 1976); Schweiker, Richard, "Health Care: Making a Good System Better," in Paul Laxalt and Richard S. Williamson, eds., *A Changing America: Conservatives View of the '80s from the United States Senate* (South Bend, IN: Regnery/Gateway, 1980), 103–131; "Schweiker, Richard S(hultz)," in Charles Moritz, ed., *Current Biography 1977* (New York: H. W. Wilson, 1977), 377–380.

MARGARET MARY O'SHAUGHNESSY HECKLER
1931–

Margaret Heckler was a congresswoman from Massachusetts for eight terms (1967–1983) before serving as secretary of health and human services. Born Margaret Mary O'Shaughnessy in Flushing, New York, on 21 June 1931, she is the daughter of John O'Shaughnessy, a doorman at a New York City hotel, and Bridget (née McKeon) O'Shaughnessy. Heckler won a scholarship to Albertus Magnus College. She majored in political science, spending a year abroad studying at the University of Leiden, the Netherlands, in 1952. She returned to Albertus Magnus and earned her bachelor of arts degree in political science. Heckler entered the Boston College Law School, the only woman in her class, and served as editor of the law review before she was awarded her LL.B. degree in 1956. She was admitted to the Massachusetts Bar the same year.

Heckler and some of her fellow students from Boston College formed their own law firm because at that time few women were hired in law firms. She also became involved in politics, serving, as a Republican, on the Republican Town Committee of Wellesley, Massachusetts, and volunteering to work on the campaigns of fellow Republicans. In 1962, she won a seat on the Massachusetts Governor's Council, where she served until 1967.

In 1966, Heckler decided to run for a seat in the U.S. House of Representatives. Her opponent in the Republican primary was Representative Joseph Martin, who had held the seat since 1925 and had served as House Republican Leader and Speaker of the House. Heckler, who did not disagree with Martin on any substantive issues, ran on the issue that the district needed energetic, continuous and full-time representation, a veiled allusion to Martin's age—he was 82. She won the primary by more than 3,000 votes and then defeated her Democratic opponent to win a House seat.

Heckler eventually served in Congress from 3 January 1967 to 3 January 1983. She was a member of the Committee on Veterans' Affairs, the Committee on Government Operations, the Committee on Banking and Currency, the Committee on Agriculture, and the Committee on Science and Technology. She was an outspoken advocate for child care for working parents and spoke harshly of President Richard M. Nixon's veto of a child development program in December 1971. She was also a supporter of the Equal Rights Amendment and helped author the Equal Credit Opportunity Act in 1974 to assist women to gain loans. She was an opponent of the federal funding for abortions.

In 1982, based on the 1980 census, voting districts in Massachusetts were redrawn, and Heckler found her district combined with the Fourth District, which Barney Frank represented. The two ran against each other in the

1982 election, and Frank won. On 12 January 1983, Heckler was named by President Reagan to succeed Richard S. Schweiker as secretary of health and human services. Her hearings before the Senate Finance Committee centered on her opposition to abortion, but her nomination was ratified by the committee and confirmed by the full Senate on 3 March 1983 by a vote of 82 to 3, and she took office as the third secretary of health and human services. Her tenure lasted until 13 December 1985. Heckler pushed through new guidelines for the disability program of Social Security and advocated more federal spending for AIDS victims and those suffering from Alzheimer's disease. In 1984, she endorsed the irradiation of some foods to kill bacteria.

However, Heckler did not get along with some of Reagan's staff, and she became an ineffective secretary, without access to the president to get the department's agenda advanced. Reagan removed her from office on 12 December 1985 and offered her the post of U.S. ambassador to Ireland, where she served until October 1989.

References: "Heckler, Margaret M(ary O'Shaughnessy)," in Charles Moritz, ed., *Current Biography 1983* (New York: H. W. Wilson, 1983), 182–185; "Margaret M. Heckler," in *Women In Congress, 1917–1990* (Washington, DC: GPO, 1991), 99–100.

OTIS RAY BOWEN
1918–

Otis Bowen is a doctor and was a former governor of Indiana when selected by President Ronald Reagan to serve as the fourth secretary of health and human services (HHS). Born in Richland Center, near Rochester, Indiana, on 26 February 1918, Bowen is the son of Vernie Bowen, a teacher, and Pearl (née Wright) Bowen. Bowen's father moved from town to town as a teacher; therefore, Bowen attended schools in several different Indiana towns, including Kewanna, Fulton, and Francesville.

He entered the University of Indiana at Bloomington and, after obtaining his bachelor's degree in chemistry in 1939, enrolled in the University of Indiana School of Medicine and received his M.D. degree in 1942. After serving for a short period as an intern at Memorial Hospital in South Bend, Indiana, Bowen joined the U.S. Army Medical Corps as a first lieutenant and rose to the rank of captain while serving in the Pacific theater. After he was discharged in 1946, Bowen opened a private medical practice in Bremen, Indiana, later serving on hospital boards across Indiana. From 1952 to 1956, he served as coroner for Marshall County, Indiana.

In 1956, Bowen was elected to a seat in the Indiana General Assembly, where he served for a term; in 1960, he was elected again and remained until 1972, serving as Republican Minority Leader in 1965 and as Speaker of the House from 1967 to 1972. In 1968, he attempted to win the Republican gubernatorial nomination, but lost. Four years later, however, he won the Republican gubernatorial nomination, defeating former Governor Matthew E. Welsh by more than 300,000 votes out of 2 million cast. In 1976, he was reelected to a second term. Historian John Raimo wrote, "The key to his re-election . . . was the successful implementation in 1973 of his property tax relief proposal. The plan not only reduced individual property taxes by 25 per cent through the creation of a fund from which deficiencies were paid, but it included controls against other uses of the dedicated revenues as well as special benefits to elderly, disabled, and low income individuals and families. Bowen's first term was identified with a significant expansion of the state's recreational facilities—parks, forests, reservoirs, and historical sites and memorials—under a revitalized Department of Natural Resources. Moreover, the governor's low-key personality and his perception by the public as a hard-working, trustworthy public servant—the family doctor image of

one who listened, learned, and responded to needs—contributed to his re-election."

Bowen left office on 13 January 1981. He accepted a post as the Lester D. Bibler Professor of Family Medicine at the Family Practice Unit of the Indiana University School of Medicine at Bloomington. In early 1982, he was named by Secretary of Health and Human Services Richard S. Schweiker as the chairman of the Advisory Council on Social Security to make recommendations on how to finance Social Security and Medicare. The Bowen Commission, as it was known, reported to the new secretary, Margaret Heckler, on 30 March 1984, with several important recommendations, including raising the age of eligibility of Social Security from 65 to 67 and increasing alcohol and tobacco taxes to fund both Social Security and Medicare.

When Secretary Heckler was shifted from HHS to become the U.S. ambassador to Ireland, those considered to replace her included Karl D. Bays, chairman and chief executive officer of the American Hospital Supply Corporation; James J. Cavanaugh, a health specialist who had served in the Nixon and Ford administrations; and David B. Swoap, a former HHS official, who at the time was serving as the secretary of health and welfare in the state of California. But Senator Dan Quayle of Indiana, supported former Governor Bowen for the position.

On 7 November 1985, Reagan selected Bowen, who later said, "I was even beginning to think about retiring, to doing a little writing and reading and fishing, taking care of my lawn, and traveling. . . . But when the president calls and asks you to do something, it's pretty hard to say no." Nominated on 4 December 1985, he was confirmed on 12 December by a vote of 93 to 2, and he took office as the fourth secretary of health and human services. His tenure lasted until the end of the Reagan administration on 20 January 1989.

Bowen was involved with such issues as the use of radiation on fruits and vegetables to control insects and expanded Medicare coverage for the elderly. At HHS Bowen played the role of the country doctor. In an interview 100 days into his tenure, he said he was feeling more comfortable with the job, and that he "hoped to impart his wisdom through 'House Calls,' a series of 60-second radio broadcasts on such topics as snuff and chewing tobacco, cocaine, parents' rights under Medicare and the risks of smoking in pregnancy."

After leaving office, Bowen retired to his home in Indiana. The Bowen Institute on Political Participation at Indiana's Ball State University was named in his honor.

References: "Bowen, Otis R(ay)," in Charles Moritz, ed., *Current Biography 1986* (New York: H. W. Wilson, 1986), 57–60; "Bowen, Otis R.," in John W. Raimo, ed., *Biographical Directory of the Governors of the United States, 1978–1983* (Westport, CT: Meckler, 1985), 79–80.

LOUIS WADE SULLIVAN
1933–

Louis Sullivan was the head of Morehouse School of Medicine in Atlanta and a controversial choice for secretary of health and human services when selected by President-elect George Bush in December 1988. Born in Atlanta, Georgia, on 3 November 1933, Sullivan is the son of Walter Wade Sullivan, an undertaker and civil rights activist, and Lubirda Elizabeth (née Priester) Sullivan, a teacher. The family moved to Blakely, Georgia, when Sullivan was young, but because of segregation and limited opportunities for black students, Sullivan was sent back to Atlanta, where he attended public schools. Sullivan attended Morehouse College in Atlanta; he earned his bachelor of science degree magna cum laude in 1954 and his medical degree cum laude from Boston University in 1958, the only African American in his class. He spent his internship and medical residency at the New York Hospital–Cornell Medical Center. In 1960, he obtained a fellowship in pathology at the Massachusetts

General Hospital in Boston and, in 1961, received a research fellowship at the Thorndike Memorial Laboratory at the Harvard University Medical School.

In 1963, Sullivan became an instructor of medicine at the Harvard Medical School. A year later, he became an assistant professor of medicine at the New Jersey College of Medicine, serving until 1966. That year, he moved to Boston University to serve as an assistant professor of medicine and as codirector of hematology at the college's medical school. Sullivan was promoted to associate professor in 1968 and, six years later, to professor of medicine and physiology.

Sullivan and a group of Morehouse alumni formed that university's Medical Education Program in 1975, and Sullivan was named as dean of the program. The program was initiated to train doctors to serve in urban areas and in areas of the South where doctors were scarce. In 1981, this program became the Morehouse School of Medicine, one of only three all-black medical schools in the United States. Sullivan was dean of the school and professor of biology and medicine. He became one of the most respected voices in the nation for black medical education.

In 1988, Vice-president George Bush was elected president, and he named Sullivan as his secretary of health and human services. Sullivan soon ran into controversy, particularly over his views regarding abortion. On 15 December 1988, seven days before Sullivan was officially named to the post, the National Right-to-Life Committee sent Bush a letter opposing the appointment. When Sullivan, in an interview in the *Atlanta Journal and Constitution* supported the right to have an abortion, it seemed that his nomination would be scuttled. However, he then stated that he felt abortion should be illegal except in the cases of rape, incest, and the health of the mother.

Bush went ahead with the nomination on 22 December, calling Sullivan "an outstanding leader in the health community." Sullivan then told a reporter that he did not favor overturning *Roe v. Wade,* the 1973 Supreme

Court decision legalizing abortion; then he stated that he supported the overturning of the decision. Sullivan's confirmation hearings were delayed over the issue, and at the hearings Sullivan created more controversy by not taking a stand on the use of fetal tissue in research. Still, Sullivan was recommended unanimously by the Senate Finance Committee and, on 1 March 1989, was confirmed, 98 to 1, as the fifth secretary of health and human services.

On 8 March 1989, Sullivan came out in favor of controversial needle-exchange programs, which attempted to halt the spread of AIDS among drug abusers by trading their used needles for clean ones. When drug czar William J. Bennett came out publicly against Sullivan's proposal, the secretary relented. Sullivan remained in his position for the remainder of the Bush administration, ending on 20 January 1993. He was a staunch advocate for minority health care advances and called for the elimination of tuberculosis in the United States by 2010. He increased spending on programs that assisted health programs and scholarships for minorities.

After leaving office in January 1993, Sullivan returned to the Morehouse School of Medicine.

References: "Sullivan, Louis W(ade)," in Charles Moritz, ed., *Current Biography 1989* (New York: H. W. Wilson, 1989), 560–563.

DONNA EDNA SHALALA
1941–

Donna Shalala was the first woman to head the University of Wisconsin at Madison when she became secretary of health and human services (HHS). Born in Cleveland, Ohio, on 14 February 1941, Shalala is the daughter of James Abraham Shalala, a real estate salesman, and Edna (née Smith) Shalala, a physical education teacher

and attorney. Donna Shalala attended local schools in Cleveland, then entered the Western College for Women in Oxford, Ohio, and received a bachelor's degree in urban studies in 1962.

Shalala then joined the Peace Corps and spent two years teaching social science and serving as the dean of women at the agricultural college of the University of Ahwaz in Lebanon. When she returned to the United States, she entered the Maxwell School of Citizenship and Public Affairs at Syracuse University in New York, and traveled to Lebanon and Syria representing the U.S. Information Agency to train teachers in English studies. In 1966, she became the assistant director of Syracuse University's urban community-development program. The following year, she was named as assistant to the chairman of the New York State Constitutional Convention's Committee on Local Government and Home Rule. In 1968, she received her master of social science degree and, two years later, a Ph.D. degree.

From 1970 to 1972, Shalala taught political science at Bernard M. Baruch College in New York and then taught politics and education at Teachers College at Columbia University. In 1975, she was appointed as director and treasurer of the Municipal Assistance Corporation for the City of New York, established to avert bankruptcy. Shalala was the only woman on the committee; she oversaw the issuance of some $6 billion in bonds to float and repay city debt. In January 1977, when President Jimmy Carter took office, Shalala joined his administration as assistant secretary of housing and urban development for policy development and research. In this position, she investigated new ways to assist women in gaining loans to pay home mortgages.

On 21 December 1979, she was named president of Hunter College in New York City. On 29 May 1987, Shalala became only the second woman to head a major American research university when she was named as chancellor of the University of Wisconsin at Madison. Because there were so few minorities at the university, Shalala, only a month after taking over, instituted a plan to increase the number of minorities on campus, setting quotas for the enrollment of blacks, Hispanics, and American Indians. She enraged many, and earned the nickname "The Queen of Political Correctness," by instituting a code against "hate speech." In 1991, a federal judge struck down the code as unconstitutional, and it was never reinstated.

In 1992, Arkansas Governor Bill Clinton was elected president, and he selected Shalala as his secretary of health and human services on 11 December 1992. At the press conference announcing her selection, she said, "My own administrative experience is in managing large complex institutions that have fiefdoms. . . . A place like HHS is a natural for me."

Confirmed on 21 January 1993, she was sworn in as the sixth secretary of health and human services. Journalists Jeffrey Trammell and Gary P. Osifchin wrote in 1994, "Shalala has identified prevention, independence, and customer service as her top priorities at HHS. As such, she has stressed the importance of making primary care, immunizations, and prenatal care key components of the new health care system. In April 1993, she also announced legislation that would pave the way for complete immunization of all American children." Shalala has pushed for more funding for AIDS research and called for welfare reform, although she opposed a Republican welfare proposal that passed the Congress in 1996 and that President Clinton signed. She took the initiative in trying to hold down health costs while insisting on cost controls over HMOs (health maintenance organizations). In 1998, she launched the Choose Your Cover campaign to bring awareness to rising skin cancer rates in the United States.

Currently, Shalala is the longest-serving secretary of health and human services.

References: *The International Who's Who of Women* (London: Europa Publications, 1992), 408; "Shalala, Donna Edna," in Charles Moritz, ed., *Current Biography 1991* (New York: H. W. Wilson, 1991), 514–518; Trammell, Jeffrey B., and Gary P. Osifchin, eds., *The Clinton 500: The New Team Running America, 1994* (Washington, DC: Almanac Publishing, 1994), 239.

HOUSING AND URBAN DEVELOPMENT

———⟐———

The first federal housing program was established in the Franklin Roosevelt administration. Congress enacted the National Housing Act , which established the Federal Housing Administration (FHA). Three years later, another congressional action, the United States Housing Act of 1937, established the U.S. Housing Authority to create low-rent housing for people affected by the Depression. This agency was taken into the Housing and Home Finance Agency under Presidential Reorganization Plan No. 3 of 27 July 1947. Three subsequent acts, the Housing Acts of 1949, 1954, and 1959, created programs to establish housing for low-to-middle-income families and the elderly.

By 1965, one of the cornerstones of President Lyndon B. Johnson's Great Society program of massive federal aid to the cities was a federal department to control housing programs and municipal expansion and improvement. Johnson sent Congress a blueprint for the first federal-level agency in the U.S. government since the Pentagon; the Department of Housing and Urban Development Act of 1965 was passed, and the act was signed into law on 9 November 1965.

The organic act establishing the department outlines its functions: "[to] provide assistance for housing and for the development of the Nation's communities; to assist the President in achieving maximum coordination of the various Federal activities which have a major effect upon urban community, suburban, or metropolitan development; to encourage the solution of problems of housing, urban development, and mass transportation through State, county, town, village, or other local and private action, including promotion of interstate, regional, and metropolitan cooperation; to encourage the maximum contributions that may be made by vigorous private homebuilding and mortgage lending industries to housing, urban development, and the national economy; and to provide for full and appropriate consideration, at the national level, of the needs and interests of the Nation's communities and of the people who live and work in them."

On the same day that he signed the act into law, Johnson named Robert C. Weaver, a Harvard-educated specialist in race relations, as his first nominee to head the new agency. Weaver was confirmed and sworn into office on 18 January 1966, making him the first black man to hold a cabinet position.

In his three years as the head of the Department of Housing and Urban Development (HUD), Weaver oversaw the passage of the Civil Rights Act of 1968, which included Section 701, known as the Fair Housing Act, outlawing race discrimination in housing, and the Housing Act of 1968, which established the Government National Mortgage Association (known as Ginnie Mae), a wholly owned subsidiary of the department, which used government-backed securities to guarantee mortgage funds for moderate-income families. Weaver was forced to deal with riots that occurred in the inner cities following the assassination of the Rev. Dr. Martin Luther King, Jr., on 4 April 1968. Weaver resigned his post at the end of 1968, when President Johnson was near the end of his term of office; he was replaced for the last weeks of Johnson's administration by educator Robert C. Wood. The third HUD secretary, George W. Romney, a former governor of Michigan, oversaw the passage of the Housing and Urban Development Act of 1970, which established the Federal Experimental Housing Allowance Program and Community Development Corporation, and the demolition of the disastrous Pruitt-Igoe housing development in St. Louis, the first sign that federal public housing programs were failing. Romney, who reorganized the department so that it became more of an administrative organ than one that initiated housing programs, was replaced, in 1973, by James T. Lynn, director of the Office of Management and Budget, an assistant to President Nixon, and former general counsel to the Department of Commerce and undersecretary of that department.

During Lynn's two-year tenure, he oversaw passage of the Housing and Community Development Act of 1974, which consolidated housing program block grants into the Community Development Block Grant (CDBG) program, Congress enacted the National Mobile Home Construction and Safety Standards Act of 1974, as well as the Consumer Home Mortgage Assistance Act of 1974. Under Lynn's successor, Carla A. Hills, the first woman to head the department, Congress enacted the Emergency Housing Act of 1975, which authorized temporary assistance to the unemployed to help them meet mortgage payments, and the Housing Authorization Act of 1976, which dealt with flood insurance.

When Georgia Governor Jimmy Carter was elected to the presidency in 1977, he selected Patricia Roberts Harris, who became the first black woman to head HUD. Under her leadership, HUD was changed into a vehicle for new housing initiatives nationwide. Congress passed such legislation during her tenure as the Supplemental Housing Act of 1977, which established the National Commission on Neighborhoods, and the Housing and Community Development Act of 1977, which changed CDBG to include the elderly and handicapped under its protections. Congress also directed the submission of an annual report on National Urban Policy and passed the Community Reinvestment Act of 1977 and the National Energy Conservation Policy Act of 1978, which authorized certain financing for conservation and other energy-related improvements in housing.

Harris then became the first secretary of the Department of Health and Human Services, and Carter named Maurice Edwin "Moon" Landrieu, the former mayor of New Orleans, Louisiana, as the seventh secretary of HUD.

During his tenure, which lasted until the end of the Carter administration in January 1981, Landrieu oversaw congressional passage of the Housing and Community Development Amendments of 1979, which were additions to numerous housing acts, including the CDBG, Action Grant, Neighborhood Self-help Development, and Urban Homesteading programs, and made substantive changes in the rent supplement program and allowed for high mortgage limits for homes financed by the FHA; the Veterans' Disability

Compensation and Housing Benefits Amendments of 1980, which provided some grants to veterans who were severely disabled, as well as increasing the maximum loan guarantees to those same veterans; the Housing and Community Development Act of 1980, which extended federal laws to community and neighborhood development programs nationwide; and the Depository Institutions' Deregulation and Monetary Control Act of 1980, passed in response to rising interest rates, which hit 19 percent in 1980.

In 1981, President Ronald Reagan named Samuel R. Pierce, Jr., a former general counsel in the Treasury Department and a Republican attorney, as the eighth secretary of HUD. Pierce would go on to serve eight full years in office. Huge cuts in the department's budget and new congressional action, such as the Housing and Urban-Rural Recovery Act; the Stewart B. McKinney Act, which assisted communities with homelessness; and the Indian Housing Act, which gave the department new responsibilities in the area of housing for Native Americans and Alaskan Indians, marked his tenure.

However, allegations of massive corruption led to the appointment of an independent counsel; Pierce was cleared of any wrongdoing but numerous officials in the department were found guilty. When Congressman Jack Kemp was named by President George Bush in 1989, he found the department to be an administrative disaster. Kemp spent his four-year tenure trying to restructure the department, cut waste and mismanagement; he focused on increasing home buying opportunities for moderate-income families and establishing enterprise zones to stimulate business in economically depressed urban areas. The Federal Housing Enterprises' Financial Safety and Soundness Act of 1992 established the Office of Federal Housing Enterprise Oversight to provide supervision over the Federal Home Loan Mortgage Corporation (also known as Freddie Mac).

In 1992, Arkansas Governor Bill Clinton was elected president, and he named former San Antonio Mayor Henry G. Cisneros as his secretary of HUD. Cisneros, the first Hispanic to head of the department, also pushed the idea of enterprise zones, and this plan became an integral part of the Empowerment Zone and Enterprise Community Program, which became law as part of the Omnibus Budget Reconciliation Act of 1993. This action authorized the establishment of enterprise zones in economically depressed rural and urban areas through a combination of tax incentives from the government and loans to businesses willing to locate in these areas. Nine empowerment zones were initially established, along with ninety-five smaller enterprise communities.

Cisneros also released a *Blueprint for the Reinvention of HUD,* a report that urged sweeping reforms in public housing and in FHA mortgages and the consolidation of all other monetary and spending programs within HUD into three distinct block grant programs to states and municipalities. Cisneros left office at the end of Clinton's first term and was replaced by his Assistant Secretary for Community Planning and Development Andrew M. Cuomo. Cuomo, the first secretary to be chosen from within the department, approved additional enterprise zones, raising the number to thirty-one by 1999, pushed his HOPE VI grants to demolish large high-rise projects in urban areas and replace them with smaller developments, and got 50,000 extra housing vouchers from Congress to assist the homeless.

References: Garonzik, Joseph, *The Department of Housing and Urban Development: A Chronology* (Washington, DC: Department of Housing and Urban Development, Office of Public Affairs, 1977); McFarland, M. Carter, *The Federal Government and Urban Problems: HUD: Successes, Failures, and the Fate of Our Cities* (Boulder, CO: Westview Press, 1978); Welfeld, Irving, *HUD Scandals: Howling Headlines* *and Silent Fiascos* (New Brunswick, NJ: Transactions Publishers, 1992); Willman, John B., *The Department of Housing and Urban Development* (New York: Praeger, 1967).

ROBERT CLIFTON WEAVER
1907–1997

Robert Weaver was called one of the architects of President Lyndon B. Johnson's Great Society series of economic programs that defined Johnson's administration. The first African American named to a cabinet office, Weaver was a civil rights pioneer who worked, from the 1930s until his death, advancing the rights of black Americans. Born in Washington, D.C., on 29 December 1907, he was the son of Mortimer Grover Weaver, a postal clerk, and Florence (née Freeman) Weaver. Weaver became an electrician, while still in high school and, in his senior year, owned his own electrical business. He entered Harvard University, his grandfather's alma mater, graduating in 1929 with a bachelor's degree cum laude in economics; he earned his master's degree in the same subject two years later. After a year as a professor of economics at the Agricultural and Technical College of North Carolina at Greensboro, he returned to Harvard as an Austin scholar. He received his Ph.D. degree in economics in 1934.

In 1933, Weaver was hired as part of President Franklin D. Roosevelt's New Deal economic program to end the Depression. He was called a member of Roosevelt's "black cabinet," a group of African Americans in subcabinet positions that included Mary McLeod Bethune of the National Youth Administration, Lawrence A. Oxley of the Department of Labor, and Joseph H. B. Evans of the Farm Security Administration. Weaver went to work initially as an adviser to Secretary of the Interior Harold L. Ickes, from 1934 to 1938; later, he worked as a special assistant to Nathan Straus of the Housing Authority, from 1938 to 1940. He worked with Sid-

ney Hillman of the National Defense Advisory Committee in 1940 and served as head of the Negro employment and training branch of the labor division in the Office of Production and Management from 1942 to 1943. After the United States entered World War II, Weaver served as director of Negro Manpower Services as a member of the War Manpower Commission.

Weaver left Washington to serve as a member of the Mayor's Committee on Race Relations for the city of Chicago. He then moved to New York, where he taught at Columbia and New York Universities. After the war, Weaver went to work as a member of the United Nations Relief and Rehabilitation Administration in the Ukraine (then part of the Soviet Union). When he returned to the United States, he wrote several works on the problems of blacks and housing, including *Negro Labor: A National Problem* (1946), and *The Negro Ghetto* (1948).

In 1949, the John Hay Whitney Foundation hired Weaver as director of its Opportunity Scholarships Fund, distributing monies from the foundation to black students who needed economic assistance to attend college. During the 1950s, Weaver served on a number of housing boards, including as the chairman of the New York State Rent Administration (1955–1959), becoming the first black to hold a cabinet office in New York State government. In late 1960, New York City Mayor Robert Wagner was prepared to name Weaver as the Manhattan borough president to replace Hulan Jack; but before the Manhattan City Council could vote on Weaver's nomination, on 31 December 1960 President-elect John F. Kennedy named Weaver as the administrator of the Housing and Home Finance Agency (HHFA), to succeed Norman P. Mason.

The HHFA was the major government agency that dealt with housing and other urban matters. After Senate confirmation on

9 February 1961, Weaver became the highest-ranking black ever in the U.S. government. During his five years as the head of this agency, Weaver oversaw the Community Facilities Administration, the Federal Housing Administration, the Federal National Mortgage Association, the Public Housing Administration, and the Urban Renewal Administration. He set as his first goal the outlawing of segregation in federally subsidized housing; in 1952, he had called for the signing of an executive order to that effect. He oversaw this amalgamation of housing departments that had a combined annual budget of $340 million.

During the 1960s, Weaver was at the forefront of the move to desegregate federal housing and to increase appropriations for such housing units. He authored two more books: *The Urban Complex* (1964) and *Dilemmas of Urban America* (1965). In 1962, Weaver was presented with the Spingarn Medal of the National Association for the Advancement of Colored People for his lifetime of service in civil rights.

Weaver was a key component of President Lyndon Johnson's Great Society of economic programs, many of which aimed to help black Americans, who were disproportionately represented among the poor. Weaver, as head of the HHFA, was one of the leaders who drafted many of the pieces of legislation. In 1964, Johnson delivered a housing and community development address to Congress, asking that Weaver's agencies be established as a cabinet-level department. In his budget message in January 1965, and, again, in his Message on the Cities in March 1965, he called for the creation of the department.

After this second speech, Representative Henry S. Reuss of Wisconsin and Representative Dante Fascell of Florida introduced legislation in the House, and Senator Abraham Ribicoff of Connecticut, introduced similar legislation in the Senate. The two bills were reconciled and passed both houses of Congress; on 9 September 1965, Johnson signed the act establishing the Department of Housing and Urban Development. He did not immediately name a secretary to head the new department; Weaver, as head of the agency being superseded by HUD, was the acting head of the department until someone could be named. In an interview, Lawrence O'Brien, who was serving as Johnson's postmaster general when Weaver was chosen, said, "Weaver was a darn good candidate if you were considering recognizing the black community at this level. He was not a civil rights leader as such. He was, as I recall, an academician. He was not one of Martin Luther King's lieutenants, which would probably have placed more of a spotlight on the whole thing. His image was of a fellow of great competency and good background, a solid resume, and qualified."

Weaver was nominated on 14 January 1966 and confirmed by the Senate, unanimously, three days later. His tenure would last until late 1968. His struggles to mold his new agency into a cabinet department are apparent in his annual reports, in which he laid out the agency's goals. In his first annual report, in 1965, Weaver explained, "In establishing this 11th executive department, Congress recognized that in our urban nation the city needed a coequal voice at the Cabinet table along with the other major functions of the Federal Government. Thus, Congress has provided the framework for more effective Federal action in two critical domestic problems—providing decent housing in a wholesome environment for every family, and the future of our cities and suburbs."

In his 1966 report, he stated, "Now we are mounting a far greater, more comprehensive attack on the urban problems than any we have previously conceived. We can no longer deal with the physical rebuilding of urban areas without regard to the human problems and the measures needed for human betterment. They must be dealt with jointly. We can no longer treat the central older city and the outlying areas of urban growth as if they were alien to each other. They are interwoven in so many ways that the ills of one compound the difficulties of the other."

James Barron wrote in 1997, "Dr. Weaver,

who said that 'you cannot have physical renewal without human renewal,' pushed for better-looking public housing by offering awards for design. He also increased the amount of money for small businesses displaced by urban renewal and revived the long-dormant idea of Federal rent subsidies for the elderly." Following the April 1968 assassination of the Rev. Dr. Martin Luther King, Jr., and the ensuing urban riots, Congress enacted the Civil Rights Act of 1968, which included the Fair Housing Act, outlawing discrimination in housing nationwide, and the Housing Act of 1968, which established the Government National Mortgage Association, which extended the availability of mortgage funds to people of moderate incomes to pay for mortgages.

In December 1968, after Republican Richard M. Nixon won the presidency, Weaver resigned from the cabinet, and was replaced by Undersecretary of Housing and Urban Development Robert C. Wood. Weaver returned to private life, serving as president of Baruch College and professor of urban affairs at Hunter College, both in New York City. In the 1970s, he was one of the original directors of the Municipal Assistance Corporation, which provided financial assistance to New York City to prevent bankruptcy.

Robert Weaver died at his home in New York City on 17 July 1997, at the age of 89. In 1999, the Housing and Urban Development Building in Washington was named the Robert C. Weaver HUD Building in his honor.

References: *Annual Report, 1965: U.S. Department of Housing and Urban Development, Robert C. Weaver, Secretary* (Washington, DC: GPO, 1966), 3; Armstrong, Robin, "Robert C. Weaver," in *Contemporary Black Biography* (Detroit, MI: Gale Research; 13 vols., 1992–1997), 8: 259–261; *HUD Second Annual Report* (Washington, DC: GPO, 1966), 5–6; "Weaver, Robert C(lifton)," in Charles Moritz, ed., *Current Biography 1961* (New York: H. W. Wilson, 1961), 474–476; Williams, Alma Rene, "Robert C. Weaver: From the Black Cabinet to the President's Cabinet" (Ph.D. dissertation, Washington University, 1978), 171; Willman, John B., *The Department of Housing and Urban Development* (New York: Praeger, 1967).

ROBERT COLDWELL WOOD
1923–

Robert Wood served for eighteen days as the second secretary of housing and urban development (HUD). He is better known for his three years as undersecretary of the department, during which time he assisted Secretary Robert C. Weaver in formulating policy and establishing the department. Wood was born in St. Louis, Missouri, on 16 September 1923, the son of Thomas Frank Wood and Mary (née Bradshaw) Wood. He served in the U.S. Army during World War II, then received a bachelor of arts degree from Princeton University in 1946. He earned a master's degree in 1947, an M.B.A. in 1948 and a Ph.D. degree in 1950, all from Harvard University.

In 1949, he was named as associate director of the Florida Legislative Bureau, where he served until 1951. That year, he was named as a management organization expert for the U.S. Bureau of the Budget (now the Office of Management and Budget), where he served until 1954. In 1954, he left government to become a lecturer, then an assistant professor of political science at the Massachusetts Institute of Technology (MIT), from 1959 to 1962, becoming a full professor in 1962. He was named as head of the political science department in 1965.

In January 1966, Wood was named by President Lyndon B. Johnson as undersecretary of the just-established Department of Housing and Urban Development. During his service as undersecretary, which ended in January 1969, Wood served as the head of the White House Task Force on Urban Problems, charged by President Johnson with establishing a governmental program for HUD. Wood was also a liaison with the presidential special assistant, Joseph Califano, Jr., another member of the task force.

In December 1968, Secretary Weaver resigned. Johnson then named Wood, on 2 January 1969, to serve as the second secretary of HUD. With Congress in recess, Wood was never formally confirmed in the position, and he served only eighteen days, until 20 January 1969.

Wood returned to Massachusetts, where he served as the head of the Massachusetts Bay Transportation Authority from 1969 until 1970. He also worked for the joint Harvard-MIT Center on Urban Studies at Cambridge until 1970, and then served as president of the University of Massachusetts from 1970 until 1977. Later, he served as superintendent of Boston Public Schools (1978–1980), and as a professor at the University of Massachusetts. In 1994, he was named as chairman emeritus of that university.

References: Willman, John B., *The Department of Housing and Urban Development* (New York: Praeger, 1967); "Wood, Robert Coldwell," in Robert Sobel, ed.-in-chief, *Biographical Directory of the United States Executive Branch, 1774–1971* (Westport, CT: Greenwood, 1971), 354; "Wood, Robert Coldwell," in *Who's Who in America: 2000 Millennium Edition* (New Providence, NJ: Marquis Who's Who; 2 vols., 2000), 2: 5365.

GEORGE WILCKEN ROMNEY
1907–1995

George Romney served as the governor of Michigan from 1963 to 1969 and was the third secretary of housing and urban development (HUD). Romney was born in near Chihuahua, Mexico, on 8 July 1907, the son of Gaskell Romney and Anna (née Pratt) Romney. Romney's family moved numerous times, eventually settling in Salt Lake City, Utah, where Romney attended the Latter-Day Saints Junior College from 1922 to 1926. He then served as a Mormon missionary to England and Scotland for two years, returning in 1928 to study at the University of Utah before he headed east, finishing his secondary education at George Washington University in Washington, D.C. At the same time, he was working as a typist for Senator David I. Walsh, Democrat of Massachusetts, and later as a researcher for the senator, working on tariff legislation.

During the 1930s, Romney worked for the Aluminum Company of America as a salesman in Los Angeles. When the company changed its name to ALCOA, Romney became their national representative in Washington, D.C. He also served as president of the Washington Trade Association Executives. In 1939, he was named as head of the Detroit office of the Automobile Manufacturers Association; in 1942, he became the general manager of the national association and, during World War II, was the auto industry's chief spokesman, serving as the managing director of the Automotive Council for War Production.

In 1948, Romney was hired by George Mason, president of the Nash-Kelvinator Corporation, as his assistant. Romney rose to become vice-president of the company in 1953, and, in 1954, when Nash-Kelvinator merged with the Hudson Motor Car Company to form American Motors, Romney became the new company's president and chairman. In his eight years (1954–1962) as head of the corporation, he helped change the face of the American automobile industry, by introducing the compact car to the public in the form of the Nash Rambler, and changed the company from a money-loser into a profitable concern.

In 1962, Romney resigned from American Motors to run for governor against the incumbent, Democrat John B. Swainson. On 6 November 1962, he defeated Swainson by 80,000 votes out of nearly 3 million cast, breaking a fourteen-year hold by the Democrats on the state house. He was reelected in 1964 and 1966.

Historians Robert Sobel and John Raimo wrote, "Governor, Romney worked for the passage of the new state constitution. Conscious of the state's financial difficulties when he took office, Romney urged the state legislature to enact a tax reform package, which included a personal and corporate income tax. Romney was never reluctant to speak out on national issues and on Republican Party matters. He urged moderation of problems of civil rights legislation, the war in Vietnam, and the left-right division in the Republican Party."

After he was reelected in 1966, many in the liberal faction of the Republican Party saw him as a potential presidential candidate. He announced his candidacy and refused to run for a fourth term as governor of Michigan. It appeared that he would give a strong challenge to the presumptive nominee, former Vice-president Richard M. Nixon. But then, during an interview, he was asked why he had changed from his earlier support of the war in Vietnam to criticizing it. He attributed this earlier support to a trip to Vietnam, in which he claimed he had been "brainwashed" by the military. When he was criticized for this remark, he said "I'm not talking about Russian-type brainwashing. I'm talking about the LBJ kind . . . the credibility gap, a snow job . . . manipulating the news."

A week before the 1968 New Hampshire primary, Romney ended his campaign. In a 1989 interview, Romney denied that his withdrawal from the race had anything to do with his comment and the firestorm that followed it. "It was because [New York Governor] Nelson Rockefeller became a candidate, and there was no way I could get the nomination fighting both Rockefeller and Richard Nixon." Despite his differences with Nixon, he campaigned for him when Nixon won the Republican presidential nomination and, after Nixon's victory over Vice-president Hubert H. Humphrey in the general election, was named to Nixon's cabinet as secretary of HUD, the first Republican to hold the office.

Calling himself a "realistic idealist" who wanted to bring a new style of Republicanism to office, Romney was confirmed as the third secretary of the department on 20 January 1969. During his service, which lasted until the end of Nixon's first term, Romney tried to bring a new direction to the agency. Under his leadership, Congress enacted the Housing and Urban Development Act of 1970, which established a national growth policy, encouraged proper growth in metropolitan areas, cities, and counties, and emphasized inner-city development. Romney pushed to have the disastrous Pruitt-Igoe housing development in St. Louis demolished—the first acknowledgment that the type of federally assisted public housing promoted in the 1950s and 1960s was a failure. Because of this realization, shortly before Romney left office, President Nixon ordered a moratorium on housing and community development assistance. During his tenure, Romney increased federal assistance to augment the amount of mortgage monies in circulation, from $1.3 billion in 1967 to $8.2 billion by 1970. In 1972, he announced a National Urban Growth Policy.

Following President Nixon's reelection in November 1972, Romney announced that he would be resigning. When his successor, James T. Lynn, was confirmed by the Senate, Romney departed on 2 February.

After leaving office, Romney founded the National Volunteer Center, an organization that promotes volunteerism, based in Arlington, Virginia. In his final years, he remained a strong force in the liberal wing of the Republican Party. On 26 July 1995, Romney suffered a massive heart attack and died. He was 88 years old.

References: Mollenhoff, Clark, *George Romney, Mormon in Politics* (New York: Meredith Press, 1968); "Romney, George," in Robert Sobel and John Raimo, eds., *Biographical Directory of the Governors of the United States, 1789–1978* (Westport, CT: Meckler Books; 4 vols., 1978), I2: 768.

JAMES THOMAS LYNN
1927–

James Lynn served as President Richard M. Nixon's director of the Office of Management and Budget, as an assistant to the president, and as Nixon's secretary of Housing and Urban Development (HUD). An attorney from Ohio, James T. Lynn also served as general counsel for the Department of Commerce. Born in Cleveland, Ohio, on 27 February 1927, Lynn is the son of Fred Lynn and Dorthea Estelle (née Petersen) Lynn. He attended local schools, then entered the Adelbert College of Western Reserve University (now Case Western Reserve University) in Cleveland, from which he earned a bachelor of arts degree in economics and political science in 1948.

He completed his education by receiving a bachelor of law degree magna cum laude from Harvard Law School in 1951; he was a case editor of the *Harvard Law Review*. Lynn served in the U.S. Naval Reserve from 1945 to 1946. After graduating from Harvard, Lynn returned to Cleveland, where he joined the law firm of Jones, Day, Cockley, & Reavis and practiced antitrust and real estate law, among other fields. In 1960, he became partner, at age 33, taking over many of the firm's international responsibilities.

Although never political, Lynn had an ambition for government service in some capacity. After former Vice-president Richard M. Nixon was elected president in 1968, Lynn visited with the president-elect and asked for a position in the new administration. His law partner, H. Chapman Rose, was a friend of Maurice H. Stans, the incoming-secretary of Commerce, and Stans asked to have Lynn named as general counsel for the Department of Commerce. Lynn served as general counsel from March 1969 until April 1971, when he became undersecretary of the Department of Commerce. Following President Nixon's reelection in November 1972, Secretary of HUD George W. Romney announced he was leaving the administration. On 5 December 1972, President Nixon named Lynn as Romney's replacement. Confirmed on 20 January 1973, Lynn took office as the fourth secretary of HUD. During his tenure, which lasted until 2 January 1975, Lynn oversaw congressional passage of several pieces of legislation directly related to operations of the department, including the

Housing and Community Development Act of 1974, which concentrated all of the department's housing block grants into one single grant, called the Community Development Block Grant Program); the National Mobile Home Construction and Safety Standards Act of 1974; and the Consumer Mortgage Home Assistance Act of 1974.

President Nixon's planned to consolidate several cabinet departments into super departments, and Lynn was to become the secretary of the new Department of Community Relations, with authority over housing and urban development, community planning and regional development, transportation, and state and local disaster relief. However, Nixon's plan never received congressional support, and it quietly died.

On 2 January 1975, Lynn resigned from HUD to become director of the Office of Management and Budget. He also acted as an assistant to President Gerald R. Ford, until the end of Ford's administration on 20 January 1977. Lynn then left government and returned to private practice. He as chairman of the board of the Aetna Life Insurance Company from 1984 to 1992 and then as a senior adviser with Lazard Freres & Company, an investment banking firm.

References: "Lynn, James T(homas)," in Charles Moritz, ed., *Current Biography 1973* (New York: H. W. Wilson, 1973), 264–266.

CARLA ANDERSON HILLS
1934–

Carla Hills became the first woman to serve as the head of the Department of Housing and Urban Development (HUD); she had been the first woman to serve as assistant attorney general and as the head of the Civil Division in the Department of Justice. Carla Anderson was born in Los Angeles, California, on 3 January 1934, the daughter of Carl Anderson and Edith (née Hume)

Anderson. She studied at the Marlborough School for Girls, then entered Stanford University and, in 1954, attended Oxford University in England. She then returned to Stanford and earned her bachelor's degree in history in 1955. Three years later, she was awarded her law degree from the Yale University Law School.

In 1959, she was admitted to the California state bar, and that same year was named as an assistant U.S. attorney in Los Angeles, serving from 1959 to 1961. In 1962, after she left the U.S. attorney's office, she and her husband, Roderick M. Hills, helped found the Los Angeles law firm of Munger, Tolles, Hills, and Rickershauser, where she worked as a major partner until 1974. She became an authority on antitrust law and coauthored a work on federal civil practice, and one on antitrust law. In 1972, she served as an adjunct professor of law at the University of California at Los Angeles.

In 1973, Attorney General Elliot L. Richardson offered Hills's husband the position of assistant attorney general. He turned down the offer because of law firm commitments, but Richardson was so impressed by Carla Hills that he offered her the same position, which she accepted, becoming the first woman to be named to that post in the Department of Justice since the 1920s. On 20 October 1973, Richardson resigned after refusing to carry out President Nixon's order to fire Special Prosecutor Archibald Cox during the Watergate scandal. Richardson's successor, William B. Saxbe, offered Hills the position of assistant attorney general in charge of the department's Civil Division. Confirmation by the Senate, on 7 March 1974, made her the highest-ranking woman in the Department of Justice. She oversaw more than 200 attorneys in the department, as well as U.S. attorneys across the country.

On 13 February 1975, President Gerald R. Ford announced that he would nominate Hills to succeed James T. Lynn as secretary of HUD. Many Democrats opposed her nomination on the grounds that she was unqualified to head a department with which she had no prior experience. Nonetheless, she was confirmed on 5 March 1975 and sworn in as the fifth secretary, becoming the first woman to serve in the cabinet in more than twenty years.

During her tenure, which lasted until the end of the Ford administration on 20 January 1977, Hills oversaw the congressional passage of such actions as the Emergency Housing Act of 1975, which authorized temporary monetary assistance for mortgage assistance to the unemployed, and the Housing Authorization Act of 1976, which changed some community housing laws relating to flood insurance. As secretary, she was sued as part of a discrimination lawsuit against the Chicago Housing Authority by several black families; the case, *Hills v. Gautreaux et al.* (1976) was decided against Hills and the department. The court held that HUD could not establish government housing exclusively in predominantly black neighborhoods but had to expand housing programs to predominantly white neighborhoods outside of city limits.

Hills returned to private practice in 1977. In 1982, she served as cochairperson of the President's Commission on Housing. In 1988, her husband's good friend, Vice-president George Bush, was elected president, and Hills was named as the U.S. trade representative. During her tenure in this office, she laid the groundwork for the passage and signing of the North American Free Trade Agreement, and worked to end farm subsidies by the European Community. In 1993, Hills returned to private practice in Washington, D.C., with her husband.

References: "Hills, Carla Anderson," in Charles Moritz, ed., *Current Biography 1975* (New York: H. W. Wilson, 1975).

PATRICIA ROBERTS HARRIS
1924–1985

Patricia Harris was the first African American woman named to a cabinet post; she went on to hold three different cabinet positions—secretary of housing and urban development (HUD), secretary of health, education, and welfare (HEW), and secretary of health and human services (HHS)—after serving as the U.S. ambassador to Luxembourg. She also was a longtime advocate of civil rights for black Americans.

Born as Patricia Roberts on 31 May 1924 in Mattoon, Illinois, she was the daughter of Bert Fitzgerald Roberts, a Pullman railroad car waiter, and Hildren Brodie (née Johnson) Harris. She grew up in Mattoon and attended school there and in Chicago. After graduating from high school, Harris worked for a year to earn enough money to attend college; in 1942, she received a scholarship to Howard University in Washington, D.C., and graduated with a bachelor's degree summa cum laude in 1945. While at Howard, she was involved in the civil right movement and participated in a sit-in at a segregated lunch counter in Washington, D.C. After graduating from Howard, she returned to Illinois, and did two years of graduate work in industrial relations at the University of Chicago. From 1946 to 1949 she worked as the program director for the YWCA in Chicago. In 1949, she returned to Washington, D.C., and did additional graduate work at American University. She also worked as the assistant director of the American Council on Human Rights, a post she held until 1953.

Harris took law classes at the George Washington University Law School and graduated first in her class in 1960. That same year, she was employed by the Department of Justice as a trial attorney in the Appeals and Research Section of the Criminal Division. However, she remained there only a short time, leaving to accept an appointment as the associate dean of students and a lecturer in the law at Howard University. By 1965, she had become an assistant professor of law at Howard, although she had resigned as associate dean in 1963. In July 1963, President John F. Kennedy named Harris as cochairwoman, with Mildred McAfee Norton, of the National Women's Committee for Civil Rights. The committee was established to coordinate peaceful activities to fight segregation on a national basis.

On 19 May 1965, President Lyndon B. Johnson named Harris as the U.S. ambassador to Luxembourg to replace the resigning William G. Rivkin, making her the first black woman to serve in an ambassadorial post. In an interview, she expressed mixed feelings on the nomination: "I feel deeply proud and grateful the President chose me to knock down this barrier, but also a little sad about being 'the first Negro woman' because it implies we were not considered before."

Harris served in Luxembourg and also was a representative of the United States at the twenty-first and twenty-second General Assemblies of the United Nations; she resigned on 22 September 1967 and returned to the United States and to Howard University as a full professor of law. In 1969, she resigned and entered private practice as a partner in the Washington and New York law firm of Friend, Frank, Harris, Shriver, and Kampelman. A staunch liberal and Democrat, she served as the chair of the credentials committee at the 1972 Democratic National Convention, the first time a Democratic convention committee was chaired by an African American. She also remained at the forefront of civil rights work, serving as a member of the executive board of the NAACP Legal Defense Fund from 1967 to 1977.

In 1976, Georgia Governor Jimmy Carter was elected president, and he chose Harris as his secretary of HUD. Harris, who had a long history of working on the national and local levels to make housing affordable for the poor, including as a chairman of the Housing Committee of the Washington Urban League from 1956 to 1960, had met Carter in 1972 at the Democratic National Convention; he was impressed by her. Following the announcement of her selection on 21 December 1976, some civil rights and feminist groups were not enthusiastic, because her work for women's rights and civil rights had been reserved and not confrontational.

Some Democrats even expressed reservations. At her confirmation hearings, Senator

William Proxmire of Wisconsin claimed that she was not in touch with the problems of the poor. In response, Harris pointedly said, "Senator, I am one of them. You do not seem to understand who I am. I'm a black woman, the daughter of a dining car waiter. I'm a black woman who even eight years ago could not buy a house in some parts of the District of Columbia. Senator, to say I'm not by and of and for the people is to show a lack of understanding of who I am and where I came from."

Harris was confirmed on 20 January 1977 as the sixth secretary of HUD. During her tenure, which lasted until 24 September 1979, she tried to bring order to the department. She oversaw congressional passage of the Supplemental Housing Act of 1977, which created the National Commission on Neighborhoods, and the establishment of Urban Development Action Grants, which offered distressed communities monies for residential or nonresidential use. Biographer Judith Johnston wrote, "She brought with her experience in providing minorities improved access to better housing, a higher standard of living, and greater economic opportunities. In particular she directed an effort to prevent discrimination against women who applied for mortgage loans."

On 20 July 1979, President Carter reorganized his cabinet; he asked for the resignation of HEW Secretary Joseph Califano, Jr., and replaced him with Harris, who was replaced by New Orleans Mayor Maurice Landrieu. Confirmed a week later, Harris turned out to be the final HEW secretary. Carter had proposed that the department's education component be made into a separate cabinet department and the remaining agency be renamed the Department of Health and Human Services. Harris oversaw the transition of HEW to HHS and was named as the first secretary of HHS when the new department was named in May 1980. She was remembered as a competent administrator who appealed cuts in her departments directly to the president.

After the Carter administration ended in January 1981, Harris returned to private life as a law professor at the George Washington National Law Center. In 1982, residents of the District of Columbia, dissatisfied with Mayor Marion Barry, recruited Harris as their candidate for mayor. She was backed by middle-class whites and blacks, but this support was not sufficient for her to defeat Barry in a bitter contest.

Harris died of cancer, on 23 March 1985, at the age of 60.

References: "Harris, Patricia Roberts," in Charles Moritz, ed., *Current Biography 1965* (New York: H. W. Wilson, 1965), 189–191; Johnson, Judith R., "Harris, Patricia Roberts," in John A. Garraty and Mark C. Carnes, gen. eds., *American National Biography* (New York: Oxford University Press, 24 vols., 1999), 10: 179–180.

MAURICE EDWIN "MOON" LANDRIEU

1930–

Moon Landrieu, a popular mayor of New Orleans, Louisiana, was named as the seventh secretary of housing and urban development (HUD) in the wake of the cabinet shake-up by President Jimmy Carter. Born in New Orleans on 23 July 1930, Landrieu is the son of Joseph Landrieu and Loretta (née Bechtel) Landrieu. Landrieu (who legally changed his name to Moon, a childhood nickname) grew up in the poorer section of New Orleans, where his parents ran a grocery store. He attended local schools, then won a scholarship to Loyola University in New Orleans. There, he majored in business administration and was the baseball team's star pitcher. After earning his bachelor's degree in business administration, Landrieu entered Loyola's law school and received his LL.B. degree in 1954. He was admitted to the Louisiana bar that same year.

Landrieu joined the U.S. Army, where he served in the office of the Judge Advocate

General with the rank of second lieutenant. After his discharge in 1957, he opened a law office in New Orleans. Landrieu joined a local affiliate of the Young Crescent City Democratic Association and, in 1959, was elected to a seat in the Louisiana state House of Representatives from Ward 12, a predominantly black and low-income district. When Governor Jimmie Davis introduced bills in the legislature to circumvent federal desegregation laws, Landrieu was the only member of either house to vote against the enactments. He was reelected to the seat and held office until 1966. In 1966, Landrieu then ran for and was elected to a seat as councilman-at-large on the New Orleans City Council. He served until 1969. In that year, Landrieu ran for mayor against Republican Ben Toledano and won by 30,000 votes, knitting together a coalition of poor whites and poor blacks. Historian Melvin C. Holli wrote, "Mayor Landrieu worked hard to rebuild the tourist industry. He opened up the city to private real estate development, and the resulting demolition of some historic buildings brought him into conflict with the preservationists. The historic French Market was refurbished with a riverside promenade, nicknamed the 'Moon Walk.' Even more daring and controversial was Landrieu's vigorous support of the construction of the $163 million dollar 'Superdome,' one of the largest enclosed sports stadiums in the nation. To critics that charged that the mammoth project was an exercise in madness, Landrieu pointed to the thousands of additional hotel rooms and other facilities that had been built to accommodate the new business from the Superdome, and that critics had also charged Bavarian castle builder King Ludwig with madness Landrieu established a record as an effective financial administrator working closely with the state legislature for additional funds and garnering from the federal government far more than a proportional share of federal aid."

Landrieu was a leading Democrat with a national reputation. In 1972, Democratic Presidential candidate Senator George S. McGovern considered him as a potential running mate. However, his second mayoral term ended on 1 May 1978, and Landrieu left office to become the president of the Joseph C. Canizaro Interests Co., a New Orleans land development firm. In mid-July 1979, President Jimmy Carter undertook a major reorganization of his cabinet and named Landrieu, on 27 July 1979, as the new secretary of HUD. During his confirmation hearings, allegations that Landrieu had taken Mafia money during his term as mayor, as well as the alleged mob ties of Canizaro Interests, threatened to derail his nomination. However, he assured the senators that he would divest himself of all interest in the company, and would recuse himself on any matter dealing with interests Canizaro had before HUD. Landrieu was confirmed on 12 September, by a vote of 97 to 0, as the seventh HUD. His tenure lasted until the end of the Carter administration on 20 January 1981.

Landrieu oversaw the congressional passage of such enactments as the Housing and Community Development Amendments of 1979, which established additions to such previous HUD programs as the Community Development Block Grant, Action Grant, Neighborhood Self-help Development, and Urban Homesteading programs; the Veterans' Disability Compensation and Housing Benefits Amendments of 1980, which offered federal assistance to veterans who were severely disabled; and the Depository Institutions' Deregulation and Monetary Control Act of 1980, which was passed due to the rise in interest rates to 19 percent in 1980.

Landrieu saw that the department could not oversee all the construction of public housing in the United States, and he wanted a system of incentives to push for private construction. In an interview in August 1979, he said, "Government doesn't build the cities of this country and it won't be able to rebuild them. They were built by the private sector. That's where the money is, the innovation is, [and] the incentive is."

In January 1981, Landrieu returned to private life. He was named as a judge to the Fourth Circuit Court of Appeals in New Orleans, where he now serves as chief judge.

His daughter, Mary Landrieu, was elected to the U.S. Senate from Louisiana in 1996.

References: Haas, Garland A., *Jimmy Carter and the Politics of Frustration* (Jefferson, NC: McFarland, 1996), 84; Holli, Melvin G., "Landrieu, Moon," in Melvin G. Holli and Peter d'Alroy Jones, eds., *Biographical Dictionary of American Mayors, 1820–1980: Big City Mayors* (Westport, CT: Greenwood, 1981), 207; Kaufman, Burton I., *The Presidency of James Earl Carter, Jr.* (Lawrence: University Press of Kansas, 1993), 147; "Landrieu, Moon," in Charles Moritz, ed., *Current Biography 1980* (New York: H. W. Wilson, 1980), 206–210.

SAMUEL RILEY PIERCE, JR.
1922–

Samuel Pierce became the fourth African American named to a cabinet post when Ronald Reagan chose him as the secretary of housing and urban development (HUD) in 1980. He served the longest term of any HUD secretary—eight full years. Born in Glen Cove, Long Island, a suburb of New York City, on 8 September 1922, Pierce was the son of Samuel Pierce Riley, Sr., a dry-cleaning store owner and real estate investor, and Hettie Elenor (née Armstrong) Pierce.

Pierce went to Cornell University on a scholarship and was elected to Phi Beta Kappa his junior year. In 1943, he left college to join the U.S. Army's Criminal Investigation Division, the only black serving in that division in North Africa and Italy. Discharged in 1946 with the rank of first lieutenant, he returned to Cornell and received a bachelor's degree with honors in 1947. He then entered Cornell's School of Law and received his law degree in 1951. He earned an LL.M. degree in taxation from New York University's school of law in 1952 and served, from 1957 to 1958, as a Ford Foundation fellow at the Yale University Law School.

In 1949, Pierce went to work in the office of Manhattan District Attorney Frank Hogan, where he served as Hogan's assistant until 1953. That year, he was named by President Dwight D. Eisenhower as the assistant U.S. attorney for the Southern District of New York. Then, in 1955, Pierce was named as the assistant to the undersecretary of labor, the first black to hold that position. The following year, he moved to the legislative branch to serve as the associate counsel, and then counsel, to the House Judiciary antitrust subcommittee.

Pierce gained the respect of Senator Kenneth Keating of New York, who hired Pierce as the treasurer for his 1958 reelection campaign. Pierce served as an informal adviser to Keating and New York gubernatorial candidate Nelson Rockefeller on issues relating to African Americans. After Rockefeller was elected, he named Pierce, in 1959 and 1960, to vacancies on the New York County Court of General Sessions. He ran for full terms to these seats but lost in heavily Democratic New York City.

Pierce then entered private law practice, becoming the first black partner in the New York firm of Battle, Fowler, Stokes & Kheel, specializing in tax law. He was named by Governor Rockefeller and New York Mayor John V. Lindsay to various panels in the city and state. Pierce was also involved in the civil rights movement, serving as an attorney for the Rev. Dr. Martin Luther King, Jr., as well as the *New York Times,* when both were sued by officials in Alabama over an advertisement in the paper that Alabama police found demeaning. Pierce argued the case before the U.S. Supreme Court, which became the landmark First Amendment case of *New York Times v. Sullivan* (1964). He also worked to expand opportunities for blacks in the construction industry and was a founder of the Freedom National Bank, the first bank in New York state led by blacks.

In 1968, Pierce headed the group Black Americans for Nixon-Agnew and, was offered the position of chairman of the U.S. Civil Service Commission in the new administration, but he declined, preferring to remain in private industry. However, two years later, he accepted the position of general counsel in the Department of the Treasury.

During his tenure, he worked on the government's $250 million loan to the Lockheed Aircraft Corporation and helped draw up the administration's wage and price controls. In 1973, he returned to his old law firm as a senior partner.

In 1980, Pierce's old friend Alfred Bloomingdale urged President-elect Ronald Reagan to name Pierce to his cabinet. Bloomingdale was serving in an unofficial capacity as part of Reagan's kitchen cabinet, a group of advisers relating to policy and cabinet selections. Reagan also considered Philip Sanchez, a Hispanic businessman, for the post. When Sanchez asked that he not be named, Reagan convinced Pierce, who wanted to be either attorney general of secretary of labor, to take the job. His nomination was announced on 22 December 1980, and he was confirmed by the Senate on 20 January 1981, by a vote of 98 to 0. He took office as the eighth secretary of HUD and served through both of Reagan's terms, the only one of Reagan's cabinet officers to do so. Pierce oversaw 14,300 employees and an annual budget of about $14 billion. Dubbed "Silent Sam" because of the inconspicuous way he went about his work, Pierce followed administration policy to cut the budget of his department.

He oversaw a number of important congressional enactments, including the Housing and Community Development Amendments of 1981, which amended the Housing and Community Development Act of 1974; the Veterans' Disability Compensation, Housing, and Memorial Benefits Amendments of 1981, which amended title 38 of the U.S. Code to allow the administrator of Veterans' Affairs to help veterans with home loans; the Housing and Urban-Rural Recovery Act of 1983 , which created a housing voucher program and the Rental Rehabilitation Program; the Stewart B. McKinney Homeless Assistance Act of 1987, which provided through HUD assistance to homeless, with special emphasis on the elderly, persons with disabilities, and families with children; the Indian Housing Act of 1988, which amended the U.S. Housing Act of 1937 to establish a program to offer assistance to American Indians to purchase or rent homes; and the Fair Housing Amendments Act of 1988, which amended Title VIII of the Civil Rights Act of 1968 to expand the reach of fair housing provisions and give the department enforcement responsibility.

In his 1981 annual report, Pierce wrote, "During 1981, I began a concerted effort to direct HUD's assistance to the persons and areas of greatest need. The Department underwent major change, with unnecessary and unsupportable costs eliminated, inefficient and ineffective programs improved or discontinued, and runaway expenditures brought under control. We are determined to help the most needy Americans meet their basic housing requirements. More responsible management can help us reach that goal." In his 1982 report, he expanded on this idea: "[One] of our primary goals is to ensure equal access to housing for all persons. . . . We used conciliation and education to develop positive solutions and to combat the ignorance which is a fundamental component of discrimination. We extended our support of voluntary compliance efforts, and we continued our development of amendments to strengthen enforcement of our fair housing laws . . . we successfully encouraged the federal government's intervention as a 'friend of the court' in . . . *Havens Realty Company v. Coleman*. In that case, the Court ruled that fair housing 'testers,' who, because of their race, did not receive accurate information on the availability of housing have standing to sue under the Fair Housing Act. . . . We continued to promote the economic growth of cities and States through our existing programs and by increasing our emphasis on partnerships among the private sector and all levels of government in community revitalization efforts."

Pierce left office in January 1989. A year later, however, rumors spread that Pierce had been involved in profiteering and influence peddling. Attorney General Richard Thornburgh asked for an independent counsel to be named. Arlin Adams, an attorney and former judge on the Circuit Court of Appeals for the Third Circuit, was named on 1 March 1990, and he served until he was replaced by Larry D. Thompson on 3 July 1995. In October 1998, Thompson released his final report, which detailed severe misconduct by several of Pierce's assistants, resulting in misappropriations of millions of dollars of housing funds. His executive assistant, Deborah Gore Dean, was convicted on twelve felony counts and sentenced to twenty-one months in prison. However, neither Adams nor Thompson found that Pierce had committed any wrongdoing, and he was cleared of any unethical conduct.

References: "1981 Annual Report U.S. Department of Housing and Urban Development" (Washington, DC: Government Printing Office, 1982), ii; "1982 Annual Report U.S. Department of Housing and Urban Development" (Washington, DC: Government Printing Office, 1983), 3; "Pierce, Samuel Riley Jr." in Charles Moritz, ed., *Current Biography 1982* (New York: H. W. Wilson, 1982), 318–322.

JACK FRENCH KEMP
1935–

Jack Kemp may be best remembered as Senator Robert J. Dole's running mate in the 1996 presidential election, but he also made his mark during his four years as secretary of housing and urban development (HUD) in the George Bush administration. Born in Los Angeles, California, on 13 July 1935, Kemp is the son of Paul R. Kemp, the owner of a trucking firm, and Frances (née Pope) Kemp, a schoolteacher and social worker. Kemp attended local schools, then completed his education at Occidental College in Los Angeles, where he majored in physical education, earning a bachelor's degree in 1957. After college, he was drafted by the Detroit Lions football team, and eventually played as the Buffalo Bills' starting quarterback. He was the American Football League's Player of the Year in 1965 and was named Most Valuable Player of that year's championship game.

In the early 1960s, Kemp, a moderate-to-conservative Republican, was influenced by conservative economic writers like Ludwig von Mises and Friedrich von Hayek, both of whom wrote that free markets, with as little government intervention as possible, made for stronger economies. He was strongly affected by Barry Goldwater's *The Conscience of a Conservative*. But Kemp developed a strong libertarian streak and sided with such writers as Irving Kristol and Jude Wanniski, former socialists who had moved to the right of the political spectrum with their ideas on using tax reform to the betterment of society, particularly areas of urban blight.

In 1967, Kemp became an adviser to Republican Governor Ronald Reagan of California and eventually served as a member of the Republican National Committee. In 1970, when Representative Richard Dean McCarthy, decided not to run for reelection, Kemp announced his intention to run for the open seat. Kemp beat Democrat Thomas P. Flaherty, by 9,000 votes out of some 190,000 cast, and entered Congress on 3 January 1971. Kemp won reelection eight more times, serving until 3 January 1989. Kemp was a member of the Committee on Appropriations, the Subcommittee on Foreign Operations, Export Financing, and Related Programs, and the Select Committee on Children, Youth and Families. He was an outspoken supporter of the Vietnam War and of civil rights initiatives. He was also one of the first advocates of what became known as supply side economics—the idea that the tax system should be used not as a punitive measure against people but as a tool to shape society; lowering taxes could actually increase revenues by stimulating economic growth.

Kemp coauthored the Kemp-Garcia Bill introduced in Congress in 1980 to establish enterprise zones, areas with low taxes to stimulate business activity, in predominantly minority areas. Kemp hoped that lowering taxes would encourage businesses to move to areas of urban blight, an idea that won little approval at first–the bill was defeated. His plan to lower the highest tax rates to stimulate investment in the economy became a key portion of the Kemp-Roth Tax Law, which was enacted by Congress and signed into law by President Ronald Reagan. In 1980, while running a second time, Reagan took Kemp's plan for a 30 percent cut in the top rates of personal income tax and made it a major part of his economic plan. The Kemp-Roth plan, coauthored by Senator William Roth, Republican of Delaware, was embodied in the Economic Recovery Tax Act of 1981.

Many considered Kemp a possible successor to Reagan, whose two terms in office ended in 1989. Kemp announced himself as a candidate for president in 1988, but his candidacy floundered because he was too independent of many of the more right-wing factions of his party, particularly in the areas of affirmative action for minorities. Kemp stated in 1986, "This is not the Grand Old Party anymore. . . . We've got to be the party of labor. Economic growth doesn't mean anything if it leaves people out. If we trust our ideas we have to take them into the ghetto, into the barrio and into the trade union hiring hall. Franklin Roosevelt made his party the party of hope, and now we must do the same thing for the party of Lincoln." Kemp's campaign never seemed to get off the ground, and he eventually pulled out of the race.

Following the election of Vice-president George Bush, as president in 1988, Bush named Kemp as his secretary of HUD. Kemp had had some relevant experience in Congress with his work on bringing business to urban areas, and on 2 February 1989, he was confirmed by the Senate by a vote of 100 to 0 and took office as the ninth secretary. As secretary, Kemp tried to clean up the corruption uncovered in the department. Richard Stengel wrote in 1996, "Hoping to use HUD to launch his own war on poverty, Kemp persuaded Bush to support a $4 billion housing program that encouraged public-housing tenants to buy their own apart-

ments. But the Democratic Congress only allocated $361 million for the program."

When Kemp took over, cuts in the department by Pierce and Reagan had left it with about 11,000 employees; Kemp brought that back up to over 14,000 by the time he left office. Budget authority in 1989 was $14billion; by 1992 it was $26 billion. Kemp also oversaw the congressional passage of such enactments as the Housing and Urban Development Reform Act of 1989, which included over fifty different reforms to ensure financial and managerial integrity in the department; the Cranston-Gonzalez National Affordable Housing Act of 1990, which created the HOME Investment Partnerships Program and provided funding to assist the homeless; the VA-HUD Independent Agencies Appropriations Act, which authorized the Capital Grants program to assist the elderly and disabled with housing; and the Housing and Community Development Act of 1992 , which established the Office of Federal Housing Enterprise Oversight to supervise the Federal National Mortgage Association ("Fannie Mae") and Federal Home Loan Mortgage Corporation ("Freddie Mac") housing loan programs.

Kemp was praised by Democrats and Republicans for his work to clean up the department. He saw the department through an independent counsel investigation that highlighted corruption in the department in the pre-Kemp years. After leaving office in 1993, Kemp helped found, with former Secretary of Education William Bennett, Empower America, a national organization that stressed individual solutions to problems usually handled by government. In 1996, Republican Presidential nominee Senator Robert J. Dole of Kansas surprised many by selecting Kemp as his running mate. Dole and Kemp had never gotten along—the two had, over the years, exchanged heated remarks over the direction of the Republican Party. Nonetheless, Kemp was seen by Dole as an exciting candidate who gave him a shot at winning the presidency. Kemp dismissed critics of his joining with Dole by saying that "unity does not require unanimity." However, Dole and

Kemp were defeated by incumbent President Bill Clinton in November 1996.

Today, Jack Kemp remains a leading voice for what he calls "bleeding heart conservatism." He appears on television as a political commentator.

References: "Kemp, Jack (French)," in Charles Moritz, ed., *Current Biography 1980* (New York: H. W. Wilson, 1980), 181–184; Stanley, Alessandra, "The Quarterback of Supply Side: Jack Kemp is Propelled by Ideas," *Time,* 13 April 1987, 25–26; Stengel, Richard, "Jack Be Nimble: Confident, Impulsive, Self-righteous, Kemp Has a Long History of Calling His Own Plays," *Time,* 19 August 1996, 28.

HENRY GABRIEL CISNEROS
1947–

Henry Cisneros was a popular mayor of San Antonio, Texas, before he served as secretary of housing and urban development (HUD) in the Clinton administration, but his career faltered when he was indicted for lying and obstruction of justice. Cisneros, the son of George Cisneros, a civilian administrator in the U.S. Army, and Elvira (née Munguia) Cisneros, was born in San Antonio on 11 June 1947. He attended local schools, then went to Texas A&M University in 1964. He received his bachelor of arts degree in English in 1968 and a master's degree in urban and regional planning in 1970. Cisneros had turned to this latter field after attending a seminar at West Point in 1967 on urban problems. After earning his bachelor's degree, Cisneros was hired as an analyst by Roy Montez, a director of the San Antonio department of the Model Cities Program, a government initiative established by President Lyndon B. Johnson as part of his Great Society economic program to assist in urban revitalization. In January 1969, he was promoted to assistant director of the program. During this time, he worked to reinvigorate the Hispanic sections of the city.

In 1970, Cisneros went to Washington, D.C. and became the executive vice-president of the National League of Cities. He applied for and was accepted to the 1971 White House fellowship program, to receive experience in how government works. He was assigned to work as an aide to Elliot L. Richardson, the secretary of health, education, and welfare. The following year, Cisneros moved to Boston, where, with a grant from the Ford Foundation, he earned a master's degree in public administration from the John F. Kennedy School of Government. He also worked as a teaching assistant at Massachusetts Institute of Technology (MIT) and completed doctoral studies. Turning down an opportunity to teach at MIT full-time, Cisneros accepted a professorship at the University of Texas at San Antonio, where he taught urban studies and labor economics. In 1975, he received his Ph.D. degree from the George Washington University in Washington, D.C.

In 1975, right after Cisneros returned to San Antonio, he was nominated to run for a seat on the San Antonio City Council. Elected, he became, at age 27, the youngest city councilman in the city's history. Reelected in 1977 and 1979, he became the leading Hispanic politician in the city. In 1981, he announced his candidacy for mayor. The incumbent, Lila Cockrell, did not to run for reelection, and Cisneros won an easy election on 4 April 1981, making him the first Hispanic mayor of San Antonio since 1842 and the first Hispanic mayor of a major American city.

Cisneros was reelected mayor three additional times, serving until 1989. He helped rebuild the city's economic base, spent more than $200 million to revitalize the city's Hispanic areas, boosted tourism, and used incentives to attract business to the city. In 1984, Democratic presidential candidate Walter Mondale interviewed Cisneros as a possible running mate. Cisneros was passed over, but many talked of him as a potential governor of Texas, perhaps even the first Hispanic president of the United States. In 1985, he was elected as president of the National League of Cities.

In 1989, however, Cisneros announced that he would be leaving politics. It had been disclosed that he had been having an affair with a former campaign aide, Linda Medlar. Rather than remain in office and subject his family to continued scrutiny, Cisneros chose to go into private business. He became chairman of the Cisneros Asset Management Company, which lent assets to tax-exempt organizations. He also appeared on television as the host of *Texans* and gave commentary in Spanish on a program called *Adelante*. He also served as deputy chairman of the Federal Reserve Bank of Dallas and as a board member of the Rockefeller Foundation.

In 1992, President-elect Bill Clinton, former governor of Arkansas, was elected president. Despite having left office under an ethical cloud, Cisneros was offered the position of secretary of HUD, because of his long career in urban affairs. After being confirmed by the Senate, unanimously, on 21 January 1993 as the tenth secretary of HUD, Cisneros served for the entire first Clinton term, until early 1997. During his four years in office, he oversaw the continuation of department backing of so-called enterprise zones, initially sought by his predecessor, Jack F. Kemp, an idea that was installed as the Empowerment Zone and Enterprise Community Program in the Omnibus Budget Reconciliation Act of 1993.

In 1995, Cisneros released *Blueprint for the Reinvention of HUD,* a major report that called for broad and comprehensive changes in the department, including the advocacy of housing reform, improvements to the Federal Housing Administration, and combining all other department programs into three major block grant initiatives. Cisneros also oversaw drastic cuts in departmental expenses, including three rounds of cuts that reduced the budget from $26 billion to $19.5 billion, in the number of department employees from 13,500 when he got into office to 10,300 when he left. Cisneros pointed out as his major accomplishment the rise in homeownership, to 65.6 percent—in all, more than 66 million Americans owned homes, up more than 4.5 million from when he took office.

Cisneros had been office only a little more than a year when the Medlar affair came back to haunt him. In July 1994, she filed a breach of contract suit, alleging that he had promised to pay for her daughter's education—in fact, Cisneros had paid Medlar more than $200,000. In preconfirmation interviews with the FBI, he had claimed that he had paid her only a small amount. More damaging were tape-recorded phone conversations in which Cisneros indicated that he would lie to the FBI during his background check. In March 1995, Attorney General Janet Reno recommended that an independent counsel be appointed to examine whether Cisneros had lied to the FBI. Cisneros remained in office during the investigation, declaring that he regretted any mistakes he had made, but that he had never violated the public's trust. After Clinton had won a second term, Cisneros offered his resignation on 21 November 1996, citing increasing debts, both from the Medlar investigation and his daughter's education, which could not be paid from his salary as a cabinet officer, as the sole reason for leaving.

After leaving the cabinet, Cisneros went to work as head of the Spanish-language Univision television network. On 11 December 1997, Cisneros, along with former aides John Rosales and Sylvia Arce-Garcia, was indicted on twenty-one counts of lying to the FBI and obstructing justice. On 7 September 1999, Cisneros pleaded guilty to one count of lying to the FBI, a misdemeanor; he was fined $10,000.

References: Catalano, Julie, "Henry Cisneros," in Joseph C. Tardiff & L. Mpho Mabunda, eds., *Dictionary of Hispanic Biography* (Detroit: Gale Research, 1996), 227–230; "Cisneros, Henry G(abriel)," in Charles Moritz, ed., *Current Biography 1987* (New York: H. W. Wilson, 1987), 93–96.

ANDREW MARK CUOMO
1957–

In 1997, at the age of 39, Andrew Cuomo became the secretary of housing and urban development (HUD), one of the youngest people ever to serve in a cabinet-level post. Born in Queens, a borough of New York City, on 6 December 1957, he is the son of Mario Cuomo, governor of New York (1983–1995), and Matilda Cuomo. He was involved in politics at an early age, assisting in his father's unsuccessful campaigns for lieutenant governor, in 1974, and for mayor of New York City, in 1977. Cuomo entered Fordham University in New York and earned a bachelor's degree in 1979; he then went to the Albany Law School in Albany, New York, and was awarded a law degree in 1982. That same year, Cuomo was the campaign manager for his father's successful campaign for governor. Two years later, he served as his father's special assistant, but left that position when he was named as assistant district attorney for Manhattan.

Over the next two years, while he served as assistant district attorney, Cuomo worked in a law firm in private practice. However, his interest was in housing for the poor, and in 1986, Cuomo established the Housing Enterprise for the Less Privileged (HELP), which developed a program of assisting the homeless not only with housing but with drug and medical treatment and job training. In 1991, New York Mayor David Dinkins named Cuomo as head of the New York Commission on the Homeless. In 1992, after the election of Democrat Bill Clinton as president, Cuomo was named as assistant secretary of HUD for Community Planning and Development, where he helped Secretary Henry G. Cisneros formulate seventy-two enterprise or empowerment zones where businesses were given incentives to relocate to create jobs and other opportunities.

In 1996, Cisneros announced that he would be resigning, and on 20 December 1996, Clinton named Cuomo to succeed Cisneros. In his Senate nomination hearings, Cuomo put forward his philosophy, "The object of our efforts must be the development of self-sufficiency—not the perpetuation of government programs . . . the pride and dignity of having a job and earning one's own bread is the best social services program that exists . . . the private sector is the engine that will drive the economic rebirth of a community and . . . real solutions will be found in the local communities—through local partnerships and local initiatives. . . . I seek to fulfill HUD's mission—a mission which begins with a simple, yet profound goal clearly proclaimed by the Housing Act of 1949: 'A decent home and a suitable living environment for every American family.'"

Cuomo was confirmed on 29 January 1997 as the eleventh secretary of HUD. In 1997, he announced a plan to fully fund Section 8 mortgages in an effort to stop abuses in the program to provide developers with financial incentives to build low-cost housing. In 1999, he released the report, *Now Is the Time: Places Left Behind in the New Economy,* which called for increased aid for economic development in depressed areas, more housing vouchers, more redevelopment of troubled housing projects, and increased funding for a variety of department programs. Cuomo continues to serve as the head of HUD.

References: "Cuomo, Andrew M.," in Judith Graham, ed., *Current Biography 1998* (New York: H. W. Wilson, 1998), 7–10; United States Congress, Senate, Committee on Banking, Housing, and Urban Affairs, *Nomination of Andrew M. Cuomo: Hearing Before the Committee on Banking, Housing, and Urban Affairs, United States Senate, One Hundred Fifth Congress, First Session, on Nomination of Andrew M. Cuomo, of New York, to be Secretary, U.S. Department of Housing and Urban Development, January 22, 1997* (Washington, DC: GPO, 1997).

INTERIOR

T he Department of the Interior, the first department added to the cabinet in the nineteenth century and the first in fifty years (after the Navy in 1798), was established to handle all of the land and resource matters in the United States. Its various bureaus were initially established in other departments, and many politicians resisted creating a sixth cabinet-level department. In 1783, Pelatiah Webster, in *A Dissertation on the Political Union and Constitution of the Thirteen United States of North-America,* called for the establishment of a "Secretary of State" who would have under his power not only external but internal affairs. In drawing up the U.S. Constitution four years later, Gouverneur Morris called for the creation of a secretary of domestic affairs, who was to "attend to matters of general policy, the state of agriculture and manufactures, the opening of roads and navigations and the facilitating communications through the United States." Although this idea was never drafted into the Constitution, Morris thought highly of it; years later, he continued to write of the need for a "Minister of the Interior" in the federal government.

Congress, however, created the Department of State mainly to conduct the foreign affairs of the nation, with bureaucratic powers over domestic matters as a secondary responsibility of the secretary at the head of the agency. On 15 December 1789, Thomas Jefferson, having been asked by President George Washington to become secretary of state, wrote to him, "But when I contemplate the extent of that office, embracing as it does the principal mass of domestic administration, together with the foreign, I cannot be insensible to my inequality to it." Jefferson took the post regardless of the extra work and, in 1790, sent an estimation of the department's expenses for one year to Secretary of the Treasury Alexander Hamilton equaling $2,625 for the running of the Foreign Office and $1,836 for the "Home Office."

Gradually, however, agencies that had been established inside the existing departments to deal with domestic matters became overwhelmed when so spread across the government. In his annual message of 3 December 1816, President James Madison called attention to "the expediency . . . of an additional department in the executive branch of the Government . . . to be charged with duties now overburdening other departments and with such as have not been annexed to any department." All of the officers in Madison's cabinet signed a letter to Congress asking for the creation of a department that would control five distinct areas: territorial governments, national highways and canals, the general post office, the patent office, and Indian affairs. (The Post Office was made into an official and separate cabinet department in 1829.) These pleas were ignored, however, and the established departments continued to sag under the weight of numerous problems with these domestic issues.

In his 1848 annual report, Secretary of the Treasury Robert J. Walker wrote that many of the agencies in his department—including the Land Office—had nothing to do with the Treasury, that the State Department had nothing to do with patents, which it controlled, and that the War Department should not have control over Indian affairs. To Congress, he called for the establishment of another department to handle all of these affairs. That same year, as Congress looked toward the management of the lands and Native American affairs that had come under U.S. control in the Mexican-American War just recently fought, it undertook to implement Secretary Walker's recommendations. After hearings in the House Agriculture Committee, a bill was drafted and passed in both houses; on 3 March 1849, Congress established a Home Department (9 Stat. 395), which, in contrast to the State Department that controlled all external matters, would be concerned directly with numerous and diverse domestic matters. Forming the core of the new department were the General Land Office, the Bureau of Indian Affairs, the Patent Office, the Pension Office, the conducting of the census, and the maintenance of public buildings in Washington, D.C.

There is considerable evidence that former Senator George Evans of Maine was selected for the new post of secretary of the Home Department. On 4 March 1849, the day following passage of the legislation, Senator Daniel Webster wrote to incoming Secretary of State John Middleton Clayton in support of Evans. However, reports historian Mary Hinsdale, Senator William H. Seward of New York, who sought to deny Webster any say in the cabinet, especially the formation and composition of the leadership of the new department, convinced President Zachary Taylor to move former Secretary of the Treasury Thomas Ewing, whom Taylor had picked to be postmaster general in the new administration, over to Home, and Taylor, who courted Seward's favor, did exactly that, while he named Senator Jacob Collamer to the Post Office. Thus, Thomas Ewing, and not George Evans, became the first secretary of the Home Department.

Ewing began work starting from scratch in bringing all of these diverse agencies under the aegis of one working bureaucratic department. His agency, with 600 employees, was spread across Washington, D.C., but its main offices were located in the Patent Office building, which occupied two blocks, fronting south on F Street, and north on G Street. As James D. McCabe wrote in 1873, "It is constructed of the plainest Doric style, of massive crystallized marble, and though devoid of exterior ornament is one of the most magnificent buildings in the city. It is grand in its simplicity, and its architectural details are pure and tasteful." In his annual report for 1849, Ewing wrote, "The act to establish the Department of the Interior was passed at the close of the last session of Congress, when the attention of that body was occupied by a large accumulation of public business, in consequence of which it was left, in some respects, imperfect. The department is named in the title 'A Home Department;' but the body of the act provides that its shall be called 'The Department of the Interior.' The title of the act, being the part last adopted in the process of enactment, is believed to express the intention of Congress as to the name, but the language of the act itself being imperative, I felt constrained to conform to it in the adoption of a seal, and in all other official acts."

Ewing resigned after just sixteen months in office, and he was succeeded by four men in the next eleven years. Perhaps the most controversial of the early secretaries was Jacob Thompson (1857–1861), who may have used the department to further the military operations of his native South just prior to the outbreak of the Civil War. Later secretaries have been more obscure than confrontational, with the exception of Harold Ickes (1933–1946), who served the longest as secretary and expanded the powers of the department more than any other secretary; Albert B. Fall (1921–1923), jailed for his role in the Teapot Dome scandal; James Watt (1981–1983), who was reviled by environmentalists for his prodevelopment policies; and Bruce Babbitt (1993–), an activist secretary in the opposite mode.

Congress added new agencies to the Interior Department in the years following its establishment. In 1867, it created a "department" of education and, six years later, transferred authority over territorial matters from the State Department to Interior. In 1879, the Geological Survey was created; in 1916, President Woodrow Wilson created the National Park Service to oversee all national parks in the United States; and in 1940, a bureau in the Department of Commerce, the Bureau of Fisheries, and one in Agriculture, the Bureau of Biological Survey, were transferred to Interior and consolidated as the Fish and Wildlife Service. Other agencies in the department were moved around. With the establishment of the Department of Justice in 1870, Interior's jurisdiction over district attorneys, marshals, and court officers was transferred to that new department. Jurisdiction over labor was given completely to the new Department of Labor in 1888 (not at that time a cabinet-level department), and, in 1903, the Census Bureau was made a part of the Department of Commerce and Labor.

By the 1930s, the need for a new Interior building became apparent. The "Old Interior Building" was the second home of the department, really a small annex, and did not have enough offices. In 1934, Secretary Harold Ickes received $1.435 million for the purchase of land between 18th and 19th Streets and C and E Streets in western Washington, D.C., with an additional $12.7 million for the construction of a structure to house the department. Dedicated on 16 April 1936, this new behemoth was not ready for occupancy until 1937.

In the history of the department, there have been, as of this writing, forty-seven secretaries, who served an average tenure of 38.3 months, or 3 years, 2 months per secretary. Terms ranged from the thirteen years of Harold Ickes to the eleven days of the second secretary, Thomas McKean Thompson McKennan.

The department has historically had "a wide range of responsibilities entrusted to it: the construction of the national capital's water system, the colonization of freed slaves in Haiti, exploration of western wilderness, oversight of the District of Columbia jail, regulation of territorial governments, management of hospitals and universities, management of public parks, the basic responsibilities for Indians, public lands, patents, and pensions. In one way or another all of these had to do with the internal development of the nation or the welfare of its people." The department's logo consists of an American buffalo standing before blue mountains and a radiant sun. The original logo, an eagle with its wings outstretched, was replaced by the present one by Secretary Ray Lyman Wilbur in 1929.

References: Daniel Webster to John Middleton Clayton, 4 March 1849, John Middleton Clayton Papers, Volume 3 (1849—15 January–29 March), Library of Congress; Forness, Norman Olaf, "The Origins and

Early History of the United States Department of the Interior" (Master's thesis, Pennsylvania State University, 1964); Hinsdale, Mary Louise, *A History of the President's Cabinet* (Ann Arbor, MI: George Ware, 1911), 140; Jefferson to Washington, 15 December 1789, in Henry S. Randall, ed., *Life of Thomas Jefferson* (New York: Derby & Jackson, 3 vols., 1858), 1: 557; Learned, Henry Barrett, "The Establishment of the Secretaryship of the Interior," *American Historical Review* 16 (1911); McCabe, James D. (Edward Winslow Martin, pseud.), *Behind the Scenes in Washington. Being a Complete and Graphic Account of the Credit Mobilier Investigation, the Congressional Rings, Political Intrigues, Workings of the Lobbies, Etc . . .* (New York: Continental Publishing Company, 1873), 332–333; *Report of the Secretary of the Interior for 1849* (Washington, DC: Government Printing Office, 1849), 1; Trani, Eugene P., "The Secretaries of the Department of the Interior, 1849–1969" (unpublished manuscript, National Anthropological Archives, Smithsonian Institution, 1975); Watkins, T. H., *Righteous Pilgrim: The Life and Times of Harold L. Ickes, 1874–1952* (New York: Henry Holt, 1990), 447–451; Webster, Pelatiah, *A Dissertation on the Political Union and Constitution of the Thirteen United States, of North-America: Which Is Necessary to Their Preservation and Happiness, Humbly Offered to the Public, by a Citizen of Philadelphia* (Philadelphia: Printed and Sold by T. Bradford, [1783]).

THOMAS EWING

1789–1871

See Secretary of the Treasury, 1841

THOMAS MCKEAN THOMPSON MCKENNAN

1794–1852

Little is known of Thomas McKennan. He served as the second secretary of the interior for only eleven days, from 15 August to 26 August 1850. Historians of the department do not mention him except in connection with his successor, Alexander Stuart; no manuscript collections have been found about him or of his letters, and no works that he may have written seem to exist. McKennan was born in New Castle, Delaware, on 31 March 1794, the son of Col. William McKennan, a soldier in the Revolutionary War, and Elizabeth (née Thompson) McKennan. McKennan moved with his family to western Virginia in 1797 and later to Washington, Pennsylvania. There he attended and graduated from Washington College (later Washington and Jefferson College) and was a tutor

in ancient languages before studying law. He was admitted to the bar in 1814.

McKennan entered political life in 1815, when he was elected for a two-year term as attorney general of Washington County, Pennsylvania. From 1818 until 1831 he was a member of Washington's town council. It was not until 1830, when he was 36, that he decided to run for a seat in the U.S. House of Representatives. He was elected and served from 4 March 1831 until 3 March 1839, as well as part of an unexpired term from 3 May 1842 until 3 March 1843.

How McKennan came to be named as the second secretary of the interior is clouded in mystery. President Fillmore had difficulty in finding a replacement for the first secretary, Thomas Ewing, following Ewing's resignation. Fillmore first offered the vacant post to Senator James Alfred Pearce of Maryland and, when Pearce declined, proffered it to McKennan, who accepted on 23 July. He was confirmed by the Senate on 15 August and took office that same day. According to Interior Department historian Eugene Trani, McKennan suffered from a peculiar nervous temperament that made him unable to handle the affairs of the department. On 26 August, after just one week and four days as secretary, McKennan resigned. He had barely any or no influence over the direction of the department's policies.

Little is known about the remainder of his life. He died in Reading, Pennsylvania, on

9 July 1852, and was buried in Washington Cemetery, in Washington, Pennsylvania.

References: Sobel, Robert, ed.-in-chief, *Biographical Directory of the United States Executive Branch, 1774–1971* (Westport, CT: Greenwood, 1971), 224–225; Trani, Eugene P., "The Secretaries of the Department of the Interior, 1849–1969" (unpublished manuscript, National Anthropological Archives, Smithsonian Institution, 1975), 20.

ALEXANDER HUGH HOLMES STUART
1807–1891

Alexander Stuart served as the third secretary of the interior from 1850 until 1853 and set the tone of the department's policies for the next several administrations. Stuart was born in Staunton, Virginia, on 2 April 1807, the son of Archibald Stuart and Eleanor (née Briscoe) Stuart. Alexander Stuart was educated at the Liberty Hale Academy at Staunton, at the College of William and Mary, and at the University of Virginia, from which he graduated in 1828. He had studied law; he received his law license and opened a law office in Staunton the same year.

A Whig by political persuasion, Stuart supported the presidential candidacy of Henry Clay in 1832 and, four years later, Stuart was elected to the Virginia House of Delegates, where he served until 1839. The following year he was elected to the U.S. House of Representatives, where he served for a single term, and he was noted for his support of overturning the gag rule imposed on Northern congressmen who wished to present petitions for the ending of slavery.

Stuart did not hold office again until August 1850, when President Millard Fillmore asked Stuart to fill the vacancy in the Interior Department secretaryship left by Thomas McKennan's resignation. Fillmore knew Stuart, having served with him in the U.S. House of Representatives. As the third secretary,

Stuart spent much of his time, as chief of territorial and Indian courts, dealing with matters involving judges and clerks. In his 1852 annual report, Stuart wrote, "In former reports I have brought to your notice many other subjects which I regarded as of public interest. Among these were the establishment of an agricultural and statistical bureau; a revision of the laws relating to the fees of marshals, attorneys, and clerks of the circuit and district courts of the United States; an increase of the salaries of the judges of the district courts of the United States; the enlargement of the functions of the Attorney General so as to make him the head of the Department of Justice, and the transfer to that department of all matters connected with the administration of justice; the construction of a national highway through our own territory to the Pacific; the more precise definition of the duties of the several executive departments; and that provision be made for the appointment of a solicitor to the Department of the Interior."

In summing up his tenure, department historian Eugene Trani writes, "Stuart was the new Department's first Secretary to establish significant policies. He introduced a civil service system for judging subordinates. He standardized the procedures and attempted to clarify the responsibilities for each position in the Department. He appealed for a commission to insure the issuance of clear and free land titles and advocated outright sale rather than the leasing of mineral lands. He renewed the plea for the creation of an agricultural bureau and the appointment of a solicitor, begun by Ewing, as well as for a building to house the entire Department." In short, Stuart was the first secretary to establish a clear line of policies that he, as well as his successors, could follow.

Stuart served from 16 September 1850 until the end of the Fillmore administration on 4 March 1853. He retired to private life. In 1856, however, when the Whig Party disintegrated and the American, or Know-Nothing, Party emerged, Stuart took up the new organization's platform as his own. He supported the election of the Know-Nothing presidential candidate—his old boss, Millard Fillmore—that same year and published a series of letters, called the Madison Letters, which championed the doctrines of the new party. Decimated in the election, however, the Know-Nothings soon went out of existence. In 1857 Stuart was elected to the Virginia state senate, and he served as chairman of the committee that investigated the raid by abolitionist John Brown into Harpers Ferry. In 1861, Stuart was a delegate to the Virginia convention that met to decide on the issue of secession over the election of Abraham Lincoln. Although Stuart did not deny the right of the state to secede, he denounced such a move as leading the state down a path it would come to regret. During the Civil War, because of his age, he did not participate in the fighting, but with the end of the conflict he reached out to reconcile with the North; his pamphlet, *The Recent Revolution: Its Causes and Its Consequences* (1866), was meant to facilitate that process. He was a key figure in helping Virginia to avoid a carpet-bag government and to keep the majority white population from being disenfranchised. Stuart was elected to Congress in 1865 but, because he was a Southerner, he was not permitted to take his seat. In 1873, he was elected to a three-year term in the Virginia House of Delegates. His final work was as rector of his alma mater, the University of Virginia, from 1876 to 1882 and again from 1884 to 1886. As a trustee of the Peabody Fund from 1871 to 1889, he called on the federal government to assist in the education of African Americans in the South. He died in the house in which he was born on 13 February 1891 at age 83.

References: Abernethy, Thomas P., "Stuart, Alexander Hugh Holmes," in *DAB* 9: 160–161; *Biography of Alexander H. H. Stuart,* Alexander Hugh Holmes Stuart Papers, Box 2, Folder "1894-Robertson," University of Virginia at Charlottesville; *Report of the Secretary of the Interior, December 4, 1852* (Washington, DC: GPO, 1852), 48–49; Robertson, Alexander F., *Alexander Hugh Holmes Stuart, 1807–1891: A Biography* (Richmond, VA: William Byrd Press, 1925); Trani, Eugene P., "The Secretaries of the Department of the Interior, 1849–1969" (unpublished manuscript, National Anthropological Archives, Smithsonian Institution, 1975), 17–22.

ROBERT MCCLELLAND
1807–1880

During Robert McClelland's storied political career, he served as a congressman, governor of Michigan, and member of his state's constitutional convention. Yet his most important work, as secretary of the interior in the administration of Franklin Pierce, has been overlooked by historians. Born in Greencastle, Pennsylvania, on 1 August 1807, he was the son of Dr. John McClellan and Eleanor Bell (née McCulloch) McClellan. There is no record of when Robert changed the spelling of his name. He attended Dickinson College in Carlisle, Pennsylvania, in 1829 and, two years later, after some legal training, was admitted to the state bar. In 1833, he moved to Monroe, Michigan and established a law practice. He would be identified with Michigan for the rest of his life.

In 1835, after only two years in Michigan, McClelland was chosen as a member of that state's constitutional convention to prepare for statehood. He was active in organizing the new government and the Democratic Party in the state. Three years after his initial work, he was elected to the state legislature and served from 1839 to 1840 and in 1843; in 1842 he was elected to the U.S. House of Representatives, in which he served for three terms (1843–1849). After leaving Congress, he served as a delegate to the Michigan Constitutional Convention; he then ran for and was elected governor of Michigan, serving for just fourteen months, from 1852 until 1853. On 7 March 1853, McClelland resigned as governor to accept an appointment offered by President Franklin Pierce to serve as the fourth secretary of the interior. Pierce biographer Larry Gara writes, "Reform and honest administration also characterized the

Interior Department headed by Robert Mc-Clelland, another stickler for rules and procedure. McClelland, who was personally low-keyed and unobtrusive, was brusque and demanding in his official capacity. He headed a department consisting of four important operations—land, Indian, pension, and patent bureaus—with offices scattered around the city. It was also a department where opportunities for graft abounded. Still, he did what he could to make its operation responsible. He was overworked and under-staffed, and his was an almost impossible assignment. Although he introduced more orderly procedures and strict work rules within the department, the interests of land speculators and illegal settlers on public land, the thousands claiming a right to a government pension, unscrupulous Indian agents, and greedy railroad promoters all worked to undermine McClelland's reforms." Because of his reputation and hard work, McClelland is considered a luminary in a cabinet that included Attorney General Caleb Cushing, Secretary of State William Learned Marcy, and Secretary of War Jefferson Davis.

McClelland worked to bring the land possessions brought under the aegis of U.S. control in the recently fought war with Mexico to be placed under the land office's authority. In his annual report for 1854, McClelland wrote, "The business of the general land office has greatly increased, but had been conducted with vigor and ability. The surveys of the public land have progressed rapidly, and the necessary preparations, as far as appropriations will permit, have been made for extending them into the new territories." In his 1855 report, McClelland discussed the state of Native Americans, under the supervision of the department: "A liberal hand should be extended to them, and every means resorted to for their improvement and elevation. Moral and religious principles, and the arts of civilized life, should be taught to them." During his tenure, Commissioner of Indian Affairs George W. Manypenny negotiated fifty-two treaties with Indian nations involving 174 million acres of land, which cost $11 million. McClelland envisioned allowing the Na-tive Americans to live on reservations while teaching them work habits and Christian doctrine.

McClelland served for the entire Pierce administration, leaving on 4 March 1857 and returning to Michigan, where he worked as an attorney in Detroit. His final service was as a member the state Constitutional Convention in 1867. McClelland died on 30 August 1880, less than a month after his seventy-third birthday, and he was buried in Elmwood Cemetery in Detroit.

References: Gara, Larry, *The Presidency of Franklin Pierce* (Lawrence: University Press of Kansas, 1991), 61–62; "McClelland, Robert," in Robert Sobel and John Raimo, eds., *Biographical Directory of the Governors of the United States, 1789–1978* (Westport, CT: Meckler Books; 4 vols., 1978), 2: 745–746; Nichols, Roy F., "McClelland, Robert," in DAB 6: 586; *Report of the Secretary of the Interior [for the Year 1855]* (Senate Executive Document No. 1, 34th Congress, 1st Session, 1855) 121, 138; "Report of the Secretary of the Interior, December 4, 1854," in *Message from the President of the United States to the Two Houses of Congress, at the Commencement of the Second Session of the Thirty-third Congress* (House Executive Document No. 1, 33d Congress, 2d Session, 1854), 28–46.

JACOB THOMPSON
1810–1885

Jacob Thompson may be the most notorious man who ever served as secretary of the interior, whose actions lead some historians to believe that he was involved with the assassination of Abraham Lincoln. During the Civil War he served as a Confederate agent in Canada trying to sabotage the Union war effort. Thompson, the son of Nicholas Thompson, a tanner from Virginia, and Lucretia (née Van Hook) Thompson, was born at Leasburg, North Carolina, on 15 May 1810. Although his father wanted Jacob to be a minister, instead he attended the Bingham

Academy in Orange County, North Carolina and graduated from the University of North Carolina in 1831, remaining as a tutor for an eighteen months. He then studied law in Greensboro and, in 1835, was admitted to the state bar. The following year, he moved to Natchez, Mississippi, the state with which he would remain identified for the rest of his life. In 1837, he and his eldest brother, Dr. James Young Thompson, moved to Ponotoc, Mississippi, where Jacob opened a law office. In 1837, he entered the political field, running an unsuccessful race for state attorney general, but became a leader in the state Democratic Party before moving to Oxford, Mississippi. In 1838, Thompson ran for and was elected to a seat in the U.S. House of Representatives, where he immediately made his mark by becoming a member of the public lands and Indian affairs committees, rising to become chairman of both committees during his six terms (1839–1851).

In 1850, Thompson was defeated for reelection by the Whigs, and he returned to Mississippi. In 1853, President Franklin Pierce offered him the post of U.S. consul to Havana, but Thompson refused. Two years later, he ran for a U.S. senate seat, but was defeated by Jefferson Davis, a former secretary of war. For his support of the party, however, in 1857, Thompson was selected by President James Buchanan as secretary of the interior. Few sources deal with his selection, although it can be surmised that Buchanan, a states' rights supporter, desired to fill his cabinet with as many proslavery sympathizers as possible. Much of Thompson's tenure at Interior (1857–1861) dealt with the management of the public lands. Thompson wrote in his 1857 annual report, "In presenting an exhibit of the operations of this department, attention is first invited to the important and diversified interests connected with the administration of our public domain, respecting which the accompanying report of the Commissioner of the General Land Office furnishes interesting details, with a gratifying view of our extended land system. American legislation has shown its superior practical wisdom by its simplicity and adaptation to the wants of our people in its code of land laws, in regard to the improvement of which few suggestions can be made."

A year later, in the 1858 narration, Thompson wrote, "In the administration of the Interior Department, there is no subject of greater magnitude or of deeper interest to the people of the United States, than that of the public lands. Our system of disposing of them is the most just and equal, and, at the same time, the most conducive to their rapid settlement and reclamation from a wild and unproductive state, that has ever been devised by any government which has possessed extensive tracts of uncultivated land. It is a system peculiar to the United States, and is based upon the simple but just principle that, as the public domain is the property of the people of all the States collectively, any individual desiring to appropriate to himself any particular portion of it, is allowed to do so by paying into the common treasury a moderate consideration."

Following the election of Abraham Lincoln as president in 1860, secessionists in the South pushed to have their respective states separate from the United States in order to preserve slavery and their antebellum way of life. Thompson was a supporter of these plans. However, President Buchanan desired to head off a potential war between the federal government and American citizens, and to this end he sent a supply ship, *Star of the West,* to resupply the troops at Fort Sumter in South Carolina. Thompson received word of this action and demanded from Buchanan that it be recalled. Buchanan refused and on 8 January 1861 Thompson resigned as secretary, using his last public office to inform the people of Charleston, South Carolina, around Fort Sumter, that a ship was coming with troops and materiel. Two days later, the ship was blocked, leading to the firing on Fort Sumter on 12 April, setting off the Civil War. Thompson, who was replaced by Chief Clerk Moses Kelly, became the last Southerner to leave Buchanan's cabinet. Heading south, the former secretary became an aide to General P. G. T. Beauregard. Thompson later served under Generals John C. Pemberton and Stephen D. Lee. In 1863, he was elected to the Mississippi legislature.

In 1864, Confederate President Jefferson Davis named Thompson as the Confederate commissioner to Canada to help fleeing Confederate prisoners escape, and to use his power to disrupt the Northern banking system. To the latter end, he was given $200,000 and, within a year, had augmented that by $330,000 from Confederates who had stolen it from trains and banks in the North. In a 3 December 1864 dispatch to Secretary of State Judah P. Benjamin Thompson wrote, "Sir— Several times I have attempted to send you communications, but I have no assurance that any one of them has been received. I have realized no effort to carry out the objects the government had in view in sending me here. I had hoped at different times to have accomplished more, but still I do not think my mission has been altogether fruitless. At all events we have afforded the Northwestern States the amplest opportunity to throw off the galling dynasty at Washington, and openly to take ground in favor of State rights and civil liberty. This fact must satisfy the large class of discontents at home of the readiness and willingness of the administration to avail itself of every proffered assistance in our great struggle for independence."

While Thompson may have spent some of the funds set aside for him in his endeavors, much of it was left untouched, perhaps as much as half a million dollars. Some historians have suggested that Thompson may have met with John Wilkes Booth or some of his associates, and given them stipends to aid them in their assassination attempt on President Lincoln. When the Confederate government collapsed, Thompson fled to France with what money remained and lived in the elegant Grand Hotel in Paris. When former Confederate Secretary of State Benjamin, the only Confederate official to escape to Europe, approached him in Paris to retrieve the money, Thompson told him that the remaining funds were remuneration for his crops in Mississippi that were destroyed. Finally, embarrassed by Benjamin, Thompson gave him £12,000. Historians have attempted to figure out how much Thompson absconded with, but to no avail. In 1868, he returned to Mississippi, but was never arrested for his wartime activities. He purchased numerous land holdings in and around Oxford and Memphis, and became a wealthy man. In 1876, a congressional committee investigated whether he had stolen funds from the Indian bureau during his tenure as secretary of the interior, but the investigation closed with no finding of guilt. Thompson died in Memphis on 24 March 1885. He was called by some "the greatest scoundrel of the Civil War."

References: Oldham, Dorothy Z., "The Life of Jacob Thompson" (master's thesis, University of Mississippi, 1930); O'Toole, George J. A., *The Encyclopedia of American Intelligence and Espionage from the Revolutionary War to the Present* (New York: Facts on File, 1988), 447–448; *Report of the Secretary of the Interior [for the Year 1857]* (Washington, DC: GPO, 1857), 1; *Report of the Secretary of the Interior [for the Year 1858]* (Washington, DC: GPO, 1858), 1; Rosenberg, Morton M., "Thompson, Jacob," in David C. Roller and Robert W. Twyman, eds., *The Encyclopedia of Southern History* (Baton Rouge: Louisiana State University Press, 1979), 1232–1233; Schultz, Fred L., "Thompson, Jacob," in Patricia L. Faust, ed., *Historical Times Illustrated Encyclopedia of the Civil War* (New York: Harper & Row, 1986), 754–755; Sifakis, Stewart, *Who Was Who in the Civil War* (New York: Facts on File, 1988), 651–652; Wakelyn, Jon L., *Biographical Dictionary of the Confederacy* (Westport, CT: Greenwood, 1977), 410–411; The Thompson reports, in "A Leaf From History. Report of J. Thompson, Secret Agent of the Late Confederate Government," *New York Herald,* 25 July 1872, 8:, "The Confederate Archives. Jacob Thompson's Mission to Canada," *New York Herald,* 28 July 1872, 5.

CALEB BLOOD SMITH

1808–1864

Caleb Smith served as the sixth secretary of the interior for eighteen months, during the tumultuous first years of the American Civil War. His service is considered by historians mainly as a caretaker, for few initiatives or reforms were instituted during his tenure. Smith was born in Boston, Massachusetts, on 16 April 1808, and when he was six years old he moved with his parents (who have never been identified) to Cincinnati, Ohio, where he grew up. He entered Cincinnati College at age 15, and continued his studies at Miami University in Ohio, leaving after two years to pursue the law. He studied law under Oliver H. Smith in Connersville, Indiana, and remained there to practice. However, he soon became interested in the political field and, in 1831, joined with Matthew Hull to publish the *Indiana Sentinel,* a Whig newspaper. After just a year he left the paper and, in 1833, was elected to the Indiana state house of representatives for three terms (1833–1837, 1840–1841). In 1835, he was elected Speaker, and controlled a massive internal improvements bill to passage; he later served as chairman of the Committee on Canals.

In 1840, Smith made a name for himself in national Whig circles by helping William Henry Harrison, the Whig presidential candidate, win the state's electoral votes that year. Smith served as an elector at the same time. That same year, he ran an unsuccessful campaign for the U.S. House of Representatives, but two years later he was successful and served three terms (1843–1849), where he was a member of the Committee on Territories. After leaving Congress, he served on the Board of Commissioners, which adjusted claims against Mexico arising from the Mexican-American War. In 1851, he returned to Cincinnati and, three years later, became president of the Cincinnati and Chicago Railroad, where he served until 1859, when he moved to Indianapolis. In 1859, Smith was named head of the state delegation to the 1860 Republican National Convention, where he urged the unanimous support of his party for Abraham Lincoln. During the convention and the subsequent campaign, he remained a staunch supporter of Lincoln and Lincoln's election. Smith accepted the post of secretary of the interior in the new administration. However, he was not happy in this position. Writes historian Eugene Trani, "From his assumption of the office on 5 March 1861, [Smith] contemplated retirement. His health was failing and he found himself unsuited to the bureaucratic routine. After quickly dispensing departmental patronage to his political allies, he left the work of the department to John Usher, who obtained the newly-created post of Assistant Secretary. It is ironic that the Homestead Act, perhaps the most celebrated land legislation in American history, became law during the terms of one of the most inactive Secretaries of the Interior." The act itself, however, had little effect because of the Civil War.

In his annual report for 1861, Smith wrote, "The report of the operations of this department during the fiscal year ending June 30, 1861, will exhibit a diminished amount of business in some of the most important bureaus connected with the department. This is attributable mainly to the insurrection which has suddenly precipitated the country into a civil war . . . the decline of business has very sensibly affected the operations of the General Land Office. Official intercourse has been entirely suspended with all the southern States which contain any portion of the public lands, and consequently no sales have been made in any of those States. In all the northern States in which any of the public lands are situated the war has almost entirely suspended sales. The demand for volunteers has called into the ranks of the army and a large number of that portion of our people whose energy and enterprise in time of peace incline them to emigrate to the west and settle upon the public lands, thus laying the foundations of future prosperous communities and States. Besides, the ordinary channels of trade and commerce have been so obstructed by the war that the sources of income, from which the settlers upon the public lands have realized the means of purchasing, have been greatly diminished."

In his second and last report, in 1862, Smith explained, "It is a source of gratification that, while the social and commercial relations of the people have been greatly deranged by the civil war which rebellion has forced upon the country, in most of the loyal States the great interests of agriculture, manufactures, and commerce have been well sustained, and have returned remunerating profits for the capital and labor invested in them." In discussing the General Land Office, he wrote, "The demand for the public lands has continued to decline since my last report. The sales for cash have not produced a sum sufficient to pay the expenses of our land system."

In October 1862, when a vacancy opened up on the Indiana Supreme Court, a post Smith very much desired, he asked President Lincoln to name him to the post and, on 31 December 1862, Smith formally resigned and handed the department over to his assistant secretary, John Palmer Usher. Smith served on the Indiana Supreme Court until he suffered a fatal heart attack in his office on 7 January 1864 at the age of 55.

References: Department of the Interior, *Report of the Secretary of the Interior [for the Year 1861]* (Washington, DC: GPO, 1861), 1; Department of the Interior, *Report of the Secretary of the Interior [for the Year 1862]* (Washington, DC: GPO, 1862) 1; "Smith, Caleb Blood," in *DAB* 9: 244–245; Trani, Eugene P., "The Secretaries of the Department of the Interior, 1849–1969" (unpublished manuscript, National Anthropological Archives, Smithsonian Institution, 1975), 34–37.

JOHN PALMER USHER
1816–1889

John Usher was the first person to hold the title of assistant secretary of the interior (1861–1862), and he was the seventh secretary of the interior. A longtime Republican Party stalwart, he was also a respected attorney. Usher saw the department through to the end of the Civil War. Born in Brookfield, New York, on 9 January 1816, he was the son of Dr. Nathaniel Usher, a physician, and Lucy (née Palmer) Usher. John Palmer Usher received a common school education, then studied law under Henry Bennett in New Berlin, New York, and he was admitted to the bar in 1839. In 1840, Usher moved to Terre Haute, Indiana, where he opened a law practice and, while riding circuit, became a friend of another attorney—Abraham Lincoln.

In 1854, after serving a one-year term in the Indiana legislature (1850–1851), Usher, an antislavery Whig, left his party to join the fledgling Republican Party, founded that year in Wisconsin. In 1856, he ran an unsuccessful campaign for Congress as a Republican. In 1861, Usher was named attorney general of Indiana. Four months later, however, he resigned to become assistant secretary of the interior in the Lincoln administration. Although Usher was the assistant at the Interior Department, the secretary, Caleb Smith, put him in charge of many of the day-to-day activities, and it was in fact Usher who ran the department. When Smith resigned, Usher succeeded him on the first day of January 1863. Biographers Elmo Richardson and Alan Farley write, "The policies of greatest significance pursued by Usher came within the principal subjects of public lands, Negro colonization, Indian affairs, and the Pacific railroad." In his 1863 report, Usher's major concern was that he found the department's library in such poor shape that certain congressional documents on laws relating to the department's activities were missing or in-

complete, which "render wholly impracticable to carry the provisions of the joint resolution into effect."

Usher, while he was against slavery, was
not a Radical like most of the Republicans in
Congress, and he incurred their wrath. When
President Lincoln named Hugh McCulloch of
Indiana as the secretary of the treasury in
1865, Usher felt that it was inappropriate to
have two cabinet members from the same
state; on 9 March 1865, he submitted his resignation, effective 15 May. However, Usher
stayed through Lincoln's assassination, and
remained for a month into the administration
of Andrew Johnson. He then returned to
Lawrence, Kansas, where he served as chief
counsel of the Kansas Pacific Railroad; later,
when he was to become the president of the
railroad, the appointment was blocked by his
successor at Interior, James Harlan, who was
fighting with the railroad's eastern division.
Instead, Usher remained as the railroad solicitor, and worked in this capacity until his
retirement in 1880. He served as mayor of
Lawrence (1879–1881), and published *Reminiscences of Abraham Lincoln by Distinguished Men of His Time* (1885). Usher died
in Lawrence on 13 April 1889 at the age
of 73.

References: Department of the Interior, *Report of
the Secretary of the Interior [for the Year 1863]*
(Washington, DC: GPO, 1863), 20; "[Obituary:]
Hon. John P. Usher," *Lawrence Daily Journal,* 14
April 1889, 4; Richardson, Elmo R., and Alan W.
Farley, *John Palmer Usher, Lincoln's Secretary of
the Interior* (Lawrence: University of Kansas Press,
1960); Sifakis, Stewart, *Who Was Who in the Civil
War* (New York: Facts on File, 1988), 669; Trani,
Eugene P., "The Secretaries of the Department of
the Interior, 1849–1969" (unpublished manuscript,
National Anthropological Archives, Smithsonian
Institution, 1975), 38–43.

JAMES HARLAN
1820–1899

James Harlan's service as the eighth secretary of the interior was as brief as his two
predecessors. He spent most of his tenure
trying to eliminate corruption in the department. The son of Silas Harlan and Mary (née
Conley) Harlan, James Harlan was born in
Clark County, Illinois, on 26 August 1820.
Descended from George Harland, a Quaker
who emigrated from England to Ireland and
then to America about 1687, Harlan and his
parents moved to the settlement called New
Discovery, Indiana, when he was about four.
Harlan received an education in the small log
cabin school in Parke County, and then
taught in a district school for a short period
time. He attended Indiana Asbury University
(now DePauw University), and graduated in
1845. After marrying, Harlan and his wife
moved to Iowa and settled in Iowa City,
where he became a principal of a small college.

In 1847, Harlan, a Whig, began his political career when he was elected as superintendent of public instruction, but the election
was overturned. He read and studied law,
and was admitted to the state bar in 1850.
That same year, he refused a nomination by
the Whigs for governor. Three years later, he
served as the head of Iowa Conference University (now Iowa Wesleyan University),
where he served until 1855. Harlan was a
member of the Whigs' antislavery wing, but
in 1855 he joined the Free-Soil movement.
He was elected to the U.S. Senate as a Free-
Soiler. In 1856, he then joined the newly
founded Republican Party and in 1860 was
reelected to the senate as a Republican. He
became a vocal supporter of the Lincoln administration. His daughter married Lincoln's
son, Robert Todd Lincoln.

When Secretary of the Interior John
Palmer Usher resigned on 9 March 1865 Pres-
ident Lincoln named Harlan to the vacancy.
The Senate took up the nomination that

same day, and confirmed Harlan, who was to take office on 15 May. He wrote to Senator James F. Wilson of Iowa in late March, "I now intend to accept the office of Secretary of the Interior if I find I can get the pack of thieves now preying on the Govt. under its auspices out of power, otherwise I will not. I do not deem it my duty to lend my name to plaster over their corruptions. The prospect of effecting this is not very good, for it happens that some of the worst of these people have the President's confidence." With Lincoln's assassination on 14 April 1865, Harlan, by law, could not remain in the cabinet unless the president renominated him; however, Lincoln's successor, Andrew Johnson, renominated Harlan for the position; he was reconfirmed by the Senate and took office on 16 May.

In his fifteen months as Secretary, Harlan worked to eliminate graft and corruption from the department. Historian Eugene Trani writes, "He began the weeding-out policy he promised. Many pensioners, employed by the Department, were doing no work and Harlan dismissed them, accusing Usher of making unnecessary appointments. He replaced three bureau chiefs, and in one day relieved eighty persons of their jobs." Harlan was denounced in William Douglas O'Connor's 1866 pamphlet, *The Good Grey Poet: a Vindication*, for firing poet Walt Whitman. Harlan advocated further additions to the Homestead Law, and in his two annual reports explained how land sales were increased. Harlan was never much in agreement with the administration of Andrew Johnson. On 27 July 1866, he resigned, effective 31 October, in protest over the policies of the administration and was immediately elected to his old senate seat by the Iowa legislature. After the elections of 1866, however, there were charges of corruption in Harlan's handling of Interior affairs, including Cherokee land sales. These were never proved, but they were used against him in 1872 when he came up for reelection, and he was defeated by Republican William Boyd Allison.

Harlan tried to win a seat in the U.S. Senate in 1875, but he was defeated, because of alleged ties to the Crédit Mobilier corruption case. He was renominated in 1881, but withdrew, and he served as the presiding judge of the Alabama Claims Commission (1882–1886), which settled shipping and damage demands against England arising from the Civil War. Harlan died in Mount Pleasant, Iowa, on 5 October 1899 at age 79, and was buried in the Forest Home Cemetery. His statue in Statuary Hall in the U.S. Capitol in Washington, D.C., represents his adopted state of Iowa; the other statue to represent Iowa is that of another secretary of the interior—Samuel Jordan Kirkwood.

References: Brigham, Johnson, *James Harlan* (Iowa City: State Historical Society of Iowa, 1913); Department of the Interior, Office of Indian Affairs, *Report of the Secretary of the Interior, with Accompanying Papers [Report of the Commissioner of Indian Affairs]* (Washington, DC: GPO, 1866), 1; Ross, Earle Dudley, "Harlan, James," in *DAB* 4: 268–269; Trani, Eugene P., "The Secretaries of the Department of the Interior, 1849–1969" (unpublished manuscript, National Anthropological Archives, Smithsonian Institution, 1975), 44–48.

ORVILLE HICKMAN BROWNING
1806–1881

Orville Browning was named secretary of the interior in the midst of Andrew Johnson's fight against Congress over which members sat in his cabinet, in particular, Secretary of War Edwin Stanton. Browning's tenure as Interior secretary was limited in its effectiveness in an administration preoccupied by impeachment. Browning, the son of Micaijah Browning, a farmer, and Sally (née Brown), was born in Harrison County, Kentucky, on 10 February 1806. Little is known about his parents, and equally little is known of Browning's early education. He did attend Augusta College in Kentucky, but because of his family's poverty he was forced to leave early and never received his degree. He studied law for a time in Cynthiana, Kentucky, and, about 1831, after being admitted to the state bar, settled in Quincy, Illinois.

Browning quickly became a leader in that community and in 1842 was elected to a seat in the lower house of the Illinois state assembly, which emboldened him to contest, unsuccessfully, Rep. Stephen A. Douglas for a seat in Congress. Browning challenged Douglas again in 1850 and 1852, but was defeated each time. Although he was a close friend of Lincoln, Browning came from the more conservative wing of the Whig Party, and when the antislavery Whigs joined with the new Republican Party in 1854, Browning was hesitant. However, in 1856, he helped draft the state Republican platform and, in 1860, he convinced other delegates to the Republican National Convention that Lincoln was an excellent choice for the party's presidential nomination. When Senator Douglas died, Governor Richard Yates of Illinois named Browning to fill the remaining two years of his term. This tenure in the U.S. Senate was a disaster for Browning. Although at the start of the Civil War he wholeheartedly backed the policies of the Lincoln administration, he gradually came to see them as a disaster for the nation and considered the emancipation of the slaves to be wrong. His opposition to Lincoln led to the Democrats winning back the state legislature in 1862, and Browning was replaced by William A. Richardson. Browning remained in Washington, and established a law practice with former Secretary of the Interior Thomas Ewing. During this period, Browning developed a scheme to ship Confederate produce across the front lines to Union stores, so he and his fellow Southerners would make money. The end of the war ended any chance of this scheme succeeding.

With Lincoln's assassination and the harsh Reconstruction policies imposed on the South by the Republicans in Congress, Browning became a dissenter and a supporter of the policies of President Andrew Johnson, a Union Democrat. In May 1866, Johnson named Browning as his adviser on patronage. This was the first step in making Browning a close counselor in governmental matters.

On 27 July 1866 when Secretary of the Interior James Harlan, resigned Johnson named Browning, who had no experience in natural resources matters, as Harlan's replacement. His tenure, which lasted until 4 March 1869, is not considered one of the more important ones in the department's history. Eugene Trani writes, "While Browning headed Interior, new divisions, including the Commissioner of Education, were added and he found this was one of the largest and most confusing government Departments. In the normal patronage rush that followed his appointment, he attempted to release Radicals and replace them with friends of the administration. His installment of Lewis V. Bogy as Commissioner of Indian Affairs was controversial. The Senate did not accept the appointment and Browning, who thought Bogy valuable, made him a special agent for the distribution of goods to the Indians. The Senate asked about Bogy's status, an investigation followed, and Bogy left the department." Browning's three annual reports are not noteworthy. He discusses such matters as Indian affairs and proposed legislation with the sense that his recommendations would get through a Congress that, at that time, was moving to impeach the president over policy differences. Browning was perhaps Johnson's most loyal cabinet member, and during Attorney General Henry Stanbery's absence to argue for the president during the impeachment proceedings, Browning stood in as attorney general ad interim.

Browning left office with Johnson and the remainder of the administration on 4 March 1869, and spent the rest of his life in Illinois. As a member of the state's constitutional convention of 1869–1870, he strongly opposed granting suffrage to blacks. He later served as counsel for several railroads and acted as the lead attorney for the Chicago, Burlington, and Quincy Railroad in the *Granger* case, which came before the U.S. Supreme Court. Browning was 75 years old when he died in Quincy, Illinois, on 10 August 1881.

References: Baxter, Maurice, *Orville H. Browning, Lincoln's Friend and Critic* (Bloomington: University of Indiana Press, 1957); Pease, Theodore Calvin, "Browning, Orville Hickman," in *DAB* 2: 175–176; Trani, Eugene P., "The Secretaries of the Department of the Interior, 1849–1969" (unpublished manuscript, National Anthropological Archives, Smithsonian Institution, 1975), 49–55.

JACOB DOLSON COX
1828–1900

Jacob Cox was secretary of the interior for only eighteen months; he resigned to protest the civil service and spoils abuses of the Grant administration, joining the short-lived Liberal Republican movement in an effort to spur reform. The son of Jacob Dolson Cox, Sr., a contractor, and Thedia Redelia (née Kenyon) Cox, he was born in Montreal, Canada, on 27 October 1828 while his father was working on the roof of the Church of Notre Dame. The family returned to New York soon after. Cox's chances of a college education ended with the financial panic of 1837. Instead, he studied law while working as a clerk in a law office in New York City. In 1842, he decided to enter the seminary at the Oberlin Collegiate Institute (now Oberlin College) in Oberlin, Ohio, and received a bachelor's degree in 1851 and later a master's degree in 1854.

In 1851, Cox moved to Warren, Ohio, where he worked as a superintendent of the public schools there until he finished his legal training, and he then opened a law practice there. He worked for the election of Whig Party presidential candidate Winfield Scott in 1852, but, being from the antislavery wing of the party, joined the Republican Party when it formed in 1854. The following year he was a delegate to the state convention. In 1858, he was elected as a Republican to the Ohio state senate, and there became friends with other antislavery activists, including James A. Garfield.

With the outbreak of the Civil War, Cox resigned his senate seat and volunteered for military duty and was named as a brigadier general of volunteers, in charge of the enlistment and recruitment of Ohio troops. He fought in the battles of Antietam, Atlanta, Franklin, and Nashville and was promoted to major general, and led the Twenty-third Army Corps. At the end of the war, he was in North Carolina paroling captured Confederate troops. Returning to Ohio, he discovered that he had been nominated for governor by the Union Party, an amalgamation of anti-slavery Republicans and antislavery Democrats. Cox was elected over his Democratic rival, George Mayan, by more than 25,000 votes. In his single two-year term (1866–1868), Cox attempted to bridge the political divide between the Radical Republicans and the Unionists, who stood on a more moderate platform. In 1868, he refused a second nomination for governor and moved to Cincinnati to become a professor of law at the University of Cincinnati. He refused an offer from President Johnson to serve as the commissioner of the Internal Revenue.

In March 1869, President-elect Ulysses S. Grant offered Cox the position of secretary of the interior. Cox wrote back his acceptance, and on 5 March 1869 became the tenth secretary of the interior. Eugene Trani writes, "[Cox] advocated Indian reservations for any tribes who lived near white men and established a Board of Indian Commissioners from the clergy. He championed Grant's peace policy, but the policy largely failed because the white population steadily invaded Indian lands. The Secretary then suggested tribes be moved to reservations. He had the government pay Indian annuities in small bills, thus eliminating the middlemen who charged high percentages to change larger bills Indians had formerly received." In his annual report for 1869, Cox explained his chief concern, civil service reform, "It would seem that the remedy is in the hands of the executive and departmental officers; but practically, the custom has become so firmly established, that members of Congress are forced to yield to the importunity of their constituents, and are unable to get relief except by urging appointments and removals upon the executive departments. Thus public business is most seriously embarrassed and retarded, and changes are sometimes made because, in that way alone, does it seem possible to get room for the ordinary action of the administrative machinery."

Cox soon became embittered with the pace of civil service reform in the Grant administration and, although he was a good friend of Grant, decided to resign. On 5 October 1870, after just eighteen months at Interior, he wrote to Grant and submitted his resignation, "My views of the necessity of reform in the civil service have brought me more or less into collision with the plans of our active political managers, and my sense of duty has obliged me to oppose some of their methods of action."

Cox returned to Cincinnati, where he resumed his law practice. He became a leader in the Liberal Republican Party, which championed civil service reform, and for a time was touted as a possible presidential candidate to run against Grant in 1872. In 1873, after the collapse of the Liberal Republican movement, Cox moved to Toledo, where he was named as receiver of the Toledo, Wabash, and Western Railroad. In 1876, he was elected to the U.S. House of Representatives, but after just one term he became dissatisfied with the slow pace of reform and returned to Cincinnati. He became dean of the Cincinnati Law School, serving from 1881 until 1897, as well as serving as president of the University of Cincinnati from 1885 to 1889. After leaving public life, he spent his last years writing his memoirs, *Military Reminiscences of the Civil War.* He died while visiting in Magnolia, Massachusetts, on 4 August 1900, at the age of 71, and was buried in Cincinnati.

References: "Cox, Jacob Dolson," in Robert Sobel and John Raimo, eds., *Biographical Directory of the Governors of the United States, 1789–1978* (Westport, CT: Meckler Books; 4 vols., 1978), 3: 1211–1212; Department of the Interior, *Report of the Secretary of the Interior [for the Year 1869]* (Washington, DC: GPO, 1869), 25–26; Ewing, James Rees, *Public Services of Jacob Dolson Cox: Governor of Ohio and Secretary of the Interior* (Washington, DC: Neale, 1902); Hockett, Homer Carey, "Cox, Jacob Dolson," in *DAB* 2: 476–478; Martin, Edward Winslow, *The New Administration; Containing Complete and Authentic Biographies of Grant and His Cabinet* (New York: George S. Wilcox, 1869), 93–121; Trani, Eugene P., "The Secretaries of the Department of the Interior, 1849–1969" (unpublished manuscript, National Anthropological Archives, Smithsonian Institution, 1975), 56–61.

COLUMBUS DELANO
1809–1896

Columbus Delano was the longest-serving secretary of the interior since its establishment up until that time, holding that position from 1870 until 1875. In those years, serious abuses in the Office of Indian Affairs were uncovered, forcing his resignation and permanently staining his career. Delano was born in Shoreham, Vermont, on 4 June 1809, the son of James Delano and Elizabeth (née Bateman) Delano. James Delano died when his son was six years old, and he and his mother moved to Mount Vernon, Ohio, where he received a primary education. He read the law in a local law office, and in 1831, was issued a license to practice law. For a period of time, he served as the prosecuting attorney for Knox county, Ohio.

In 1844, Delano was elected to Congress as a Whig, in a strongly Democratic district that encompassed Knox, Licking, and Franklin counties. He served a single two-year term, preferring not to run for reelection. In 1847, he ran an unsuccessful campaign to become governor of Ohio. He then moved to New York City, where he became a member of the banking firm of Dunlevy & Company, which in 1850 became Delano, Dunlevy & Company. He returned to Mount Vernon in 1855, leaving no history of his life in New York. He worked as a lawyer and a farmer and, during the next five years, moved from the Whig Party to the new Republican Party, which suited his antislavery opinions. In 1860, he was elected as a delegate to the Republican National Convention, supporting Abraham Lincoln for the nomination for president.

At the outbreak of the Civil War, Delano was named commissary general of Ohio, in charge of supplying the soldiers with guns and other materiel. In 1862, he was defeated for a seat in the U.S. Senate, but in 1863, he was elected to a single term in the Ohio state house of representatives. In 1864, he was elected again to a seat in the U.S. House of Representatives, where he served for two terms (1865–1869) and became a member of the so-called Radical or antislavery wing of the Republican Party, and voted to impose harsh Reconstruction policies on the defeated South. In 1869 President Ulysses S. Grant appointed him commissioner of Internal Revenue, and he spent a year in that position uncovering massive whiskey frauds, which were blamed on him although he had nothing to do with them. Nonetheless, following the resignation on 31 October 1870 of Secretary of the Interior Jacob D. Cox, Grant named Delano to the vacancy, and he was confirmed by the Senate and sworn in on 1 November as the eleventh secretary.

During his nearly five years at Interior, ending on 30 September 1875, Delano tried to deal specifically with the problems affecting American Indians, utilizing the services of the Board of Indian Commissioners, which had been constituted under his predecessor, Jacob Cox. In his annual report for 1871, Delano explained, "The humane and peaceful policy which has been inaugurated by the Government in the conduct of Indian affairs for the past two years has been productive of gratifying results. The board of commissioners authorized by the law of April 10, 1869, composed of citizens distinguished for intelligence and philanthropy, and serving without pay, has assisted in withdrawing from the Indian service much that has been heretofore regarded as the source of evil and injustice, and which is supposed to have prevented the success of public measures intended as a means of civilization. The services of that board have exercised a wholesome influence in establishing the new policy, and its active aid and cooperation in carrying out measures of the Government in that behalf have been valuable to this Department." However, not all was as Delano portrayed. Eugene Trani writes, "The scandal which followed Delano from the Internal Revenue Service obliterated all constructive attempts in his earlier years at Interior. He also lacked the ability to circumvent schemers who tried to exploit the Department, and could not cope with the bureaucratic process." In August 1875, five commissioners from the Board of Indian Commissioners resigned, claiming that Delano had refused to remove a number of crooked suppliers from working with the department—suppliers they called the Indian Ring. In one case, investigated by Congress, the Red Cloud reservation was left virtually without food because of massive corruption. Although Congress did not implicate Delano directly in their inquiry, he was scolded for lax administration of the supply system. His reputation soiled, he resigned on 30 September 1875. An article in the *Nation* magazine stated, "He succeeded an honest and capable Secretary of the Interior, who resigned because he would not allow politicians to meddle with the affairs of the Department, and that he in turn resigned long after it was evident that he was not capable, and at a time when his going, unlike Secretary Cox's, added strength to the Administration by removing a burden."

Delano retired to his farm in Mount Vernon, Ohio, serving as the president of the National Wool Growers' Association and as a trustee of Kenyon College in Ohio. Delano died in Mount Vernon on 23 October 1896 at age 87 and was interred in Mound View Cemetery in Mount Vernon, Ohio.

References: Benton, Elbert J., "Delano, Columbus," in *DAB* 3: 217–218; Department of the Interior, *Report of the Secretary of the Interior [for the Year 1871]* (Washington, DC: GPO, 1871), 1; Department of the Interior, *Report of the Secretary of* the Interior [for the Year 1872] (Washington, DC: GPO, 1872), 3; *Investigation of Conduct of Indian Affairs,* House Report No. 778, 43d Congress, 1st Session [serial 1627], 1874; *Investigation of Indian Frauds,* House Report No. 98, 42d Congress, 3d Session [serial 1578], 1874; *Report of the Special Commission Appointed to Investigate the Affairs of the Red Cloud Indian Agency,* House Miscellaneous Document No. 167, 44th Congress, 1st Session [serial 1702], 1876; Trani, Eugene P., "The Secretaries of the Department of the Interior, 1849–1969" (unpublished manuscript, National Anthropological Archives, Smithsonian Institution, 1975), 62–67; Vickers, Dorothy P., *The Career of Columbus Delano* (master's thesis, Ohio State University, 1946); Waltmann, Henry G., *The Interior Department, War Department, and Indian Policy, 1865–1887* (master's thesis, University of Nebraska, 1962).

ZACHARIAH CHANDLER

1813–1879

Zachariah Chandler served as the twelfth secretary of the interior. Historian Eugene Trani writes, "Zachariah Chandler was a shrewd politician whose public life was surrounded by controversy." Born in Bedford, New Hampshire, on 10 December 1813, he was the son of Samuel Chandler and Margaret (née Orr) Chandler. Zachariah Chandler attended common schools in Vermont, then moved to Detroit when he was about 20, where, he opened a general store and invested in banks and land. He became one of the richest men in Michigan. This enormous wealth allowed him to run and win election as the mayor of Detroit, serving from 1851 to 1852. A gubernatorial race in 1852, as a Whig, ended in defeat.

In 1854, as he became increasingly conservative, Chandler was one of several Michigan politicians to call for an assemblage of antislavery Whigs to leave their party and form a new, antislavery political entity. Appearing at a convention in Jackson, Michigan, on 6 July 1854, they formed the rudiments of what would soon become the

Republican Party. In 1856, he attended the Pittsburgh convention that nominated the first national ticket for the Republicans, and Chandler was nominated for the U.S. Senate. He was elected the following January to succeed former Secretary of War Lewis Cass. Chandler aligned himself with the increasingly radical members of the Republican Party, who demanded an end to slavery at all costs. In March 1861, at the start of the Civil War, he was named chairman of the Senate Commerce Committee. A member of the Joint Committee on the Conduct of the War, Chandler sponsored legislation to have the federal government administer abandoned property of Southerners. He stated, "Without a little bloodletting, this union will not, in my estimation, be worth a rush." After the war, he supported the Reconstruction Acts, although he saw them as too weak on the Southern states.

In 1874, Chandler was defeated for reelection despite controlling much of the patronage for the state in Washington. He returned home to Detroit in January 1875, but President Grant asked him to accept a government position. There were rumors that Chandler would be named as the U.S. minister to St. Petersburg, or succeed Benjamin Bristow as secretary of the Treasury. However, following the resignation of Secretary of the Interior Delano, Chandler was offered the position, and he accepted, taking office on 19 October 1875. During his tenure, which lasted until Grant left office on 4 March 1877, he spent much of the time eliminating corruption that had flourished in the Interior Department during Delano's term of office. A month after Chandler took office, all of the clerks in the Patent Bureau were fired, for being involved in graft. In the Indian Office, Chandler refused to deal with so-called Indian Attorneys who were set up to represent Native Americans in official department matters but instead cheated them. He then sent an order to the Commissioner of Indian Affairs on 6 December 1875, "Hereafter no payment shall be made and no claim shall be approved for services rendered for or in behalf of any tribe or band of Indians in the procurement of legislation from Congress or from any State Legislature, or for the transaction of any other business for or in behalf of such Indians before this Department or any bureau thereof, of before any other Department of the government, and no contract for the performance of such services will hereafter be recognized or approved by the Indian Office or the Department." When Interior Department employees resisted carrying out Chandler's orders to fire en masse workers who the Secretary felt were not doing their job, Chandler received support from the president to fire anyone who did not carry out his orders, even career employees. Chandler's strict adherence to principle, even in unpopular decisions, earned him praise by historians of the department. Years after he left Interior, his successor, Carl Schurz, remarked that Chandler's actions in attempting to clean up the department and make its organization run better made his job far easier.

Although Chandler returned to Michigan after leaving government, he was not home for long. In 1878, the Michigan legislature elected him to the U.S. Senate to fill the vacancy left by the resignation of Senator Isaac P. Christiancy. Chandler had served barely a year when he died suddenly on 1 November 1879, six weeks shy of his sixty-sixth birthday.

References: Chandler, George, *The Chandler Family: The Descendants of William and Annis Chandler, Who Settled in Roxbury, Massachusetts, 1867* (Boston: D. Clapp, 1872), 818; MacDonald, William, "Chandler, Zachariah," in *DAB* 2: 618; Trani, Eugene P., "The Secretaries of the Department of the Interior, 1849–1969" (unpublished manuscript, National Anthropological Archives, Smithsonian Institution, 1975), 68; *Zachariah Chandler: An Outline Sketch of His Life and Public Services* (Detroit, MI: Post and Tribune, 1880), 20–37, 337–355.

CARL SCHURZ
1829–1906

Carl Schurz was the first foreign-born secretary to serve in the cabinet, and although caught up in many controversies in his life, he nonetheless was considered one of the finest secretaries of the interior. Carl Schurz, the son of Christian Schurz and Marianne (née Jüssen), was born in the village of Liblar, near Cologne, Germany, on 2 March 1829. Christian Schurz was a schoolmaster in Liblar, and his wife was the daughter of a farmer. Carl Schurz wanted to grow up to become a professor of history; he instead turned into a revolutionary. At age 19, Schurz became the student leader of a revolutionary movement to reform the government; he came under the influence of Professor Gottfried Kinkel, one of the leaders of the movement, and he took part in several battles against the Prussian authorities. He was nearly captured in one battle, fled to France, and eventually sailed for America, never to see his homeland again.

Schurz, who married a German woman while in Paris, settled in Philadelphia for a time before moving to Wisconsin. In 1856, he purchased a small farm and with his fiery rhetoric now aimed toward freeing the slaves, he joined the newly founded Republican Party. The following year, while a delegate to the Republican state convention, he was nominated for the post of lieutenant governor even though he could not speak much English and was not an American citizen. This point led to his slim defeat by 100 votes. In 1858, however, he campaigned in Illinois for Abraham Lincoln's abortive U.S. Senate race. A delegate to the Republican National Convention in 1860, Schurz was named to the committee that informed Lincoln of his presidential nomination; Schurz then campaigned for him. Lincoln appointed Schurz U.S. minister to Spain.

In his year in Madrid, Schurz worked with the U.S. minister to the Court of St. James, Charles Francis Adams, to secure support abroad for the U.S. government's position during the Civil War. Angered that the issue of slavery was not being discussed, he returned to the United States in January 1862 and, that April, resigned his ministership. He was appointed a brigadier general of volunteers, and was at the battles of the First Bull Run and Gettysburg, and eventually rose to the rank of major general. Following the war and the assassination of Lincoln, President Johnson asked Schurz to tour the defeated Southern states and report on conditions there. However, when Schurz recommended that no Southern state should be readmitted to the Union without granting the right to vote to the former slaves, Johnson suppressed the report, only releasing it when Congress demanded it.

In 1866, Schurz became the Washington correspondent for Horace Greeley's *New York Tribune;* after just a year, he resigned to become the editor-in-chief of the *Detroit Post,* then moved to St. Louis, where, with journalist Emil Preetorius, he founded the *St. Louis Westliche Post,* a German-language newspaper. In 1868, he was the keynote speaker at the Republican National Convention.

In 1869, Schurz was elected by the Missouri legislature for a term in the U.S. Senate. A reformer, he introduced a bill to establish a civil service system in the government to end patronage and corruption. Gradually, he parted company with many Republicans over their support for President Ulysses Grant, and, because he felt he could not support the Democrats, he decided that the formation of a new party was in order. In 1871, he was a key leader in the establishment in Missouri of the Liberal Republican Party. He served as the president of the convention in Cincinnati that nominated Horace Greeley for president and Governor Benjamin Gratz Brown of Missouri for vice-president. The election ended in Greeley's disastrous defeat, and the Liberal Republican Party collapsed soon thereafter. In 1876, Schurz backed the Republican presidential nominee, Rutherford B. Hayes, because he felt Hayes was in favor of civil service reform.

Hayes won the election, which gave the Republicans another chance to name the top posts in the government. Hayes offered Schurz a post in his cabinet. Historian Kenneth Davison relates that "Schurz . . . offered his choice of the Post Office or Interior portfolio, accepted the latter." On 25 February 1877, Hayes wrote to Schurz, "I do not, or have not desired to be committed on Cabinet appointments until the issue was reached. But it is proper to say that, if elected, it has for a long time been my wish to invite you to take a place in the Cabinet. I think it would be fortunate for the country, and especially so for myself, if you are one of the members of the Cabinet. I am not likely to change that opinion. The Interior Department is my preference for you. The Post-Office would come next." Schurz consented, and was confirmed on 10 March 1877 by a vote of 55 to 1.

In his first annual report, that for 1877, Schurz spent a considerable amount of time discussing a fire that had destroyed some of the Interior department offices in the Patent Building, and what should be done to ameliorate the situation for new offices. He wrote, ". . . all of the valuable records of the department were preserved, they having been stored in rooms that have proven practically fire-proof." Schurz is best known during his tenure for his Indian policy, which was very different than his predecessors.

In his 1878 report, Schurz went into great detail to outline this policy: "In my last annual report, I sketched a plan of an 'Indian policy,' the principal points of which were the following:

1. The permanent location of the Indians on a smaller number of reservations containing a fair proportion of arable and pasture lands;

2. Encouragement of agricultural and pastoral pursuits by the furnishing of agricultural instruments and domestic animals, and proper instruction by practical farmers;

3. The gradual allotment of small tracts of land to the heads of families, to be held

in severalty under proper restrictions;

4. The discouragement of hunting, proper restrictions as to the possession of arms and ammunition by Indians, and a gradual exchange of ponies for cattle;

5. The extension of the laws of the United States over Indian reservations, to be enforced by proper tribunals, and the organization of an Indian police;

6. The labor of white men on Indian reservations as much as possible to be dispensed with, and proper discrimination to be made in the distribution of supplies and annuity goods and the granting of favors between Indians who work and those who live as idle vagabonds;

7. The establishment of schools for the instruction of Indian children in the English language, the elementary branches of knowledge, and especially in practical work;

8. Sufficient provision for the wants of the Indians until they become self-supporting.

This plan, put forth without any pretension to novelty, seemed to meet with general approval, as far as public opinion expressed itself, and I firmly believe that its execution, if properly aided by Congress and not interfered with by the white population of the Western States and Territories, would, in the course of time, bring forth satisfactory results."

In his 1879 report, Schurz explained, "It is believed that the normal condition of the Indians is turbulence and hostility to the whites; that the principal object of an Indian policy must be to keep the Indians quiet; and that they can be kept quiet only by the constant presence and pressure of force. This is an error. Of the seventy-one Indian agencies, there are only eleven which have military posts in their immediate vicinity, and fourteen with a military force within one to three days' march. Of the 252,000 Indians in the United States, there have been since the pacification of the Sioux at no time more than a few hundred in hostile conflict with the whites." In his final report, in 1880, he concluded, "When I took charge of this department the opinion seemed to be generally prevailing that it was best for the Indians to be gathered together upon a few large reservations where they could be kept out of contact with the white population, and where their peaceful and orderly conduct might be enforced by a few strong military posts . . . more extensive observation and study of the matter gradually convinced me that this was a mistaken policy; that it would be vastly better for the Indians and more in accordance with justice as well as wise expediency to respect their home attachments, to leave them upon the lands they occupied, provided such lands were capable of yielding them a sustenance by agriculture or pastoral pursuits, and to begin and follow up the practice of introducing them among the habits and occupations of civilized life on the ground that they inhabited. It also became clear to me that the maintenance of the system of large reservations against the pressure of white immigrations and settlement would in the course of time become impracticable. The policy of changing, shifting, and consolidating reservations for the purpose above stated was therefore abandoned, except in cases where the lands held by the Indians were not capable of useful development, and other lands better adapted to their advancement could be assigned to them." Perhaps Schurz's most enduring legacy is his enlightened treatment of Native Americans.

Schurz left office on 4 March 1881, and returned to journalism. He purchased, with Henry Villard, the *New York Evening Post,* and became an important voice in American journalism. In 1892, he began writing editorials for *Harper's Weekly,* but this ended with his unpopular opposition to the war against Spain in 1898. Schurz supported Democrat William Jennings Bryan for president in 1900 because he was an anti-imperialist. Schurz died at his home in New York on 14 May 1906 after a week's illness at age 77. He was interred in Sleepy Hollow Cemetery in Tarrytown, New York.

References: Covering the Disputed Election, the End of Reconstruction, and the Beginning of Civil Service (New York: David McKay, 1964), 78–79; Davison, Kenneth E., *The Presidency of Rutherford B. Hayes* (Westport, CT: Greenwood, 1972), 96; T. Harry Williams, ed., *Hayes: The Diary of a President, 1875–1881* (New York: David McKay, 1964) (Hayes memo); Schurz, Carl (Frederic Bancroft, ed.), *Speeches, Correspondence and Political Papers of Carl Schurz* (New York: G. P. Putnam's Sons, 6 vols., 1913), 3: 403; Trefousse, Hans L., *Carl Schurz: A Biography* (Knoxville: University of Tennessee Press, 1982); Villard, Oswald Garrison, "Schurz, Carl," in *DAB* 8: 466–470.

SAMUEL JORDAN KIRKWOOD

1813–1894

Samuel Kirkwood was an Iowa farmer who had served his state both as governor and as one of its U.S. senators. When selected to serve as James A. Garfield's secretary of the interior in 1881, he was a respected politician known, as biographer Eugene Trani writes, "[for] his shapeless slouch hat, his loose-fitting, well worn-clothes, [and] his dangling cigar." Born in Harford County, Maryland, 20 December 1813, Kirkwood was the son of Jabez Kirkwood and Mary (née Alexander) Kirkwood, middle class farmers of Scotch and Irish backgrounds. Kirkwood's only primary education, according to a statement he wrote in 1887, was "received . . . at an Academy kept in Washington City [now Washington, D.C.] by John McLeod . . . my attendance ended when I was about fourteen years of age." Kirkwood then worked as a clerk in a drug store before returning to his family's farm. Financial reverses left the family destitute, and, in 1835, they moved to Richland County, Ohio, where Kirkwood worked as a teacher and deputy county assessor. He read the law, and was admitted to the Ohio state bar in 1943. From 1845 to 1849, he served as the prosecuting attorney for Richland County.

After serving as a member of the state convention of 1850–1851, which drafted the Ohio Constitution, Kirkwood moved to Iowa in 1855 to become a farmer and a miller. He joined the Iowa Republican Party in 1856, and was elected to the Iowa state senate. In 1858, he was named as the director of the State Bank of Iowa and, the following year, was nominated by the Republicans for governor of the state. In the general election, Kirkwood defeated Democrat Augustus Caesar Dodge by almost 3,000 votes and, in 1861, was reelected by more than 11,000 votes. During his term as governor, which lasted until 1864, Kirkwood attempted to solve a major crisis over a bankrupt state treasury and keeping the state in the Union. In 1863, he did not seek reelection, but three years later was elected by the state legislature to the U. S. Senate to succeed James Harlan, who had resigned to become secretary of the interior in the Andrew Johnson administration. Kirkwood served only a year, for in 1867 Harlan resigned and desired his old Senate seat back, and Republicans in the state legislature elected Harlan over Kirkwood. He then retired to his farm in Iowa.

In 1875, against his wishes, the state Republicans nominated him a third time for governor, and Kirkwood was elected. In 1877, he was reelected to the U.S. Senate. His term was cut short in 1881, when he left to become secretary of the interior. According to historian Theodore Clarke Smith, Kirkwood's name was not added to the list of potential cabinet appointees until 14 February 1881—less than three weeks before Inauguration Day. His name was not included because the other U.S. senator from Iowa, William Boyd Allison, was being considered for secretary of the Treasury. Once Allison declined, Kirkwood became a possible selection. On 28 February, however, Garfield completed his cabinet list—and Allison was selected for Interior. Allison again declined a cabinet post, and, on 5 March, the day after becoming president, Garfield sent to the Senate a list that included Kirkwood at Interior. Kirkwood's name was sent to the Senate on 8 March, and on that same day he was confirmed.

Kirkwood spent much of his time trying to reform the Indian bureau. Biographer Eugene Trani writes, "He requested increased funds for Indian education, instructed Indians agents to make frequent reports, and suggested that Indian reservations be reduced in size and number, but made permanent." Kirkwood's only annual report was issued in 1882.

After the death of President Garfield on 19 September 1881, Kirkwood offered his resignation, which was not accepted by President Chester A. Arthur, until 17 April 1882. When he left the Interior Department, he was 68 years old. He returned to Iowa, where in 1886 he was an unsuccessful candidate for the U.S. House of Representatives. Kirkwood died in Iowa City, Iowa, on 1 September 1894, at the age of 80, and was interred in Oakland Cemetery, Iowa City. He is commemorated by his statue, representing his adoptive state of Iowa, in Statuary Hall in the Capitol in Washington, D.C.

References: "Biographical Statement for World's Fair Biographical Dictionary," in Box 1, folder 19A, Samuel Jordan Kirkwood Papers, State Historical Society of Iowa, Iowa City; "Kirkwood, Samuel Jordan," in Robert Sobel and John Raimo, eds., *Biographical Directory of the Governors of the United States, 1789–1978* (Westport, CT: Meckler Books, 4 vols., 1978), 2: 432–433; Horack, Frank E., "Kirkwood, Samuel Jordan," in *DAB* 5: 436–437; Smith, Theodore Clarke, *The Life and Letters of James Abram Garfield* (New Haven, CT: Yale University Press; 2 vols., 1925), 1098.

HENRY MOORE TELLER

1830–1914

Henry Teller has been called "The Defender of the West" (a nickname given to him by his biographer, Elmer Ellis) because historian G. Michael McCarthy said that he was "an outspoken proponent of maximum land use all his political life, especially as Secretary of the Interior under Chester A. Arthur." Teller was born on his family's farm in Allegheny County, New York, on 23 May 1830, the eldest son of John Teller and Charlotte (née Moore) Teller. Teller attended local schools, as well as academies at Rushford and Alfred in New York. He taught school and, after reading the law in the office of a lawyer in Angelica, New York, was admitted to the New York state bar in 1858.

Teller moved to Morrison, Illinois, where he practiced law. In 1861, shortly before the Civil War broke out, he relocated to Colorado, a state with which he would be identified for the remainder of his life. A Unionist, he raised a militia in Denver for anticipated Indian attacks in sympathy with the Southern rebellion. After the war, he became a noted attorney in Denver, rising in influence as a corporate attorney and as a counselor for the Colorado Central Railroad from 1872 to 1876.

In 1876, when Colorado was admitted to the Union, Teller was elected to the U.S. Senate by the state legislature as a Republican. In the Senate, he was a staunch defender of western interests, calling attention to mining interests and public land use. He deviated from the Republican Party when he became a Silverite—someone who advocated coinage backed by silver rather than gold.

The resignation of Samuel J. Kirkwood on 17 April 1882 created a vacancy in President Arthur's cabinet. Many speculate that Arthur reached out to Teller because Teller was so widely respected in his stands on issues directly important to the West. Historian Eugene Trani writes that Teller initially supported the selection of the other senator from Colorado, Jerome Chaffee and when Arthur asked Teller to take the spot, "Teller was reluctant because of the commitment to Chaffee. Still, he accepted the appointment. Westerners were elated."

During his nearly three years at Interior, lasting until the end of the Arthur administration on 4 March 1885, Teller tried to deal with Indian attacks against settlers in the American West. In his annual report for 1882, Teller wrote that there had been "no disturbances among the Indians at this time, although during the past year there has been much dissatisfaction, and in some sections open outbreaks . . . these raids find the people unprepared for war, and the settler at his daily work is not prepared to cope with this wily foe, who is better armed than he." Teller formed an Indian school fund to pay for the education of Indian youth and established the Court of Indian Offenses. Regarding the former, he noted in his 1883 annual report, "An increased public interest has been aroused concerning the duty of the Government in this behalf. The success of attending all efforts in that direction, whether put forth by the Government or through the aid of charitable persons and associations, is most encouraging. The fact that the attempt to educate the Indian is not confined to a knowledge of books, but that the effort is being made to give him a practical education that will enable him to supply his own wants by his own labor, has won to the cause of Indian education many who saw but little advantage to the Indian in a literary education alone."

In regard to land matters, Teller asked Congress to rescind the Timber Culture laws, designed to protect timber from overuse, and preemption laws, which prohibited settlers from going on certain public lands. Teller overruled the commissioner of the General Land Office, allowing settlers to farm, cultivate and even settle on public lands that had been sectioned off, earning him wide criticism.

After leaving Interior at the end of the Arthur administration, Teller was again elected to the U.S. Senate, where he served until 1909. Serving on committees with interests important to the West, including Public Lands and Mining and Mines, he was the leading spokesman for the settler. As the Republican Party moved toward supporting the gold standard, Teller backed silver, and at the 1896 Republican National Convention he and other Silverites formed the Silver Republican Party. Many believed that the Democrats, to initiate fusion with the dissenters, would nominate Teller for president, but they turned to William Jennings Bryan instead.

Teller supported Bryan, who went down to defeat against Republican William McKinley. In 1898, Teller introduced the Teller Amendment to the war resolution against Spain, one that advocated a protectorate be made of Cuba until it could achieve independence. When the Silver Republican Party dissolved in 1900, Teller joined the Democratic Party. In the minority in his final years in the Senate, he was nonetheless considered an elder statesman. He left the Senate in 1909 at the age of 79, and returned to Colorado. Teller died at the home of his daughter in Denver on 23 February 1914 at age 84.

References: Ellis, Elmer, *Henry Moore Teller: Defender of the West* (Caldwell, ID: Caxton Printers, 1941); Ellis, Elmer, "Teller, Henry Moore," in *DAB* 9: 362–363; McCarthy, G. Michael, "The Forest Reserve Controversy: Colorado under Cleveland and McKinley," *Journal of Forest History* 70: 2 (April 1976), 80–90; Department of the Interior, *Report of the Secretary of the Interior for the Fiscal Year Ending June 30, 1882* (Washington, DC: GPO, 1882), 1; Department of the Interior, *Report of the Secretary of the Interior for the Fiscal Year Ending June 30, 1883* (Washington, DC: GPO, 1883), 6–7; *Message of the President of the United States, Transmitting [a] Letter of the Secretary of the Interior Relative to Pending Legislation Providing for the Opening Up to Settlement of Certain Lands in the Indian Territory* (Washington, DC: GPO, 1885).

LUCIUS QUINTUS CINCINNATUS LAMAR
1825–1893

It is often said that Lucius Lamar was the first Southerner to sit in the cabinet following the end of the Civil War; in fact, that honor goes to David McKendree Key, who was postmaster general in the cabinet of Rutherford B. Hayes from 1877 to 1880. Nonetheless, Lamar was an important judicial figure in the nation's history, whose service as secretary of the interior was an interregnum before his tenure on the U.S. Supreme Court. Born near Eatonton, Georgia, 17 September 1825, the son of Lucius Quintus Cincinnatus Lamar, Sr. and Sarah William (née Bird) Lamar, he was part of the landed aristocracy of Georgia. His father was a circuit court judge in Georgia who committed suicide in 1834. At that time, his mother moved with her children to Covington, Georgia, where she placed Lucius in the Georgia Conference Manual Labor School, a Methodist institution of higher learning. He graduated in 1841, and continued his studies at Emory College (now Emory University) and received a degree in 1845. He then studied law in his uncle's office in Macon, was admitted to the Georgia bar in 1847, and served as a professor of mathematics at the University of Mississippi at Oxford.

Inspired by the thinking of his father-in-law, the Rev. Augustus Longstreet, who was the president of the University of Mississippi, Lamar entered the political arena in Mississippi with strong states' rights and sectionalist stands. He returned to Covington to open a law practice with a friend but, in 1853, was elected as a Democrat to the Whig-dominated lower house of the state legislature. After serving for a single one-year term, he moved his law practice to Macon, Georgia. In 1855, after failing to win the Democratic nomination for Congress, he moved back to Mississippi. He bought a plantation called Solitude and with it numbers of slaves and became a gentleman farmer.

Less than a year later, however, he was nominated by the Mississippi Democrats for a seat in Congress on a states' rights and slaveowners' rights platform. Elected for the first of two terms, he used his first opportunity to speak before the House in support of Southern sectionalism. He was a delegate to the 1860 Democratic National Convention, supporting Senator Jefferson Davis of Mississippi for president. When moderate Senator Stephen A. Douglas of Illinois won the presidential nomination, Lamar and other Southerners walked out, leaving a split in the party which resulted that November in the election of Republican Abraham Lincoln. Lamar re-

signed from Congress in January 1861, to accept a position as a professor of ethics and metaphysics at the University of Mississippi. He attended the Mississippi Secession Convention as a delegate, and drew up the secession ordinance.

Lamar was made a colonel in the Nineteenth Mississippi Regiment and was at the Battle of Williamsburg in May 1862, but an acute case of apoplexy, which had affected him since childhood, removed him from further fighting. That November, Confederate President Jefferson Davis named him as the special Confederate envoy to Russia to encourage that nation to formally recognize the Confederacy. When Russia refused, Lamar spent his time shuttling between London and Paris trying to gather support for the Southern cause. He returned home in 1863, and spent the remainder of the war as an aide to Davis and as a judge advocate for the Army of Northern Virginia.

With the end of the war, Lamar was financially and mentally destroyed. His property was gone, two of his brothers had been killed in the war, and he was prohibited from holding a federal office. He returned to his position as professor of ethics and metaphysics at the University of Mississippi and then became a professor of law. He resigned in 1870 and opened his own law office. In 1872, he was elected to the U.S. House of Representatives, and he was granted a special waiver by the Congress to serve. Lamar became a spokesman for reconciliation among the North and South; with the death of Massachusetts Senator Charles Sumner, a foe of slavery, he delivered a masterly oration praising Sumner and asking for an end to hatred between the sections. Despite continuing opposition from Radical Republicans and Southerners who felt he had turned against all of his principles, Lamar was elected by the state legislature to the U.S. Senate in 1876.

The election of Democrat Grover Cleveland in 1884, the first of his party to win the White House since 1856, gave Democrats the first chance in thirty years for federal offices. Cleveland asked Lamar to fill the position of secretary of the interior to reward the former Confederate for his conciliatory attitude and to balance the cabinet geographically. Lamar accepted the position with "the best and highest interests of a common country." His appointment was criticized in some Northern circles, but in the end Lamar was confirmed by the Senate and served for three years at Interior. Eugene Trani writes, "A typical 'genteel liberal,' Lamar believed the key to the Indian problem was the elimination of corruption among Indian agents. He instituted proceedings to expel ranchers from lands they had leased from the tribes at minimal cost. He recommended tighter controls over land allotment, the disposition of tribal trust funds, and the improvement of Indian schools. A champion of the policy of diminished reservations and land allotment, Lamar believed that land ownership would teach the Indians individual responsibility and the habit of thrift." In his 1886 annual report, Lamar wrote, "The only alternative now presented to the American Indian race is speedy entrance into the pale of American civilization, or absolute extinction. In order to escape the latter and attain the former, three conditions of preparation are indispensable. The first is to get established in this race the idea and habitude of individual property-holding, through reliance upon its inviolability and a perfect sense of security in the enjoyment of its benefits. Second, an education of the entire mass of the youth of this race, embracing a thorough knowledge of the use of the English language in the daily affairs of life, arithmetic, and the mechanical arts among the males, and among the females the domestic arts in use with that sex. Third, a substitution of the universal operation of law among them in the enforcement of justice and the protection of person and property, and the punishment of crimes for the agencies of forces and superstition."

Lamar also dealt with the problem of public lands. In his 1887 report, he wrote, "Perhaps the most difficult and important duty with which this Department is charged is the administration of the public land system. The theater of its operations embraces nearly three-fourths of the area of the American States and Territories, and the vital influence exercised by the distribution of land ownership among the people renders the proper administration of the system of profound importance to the present and future prosperity of the country."

The death of Supreme Court Associate Justice William Burnham Woods on 14 May 1887 allowed President Cleveland to make his first Supreme Court appointment; Cleveland named Lamar, believing the Interior secretary to be an able administrator. Some Republicans sought to defeat the nomination, but, on 16 January 1888, Lamar was confirmed by a 32 to 28 vote, and took the oath two days later. During his service, 1888–1893, Lamar spent much of his time trying to learn the ways of the court. He wrote a friend in 1889, "I would be an impostor . . . if I were to allow you to believe that I am doing anything useful or even with moderate ability." The two most important opinions he delivered were *Kidd v. Pearson* (1888), in which he held that the definition of "commerce" excluded manufacturing, and *McCall v. California* (1890), in which he decided that interstate commerce was protected by the Constitution from state interference.

Almost from the time he began work on the court, Lamar's health began to fail. In early 1893 he suffered a series of strokes, and, on 23 January 1893, he died while visiting in Macon, Georgia, at age 67. He was originally interred in Riverside Cemetery, Macon, Georgia, but in 1894 was reinterred in St. Peter's Cemetery in Oxford, Mississippi. Lamar counties in Alabama, Georgia, and Mississippi are named after him.

References: Cate, Wirt Armistead, *Lucius Q. C. Lamar: Secession and Reunion* (Chapel Hill: University of North Carolina Press, 1935), 8–19; Department of the Interior, *Report of the Secretary of the Interior for the Fiscal Year Ending June 30, 1886* (Washington, DC: GPO, 1886), 4; Department of the Interior, *Report of the Secretary of the Interior for the Fiscal Year Ending June 30, 1887* (Washington, DC: GPO, 1887), 3; Halsell, Willie D., "The Appointment of L. Q. C. Lamar to the Supreme Court," *Mississippi Valley Historical Re-*

view, 28: 3 (December 1941), 399–412; Mayes, Edward, *Lucius Q. C. Lamar: His Life, Times and Speeches* (Nashville, Tennessee: Methodist Episcopal Church, 1896); Murphy, James B., *L. Q. C. Lamar: Pragmatic Patriot* (Baton Rouge: Louisiana State University Press, 1973); Pearce, Haywood J., Jr., "Lamar, Lucius Quintus Cincinnatus," in *DAB* 5: 551–553; Pride, David T., "Lamar, Lucius Q. C.," in Clare Cushman, ed., *The Supreme Court Justices: Illustrated Biographies, 1789–1995* (Washington, DC: Congressional Quarterly, 1995), 241–245.

WILLIAM FREEMAN VILAS
1840–1908

See Postmaster General, 1885–1888

JOHN WILLOCK NOBLE
1831–1912

Historian Eugene Trani writes of the eighteenth secretary of the interior, "John W. Noble was a prominent lawyer in late nineteenth century St. Louis. Although he was active politically, he held only one office—as Secretary of the Interior. What qualified a man of little political experience for a cabinet post?" Born in Lancaster, Ohio, on 26 October 1831, he was the son of John Noble and Catherine (née McDill) Noble. Raised in Miami and Columbus, Ohio, he attended local schools, then went to Miami College in Cincinnati for three years before going to Yale University to complete his education. He graduated from Yale with honors in 1851, having served as the editor of the *Yale Literary Magazine*. He returned to Ohio to study the law at the Cincinnati Law School and in the office of Ohio attorney Henry Stanbery, who later served as U.S. attorney general from 1866 to 1868. Noble was admitted to the Ohio bar in 1853 and opened a law office.

Noble moved to St. Louis in 1855 and his political stance became more radical. He moved from being a Free-Soiler to the Republican Party and, disgusted with the proslavery activity in St. Louis, moved to Keokuk, Iowa, in 1856. In 1859, he was elected to a two-year term as city attorney for Keokuk, and became one of the best lawyers in the state. In August 1861, he volunteered for duty in the Union army, and was enlisted in the Third Iowa Cavalry, seeing action in several southwestern battles and rising from lieutenant to colonel, eventually becoming the judge advocate general of the Army of the Southwest. In 1865, near the close of the war, he was brevetted a brigadier general for gallant and meritorious services. Following the end of the war, Noble returned to St. Louis and was appointed U.S. district attorney for the eastern district of Missouri in 1867. Over the next two decades, he became a prominent and successful attorney.

During his administration, President Grover Cleveland vetoed a number of pension bills for Civil War veterans, angering many former soldiers and helping Republican Benjamin Harrison to win the presidency in 1888. In forming his cabinet, Noble was Harrison's sole choice for the Interior Department. Historians Homer Socolofsky and Allan Spetter write that "[Noble] had established a unique reputation in the Gilded Age—he appeared to be incorruptible—the perfect man to deal with very sensitive issues that came under the jurisdiction of the Department of the Interior: namely, railroad land grants and pensions for Civil War veterans." Historian Harry Sievers adds, "Noble . . . enjoyed a 'high reputation of probity, learning and industry.' . . . His prosecution of the Whiskey Ring in St. Louis won him such admirers as Supreme Court Justice Samuel F. Miller and former Attorney General Benjamin Bristow. Before Harrison departed from Washington, Noble had accepted the office of Secretary of the Interior."

Noble served through the entire Harrison administration—from 7 March 1889 until 4 March 1893. Although he chiefly dealt with pensions, Noble also tackled the other areas inherent to the department—namely, public lands and the administration of Native American affairs. In his annual report for 1889, his first, Nobel wrote, "Your attention is first called to these as they successively occurred: the opening of Oklahoma; the successful negotiation of a treaty with the Sioux Indians of Dakota; and the advent into the Union of the four new States, North Dakota, South Dakota, Washington, and Montana, none having entered previously for thirteen years." In his 1891 annual report, he explained, "the years of the present administration have been marked to a notable degree by the expansion of the public domain for private settlement." Perhaps Noble's most positive contribution to land law was his support of the Forest Reserve Act of 1891, which allowed the president to set aside forest reserves to be made into national parks.

Noble left office after Harrison's defeat in 1892 and returned to a lucrative law practice in St. Louis. Nobel was sick for a month before he succumbed on 22 March 1912 at the age of 70.

References: Barclay, Thomas S., "Noble, John Willock," in *DAB* 7: 539–540; Department of the Interior, *Report of the Secretary of the Interior for the Fiscal Year Ending June 30, 1889* (Washington, DC: GPO, 1889), 3; Department of the Interior, *Report of the Secretary of the Interior for the Fiscal Year Ending June 30, 1891* (Washington, DC: GPO, 1891), 3; Forest reserve information in Hage, Wayne, *Storm over Rangelands: Private Rights in Federal Lands* (Bellevue, WA: Free Enterprise Press, 1989), 96–98; Sievers, Harry J., *Benjamin Harrison, Hoosier President: The White House and After* (Indianapolis: Bobbs-Merrill, 1968), 19; Socolofsky, Homer E., and Allan B. Spetter, *The Presidency of Benjamin Harrison* (Lawrence: University Press of Kansas, 1987), 27; Trani, Eugene P., "The Secretaries of the Department of the Interior, 1849–1969" (unpublished manuscript, National Anthropological Archives, Smithsonian Institution, 1975), 110.

MICHAEL HOKE SMITH
1855–1931

Hoke Smith was a giant in Georgia politics, rising to serve as governor and as a U.S. senator from the state; the *New York Times* said of him upon his death, "Senator Smith's record is one of the most brilliant in Southern statesmanship." He was born on 2 September 1855 in Newton, North Carolina, the son of Hosea Hildreth Smith, a teacher and native of New Hampshire, and Mary Brent (née Hoke) Smith, a graduate of Dartmouth College. Hosea Smith conducted much of his son's schooling, and Smith did not attend college but, after studying law in the offices of Collier, Mynatt, & Collier in Atlanta, he was admitted to the Georgia bar in 1873.

Smith then taught school for a short time, but eventually he opened a law practice in Atlanta, which became one of the state's most prestigious firms. He joined the Fulton County (Atlanta) Democratic Committee and, in 1887, he purchased the *Atlanta Journal,* which he turned into a Democratic organ. In 1888, and again in 1892, he supported the Democratic presidential candidate, President Grover Cleveland. A delegate to the 1892 Democratic National Convention, Smith helped carry the state in a victorious campaign.

On 15 February 1893, two weeks before the inauguration, Cleveland chose Smith as secretary of the interior. Although he was a fervent supporter of the president, Smith was not well known to Cleveland. The *Washington Post,* discussing Smith's appointment, reported that Smith had not spoken with Cleveland about a cabinet post until the day of the selection. Nominated on 6 March, Smith was unanimously confirmed, and he took office the same day. He was one of three Southerners in Cleveland's second cabinet, including Hilary A. Herbert at the Navy Department and Walter Q. Gresham at the State Department. Of his tenure, which lasted almost the entire second Cleveland administration (1893–1897), historian Eugene Trani writes, "Smith concentrated on several areas during his Secretaryship: the pension system, Indian affairs, public domain, railroads, and conservation. One of his first acts was to annul the rule that allowed pensioners with minor injuries, not of service origin, to collect money. He established a board of revision in the Pension Bureau, which lowered many benefits or dropped names from the pension rolls and this arrested the spiraling costs of the pension system. These reforms were not popular and many attacked Smith." Smith also concentrated on the affairs of Native Americans. In his 1894 report, Smith wrote, "The work of the Indian bureau becomes more interesting as it is better understood. Its task is that of developing a people no longer savage, but still far from civilized, into beings fit for American citizenship and capable of self-support. . . . I urge a treatment of Indian land based solely upon the purpose of realizing from it for the owners the highest possible value. What is best for the Indians—to keep their land or to sell it?" Although he served an entire four-year term as secretary, Smith's tenure is little recognized.

A backer of Grover Cleveland and the more conservative wing of the Democratic party, Smith was angered when the Democrats nominated William Jennings Bryan for president in 1896. Bryan, who backed the issuance of silver over gold monetary reserves, was at odds with many in his party. To show his indignation at the nomination Smith resigned from the government on 1 September 1896. He returned to Georgia, where he became the editor of the *Atlanta Journal,* in whose pages he took a prosegregation and antiblack stance. In 1900, he sold the paper. In 1906, he became a candidate for governor of Georgia and won the Democratic nomination. Capturing the Democratic nomination was enough to be elected; the Republican opposition was purely token. Smith sought reelection in 1908, but was defeated by Democrat Joseph Mackey Brown. Two years later, however, Smith ran against Brown again and won. Assuming the governorship a

second time, in July 1911, he was then elected by the state legislature to the U.S. Senate seat vacated by former Governor Joseph Meriwether Terrell. Smith did not resign as governor until 15 November, then headed to Washington. In his two terms in the Senate, Smith made education his key priority. He was a cosponsor of the Smith-Lever Act, which brought educational agricultural programs under federal control, the Smith-Hughes Act, which allocated federal funds for vocational education, and the Smith-Sears Act, which allowed for vocational education in the armed forces.

A close ally of President Woodrow Wilson in his first years in the Senate, Smith gradually became disillusioned with the more liberal Wilson and by 1919 was in full revolt against the administration, having voted against wartime legislation advocated by Wilson that Smith felt violated civil liberties. When Smith opposed Wilson on American entry into the League of Nations, the split was final. Smith lost his seat in 1920, when he was defeated by fellow Democrat and segregationist Tom Watson, but remained in Washington until 1924 as a lawyer and lobbyist. He then returned to Atlanta, where he continued to work almost until his death. Smith died in Atlanta on 27 November 1931 at the age of 76 and was buried in Oakland Cemetery in Atlanta

References: Carageroge, Ted, "An Evaluation of Hoke Smith and Thomas E. Watson as Georgia Reformers" (Ph.D. dissertation, University of Georgia, 1963); Department of the Interior, *Report of the Secretary of the Interior for the Fiscal Year Ending June 30, 1894* (Washington, DC: GPO, 1894), 3; Department of the Interior, *Report of the Secretary of the Interior for the Fiscal Year Ending June 30, 1896* (Washington, DC: GPO, 1896), 3; Grantham, Dewey W., Jr., *Hoke Smith and the Politics of the New South* (Baton Rouge: University of Louisiana Press, 1958); "The New Secretary of the Interior," *American Law Review* 27 (1893); "Smith, Hoke," in Robert Sobel and John Raimo, eds., *Biographical Directory of the Governors of the United States, 1789–1978* (Westport, CT: Meckler Books; 4 vols., 1978), 1: 310–311; Trani, Eugene P., "The Secretaries of the Department of the Interior, 1849–1969" (unpublished manuscript, National Anthropological Archives, Smithsonian Institution, 1975), 116; Vinson, J. Chalmers, "Hoke Smith, Cleveland's Secretary of the Interior" (master's thesis, University of Georgia, 1944).

DAVID ROWLAND FRANCIS
1850–1927

David Francis's tenure as secretary of the interior lasted seven months, from September 1896 to March 1897, and is little noted in the histories of the department. Born in Richmond, Kentucky, on 1 October 1850, he was the son of John Broaddus Francis, a sheriff, and Eliza Caldwell (née Rowland) Francis. David Francis received his primary education in the Academy for Girls. Francis attended Washington University in St. Louis, and he graduated with a bachelor's degree in 1870. Desiring to study the law, but unable to find the funds, he returned to the family farm. A short time later his uncle, David Pitt Rowland, got him a job as a clerk in the St. Louis merchant house of Shyrock & Rowland. Within six years, Francis had saved enough money to open his own merchant business, D. R. Francis & Brother, Grain Merchants.

Francis became the president of the Merchants' Exchange in 1884, and he decided to enter the political arena. That same year, he was selected as a delegate-at-large to the Democratic National Convention in Chicago, which nominated New York governor Grover Cleveland for president. Francis returned home, and was nominated by the Democrats for mayor of St. Louis. He was elected and served a four-year term. His administration was highly regarded as efficient and free from corruption, and at the end of his term he was nominated by the Democrats for governor of Missouri. On 6 November 1888, Francis was elected governor over Republican E. E. Kimball. In his four-year term, from 1889 to 1893, Francis helped establish a board of mediation and arbitration to end strikes and the Barnes Medical School. Francis was constitutionally prohibited from running for a second term, and he left office on 9 January 1893. He returned to his merchant firm in St. Louis.

On 22 August 1896, President Cleveland, who had been elected in 1892, accepted the resignation of Secretary of the Interior Hoke Smith, to be effective on 31 August. In 1895, upon the resignation of Postmaster General Wilson Bissell, Cleveland had desired to name Francis to the vacancy, but Francis turned down the opportunity. Francis was in Washington, D.C., on the day Smith resigned, and after meeting with Secretary of the Treasury John G. Carlisle, rumors rose that Francis would take the position. On 24 August, President Cleveland announced his selection of Francis for the post. Press reaction was favorable—many saw Francis as a "sound money man" from the more conservative wing of the Democratic party. Although he was sworn in on 1 September, Francis's nomination was not forwarded to the Senate until 8 December. On 18 January he was confirmed and served the remainder of his term, leaving office on 4 March. In his 1896 annual report, he briefly outlined his vision of the department, assured that few if any of these recommendations would be taken up by his successor. He wrote, "The brief time that has elapsed since I assumed this trust has not admitted of my becoming thoroughly familiar with its duties and opportunities, but its importance and possibilities have so impressed and interested me that I have given to it all the time and thought at my command." Because of his support of a gold standard, and his opposition to a silver standard, Francis did not support the Democrats' nominee for president in 1896, William Jennings Bryan, and for this he was excluded from the political scene in Missouri for more than a decade after he left office.

At the 1908 Democratic National Convention in Denver, Francis spoke to the delegates and declared that the issue of a silver standard instead of gold was dead and nominated Bryan for the presidency. Francis was offered the second spot on the ticket, but he refused. In 1910, he was a candidate for the U.S. Senate, but was defeated in the Democratic primary by James A. Reed. In 1916, President Woodrow Wilson named Francis U.S. ambassador to Russia, where he served during the collapse of the czarist government, the installation and short life of the government of Alexandr Kerensky, and the commencement of Lenin's Bolshevik regime. He also used his office to aid German and Austrian prisoners of war held in Russia during World War I. On 6 November 1918 he collapsed and was removed by stretcher to an American warship and taken to London for an operation, from which he never fully recovered. He returned to St. Louis, but was in ill health for nearly a decade. He finally succumbed on 15 January 1927 at the age of 76.

References: "Francis, David Rowland," in Robert Sobel and John Raimo, eds., *Biographical Directory of the Governors of the United States, 1789–1978* (Westport, CT: Meckler Books; 4 vols., 1978), 2: 855–56; Pusateri, Cosmo Joseph, "A Businessman in Politics: David R. Francis, Missouri Democrat," (master's thesis, St. Louis University, 1965); *Report of the Secretary of the Interior [For 1896]* (Washington, DC: GPO, 1896), 3–4; Stevens, Walter B., "Francis, David Rowland," in *DAB* 3: 577–578.

CORNELIUS NEWTON BLISS
1833–1911

Cornelius Bliss was a longtime Republican insider, serving as treasurer of the party for many years while he made a living as a successful New York merchant. He entered politics only once—to serve from 1897 to 1899 as secretary of the interior. Bliss, the son of Asahel Newton Bliss and Irene Borden (née Luther) Bliss, was born in Fall River, Massachusetts, on 26 January 1833. His father died when he was very young, and his mother remarried and moved to Louisiana. Cornelius stayed with his maternal grand-

mother in Fall River, where he attended Fisher's Academy. In 1847, he moved to New Orleans, where he worked in his stepfather's dry goods store before he became dissatisfied and returned to Massachusetts after just a year, settling in Boston. He went to work for the dry goods proprietor J. M. Beebe, and began a long career in the dry goods business.

In 1866, Bliss became a partner in the dry goods and milling firm of J. S. and E. Wright of Boston, eventually becoming the head of their New York office. the company was restructured as Wright, Bliss, and Fabyan, and, when the Wright brothers died, Bliss became the head of the company, serving in that capacity until his death. Bliss also became involved in politics and was named to the New York Chamber of Commerce in 1871. He soon became a leading New York member of the Republican Party. While he refused offers to run for mayor of New York City or governor of the state, he did serve as chairman of the Republican State Committee from 1887 to 1888 and, after refusing a cabinet post in the Benjamin Harrison administration, served as treasurer of the Republican National Committee from 1892 until 1904.

Upon his election as president in November 1896, William McKinley offered Bliss the position of secretary of the Treasury in his new cabinet. Bliss refused. Historian Lewis Gould writes, "New Yorkers pressed forward for a cabinet slot and competed with equal intensity for the coveted ambassadorship to the Court of St. James in London. Seeking a middle ground, McKinley first offered a portfolio, perhaps Secretary of the Navy, to Cornelius Bliss in early January. Acceptable to both extremes but close to neither, Bliss, a veteran fund raiser for the party, was an adroit choice, but his wife's health and his own business commitments led him to decline. . . . To recognize the West, McKinley thought of an old friend from the House, federal judge Joseph McKenna of California, for the Interior Department. . . . [When McKenna's religion collided with Interior's Indian policy], McKinley switched McKenna to the Justice Department and then began to try to find a New Yorker for the Interior Department. the place was offered to John J. McCook, a friend of McKinley's who was a Manhattan corporation lawyer and a busy backstage presence in the GOP. He said no, and on March 3, under the urging of McKinley and friends such as Elihu Root, Bliss reconsidered and came in as secretary of the Interior." Bliss was nominated and confirmed on 5 March 1897, and took office the same day.

During his nearly two-year long tenure, Bliss concentrated in two specific areas: forestry and Native American affairs. Eugene Trani writes, "The new Secretary heralded in 1897 a law to prevent forest fires on the public domain by the use of preventative measures. He called for a separate Forest Bureau, bolstered by additional appropriations, and in 1898 received these funds. For the first time, there was an adequate forest system with a graded force of officers in control." Bliss also continued to oversee the rapid expansion of the department that had started with his predecessors. In his 1898 report, he discussed the Indian situation. "The progress of the Indians during the past year, in civilization as well as education, has been gradual, though substantial. There has been but one disturbance or outbreak of a serious character, and that was among the Chippewa Indians of Minnesota. It was of very recent occurrence, however, and happily has been suppressed." Bliss, however, came to dislike the day-to-day management of the Interior Department and by early 1899 was prepared to leave office and return to his private business. Assured that he would be succeeded by the highly regarded Ethan Hitchcock, Bliss resigned on 19 February 1899. He returned to New York, where he continued to work as the Republican treasurer. In 1900, Vice-president Garret Hobart died, and McKinley asked Bliss to run with him as vice-president in the national election that year. Bliss declined, and New York Governor Theodore Roosevelt was selected instead. Bliss and Roosevelt formed a congenial relationship, and Bliss handled Roosevelt's campaign for election in 1904.

In the final years of his life, Bliss worked as president of the Fourth National Bank, and director of the Central Trust Company and director of the Equitable Life Assurance Society. He died at his home in New York City on 9 October 1911 at age 78.

References: "Bliss, Cornelius Newton," in *NCAB* 11: 15–16; Churchill, Allen L., "Bliss, Cornelius Newton," in *DAB* 1: 369; Gould, Lewis L., *The Presidency of William McKinley* (Lawrence: University Press of Kansas, 1980), 16; Trani, Eugene P., "The Secretaries of the Department of the Interior, 1849–1969" (unpublished manuscript, National Anthropological Archives, Smithsonian Institution, 1975), 124–127.

ETHAN ALLEN HITCHCOCK
1835–1909

Ethan Hitchcock served as secretary of the interior from 20 February 1899 to 4 March 1907. His tenure was marked by efforts to eliminate fraud and waste in the department. The son of Henry Hitchcock and Anne (née Erwin) Hitchcock, Ethan Allen Hitchcock was born in Mobile, Alabama, on 19 September 1835. He was a grandson of the Revolutionary War hero Ethan Allen, and nephew of the Civil War general Ethan Allen Hitchcock. His father, Henry Hitchcock, was a Vermonter by birth who moved to Alabama, became a noted attorney, and rose to become chief justice of the Alabama Supreme Court. During the financial panic of 1837, Henry Hitchcock became ill and died, and his widow and her two sons moved, first to New Orleans, Louisiana, and then to Nashville, Tennessee, where the two boys attended school. Ethan completed his studies at a private military academy in New Haven, Connecticut, in 1855. He then returned to his family, who were now in St. Louis, and he began to work in the mercantile business. In 1860, he was hired by the St. Louis firm of Olyphant & Company to head their office in Hong Kong, and he moved to China. In

1866, Hitchcock became a partner in the firm, and in 1872, he retired with a sizable fortune.

Hitchcock then spent the next two years traveling in Europe, and then returned to the United States, where he began a career as the president of several manufacturing, mining, and railway companies. He was not involved in politics, instead becoming one of the leading businessmen in St. Louis. On 16 August 1897, President William McKinley appointed him envoy extraordinary and minister plenipotentiary to Russia to advance American trade interests. the following year, the mission in Russia became an embassy and, on 11 February 1898, Hitchcock became ambassador extraordinary and minister plenipotentiary to St. Petersburg, where he served as the first American diplomat to the court of the Czars.

On 21 December 1898, following Secretary of the Interior Cornelius Bliss's resignation, President McKinley named Hitchcock to the position. The Senate confirmed him the same day, even though Hitchcock was in Russia. He did not sail for home until January, and on 20 February 1899 he took office at Interior. During his tenure, which lasted until 4 March 1907, the second longest at eight years two weeks, Hitchcock became well known for his prosecution of land frauds and aid to American Indian tribes. In many ways, Hitchcock was the most successful secretary in the department's first half century. Historian Eugene Trani explains, "Interested in the Indians, he fought to preserve oil and gas lands as well as valuable mineral and timber cutting rights on lands of the Five Tribes, when threatened by corporate interests. He defended them before the Senate Select Committee on Affairs in the Indian Territory. . . . the Newlands Reclamation Act of 1902 became law during his term, though he had little to do with its passage. . . . There also was scandal in the department. Hitchcock came to believe individuals were robbing the government of lands and resources, and he instituted an intensive investigation. With Theodore Roosevelt's full support, he dismissed Land Commissioner Binger Herman—who had attempted to cover fraud by asking for the abolition of all forest preserves . . . over one thousand people were [eventually] indicted, in twenty states, for timber and land frauds. When Hitchcock left office, convictions numbered one hundred and twenty-six." With Hitchcock's approval, forestry was placed under the jurisdiction of the Department of Agriculture, where it remains to this day.

In a document prepared by the department describing "the activities of Hon. E. A. Hitchcock during his incumbency of the office of the Secretary of the Interior," the following were put forth as Hitchcock's main goals during his tenure: "First: Prosecution of grafters, meaning thereby those who sought to defraud the Government of its public lands. Second: Prosecution of those maintaining unlawful inclosures of public lands, under the act of February 25, 1885, known as 'the Fence Law.' Third: Securing amendments to existing legislation, such for instance as the law in relation to the disposal of the ceded Chippewa lands in Minnesota, so as to render more equitable the administration of said laws, with resultant greater benefits to the Indians. Fourth: the allotment of lands in existing Indian reservations to the Indians under the general allotment act or under special laws passed for the purpose, and the restoration of the unallotted lands to the public domain and to disposition under the homestead and other public land laws."

Never close to Roosevelt, and not a member in the president's "tennis cabinet" of close advisers, he ruthlessly went about prosecuting land frauds. When the frauds reached into Congress, and implicated leading Republicans, Hitchcock exposed them regardless of party. Roosevelt needed these Republicans to pass his domestic legislation and Hitchcock was persuaded to leave on 3 December 1906, with his resignation to take effect on 4 March 1907. Hitchcock retired in Washington. On 9 April 1909, almost exactly two years after leaving Interior, he died following a trip to the western United States in which he contracted a severe cold, although the final cause of death was heart failure.

Hitchcock, who was 74, was buried in the Bellefontaine Cemetery in St. Louis.

References: Barclay, Thomas S., "Hitchcock, Ethan Allen," in *DAB* 5: 74–75; Department of the Interior, *Report of the Secretary of the Interior for the Fiscal Year Ended June 30, 1899* (Washington, DC: GPO, 1899), 3; Department of the Interior, *Report of the Secretary of the Interior for the Fiscal Year Ended June 30, 1900* (Washington, DC: GPO, 1900), 3; "Ethan Allen Hitchcock of Missouri, Secretary of the Interior," in Ethan Allen Hitchcock Papers, RG 200, National Archives; "Hitchcock, Ethan Allen," in *NCAB* 11: 16; Trani, Eugene P., "The Secretaries of the Department of the Interior, 1849–1969" (unpublished manuscript, National Anthropological Archives, Smithsonian Institution, 1975), 128–134.

JAMES RUDOLPH GARFIELD
1865–1950

James Garfield was the son of the second president of the United States to be assassinated, James A. Garfield, and became the second son of a former president to serve in a cabinet position (Robert Todd Lincoln was the first). Many historians of the Department of the Interior consider him to be one of the greatest secretaries in the department's history. Born the second son of James Abram Garfield and Lucretia (née Randolph) Garfield in Hiram, Ohio, on 17 October 1865. He grew up when his father was serving as a congressman from Ohio. In 1880, when James was 15, James A. Garfield was elected as the twentieth president of the United States. His service, however, was short. On 2 July 1881, he was shot and eventually died of his wounds. The younger Garfield had spent much of his youth shuttling between Ohio and Washington to attend school; in 1878, he moved to Concord, New Hampshire, to attend St. Paul's School. In 1880, he returned to Washington and, for the short time that his father was president, was taught by a private tutor. After his father's death, he

and his brother went to Williams College in Massachusetts, and, in 1886, Garfield started two years of law study at Columbia University in New York.

In 1888, after graduating from Columbia, Garfield returned to Ohio, passed the state bar, and opened the Cleveland law office of Garfield & Garfield with his brother. He served as part of the firm until 1896, when he was elected to the Ohio state senate, serving for three years. A reformist Republican, from the more progressive wing of the party, he ran unsuccessfully for seats in Congress in 1898 and 1900. His political career seemed to be over, until President Theodore Roosevelt named him as a member of the U.S. Civil Service Commission in 1902. This appointment commenced a long and close political association between Roosevelt and Garfield, both of whom were from the progressive wing of their party. Garfield became a member of Roosevelt's "tennis cabinet," the inner circle of advisers who played tennis with the president. In 1903, Garfield was named by Roosevelt as the commissioner of the Bureau of Corporations. Working hand in hand with the Justice Department, Garfield investigated trusts, including those of beef, steel, and oil corporations, and asked Congress for legislation to break up the massive corporations.

On 4 March 1907, Secretary of the Interior Ethan Hitchcock left office. Roosevelt had nominated Garfield on 3 December 1906, when Hitchcock resigned. At first, there was some question about the qualifications of Garfield, and Roosevelt withdrew the nomination. However, on 13 December 1906, he renominated Garfield, having secured the needed votes in the Senate to get him confirmed, which occurred on 15 January 1907, to take effect on 4 March. His tenure lasted exactly two years, until the end of the Roosevelt administration on 4 March 1909. Garfield, while wholly inexperienced in the field of natural resources and conservation, nonetheless strode to carry forth the views of Roosevelt, the first "environmental President." He established numerous national parks, improved the quality of waterways, and reclaimed arid lands under the Newlands Act of 1902. In his 1907 report, Garfield wrote, "The great increase in work of the Department during recent years, due to the imposition of new duties, the protection and development of natural resources upon the public domain, the disposition and care of Indian lands, and the growth of the Territories, has necessitated a radical change in the organization of the Department. the purposes of the changes made were to free the Secretary's office from all detail work, which could better and more properly be done by the bureaus or offices, to clear away work in arrears, to introduce the most improved business methods, to throw upon the heads of the great bureaus and offices full responsibility and to hold them strictly accountable for results, and finally to so coordinate the work of the different offices and bureaus, by conference and cooperation between the Secretary and the heads of the offices and bureaus, as to avoid duplication of work and give to each officer the full benefit of the experience of other officers in the Department engaged upon allied or similar work." Much of Garfield's work was administrative in nature. Eugene Trani writes, "His term as Secretary of the Interior was one of the most important of the middle period of the Department, and his organizational reforms proved some of the most far-reaching."

Garfield finished his term in March 1909, after the election of William Howard Taft in 1908, and returned to Ohio. He was considered a leading candidate for governor in 1910, but the progressive wing of the party was overwhelmed by the conservatives at a state convention, and Garfield was not nominated. When former President Roosevelt broke from the regular Republican party to himself run for a third term as president, Garfield was one of the first national leaders to endorse his candidacy. He spoke widely for Roosevelt in a losing cause, but attracted a following for his support of the former president.

In 1914 Garfield was nominated by the Progressives in Ohio for governor, but he was defeated. This loss convinced the Progressives to rejoin the Republican Party.

Garfield concentrated on his law practice as a partner in the firm of Garfield, MacGregor, and Baldwin. President Herbert Hoover named him as chairman of the Presidential Commission on Conservation and the Public Domain in 1929. In 1940, in his last political act, he denounced President Franklin Delano Roosevelt for his conduct over judicial tribunals.

Garfield spent his remaining years in a nursing home in Cleveland. He died of pneumonia on 24 March 1950 at the age of 84, the last of the turn-of-the-century conservationists and environmental reformers.

References: Department of the Interior 1907 annual report in *the Abridgment, 1907: Containing the Annual Message of the President of the United States to the Two Houses of Congress, 60th Congress, 1st Session, With Reports of Departments and Selections from Accompanying Papers, in Two Volumes* (Washington, DC: GPO; 2 vols., 1908), 2: 1455–1456; "Garfield, James Rudolph," in *NCAB*), 14: 35–36; "James R. Garfield," and "James Rudolph Garfield," in James Rudolph Garfield Papers, Library of Congress; *Reports of the Department of the Interior, For the Fiscal Year Ended June 30 1908: Administrative Reports in 2 Volumes* (Washington, DC: GPO, 1908), 1: 3; Thompson, Jack, "James R. Garfield: The Career of a Rooseveltian Progressive, 1895–1916," (master's thesis, University of South Carolina, 1959); Trani, Eugene P., "The Secretaries of the Department of the Interior, 1849–1969" (unpublished manuscript, National Anthropological Archives, Smithsonian Institution, 1975), 140; Warner, Hoyt Landon, "Garfield, James Rudolph," in *DAB* 3: 316–18.

RICHARD ACHILLES BALLINGER
1858–1922

Richard Ballinger's resignation as secretary of the interior split the Republican Party in two, which led to the disastrous defeat of William Howard Taft in 1912. Yet, few people know the name of the man who served as the twenty-fourth secretary, nor what he did while in office. Born in Boonesboro (now Boone), Iowa, on 9 July 1858, he was the son of Col. Richard H. Ballinger, an attorney and Civil War veteran, and Mary (née Norton) Ballinger. He attended the University of Kansas in Lawrence and Washburn University in Topeka, Kansas, before he graduated from Williams College in Massachusetts in 1884, where he was a classmate of James R. Garfield. He then studied law for two years, and was admitted to the Massachusetts bar. He began a law practice in New Decatur, Alabama, where he was elected city attorney and began a rapid rise in politics with a reputation as a man of wholesome honesty. He moved to the new state of Washington, where he first settled in Port Townsend, and ended up in Seattle, where he spent, except for his years in Washington, D.C., the remainder of his life. He opened a law practice that soon thrived, and in 1894 was elected a superior court judge for Jefferson County. He became an expert in mining law and wrote *A Treatise on the Property Rights of Husband and Wife under the Community or Ganancial System* (1895) and *Ballinger's Annotated Codes and Statutes of Washington* (1897).

Considered a reformer, Ballinger ran for mayor of Seattle and was elected, serving from 1904 to 1906. In 1907, when James R. Garfield, was named by President Theodore Roosevelt as secretary of the interior, Garfield wrote to Ballinger, asking him to come to Washington and use his skills in land and mining law as commissioner of the General Land Office. The president wrote to him, "Any man who could clean up Seattle as you did can clean up that Land Office." Ballinger instituted several reforms in the Land Office, including new accounting methods, and merit pay for workers. In 1908, he served as a member of the state delegation to the Republican National Convention, where he backed Secretary of War William Howard Taft for president.

Ballinger tired of Washington, D.C., resigned his office soon after Taft was elected, and returned to Seattle. Taft summoned him back and asked him to serve as secretary of the interior to succeed Garfield. The failure

of the new president to retain Garfield, a popular figure among Republican Progressives and environmentalists alike, was the first crack in the alliance between the supporters of Roosevelt and Taft. Ballinger accepted the position, which was followed by two of the worst years in the history of the Interior department. Almost immediately, he announced that he would be changing from the stewardship policy of Garfield. He said that the new department policy would go forward in "a safe, sane, and conservative way without impeding the development of the great West and without hysteria in one direction or another." Several facets of Garfield's policies were tossed aside, angering members of the previous administration.

The alliance quickly ruptured. In mid-1909, a field officer for the Land Office, Louis R. Glavis, charged that Ballinger, both as head of the Land Office and as secretary of the interior, had deliberately overlooked fraudulent land and coal-mine claims in Alaska by Clarence Cunningham. When Ballinger approved the land claims, Glavis went directly to Taft, who ordered Ballinger to fire Glavis for insubordination. Glavis soon became a cause célèbre among environmentalists for his strong stand. Glavis published his charges in a lengthy article in *Collier's* magazine. An investigation showed that Chief Forester Gifford Pinchot had aided Glavis with writing the article and getting it published. Taft then ordered Ballinger to fire Pinchot, who was also popular with environmentalists. A congressional investigation ensued; the attorney for *Collier's,* Louis Brandeis, charged that Ballinger had covered up massive wrongdoing in the Interior Department. the committee cleared Ballinger of any transgressions. Although found innocent of the charges Glavis had leveled, Ballinger's ability to lead the department was badly damaged.

In his 1910, Ballinger wrote, "If, as originally intended, the Interior Department was to possess the bureaus and institutions relating to domestic affairs, it has lost that distinctive feature by the creation of two other departments which have taken over parts of its functions, viz, the Department of Agriculture and the Department of Commerce and Labor. If I may venture an opinion, it would have been more logical to have consolidated the Interior Department and Department of Agriculture at the time of the creation of the Department of Commerce and Labor and transferred from them certain functions to the Department of Commerce and Labor and other departments, as, for instance, the Patent Office in the Department of Commerce and Labor; the Pension Office to the War and Navy Departments, where it was originally lodged." He also called attention to the fact that at the time, the department's business was conducted out of three buildings: the Patent Office building, the old Post-Office Building, and the Pension building, with further offices in the Government Hospital for the Insane and the Freedmen's Hospital. He wrote, "It would be economy for the Government to build the necessary structures to care for all the bureaus which can not be accommodated in the three buildings of the Government, and the congested condition of the Patent Office and the Secretary's office makes some action in this direction necessary in the near future."

In the end, however, Ballinger's troubles with the environmentalists, and the affair over the firing of Glavis and Pinchot, damaged his health and his tenure. On 19 January, 1911, he sent a letter of resignation to President Taft. A few days later, Taft wrote back, asking that he delay such a move. Taft felt that time would allow Ballinger's reputation to grow. It did not. On 6 March 1911 Ballinger once again sent a letter of resignation and, on 7 March, Taft reluctantly accepted it. Ballinger formally left office on 13 March 1911, a broken man. Historian James Penick Jr., writes, "The controversy with Ballinger was really Pinchot's bid to perpetuate the system of the previous administration. He failed and the movement subsequently fragmented into its individual components." In 1940, then-Secretary of the Interior Harold Ickes, who had sided with Glavis against Ballinger, came forward and repented for what he believed was a wrong committed against Ballinger. In a *Saturday Evening Post* article, he wrote, "This article is by way of confession and penance. In writing it, I am hoping that a grave wrong may be righted. For thirty years I have clung to the commonly held opinion that . . . Richard A. Ballinger, was a dishonest and unworthy public official. For three decades I have believed Ballinger guilty; possibly because my friends were among those who broke Ballinger, and my political enemies were among those who supported him. . . . I had the departmental records—both printed and unprinted—brought down from the heavily laden shelves and gone thoroughly gone over by fresh minds that had no prejudices or preconceived notions. The result of this research is enough to show that in the Ballinger case, which was a principal factor in the destruction of the Taft Administration and broke Secretary Ballinger's life and career, we have a veritable American Dreyfus affair. President William Howard Taft called the conspiracy against Ballinger 'the most cruel persecution that I am familiar with in modern times.' Today, thirty years after those words were written, I am inclined to agree."

The Ballinger tenure had a great impact on the administration. In 1912, Progressives who were angered with Taft and how the entire affair was handled nominated Theodore Roosevelt for president, and Roosevelt split the Republican vote with Taft, allowing Democrat Woodrow Wilson to be elected. Ballinger had returned to Seattle, where he practiced law until his death on 6 June 1922, a month shy of his sixty-fourth birthday.

References: Ickes, Harold L., "Not Guilty! Richard A. Ballinger—An American Dreyfus," *Saturday Evening Post* 212: 48 (25 May 1940), 9–10, 123–128; Paxson, Frederic Logan, "Ballinger, Richard Achilles," in *DAB* 1: 555–556; Penick, James, Jr., *Progressive Politics and Conservation: The Ballinger-Pinchot Affair* (Chicago: University of Chicago Press, 1968), 196; Trani, Eugene P., "The Secretaries of the Department of the Interior, 1849–1969" (unpublished manuscript, National Anthropological Archives, Smithsonian Institution, 1975), 144–151; United States Congress, Senate, *Investigation of the Interior Department and*

Forestry Bureau Policies on Coal Lands of Alaska and Water-Power Sites in the United States, Senate serials 5892–5902: Document No. 719, 61st Congress, 3d Session (13 vols., 1911).

WALTER LOWRIE FISHER
1862–1935

Fisher was nominated for secretary of the interior in March 1911, to heal the wounds caused by the tenure of Richard Ballinger. In his two years in office, he was known for being an able administrator who focused the department's activities on conservation and national parks. the son of Daniel L. Fisher, a Presbyterian clergyman, and Amanda (née Kouns) Fisher, Walter Lowrie Fisher was born on 4 July 1862 in Wheeling, Virginia (now in West Virginia). His mother was a member of a prosperous farming family in West Virginia. Fisher's father served as the president of Hanover College in Indiana. Fisher after receiving his primary education in Indiana, attended Marietta College in Ohio, before transferring to Hanover, where he received his bachelor's degree in 1883. He then studied the law, and was admitted to the Indiana bar in 1888. Fisher moved to Chicago and was named a special assessment attorney for the city. He left that office after a year to open his own law practice.

For several years, Fisher worked at expanding his law practice. In 1901, he was elected as secretary of the executive committee of the Municipal Voters League of Chicago, a reformist organization. Fisher served as secretary until 1906, when he was elected president of the organization. Considered a Progressive Republican, Fisher used his influence to clean up municipal voting, and he railed against so-called grey wolves, aldermen he believed to be corrupt. Fisher's campaign became so successful that candidates who desired to be elected needed

to sign the league's pledge. Fisher also worked as the city traction counsel to clean up Chicago's transportation system, which was corrupt. Fisher's plan, to lease railways to companies with strict oversight, was endorsed by the city council and passed by referendum. Later, Fisher served on the Merriam Commission, which investigated corruption in city government. It was as president of the Conservation League of America that Fisher received his reputation that later earned him a cabinet post. Working closely with Gifford Pinchot, Fisher drew up the principles of the National Conservation Association, which was established in 1909, and which he served as vice-president from 1910. President William Howard Taft named Fisher as a member of the Railroad Securities Commission. Taft had long known Fisher, having worked with him when he served as secretary of War and Fisher had represented the city of Chicago.

In 1911 Ballinger resigned as secretary of the interior. Taft, in order to reach out to the Progressives, named Fisher to the vacancy on 10 April; he was confirmed by the Senate a week later on 17 April and was sworn into office the same day. Historian Alan Gould writes, "Taft's appointment of a progressive to fill the vacancy was generally misinterpreted by contemporary political leaders as both an unqualified repudiation of the administration's position on resource policies and as one more indication of Taft's political naïveté. Former Secretary of the Interior James Garfield, speaking for the majority of the progressives, revealed this misinterpretation when he spoke of the Fisher appointment as 'just another one of Taft's incomprehensible actions displaying again his absolute lack of political sagacity.'" A writer for *Leslie's Weekly* magazine notes, "In Chicago they call Walter Lowrie Fisher, Mr. Ballinger's successor, a practical uplifter and crusader. Not all uplifters, as we have reason to know, really uplift. Mr. Fisher appears to be different. In reform matters he has kept his head, as was shown by his connection with the conservation movement. Even when he was president of the National Conservation Congress, the Chicago lawyer did not allow the idea to run away with him. In the later bitter controversy between Secretary Ballinger and Gifford Pinchot, Mr. Fisher kept strictly out of the fight, so far as personalities or radical issues were concerned."

During his tenure, which lasted from 17 April 1911 until 4 March 1913, Fisher was an able administrator, overseeing the department more in a healing capacity than as a policy maker. He took a middle course between the pure environmentalism of Garfield and the pure business sense of Ballinger: Fisher proposed that coal lands in Alaska be leased, but with governmental controls, and that a railroad be built across Alaska by the government-owned Panama Canal Construction Company. Neither proposal was accepted by Congress while he was in office; they were acted on by his successor, Franklin K. Lane, and passed into law. Eugene Trani notes, "Fisher's greatest contribution—a very important one—was shaking the Department out of the doldrums caused by the Ballinger-Pinchot controversy and getting it moving as a protector of natural resources. He "wisely steered clear of either side of the conflict."

Fisher campaigned for Taft in 1912, even though many of his friends and political allies favored Theodore Roosevelt. the Taft-Roosevelt feud split the Republican vote, and allowed Democrat Woodrow Wilson to capture the presidency. Fisher did not desire to be retained in the new administration, and was pleased when the new president selected Franklin Lane as his successor. Fisher returned to Chicago and resumed the practice of law, serving as special counsel to the mayor's office for transportation issues. He died at his home in Winnetka, Illinois, on 9 November 1935 of a coronary thrombosis at the age of 73.

References: Gould, Alan B., "'Trouble Portfolio' to Constructive Conservation: Secretary of the Interior Walter L. Fisher, 1911–1913," *Forest History* 16: 4 (January 1973), 4–12; Heinl, Robert D., "Another Great Lawyer for Taft's Cabinet," *Leslie's Weekly,* undated clipping in Fisher Papers, Box 30, File "Clippings, 1911," Library of Congress; McKee, Oliver, Jr., "Fisher, Walter Lowrie," in *DAB*

1: 299–300; "Walter L. Fisher," in Box 24, File "genealogy," Walter Lowrie Fisher Papers, Library of Congress.

FRANKLIN KNIGHT LANE
1864–1921

Franklin Lane served ably as the first of two of Woodrow Wilson's secretaries of the Interior. Lane, the son of Christopher Lane and Carolina (née Burns) Lane, was born on 15 July 1864 near Charlottetown, on Prince Edward Island, Canada. His father was a Presbyterian minister who traveled often. When Franklin was three, and his father was suffering from bronchitis, they moved to the Napa Valley area of California to improve his father's health. Franklin Lane attended public schools in the Napa Valley, as well as a private school, Oak Mound. In 1876, when he was 13, the family moved to Oakland, California, and, in 1884, Lane entered the University of California. Lane studied law at the Hastings College of Law in San Francisco, and was admitted to the state bar in 1888.

Lane worked for several newspapers in the San Francisco area while attending college, and after he was admitted to the state bar he continued to work as a correspondent for the San Francisco *Chronicle*. In 1891, he moved to Washington state, where until 1895, he worked as the editor of the Tacoma *Daily News.* After the sale of the paper he returned to San Francisco, where he began a private law practice. He acquired a reputation as a fine attorney, and from 1899 until 1904 served as first city attorney, then county attorney, for the San Francisco area. During the Great Earthquake of 1906, he worked with the relief squads that helped those in need of assistance. That same year, he traveled to Washington, D.C., to speak with President Theodore Roosevelt about plans for the Hetch Hetchy water supply in Yosemite National Park. Roosevelt was so impressed with the young attorney that he hired him to sit on the Interstate Commerce Commission (ICC) even though Lane was a Democrat. He became an outstanding member of that commission and on 1 January 1913, Lane became the chairman of the commission.

The previous November, Democrat Woodrow Wilson had been elected president. In formulating his cabinet, Wilson selected the little-known Lane for a cabinet post. Biographer August Heckscher writes, "Given the propensity of Democrats to adhere to a states'-rights philosophy, the choice of a Secretary of the Interior was especially delicate. Wilson wanted to stand by his party's commitment to conservation, yet he knew the danger of outraging traditional Democratic concepts. On [Colonel Edward Mandell] House's [chief aide to Wilson] suggestion he named a westerner, Franklin K. Lane, who had a progressive record and had been appointed by Theodore Roosevelt to the Interstate Commerce Commission." Arthur W. Page, of the *World's Work* magazine, writes, "House recommended Lane, as perhaps the one man available, adapted to any Cabinet position from Secretary of State down. At one time Lane was slated for the War Department, at another time another department, and finally placed as Secretary of the Interior because being a good conservationist, as a Western man, he could promote conservation with more tact and less criticism than an Eastern man."

Although he had desired to remain as chairman of the ICC, Lane accepted the Interior portfolio and went to work on several environmental topics that interested him, most notably the Hetch Hetchy Valley controversy in California. Opposed by environmentalists because it would flood the Hetch Hetchy Valley in Yosemite, Lane's predecessor, Richard Ballinger, had ordered the project to go forth. Lane agreed, but decided instead for government, rather than private, control of the program. In 1916, working with President Wilson, Lane established the National Park Service, with control over the nation's national park system, and he placed environmentalist Stephen Mather as the organization's chief. He also oversaw the end of

the Cherokee Nation, which went out of existence in 1914. In his annual report for that year, he wrote, "Three things of unusual purport have marked the life of this department during the past year—the passing of the Cherokee Nation, the opening of Alaska, and the advancement of a series of measures aimed to promote the further development of the West. These things are apparently unrelated, yet they have made an appeal to me as alike illustrative of the newness of our country, the novelty of its problems, and the responsiveness of our Government. There is such a significance in these policies, they evidence a faith so robust, as to give them distinction. And if it is true that 'in America each is to have his chance,' the events of this year are well designed to give a sure confidence to the Alaskans and those who look to that Territory as a land of opportunity, to the Indians and those who are concerned as to their future, to the home maker and miner of the West and all whose interests are allied with theirs."

Lane served from 1913 until 1920. Some historians call him one of the most effective Interior secretaries of the twentieth century. Department historian Eugene Trani writes, "Lane's accomplishments covered many areas. He advocated a government-constructed railroad in Alaska. His philosophy of democratic, antimonopolistic, efficient development of resources was clear. . . . Lane created the Alaskan Commission to help development and withdrew acres for natural beauty parks. . . . He also brought passage of legislation concerning hydroelectric power and leasing of public oil lands. Despite opposition, he retained government power to revoke leases if monopolistic practices existed. Acts passed in 1920 set time limitations on hydroelectric and oil leases." He was so widely respected that when Secretary of War Lindsey Garrison resigned in 1916, Lane, as well as Secretary of Agriculture David F. Houston, were considered to fill the vacancy before Newton D. Baker was finally selected.

Although he began his tenure as a close friend of President Wilson, over the years their relationship became strained. When

Secretary of State Robert Lansing resigned, Lane backed the former secretary rather than the president. Further, press leaks with information inside cabinet conferences were alleged by the president's allies to have come from Lane. By 1920, he was in declining health, and the salary of the Interior secretary was not enough to support his family. On 15 February 1920, he resigned, effective 1 March, to become the vice-president of the Pan-American Petroleum Company. He told close friends that service in Washington had left him so destitute that he did not have enough for train tickets for him and his family back to California. On 18 May 1921, he checked into the Mayo Clinic in Rochester, Minnesota, for a heart bypass operation. He suffered a heart attack on the operating table and died, at age 56. He was mourned by Democrats and Republicans alike.

References: Canfield, Leon H., *The Presidency of Woodrow Wilson: Prelude to a World in Crisis* (Rutherford, NJ: Fairleigh Dickinson University Press, 1966), 22; Heckscher, August, *Woodrow Wilson* (New York: Charles Scribner's Sons, 1991), 271; Hendrick, Burton J., "The American 'Home Secretary' . . . Mr. Franklin K. Lane," *World's Work* 26: 4 (August 1913), 396–405; Lane, Anne Wintermute; and Louise Herrick Wall, eds., *The Letters of Franklin K. Lane, Personal and Political* (Boston: Houghton Mifflin, 1922), 129–130; McKee, Oliver, Jr., "Lane, Franklin Knight," in *DAB* 5: 572–573; Olson, Keith W., "Franklin K. Lane: a Biography," (master's thesis, University of Wisconsin, 1964); *Report of the Secretary of the Interior for the Fiscal Year Ended June 30 1914* (Washington, DC: GPO, 1914), 1; Trani, Eugene P., "The Secretaries of the Department of the Interior, 1849–1969" (unpublished manuscript, National Anthropological Archives, Smithsonian Institution, 1975), 160–161.

JOHN BARTON PAYNE
1855–1935

Payne served as secretary of the interior for a year and a week, and in that time he vigorously opposed the construction of reclamation dams in Yellowstone National Park. He is better remembered for his later work as chairman of the American Red Cross. Payne was born on 26 January 1855 in Pruntytown, Virginia (now in West Virginia), the son of Dr. Amos Payne, a physician, and Elizabeth Barton (née Smith) Payne. When the Civil War broke out, Amos Payne moved his family away from the fighting to a farm in Orleans, Virginia. John Payne was educated in the schools of Orleans and was attended by a private tutor as well. This appears to be his only education. He went to work as a clerk in a general store in Warrenton, Virginia, and later worked as the assistant to Adolphus Armstrong, the clerk of the courts of the circuit court of Taylor County. It was here that he became interested in law, and read the law at night. He was admitted to the Virginia bar in September 1876.

That same year, Payne entered the political field, and stumped for the Democratic presidential ticket of Samuel Tilden and Thomas Hendricks. His work won him the seat of chairman of the Taylor County Democratic Committee. He then moved to Kingwood, in Preston County, West Virginia, to practice the law. He eventually served in several positions in the state Democratic Party, and in 1880, worked to support the Democratic presidential candidate, General Winfield Scott Hancock. the following year, Payne was chosen by the West Virginia bar as a special judge of the circuit court of Tucker County. In 1882, Payne was elected as mayor of Kingwood, serving until November of that year and then he moved to Chicago, a town with which he was identified for the remainder of his life.

Payne was elected as president of the Chicago Law Institute in 1889 and, in November 1893, he was elected as a judge of the superior court of Cook County, Chicago, where he served until he resigned on 5 December 1898 to return to his law practice. In 1902, he became a partner in the firm on Winston, Payne, Strawn & Shaw, staying with them until 1917. President Woodrow Wilson offered him the position of solicitor general in 1913, but Payne declined. In October

1917, he was summoned to Washington by President Wilson to serve as general counsel for the U.S. Shipping Board, where he settled contracts and made decisions about ships that had been requisitioned for military during World War I. In January 1918, Wilson named him as general counsel of the U.S. Railroad administration, where Payne was responsible for handling the legal affairs of railroad lines placed under government control during the war. In July of 1919, Wilson made him chairman of the U.S. Shipping Board, to replace the retiring Edward N. Hurley, and Payne spent the next seven months reorganizing the domestic shipping program of the United States to a postwar setting.

The resignation of Secretary of the Interior Franklin Lane on 15 February 1920 left the president with a vacancy in his cabinet with a little more than a year until he left office. It was speculated that Senator John Franklin Shafroth of Colorado was being considered for the post, but he was passed over. On 17 February, Wilson announced that Payne, who had no experience with conservation matters, would serve as Lane's replacement. Payne released a statement, "I will accept this Cabinet position—should I be confirmed—simply because the President has named me. I am afraid my heart is in the Shipping Board. There shall be no change in that. I have asked the President to continue me here until the present program is so far along, that my successor will find it fairly easy. . . . This will take perhaps a couple of weeks." Payne was confirmed on 28 February, and took office that same day, serving fifty-three weeks in office. Eugene Trani writes, "At Interior, Payne carried out policies instituted by his predecessors. He continued construction of the Alaskan Railroad and supervised the new policies on resource and hydroelectric leasing established in Lane's term." Trani adds, "Payne was more than an interim Secretary. He vigorously opposed efforts to build reclamation dams in Yellowstone National Park, believing the parks would never be commercial. His opposition was instrumental in the plan's congressional defeat. He devoted much of his time to the conservation of naval petroleum reserves, reserves destined for notoriety in the next decade." On 4 March 1921, with Wilson's term finished, Payne left office.

Although he was a Democrat, who had served in the cabinet of a Democratic administration, Payne was nonetheless asked by the new president, Republican Warren G. Harding, to serve as the head of the American Red Cross. It was his service to the Red Cross where Payne was to receive much of the notice in his life. He accepted the chairmanship without pay, and was reappointed by Presidents Coolidge, Hoover, and Roosevelt. Payne expanded the Red Cross to an international relief organization. He remained as head of the Red Cross up until his death. John Payne died in Washington of appendicitis on 24 January 1935—two days before his eightieth birthday.

References: McKee, Oliver, Jr., "Payne, John Barton," in *DAB* 7: 594; Payne biographical file in the American Red Cross Library, Washington, DC; Trani, Eugene P., "The Secretaries of the Department of the Interior, 1849–1969" (unpublished manuscript, National Anthropological Archives, Smithsonian Institution, 1975), 166–169.

ALBERT BACON FALL
1861–1944

Albert Fall became the first cabinet member to serve time in prison; he was implicated in the Teapot Dome scandal, much of which he helped bring about by helping two political cronies cash in cheaply on government oil reserves with the payment of a bribe. Fall, a noted U.S. senator from New Mexico and friend of President Warren G. Harding, spent his last days in disgrace. Fall was born in Frankfort, Kentucky, on 26 November 1861, the eldest of three children of Williamson Ware Robertson Fall and Edmonia (née Taylor) Fall, both schoolteachers. When his father became a soldier in the Confederate army during the first years of the

Civil War, Albert went to live in Nashville, Tennessee, with his paternal grandfather. After the war Fall returned to his parents and worked in a cotton mill. When his father taught school, he attended classes with him and received instruction from him. It is not known whether he received anything more than a primary school education.

Fall taught school for a time and read the law. In 1881, when he was twenty, he headed West to find new opportunities, settling first as a bookkeeper in Clarksville, Texas. For a time he became a cowboy, but he tired of that life and returned to Clarksville to run a general store. Fall then worked at numerous odd jobs, including as a miner and a foreman in Mexico. He became fluent in Spanish, and was able to travel through the Southwest. During a stop in Kingston, New Mexico, he met Edward L. Doheny, a businessman who would be part of his downfall. His family relocated to Kingston, eventually moving to Las Cruces where he intended to become an attorney. Instead, he entered local politics in the New Mexico Territory. He bought a small local newspaper, and turned it into the Las Cruces *Independent Democrat*. Before long, Fall was elected to a seat in the territorial legislature and served from 1890 until 1892 and later three times in the Territorial Council (1892–1893, 1896–1897, 1902–1904). In 1893, he was appointed by President Grover Cleveland as an associate justice on the New Mexico Territorial Supreme Court, where he served until 1895. In 1897, and later in 1907, he served for short periods as territorial attorney general.

Fall was a Democrat until 1904, when he became a Progressive Republican. In 1908, Fall served as a delegate from New Mexico Territory to the Republican National Convention that nominated Secretary of War William Howard Taft for president. In 1912, when New Mexico entered the Union as the forty-seventh state, the state legislature was ready to pick two U.S. senators to send to Washington. Fall was elected. He was a leading proponent of action to preserve American interests in Mexico. Fall became a harsh critic

of President Woodrow Wilson's Mexican policy and, following the end of World War I, a severe opponent of Wilson's Treaty of Versailles. Fall was the consummate westerner and looked the part. Biographer, Francis Russell, writes, "Pugnaciously erect, with mustache and goatee, gambler's bow tie, black, broad-brimmed Stetson hat, and a mean little cigar the size of a lead pencil clamped in the jaw, he looked the incarnation of the West. His eyes were a disconcerting blue, and he had been known to carry the six-shooter of his frontier days even on the floor of the Senate. His beliefs were as much of the frontier as his appearance. He believed that northern Mexico should be annexed by the United States, that conservationists were akin to Eastern bird-watchers, and that public lands should be disposed of immediately and without restrictions."

Fall and Harding were close friends in the U.S. Senate; the men were partners in a regular Senate poker game. They also served together on the Senate Foreign Relations Committee. In 1920, Harding was unexpectedly nominated for president by the Republicans. Fall helped Harding write some of his speeches, but otherwise he stayed away from the campaign trail. When Harding was elected, he approached Fall and asked him to be his secretary of state. When word of this leaked out, there were protests even from staunch Republicans, and instead, former supreme court justice and 1916 Republican presidential candidate Charles Evans Hughes was selected. Harding wanted Fall to serve in his cabinet, and offered him the Interior portfolio. Harding desired a westerner in that position and, with Fall having been a friend of former President Roosevelt, the new president saw this as an opportunity to reward that wing of the party. On 4 March 1921 Fall's name was put in nomination. Fall, along with the rest of Harding's cabinet, was confirmed that same day, and Fall moved into his new offices.

Within three months of beginning work at Interior, Fall was approached by Doheny, head of the Pan-American Petroleum Company, and Harry F. Sinclair, head of the Mammoth Oil Company. They wanted to get the leases to two government petroleum preserves. To protect against a shortfall in the American petroleum market, reserves were constructed at Elk Hills, California, and Teapot Dome, Wyoming. The two men paid Fall a bribe to gain control of the leases. Fall went to Secretary of the Navy Edwin Denby (who controlled the leases) and President Harding and convinced them to move control to the Interior Department. Once this was done, Fall sold the leases to Doheny and Sinclair. Fall then pushed to have the Forest Service, part of the Agriculture Department, moved to the Interior Department, so that he could sell off large tracts of forestry reserves. On the advice of former forester Gifford Pinchot, a disgusted bureaucrat, Harry Slattery, investigated Fall's role in the transfer of the agency and discovered the sale of the leases to Doheny and Sinclair. Slattery went to Senator Robert LaFollette of Wisconsin and asked him to begin an investigation. LaFollette introduced the bill in the Congress to start an inquiry to "investigate the entire subject . . . and to report its findings and recommendation to the Senate," which was expanded into a Senate Select Committee under the control of Senator Thomas Walsh. On 4 March 1923 Fall resigned, and returned to New Mexico.

Gradually, however, through the Walsh committee hearings, the bribery was exposed. Fall was called to testify and denied that Doheny had ever paid him, and that the $100,000 he received was a loan from newspaper publisher Edward McLean. The death of President Harding, and the resignations of Attorney General Harry M. Daugherty and Secretary of the Navy Denby, both of whom were implicated in the scandal, did not end the controversy. The courts canceled the two leases in 1927 and, in 1929, Fall was indicted and convicted of receiving a bribe—the first cabinet official to be convicted of a crime. Doheny was acquitted of giving the bribe to Fall, and Sinclair was convicted merely of contempt of Congress. Fall served nearly a year in prison, and was released in 1932, a sickly and broken man. He spent his remaining years in poverty and declining health. On 30 November 1944, he died at the Hotel Dieu Hospital in El Paso, Texas, where he had lived since the government confiscated his ranch in New Mexico in 1936. He was 83 and was buried in the Evergreen Cemetery in El Paso.

References: Fall, Albert Bacon (David H. Stratton, ed.), *The Memoirs of Albert B. Fall* (El Paso, TX: Western Press, 1966); Noggle, Burl, *Teapot Dome: Oil and Politics in the 1920s* (Baton Rouge: Louisiana State University Press, 1962); Russell, Francis, *The Shadow of Blooming Grove: Warren G. Harding in His Times* (New York: McGraw-Hill, 1968), 264; Sinclair, Andrew, *The Available Man: The Life behind the Masks of Warren Gamaliel Harding* (New York: Macmillan, 1965), 188; Stratton, David H., "Fall, Albert Bacon," in *DAB* 2: 258–260; Trani, Eugene P., "The Secretaries of the Department of the Interior, 1849–1969" (unpublished manuscript, National Anthropological Archives, Smithsonian Institution, 1975), 170–176; Werner, Morris Robert, and John Starr, *Teapot Dome* (Clifton, NJ: A. M. Kelley, 1950).

HUBERT WORK
1860–1942

See Postmaster General, 1922–1923

ROY OWEN WEST
1868–1958

Roy West was one of the most controversial nominees for secretary of the interior, and because of the controversy, he spent much of his tenure as an interim appointment, being confirmed only five weeks before he left office. His term at Interior came during the 1928 presidential election and had little impact on the department or its policies. the son of Pleasant West, a businessman, and Helen Anna West, Roy West was born in

Georgetown, Illinois, on 27 October 1868. He attended local schools, then DePauw University in Indiana, where he received a bachelor's degree and a law degree in 1890, and, three years later, a master's degree. He moved to Chicago and, with Charles S. Deneen, also an attorney, began a law practice.

West soon became a prominent attorney in Chicago, and in 1894 was named assistant county attorney for Cook County, Chicago, and, he served as Chicago's city attorney, from 1895 to 1897. He served as a member of the Cook County Board of Review from 1898 to 1914. In 1904, West worked as Deneen's campaign manager for governor of Illinois; Deneen was elected, and served two terms, from 1905 to 1913. The election helped build West's reputation in national Republican politics; he served as delegate to the Republican National Conventions in 1908, 1912, 1916, and 1928. In 1924, West helped get Deneen elected to the U.S. Senate; for his work, President Calvin Coolidge named West as secretary of the Republican National Committee.

On 20 July 1928, following the resignation of Secretary of the Interior Hubert Work, Coolidge named West to succeed him. the appointment was met with brutal opposition, especially from Democrats, who charged West with a conflict of interest. When in private law practice, West represented Samuel Insull, the owner of several utilities. West was paid with shares in some of Insull's utilities. As Insull still had utilities permit applications before the Federal Power Commission, it was thought he might receive favored treatment. Hearings opened on West's appointment, and he served in an interim capacity. West said that he had sold the shares years earlier and had done very little business for Insull. West was confirmed on 21 January 1929, five weeks before he left office. He had little impact on the department's policies.

West left office on 4 March 1929, and was succeeded by Ray Lyman Wilbur. President Herbert Hoover offered West the post of U.S. ambassador to Japan, but West declined. During World War II, West served as a spe-cial adviser to the U.S. Justice Department on the cases of conscientious objectors. He retired in 1952, continuing, until his death, to be involved in political and civic affairs in Chicago. He died there on 29 November 1958, a month past his ninetieth birthday. The library at DePauw University is named in his honor.

References: Rawley, James A., "West, Roy Owen," in *DAB* 3: 683–684; Trani, Eugene P., "The Secretaries of the Department of the Interior, 1849–1969" (unpublished manuscript, National Anthropological Archives, Smithsonian Institution, 1975), 185–188; United States Senate, Committee on Public Lands and Surveys, *Nomination of Honorable Roy O. West to Be Secretary of the Interior* (Washington, DC: GPO, 1928).

RAY LYMAN WILBUR
1875–1949

Ray Wilbur is barely remembered for his service as secretary of the interior during the Hoover administration. Wilbur was born in Boonesboro (now Boone), Iowa, on 13 April 1875, the son of Dwight Locke Wilbur, a lawyer and Union soldier, and Edna Maria (née Lyonan). Ray Wilbur was also the brother of Secretary of the Navy Curtis Dwight Wilbur. In 1883, when Ray Wilbur was eight, his family moved to Jamestown, in the Dakota Territory, where his father worked as a land agent for the Northern Pacific Railroad. After five years, the Wilburs moved to Riverside, California, where Ray received much of his primary education. He entered Stanford University in Palo Alto, California, intending to study medicine. In his freshman year, he met Herbert Hoover, and the two men developed a life-long friendship. Wilbur received his bachelor's degree from Stanford in 1896, then remained as a graduate student in physiology and earned his master's degree in 1897. He then attended the Cooper Medical College in San

Francisco and earned his M.D. degree in 1899.

Wilbur worked in San Francisco as a physician, but in 1900 returned to Stanford as an assistant professor in physiology and studied for his Ph.D., which he quit pursuing in 1903. He then spent several years in Europe and the eastern United States. In 1908, Wilbur returned to Stanford and became a clinical professor of medicine. the following year, he was appointed chairman of the Stanford Medical School. In 1911, Wilbur became the dean of the medical school and in 1916, was named Stanford University's third president. He would serve as the president of Stanford for twenty-three years, until his retirement in 1943.

During the first years of World War I, Wilbur, while in Washington, D.C., recommended Herbert Hoover for the position of wartime food administrator Hoover was chosen and made Wilbur his assistant. Wilbur returned to Stanford, however, the postwar changes to the nation, and to Stanford, disturbed him and he desired a change. At this time, Herbert Hoover was elected president of the United States, and asked Wilbur to serve as secretary of the interior. Initially, Wilbur resisted on the grounds that his work at Stanford was too important for him to leave. So Hoover asked the Stanford Board of Trustees to grant Wilbur a leave of absence. The board agreed, and Wilbur was officially nominated and confirmed on 5 March 1929, as the thirty-first secretary of the interior.

In his four years at Interior, Wilbur tried to manage the department as he had Stanford. He refused the spacious office of the secretary, instead taking a small room that became known as the secretary's cubbyhole. When Wilbur took office, the emblem of the department had been an eagle with its wings outstretched—Wilbur changed this to a standing bison. He wrote, "It was surprising to see what a difference was made by a such a minor change as new stationary for the Department. It seemed to me that the coat of arms of the Interior Department, an eagle with outspread wings, was not particularly

characteristic of the Department and its responsibilities. I selected one of the best pictures I could find of an American bison and had that put on our stationary and official correspondence. It was very attractive . . . the revamped letterhead gave a lift to staff morale, emphasizing as it did a fresh start, making us more aware of the fact that ours was a distinctive department with unique and characteristic functions to perform."

In his annual report for 1929, Wilbur wrote, "This is a period of changing emphasis in the work of this department. Some of the great bureaus, particularly the Bureau of Pensions and the General Land Office, have overtaken the peak of their administrative load under existing legislation. Other bureaus, such as the Geological Survey and the Bureau of Reclamation, have ahead of them large tasks for completion. One activity, that of the Indian Service, has before it a definite and unique goal—that of working itself out of a job. Its program calls for a large economic saving to the country by increased expenditures to enable the Indian population to eventually become self-supporting. On the other hand, the National Park Service and the Office of Education look forward to constantly increasing fields of activity." In his 1930 report, he wrote, "Continental conservation is the key to the future of this Nation and is the present problem of this department; nearly all of its functions center about it." He also worked during his tenure to cure syphilis nationally and reduce illiteracy. Perhaps his most enduring work was the construction of the Boulder Canyon dam, which he named Hoover Dam.

Hoover was defeated in 1932 and in March 1933 Wilbur returned to Stanford, where he remained until his retirement in 1943. He died at Palo Alto on 26 June 1949 at the age of 74. A chair in the political science department, as well as a dormitory at Stanford, are named in Wilbur's honor.

See also Curtis Dwight Wilbur

References: Robinson, Edgar Eugene, and Paul Carroll Edwards, eds., *The Memoirs of Ray Lyman*

Wilbur, 1875–1949 (Stanford, CA: Stanford University Press, 1960); "Wilbur, Ray Lyman," in *NCAB* 51: 337–338, C: 12; Swain, Robert E., "Ray Lyman Wilbur: 1875–1949," *Science,* 3: 2883 (31 March 1950), 324–327; Trani, Eugene P., "The Secretaries of the Department of the Interior, 1849–1969" (unpublished manuscript, National Anthropological Archives, Smithsonian Institution, 1975), 189–196; Veysey, Laurence, "Wilbur, Ray Lyman," in *DAB* 2: 891–895.

HAROLD LeCLAIRE ICKES
1874–1952

Harold Ickes served as secretary of the interior from 1933 until 1946 Ickes was born near Hollidaysburg, Pennsylvania, on 15 March 1874, the son of Jesse Boone Williams Ickes, a tobacconist, and Martha (née McCune) Ickes. His grandfather, founded Ickesville, Pennsylvania; Harold Ickes spent the first years of his life there. When his mother died, he and a sister went to live with an aunt in Chicago. Harold received his primary school education there and entered the University of Chicago. He graduated in 1897, and became a reporter for the Chicago *Record,* rising to assistant sports editor and then assistant political editor. He covered the 1900 Republican and Democratic National Conventions. Ickes returned to the University of Chicago to study the law and, in 1907, graduated, was admitted to the Illinois bar, and became an attorney in Chicago.

An admirer of Theodore Roosevelt, Ickes swung away from the Regular Republican party in 1912 when Roosevelt bolted and formed the Progressive, or "Bull Moose," Party. Ickes returned to the Republican fold in 1916 when the party nominated Supreme Court Justice Charles Evans Hughes for president, but thereafter Ickes voted for Democrats. An advocate of civil liberties, Ickes served on various reform commissions in Chicago, including the People's Traction League and the Utility Consumers' and Investors' League.

Ickes supported Franklin Roosevelt's candidacy in the 1932 presidential race. After the election, the new president-elect desired a Republican in his cabinet and offered the post of secretary of the interior first to Senator Hiram W. Johnson of California and then to Senator Bronson Cutting of New Mexico. Both men turned him down, preferring to remain in the Senate. Roosevelt then turned to Ickes who was considered an Independent Republican. Historian Barry Mackintosh writes, "He was not from the western states that traditionally supplied secretaries of the interior, and he had no personal familiarity with the successful candidate. He made his interest known [for the Interior portfolio] through mutual acquaintances, however, and eagerly accepted the post upon his call to Roosevelt's Hyde Park home." Roosevelt himself later wrote of his nominee, "I liked the cut of his jib." Ickes was formally nominated and confirmed on 4 March 1933.

During his tenure, which lasted a record 12 years 49 weeks, Ickes changed the department. As one of his first acts, he refused to name a political appointee for commissioner of Indian Affairs, instead selecting John Collier, a lifelong white reformer who helped usher in what historians called a New Deal in Indian affairs. Ickes also brought back Louis R. Glavis, who had been fired during Ballinger appointment and named Oscar L. Chapman, a Colorado lawyer and reformer, assistant secretary of the interior, a post he would hold for 16 years. During Ickes's tenure, the Taylor Grazing Act of 1934 was passed, which allowed for 80 million acres of grasslands to be used for grazing. the Wheeler-Howard, or Indian Reorganization, Act, of 1934 also was passed, which extended constitutional rights and self-determination to Native Americans. One of his most enduring accomplishment was the construction of a complex to hold all of the Interior department's major offices.

Unlike his predecessors, Ickes did not write detailed annual reports. However, in 1936, he wrote, "Once again, I commend to your consideration the desirability of changing the name of the Department of the Interior to that of the Department of Conservation—a name more expressive of its fundamental purpose and nature. Such a designation would give conservation an authority heretofore lacking, it would promote an increased consciousness of conservation as a Government policy, not only in the minds of officials but among the people of the United States generally, and it would place upon the personnel of the Department a definite responsibility for advancing the cause of conservation to the end that the resources of the United States may be used for the maximum benefit of every citizen of the country." There is no evidence that such a recommendation was ever considered. In his 1938 report, Ickes concluded, "From the accompanying reports of the bureaus and divisions of the Department, most of which deal with some important phase of conservation, and as a result of my own first-hand observations and information, I believe that a great advance in sentiment for conservation has been made during the past year."

Eugene Trani writes, "Ickes' greatest accomplishments as Secretary occurred in Roosevelt's third and fourth terms. Throughout the Second World War he served as custodian of natural resources. He had refused to sell helium to Nazi Germany in 1938 (Ickes from the beginning was strongly anti-Hitler), and had headed the Federal Oil Administration in the days of the National Recovery Administration. So the President named him Petroleum Coordinator for National Defense in May 1941, making him the czar of American oil. Ickes moved quickly, calling for more effective use of petroleum."

When Franklin Roosevelt died in April 1945, Vice-president Harry S Truman became president. Ickes and Truman did not have much in common, and relations between the two men became strained. In late 1945, Truman nominated Edwin W. Pauley for the post of under secretary of the Navy. Ickes testified before the Senate committee that Pauley, while serving as treasurer of the Democratic National Committee, had asked Ickes to refrain from seeking offshore oil rights in California in exchange for $300,000

for the party. Pauley denied the charge, and President Truman reported that he believed Ickes to be mistaken. On 12 February 1946, angered by the president's siding with Pauley, Ickes wrote to Truman that he did not care to "commit perjury for the sake of the party" and resigned. Truman accepted the resignation after leaking the letter to the press. At Pauley's own request, Truman soon withdrew his nomination for the Navy position.

Ickes spent the final years of his life devoted to writing his memoirs and a newspaper column. On 3 February 1952, while he was hospitalized in Washington, D.C., for an arthritic condition, he died. Ickes was 77 years old.

References: Ickes, Harold L., *The Autobiography of a Curmudgeon* (New York: Reynal and Hitchcock, 1943); Mackintosh, Barry, "Harold L. Ickes and the National Park Service," *Journal of Forest History,* 29: 2 (April 1985), 78–84; Trani, Eugene P., "The Secretaries of the Department of the Interior, 1849–1969" (unpublished manuscript, National Anthropological Archives, Smithsonian Institution, 1975), 197–209; Watkins, T. H., *Righteous Pilgrim: the Life and Times of Harold L. Ickes, 1874–1952* (New York: Henry Holt, 1990).

JULIUS ALBERT KRUG
1907–1970

Julius Krug was selected to replace Harold Ickes as secretary of the interior. He was 38, the youngest cabinet member since Alexander Hamilton. Krug was not prepared for the position, however. His tenure was hectic and controversial, and he left after three years. Born in Madison, Wisconsin, on 23 November 1907, he was the son of Julius John Krug, a policeman, and Emma (née Korfmacher) Krug. Julius weighed so much at birth that his father apparently said, "Julius is no name for him! I ought to call him Captain Kidd!" Krug was called Cap by his family and close friends for the remainder of his life. He attended local schools in Madison, then went to the University of Wisconsin at Madison, and he graduated in 1929 with a bachelor's degree. The following year, he earned a master's degree in utilities management and economics.

In 1930, Krug went to work for the Bell Telephone System in Milwaukee as a research statistician. After a year and a half in this position he went to work for the Wisconsin Public Service Commission and served as a technician on utility rates and evaluations. He rose to become chief of the depreciation section of the commission. In 1935, Krug was hired by the Federal Communications Commission in Washington, D.C., to serve as a public utilities expert. He conducted the first government investigation into the business practices of the Long Lines Department of the American Telephone & Telegraph Company. In 1938, Governor Albert ("Happy") Chandler reorganized the Kentucky Public Service Commission and hired Krug to serve as chairman. Late that same year, President Franklin Roosevelt asked Krug to serve as the head of power operations for the Tennessee Valley Authority. Krug established a program to purchase private power lines from the Tennessee Electric Company, a business owned by Wendell Willkie. In 1940, Krug was asked by President Roosevelt to go to Costa Rica to manage that nation's utilities. From 1941 until 1944, Krug worked at the Office of Production Management, and then the War Production Board (WPB), during the World War II, handling production and power problems. Krug served as chief of the power branch, deputy director general for priorities control, and deputy director general for distribution, rising to become director of the Office of War Utilities.

In April 1944, Krug left the WPB to serve as a lieutenant commander in the U.S. Navy Reserve. When he returned, in August 1944, he was named as chairman of the WPB. In August 1945, Krug quit. After leaving the WPB, Krug was offered a position in Hollywood as a consultant. Secretary of the Interior Harold Ickes resigned on 12 February

1946. On 26 February President Truman nominated Krug for the post and, on 6 March, Krug was confirmed. The *Washington Examiner* reported on the change at the top at Interior, "Almost overnight, Interior was a different place. You can sense the change in the labyrinth of the department's corridors; feel it, it seems, in the attitude of the elevator operators—at least they no longer have to worry about getting their heads chopped off for failing to recognize the agency's princelings, as happened at least once under the 'Curmudgeon.' . . . What for 14 years was a hornet's nest of politics, both public and personal, a backdrop for a one-man show, has become a place of public business. Doors are opened for the doers instead of the ax-grinders. Subordinates concentrate on their jobs instead of trying to outguess the changing moods of 'the chief'; office holders act like servants of the public, less like lords of the public domain."

Almost from the beginning, however, Krug's tenure ran into trouble. As head of the department, he oversaw the operations of mines. In the 1930s, the United Mine Workers of America (UMWA) demanded new services be included in their contracts. By 1946, health care for the miners became a crucial issue blocking a new contract. John L. Lewis, head of the UMWA, met with Krug. At that conference, Lewis charged Krug with labor violations. Krug seemed to settle the situation and left for vacation. Then Lewis announced that if the government refused to negotiate for a new contract the old one was void and the miners would strike. President Truman issued an Executive Order directing Krug to take possession of the mines and to negotiate "appropriate changes in the terms and conditions of employment." Lewis, panicked, met with Krug and negotiated the historic Krug-Lewis Agreement, which settled the strike before it could injure the American economy. Truman was hailed a hero, but it was Krug who did all of the work.

Secretary of State George Marshall developed the European Recovery Program (the Marshall Plan) to get postwar Western Europe back on its feet. Krug surveyed national resources to see what impact massive exports would have on them. His report, *National Resources and Foreign Aid: Report of J. A. Krug, Secretary of the Interior, October 9, 1947,* documented what could and could not be exported in large quantities. Historian Eugene Trani later said of his service at Interior, "The tone of his tenure as Interior Secretary was one of quiet efficiency with Mr. Krug working behind the scenes to get support for his programs. Among them was desegregation of the Washington recreation facilities that were then under his office. Spurred by overall federal desegregation guidelines and Mr. Krug's insistence, Washington began an open pool and playground policy in the early 1950s." However, Krug was not close to Truman, and was shut out of many policy decisions. He was not well acquainted with the problems of the American West or Native Americans, although he sympathized with the plight of the latter, and in many areas depended upon his assistant secretary, Oscar Chapman. By 1949, his health deteriorating, Krug offered his resignation on 25 November 1949. He was just 42 years old.

Krug remained in Washington, D.C., as a consultant on power issues. In 1969, he moved to Knoxville, Tennessee, where he was co-owner of the Volunteer Asphalt Company. At that time, he became the chairman of the board of Brookside Mills. On 26 March 1970, at the age of 62, he suffered a fatal heart attack.

References: "Biographical Sketch [of] J. A. Krug," in Box 113, folder 1, "Biographical Papers," Julius A. Krug Papers, Library of Congress; Ickes, Harold, "Farewell, Secretary Krug," *New Republic* 121: 22 (28 November 1949), 17; Trani, Eugene P., "the Secretaries of the Department of the Interior, 1849–1969" (unpublished manuscript, National Anthropological Archives, Smithsonian Institution, 1975), 210–217; Truman, Harry S, *Year of Decisions: Memoirs by Harry S Truman* (New York: Signet, 1965).

OSCAR LITTLETON CHAPMAN
1896–1978

Chapman had served for more than twenty years at the Department of the Interior, as deputy secretary, assistant secretary, and secretary. Yet he remains barely known. He was born in Omega, Virginia, on 22 October 1896, the son of James Jackson Chapman and Rosa Archer (née Blount) Chapman. He attended the Randolph Macon Academy in Bedford, Virginia, before entering the University of Denver in Colorado and the University of New Mexico. During World War I, he served in the U.S. Navy as a pharmacist's mate. He was injured in the line of duty and was sent to recuperate in a Denver hospital. There he met Benjamin B. Lindsey, a local judge, who named Chapman to the post of assistant, and later, chief probation officer, of the Juvenile Court. In 1929, Chapman earned an LL.B. degree from the Westminster Law School in Denver, and the same year was admitted to the Colorado bar.

Soon after being admitted to the bar, Chapman joined Edward Costigan, a noted Denver attorney, in a private law practice. In 1930, Costigan ran for the U. S. Senate, and Chapman handled his successful campaign. During this period, Chapman became involved in Democratic politics in Colorado, and he served as the chairman of the state child welfare committee, where he championed social welfare work. In 1932, he served as a delegate to the Democratic National Convention in Chicago, and ran the successful U.S. Senate campaign of Alva B. Adams, who ran on a New Deal reform ticket. When Franklin Roosevelt was elected to the White House, Chapman's old law partner Senator Costigan recommended Chapman for an appointment in the new administration. When asked what he desired, Chapman selected Interior, because it was there where he felt he could work in the assistance of minority groups, particularly the Native Americans, Hawaiians, and Filipinos. Roosevelt named Chapman to the post of assistant secretary of the interior, serving under Secretary Harold L. Ickes. When he took office in May 1933, he was just 36 years old, an intimate member of Roosevelt's Little Cabinet of secondary department advisers. During his thirteen-year tenure as Ickes's assistant, he handled the affairs of all of the department's numerous bureaus. When in 1939 the Daughters of the American Revolution refused to allow Marian Anderson, an African American singer, to perform in their hall, Ickes, with the assistance of Chapman, helped arranged for the land in front of the Lincoln Memorial to be set aside for an outdoor concert, where 75,000 heard her sing. On 12 February 1946, when Ickes resigned, President Truman named Chapman as acting secretary of the interior. While many inside the agency felt that Chapman should be named on a permanent basis, Truman selected Julius A. Krug instead. Chapman worked closely with Krug to get department programs enacted in Congress, and coordinate departmental policy. Chapman served as Krug's second-in-command from 1946 until 1949.

On 25 November 1949, Krug submitted his resignation. On 1 December 1949, President Truman named Chapman secretary, the culmination of a career that had begun nearly seventeen years earlier. His appointment to the position was no surprise to watchers of the Interior Department, and insiders in the agency were glad he finally was rewarded for years of loyal service. Yet in his three years of service as head of Interior, little policy making was accomplished. Eugene Trani explains, "As Secretary, Chapman completed the reorganization started by Krug. He championed decentralization, knowing the inefficiencies of Ickes's administration. In long years with the Department, he had come to know most of the bureau heads, and he let these men make decisions. Chapman advocated, in fact demanded, staff assistance, and he delegated anything he thought the bureaus could handle. He did, however, insist on handling controversial

questions, with decisions stemming from the Secretary's office." At the end of his term, in January 1953, the department published *Years of Progress: 1945–1952,* about the tenures of Krug and Chapman.

After leaving office, Chapman formed the Washington, D.C. law firm of Chapman, Duff & Paul, which specialized in energy and trade law. He remained active at his practice until the summer of 1977, when his health began to fail. Chapman died in Washington on 8 February 1978 at the age of 81. The *New York Times* said of him, "Oscar Chapman was always quiet, always smiling—and always there. Whenever the Democratic Party needed a troubleshooter in the Roosevelt and Truman eras, he was on the job. And although he served as Assistant Secretary, Under Secretary and Secretary of the Interior, it is as one of the shrewdest politicians of the century that his party and his nation are likely to remember him best."

References: "Chapman, Oscar L(ittleton)," in Charles Moritz, ed., *Current Biography 1949* (New York: H. W. Wilson, 1949), 101–104; "Chapman, Oscar Littleton," in *NCAB* H: 17–18; Trani, Eugene P., "The Secretaries of the Department of the Interior, 1849–1969" (unpublished manuscript, National Anthropological Archives, Smithsonian Institution, 1975), 218–224.

JAMES DOUGLAS MCKAY
1893–1959

Douglas McKay was a highly successful governor of Oregon, who supported Dwight D. Eisenhower for the presidency in 1952 and was named secretary of interior, serving from 1953 until 1956. The son of E. D. McKay, a carpenter, and Minnie (née Musgrove) McKay. McKay left high school in 1911 when his father died to help support his family. He entered Oregon Agricultural College at Corvalis in 1913 to study agriculture and graduated with a bachelor of science degree in 1917. He then volunteered for service in the U.S. Army and was wounded at the battle of Sedan during the Meuse-Argonne offensive, an injury that forced him, once he returned home, to give up any chance of a career in agriculture.

McKay worked in a series of jobs, including insurance salesman and car dealer, to support his wife and children. He became the head of a car dealership in Salem and saved enough money to open his own dealership. At the same time, McKay entered the local political scene as a Republican, and in 1932, was elected mayor of Salem. His tight fiscal policies during the years of the Depression earned him a reputation as a responsible administrator. In 1934, he was elected to the Oregon state senate, and served for four terms. In 1948, on a platform of fiscal responsibility, he was elected governor of Oregon. Although he denounced any federal intrusion into state matters as socialistic, he was nonetheless reelected in 1950. In 1952, although a firm supporter of Senator Robert A. Taft of Ohio, who represented the conservative wing of the Republican Party, McKay felt that Taft could not win the presidential nomination. Instead, McKay shifted his loyalty to the more liberal General Dwight D. Eisenhower, and campaigned in the state for him once he got the presidential nomination. Once elected, Eisenhower sought to reward McKay by naming him secretary of the interior. The choice was ridiculed by the media, as McKay had no experience with Interior-related issues. In his hearing before the Senate Committee on Interior and Insular Affairs, McKay said that he disagreed with the philosophy behind the Tennessee Valley Authority and the Rural Electrification Administration. Nonetheless, he was confirmed, and began work as more of a middle-of-the-roader than as the plunderer his political opponents labeled him. Biographer Herbert Parmet writes, "As Secretary, McKay helped to block such Democratic concepts as the Columbia Valley Authority and public development of the Hells Canyon project. Despite the heated opposition of preservationists concerned with maintaining the beauty of natural sites, he favored building the dam at Echo Park, a project that would have created a vast reservoir at Dinosaur National Monument." When an Alabama mining company received access to harvest Oregon timber, McKay was derided by environmentalists as Giveaway McKay.

On 9 May 1956, McKay resigned as secretary to run as a Republican for a U.S. Senate seat against Republican-turned-Democrat Wayne Morse. President Eisenhower supported McKay, but McKay lost to Morse by 50,000 votes when voters rebelled against the "giveaway" scheme that had haunted him at Interior. President Eisenhower then named him chairman of the U.S. section of the International Joint Commission to settle resource questions between the United States and Canada along the Columbia River. On 22 July 1959 he suffered a heart attack in Salem and died at the age of 66. McKay's funeral was held in the state house of representatives, and he was buried in Bellcrest Memorial Park in Salem.

References: David, Glenn B., "McKay, Douglas," in Eleanora W. Schoenebaum, ed., *Political Profiles: The Eisenhower Years* (New York: Facts on File, 1980), 402–403; Mahar, Franklyn Daniel, "Douglas McKay and the Issues of Power Development in Oregon, 1953–1956" (Ph.D. dissertation, University of Oregon, 1968); "McKay, James Douglas," in Robert Sobel and John Raimo, eds., *Biographical Directory of the Governors of the United States, 1789–1978* (Westport, CT: Meckler Books; 4 vols., 1978), 3: 1284–1285; Parmet, Herbert S., "McKay, Douglas," in *DAB* 6: 416–417; Richardson, Elmo, "The Interior Secretary as Conservation Villain: The Notorious Case of Douglas 'Giveaway' McKay," *Pacific Historical Review* 41: 3 (August 1972), 333–345.

FREDERICK ANDREW SEATON
1909–1974

Frederick Seaton was involved in the political arena for most of his life, starting off in the nation's capital and ending with a five-year term as secretary of the interior under Dwight D. Eisenhower. Born in Washington, D.C., on 11 December 1909, he was the son of Fay Noble Seaton, the secretary to Senator Joseph L. Bristow, and Dorothea Elizabeth (née Schmidt) Seaton. When Frederick was six, the family moved to Manhattan, Kansas, where Fay Seaton was the publisher of the Manhattan *Mercury*. Fred attended local schools before entering the Kansas State Agricultural College (now Kansas State University) in 1927 to study journalism. A Republican, he was the head of the campus Hoover for President Club in 1928. After leaving college in 1931, he went to work for his father's newspapers, as the wire news editor for the *Morning Chronicle* and, in 1933, as city editor of the *Mercury,* and then as associate editor of the Seaton chain of newspapers.

During the 1930s, Seaton became more involved with the Republican Party. He served as vice-chairman of the Kansas delegation to the Republican National Convention in 1936, and worked as a secretary for Governor Alf Landon, the Republican presidential nominee. From 1936 until 1940, he served as a member of the Republican National Speakers' Bureau.

In 1937, Seaton moved to Hastings, Nebraska, where he became the publisher of the *Daily Tribune* and advanced to president of the Seaton Publishing Company. He devoted several years to this enterprise before being elected to the first of two terms in Nebraska's legislature in 1945. Although he failed for reelection to a third term, on 10 December 1951 Governor Val Peterson named Seaton to a vacant U.S. senate seat. His voting record during his thirteen months in Washington was conservative During the 1952 election, he backed Republican presidential nominee General Dwight D. Eisenhower, and served as a principal adviser to the general during the campaign. In September 1953, Eisenhower named Seaton as assistant secretary of Defense for Legislative Affairs, working under Secretary of Defense Charles E. Wilson. Seaton was able to secure

firm contacts on Capitol Hill and got Wilson to hold regular press conferences. When Senator Joseph McCarthy offered Seaton a list of people who he felt were subversives, Seaton accepted it, but said that he would not keep the list secret. Eisenhower was impressed by Seaton's work and, on 19 February 1955, named him the president's administrative assistant for Congressional liaison. On 15 June 1955, Eisenhower promoted Seaton to the post of deputy assistant to the president.

On 9 May 1956, Secretary of the Interior James Douglas McKay resigned. Although many believed that Undersecretary Clarence Davis would be named to the vacancy, Eisenhower named Seaton to the post, even though Seaton had no experience in that area. Nonetheless, the selection received wide praise. Seaton spoke of creating a partnership in the department, of initiating a new era of cooperation. Seaton was one of the most activist secretaries of the modern period. A supporter of Mission 66, a National Park Service plan to renovate and update the national park system, Seaton also invited industry and conservationists in to his office and asked to be told of their plans and goals and to share his vision of the department. Seaton pledged to hold weekly conferences, and was equally available to the press at all times. Historians Chester Pach and Elmo Richardson write, "Seaton shrewdly used his knowledge of Capitol Hill to avoid the brouhaha over water and resource development that regularly engulfed his embattled predecessor. He managed, for example, to quiet the controversy that had lasted for years over McKay's decision to allow private construction of three dams in Hells Canyon, Idaho. He also succeeded in mollifying both resource developers and wilderness preservationists. In the president's eyes, Seaton's effective management and moderate policies epitomized Modern Republicanism."

In his first annual report, for 1956, Seaton stressed where his interests lay: "'CONSERVATION' is a magic word of many meanings, but the common denominator of most definitions is the concept that sound conservation demands wise and prudent use—without either waste or abuse—of our natural resources. . . . Within the framework of this concept, the Department of the Interior has promulgated the policies to which it adheres in carrying out the resource programs which are its responsibility. Judicious use of our natural resources is of paramount concern to all Americans. Each succeeding generation faces the ever-present responsibility to put natural resources to their most beneficial use, all the while employing conservation practices that will assure future generations of abundant supplies for their own use and enjoyment." In his 1957 report, he explained, "Our Nation . . . must work creatively to provide for the realistic development of its natural resource base in order to meet the growing demands of today's citizens and to pass along our resource heritage to generations of unborn Americans. . . . This is the task of the Department of the Interior, which has centered its activities on helping meet constructively both the immediate and long-range requirements of our expanding economy. Although directed toward harnessing natural resources for the peaceful pursuits of our people, the contribution of the Department's efforts to our national security in a troubled world cannot be overestimated." Seaton continued to speak out about the condition of the nation's natural resources. Seaton left office on 20 January 1961, with the end of the Eisenhower administration, and returned to his newspaper publishing business. In 1962, he ran for governor of Nebraska, but was defeated. He remained an active participant in the Republican Party, serving as the chairman of President Richard Nixon's Committee on Timber and Environment.

Seaton died on 16 January 1974 in Minneapolis, Minnesota. He was 64.

References: "Meet Secretary Seaton," *American Forests* 62: 7 (July 1956), 8, 63; Pach, Chester J., Jr., and Elmo Richardson, *The Presidency of Dwight D. Eisenhower* (Lawrence: University Press of Kansas, 1991), 182–183; "Seaton, Fred(erick) A.(ndrew)," in Charles Moritz, ed., *Current Biography 1956* (New York: H. W. Wilson, 1956), 559–561; Trani, Eugene P., "The Secretaries of the Department of the Interior, 1849–1969" (unpublished manuscript, National Anthropological Archives, Smithsonian Institution, 1975), 232–236.

STEWART LEE UDALL
1920–

Many were surprised by the choice of Representative Stewart Udall of Arizona to be the secretary of the interior in the Kennedy administration. Yet the selection of Udall, the scion of a pioneering Arizona family, which took into account his long history of defending the environment, was not so surprising, and he became one of the leaders and major stars of the administration. Udall was born in St. John's, Arizona, on 31 January 1920, the son of Levi Stewart Udall, an attorney and justice on the Arizona Supreme Court, and Louise (née Lee) Udall. Stewart spent his early years on his father's farm north of St. John's. After attending a small local school, he entered the Eastern Arizona Junior College in Thatcher, then went to the University of Arizona in Tucson, but did not graduate. Instead, he left school and became a Mormon missionary, traveling the nation.

During World War II, Udall enlisted in the U.S. Army Air Forces and served as a gunner on a B-24 in Italy with the Fifteenth Air Force. He returned to the University of Arizona after the war and earned a law degree. He then formed a law partnership in Tucson with his brother Morris.

In an oral history interview in 1979, Udall said of his political roots, "I guess, to type myself as a 'New Deal liberal' would have been fairly accurate. I was a great admirer of Franklin Roosevelt, and I felt that the changes that he instituted, the things that he proposed were something very fine and good for the country. I felt also at home with the New Deal coalition—labor unions, schoolteachers, the traditional groups that were allied with the Democratic party. My interests and convictions were allied with theirs, although Arizona began changing when I became a congressman—it was becoming more conservative and we were moving into a period when the New Deal wasn't all that relevant. I think that's where my roots were, to be very honest about it." In 1954, when Congressman Harold A. Patten decided to retire, Udall ran for his seat and was elected, serving the first of three terms. A strong environmentalist, he argued for increased federal funds for environmental programs, and supported such projects as the Colorado River Project. He said, "the one overriding principle of the conservation movement is that no work of man (save the bare minimum of roads, trails, and necessary public facilities in public areas) should intrude into the wonder places of the National Park System."

On 7 December 1960, following the election of Senator John F. Kennedy to the presidency, Udall was selected to serve as secretary of the interior. During his tenure, from 21 January 1961 until 20 January 1969, Udall initiated a new era. He closed the sale of public lands for eighteen months to revise departmental policies, and to reinvigorate the public power sector. During his time in office, Congress enacted the Wilderness Act (1964), the Highway Beautification Act (1965), the Endangered Species Act (1966), the National Trails System Act (1968), and the Wild and Scenic Rivers Act (1968).

In his 1961 annual report, Udall explained, "The Department of the Interior has the prime function of planning for the future of America and working to conserve the natural resources which sustain its life. But because so much of what is happening inside America today is drowned out by the clamor of an embattled world, it is only recently that we have become aware of a growing internal crisis which deeply affects the lives of all Americans. This 'Quiet Crisis' concerns a battle being waged against us from within by the forces of natural progress and explosive growth. In its wake across America this battle has left polluted rivers and lakes, disappearing open space, overcrowded parks, de-clining resources, the threatened extinction of certain species of our wildlife, and dwindling opportunities for the outdoor experiences which through the years have had such a profound influence in shaping the national character of America."

In his 1962 report, Udall discussed the White House Conference on Conservation, which had been held under his auspices in Washington in May 1962. In his 1963 report, he wrote, "Science must become the servant of conservation. It is our responsibility to the future to generate a third great wave of conservation which will be a worthy successor to the forward thrust supplied by the two great Roosevelts—to devise new programs that will enable us to preserve this green environment which means so much to us all." During this period, Udall established seashore national parks at Cape Cod, Point Reyes in California, and Padre Island in Texas, the largest amount of land added to the National Park System by any administration. In November 1963, Udall published *The Quiet Crisis,* a history of the conservation and environmental movements in the United States, and their attempts to end pollution and preserve wildlife and the environment. After the assassination of President Kennedy on 22 November 1963, President Lyndon Johnson asked Udall to remain in his post. Udall served until the end of Johnson's tenure in January 1969, continuing to oversee landmark legislation passed by Congress. His "beautification" strategy was considered an integral part of Johnson's domestic plan called "the Great Society."

Udall left office on 20 January 1969 and since that time has been an outspoken supporter of increased environmental awareness. As an attorney, he represented Native American uranium miners in Arizona, New Mexico and Utah in numerous lawsuits against the U.S. government. Udall is also an acclaimed writer and lecturer.

References: Box 80, Files 1 and 2–7 (clippings and notes on Udall selection), Stewart Lee Udall Collection (Manuscript collection AZ 372), University of Arizona Library, Special Collections Department; Stewart Lee Udall Oral History Interview, Box 10, Former Members of Congress Oral History Project, Library of Congress; "Udall, Stewart L(ee)," in Charles Moritz, ed., *Current Biography 1961* (New York: H. W. Wilson, 1961), 464–466.

WALTER JOSEPH HICKEL

1919–

Walter Hickel was a controversial choice for secretary of the interior, opposed by environmental groups. Yet within two years was hailed as an "environmental populist." He was dismissed by President Richard Nixon because of his outspoken stand against the killing of students at Kent State University in 1970. Walter Hickel was born in Ellinwood, Kansas, on 18 August 1919,the son of Robert A. Hickel and Emma (née Zecha) Hickel, tenant farmers. He attended local schools in nearby Claflin, Kansas, but only went until he was 16 so that he could work on the family farm. When he became 19, he moved to California, where he saved some money as a carpenter so that he could move to Australia. When he learned that he could not get a passport until he turned 21, he instead went to Alaska.

Hickel arrived in Alaska at age 20 with thirty-seven cents in his pocket. He washed dishes, slept in a cabin to conserve money, and later worked as a bartender, on the Alaska Railroad, and as a construction worker. He then built his own home, sold it at a profit, then repeated the enterprise, and, by 1946, had made his name in the construction business. In 1947, he founded the Hickel Construction Company of Anchorage and eventually became a multimillionaire developer of hotels, homes, and shopping centers. By 1969, his estimated worth was purported to be $14 million. He also involved himself in the political scene, serving as Alaska's Republican National committeeman from 1954 to 1964. In 1959, he was a major supporter of statehood for Alaska, which cul-

minated in the territory being admitted as the forty-ninth state. In 1964, Hickel backed the presidential nomination of Richard Nixon, the former vice-president, but when Senator Barry Goldwater of Arizona was nominated instead, Hickel resigned from the party. In 1966, he challenged two-term Alaska Governor William A. Egan and won by 1,000 votes out of 65,000 cast. During his four-year term, he established a commission that recommended that a system of roads and highways be built across Alaska, and he asked for the right to drill for oil and gas in the Arctic Wildlife Range, but was refused by the Department of the Interior.

During the 1968 presidential campaign, when the Republican Party did nominate Richard Nixon, Hickel served as the national cochairman of Nixon's campaign committee. Following Nixon's election, on 11 December 1968 the president-elect, in a television broadcast, announced his cabinet to the nation—among the selections was Hickel as secretary of the interior. His nomination was very controversial; his Senate confirmation hearings lasted for days, and the transcript of the report composes a huge volume of testimony. In the end, however, Hickel was confirmed on 23 January 1969 by a vote of 73 to 16, and he took office as the thirty-eighth secretary of the interior. His tenure, which lasted until 25 November 1970, was marked by a drastic change from one who despised environmentalists to one who embraced them.

Journalist E. W. Kenworthy of the *New York Times* wrote, "Overnight, Mr. Hickel began to accumulate a constituency among the conservation groups that had opposed him. And the constituency grew as he made decision after decision that demonstrated concern for environment. . . . He came into office convinced that it was safe to proceed with an oil pipeline across Alaska. But he listened to the scientific doubts of geologists and agreed that the pipeline should not get a permit until the companies had come up with a satisfactory plan" to handle potential environmental damage. Hickel championed congressional legislation that mandated that oil companies, and not the federal government, clean up oil spills, and advocated that serious pollutants be removed from everyday household items. However, Hickel's biggest problem was with the administration itself. Always outspoken, he decided on 20 May 1970 to send a letter to the president calling attention to the government's military policy in Vietnam, which Hickel felt was alienating American youth. The letter embarrassed Nixon personally, especially when it was leaked to the press, and he began to look for ways to get Hickel to resign. Instead, Hickel remained steadfast. "The president hired me, and he will have to fire me," he claimed. On 25 November 1970, Hickel was called to the White House for a private meeting with President Nixon. According to press secretary Ron Ziegler, Nixon told Hickel that he felt "that the required elements for a good and continued relationship which must exist between the President and his Cabinet did not exist in this case," and fired Hickel on the spot. Later that afternoon, at a press conference, Hickel explained, "Well, the President personally terminated me about two hours ago, and there's really nothing I can say to help the situation and nothing I would say to hurt. Given the hostility toward me when I first arrived—as you people well know—and some of those incredible decisions I had to make immediately thereafter, and trying to do a job for the President and all Americans, and still survive as an individual, I had to do it my way."

Hickel returned to his private business in Alaska, and made millions in real estate deals. In 1974, 1982, and 1986, he was defeated in elections to become governor. In 1990, however, he ran for governor on the ticket of the fringe Alaska Independence Party and was elected with 37 percent of the vote. He was controversial in this second term, suing the U.S. government for setting aside 100 million acres of the state in violation of the Alaska charter and constitution. However, when Hickel allowed the hunting of Alaskan wolves from helicopters, he lost the support of some in his own party, and in 1994 he did not run for reelection. In 1996,

having returned to the Republican Party, Hickel served as the Alaska state chairman of the Dole-Kemp presidential campaign.

References: "Hickel, Walter Joseph," in Robert Sobel and John Raimo, eds., *Biographical Directory of the Governors of the United States, 1789–1978* (Westport, CT: Meckler Books; 4 vols., 1978), 1: 44; Rauber, Paul, "Golly, Wally! Alaska's Governor Thinks Big—But a Wild and Pristine State Is the Last Thing on His Mind," *Sierra* 77: 3 (May/June 1992), 38–42.

ROGERS CLARK BALLARD MORTON
1914–1979

Rogers Morton held cabinet posts in two administrations and served as a Republican member of Congress and as Republican Party national chairman. The son of Dr. David Cummins Morton and Mary Harris (née Ballard) Morton, he was born in Louisville, Kentucky, on 19 September 1914. Morton received his primary education at Woodberry Forest School near Orange, Virginia, and attended Yale University, graduating in 1937.

After leaving Yale, Morton went to the College of Physicians and Surgeons at Columbia University, New York, but decided against a career in medicine and left. He then managed the family business, Ballard & Ballard Milling. He volunteered for service in the U.S. Navy, but was discharged because of a back affliction. Instead, when World War II started, he enlisted in the U.S. Army a private and rose to the rank of captain. He returned to the United States and became vice-president of Ballard & Ballard, serving until it was sold to Pillsbury in 1951. The following year, Morton moved, with his wife and children, from Louisville to the Chesapeake Bay region of Maryland, where he built an estate he called Presqu'ile.

Starting in 1946, Rogers Morton was the campaign manager for his brother, who was elected to the U.S. House of Representatives. He reentered politics in 1960, managing the unsuccessful congressional campaign of Republican Edward T. Miller. Two years later, however, Morton ran for the same seat, representing Maryland's First Congressional District, and was elected to the first of five terms. A staunch advocate of wilderness and the outdoors, Morton served on the House Committees on Interior and Insular Affairs, and Merchant Marines and Fisheries. His business acumen was illustrated in his sitting for a short period on the Select Committee on Small Business. He assisted, during the 1960s, in helping to enact several pieces of legislation to protect the Eastern Shore and the Chesapeake Bay areas of Maryland. In 1969, after he was reelected to a fourth term, Morton relinquished all seats on these other committees for a chance to sit on the important Ways and Means Committee, which drew up legislation surrounding budgetary matters.

From 1968, when former Vice-president Richard Nixon was elected president, Morton was a strong supporter of the administration. Morton had served as Nixon's campaign manager and floor manager at the 1968 Republican National Convention, and, a month following Nixon's inauguration, Republican National Committee chairman Ray C. Bliss resigned, Nixon named Morton to head the council. Morton served as chairman from 1969 until 1971, while at the same time holding on to his congressional seat.

Morton had been hoping for a cabinet position once Nixon was elected in 1968, desiring the Interior portfolio. Instead, Nixon named Walter J. Hickel to the post. Hickel was fired, and according to the *Washington Post*, Morton had been told a week earlier that once Hickel was fired, he would be his replacement. He was nominated on 25 January 1971, and confirmed by voice vote three days later, becoming the thirty-ninth secretary of the interior and the first easterner to hold that office. During his tenure, which lasted until 30 April 1975, through the remainder of the Nixon administration and part of the Gerald Ford administration, Morton served in a caretaker capacity. Almost immediately, he ran into trouble when he approved a permit for the building of the Trans-Alaska Pipeline. Morton also had difficulty dealing with Native American issues. For years, Native Americans had been starting to assert their rights, decrying government control of their lives and reservations. In November 1972, this exploded when a faction of the American Indian Movement seized the offices of the Bureau of Indian Affairs at the Interior Department. The following March, the siege by two factions of the movement clashed at Wounded Knee, South Dakota.

On 9 August 1974, when Nixon was forced to resign, Morton was selected with others as a secret transition team for Ford. Morton thus became a close adviser to the new president. On 26 March 1975, Secretary of Commerce Frederick Baily Dent resigned. On 7 April, President Ford asked Morton to accept the commerce position and formally nominated him. The Senate confirmed Morton on 25 April, and, on 1 May, he took office as the secretary of Commerce. On 2 February 1976, after just nine months in office, Morton resigned to become the chairman of President Ford's election committee. Ford's narrow loss to Governor Jimmy Carter of Georgia left Morton out of government for the first time in fifteen years.

Morton retired to his estate. On 19 April 1979, at the age of 64, Morton died of prostate cancer. Former President Ford called him "one of the most decent, honorable, constructive, unselfish, and lovable persons I've ever known. He gave so much and expected nothing but friendship. The nation has lost a real man."

References: "Morton, Rogers C. B.," in Charles Moritz, ed., *Current Biography 1971* (New York: H. W. Wilson, 1971), 287–289.

STANLEY KNAPP HATHAWAY
1924–

Stanley Hathaway served as the fortieth secretary of the interior for a mere six weeks, resigning because of physical exhaustion and severe depression. Born in Osceola, Nebraska, on 19 July 1924, he is the son of Franklin E. Hathaway and Velam (née Holbrook) Hathaway. He served in the United States Army Air Corps from 1943 to 1945, and when he returned to the United States at the end of World War II, he entered the University of Nebraska and earned a bachelor's degree in 1948 and his law degree in 1950. Admitted to the Wyoming bar, he served as the prosecuting attorney for Goshen County, Wyoming, from 1954 to 1962.

A Republican, Hathaway served as a member of the Wyoming Republican Party and as its chairman from 1962 to 1964. In 1966, he ran for governor of Wyoming and was elected over Democrat Ernest Wilkinson by 10,000 votes out of some 110,000 cast. Biographers Robert Sobel and John Raimo write, "As governor, he sponsored efforts toward reorganizing state government and developing the Wyoming Quality Growth Plan, which included environmental protection standards and selective development of Wyoming's economy." Reelected in 1970, he returned to his law practice at the end of his term.

On 7 April 1975, President Gerald Ford asked Secretary of Commerce Rogers Morton to become the secretary of commerce; at the same time, Ford named Hathaway to replace Morton at Interior. Hathaway was criticized by environmental groups for his "regrettable suppliance to the will of big oil," but he was confirmed on 11 June 1975 by a vote of 60 to 36. However, soon after taking office, Hathaway developed fatigue and mental depression; six weeks after being sworn in, he resigned for "reasons of my personal health." His was the second shortest tenure at Interior. He returned to Wyoming, where he practiced law.

References: "Hathaway, Stanley K.," in Robert Sobel, ed.-in-chief, *Biographical Directory of the United States Executive Branch, 1774-1989* (Westport, CT: Greenwood, 1990), 169; "Hathaway, Stanley Knapp," in Robert Sobel and John Raimo, eds., *Biographical Directory of the Governors of the United States, 1789-1978* (Westport, CT: Meckler Books; 4 vols., 1978), 4:1783–1884.

THOMAS SAVIG KLEPPE
1919–

Thomas Kleppe was little known when selected by President Gerald Ford to serve as secretary of the interior to succeed Stanley Hathaway. During his fifteen-month tenure, he acted as a caretaker of the department. Thomas Savig Kleppe was born in the Kintyre, North Dakota, on 1 July 1919, the son of Lars Kleppe and Hannah (née Savig) Kleppe. Lars Kleppe, a homesteader, ran the Farmers Company, a grain-elevator business, and, by the time he was 17, Thomas was his father's right-hand man. He graduated from Valley City High School, then attended Valley City State College for only one year, leaving in 1937 to work full time for his father during the Depression. He later went to work as a bookkeeper at a local bank before he served in the U.S. Army as a warrant officer during World War II. He then went to work for a friend of his father's who manufactured cleaning products; Kleppe became president of the company in 1958.

In 1950, Kleppe ran and was elected mayor of Bismarck, North Dakota, where he served until 1954. In 1963, he became treasurer of the state Republican Party, and the following year he unsuccessfully challenged Senator Quentin Burdick for his Senate seat. Two years later, Kleppe ran for the U.S. House of Representatives. Former Vice-president Richard Nixon toured the area in support of Kleppe's candidacy. Kleppe was elected, and in the House sat on the Agriculture Committee. He was reelected in 1968, but, in 1970 gave up his seat to challenge Burdick a second time. Again, Kleppe lost, and, to compensate him, President Nixon appointed Kleppe as head of the Small Business Administration. During his tenure, allegations of abuses of the loan system came about, although Kleppe was not implicated in any of these.

On 9 September 1975, Secretary of the Interior Stanley Hathaway resigned. President Ford named Kleppe to the vacant spot. Rep. Morris K. Udall of Arizona, whose brother had served as secretary of the interior in the Kennedy and Johnson administrations, said, "Tom Kleppe is qualified for a lot of jobs, but not Secretary of the Interior." Nonetheless, Kleppe was confirmed unanimously by the Senate on 9 October 1975, and sworn into office on 17 October as the forty-first secretary of the interior and the first North Dakotan ever to serve in the cabinet. During his short tenure, Kleppe angered environmentalists by approving the sale of offshore oil and gas leases in the Northern Gulf of Alaska, although he reduced the area to be sold from 1.8 million acres to 1.1 million. His other key accomplishment was his oversight of the *Argo Merchant* ship disaster off the Nantucket Coast of Massachusetts.

Kleppe left office at the end of the Ford administration on 20 January 1977 and returned to private business in North Dakota.

References: Green, John Robert, *The Presidency of Gerald R. Ford* (Lawrence: University Press of Kansas, 1995); "Kleppe, Thomas S(avig)," in Charles Moritz, ed., *Current Biography 1976* (New York: H. W. Wilson, 1976), 218–221.

CECIL DALE ANDRUS
1931–

Cecil Andrus was a national spokesman for his state's chief crop, potatoes, on television, long before he came to prominence as Jimmy Carter's secretary of the interior. His tenure, which lasted throughout the Carter administration, has been considered by historians of the department as the most stable in the last thirty years of that agency. Born in Hood River, Oregon, on 25 August 1931, the son of Hal Stephen Andrus, a sawmill operator, and Dorothy (née John) Andrus. Andrus spent much of his boyhood on his family's farm before going to work in the timber industry. He attended local schools before entering Oregon State University in Corvallis in 1948, but he left the following year without graduating. In 1951 he volunteered for duty in the U.S. Marines and in 1955, was discharged with the rank of aviation electronic technician second class. He returned to Oregon, where he went to work as a lumberjack at the Tru-Cut Lumber Corporation in Orofino, Idaho, rising to become production manager.

In 1961, Andrus entered the political arena when, at age 29, he ran for a seat in the Idaho state senate and was elected (becoming the youngest state senator in Idaho history), serving in that body until 1966, and again from 1968 to 1970. In 1966, he ran for the Democratic nomination for governor, but lost narrowly in the Democratic primary to John Charles Herndon. When Herndon was killed in a plane crash, Andrus was substituted as the Democratic nominee, but he lost in the general election to Republican Don Samuelson. Andrus went to work as an insurance agent. He was reelected to the state senate in 1968, and served a single term. In 1970, he challenged Samuelson for the governorship, running on a platform of saving the Castle Peak in the Challis National Forest from a smelting mine, which Samuelson supported. Backed by environmentalists, Andrus won by nearly 11,000 votes to become the first Democratic governor of Idaho in 24 years. He was able to get increased funding for schools, established child development centers, and got a reduction in taxes for senior citizens. Perhaps his most enduring accomplishment were his television commercials for Idaho potatoes. Andrus easily won reelection in 1974 for a second four-year term.

On 18 December 1976, President-elect Jimmy Carter announced that he was appointing Andrus as secretary of the interior. When he had been asked earlier if he desired such a post, he replied, "If not me, I hope a Cecil Andrus 'type.'" As the *New York Times* noted upon his selection, "Governor Andrus is regarded as an environmental pragmatist who manages to remain in good standing with conservation and business interests"(18 December 1976). Officially nominated on 20 January 1977, he was confirmed by voice vote four days later, resigned the governorship that same day, and took office as the forty-second secretary of the interior. Biographer Marie Marmo Mullaney wrote, "Andrus strove for a sense of balance in the development and protection of the nation's resources. During his four-year tenure, his leadership was decisive in resolving the bitter Alaska lands dispute. That settlement protected 103 million acres of virgin public land for parks, wildlife habitat, and forest land, as well as opening up more than 250 million acres of federal land for development." In 1997, Andrus wrote, "What do I consider my greatest achievement in office? . . . I would say . . . that passage of the Alaska Lands Act was a major accomplishment, as was the Surface Mining Act, which made it possible to mine coal on federal lands with stringent environmental controls. Also, offshore oil and gas exploration had been stymied for many years, and we created a program that made it possible to sell and develop oil and gas leases but, again, with stringent environmental controls, which had never existed before." When Jimmy Carter left office in January 1981, Andrus returned to Idaho and established a consulting firm on natural resources

issues. In 1986 and 1990, Andrus was reelected governor, becoming the first man in Idaho history to be elected to four separate gubernatorial terms. In 1995, Andrus left office for the second time in twenty-five years, and retired. Today, he is the chairman of the Andrus Center for Public Policy at Boise State University in Idaho.

References: "Andrus, Cecil D.," in Charles Moritz, ed., *Current Biography 1977* (New York: H. W. Wilson, 1977), 29–32; "Andrus, Cecil Dale," in Robert Sobel and John Raimo, eds., *Biographical Directory of the Governors of the United States, 1789–1978* (Westport, CT: Meckler Books; 4 vols., 1978), 1:360–361; Mullaney, Marie Marmo, *Biographical Directory of the Governors of the United States, 1988–1994* (Westport, CT: Greenwood, 1994), 107–110; Letter from Andrus to author, 28 May 1997; U.S. Congress, Senate, Committee on Interior and Insular Affairs, *Interior Nomination: Hearings Before the Committee on Interior and Insular Affairs, United States Senate, Ninety-fifth Congress, First Session, on the Proposed Nomination of Governor Cecil D. Andrus to be Secretary of the Interior, January 17 and 18, 1977* (Washington, DC: GPO, 1977).

JAMES GAIUS WATT
1938–

About James Watt's resignation as secretary of the interior in October 1983, the *New York Times* wrote, "With the departure of James Watt, the Department of Interior loses its most active secretary probably since Harold Ickes. Mr. Watt has been a mover and a shaker." However, Watt was highly controversial, and several statements and actions that he made served to cut short his tenure. Born on 31 January 1938 in Lusk, Wyoming, he is the son of William G. Watt, a lawyer and rancher, and Lois (née Williams) Watt. As a young man, Watt worked on his family's ranch. When he was eight, the family moved to Wheatland, Wyoming, where his father opened a law practice and his mother managed the Globe Hotel. Watt, after attending local schools, entered the College of Commerce and Industry at the University of Wyoming, and earned a bachelor of science degree with honors in 1960.

For a time after graduating Watt worked as an interviewer for the Small Business Administration; however, in the fall of 1960 he entered the University of Wyoming's School of Law, and received his law degree in 1962. That same year, he became a personal assistant to Milward L. Simpson, a Republican candidate for the U. S. Senate. When Simpson was elected in November, Watt accompanied him to Washington and served as both his legislative assistant and chief counsel until leaving in 1966. He then went to work as a secretary to a chamber of commerce committee on natural resources and environmental pollution control policies. In 1969, he was named a deputy assistant secretary of the interior for water power and development by President Richard Nixon, and he held the post until he was named director of the Bureau of Outdoor Recreation. In 1975, President Gerald Ford named him as a member of the Federal Power Commission, a position he held until January 1977. That year, he returned to the western United States and became the head of the Mountain States Legal Foundation, headquartered in Denver, Colorado. In the 1970s, resistance to federal mandates over land management and natural resources began in the western states, and was dubbed the "Sagebrush Rebellion." Established by Joseph Coors, the head of one of the nation's largest breweries, the Mountain States Legal Foundation was created to defend the rights of people opposed to federal mandates and other dictates. As the head of the firm, Watt became closely tied to the tide of anti-environmentalism in the West.

With the 1980 election of former California governor Ronald Reagan, a revolution swept over Washington. One of Reagan's most controversial selections for a cabinet post came on 22 December 1980 when he selected Watt to be his secretary of the interior. Historian Ron Arnold reports that former

Senator Clifford Hansen of Wyoming had been Reagan's first choice for Interior, but Hansen's family had held leases with the Bureau of Land Management, which he would oversee if chosen, a conflict of interest. On 2 December 1980, he phoned President-elect Reagan and declined the position. On 3 December, Reagan's transition team was ordered to find a new face. They came up with several names, among them Watt's. Watt was asked to fly to Washington for an interview. Senator Paul Laxalt of Nevada had a lengthy interview with him, then called Reagan and said, "I've found the man for Interior. His name is Jim Watt—you haven't met him—and he's razor sharp. He's a steely manager who knows the Department, and he can take the pressure—he's got the hide of a rhino. What's more, he's clean as a whistle. He's our man." Watt's nomination was immediately condemned by environmentalists, who cited his record at Interior in the 1970s and his work for the Mountain States Legal Foundation as proof of his animosity toward conservation issues. Nonetheless, on 22 January 1981, Watt was confirmed, 83 to 12, and he took office as the forty-third secretary of the interior.

In nearly three years as Interior secretary, Watt may have become the most controversial man to ever hold that post. Almost immediately, he angered environmentalists by cutting in half the federal funding for the purchase of parklands in cities and towns, and advocated ending all such funding the following year. He offered to lease 1.3 million acres off the shore of northern California for gas and oil exploration. In 1982, he proposed selling 35 million acres, or 5 percent, of all federal land to help pay down the deficit for that year. He attempted to sell off 800,000 acres that had been designated as wilderness areas, and advocated doubling the price of duck stamps to raise more revenue for wetlands preservation. In April 1983, he even angered Reagan when he refused the use of federal lands for a concert by the Beach Boys, a group he denounced. Reagan, who liked the group's music, rescinded Watt's decision and awarded the secretary a plaster foot to remind him to avoid similar remarks in the future.

But what finally ended Watt's service was a remark he made concerning the ethnic makeup of a panel he had just established. "I have a black, a woman, two Jews and a cripple," he told reporters. Watt was condemned for his comments, and on 9 October 1983, he issued a letter of resignation to President Reagan, which was accepted. Watt wrote, "It is time for a new phase of management, one to consolidate the gains we have made. It is my view that my usefulness to you in this Administration has come to an end. A different type of leadership at the Department of the Interior will best serve you and the nation."

After leaving office, Watt worked as a consultant, lobbying the Department of Housing and Urban Development. In 1990, during a criminal investigation of influence-peddling in the department, Watt received a subpoena for documents relating to his lobbying; during his testimony before the grand jury, he withheld some of the documents. He was charged with more than fifty counts of lying to a grand jury, but on 12 March 1996 pleaded guilty to some of the charges and was sentenced to five years' probation, a $5,000 fine, and 500 hours of community service.

References: Arnold, Ron, *At the Eye of the Storm: James Watt and the Environmentalists* (Chicago: Regnery Gateway, 1982), 25–27; "Watt, James G(aius)," in Charles Moritz, ed., *Current Biography 1982* (New York: H. W. Wilson, 1982), 431–434.

WILLIAM PATRICK CLARK
1931–

William Clark was a close adviser of Ronald Reagan's when Reagan was governor of California, and became a justice on the California Supreme Court. When Reagan became president in 1981, Clark served as deputy secretary of state, assistant to the president for national security affairs and, in 1983, as the forty-fourth secretary of the interior. Clark, the son of William Pettit Clark, a cattleman and fourth-generation Californian, and Bernice (née Gregory) Clark, was born in Oxnard, California, on 23 October 1931. William Clark attended local schools before entering the Villanova Preparatory School in Ojai. He enrolled in Stanford University. However, after a year, he left Stanford to enter the Augustinian Novitiate in New Hamburg, New York, in 1950. After just a year there, he quit and returned to Stanford, but continued his studies at the University of Santa Clara. Before earning a degree, he attended the Loyola Law School in Los Angeles. In December 1953, Clark was drafted into the U.S. Army and served as a counterintelligence agent and spent the next two years in Germany. In 1955, Clark returned to the United States and, while working during the day as an insurance adjuster, spent nights at law school. Although he never earned a law degree, he took the state bar in 1958 and was able to practice law.

Clark returned to Oxnard, where he helped to establish the law firm of Clark, Cole & Fairfield, and was a senior partner from 1958 until 1966. A Democrat, he nonetheless became disillusioned with the direction of the party in the 1960s under the direction of Governor Edmund G. Brown of California. In 1964, Clark went to a dinner for Republican Presidential candidate Senator Barry Goldwater of Arizona, and met Ronald Reagan, who was speaking on behalf of Goldwater. the two men became friends. In 1965, when Reagan was considering challenging Brown for the governorship, Clark hosted fund-raising parties for him and served as one of his campaign managers. Reagan was elected in 1966, and named Clark as a member of the state government reorganization task force; when Reagan took office in January 1967, Clark was named as his chief of staff. Here he worked with such men as Edwin Meese III and Michael K. Deaver, men who would play an integral role in Reagan's later political life. As chief of staff, Clark personally briefed Reagan each day on important issues, turning the office into "a smoothly running operation," as *U.S. News & World Report* later said.

In January 1969, Reagan named Clark to the first of a series of judicial appointments, starting with a seat on the California Superior Court in San Luis Obispo, followed by seats as an associate justice on the State Court of Appeals in August 1971 and in 1972, as an associate justice on the California Supreme Court. Although his nomination was controversial because he had never earned a law degree, Clark worked during his tenure on the state's highest court as one of the leading conservatives on the court, often coming into conflict with the liberal chief justice, Rose Bird. He was considered honest and trustworthy even by his political opposition.

When Reagan was elected president in 1980, several of his lists for cabinet appointments included the name of William Clark for secretary of Agriculture, attorney general, and even director of the Central Intelligence Agency, but Clark refused all of them, instead accepting the post of deputy secretary of state under Alexander Haig, but only after Edwin Meese, selected as presidential counsel, came to Clark with a plea from Reagan to be in his administration. This appointment caused new controversy, mainly because Clark had no foreign policy experience. Nonetheless, the Senate Foreign Relations Committee approved his nomination and, on 24 February 1981, he was confirmed by the Senate, 70 to 24. Clark soon became involved in all areas of foreign affairs. Clark was put in charge of department policy in El Salvador, and he substituted for Haig at a Paris meeting of the Organization for Economic Cooperation and Development. By late 1981, *Newsweek* was reporting the Clark "added elements of wisdom and restraint" to the State Department.

In late 1981, allegations that National Security Adviser Richard Allen had accepted small gifts from a South Korean delegation led to a criminal investigation. Even though Allen was cleared on any wrongdoing, on 4 January 1982 Reagan announced the resignation of Allen and his replacement by Clark. Clark brought in conservatives Clare Boothe Luce and William F. Buckley as advisers to the president. As such, during Clark's tenure the hard line of the Reagan administration against the Soviet Union was reinforced, so much so, that when Secretary of State Haig did not approve of the way Clark was advising the president, Clark convinced Reagan to get rid of Haig and replace him with the more temperate George Shultz. Clark served in this capacity until 1983.

On 9 October 1983, Secretary of the Interior James G. Watt resigned. A *New York Times* report speculating about who was to replace him centered on Norman Livermore, who served as California's secretary of natural resources while Ronald Reagan was governor; Russell Train, the former head of the Environmental Protection Agency; and former Senator James L. Buckley of New York. On 13 October 1983, just four days after Watt left office, Reagan announced that he had selected Clark and was moving Clark's aide, Robert McFarlane, into the post of national security adviser. Reagan said, "He is a God-fearing Westerner, a fourth-generation rancher and a person I trust. And I think he will be a great Secretary of the Interior." Because he had no experience in the area of natural resources and the environment, Clark's appointment was strongly criticized, particularly by environmental groups. However, Clark was supported by Republicans on Capitol Hill, and, on 18 November 1983, he was confirmed, 71 to 18, as the forty-fourth secretary of the interior. Clark's tenure, which lasted until 6 February 1985, was merely a caretaker one in which he sought to undo the political damage caused by his predecessor. The *New York Times* wrote in 1985 that his chief accomplishments in his fifteen months at Interior included "restoring communications with Congress, conservationists, and other outside groups ... changes in coal and offshore oil leasing programs ... [and] a return to [the] acquisition of National Park and wildlife refuge land after a moratorium imposed by Watt."

On 1 January 1985, Clark announced his

intention to resign and retire in California, adding that he would stay on until his replacement was confirmed. On 6 February, when Energy Secretary Donald Hodel was confirmed, Clark left and returned to his ranch near San Luis Obispo, California.

References: "Clark, William P(atrick)," in Charles Moritz, ed., *Current Biography 1982* (New York: H. W. Wilson, 1982), 68–71.

DONALD PAUL HODEL
1935–

See Secretary of the Energy, 1982–1985

MANUEL LUJÁN, JR.
1928–

The first Hispanic to serve as secretary of the interior, Manuel Luján was elected to Congress from a rural New Mexico district, where he championed free enterprise and the use of natural resources. Although he was the first Interior head to serve a four-year term in nearly a decade, and the second in nearly twenty years, his tenure received little notice from the media. Born on a small farm near the Indian pueblo of San Ildefonso, New Mexico, on 12 May 1928, Luján was the eighth of eleven children of Manuel Luján, Sr., and Lorenzita (née Romero) Luján. Luján Sr. was the owner and operator of a successful insurance agency in Santa Fe and was later elected mayor of that city. In the 1940s he ran unsuccessfully for a seat in Congress and for governor of New Mexico. His son attended local schools in San Ildelfonso, then spent a year as a business administration student at St. Mary's College in San Francisco, transferring to the College of Santa Fe, where he received his bachelor's

degree in 1950. In 1948, he went to work for his father's insurance business and, except for a brief and unsuccessful run for the New Mexico state senate in 1964, remained at that post for twenty years.

In 1968, Luján moved the family insurance business to Albuquerque. He served for a short time as vice-chairman of the state Republican Party and decided to run for Congress. Running against Rep. Thomas Morris in the first New Mexico congressional district, Luján won a narrow victory to become the first Hispanic to represent New Mexico in Congress and the first Republican Hispanic ever to serve in that body. Luján served in the House from 3 January 1969 until 3 January 1989. There, as journalist Martin Tolchin explained, he "focused on serving his constituents in New Mexico rather than on making legislative history." Serving on the House Interior Committee, he opposed environmental policies, which earned him low ratings from the League of Conservation Voters. He was a strong supporter of nuclear energy development but stood firm against the use of New Mexico territory for the storage of nuclear waste, instead preferring that existing sites be used. An advocate of opening federal lands to mining, logging, grazing, and recreation, Luján also worked to return certain lands to the Native Americans in New Mexico. In 1985, he gave up his seat on the Interior Committee, where he was ranking Republican, to take a seat on the Science, Space and Technology Committee, where he became ranking Republican. His only real challenge in twenty years was from William Richardson, whom he beat in 1980 by a slim margin.

A strong supporter of the policies of President Ronald Reagan, on three occasions Luján was considered for the post of secretary of the interior, but was passed over for James Watt, William Clark, and Donald Hodel. However, with the election of George Bush in 1988, another opportunity was presented. This time, Bush wanted to include Hispanics in his cabinet, and on 22 December 1988 he named Luján as his choice for secretary of the interior. The pick was not without controversy, Many environmental groups decried Luján's selection, citing his voting record in Congress, but it was applauded by the business community and industries. On 2 February 1989, Luján was approved unanimously by the Senate, and he took office on 8 February as the forty-sixth secretary of the interior. During his tenure, Luján was widely criticized for putting industry before the environmental needs of the nation. He advocated increased logging in areas where the endangered northern spotted owl had its habitat; proposed to sell or lease six wildlife refuges in New York state; and sided with coal companies to challenge the 1977 Surface Mining Control and Reclamation Act, which required coal companies to restore land to areas that had been strip-mined. In 1992, the environmental group Defenders of Wildlife sued Luján, seeking to have the Interior Department apply the Endangered Species Act to foreign nations where the United States conducted commerce. In 1992, the U.S. Supreme Court ruled in favor of Luján. Luján was never on the "inside" of administration policy; in March 1989, when the *Exxon Valdez* spilled some 11 million gallons of oil in the Prince William Sound off Alaska, President Bush sent Secretary of Transportation Samuel Skinner and EPA administrator William Reilly to the scene, while Luján was left in Washington to coordinate affairs. In histories of the Bush administration, Luján is barely mentioned.

Luján left office in January 1993, after Bush's defeat, and returned to New Mexico. The Manuel Lujan Jr. Neutron Scattering Center at the Los Alamos National Laboratory in Los Alamos, and the Manuel Lujan Jr. Center for Space Telemetering and Telecommunications at New Mexico State University at Las Cruces are named in his honor.

References: Greve, Michael S., *The Demise of Environmentalism in American Law* (Washington, DC: American Enterprise Institute, 1996); *Luján v. Defenders of Wildlife,* 504 U.S. 555 (1992), 565; "Lujan, Manuel, Jr.," in Charles Moritz, ed., *Current Biography 1989* (New York: H. W. Wilson, 1989), 354–358; Parmet, Herbert S., *George Bush:*

The Life of a Lone Star Yankee (New York: Scribner, 1997), 358–359.

BRUCE EDWARD BABBITT
1938–

Bruce Babbitt was called by a Florida newspaper in 1988 a "neo-liberal of the right" for his advocacy as governor of Arizona of programs that many outside his political circle found popular. Tom Kenworthy of the *Washington Post* labeled him a "pragmatic critic" of the political system. Born in Los Angeles, California, on 27 June 1938, he is the son of Paul Babbitt, Jr., an amateur anthropologist who later became the mayor of Flagstaff, Arizona, and Frances Babbitt. His grandfather, Charles Babbitt, was one of five Babbitt brothers who moved west, ending up in Flagstaff, where they built an empire, becoming one of the state's prominent pioneer families. Bruce Babbitt attended local schools in Flagstaff, then entered the University of Notre Dame in Indiana, where he was awarded a bachelor's degree in geology in 1960. Subsequently he earned a master's degree in geophysics at the University of Newcastle in England and in 1965, a law degree from Harvard University.

A trip to Bolivia soon after graduation convinced Babbitt that he should work to alleviate the misery of the poverty he saw there. While earning his law degree at Harvard, he spent some time working for civil rights activists in Selma, Alabama, and, after graduation, he got a position working for President Lyndon B. Johnson's New Society antipoverty program as a civil rights attorney. He then went to work as a special assistant to the director of VISTA (Volunteers in Service to America) until 1967, when he returned to Arizona to join the Phoenix law firm of Brown & Bain. Babbitt worked as a counsel for the Navajo Indians of Arizona, and he aided them in a lawsuit that resulted in Native Americans' being allowed to serve in the state legislature. He also worked as counsel for the Arizona Wildlife Federation and became an expert in wildlife matters. From 1974 to 1978, he served as the state's attorney general.

In 1977, Arizona Governor Raul Castro was named as U.S. ambassador to Argentina. Succeeding to the office of governor was Secretary of State Wesley Bolin, which made Babbitt first in the line of succession. Less than five months later, on 4 March 1978, Bolin died of a heart attack, and Babbitt, 39 years old, became the youngest governor in state history. During his nearly nine years as governor, Babbitt helped enact into a law a 1980 bill to protect state groundwater supplies, established the Arizona Health Care Cost Maintenance System (AHCCM), a state Medicare system, and attempted to change the system of county government that had operated in the state since the late nineteenth century. While he began in office as a liberal, he came to sense that liberal approaches to most problems were not working and moved to the right on many issues, particularly after Ronald Reagan became president in 1981. Babbitt was a leader in supporting Reagan's notion of a "new federalism." In 1986, instead of running for the open seat of retiring Senator Barry Goldwater, Babbitt readied himself for the presidential run in 1988. That campaign, however, ended in disaster for Babbitt, and he dropped out of the race early. Babbitt then became the president of the League of Conservation Voters and was outspoken on environmental matters.

When President-elect Bill Clinton presented Babbitt's name for Interior, Hispanics demanded that Representative Bill Richardson of New Mexico be given the position instead. For several days, Babbitt was being touted as a possible candidate for U.S. trade representative. Instead, on 22 December 1992, Clinton named Babbitt as Interior secretary. Tom Kenworthy wrote, "Babbitt's views about the fragility of the arid West were nurtured by writers such as Aldo Leopold and Wallace Stegner, and he developed his early ideas about the role of government in the civil rights and anti-poverty

movements." Prior to his confirmation hearing, Babbitt's friend former Senator Barry Goldwater wrote to his former Senate colleagues, calling Babbitt "a highly competent expert. . . . I give him my highest recommendation." Babbitt was confirmed and sworn in on 20 January 1993 as the forty-seventh secretary of the interior.

During his tenure, which continues as this is being written, Babbitt has become one of the most activist secretaries in recent Interior history. He initiated a plan to restore the ecosystem of southern Florida, including the Everglades, to their original status; he changed nearly two decades of federal policy by setting aside old-growth timber forests in the Pacific Northwest, while at the same time allowing for a sustainable level of timber harvesting by lumber companies; and he established Habitat Conservation Plans to set aside areas thought to be vital to the ecosystem. When he took office, he said in an interview, "Making the Endangered Species Act work and making it workable is really the number one issue." In another interview, he addressed the concerns of those in the so-called Wise Use movement, which supported the policies of Babbitt's four predecessors at Interior. "I think the Wise Use movement has discovered the takings issue and used it to unite all kinds of users of public lands with a message of fear and paranoia. But while I speak against the excesses of the movement, I think it's also important to deal very thoughtfully and carefully with the takings issue. the place where I think there are some legitimate concerns is the Endangered Species Act. We have to be very careful to administer the act in a proactive way, so you can anticipate problems and reassure private-property owners that the administration of the act is not going to eliminate their ability to use the land in a reasonable fashion."

Babbitt may be considered, by friends and foes alike, as one of the most controversial secretaries of the Interior. *Washington Times* writer Valerie Richardson wrote on 14 November 1993, "Interior Secretary Bruce Babbitt and an earlier holder of the office, James Watt, have one thing in common—a knack for making enemies." Babbitt's plans to cut back on the use of public lands for grazing, for mining, and for other industrial uses earned him great enmity from commercial interests. In 1993, when Supreme Court Justice Harry Blackmun retired from the court, Babbitt was considered for the vacancy, but his controversial stands on many issues forced President Clinton to reconsider.

In 1997, Babbitt, always considered honest, became ensnared in the scandal over fundraising for the 1996 Clinton campaign. An old friend accused him of accepting donations to the Democratic National Committee from Native Americans interested in keeping casino rights to themselves at the expense of other Indians who had donated to the Republican Party. Called before Congress, Babbitt became entangled in a series of contradictions that pained his closest allies. However, in September 1999, the independent counsel appointed to look into the allegations against Babbitt found no wrongdoing on Babbitt's part and closed the investigation.

References: "Babbitt, Bruce Edward," in John W. Raimo, ed., *Biographical Directory of the Governors of the United States, 1978–1983* (Westport, CT: Meckler, 1985), 21–22; Cohn, Roger, and Ted Williams, "Interior Views: In His First Major Interview since Taking Office, Interior Secretary Bruce Babbitt Talks about the Sweeping Changes He's Planning," *Audubon* 95: 3 (May–June 1993), 78–84; Nobbe, George, "Interview with Interior Secretary Babbitt," *Wildlife Conservation* 96: 6 (November–December 1993), 76–77, 80–81; Tate, Donald J., "Bruce Babbitt," in John L. Myers, ed.-in-chief, *The Arizona Governors, 1912–1990* (Phoenix: Heritage, 1989), 159–166.

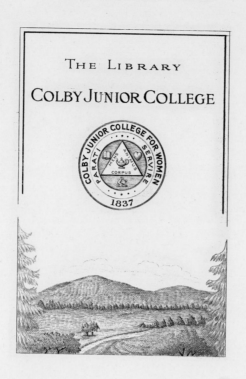

ART OF THE SOUTH PACIFIC ISLANDS

CEREMONIAL BOARD. Papuan Gulf, New Guinea. *Collection Eliot Elisofon. (Color Photo Eliot Elisofon.)*

ART OF THE
SOUTH PACIFIC
ISLANDS

Paul S. Wingert

Assistant Professor of Fine Arts and Archaeology
Columbia University

THE BEECHHURST PRESS · NEW YORK

The material in this book was first used in the Catalogue issued
for the 1953 Loan Exhibition of the Art of the South Pacific
Islands held at the M. H. de Young Memorial Museum, San
Francisco. Readers will find that a number of references to the
exhibition and a complete catalogue of the exhibits have been
retained in these pages. The book thus serves as a permanent
record of one of the most comprehensive and remarkable exhi-
bitions of its kind ever to be assembled.

PRODUCED BY THAMES AND HUDSON LTD LONDON 1953
PRINTED AND BOUND BY JARROLD AND SONS LTD NORWICH ENGLAND
ALL RIGHTS RESERVED

CONTENTS

5

LIST OF ILLUSTRATIONS

Numbers in parentheses refer to the Catalogue of the Exhibition, pages 47–64

FIGURES IN THE TEXT

LIST OF ILLUSTRATIONS

Numbers in parentheses refer to the Catalogue of the Exhibition, pages 47–64

PHOTOGRAVURE PICTURES

7

27. Sepik River, New Guinea. Miniature mask. (65)

28. Tchambuli, Sepik River, New Guinea. Basketry mask. (77)

29. Sepik River, New Guinea. Gable mask for ceremonial house. (76)

30. Tchambuli, Sepik River, New Guinea. Carved and painted shield. (95)

31. Tchambuli, Sepik River, New Guinea. Suspension hook. (92)

32. Mundugumor, Sepik River, New Guinea. Suspension hook. (93)

33. Tchambuli, Sepik River, New Guinea. Mask. (72)

34. Sepik River, New Guinea. Shield with pierced design. (94)

35. Sepik River, New Guinea. Suspension hook with bird form. (91)

36. Sepik River, New Guinea. Sago scoop. (102)

37. Sepik River, New Guinea. Breast ornament. (120)

38. Sepik River, New Guinea. Ceremonial carving. (111)

39. Sepik River, New Guinea. Bowl with carved figures as handles. (100)

40. Sepik River, New Guinea. Lime tube stopper. (107)

41. Huon Gulf⁄Tami Island, New Guinea. Figure. (122)

42. Huon Gulf⁄Tami Island, New Guinea. Drum. (128)

43. Huon Gulf⁄Tami Island, New Guinea. Bowl. (130)

44. Papuan Gulf, New Guinea. Carved and painted shield. (132)

45. Papuan Gulf, New Guinea. Bark⁄cloth mask. (140)

46. Papuan Gulf, New Guinea. Bark⁄cloth mask. (139)

47. Papuan Gulf, New Guinea. Ceremonial board. (135)

48. Torres Straits, New Guinea. Wooden mask. (146)

49. Fly River, New Guinea. Painted carved pith heads. (147; 148)

50. Trobriands, Massim Area, New Guinea. Incised club. (173)

51. Trobriands, Massim Area, New Guinea. Painted war shield. (174)

52. Trobriands, Massim Area, New Guinea. "Kai⁄diba", dance shield. (160)

53. Massim Area, New Guinea. Figure, spatula handle. (163)

54. Trobriands, Massim Area, New Guinea. Figure, spatula handle. (168)

55. Solomon Islands. Mortar with figure. (178)

56. Central Solomon Islands. "Musumusu", canoe bow figure. (175)

57. Central Solomon Islands. Head carved in coral. (183)

58. Eastern Solomon Islands. Bowl shaped as bird. (186)

PREFACE AND ACKNOWLEDGEMENTS

THIS EXHIBITION PRESENTS OUTSTANDING EXAMPLES OF THE highest achievements of South Pacific Island artists. It has been assembled, with the exception of important material from the Royal Ontario Museum of Archaeology in Toronto, Canada, entirely from American museum and private collections. The purpose is to represent as comprehensively as possible the aesthetic qualities that are to be found in the varied art of this enormous area. No attempt has been made to attain ethnological completeness, and, consequently, unembelished objects are not included. The exhibition is also not intended to show the full range of variations within a style. Each work was, instead, carefully selected as a masterpiece of a tribe or region. The richness of the collections in this country has made it possible to represent all of the major styles in the art of this great island world.

Known also as Oceania or the South Seas, this island world is scattered throughout the wide expanses of the Pacific Ocean. The Hawaiian Islands lie near its northernmost limits and the South Island of New Zealand its southernmost. The exploration of this vast area has been continuing for over four hundred years and there still remains today a number of unexplored regions. Adventurers, traders, missionaries, and scientists have been attracted as by a magnet to these islands. Deeds of bravery, treachery, and self-sacrifice have provided material for a very extensive literature, some of it romantic and fictitious, but much of it documentary and scientific. As a consequence, the area became known to many people through these books, a knowledge often inciting dreams and hopes. But World War II and the recent fighting in Korea have given these islands another reality through grim experiences. They now have for us a truer and more tangible existence. But a real understanding of the South Pacific world can only come from a knowledge of the people and their way of life. It is felt that an exhibition of their art, which tells so much about them, will provide an excellent beginning to a greater understanding of these people.

The art stands on its own merits and must be judged by its own criteria. Since all art is an expression of a culture, it is obvious that a culture so different from our own will have a very different art. Moreover, even a cursory examination of Oceanic art reveals a close relationship between form and content, so close, in fact, that some knowledge of its cultural background is necessary before it can be understood. While the content varies, much of it is charged with a directness, intensity, and power which are revealed through often spectacular forms and varied materials and techniques. For these reasons this art, many years ago, attracted the attention of modern artists who were the first to recognize its aesthetic quality and expressive power. The interest in South Pacific Island art is no longer restricted to a few artists, critics, and culture historians, but has recently been expanding to include those persons who view art as an enriching experience.

The exhibition includes examples from the five divisions of Oceania. These are arranged in the following sequence: Indonesia, Melanesia, Australia, Micronesia, and Polynesia. The art of Indonesia includes only that art which has not been influenced by the historic styles of the Asiatic mainland. The arrangement of the material is intended to make clear the important art styles that were developed in the five major areas, and in this way to aid in the understanding of specific styles and their relationships. This, it is believed, will contributed to an appreciation of the richness and variety of forms in South Pacific Island art.

ACKNOWLEDGEMENTS. Recent research which contributed to the formulation of some of the conclusions expressed in the text was made possible in 1952 by a grant for travel and study in the South Pacific from the Wenner-Gren Foundation for Anthropological Research in New York. Sincere thanks are extended to the Foundation and to its

Director, Dr. Paul Fejos. Without the generous co-operation of the following persons and institutions in lending material from their collections this exhibition would not have been possible: Dr. George E. Altman, Los Angeles; Mr. and Mrs. Ralph C. Altman, Los Angeles; Mr. Julius Carlebach, New York; Mr. Herschel Chipp, New York; Mr. Donald Deskey, New York; Mr. Eliot Elisofon, New York; Mrs. Vaid McHattie Forbes, Honolulu; Mr. Nasli Heeramaneck, New York; Mr. John J. Klejman, New York; Dr. Ralph Linton, New Haven, Connecticut; Mr. William Moore, Los Angeles; Mr. Vincent Price, Beverly Hills; Mr. Nelson A. Rockefeller, New York; Miss Helen Tamiris, New York.

American Museum of Natural History, New York; Brooklyn Museum; Washington State Museum, Seattle; Denver Art Museum; University Museum, Philadelphia; Peabody Museum, Harvard University; Seattle Art Museum; Milwaukee Public Museum; Los Angeles County Museum; Bernice P. Bishop Museum, Honolulu; Newark Museum; Cincinnati Museum of Natural History; Royal Ontario Museum of Science; Museum of Archaeology, Toronto, Canada; Buffalo Museum of Science; M. H. de Young Memorial Museum, San Francisco; Detroit Institute of Arts; Honolulu Academy of Arts; Peabody Museum, Salem, Massachusetts; Anthropology Museum, University of California, Berkeley; Cleveland Museum of Art.

Gratitude is due to the following persons for information and assistance: Dr. John O. Brew; Mrs. Willena Cartwright; Miss Katherine Coffey; Miss Virginia Cummings; Mr. Jean Delacourt; Mr. Ernest S. Dodge; Mr. Frederic H. Douglas; Mr. Ralph Dury; Dr. Edward W. Gifford; Mr. Robert P. Griffing, Jr.; Dr. Erna Gunther; Dr. Kenneth Kidd; Dr. Ralph Linton; Mr. Herbert Matter; Mr. William Milliken; Dr. Thomas Munro; Miss Caroline Osborne; Mr. Fred Pleasants; Dr. Froelich Rainey; Dr. Robert P. Richardson; Dr. Robert Ritzenthaler; Dr. Harry Shapiro; Dr. Alexander Spoehr; Miss Emily Hartwell Tupper; Mr. Stephen Williams.

13

Very special thanks for their generous help in assembling the material are extended to the following persons: Mr. Ralph C. Altman; Miss Geraldine Bruckner; Mr. Julius Carlebach; Mr. Eliot Elisofon; Miss Carol Kinzel; Mr. Fred Orchard; Miss Erica Pauli; Miss Flora Seigel; Colonel Smith; Miss Bella Weitzner.

A debt of gratitude for invaluable assistance in many phases of the exhibition is extended to Miss Marion Sehnert.

With the exception of the following, credit for illustrations is due to the museum or the person lending the work to the exhibition: Miss Berenice Abbott—27, 29, 52, 65, 77; Mr. Eliot Elisofon—111, 138 (frontispiece and detail on cover in colour), 318; Mr. Charles Uht—130, 146, 175, 183, 263; Dr. Paul S. Wingert—20, 78, 80, 122, 141, 320, 321, 324, 325.

Credit is due and sincere thanks are expressed to Mr. Gilbert F. Carpenter for his excellent drawing of the vignettes in the text and for making the fine maps.

PAUL S. WINGERT

Columbia University
New York
September 1953

ART OF THE SOUTH PACIFIC ISLANDS

1. Backgrounds

IN THE VAST EXPANSES OF THE SOUTH PACIFIC OCEAN MANKIND, living on a comparatively primitive level, has developed many amazingly varied and rich cultures. The great diversity existent among these cultures is strikingly apparent in an almost limitless variety of art forms. When examined within the context of its background the art reflects the geographical, physical, as well as cultural variations so characteristic of this extensive region as a whole.

The South Pacific is customarily divided into five areas: Indonesia, Melanesia, Australia, Micronesia, and Polynesia (Map 1). Of these, Australia is a sub-continent and the other four are composed of literally hundreds of islands. Although these lie, with few exceptions, within the tropics, life on them differs considerably, depending upon the natural resources at hand. The people themselves represent three of the major groups of man: Caucasoid or white, Negroid or black, and Mongoloid or yellow. In practically all areas these groups have to some extent intermingled. Life is largely sustained by agriculture, often of the small garden variety, although food-gathering and hunting exist in a few regions and fishing in many.

Indonesia, the word meaning Indian (Indo) Islands (nesia), comprises a large number of islands extending to the east and north-east as a wide crescent off the south-easternmost tip of Asia. They are situated relatively close to each other, are of mountainous structure, and vary in size from small to such large ones as Sumatra, Java, Borneo, and Luzon in the Philippines. They may be considered the gateway through which the first groups of people entered the South Pacific world to the east. For thousands of years waves of migrants swept into Indonesia from the

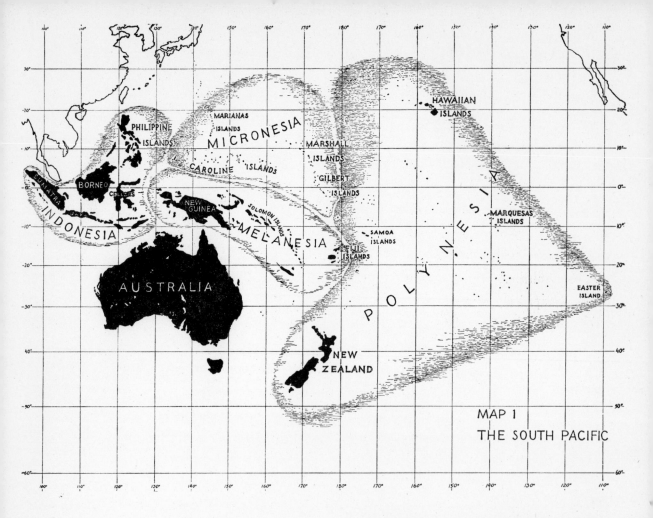

MAP 1

THE SOUTH PACIFIC

Asiatic mainland, each wave after a time forcing eastwards its predecessor. One of the earliest of these racial groups were the Australoids, an
ancient and specialized Caucasoid branch, who still survive as the
Australian Aborigines. In point of time, the next to arrive were the
Negroid Papuans who later moved eastwards and inhabited parts of
western Melanesia. The Papuans may still have been dominant in these
islands when the so-called Indonesian peoples arrived from the mainland of Asia. It is believed that the Indonesians were basically of
Caucasoid stock with Negroid and Mongoloid admixtures, and that
they brought with them the Malayo-Polynesian languages, as well
as a number of new culture traits. The inter-mixture of the

16

Indonesians with the Papuans gave rise to a Negroid group speaking Malayo-Polynesian who moved eastwards and became the most numerous group in Melanesia. These peoples are the Melanesians. Still later another group of Indonesians, predominantly Caucasoid in type, migrated in several waves and easy stages into the central and eastern South Pacific. These are the Polynesians. The last peoples to settle in the Pacific were the Micronesians, a somewhat later offshoot of the Indonesians who were more Mongoloid in type than the Polynesians. Evidences of these various groups are still found today in Indonesia, where they now constitute, except in the eastern islands, a minority group among the dense Malay population.

The art of those Indonesian peoples who have maintained to a degree their cultural identity is Oceanic rather than Asiatic in its affiliations. Examples of this art come from the Island of Nias, off the south-west coast of Sumatra; from the Batak tribes of Sumatra; the South West Islands, particularly Leti; Borneo; and from some of the inland tribes on Luzon Island in the Philippines (Map 2). A good deal of it derives its content from the spirit world, supernatural beings, and magical concepts.

The Melanesian (black) Islands, so named because of their Negroid Papuan and Melanesian inhabitants, extend in a south-east direction for almost three thousand miles into the South Pacific. They contain a great number of small and large islands, the largest, New Guinea, over 1300 miles long, and are of rugged volcanic formation, although fertile lowlands and swamps abound. Of the numerous cultures developed in Melanesia some are related, but many are very different in character. Cultural variations often exist even on a small island. The presence throughout Melanesia of a clan organization of society and a number of basically common institutions and practices suggests that these islands were settled by small groups who banded together

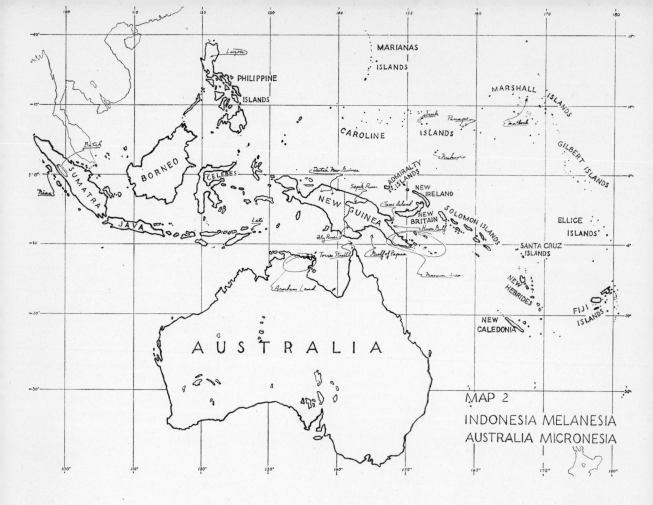

MAP 2

INDONESIA MELANESIA
AUSTRALIA MICRONESIA

co-operatively in small villages for protection and subsistence. Warfare, cannibalism, and head-hunting, together with language differences, further tended to isolate one area or even one village from another. The numerous cultural variations are therefore explainable as local develop-ments and interpretations of a common heritage.

Hurricanes, active volcanoes, and tidal waves give the Melanesian Islands a quality of violence that often re-echoes in the lives of the people. Their religious beliefs center in supernatural spirits, often of fearsome character, mythological beings, the power of the ancestors, and magical practices. Elaborate dramatic ceremonies, some lasting for days or months or even years, are enacted as part of the religious and social

18

life. Secret societies are numerous, and in some areas large men's club-houses are built within which ceremonial objects are set up and rites performed. Everywhere throughout Melanesia an abundance of art is required for use in religious and secular ceremonies. In its amazing variety of dramatic statement this art is a true reflection of the diversity of culture patterns. The most important of these islands are: New Guinea, the Admiralty Islands, New Ireland, New Britain, the Solomon Islands, New Hebrides, New Caledonia, and the Fiji Islands (Map 2).

To the south of New Guinea is the large sub-continent of Australia. In the central and northern deserts and wastelands the non-Negroid but dark-skinned Australoids still survive as nomadic hunters and food-gatherers. The flora and fauna of the Continent is such that subsistence has been arduous for them. As a consequence, their material culture, the types of objects they produce, their implements and weapons are meager and of very simple kind. Divided into many dispersed small tribes, they have nevertheless developed a complex social system and ceremonial life in which a unique type of totemism plays a leading role. Frequently associated with the totems is the concept of supernatural power and mythological beings. Although not as arresting as that of Melanesia, the art of Australia, much of it produced for ceremonial use, has a distinctive quality and appeal.

The Micronesian Islands to the north of Melanesia and east of the Philippines are aptly named "small islands". The major groups—Palau, Carolines, Marshalls, Marianas, and Gilberts—are widely scattered, small, flat coral atolls. Natural resources are the most limited of any area in the South Pacific. These people are skilled navigators and have maintained trade contacts between the various groups, a circumstance which has contributed to a marked homogeneity throughout much of Micronesia. Some of the elements of this culture suggest analogy with those of both Melanesia and Indonesia, such as large decorated ceremonial or club-houses, the presence of clans and of a class system, and the belief in nature spirits and the power of certain ancestors. Craftsmanship was highly developed and appears in textiles (made with the true loom), in house-building and decoration, and especially in designing and fashion-ing canoes. Much of their art is expressed in this craftsmanship, some of it intended for ceremonial use, but the greater part of it decorative or utilitarian.

East and south-east of Micronesia the Polynesian Islands are spaced in an immense area of the Pacific (Map 3). They consist of many islands both large and small, some of them volcanic and mountainous in formation, and others of the low coral atoll variety. A roughly equi-lateral triangle, almost 5000 miles along each side, with its apex at Hawaii and its base extending between New Zealand and Easter Island, defines the area in which these islands are located. In the central part of this great area are situated from west to east the Samoan, Tongan, Cook, Austral, and Society Islands. Marginal to these are Hawaii, the Marquesas, New Zealand, and Easter Island. The great distances separating many of the islands and groups tended to isolate them from each other, although there were occasional contacts. Consequently, there developed throughout the islands variations of basically similar culture elements.

The importance of ancestors was the dominant factor in practically all facets of Polynesian life. Ancestry was traced back to very early legendary times and these ancestors were worshipped as deities. Even the revered gods of various crafts were often deified early craftsmen. The social system too was based on ancestor worship. Society was stratified according to seniority of birth, the highest rank being claimed by those who could trace descent back through a line of first-born to an early ancestor. Such a system of rank had therefore religious sanction. Because of the importance of descent genealogies were carefully kept. Of

20

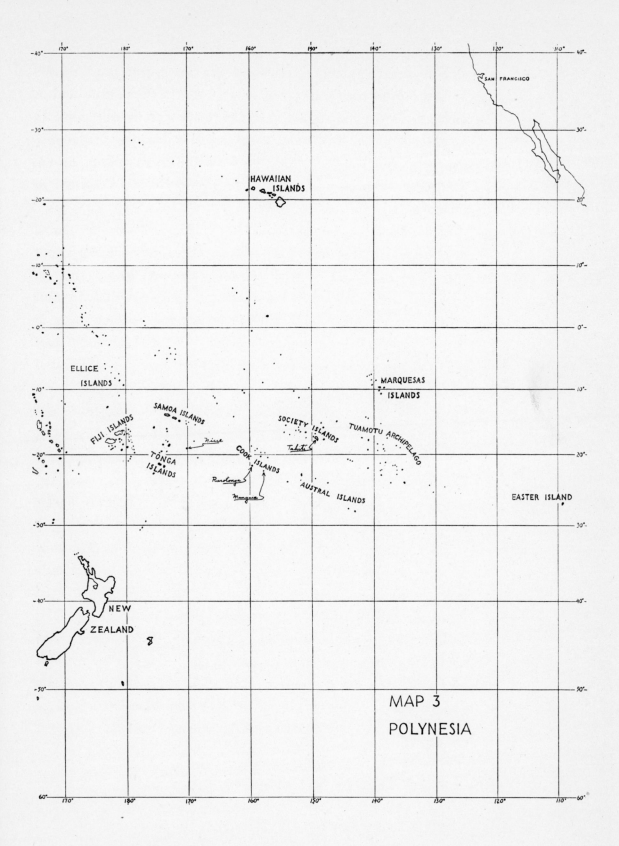

MAP 3

POLYNESIA

secondary importance in Polynesian religion were the great gods who had control of their own special spheres, such as sky, earth, sea, or war. In some areas they were worshipped formally under the direction of a priesthood.

The concept of mana and its corollary taboo was as culturally pervasive as ancestor worship with which it was closely associated. Mana was the belief in the presence of a universal power. In differing degrees it was contained in all animate and inanimate things. The degree and potency of mana in an object, such as a weapon, was determined or revealed by its performance or efficacy, and in a person by his high birth or skill in his vocation. Gods also had mana depending upon their rank. Since objects and persons of great mana were dangerous to those with less, taboos or bans were established to protect against it. To break a taboo was fatal.

Polynesian culture was largely one of specialization. All activities were under the control of those trained specialists who possessed requisite mana. That the artist was such a specialist is evidenced by the high degree of technical excellence in his work. While it is both decorative and expressive, Polynesian art does not emphasize dramatic effects as does that of Melanesia.

South Pacific Island art as a whole includes architecture, sculpture, painting, and many of the so-called minor arts and crafts. Sculpture is, however, dominant. The artist utilized a wide variety of materials, at times combining them in various ways. He was with few exceptions a trained craftsman who was esteemed for his skill. The efficient tools which he devised were, except in Indonesia where metal was used, fashioned in stone, shell, or bone. In the greater number of these islands art occupied an important place in the lives of the people. It was indeed one of the basic facets of their culture and was closely interrelated with their social customs, religious beliefs, and economic practices, these serving as the main forces or motivations which led to this art.

22

2. Art Forms

THERE ARE THROUGHOUT THE SOUTH PACIFIC ISLANDS A GREAT number of art styles. The almost bewildering diversity of these styles makes its difficult at first to recognize any forms or patterns as recurrent and as basic to the art of this vast area as a whole. But a closer examina⁄ tion does reveal the presence of certain important basic forms and concepts, even though these are rendered in many different styles. The great distances frequently separating the areas where such forms appear make it quite unlikely that they are the consequence of direct contacts or interchange. But, the very existence of these forms seems to indicate their persistence through time and their origin from a common center.

Essential for an understanding of the art is the preliminary considera⁄ tion of such generalities as medium, color, size, and subject⁄matter. The way in which the subject⁄matter is presented must be carefully observed. In the visual pursuit of this, account should be taken of the proportioning and arrangement of parts; the type of symmetry employed in their distribution; the emphasis achieved through repetition, variation, or alteration of motives; and the rhythmical relationships established between certain shapes, lines, or details. It will be found that some forms in a design are structural or functional, that is, they are necessary to describe the subject⁄matter. But in many instances the particular rendering of these forms is not controlled by such practical require⁄ ments. It was instead dictated by expressive or aesthetic aims. A greater appreciation of this art will be attained when it is examined in this way.

In Oceanic, as in all art, the subject most commonly encountered is the human figure. Through it concepts, psychological and emotional states, and the world of reality are expressed. The human form is often

23

Fig. 1

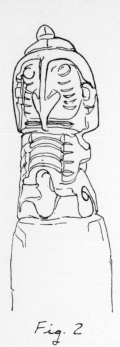

Fig. 2

Fig. 3

closely akin to reality and is based on the artist's knowledge and experience of the physiological existence of his fellow beings. These representations are essentially naturalistic and are clearly recognizable as such. Good examples appear in the ancestor figures from Nias and the Sepik River, New Guinea, and the sculptured forms from the Philippines, the Admiralty and Solomon Islands, and from Tahiti and Hawaii.

In other forms the human figure is distorted, sometimes greatly so, or certain parts are exaggerated. Easter Island skeletal figures and some Hawaiian, Sepik River, Admiralty and Solomon Island carvings demonstrate exaggeration. In many instances this is confined to the rendering of the head and is associated with distortion. Although distorted forms are semi-human in appearance, they often go beyond this realm and approach or achieve the fantastic. Found in many South Pacific areas, fantastic forms are more typical of certain regions of Melanesia, as the Sepik River and Papuan Gulf, New Ireland and New Britain, Dutch New Guinea and New Hebrides, and to some extent the central Solomons, Hawaii, Easter Island, New Zealand, and Borneo. The basis for them is in abnormal emotional states when, through halucinations, paranoid fears and delusions, and psychic oppressive states, the real world gives way to one of fantasy and the grotesque. In Melanesian art the appearance given supernatural and mythological spirits was initially arrived at through these circumstances.

The crocodile and birds are the most frequently represented zoomorphic forms, especially in Melanesia. They are prominent in the art of the Admiralty Islands, Sepik River and Massim Areas of New Guinea, the eastern Solomon Islands, and in New Ireland. The pig, fish, and snake are also found in the art of the same areas. Animal, as well as human forms, run the gamut from essential naturalism through

24

complex distortion and at times approach complete distortion, as in the carvings from the Massim Area. Floral or plant forms appear in the decorative vocabulary of certain areas, a vocabulary often richly developed and including both angular and curvilinear geometric elements. Geometric decorative art was extensively developed in the central islands of Polynesia and in Micronesia and Australia. Some of the motives in decorative designs are, although without meaning, identical to those found in the representational and expressive art of the same area. They well illustrate the extent to which traditional forms dominate the art of the various regions of the South Pacific world.

The aesthetic concepts developed in these islands are expressed in five major categories of art forms. These are encountered so consistently throughout the area that they must be considered as basic or fundamental. They are the common denominators of Oceanic art. But, since they are rendered within the traditional style of an area, they are very diverse in appearance. It is rewarding to recognize and study these basic forms since they add to the understanding of this rich and varied art.

The five major categories of art forms may be identified as follows: (1) the contained form expressed entirely by its own sculptural shapes (2, 97);* (2) the expansive polychromed form, with the painted areas or designs often referring to concepts or relationships other than those given by its own sculptural shapes (25); (3) related forms, usually superposed but always, whether polychromed or not, expressing an assemblage of shapes and ideas (38); (4) aerial forms, those pierced designs which result from the cutting away of the entire background surrounding linear shapes, these forms often being a complex compositional statement (17, 34); and (5) two-dimensional surface delineations, either incised or carved in low relief, or painted on the surface, and of geometric or representational character (43). In any one of the five

* Numbers in parentheses, unless otherwise noted, refer to the illustrations following page 64.

Fig. 4

groups materials, such as shells, teeth, feathers, etc., are frequently added to contribute to a more complete statement of subject-matter.

Contained sculptural forms of the first category appear in the art of all the major South Pacific areas with the exception of Australia. Outstanding examples are the ancestor figures of Nias and the coastal area of the Sepik River, the standing figures from Nukuoro, and the generic portrait figures from Hawaii.

The expansive polychromed forms of the second category dominate the art of Melanesia, appear in a few instances in both Indonesia and Polynesia, and are practically non-existent in Micronesia and Australia. These forms, as those of the first group, include both masks and figures. Excellent examples appear in the art of the Sepik River, where this tradition is highly developed.

Related or superposed forms occur in many sculptures from Indonesia, Melanesia, and Polynesia, and to an extent in house carvings from Micronesia, but are again absent in Australian art. Representative of this category are magicians' staffs from the Batak of Sumatra, canoe prow carvings from the Sepik River, and house posts from the Maori of New Zealand.

Although a few examples of aerial forms are found everywhere in Oceania except Australia, they too receive their greatest development in Melanesia. But fine renderings of them do appear as large ears or wings attached to Borneo masks and as Maori war-canoe prow and stern carvings. In Melanesia, particularly in the western half of the area, aerial forms constitute the most exciting, aesthetic achievements. Noteworthy are the mortuary carvings from New Ireland and the shields and canoe prows from South Dutch New Guinea and the Massim Area.

Two-dimensional surface delineations were produced in all five of the South Pacific areas. Within this category the incised and low-relief carved examples are the most numerous. Representative are the

26

Fig. 5

boomerangs and shields from Australia, house decorations from the Batak, Ponape Island dance wands, Huon Gulf bowls, and the clubs from Tonga, Samoa, and other central Polynesian islands. Flat painted surface designs also appear on Borneo shields, Trobriand Island war shields from the Massim Area, sheets of bark from Arnhem Land, Australia, and tapa cloth from many parts of Polynesia. Important achievements within this category are the shell pendants (kapkaps) from Melanesia in which cut-out flat tortoise shell designs are attached to a circular disk of white tridacna shell. Many examples of two-dimensional delineation occur as decorations on implements and utensils.

But, subject-matter in Oceanic art was not restricted to specific categories of art forms. Instead, art forms of different types might be used to convey similar subject-matter, even within the confines of a single small island. Contained sculptural forms as well as related superposed forms tend to receive a more naturalistic treatment than polychromed and aerial forms which are often dramatic expressions of the supernatural.

The major art styles in the South Pacific can best be characterized by discovering the unique elements used in the rendering of forms within the various categories. Since the art styles are so numerous and so diverse, this characterization can therefore only be achieved by considering the art of each group or area separately. For geographical and historical reasons it is logical to proceed in this examination from area to area in the following order: Indonesia, Melanesia, Australia, Micronesia, and Polynesia.

In Indonesia sculptural contained forms are particularly strong in the art of Nias, Leti, and the Philippines. Accomplished examples are the ancestor figures of Nias. Carefully carved, they were made after death as containers for the spirits of departed ancestors. They were

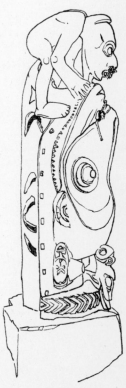

Fig. 6

revered and honored, and indicate a firmly rooted ancestor worship. The figures are types and in no sense of the word even generic portraits. Whether represented as seated or squatting, they are frontally posed and static with fully rounded shapes. All of the forms are separated by free space and the figures have a satisfying existence as wood sculpture. There is no surface decoration and the carvings present an organic unity of parts. Leti ancestor figures, rendered in a related style, represent the human form in simpler shapes with sharper accents on the separate parts. The often naturalistic figure sculptures from the northern Philippines are also within this style group.

Polychromy in Indonesian art is best seen in the architectural sculptures of the Batak and in Borneo masks. For the gables of their houses the Batak carved depictions of protective spirits whose features were dominated by large staring eyes rendered as concentric circles. Curvilinear surface patterns flank these heads, the entire carving given an extra dimension expressively by being painted black, red, and white. Although not large in size these heads are heroic in scale and dynamic in appearance. Concentric circular eyes are used as expressive features in the art of a number of areas of Melanesia, as in the masks of New Britain, the figurative sculpture and masks of the middle Sepik River region, the bark-cloth masks of the Papuan Gulf, and in figures and masks in the New Hebrides. They also appear in a somewhat modified form in carved and painted Polynesian representations in Easter Island.

Borneo masks are less fearsome in expression and more fantastic than Batak carvings. Not only paint but also attached materials are used to represent eyelids, ears, and protruding tongues in the characterization of spirits. This use of a variety of materials in the same object to produce a spectacular effect is a common trait in much of Melanesian art. In New Ireland, for example, valves of sea-snails, fiber, clay, and bark-cloth are attached to sculptured masks and figures. The use of combinations of varied materials is also particularly characteristic of the sculpture of the Sepik River area.

Superposed forms involving a number of human and animal figures are carved on the magicians' staffs of the Batak (Fig. 1). These depict reality in a direct and simplified way and the designs are interrelated by a vertical repetition and alternation of rhythmic lines and shapes. Important tribal heirlooms, they were stuck in the ground at ritual occasions. Superposed figures in high relief and in the round are also carved as handles on Igorot spoons and ladles.

Two-dimensional carved and painted patterns appear commonly in the art of Indonesia. These are often composed of curvilinear elements derived from plant forms or the protective water-buffalo horn motive. Some of them depict conventionalized dog, human, and spirit forms; while others are purely geometric in character. Painted shields from Borneo are good examples of this style. Although some of the two-dimensional forms have a spatial setting, the majority of them, as in other parts of the South Pacific, are composed of small units which cover the entire surface.

Indonesian art is not dominated by a single style, design tradition, or preferred subject-matter. As in other Oceanic areas, it consists of a number of local or regional styles. Perhaps the most notable single feature of this art is its constant use of curvilinear lines and surfaces and the infrequent appearance of strongly angular shapes. All of the basic art forms of Oceania appear in Indonesia.

In its fourteen major areas and island groups Melanesia has produced an amazing number of styles and an enormous quantity of art works. The majority of these are wood sculptures, although some outstanding examples of stone carving have been found. Other techniques include fabrication, using bark-cloth, raffia, and the

29

Fig. 7

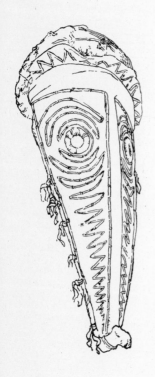

Fig. 8

pith of reeds, and piercing and engraving of shell and bone. It is impossible to single out any shared elements in an art composed of so many heterogeneous styles. But on the basis of strongly dominating art forms these styles may be divided into two reasonably clear-cut groups. In one the art is dominated by a spectacular expressive polychromy (frontispiece); while in the other the strongest element is an emphatic sculptural statement of content (57). In both of these groups the dominant art forms are often richly combined with others.

The polychromed group in Melanesian art is represented by objects from New Ireland, New Britain, Sepik River, Huon Gulf, Papuan Gulf, and New Hebrides. In these islands and areas very numerous spectacular and prolonged ceremonies were distinctive culture elements. They were held at stated times and required an abundance of art objects of various kinds. While in some regions these were used repeatedly until they had to be replaced by new ones, in other areas they were made anew for every ceremony. Specific supernatural, mythological, or ancestral spirits were dramatized by the art which was intended to enact a role in an assemblage of other objects. Regardless of its basic design, this art was usually expressively enriched by painting in bright contrasting colours and by appending a variety of materials.

In New Ireland this polychromed style was given its particular character by combining it with aerial forms. The art was used in lengthy mortuary ceremonies which were performed periodically to honor the recent dead and the mythological and legendary ancestors. A variety of masks, single figures, columnar carvings with superposed forms, and other objects were required for these rites (Fig. 4). While all of the forms are derived from nature, they are distorted to achieve an intense, dynamic, often fierce appearance. An open cage-like structure surrounds figures and columns creating an aerial design. Carved and painted details, such as crescent, wheel, and wing patterns, and bird

30

forms refer symbolically to the dead. Complex compositions are typical of this art. A boar's head, human figures and heads, and bird and snake forms are often interrelated in the same design. New Ireland sculptures were painted in red, white, yellow, black, and occasionally blue, often in small scattered units which tend to give an even greater transparency and a visually broken surface movement to the aerial forms. Few analogies associate this style with those of any other Melanesian art.

Pith covered and vividly painted fantastic masks from New Britain represent jungle supernatural spirits and were worn in often brutal initiation ceremonies when the youth were admitted to tribal standing. They are generally based on conical, columnar, and circular geometric shapes with human features imposed on the surface. For other cere-monies masks were modelled over the human skull and small figures of a more naturalistic mien were carved in chalk. Carved and brightly painted designs derived from the human face embellished the surfaces of large shields. In these, concentric circles and sinuous lines are conspicuous. New Britain art stresses curvilinear lines and surfaces, composed into weird, almost surrealistic designs (Fig. 5).

The polychrome Melanesian style dominates the art of the Sepik River. The art of this area is not only the most prolific in the South Pacific but also within the entire primitive world. Various motivations lay behind it, but the strongest were derived from the socio-religious ceremonies and those of the men's societies. In this area many cere-monies and the requisite art forms were traded or purchased by one tribe from another. Certain tribes did not make their own art objects but bought them from or had them made by members of another tribe. Of the tribes who produced their own art, the Tchambuli, Mundugu-mor, and Abelam in particular developed tribal styles. But, because of the cultural flux and interchange, a characterization may be given to Sepik River art as a whole.

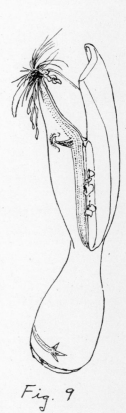

Fig. 9

31

Masks, figures, drums, flutes, and many other ceremonial objects were often so sacred that they could only be seen by members of the men's society; other similar sculptures were used in public communal ceremonies. Supernatural and legendary spirits who were founders, protectors, or benefactors of a society or of a tribe provided the subject matter for this art. Spirit beings were given human or semi-human appearance or were rendered as bird forms. A conspicuous tendency is the elongation of the human nose which terminates in a sharp point or a bird's head. Color was used extensively as an adjunct to sculptured parts or as surface designs.

Large eyes, accented by concentric circles, serve as the focal expressive elements of Sepik River figures and masks. They produce an intense, startling, and emotionally charged effect. Distortion, sometimes becoming fantastic, is freely employed in this art. Elaborate symbolic and decorative designs are painted on many figures and masks. Freely used circular patches and scroll and sinuous surface lines intensify the dynamic expression of carved forms. Sepik River art, whether simple or complex, excites the eye and stimulates the imagination (Fig. 6). This is often the consequence of the rhythmic interplay of curved surfaces and flowing lines.

In contrast, a heaviness and an angularity characterizes much of the art of the near-by Huon Gulf-Tami Island area. Human forms and clan-owned designs depict ancestor and mythological spirits. Huge heads, set without a neck into the upper part of the body, dominate the greatly distorted forms which are inorganically articulated and at times four-sided. Boneless, rubbery shapes define the legs and arms (Fig. 7). The surface designs and details are almost entirely sharp and angular. Finely decorated bowls from this area evidence

32

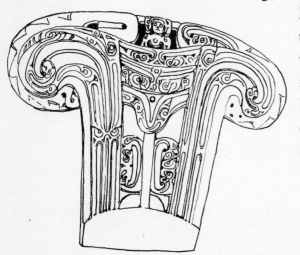

Fig. 10

the same style elements. This sculpture is often only lightly painted red, white, and black.

The art of both the Papuan Gulf area and New Hebrides Islands was motivated by the most prolonged ceremonies performed in Melanesia. In the Papuan Gulf these centered around supernatural jungle and sea spirits who were considered benefactors. The ceremonies required many bark-cloth covered and painted masks of different types. The masks portray the spirits as they appeared when seen by certain members of the tribe. They are given a fantastic appearance, partly human, partly crocodile (Fig. 8). As many as a hundred of these masks were worn at a ceremony and afterwards destroyed. Geometric surface designs are delineated with appliqued strips of reed and are painted in delicate pastel colors. The stirring aspect of these masks is comparable to that of many Sepik River representations. Papuan Gulf designs identical with those on the masks are also carved on shields, ceremonial boards, bullroarers, and other objects. A remarkable homogeneity characterizes this strikingly exotic art.

Numerous graded religious and secular societies dominate life in the New Hebrides. Custom demanded that a man advance from grade to grade within them throughout his life. For each advancement he had to provide the masks, figures, and other objects needed in the accompanying ceremonies. The figures and masks were used only once. They represented various ancestor spirits and have an unreal appearance which is intensified by polychromy in brilliant earth pigments. A conspicuous feature of this style is the long oval or diamond shaped head, sometimes carved with huge circular eyes and surrounded by carefully rendered notches (Fig. 13). New Hebrides art is an excellent example of the spectacular strain so prominent in Melanesia.

The sculptural or second group of Melanesian styles is prominent in the art of the Admiralty Islands, Dutch New Guinea, Torres Straits,

Fig. 11

Fig. 12

Fig. 13

Massim Area, Solomon Islands, Santa Cruz, New Caledonia, and Fiji. Ancestor spirits and totems were represented in this group by contained sculptural forms.

Human and zoomorphic figures in this art are often comparatively naturalistic, although they are at times conventionalized and even distorted. The korovar, the ancestor spirit-container figures of northern Dutch New Guinea are examples of distortion (Fig. 2). In comparison the ancestor and figurative sculpture of the Admiralty Islands is more organically conceived (Fig. 3). Although at times decorated with geometric surface patterns, it is essentially a sculptural interpretation of natural form. The finest sculptures from the Admiralty Islands, however, are the large decorated food bowls. These are sometimes given the shape of a bird, and sometimes have handles of pierced and spiral patterns which are excellent examples of aerial forms.

Aerial forms are also magnificently rendered in the art of the Massim Area (Fig. 10). This remarkably curvilinear art represents totemic forms, frequently birds, often conventionalized to the point of abstraction. Elegance of technique and design are important features of this style. Color is used sparingly and the effects are achieved entirely by sculptural means. Two-dimensional surface patterns are also common in the Massim Area. These too are predominantly curvilinear. Particularly arresting in Massim two-dimensional art are the painted war shields.

Totemic forms, primarily fish, figure prominently in Torres Straits art. These are often rendered as incised motives on such ceremonial objects as drums (Fig. 9). Wooden masks with flat-angled planes are carved in this area for use in harvest and fertility rites. On the adjacent coast of New Guinea in the Fly River area spirits are given specter-like expression in small carved and painted pith heads.

Fine examples of aerial forms appear in the art of south Dutch New

34

Guinea (8, 9). These too are largely composed of curvilinear elements, the curves being less free and moving than those in Massim art. In some parts of south Dutch New Guinea dramatic mythological figures were rendered. These belong within the first group of Melanesian styles.

The most organically conceived sculptural style in Melanesia is that of the Solomon Islands. The human figure, although at times distorted or exaggerated, as in the large-headed canoe carvings, is often given a naturalistic interpretation (Fig. 11). This is essentially a descriptive interpretation of reality. Santa Cruz figures are rendered similarly (Fig. 12). A distinctive feature of Solomon Island art is its fine shell-inlay work. It is used either to define further structural details of a form or as decoration. Shell-inlay is extensively used to decorate large and small food bowls in the eastern Islands of the Group. Of ceremonial importance, some of these bowls are given the shape of birds, on others birds, fish, and human figures are interrelated. The two-dimensional surface art of the Solomons also appears in finely incised or carved and painted ceremonial paddles and clubs.

New Caledonian art was largely motivated by ancestor worship centering in the ancestor of a clan or group. To honor an ancestor, the door jambs and roof spires of clan houses were carved with large heads and half-figures (Fig. 14). These follow a fixed style which emphasizes by swelling surfaces the volumes of cheeks and heads. They are often roughly carved without much concern with refinement of shape or surface. In contrast, the hook-nosed masks, which represent aquatic spirits, and the very simply but effectively shaped bird head clubs are carefully rendered.

Fiji art fulfilled both religious and bellicose needs. Elegantly designed shallow dishes were made to hold oil with which the priests were anointed (Fig. 15). Great, heavy war clubs of iron-wood were decorated with deeply carved, cross-hatched lines. Fijian art in both of these forms

Fig. 14

35

Fig. 15

Fig. 16

anticipates Polynesian and Micronesian styles. The bark-cloth, however, is painted in bold, vigorous designs reminiscent of those of other parts of Melanesia.

Melanesian art is certainly the most varied in styles, techniques, and motivations of the entire South Pacific. Memorable among its forms are the spectacular and often dynamic representations of spirit beings. Their dramatization of other-worldliness is stated vigorously in color and shapes. But delicate pierced designs and organic sculptural forms are also important examples of the rich art from this area.

Although historically and geographically Australia is part of the Oceanic world, it is culturally distinct and artistically, at the best, only marginal. The greater part of its art consists of incised or engraved geometric designs in wood and shell on weapons, implements, and a few simple objects used in initiation and totemic ceremonies. The designs, using both angular and curvilinear elements, are usually composed of concentric and parallel lines and grooves (Fig. 16). Rock engravings and some paintings are found in various parts of the continent. Only in the bark paintings of eastern and northern Australia and in the rudimentary carved and painted mythological figures from Arnhem Land in northern Australia is there any suggestion of similarities with Melanesia, and these are of tenuous character. Australia must be viewed as an isolated art province in Oceania.

Micronesia too is an area of sparse art. But certain relationships between this art and that of Melanesia and Polynesia bring it completely within the orbit of the South Pacific. Typical of Micronesia is the reliance upon simplified shapes which are often so frankly designed as to have a quality of elegance. Bowls and dishes of modern aspect are good examples of this style, which is quite within the contained sculptural tradition of Oceania. Bowls of this style suggest comparison with those from the eastern Solomons and from Hawaii. The chaste

36

manikin-like figures from Nukuoro, so reminiscent of the "mechanistic" forms of de Chirico, are also further examples of this style (78). The flat surface designs lightly carved and painted on Ponape dance paddles represent a geometric surface style which reaches its climax in the fine plaited pandanus mats. The aerial tradition is also found in the con-fronted, simplified birds on Truk canoe prows (Fig. 17), somewhat analogous in the treatment of the bird form to Solomon Island style, and in the numerous shark's-tooth edged weapons from the Gilberts. Although these forms are aesthetically interesting, Micronesia is never-theless an art area of secondary importance as compared with Indonesia and Melanesia.

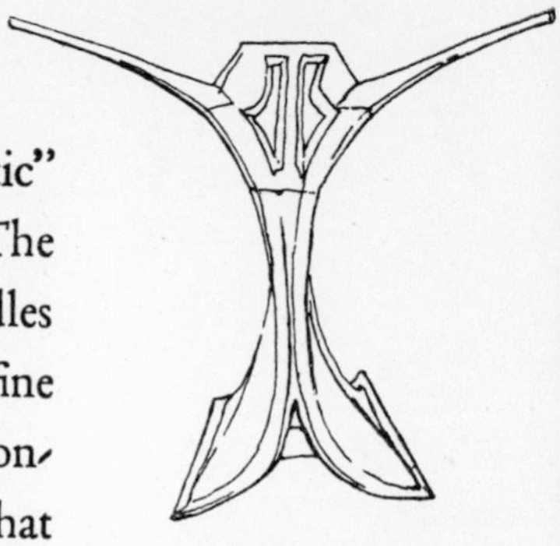

Due to the accidents of discovery the art of the Polynesian islands was the first to reach this country from the South Pacific. For similar reasons the art of Polynesia became acculturated or disappeared earlier, with the exception of that of Indonesia, than in other Oceanic areas. Much of the art from Polynesia, therefore, is of earlier date than that from Melanesia and Micronesia. A proportion of this art consists of two-dimensional surface delineations on clubs, utensils, and tapa cloth. These objects were primarily decorated for persons of high rank. Although they are common to all areas of Polynesia, they are most abundant in the central region.

Clubs of various shapes from Tonga and Samoa have either the striking surface or the entire length decorated with parallel low relief carved angular designs. These are arranged in zones into which the surface is first divided. In some examples, particularly those from Tonga, zoomorphs and anthropomorphs of tiny stick-like or linear shapes are included within the geometric design (Fig. 18). The clubs were generally carved from iron-wood, stained a deep reddish-brown or black, and very highly polished. The carving was very carefully done, a shark's tooth serving as a tool.

Fig. 17

Fig. 18

37

In contrast to these angular patterns, ceremonial paddles from the Austral Islands were elaborately and completely decorated with both angular and curvilinear designs (80). These too are arranged in organized space areas and many of the motives are composed of concentric forms. Around the circumference of the knob-like handles of the paddles tiny figures in high relief are carved. The heads of these figures are rendered as spherical triangles, the bodies suggested by segments of swinging circular lines; while the only facial features are enormously scaled frog-like eyes. As the majority of Polynesian paddles, these were usually stained a black-brown and polished.

Highly conventionalized figure representations from central Polynesia also appear on the ceremonial adzes from Mangaia in the Cook Islands. On the handles, which are often pierced, the human figure is reduced to crossing diagonals bisected vertically by a straight line. At the end of the handle more complete forms are sometimes carved. The adzes are symbols of Tane, the god of craftsmen. Carved in a less conventionalized manner, the so-called District God from Raratonga also in the Cook Islands (79) and the fly-whisk handle from Tahiti (83) depict stocky human figures with large narrow heads and huge ovoid eyes.

Examples of an organic, simplified naturalism appear in a few sculptured figures from Tahiti (82). In these, body shapes are full and rounded and a slightly enlarged head is expressed as an almost pure ovoid. There is strong suggestion of muscular definition in such figures. Calm, even introspective in mood, they may represent deities or they may be generic portraits of ancestors.

Utilitarian objects, as neck-rests and bowls, were made throughout the central Islands. They have simplified elegant shapes comparable to those of Micronesia. Tapa cloth was decorated everywhere in this area

38

with a variety of mostly geometric designs. These designs were rendered in color.

The art of the Marquesas Islands is, in many respects, closely related to that of Central Polynesia. Three-dimensional forms appear in both large and small sculptures in wood and stone.* Marquesan human figures have a short body, massive legs, and a large overhanging head set on an extremely short neck. Facial features, delineated in very low relief, are dominated by large ovoid eyes, very wide nostrils, and a long narrow oval mouth. These figures were carved as free-standing and appear as three-quarter round forms in the decoration of stilt-steps (Fig. 19). The surface of the small stilt-step forms is covered with an all-over design of shallow parallel grooves. Human forms of like kind were also carved practically in the round on bone and wooden handles of fans. Half-figures with enormously proportioned heads, typical of Marquesan style, were cut in low relief on small bone tubes used as hair decorations. Very tiny and simplified or stylized figures were also carved in bone as ear ornaments.

Human facial features of characteristic Marquesan design were used extensively in low relief and incised decorations. Spectacular examples are found on the striking heads of long, heavy clubs. Faces are carved on both sides. On the projecting knobs which serve as eye pupils and nose tiny faces are cut. The eyes containing these pupils are shaped as huge ovoids which are encircled by incised, radiating parallel lines. They resemble in appearance the intent and aggressive expression of many Melanesian sculptures. Below the striking heads of clubs a decorative band was carved with motives derived from facial features, such as eyes, ears, nose. These clubs were stained a dark black and highly polished. The outer surface of wooden bowls was divided into zones and completely decorated with geometric motives and details of

Fig. 19

* Stone figures are also characteristic of various regions, especially Tahiti, in Central Polynesia.

39

human features. Large and small stone pounders often had janus-like heads carved on the handles as terminal knobs.

Marquesan art combines surface delineation with massively scaled sculptural shapes. The forms tend to be angular and heavy, even the more curvilinear elements having a degree of angularity. This is the only area in Polynesia where tapa cloth was not decorated.

The Polynesian Maori peoples of New Zealand developed an elaborate and complex art. The primary forces behind it were closely related to the warlike proclivities of the Maori and to the importance of rank and ancestry. Ancestors, legendary and recent, appear carved as architectural decorations for the exterior and interior of special houses; while long and short fighting clubs and stern and prow pieces for the large war canoes were lavishly sculptured and decorated. Canoe bailers, boxes, flutes, breast pendants, and other objects were also carved and enriched with decoration (Fig. 20).

In its details and general character Maori art constitutes a unique Polynesian style. Large headed, heavily proportioned figures had an aggressive, almost menacing expression. A tongue often protruded from a snarling mouth which was shaped as a horizontal figure-eight. The surface of the forms was completely covered with an intricate decorative design dominated by concentric spirals. Big double spirals were used to mark the points of articulation. In house-carvings the figure was carved against a background completely covered with a comparable overall design carved in planes of different depth. The majority of figures were painted a monochrome red ochre, the eyes inlaid with paua shell.*
Heads with similar grotesque features were carved on the long taiaha or fighting stave, the protruding tongue extended and enlarged to form a sharp point. Canoe bailers and feather boxes were also often embellished with sculptured heads. Figures and heads of this type admirably

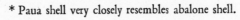

* Paua shell very closely resembles abalone shell.

40

Fig. 20

express the aggression and prowess of the legendary ancestors. Their intense, dynamic appearance suggests comparisons with Melanesia. The more immediate ancestors were given simpler, less fearsome expression, with moko or tattooing designs delineated on the face. A sensitive, almost personalized representation is sometimes apparent in the facial rendering.

Aerial forms are characteristic of Maori art. They were carved as war canoe and stern pieces and as house façade gable boards. Light and space, with the background of the complex Maori designs cut away, thus became important style elements. Superposition of forms, particularly in architectural carvings, was also common in this art; while small grotesque figures were cut in greenstone (nephrite) and bone as neck ornaments, the much prized hei-tiki.

The Maori developed one of the most elaborate and intricate art styles in the entire South Pacific. It has an almost Oriental quality in the complex luxuriance of its surface designs. Although curvilinear elements are prominent in the decorative art, rectilinear forms and parallel straight lines are also extensively used.

The mystery of Easter Island—who the people were, where they came from, what happened to them—has for some time been dispelled. The people, their culture, and their art are all clearly Polynesian. The most publicized of their art are the large, often huge brooding heads and half-figures carved in volcanic stone. These are rendered in a few simple and bold shapes and planes arranged to emphasize the depth of form. In contrast to the stone sculptures, small skeletalized ancestor figures, lizard and bird forms, and some grotesques were carved in wood with attenuated shapes, stressed outlines, and carefully carved and elaborate descriptive detail. Wood and tapa were so scarce on Easter Island that they were precious materials. Wood was even used for breast pendants which were shaped as crescents and decorated with carved heads

41

Fig. 21

comparable to those of the wooden ancestor figures. It is likely that the stone sculptures represented generically important clan members to commemorate whom they were set up. The small grotesque painted tapa figures may depict spirits and in expression and form have Melanesian affiliations (Fig. 21). Aside from the meticulous carving of detail on the skeletalized figures and the heads of clubs Easter Island art is without any two-dimensional surface designs.

Easter Island style is largely confined to contained sculptural forms. The expression is less intense and aggressive, despite the obsidian and fish-bone inlay for eyes, than that of the Maori. It is far closer expressively and in many of its forms to Marquesan art.

The strongest sculptural style in Polynesia was developed in Hawaii. Figures both large and small range expressively from the naturalistic to the strongly conventionalized. They were carved to represent public and household deities, and some seem to have been generic portraits. Hawaiian figure style is remarkable for its expression of actively posed heavy forms set completely in space. This spatial setting is fully expressed by the contained or negative spaces between the separated parts of the forms. Sharp angles and plains contrast with flowing curved surfaces and outlines to express the tension of a pose and the organic unity of the figure (Fig. 22). These forms have an amazing vitality of sculptural statement. They are often aggressive in pose, and the pulled-up corners of their large open mouths give them an almost snarling appearance.

A distinctive feature of Hawaiian art is the complete lack of carved surface decorative patterns, either on their figures or on their finely shaped wooden bowls. In this respect it differs from that of other Polynesian areas. Only on gourd water-bottles do incised surface designs appear. With the exception of painted tapa and featherwork, Hawaiian art is entirely sculptural, more so than that of any other Polynesian area.

Of the five South Pacific areas, Melanesia is by far the richest in its art forms. Polynesia, far more homogeneous in the style of its art, would have to be ranked second; Indonesia, although of great importance as a source of origin for Oceanic styles, would be third; Micronesia, of far less importance, would be fourth; and Australia, of marginal significance, would be fifth. The art of this vast area is astounding in the diversity of its style and forms. It is also of commanding importance aesthetically.

3. Summation

THE ONLY COMMON FEATURE IN SOUTH PACIFIC ISLAND ART IS the use of the human form or facial features as an expressive medium. The strongest aesthetic qualities in this art are therefore revealed through the human form.

The artists of Oceania understood that the human figure is by nature an assemblage of separate forms which are articulated into an organic unity. The joints or points of articulation both separate the forms and permit their mobility. The major shapes are essentially cylindrical or ovoid and are arranged in a vertical alignment, but their proportions in this alignment are extremely varied, differing almost from person to person. The weight and bulk of these parts is also varied and is of particular significance. In a slender figure, for example, they may be almost geometrically shaped, producing a somewhat flowing surface; while in a more heavily muscled figure the forms are irregularly shaped and the surface planes more varied. The most distinctive part of the human figure is the head with its expressive individualized facial features.

43

Fig. 22

From his knowledge of life the Oceanic artist understood the value of continuous curving surfaces and flowing outline patterns inherent in the human figure. By enlarging the forms and accenting the separation of parts the figure could be expressed as an assemblage of forms. Unity could be achieved through a re-statement of shapes and line patterns. By attenuating the form and by using tight continuous outlines verticality could be expressed. Free distortion of forms and facial features and an exotic set of proportions could make the human figure a spectacular statement of an intense emotional state. Through tensions of pose and an assymmetrical balancing of forms a physically disturbing response could be elicited from the spectator. Finally, the artist recognized that through the emphasis of free or negative spaces between the parts of the figure space could be made a positive aesthetic and expressive force, since it would stress the form pattern by reference to its obverse, empty space. Typical of Melanesian art in particular was the knowledge that the visual impact of bright contrasting colors could heighten the expression of sculptured shapes. Drama could be intensified by the use of materials of varied texture and character. The South Pacific artist could also count heavily on the actual participation or identification of the spectator with the object in a ceremony or through its emotional impact. In this he was aided by the dominant role art played in the lives of the people and, as a consequence, their attitude towards and under-standing of an object.

In all art, regardless of the time and place of its creation, the sensitivity and perception of the artist to the life around him is of major significance. The art tradition within which he creates determines the particular aspect of the subject-matter to be stressed—that is, the basic conformation of a work is fixed within a culture. But, the artist gives to that pattern the cumulative consequence of his experience with life. If his perception is acute and his sensibilities refined he will be able to create within the limits of his tradition frequent masterpieces. In South Pacific Island art masterpieces are frequent. The real test of a great work of art in every culture is its ability to sustain or add to the initial impact when it is re-viewed. Pacific Island art has that ability and requires, in fact, repeated observation to appreciate fully its aesthetic qualities.

Note—Some of the ideas expressed in this "Summation" have appeared in the following article: Wingert, Paul S.—"Some Aesthetic Aspects of Pacific Island Art," *Honolulu Academy of Arts News Bulletin and Calendar*, 14, November, 1952, pp. 2–5.

BIBLIOGRAPHY

ARCHEY, GILBERT, South Sea Folk. Handbook of Maori and Oceanic Ethnology, Auckland, N.Z., 1949, 2nd ed.

BEAGLEHOLE, J. C., The Exploration of the Pacific, London, 1934

BRITISH MUSEUM, Handbook to the Ethnographical Collections, London, 1925, 2nd ed.

CHAUVET, STEPHAN, Les Arts Indigenes en Nouvelle Guinée, Paris, 1930

DAVIDSON, D. S., A Preliminary Consideration of Aboriginal Australian Decorative Art, *Memoirs, American Philosophical Society*, IX, 1937

EDGE-PARTINGTON, J., An Album of the Weapons, Tools, Ornaments, Articles of Dress of the Natives of the Pacific Islands, Manchester, 1890-1898, 3 vols.

FINSCH, O., Südseearbeiten, Hamburg, 1914

FIRTH, R. W., Art and Life in New Guinea, London, 1936

FURNAS, J. C., Anatomy of Paradise, N.Y., 1948

GREINER, RUTH, Polynesian Decorative Designs, *Bulletin, Bernice P. Bishop Museum*, 7, 1923

HADDON, A. C., The Decorative Art of British New Guinea, London, 1894

HAMILTON, A., The Art Workmanship of the Maori Race of New Zealand, Wellington, 1896-1901

HANDY, E. S. C., Polynesian Religion, *Bulletin, Bernice P. Bishop Museum*, 34, 1927

HANDY, W. C., L'Art des Iles Marquises, Paris, 1938

INDONESIAN ART, The Asia Institute, N.Y., 1948

L'ART DES OCEANIENS, *Cahiers d'Art*, 2-3, Paris, 1929

LEENHARDT, MAURICE, Arts de L'Oceanie, Paris, 1947

LINTON, RALPH, PAUL S. WINGERT and RENE D'HARNONCOURT, Art of the South Seas, New York, Museum of Modern Art, 1946

LUQUET, G. H., L'Art Neo-Caledonien, Paris, 1926

LUQUIENS, H. M., Hawaiian Art, Honolulu, 1931

MCCARTHY, F. D., Australian Aboriginal Decorative Art, Sydney, 1952.

NEVERMANN, HANS, Suedseekunst, Berlin, Staatliches Museum, 1933

PRIMITIVE KONST, Statens Ethnografiska Museum, Stockholm, 1947

REICHARD, G. A., Melanesian Design, New York, 1933, 2 vols.

ROBSON, R. W., The Pacific Islands Handbook, 1944, New York, 1945

ROUSSEAU, MADELEINE (ed.), L'Art Oceanien, No. 38. *Collection "Le Musee Vivant"*, Paris, 1951

SKILLED HANDWORK OF THE MAORI, The Oldman Collection. *Memoirs of the Polynesian Society*, 14, Wellington, 1946

STEPHAN, E., Südseekunst, Berlin, 1907

THE OLDMAN COLLECTION OF POLYNESIAN ARTIFACTS, *Memoirs of the Polynesian Society*, 15, Wellington, 1943

WINGERT, PAUL S., Outline Guide to the Art of the South Pacific, N.Y., 1946

CATALOGUE

CATALOGUE

Items marked with an asterisk (*) are illustrated in the picture section following page 64; those marked with a dagger (†) appear as figures in the text.

I. INDONESIA

*1. ANCESTOR FIGURE. Nias. Wood, 27½ inches high. Collection Mr. and Mrs. Ralph C. Altman, Los Angeles. *Picture 2.*

2. ANCESTOR FIGURE. Nias. Wood, 22¾ inches high. Brooklyn Museum (34.6073).

3. ANCESTOR FIGURE. Nias. Wood, ca. 22 inches high. Carlebach Gallery, New York (18075).

*4. HOUSE DECORATION. Batak, Sumatra. Polychromed wood, 24 inches high. Seattle Art Museum. *Picture 1.*

5. MAGICIAN'S STAFF. Batak, Sumatra. Wood, ca. 65 inches high. Nasli Heeramaneck Collection, New York.

†6. MAGICIAN'S STAFF. Batak, Sumatra. Wood, ca. 68 inches high. Carlebach Gallery, New York (17711b). *Fig. 1.*

*7. ANCESTOR FIGURE. Leti, South West Islands. Wood, 16 inches high. Collection Helen Tamiris, New York. *Picture 3.*

8. ANCESTOR FIGURE. Leti, South West Islands. Wood, 6 inches high. University Museum, Philadelphia (P⁻2191).

*9. SHIELD. Kenyah⁻Kayan, Borneo. Polychromed wood, human hair, 47¼ inches high. Peabody Museum, Harvard University (85625). *Picture 4.*

10. SHIELD. Kenyah⁻Kayan, Borneo. Polychromed wood, 53½ inches high. Denver Art Museum (231⁻QI⁻EX).

11. MASK. Borneo. Polychromed wood, 20 inches high. Peabody Museum, Harvard University (63128).

*12. MASK. Borneo. Wood, 20 inches high. Milwaukee Public Museum (3190). *Picture 5.*

13. STANDING FEMALE FIGURE. Igorot, Philippines. Wood, 10 inches high. Peabody Museum, Harvard University (74184).

14. SEATED FEMALE FIGURE. Igorot, Philippines. Wood, 3½ inches high. Collection Vincent Price, Beverly Hills.

*15. LADLE. Igorot, Philippines. Wood, 15 inches long. Denver Art Museum (154⁻QI⁻P). *Picture 6.*

16. SHIELD. Igorot, Philippines. Wood, ca. 40 inches high. Washington State Museum, Seattle (5⁻13534).

17. RICE BEER LADLE. Ifugao, Philippines. Wood and bone, 47 inches long. Milwaukee Public Museum (43622).

18. CARVED SPOON. Philippines. Wood, 13½ inches long. University Museum, Philadelphia (P⁻2074).

19. CARVED SPOON. Philippines. Wood, 7¾ inches long. University Museum, Philadelphia (P⁻2076).

II. MELANESIA

*20. "KOROVAR", ANCESTOR FIGURE. Dutch New Guinea. Wood, 15 inches high. Bernice P. Bishop Museum, Honolulu (C⁻9676). *Picture 10.*

21. "KOROVAR", ANCESTOR FIGURE. Dutch New Guinea. Wood, ca. 8 inches high. Collection John J. Klejman, New York.

†22. "KOROVAR", ANCESTOR FIGURE. Dutch New Guinea. Wood, 3 inches high over⁻all. Collection Nasli Heeramaneck, New York. *Fig. 2.*

23. "KONEIM-ANIM", MYTHOLOGICAL BEING. South Dutch New Guinea. Wood, seeds, skin, 53½ inches high. Los Angeles County Museum (A-1931-61).

24. CANOE PROW CARVING. Geelvink Bay, Dutch New Guinea. Wood, 28½ inches high. Peabody Museum, Harvard University (72755).

25. CARVED CANOE PROW. Humboldt Bay, Dutch New Guinea. Polychromed wood, 22 inches high. American Museum of Natural History, New York (S-1093).

26. CARVED CANOE PROW. Dutch New Guinea. Polychromed wood, 33 inches high. Peabody Museum, Harvard University (72675).

*27. PIERCED CANOE PROW DECORATION. South Dutch New Guinea. Wood, ca. 50 inches high. Carlebach Gallery, New York (19640). Picture 9.

28. SHIELD. Dutch New Guinea. Polychromed wood, 41 inches high. Peabody Museum, Harvard University (72696).

*29. CARVED SHIELD. South Dutch New Guinea. Polychromed wood, ca. 68 inches high. Carlebach Gallery, New York (19663). Picture 8.

30. DRUM. South Dutch New Guinea. Wood, 54 inches high. Los Angeles County Museum (A-1931-54).

*31. PAINTED BARK-CLOTH. North Dutch New Guinea. Designs in black and red, 60 inches high by 34 inches wide. Cincinnati Museum of Natural History. Picture 7.

32. PAINTED BARK-CLOTH. North Dutch New Guinea. Designs in black and red, 57 inches high by 38 inches wide. Cincinnati Museum of Natural History.

33. CARVED BOWL. Admiralty Islands. Polychromed wood, 10 inches high, 12 inches diameter. American Museum of Natural History, New York (80.0-5327).

34. BOWL IN SHAPE OF BIRD. Admiralty Islands. Wood, 18 inches long. Peabody Museum, Harvard University (D-1245).

*35. CARVED BOWL. Admiralty Islands. Wood, ca. 20 inches long. Newark Museum (24.794). Picture 11.

36. LADLE. Admiralty Islands. Wooden handle, gourd bowl, 16 inches long. American Museum of Natural History, New York (80.0-273). Picture 13.

37. DAGGER, DECORATED HANDLE. Admiralty Islands. Obsidian blade, wooden handle ca. 10 inches long. Royal Ontario Museum of Archaeology, Toronto, Canada (HB-1597).

38. DAGGER, DECORATED HANDLE. Admiralty Islands. Obsidian blade, wooden handle ca. 11 inches long. Buffalo Museum of Science (C-10763).

*39. FIGURE, SPEAR DECORATION. Admiralty Islands. Wood, sting-ray spines, 22¾ inches high. American Museum of Natural History, New York (80.0-244). Picture 12.

40. SPATULA, FIGURE AS HANDLE. Admiralty Islands. Wood, 17½ inches long over-all. American Museum of Natural History, New York (80.1-1249).

41. SPATULA, FIGURE AS HANDLE. Admiralty Islands. Wood, 17 inches long over-all. American Museum of Natural History, New York (80.0-5412).

†42. SPATULA, FIGURE AS HANDLE. Admiralty Islands. Wood, 13 inches long over-all. American Museum of Natural History, New York (80.0-5385). Fig. 3.

43. "KAPKAP", BREAST ORNAMENT. Admiralty Islands. Tridacna shell with tortoise-shell decoration, ca. 4 inches diameter. Carlebach Gallery, New York (18157).

44. "KAPKAP", BREAST ORNAMENT. Admiralty Islands. Tridacna shell with tortoise-shell decoration, ca. 2 inches diameter. Carlebach Gallery, New York (17723C).

45. CANOE-SHAPED VESSEL. Hermit Islands. Wood, ca. 18 inches long. Collection John J. Klejman, New York.

*46. "MALAGAN", COLUMNAR MORTUARY CARV-ING. New Ireland. Polychromed wood, 66 inches high. Carlebach Gallery, New York. *Picture 17.*

*47. CEREMONIAL CARVING. New Ireland. Poly-chromed wood, 41½ inches high. M. H. de Young Memorial Museum, San Francisco. *Picture 18.*

*48. CARVING USED IN MORTUARY CEREMONIES. New Ireland. Polychromed wood, 30 inches long. Newark Museum (24.688). *Picture 4.*

*49. MASK USED IN MORTUARY CEREMONIES. New Ireland. Polychromed wood, 38 inches high. Collection Mr. and Mrs. Ralph C. Altman, Los Angeles. *Picture 15.*

†50. MASK. New Ireland. Polychromed wood, ca. 20 inches high. Collection John J. Klejman, New York. *Fig. 4.*

51. MASK USED IN MORTUARY CEREMONIES. New Ireland. Polychromed wood, 42 inches high. Milwaukee Public Museum (785).

*52. MASK. New Ireland. Polychromed wood, ca. 14 inches high. Carlebach Gallery, New York (19996/3). *Picture 16.*

53. WING OF MASK. New Ireland. Polychromed wood, 26¾ inches high. Collection Mr. and Mrs. Ralph C. Altman, Los Angeles.

54. "SAKABUL", MORTUARY DANCE OBJECT. New Ireland. Polychromed wood, 18¼ inches long. Brooklyn Museum (37.2892).

55. FEMALE FIGURE. New Ireland. Polychromed chalk, 20 inches high. Denver Art Museum (229-QM-EX).

56. "KAPKAP", BREAST PENDANT. New Ireland. Tridacna shell, tortoise-shell decoration, ca. 3¾ inches diameter. Carlebach Gallery, New York (17723b).

*57. CARVED AND PAINTED SHIELD. New Britain. Wood, 47⅞ inches high. Peabody Museum, Harvard University (33-32-70/130). *Picture 19.*

58. CARVED AND PAINTED SHIELD. New Britain. Wood, 54 inches high. Newark Museum (24.345).

*59. MASK. Sulka, New Britain. Pith over light wood frame, 42 inches high. Denver Art Museum (4-NM-P). *Picture 20.*

60. MASK. New Britain. Modeled human skull, 11½ inches high. Peabody Museum, Harvard University (47843).

61. FIGURE. New Britain. Polychromed chalk, 13½ inches high. Buffalo Museum of Science (C-9438).

62. FIGURE. New Britain. Polychromed chalk, 9¼ inches high. Buffalo Museum of Science (C-9439).

63. NECKLACE. New Britain. Nassa-shells, 16¾ inches across. Buffalo Museum of Science (C-10782).

64. MINIATURE MASK. Sepik River, New Guinea. Wood, 3⅜ inches high. Peabody Museum, Harvard University (47-72-70/2738).

*65. MINIATURE MASK. Sepik River, New Guinea. Wood, ca. 3 inches high. Carlebach Gallery, New York (18809). *Picture 27.*

66. MASK. Kaup, New Guinea. Wood, 14 inches high. American Museum of Natural History, New York (80.0-8897).

67. MASK. Kaup, New Guinea. Wood, 26 inches high. American Museum of Natural History, New York (80.0-4740).

*68. MASK. Abelam, New Guinea. Polychromed wood, 14 inches high. American Museum of Natural History, New York (80.0-6682). *Picture 26.*

69. MASK. Abelam, New Guinea. Painted basketry, 9 inches high. Brooklyn Museum (42.114.11).

70. MASK. Mundugumor, New Guinea. Polychromed wood, 11 inches high. Brooklyn Museum (42.114.8).

71. MASK. Mundugumor, New Guinea. Polychromed wood, 19 inches high. American Museum of Natural History, New York (80.0/8287).

*72. MASK. Tchambuli, Sepik River, New Guinea. Polychromed wood, cowrie-shell eyes, 25½ inches high. American Museum of Natural History, New York (80.0/8101). *Picture 33.*

73. MASK. Tchambuli, Sepik River, New Guinea. Polychromed wood, 12 inches high. American Museum of Natural History, New York (80.0/7373).

74. MASK. Tchambuli, Sepik River, New Guinea. Polychromed wood, 14 inches high. Brooklyn Museum (42.114.1).

75. MASK. Tchambuli, Sepik River, New Guinea. Polychromed wood, cowrie-shell eyes, 22½ inches high. American Museum of Natural History, New York (80.0/7385).

*76. GABLE MASK FOR CEREMONIAL HOUSE. Tchambuli, Sepik River, New Guinea. Polychromed wood, 51⅛ inches high. University Museum, Philadelphia (29/50/615). *Picture 29.*

*77. MASK. Tchambuli, Sepik River, New Guinea. Painted basketry, ca. 26 inches high. Carlebach Gallery, New York (18544). *Picture 28.*

*78. MALE FIGURE. Sepik River, New Guinea. Wood, 25½ inches high. Bernice P. Bishop Museum, Honolulu (B-9863). *Picture 21.*

79. FIGURE. Sepik River, New Guinea. Wood, 6½ inches high. University Museum, Philadelphia (29/50/637).

*80. FIGURE. Sepik River, New Guinea. Wood, 9¾ inches high. Bernice P. Bishop Museum, Honolulu (B-9866). *Picture 23.*

81. SEATED FIGURE. Sepik River, New Guinea. Wood, 6 inches high. Seattle Art Museum.

82. FIGURE. Sepik River, New Guinea. Wood, 7⅞ inches high. Bernice P. Bishop Museum, Honolulu (B-9864).

83. FIGURE. Kaup, Sepik River, New Guinea. Wood, 27 inches high. American Museum of Natural History, New York (80.0/9055).

84. FIGURE. Arapesh, Sepik River, New Guinea. Polychromed wood, 58 inches high. American Museum of Natural History, New York (80.0/6723).

*85. FIGURE. Mundugumor, Sepik River, New Guinea. Polychromed wood, 19 inches high. American Museum of Natural History, New York (80.0/8248). *Picture 22.*

86. FIGURE FOR TOP OF SACRED FLUTE. Mundugumor, Sepik River, New Guinea. Wood, 19½ inches high. American Museum of Natural History, New York (80.0/8243).

87. SUSPENSION HOOK CARVED WITH FIGURE. Abelam, Sepik River, New Guinea. Polychromed wood, 19 inches high. American Museum of Natural History, New York (80.0/6643).

88. CARVED SUSPENSION HOOK. Tchambuli, Sepik River, New Guinea. Polychromed wood, 18 inches high. American Museum of Natural History, New York (80.0/7481).

89. CARVED SUSPENSION HOOK. Tchambuli, Sepik River, New Guinea. Polychromed wood, 17 inches high. American Museum of Natural History, New York (80.0/7481).

*90. SUSPENSION HOOK. Sepik River, New Guinea. Polychromed wood, 29 inches high. University Museum, Philadelphia (29/50/338). *Picture 25.*

*91. SUSPENSION HOOK WITH BIRD FORM. Sepik River, New Guinea. Polychromed wood, 18 inches high. American Museum of Natural History, New York (80.0/7464). *Picture 35.*

*92. SUSPENSION HOOK. Tchambuli, Sepik River, New Guinea. Polychromed wood, 49 inches high. American Museum of Natural History, New York (80.1⁄1093). *Picture 31.*

*93. SUSPENSION HOOK. Mundugumor, Sepik River, New Guinea. Polychromed wood, 49 inches high. American Museum of Natural History, New York (80.0⁄8127). *Picture 32.*

*94. SHIELD WITH PIERCED DESIGN. Sepik River, New Guinea. Wood, ca. 60 inches high. Detroit Institute of Arts (26.370). *Picture 34.*

*95. CARVED AND PAINTED SHIELD. Tchambuli, Sepik River, New Guinea. Wood, 69 inches high. American Museum of Natural History, New York (80.0⁄8137). *Picture 30.*

96. CARVED AND PAINTED SHIELD. Tchambuli, Sepik River, New Guinea. Wood, 55 inches high. University Museum, Philadelphia (29⁄50⁄490).

97. CARVED STOOL. Sepik River, New Guinea. Polychromed wood, 29 inches high. American Museum of Natural History, New York (80.0⁄8131).

*98. SEAT SHAPED AS BIRD. Sepik River, New Guinea. Polychromed wood, 50 inches long. University Museum, Philadelphia (29⁄50⁄317). *Picture 24.*

99. SEAT SHAPED AS BEAKED BIRD HEAD. Sepik River, New Guinea. Polychromed wood, 23 inches high. University Museum, Philadelphia (29⁄50⁄321).

*100. BOWL WITH CARVED FIGURES AS HANDLES. Sepik River, New Guinea. Wood, 22 inches long. Collection William Moore, Los Angeles. *Picture 39.*

101. LIME MORTAR. Sepik River, New Guinea. Polychromed wood, $5\frac{1}{2}$ inches long. University Museum, Philadelphia (29⁄50⁄584).

*102. CARVED SAGO SCOOP. Sepik River, New Guinea. Wood, $14\frac{1}{8}$ inches long. Peabody Museum, Harvard University (47⁄72⁄70/2726). *Picture 36.*

103. DECORATED BOWL. Sepik River, New Guinea. Polychromed pottery, 8 inches high by 9 inches diameter. University Museum, Philadelphia (29⁄50⁄348).

104. LIME TUBE STOPPER. Sepik River, New Guinea. Wood, 27 inches long. Cincinnati Museum of Natural History (417).

105. LIME TUBE STOPPER. Sepik River, New Guinea. Polychromed wood, 30 inches long overall, stopper 21 inches long. University Museum, Philadelphia (29⁄50⁄552).

106. LIME TUBE STOPPER. Sepik River, New Guinea. Polychromed wood, 30 inches long overall, stopper $17\frac{1}{2}$ inches long. University Museum, Philadelphia (29⁄50⁄557).

*107. LIME TUBE STOPPER. Sepik River, New Guinea. Polychromed wood, $16\frac{1}{2}$ inches long. Honolulu Academy of Arts (4196). *Picture 40.*

108. CANOE PROW SHAPED AS CROCODILE HEAD. Sepik River, New Guinea. Wood, $60\frac{1}{2}$ inches long. University Museum, Philadelphia (29⁄50⁄625).

109. CANOE PROW SHAPED AS FIGURE AND BIRD. Kaup, Sepik River, New Guinea. Wood, 23 inches high. American Museum of Natural History, New York (80.0⁄8919).

†110. DECORATIVE CARVING, POSSIBLY FROM A CANOE PROW. Sepik River, New Guinea. Wood, 36 inches high. Cincinnati Museum of Natural History (900). *Fig. 6.*

*111. CEREMONIAL CARVING. Sepik River, New Guinea. Polychromed wood, ca. 36 inches high. Collection Donald Deskey, New York. *Picture 38.*

112. CARVED DRUM. Tchambuli, Sepik River, New Guinea. Wood, 24 inches high. American Museum of Natural History, New York (80.0⁄8114).

113. CARVED AND PAINTED NECK⁄REST. Sepik River, New Guinea. Wood, 28 inches long. University Museum, Philadelphia (29⁄50⁄300).

114. SPATULA DECORATED WITH CARVED HEAD. Sepik River, New Guinea. Wood, ca. 11½ inches long. Cincinnati Museum of Natural History (202).

115. SMALL HUMAN HEAD, Mundugumor, Sepik River, New Guinea. Polychromed stone, 5 inches high. American Museum of Natural History, New York (80.0/8422).

116. DAGGER WITH INCISED DECORATION. Tchambuli, Sepik River, New Guinea. Cassowary leg bone, 10½ inches long. American Museum of Natural History, New York (80.0/7943).

117. DAGGER WITH INCISED DECORATION. Abelam, Sepik River, New Guinea. Cassowary leg bone, 10¼ inches long. American Museum of Natural History, New York (80.0/7078).

118. DAGGER SHAPED AS A BIRD. Sepik River, New Guinea. Cassowary leg bone, 10¼ inches long. American Museum of Natural History, New York (80.0/7952).

119. PAINTED DECORATIVE CARVING. Sepik River, New Guinea. Wood, feathers, shell, 29½ inches wide by 18 inches high. University Museum, Philadelphia (29/50/667).

*120. PENDANT BREAST ORNAMENT. Sepik River, New Guinea. Raffia fiber, shell, 16 inches long. University Museum, Philadelphia (29/50/35). Picture 37.

121. FEATHER HEADDRESS. Sepik River, New Guinea. 62 inches wide by 56 inches high. Los Angeles County Museum (L/1444/31).

*122. FIGURE. Huon Gulf/Tami Island, New Guinea. Polychromed wood, 9¾ inches high. Bernice P. Bishop Museum, Honolulu (B/1018). Picture 41.

123. FIGURE. Huon Gulf/Tami Island, New Guinea. Polychromed wood, 8½ inches high. American Museum of Natural History, New York (80.11/607).

124. FIGURE. Huon Gulf/Tami Island, New Guinea. Polychromed wood, ca. 40 inches high. Collection Herschel Chipp, New York.

125. MORTAR CARVED WITH FIGURE. Huon Gulf/Tami Island, New Guinea. Polychromed wood, 6 inches high. Peabody Museum, Salem, Mass. (19504).

†126. NECK/REST. Huon Gulf/Tami Island, New Guinea. Polychromed wood, 5¾ inches long by 6 inches high. Buffalo Museum of Science (C/11713). Fig. 7.

127. NECK/REST. Huon Gulf/Tami Island, New Guinea. Polychromed wood, 7¼ inches long by 6 inches high. American Museum of Natural History, New York (80.1/1606).

*128. CARVED DRUM. Huon Gulf/Tami Island, New Guinea. Wood, 26½ inches high. American Museum of Natural History, New York (S/651). Picture 42.

129. DECORATED BOWL. Huon Gulf/Tami Island, New Guinea. Wood, ca. 18 inches long. Honolulu Academy of Arts (4184).

*130. DECORATED BOWL SHAPED AS BIRD. Huon Gulf/Tami Island, New Guinea. Wood, 16⅝ inches long. Collection Nelson A. Rockefeller, New York (4/39). Picture 43.

131. DECORATED BOWL SHAPED AS BIRD. Huon Gulf/Tami Island, New Guinea. Wood, 21⅞ inches long. Collection Eliot Elisofon, New York.

*132. CARVED AND PAINTED SHIELD. Papuan Gulf, New Guinea. Wood, ca. 36 inches high. Royal Ontario Museum of Archaeology, Toronto, Canada (HB/510). Picture 44.

133. CARVED AND PAINTED SHIELD. Papuan Gulf, New Guinea. Wood, ca. 38 inches high. Brooklyn Museum (00.136).

134. CEREMONIAL BOARD. Papuan Gulf, New Guinea. Polychromed wood, 40 inches high. Detroit Institute of Arts (B-4303).

*135. CEREMONIAL BOARD. Papuan Gulf, New Guinea. Polychromed wood, 41½ inches high. Buffalo Museum of Science (C-8175). *Picture 47.*

136. CEREMONIAL BOARD. Papuan Gulf, New Guinea. Polychromed wood, 30¾ inches high. Honolulu Academy of Arts (3573).

137. CEREMONIAL BOARD. Papuan Gulf, New Guinea. Polychromed wood, 35 inches high. Milwaukee Public Museum (26005).

138. CEREMONIAL BOARD. Orokolo, Papuan Gulf, New Guinea. Polychromed wood, 55 inches high. Collection Eliot Elisofon, New York.

*139. BARK-CLOTH MASK. Papuan Gulf, New Guinea. Polychromed, cane appliqué design, 30 inches high. Collection Mr. and Mrs. Ralph C. Altman, Los Angeles. *Picture 46.*

*140. BARK-CLOTH MASK. Purari, Papuan Gulf, New Guinea. Polychromed, cane appliqué design, 26 inches high. University Museum, Philadelphia (P-4089). *Picture 45.*

141. BARK-CLOTH MASK. Papuan Gulf, New Guinea. Polychromed, cane appliqué design, 20 inches high. Peabody Museum, Harvard University (50529).

†142. BARK-CLOTH MASK. Papuan Gulf, New Guinea. Polychromed, cane appliqué design, 59 inches high. Peabody Museum, Harvard University (50514). *Fig. 8.*

143. INCISED BULL-ROARER. Papuan Gulf, New Guinea. Wood, 13 inches long. Brooklyn Museum (51.118.15).

144. DECORATIVE BELT. Papuan Gulf, New Guinea. Incised bark, ca. 50 inches long. Buffalo Museum of Science (C-9165).

145. FIGHTING CHARM. Papuan Gulf, New Guinea. Raffia, shells, seeds, 11 inches high by 12 inches wide. Buffalo Museum of Science (C-10985).

*146. MASK. Torres Straits, New Guinea. Wood, shell inlay eyes, 20 inches high. Collection Nelson A. Rockefeller, New York (4-64). *Picture 48.*

*147. CARVED HEAD. Fly River, New Guinea. Polychromed pith, ca. 9 inches high. Detroit Institute of Arts (14.885). *Picture 49a.*

*148. CARVED HEAD. Fly River, New Guinea. Polychromed pith, ca. 9 inches high. Detroit Institute of Arts (14.886). *Picture 49b.*

149. ARROW CARVED WITH HUMAN FORM. Torres Straits, New Guinea. Wood, ca. 55 inches long. Royal Ontario Museum of Archaeology, Toronto, Canada (HB-395).

150. ARROW CARVED WITH CROCODILE FORM. Torres Straits, New Guinea. Wood, ca. 55 inches long. Royal Ontario Museum of Archaeology, Toronto, Canada (HB-449).

151. ARROW CARVED WITH HUMAN FORM. Torres Straits, New Guinea. Wood, 60 inches long. Buffalo Museum of Science (C-6990).

152. ARROW CARVED WITH CROCODILE FORM. Torres Straits, New Guinea. Wood, 60 inches long. Buffalo Museum of Science (C-6983).

†153. CARVED DRUM. Torres Straits, New Guinea. Wood, shells, cassowary feathers, 38½ inches high. Collection Nelson A. Rockefeller, New York (4-60). *Fig. 9.*

154. CARVED AND INCISED CLUB. Torres Straits, New Guinea. Wood, 32 inches long. Buffalo Museum of Science (C-6680).

155. CANOE PROW. Louisiades, Massim Area, New Guinea. Wood, 14 inches long. Buffalo Museum of Science (C-11029).

156. CANOE PROW. Milne Bay, Massim Area, New Guinea. Wood, ca. 20 inches high. Washington State Museum, Seattle (3368⁄60).

†157. CANOE PROW CARVING. Trobriands, Massim Area, New Guinea. Wood, 20 inches long by 24 inches wide. Peabody Museum, Harvard University (83777). *Fig. 10.*

158. CANOE PROW CARVING. Trobriands, Massim Area, New Guinea. Wood, ca. 22 inches long. M. H. de Young Museum, San Francisco.

159. CANOE PROW FIGURE. Massim Area, New Guinea. Wood, 9½ inches long by 8½ inches high. Bernice P. Bishop Museum, Honolulu (8784).

*160. "KAI⁄DIBA", DANCE SHIELD. Trobriands, Massim Area, New Guinea. Wood, 28 inches high. Newark Museum (24.661). *Picture 52.*

161. CARVED DRUM. Massim Area, New Guinea. Wood, 27 inches high. Peabody Museum, Salem, Mass. (E⁄24649).

162. FIGURE, SPATULA HANDLE. Massim Area, New Guinea. Wood, 15¾ inches long. Buffalo Museum of Science (C⁄8335).

*163. SEATED FIGURE, SPATULA HANDLE. Massim Area, New Guinea. Wood, 14 inches long over⁄all, figure 8½ inches. Collection Vincent Price, Beverly Hills. *Picture 53.*

164. SPATULA, INCISED HANDLE. Massim Area, New Guinea. Wood, 17½ inches long. Collection William Moore, Los Angeles.

165. SPATULA, CARVED HANDLE. Massim Area, New Guinea. Wood, 12 inches long. Collection William Moore, Los Angeles.

166. SPATULA, CARVED HANDLE. Massim Area, New Guinea. Wood, ca. 8 inches long. Buffalo Museum of Science (C⁄12368).

167. SPATULA, CARVED HANDLE. Massim Area, New Guinea. Wood, 11 inches long. University Museum, Philadelphia (P⁄2604).

*168. SPATULA, CARVED HANDLE. Massim Area, New Guinea. Wood, 12 inches long. Los Angeles County Museum (A⁄5119.5). *Picture 54.*

169. SPATULA, CARVED HANDLE. Massim Area, New Guinea. Wood, ca. 9 inches long. Buffalo Museum of Science (C⁄8571).

170. DECORATED COMB. Milne Bay, Massim Area, New Guinea. Wood, ca. 6 inches high. Washing⁄ton State Museum, Seattle (4⁄12870).

171. AXE, CARVED HANDLE. Massim Area, New Guinea. Wood, 27¼ inches long. Peabody Museum, Salem, Mass. (E⁄5221).

172. INCISED CLUB. Massim Area, New Guinea. Wood, ca. 27 inches long. Collection Ralph Linton, New Haven, Conn.

*173. CLUB, INCISED DECORATION. Massim Area, New Guinea. Wood, 32 inches long. Buffalo Museum of Science (C⁄8281). *Picture 50.*

*174. PAINTED WAR SHIELD. Trobriands, Massim Area, New Guinea. Wood, 31 inches long by 15½ inches wide. Buffalo Museum of Science (C⁄8163). *Picture 51.*

*175. "MUSUMUSU", CANOE PROW FIGURE. Central Solomon Islands. Wood, mother⁄of⁄pearl shell inlay, 9⅝ inches high. Collection Nelson A. Rockefeller, New York (4⁄17). *Picture 56.*

†176. "MUSUMUSU", CANOE PROW FIGURE. Central Solomon Islands. Wood, ca. 11 inches high. Milwaukee Public Museum. *Fig. 11.*

177. "MUSUMUSU", CANOE PROW FIGURE. New Georgia, Solomon Islands. Wood, mother⁄of⁄pearl shell inlay, 11 inches high. Buffalo Museum of Science (C⁄12041).

*178. MORTAR, CARVED FIGURE. Solomon Islands. Wood, ca. 6 inches high. Buffalo Museum of Science (C⁄10720). *Picture 55.*

179. CLUB. Bougainville, Solomon Islands. Wood, 50 inches long. American Museum of Natural History, New York (S⁄2646).

180. CLUB. Bougainville, Solomon Islands. Wood, 50 inches long. American Museum of Natural History, New York (S⁄2648).

181. CLUB, INCISED BLADE. Bougainville, Solomon Islands. Wood, 45½ inches long. University Museum, Philadelphia (29⁄58⁄42).

182. CARVED HEAD. Solomon Islands. Stone, 5½ inches high. Cincinnati Museum of Natural History (218).

*183. CARVED HEAD. Solomon Islands. Coral, 10¾ inches high. Collection Nelson A. Rockefeller, New York (4⁄81). *Picture 57.*

184. MODELED HUMAN SKULL. Solomon Islands. Mother⁄of⁄pearl shell inlay, life⁄size. Washington State Museum, Seattle (4⁄12626).

*185. INLAID FOOD BOWL. Eastern Solomon Islands. Wood, conus and tridacna shell, 68 inches long. Peabody Museum, Harvard University (47⁄54⁄70/2466). *Picture 59.*

*186. BOWL SHAPED AS BIRD. Eastern Solomon Islands. Wood, ca. 18 inches long. Washington State Museum, Seattle (4⁄12660). *Picture 58.*

187. BOWL SHAPED AS BIRD. Eastern Solomon Islands. Wood, ca. 11 inches long. Carlebach Gallery, New York (17780).

188. CANOE PROW CARVING. Solomon Islands. Wood, ca. 12 inches high. Washington State Museum, Seattle (4⁄12645).

189. CARVED AND PAINTED CANOE PADDLE. Buka, Solomon Islands. Wood, 47 inches long. University Museum, Philadelphia (P⁄3154).

190. CARVED AND PAINTED CANOE PADDLE. Buka, Solomon Islands. Wood, 61 inches long. University Museum, Philadelphia (P⁄4874).

191. DETAIL, SKULL HOUSE FAÇADE. Rubiana, Solomon Islands. Tridacna shell, 12 inches wide by 16½ inches high. Buffalo Museum of Science (C⁄11751).

192. INCISED PENDANT. Solomon Islands. Tridacna shell, 2 inches diameter. Buffalo Museum of Science (C⁄11736).

*193. CARVED PENDANT AS BIRDS. Solomon Islands. Mother⁄of⁄pearl shell, 6⅜ inches wide. Cincinnati Museum of Natural History (173). *Picture 60.*

*194. CARVED PENDANT. Solomon Islands. Tridacna shell, 2¼ inches diameter. Cincinnati Museum of Natural History (163). *Picture 60.*

*195. INCISED PENDANT. Solomon Islands. Tridacna shell, 2½ inches diameter. Cincinnati Museum of Natural History (184). *Picture 60.*

*196. "KAPKAP", PENDANT. Solomon Islands. Pierced tortoise shell on tridacna shell base, 5¼ inches diameter. Cincinnati Museum of Natural History (132). *Picture 61.*

*197. LIME TUBE. Solomon Islands. Engraved bamboo, 11⅝ inches long. Milwaukee Public Museum (46190). *Picture 62.*

*198. LIME TUBE. Solomon Islands. Engraved bamboo, 9½ inches long. Milwaukee Public Museum (46192). *Picture 62.*

*199. LIME TUBE. Solomon Islands. Engraved bamboo, 9¼ inches long. Milwaukee Public Museum (46193). *Picture 62.*

†200. STANDING MALE FIGURE. Santa Cruz Islands. Wood, 12 inches high. Bernice P. Bishop Museum, Honolulu (6989). *Fig. 12.*

201. DANCE STICK. Santa Cruz Islands. Carved and painted wood, 39⅜ inches long. Denver Art Museum (209-QM-EX).

202. DANCE STICK. Santa Cruz Islands. Carved and painted wood, 51 inches long. Denver Art Museum (177-QM-EX).

203. "KAPKAP", PENDANT. Santa Cruz Islands. Tortoise shell on tridacna shell base, 6½ inches diameter. Buffalo Museum of Science (C-10723).

204. "KAPKAP", PENDANT. Santa Cruz Islands. Tortoise shell on tridacna shell base, 6½ inches diameter. Newark Museum (24.809).

*205. MASK. New Hebrides. Wood, 15½ inches high. Newark Museum (25.465). Picture 63.

*206. MASK. Malekula, New Hebrides. Painted bark-cloth, fiber, ca. 24 inches high. Buffalo Museum of Science (C-8083). Picture 65.

207. HEAD. New Hebrides. Polychromed lime-stone, ca. 9 inches high. Buffalo Museum of Science (C-9441).

208. CARVED ADZE. New Hebrides. Wood, ca. 16 inches high. Washington State Museum, Seattle (4-12736).

*209. PIG-KILLER, ADZE-SHAPED CLUB. New Hebrides. Wood, 51 inches long. Washington State Museum, Seattle (4-12736). Picture 69.

†210. CARVED CEREMONIAL STAFF. New Hebrides. Wood, ca. 55 inches long. Washington State Museum, Seattle (4-12740). Fig. 13.

*211. STAFF OR SPEAR WITH CARVED HEADS. New Hebrides. Wood, 43¾ inches long. Peabody Museum, Harvard University (47-54-70/2555). Picture 64.

212. CLUB WITH CARVED HEAD. New Hebrides. Wood, 39⅞ inches long. Peabody Museum, Harvard University (47-54-70/2520).

213. CARVED CLUB. New Hebrides. Wood, 42 inches long. Denver Art Museum (101-QM-EX).

214. TURTLE-SHAPED PLATTER. New Hebrides. Wood, 24 inches long. Buffalo Museum of Science (C-13371).

*215. CARVED FOOD PLATTER. New Hebrides. Wood, 35 inches long by 17 inches wide. American Museum of Natural History, New York (80.1-915). Picture 66.

216. MALE FIGURE. New Caledonia. Wood, 45 inches high. University Museum, Philadelphia (P-3151).

*217. MASK. New Caledonia. Wood, 11 inches high. Brooklyn Museum (42.243.19). Picture 70.

*218. "TALE", CARVED DOOR JAMB. New Caledonia. Wood, 64 inches high by 26 inches wide. Denver Art Museum (237-QM-P). Picture 69.

†219. ROOF SPIRE. New Caledonia. Wood, 59 inches high. Peabody Museum, Harvard University (63044). Fig. 14.

*220. CLUB SHAPED AS BIRD HEAD. New Caledonia. Wood, 28 inches long. American Museum of Natural History, New York (80.1-906). Picture 67.

221. CLUB SHAPED AS BIRD HEAD. New Caledonia. Wood, 30 inches long. University Museum, Philadelphia (P-2306).

†222. PRIEST'S OIL DISH. Fiji. Wood, 11 inches diameter. Peabody Museum, Salem (E-10441). Fig. 15.

223. PRIEST'S OIL DISH. Fiji. Wood, 17 inches long. Peabody Museum, Salem, Mass. (E-19254).

*224. TURTLE-SHAPED KAVA BOWL. Fiji. Wood, ca. 20 inches diameter. Washington State Museum, Seattle (4-12593). Picture 73.

225. CANNIBAL FORK. Fiji. Wood, ca. 12 inches long. Washington State Museum, Seattle (4⁄12582).

*226. WIDE⁄BLADED CLUB. Fiji. Wood, 48¾ inches long. Denver Art Museum (89.⁄QM⁄EX). *Picture 72.*

227. WAR CLUB. Fiji. Wood, ca. 45 inches long. Royal Ontario Museum of Archaeology, Toronto, Canada (HB⁄7).

228. WAR CLUB. Fiji. Wood, ca. 45 inches long. Royal Ontario Museum of Archaeology, Toronto, Canada (HB⁄5).

*229. WAR CLUB. Fiji. Wood, 48 inches long. University Museum, Philadelphia (P⁄3186⁄b). *Picture 71.*

III. *AUSTRALIA*

*230. INCISED SPEAR⁄THROWER. Western Australia. Wood, 28 inches long. M. H. de Young Memorial Museum, San Francisco (50⁄32⁄141). *Picture 75.*

231. INCISED BOOMERANG. Central Australia. Wood, 28½ inches long. M. H. de Young Memorial Museum, San Francisco (50⁄32⁄88).

*232. INCISED BOOMERANG. Australia. Wood, 25¼ inches long. Buffalo Museum of Science (C⁄11597). *Picture 76.*

233. INCISED BOOMERANG. Australia. Wood, 28 inches long. Buffalo Museum of Science (C⁄11596).

234. ENGRAVED PENDANT. Western Australia. Shell, 7½ inches high by 5½ inches wide. University Museum, Philadelphia (P⁄2414).

†235. ENGRAVED PENDANT. Western Australia. Shell, 5¼ inches high by 4 inches wide. University Museum, Philadelphia (P⁄3091⁄a). *Fig. 16.*

236. ENGRAVED PENDANT. Western Australia. Shell, 7½ inches high by 5½ inches wide. University Museum, Philadelphia (31⁄33⁄41).

*237. PAINTED AND CARVED SHIELD. Western Australia. Wood, 26¾ inches high. M. H. de Young Memorial Museum, San Francisco (50⁄32⁄144). *Picture 74.*

238. CARVED SHIELD. Western Australia. Wood, 32⅜ inches high. M. H. de Young Memorial Museum, San Francisco (50⁄32⁄149).

239. PAINTED BARK. Arnhem Land, Northern Australia. 30 inches long by 14 inches wide. University Museum, Philadelphia (52⁄13⁄1).

IV. *MICRONESIA*

240. DANCE PADDLE. Ponape, Caroline Islands. Painted wood, 36 inches high. Peabody Museum, Harvard University (53478).

241. DANCE PADDLE. Ponape, Caroline Islands. Painted wood, 35½ inches high. Collection Eliot Elisofon, New York.

†242. CANOE PROW. Truk, Caroline Islands. Carved and painted wood, 14 inches high by 17 inches wide. Peabody Museum, Harvard University (55756). *Fig. 17.*

243. PAINTED BOWL. Mortlock, Caroline Islands. Wood, 11 inches long by 12½ inches wide. Peabody Museum, Salem, Mass. (E⁄14201).

244. DISH. Matty Island. Wood, 18¼ inches long. University Museum, Philadelphia (P⁄3482⁄b).

245. BELT. Marshall Islands. Shell, 34½ inches long. Los Angeles County Museum (A⁄5453.9).

*246. SWORD. Gilbert Islands. Coconut wood edged with shark's teeth, ca. 38 inches long. Washington State Museum, Seattle (4⁄12632). *Picture 77.*

*247. FEMALE FIGURE. Nukuoro Island. Wood, 15½ inches high. Honolulu Academy of Arts (4752). *Picture 78.*

V. POLYNESIA

248. NECK-REST. Tonga Islands. Wood, 19¾ inches long by 6 inches high. Denver Art Museum (67-QP-EX).

†249. PADDLE-CLUB. Tonga Islands. Wood, 42¼ inches long. Peabody Museum, Salem, Mass. (E-4813). *Fig. 18.*

250. PADDLE-CLUB. Tonga Islands. Wood, 46½ inches long. Peabody Museum, Harvard University (53438).

251. PADDLE-CLUB. Tonga Islands. Wood, 43 inches long. University Museum, Philadelphia (P-3360).

252. TAPA, PAINTED BARK-CLOTH. Tonga Islands. 88 inches long by 55 inches wide. Peabody Museum, Harvard University (83934).

†253. NECK-REST. Samoa Islands. Wood, ca. 18 inches long. Buffalo Museum of Science (C-13532).

254. CLUB. Samoa Islands. Wood, 28 inches long. Peabody Museum, Salem, Mass. (E-19564).

255. CARVED SPEAR. Samoa Islands. Wood, 72 inches long. Peabody Museum, Harvard University (63047).

256. KAVA BOWL. Samoa Islands. Wood, 18½ inches diameter. Peabody Museum, Salem, Mass. (E-20979).

257. TAPA, PAINTED BARK-CLOTH. Niue Island. 88 inches long by 67 inches wide. Peabody Museum, Harvard University.

*258. DISTRICT GOD. Raratonga, Cook Islands. Wood, 25 inches high. Peabody Museum, Harvard University (1390). *Picture 79.*

259. CEREMONIAL ADZE. Mangaia, Cook Islands. Wood, 23¾ inches high. Peabody Museum, Salem, Mass. (E-18781).

*260. CEREMONIAL ADZE. Mangaia, Cook Islands. Wood, 35 inches high. Peabody Museum, Harvard University (53510). *Picture 81.*

261. CEREMONIAL PADDLE. Austral Islands. Wood, 33¼ inches long. Peabody Museum, Salem, Mass. (7132A4).

*262. CEREMONIAL PADDLE. Austral Islands. Wood, 33¾ inches long. Peabody Museum, Harvard University (46-78-70/2447). *Picture 80 a and b.*

*263. MALE FIGURE. Tahiti, Society Islands. Wood, 40 inches high. Collection Nelson A. Rockefeller, New York (4-72). *Picture 82.*

*264. CARVED FLY-WHISK HANDLE. Tahiti, Society Islands. Wood, 14 inches long. Peabody Museum, Salem, Mass. (E-13216). *Picture 83.*

265. KAVA BOWL. Tahiti, Society Islands. Wood, 25¾ inches long. Peabody Museum, Salem, Mass. (E-28854).

266. STAMP FOR DECORATING TAPA. Central Polynesia. Coconut mid-ribe of fronds, 17½ inches long by 13 inches wide. Los Angeles County Museum (A-2209-39).

267. FISH-HOOK. Central Polynesia. Pearl and tortoise shell, ca. 2½ inches long. Cincinnati Museum of Natural History (220).

268. FISH-HOOK. Central Polynesia. Pearl and tortoise shell, ca. 2½ inches long. Cincinnati Museum of Natural History (221).

269. MALE FIGURE. Marquesas Islands. Wood, 14 inches high. Buffalo Museum of Science (C-13364).

270. CARVED CLUB. Marquesas Islands. Wood, 55½ inches long. Peabody Museum, Salem, Mass. (E-5032).

271. CARVED CLUB. Marquesas Islands. Wood, 55½ inches long. Peabody Museum, Salem, Mass. (E⁄2154).

*272. CARVED CLUB. Marquesas Islands. Wood, ca. 58 inches long. Brooklyn Museum (35.2183). *Picture 85.*

†273. STILT⁄STEP. Marquesas Islands. Wood, 11 inches high. Peabody Museum, Salem, Mass. (E⁄5081).

274. STILT⁄STEP. Marquesas Islands. Wood, 15 inches high. University Museum, Philadelphia (P⁄5045).

275. FAN, CARVED HANDLE. Marquesas Islands. Bone, 17½ inches high, handle 5 inches high. Peabody Museum, Salem, Mass. (E⁄5099). *Fig. 19.*

276. FAN, CARVED HANDLE. Marquesas Islands. Wood, 16¾ inches high, handle 4¾ inches high. Peabody Museum, Salem, Mass. (E⁄5351).

277. CARVED FAN HANDLE. Marquesas Islands. Bone, ca. 5 inches high. Collection Nasli Heera⁄maneck, New York.

278. HEADBAND. Marquesas Islands. Tridacna and tortoise shell, 18½ inches long. Denver Art Museum (116⁄QP⁄G).

279. CARVED HAIR TUBE. Marquesas Islands. Bone, 1½ inches high. Buffalo Museum of Science (C⁄13089).

280. CARVED HAIR TUBE. Marquesas Islands. Bone, 1½ inches high. Buffalo Museum of Science (C⁄12751).

281. CARVED HAIR TUBE. Marquesas Islands. Bone, ca. 1½ inches high. Collection Nasli Heera⁄maneck, New York.

*282. EAR ORNAMENT. Marquesas Islands. Bone, 1¾ inches long. Cincinnati Museum of Natural History (162). *Picture 84.*

*283. EAR ORNAMENT. Marquesas Islands. Bone, 1¾ inches long. Cincinnati Museum of Natural History (162). *Picture 84.*

284. STRANGLING CORD. Marquesas Islands. Bone attachments, 23 inches long. Brooklyn Museum (38.638).

*285. SALT POUNDER. Marquesas Islands. Stone, 3½ inches high. Cincinnati Museum of Natural History (901). *Picture 86.*

286. POUNDER. Marquesas Islands. Stone, 6¼ inches high. University Museum, Philadelphia (18011).

287. CARVED HOUSE POST. Maori, New Zealand. Wood, 47 inches high. Royal Ontario Museum of Archaeology, Toronto, Canada (HB⁄1278).

*288. FIGURE. Maori, New Zealand. Wood, 20¼ inches high. Peabody Museum, Harvard University (40⁄54⁄70/3199). *Picture 87.*

289. HEAD, HOUSE DECORATION. Maori, New Zealand. Wood, 19½ inches high. Brooklyn Museum (03.217).

*290. "TAIAHA", FIGHTING STAVE. Maori, New Zealand. Wood, 73¾ inches long. Peabody Museum, Salem, Mass. (E⁄5495). *Picture 90.*

291. "TAIAHA", FIGHTING STAVE. Maori, New Zealand. Wood, 82½ inches long. Peabody Museum, Harvard University (48⁄49⁄70/3199).

292. "TAIAHA", FIGHTING STAVE. Maori, New Zealand. Wood, 69½ inches long. Peabody Museum, Harvard University (47⁄54⁄70/2925).

293. CARVED CANOE PROW. Maori, New Zealand. Wood, 42 inches long over⁄all. Denver Art Museum (51⁄QP⁄P).

*294. CARVED WAR CANOE STERN⁄PIECE. Maori, New Zealand. Wood, 63 inches high. M. H. de Young Memorial Museum, San Francisco. *Picture 88.*

*295. CANOE PADDLE, CARVED HANDLE. Maori, New Zealand. Wood, 66½ inches long. University Museum, Philadelphia (P⁄3120). *Picture 89.*

296. CARVED CANOE BAILER. Maori, New Zealand. Wood, 18½ inches long by 10 inches wide. University Museum, Philadelphia (P⁄2316).

*297. CARVED FEATHER⁄BOX. Maori, New Zealand. Wood, 18 inches long. Museum of Anthropology, University of California, Berkeley (11.2196). *Picture 91.*

298. CARVED FEATHER⁄BOX. Maori, New Zealand. Wood, 18½ inches long. Brooklyn Museum (41.81).

*299. CARVED FEATHER⁄BOX. Maori, New Zealand. Wood, ca. 20 inches long. Peabody Museum, Harvard University (53495). *Picture 92.*

300. "TEWHATEWHA", FIGHTING CLUB. Maori, New Zealand. Wood, ca. 65 inches long. Royal Ontario Museum of Archaeology, Toronto, Canada (HB⁄164).

†301. CARVED NOSE FLUTE. Maori, New Zealand. Wood, 4 inches long. Peabody Museum, Harvard University (53500). *Fig. 20.*

302. "HEI⁄TIKI", BREAST PENDANT. Maori, New Zealand. Nephrite, 3¼ inches high. Peabody Museum, Harvard University (55996).

303. "HEI⁄TIKI", BREAST PENDANT. Maori, New Zealand. Nephrite, 4½ inches high. Brooklyn Museum (03.210).

304. "HEI⁄TIKI", BREAST PENDANT. Maori, New Zealand. Nephrite, ca. 4 inches high. Buffalo Museum of Science (JZ⁄117).

305. "HEI⁄TIKI", BREAST PENDANT. Maori, New Zealand. Nephrite, 4 inches high. Carlebach Gallery, New York.

306. "HEI⁄TIKI", BREAST PENDANT. Maori, New Zealand. Bone, 2½ inches high. Collection Nasli Heeramaneck, New York.

307. "MERE", SHORT CLUB. Maori, New Zealand. Nephrite, 14 inches long. Los Angeles County Museum (A⁄2954⁄292).

*308. ANCESTOR FIGURE. Easter Island. Wood, 18 inches high. Peabody Museum, Salem, Mass. (E⁄5306). *Picture 93.*

309. ANCESTOR FIGURE. Easter Island. Wood, 7½ inches high. Peabody Museum, Harvard University (53593).

310. ANCESTOR FIGURE. Easter Island. Wood, 17 inches high. University Museum, Philadelphia (18059).

*311. LIZARD FIGURE. Easter Island. Wood, 18½ inches high. Brooklyn Museum (50.78). *Picture 95.*

†312. GROTESQUE FIGURE. Easter Island. Painted tapa cloth covering, 19 inches high. Peabody Museum, Harvard University (53542). *Fig. 21.*

313. GROTESQUE FIGURE. Easter Island. Painted tapa cloth covering, 16 inches high. Peabody Museum, Harvard University (53543).

*314. PAINTED HEADDRESS OR HEAD MASK. Easter Island. Tapa cloth covering, 11¾ inches diameter. Peabody Museum, Harvard University (53541). *Picture 96.*

315. "REI⁄MIRO", BREAST PENDANT. Easter Island. Wood, 21 inches wide. Buffalo Museum of Science (C⁄12753).

316. CLUB WITH CARVED HEADS. Easter Island. Wood, 71 inches long. University Museum, Philadelphia (P⁄4806).

317. CLUB WITH CARVED HEADS. Easter Island. Wood, 41 inches long. University Museum, Philadelphia (P⁄3142⁄a).

*318. CLUB OR STAFF. Easter Island. Wood, 39 inches long. Collection Eliot Elisofon, New York. *Picture 94.*

*319. FEMALE FIGURE. Hawaii. Wood, 27 inches high. Collection Mrs. Vaid McHattie Forbes, Honolulu, on loan to Honolulu Academy of Arts. *Picture 97.*

*320. MALE FIGURE. Hawaii. Wood, 21½ inches high. Bernice P. Bishop Museum, Honolulu (1363). *Picture 99.*

*321. MALE FIGURE. Hawaii. Wood, 29 inches high. Bernice P. Bishop Museum, Honolulu (B-6921). *Picture 98 a and b.*

322. MALE FIGURE. Hawaii. Wood, 36 inches high. Honolulu Academy of Arts (351.1).

323. FIGURE. Hawaii. Wood, about 20 inches high. Cleveland Art Museum.

*324. AGGRESSIVE FIGURE. Hawaii. Wood, 8¾ inches high. Bernice P. Bishop Museum, Honolulu (1362). *Picture 101.*

*325. FRAGMENTARY CARVING. Hawaii. Wood, 9 inches high. Bernice P. Bishop Museum, Honolulu (187). *Picture 100.*

†326. DRUM BASE FIGURE. Hawaii. Wood, 12½ inches high. Bernice P. Bishop Museum, Honolulu (11017). *Fig. 22.*

327. CARVED FISH-POLE RACK. Hawaii. Wood, 10 inches wide. Bernice P. Bishop Museum, Honolulu (3906).

*328. "KONANE" GAME BOARD, WITH CARVED FIGURES. Hawaii. Wood, 13¼ inches long by 10½ inches wide by 8 inches high. Collection Mrs. Vaid McHattie Forbes, Honolulu, on loan to Honolulu Academy of Arts. *Picture 102.*

329. BOWL WITH FIGURES. Hawaii. Wood, 12 inches long by 6 inches wide. Peabody Museum, Harvard University (53571).

330. BOWL. Hawaii. Wood, 10¼ inches high by 8 inches diameter. Honolulu Academy of Arts (2050).

331. SPITTOON. Hawaii. Wood, 6½ inches long by 5½ inches wide by 3 inches high. Bernice P. Bishop Museum, Honolulu (698).

332. FINGER-BOWL. Hawaii. Wood, 10½ inches long by 7 inches wide by 3½ inches high. Bernice P. Bishop Museum, Honolulu (624).

333. WATER BOTTLE. Hawaii. Painted gourd, 11 inches high. Honolulu Academy of Arts (331.1).

334. FEATHER CAPE. Hawaii. 26 inches wide. Honolulu Academy of Arts (4095).

335. FEATHER LEI, NECK ORNAMENT. Hawaii. 24 inches long. Honolulu Academy of Arts (1439.1).

336. FEATHER LEI, NECK ORNAMENT. Hawaii. 24 inches long. Honolulu Academy of Arts (1440.1).

337. FEATHER LEI, NECK ORNAMENT. Hawaii. 24 inches long. Honolulu Academy of Arts (2830).

338. PAINTED TAPA. Hawaii. 25 inches long by 15 inches wide. Peabody Museum, Harvard University (2899).

339. PAINTED TAPA CLOTH. Hawaii. 36 inches long by 20 inches wide. Peabody Museum, Harvard University (45.1285).

340. PAINTED TAPA CLOTH. Hawaii. 54 inches square. Peabody Museum, Harvard University (48.436).

341. PAINTED TAPA CLOTH. Hawaii. 36 inches long by 18 inches wide. Peabody Museum, Harvard University (122-BA).

342. TAPA BEATER. Hawaii. Wood, 14 inches long. Bernice P. Bishop Museum, Honolulu (371).

343. TAPA BEATER. Hawaii. Wood, 14¾ inches long. Bernice P. Bishop Museum, Honolulu (204).

344. TAPA STAMP. Hawaii. Bamboo, 18½ inches long. Bernice P. Bishop Museum, Honolulu (20).

345. TAPA STAMP. Hawaii. Bamboo, 14½ inches long. Bernice P. Bishop Museum, Honolulu (8821-C).

346. TAPA STAMP. Hawaii. Wood, 14½ inches long. Bernice P. Bishop Museum, Honolulu (A-29).

347. "LEI NIHO PALAOA", BREAST PENDANT. Hawaii. Whale tooth ivory, human hair, 10½ inches long, hook 3¾ inches long. Peabody Museum, Salem, Mass. (E-21346).

348. DECORATED FAN. Hawaii. Dyed coconut fiber, 19½ inches wide. Peabody Museum, Salem, Mass. (E-19307).

1. CARVED AND PAINTED HOUSE DECORATION. Batak, Sumatra. *Seattle Art Museum.*

2. ANCESTOR FIGURE. Nias. *Collection Mr.
and Mrs. Ralph C. Altman, Los Angeles.*

3. ANCESTOR FIGURE. Leti. *Collection Helen
Tamiris, New York.*

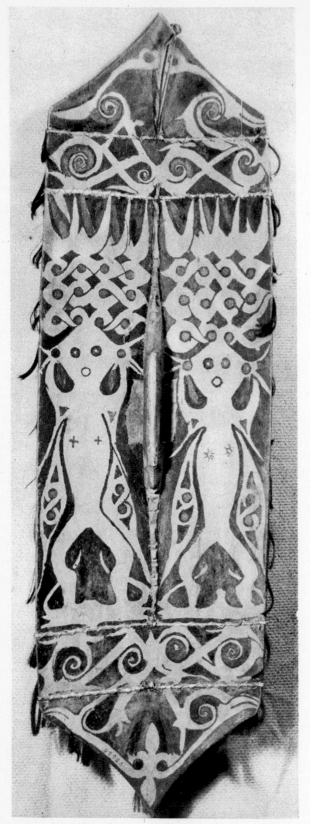

4. SHIELD. Kenyah-Kayan, Borneo. *Peabody Museum. Harvard University.*

5. MASK. Borneo. *Milwaukee Public Museum.*

6. LADLE. Igorot, Philippines. *Denver Art Museum.*

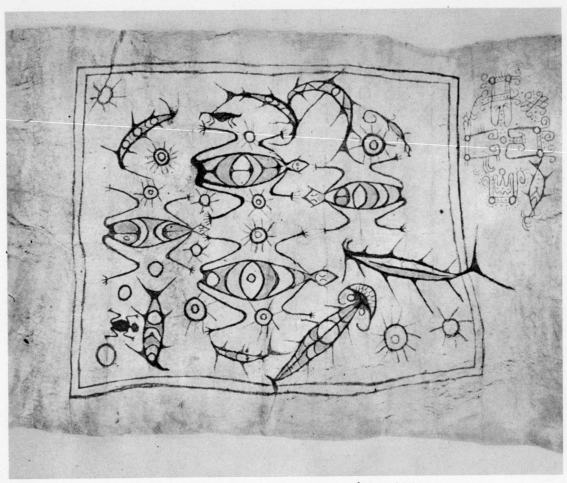

7. PAINTED BARK-CLOTH. Dutch New Guinea. *Cincinnati Museum of Natural History.*

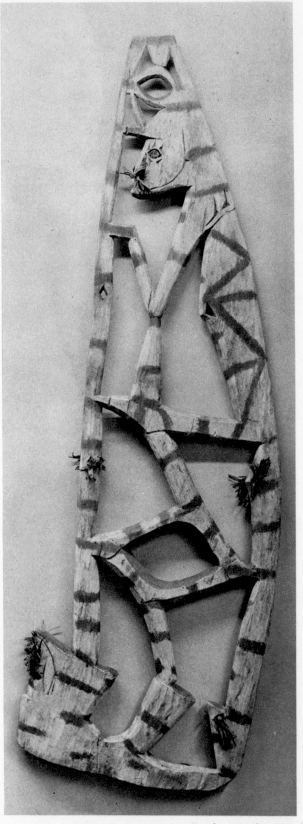

8. CARVED AND PAINTED SHIELD. South Dutch New Guinea. *Carlebach Gallery, New York.*

9. CANOE PROW DECORATION. South Dutch New Guinea. *Carlebach Gallery, New York.*

10. "KOROVAR", ANCESTOR FIGURE. Dutch New Guinea. *Bernice P. Bishop Museum, Honolulu.*

II. CARVED BOWL. Admiralty Islands. *Newark Museum.*

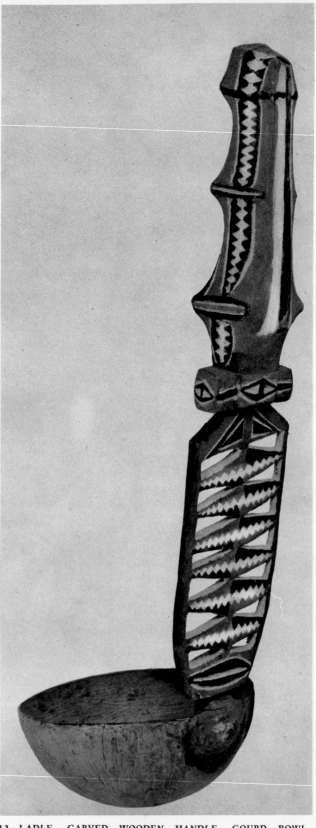

12. FIGURE, SPEAR DECORATION.
Admiralty Islands. *American Museum of Natural History, New York.*

13. LADLE, CARVED WOODEN HANDLE, GOURD BOWL. Admiralty Islands. *American Museum of Natural History, New York.*

14. CARVING USED IN MORTUARY CEREMONIES. New Ireland. *Newark Museum.*

15. MASK USED IN MORTUARY CEREMONIES. New Ireland. *Collection Mr. and Mrs. Ralph C. Altman, Los Angeles.*

16. MASK. New Ireland. *Carlebach Gallery, New York.*

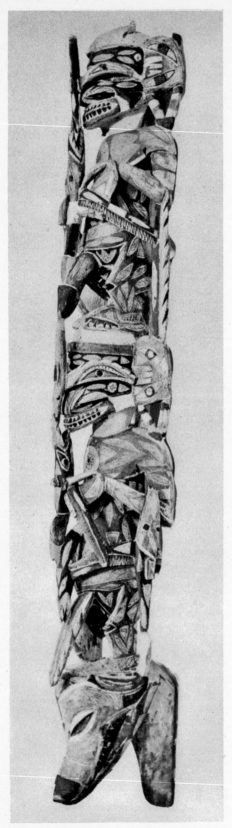

17. "MALAGAN", COLUMNAR MORTUARY CARVING. New Ireland. *Carlebach Gallery, New York.*

18. CEREMONIAL CARVING. New Ireland. *de Young Memorial Museum, San Francisco.*

19. POLYCHROMED SHIELD. New Britain. *Peabody Museum, Harvard University.*

20. MASK, PITH OVER LIGHT FRAME. New Britain. *Denver Art Museum.*

23. FIGURE. Sepik River, New Guinea. *Bernice P. Bishop Museum, Honolulu.*

22. MALE FIGURE. Mundugumor, Sepik River, New Guinea. *American Museum of Natural History, New York.*

21. MALE FIGURE. Sepik River, New Guinea. *Bernice P. Bishop Museum, Honolulu.*

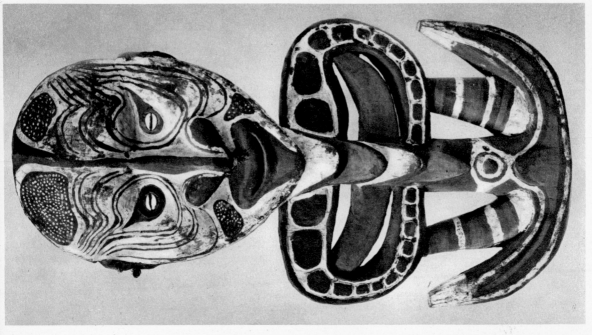

25. CARVED AND PAINTED HOOK. Tchambuli, Sepik River, New Guinea. University Museum, Philadelphia.

24. SEAT SHAPED AS BIRD. Sepik River, New Guinea. University Museum, Philadelphia.

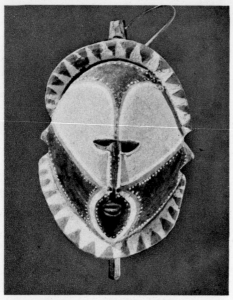

26. POLYCHROMED MASK. Abelam, Sepik River, New Guinea. *American Museum of Natural History, New York.*

27. MINIATURE MASK. Sepik River, New Guinea. *Carlebach Gallery, New York.*

28. BASKETRY MASK. Tchambuli, Sepik River, New Guinea. *Carlebach Gallery, New York.*

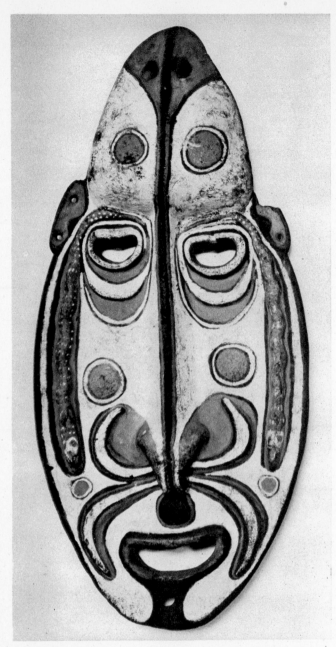

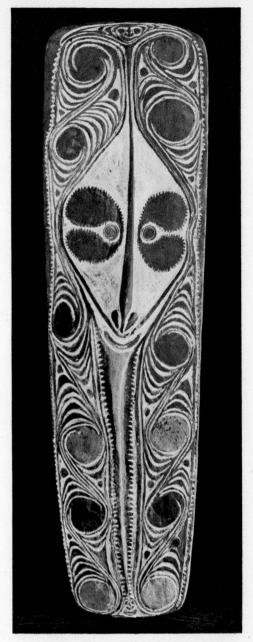

29. GABLE MASK FOR CEREMONIAL HOUSE. Sepik River, New Guinea. *University Museum, Philadelphia.*

30. CARVED AND PAINTED SHIELD. Tchambuli, Sepik River, New Guinea. *American Museum of Natural History, New York.*

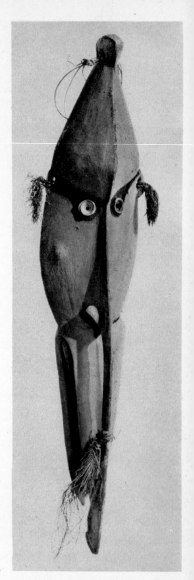

33. MASK. Tchambuli, Sepik River, New Guinea. *American Museum of Natural History, New York.*

31. SUSPENSION HOOK. Tchambuli, Sepik River, New Guinea. *American Museum of Natural History, New York.*

32. SUSPENSION HOOK. Mundugumor, Sepik River, New Guinea. *American Museum of Natural History, New York.*

34. SHIELD WITH PIERCED DESIGN. Sepik
River, New Guinea. *Detroit Institute of Arts.*

35. SUSPENSION HOOK WITH BIRD FORM. Sepik River, New
Guinea. *American Museum of Natural History, New York.*

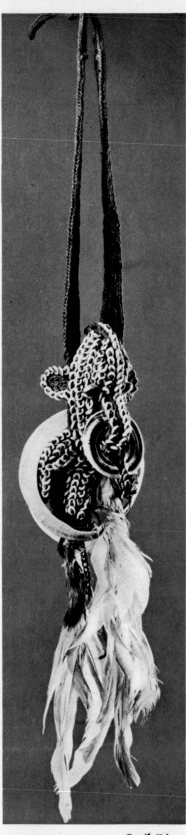

36. SAGO SCOOP. Sepik River, New Guinea. *Peabody Museum, Harvard University.*

37. BREAST ORNAMENT. Sepik River, New Guinea. *University Museum, Philadelphia.*

38. CEREMONIAL CARVING. Sepik River, New Guinea. *Collection Donald Deskey, New York.*

39. BOWL WITH CARVED FIGURES AS HANDLES. Sepik River, New Guinea. Collection William Moore, Los Angeles.

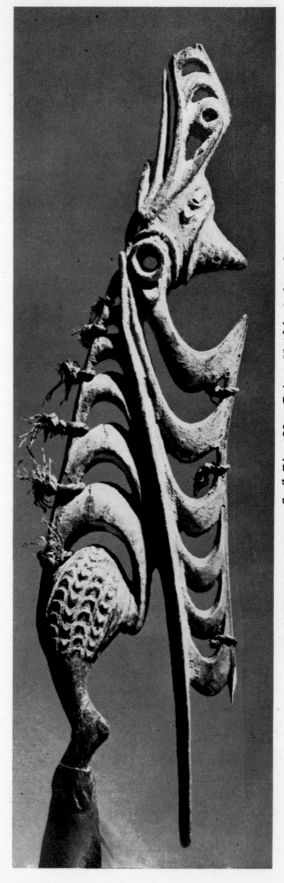

40. LIME TUBE STOPPER. Sepik River, New Guinea. Honolulu Academy of Arts.

41. FIGURE. Huon Gulf-Tami Island, New Guinea. *Bernice P. Bishop Museum, Honolulu.*

43. BOWL. Huon Gulf Tami Island, New Guinea.
Collection Nelson A. Rockefeller, New York.

42. DRUM. Huon Gulf Tami Island, New
Guinea. *American Museum of Natural
History, New York.*

44. CARVED AND PAINTED SHIELD. Papuan Gulf, New Guinea. *Royal Ontario Museum of Archaeology, Toronto, Canada.*

45. BARK-CLOTH MASK. Papuan Gulf, New Guinea. *University Museum, Philadelphia.*

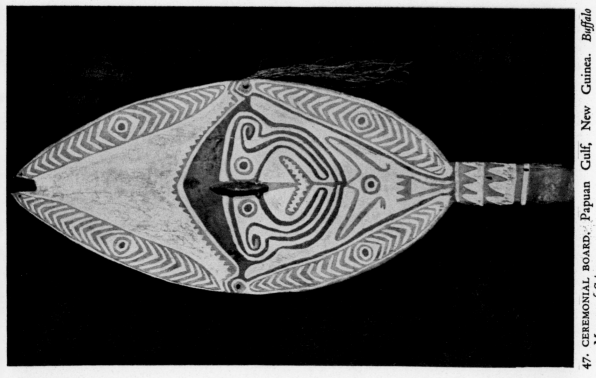

47. CEREMONIAL BOARD. Papuan Gulf, New Guinea. *Buffalo Museum of Science.*

46. BARK-CLOTH MASK. Papuan Gulf, New Guinea. *Collection Mr. and Mrs. Ralph C. Altman, Los Angeles.*

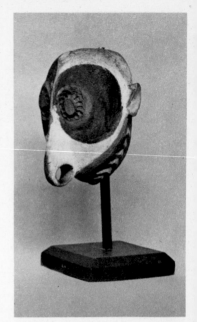

48. WOODEN MASK. Torres Straits, New Guinea. *Collection Nelson A. Rocke-feller, New York.*

49 (*a and b*). PAINTED CARVED PITH HEADS. Fly River, New Guinea. *Detroit Institute of Arts.*

50. INCISED CLUB. Trobri
ands, Massim Area, New
Guinea. *Buffalo Museum
of Science.*

51. PAINTED WAR SHIELD. Trobriands, Massim Area, New Guinea. *Buffalo Museum
of Science.*

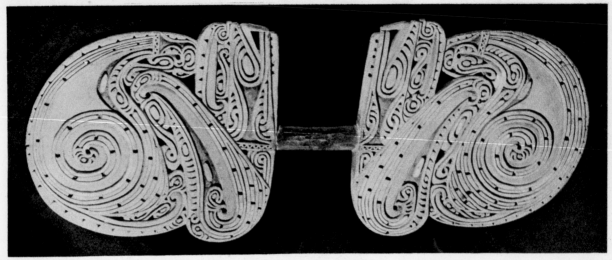

52. "KAI-DIBA", DANCE SHIELD. Trobriands, Massim Area, New Guinea. *Newark Museum.*

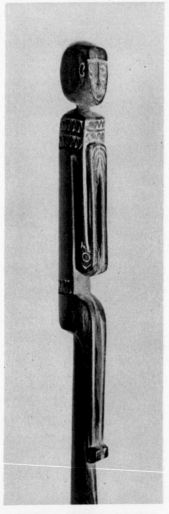

53. FIGURE, SPATULA HANDLE. Massim Area, New Guinea. *Collection Vincent Price, Beverly Hills, California.*

54. FIGURE, SPATULA HANDLE. Trobriands, Massim Area, New Guinea. *Los Angeles County Museum.*

55. MORTAR WITH FIGURE. Solomon Islands. *Buffalo Museum of Science.*

56. "MUSUMUSU", CANOE BOW FIGURE. Central Solomon Islands. *Collection Nelson A. Rockefeller, New York.*

57. HEAD CARVED IN CORAL. Central Solomon Islands. *Collection Nelson A. Rockefeller, New York.*

58. BOWL SHAPED AS BIRD. Eastern Solomon Islands. *Washington State Museum, Seattle.*

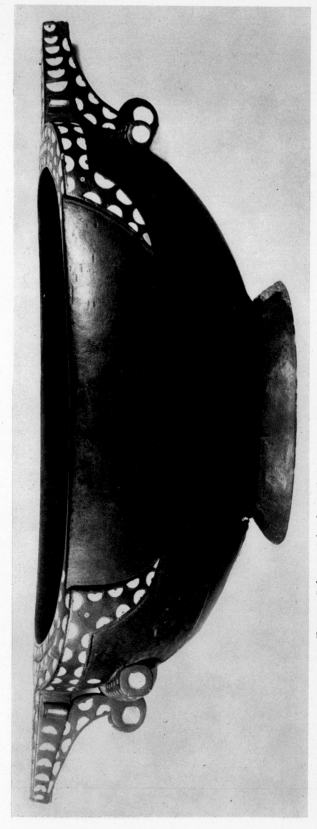

59. SHELL INLAID FOOD BOWL. Eastern Solomon Islands. *Peabody Museum, Harvard University.*

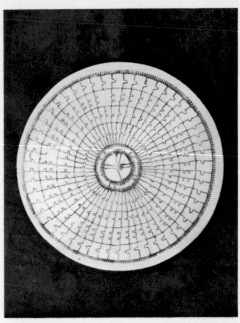

60. CARVED SHELL BREAST ORNAMENTS. Solomon Islands. *Cincinnati Museum of Natural History.*

61. "KAPKAP", TORTOISE AND TRIDACNA SHELL BREAST ORNAMENT. *Cincinnati Museum of Natural History.*

62. ENGRAVED BAMBOO LIME TUBES. Solomon Islands. *Milwaukee Public Museum.*

63. MASK. New Hebrides. *Newark Museum.*

64. CARVED DETAIL ON SPEAR. New Hebrides. *Peabody Museum, Harvard University.*

65. BARK-CLOTH AND FIBER MASK. New Hebrides. *Buffalo Museum of Science.*

66. WOODEN PLATTER. New Hebrides. *American Museum of Natural History, New York.*

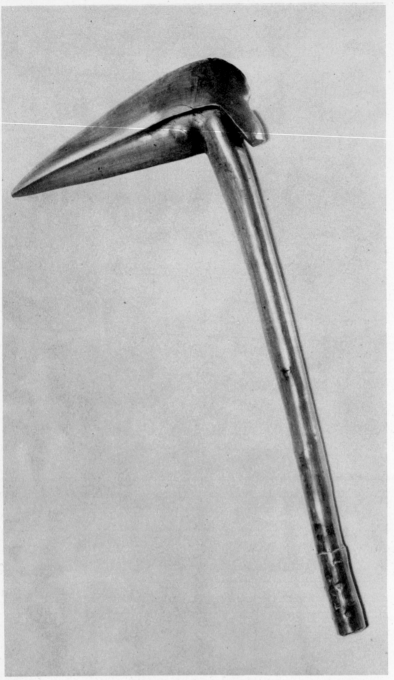

67. CLUB SHAPED AS BIRD HEAD. New Caledonia. *American Museum of Natural History, New York.*

68. PIG-KILLER. New Hebrides. *Collection Vincent Price, Beverly Hills, California.*

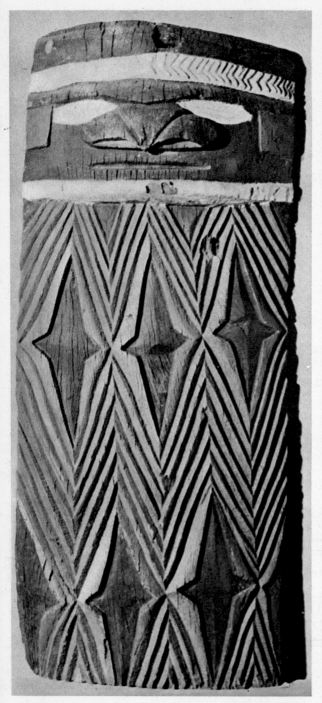

69. CARVED DOORPOST, "TALE". New Caledonia. *Denver Art Museum.*

70. MASK. New Caledonia. *Brooklyn Museum.*

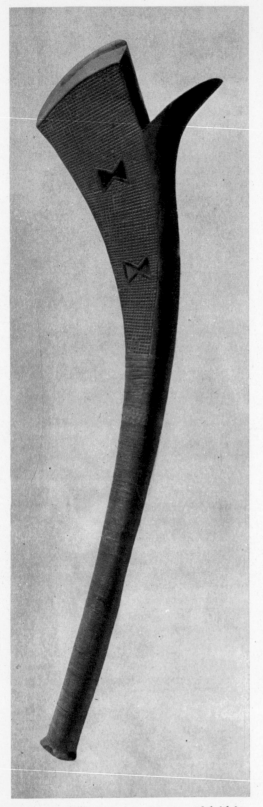

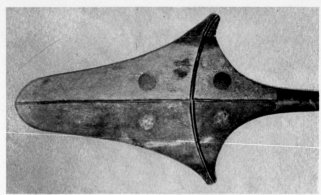

72. DETAIL OF CLUB BLADE. Fiji. *Denver Art Museum.*

71. CLUB. Fiji. *University Museum, Philadelphia.*

73 (a and b). TURTLE-SHAPED KAVA BOWL. Fiji. *Washington State Museum, Seattle.*

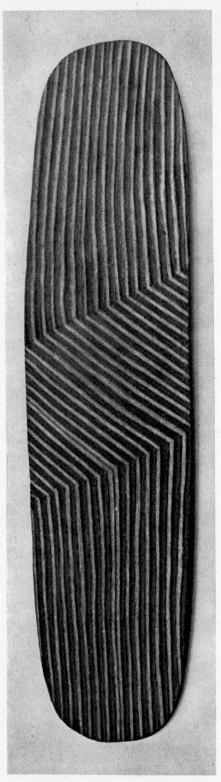

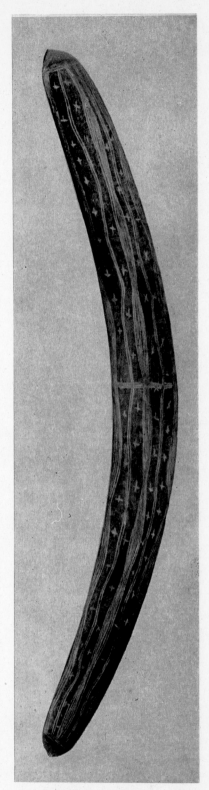

74. CARVED AND PAINTED SHIELD. Murchison River, Western Australia. *de Young Memorial Museum, San Francisco.*

75. ENGRAVED SPEAR-THROWER. Gold-field District, Kalgoorlie, Western Australia. *de Young Memorial Museum, San Francisco.*

76. ENGRAVED BOOMERANG. Australia. *Buffalo Museum of Science.*

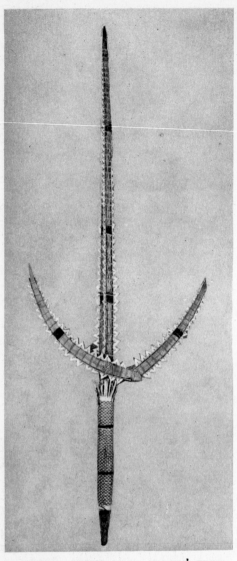

77. SWORD, EDGED WITH SHARKS' TEETH. Gilberts, Micronesia. *Washington State Museum, Seattle.*

78. FEMALE FIGURE. Nukuoro (a Polynesian outlier), Micronesia. *Honolulu Academy of Arts.*

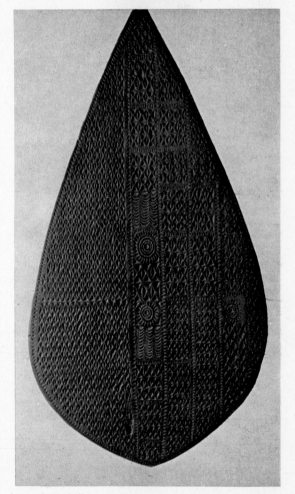

79. DISTRICT GOD. Raratonga, Cook Islands, Polynesia. *Peabody Museum, Harvard University.*

80 (*a and b*). CEREMONIAL PADDLE, DETAILS. Austral Islands, Polynesia. *Peabody Museum, Harvard University.*

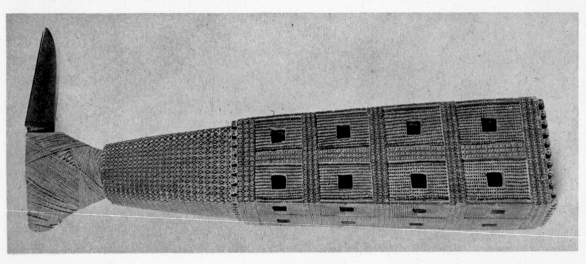

83. FLY-WHISK HANDLE. Tahiti, Society Islands, Poly-

82. MALE FIGURE. Tahiti, Society Islands. Polynesia. *Collection Nelson A. Rockefeller, New York.*

81. CEREMONIAL ADZE. Mangaia, Cook Islands, Polynesia. *Peabody Museum, Harvard*

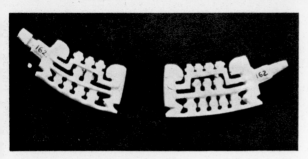

84. BONE EAR ORNAMENTS. Marquesas Islands. *Cincinnati Museum of Natural History.*

85. HEAD OF CLUB, DETAIL. Marquesas Islands. *Brooklyn Museum.*

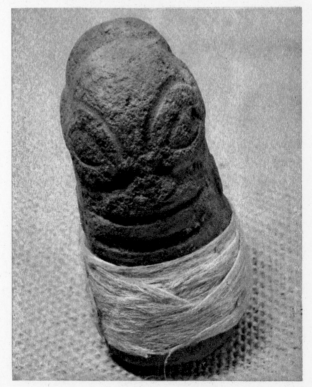

86 (*a and b*). SALT POUNDER. Marquesas Islands. *Cincinnati Museum of Natural History.*

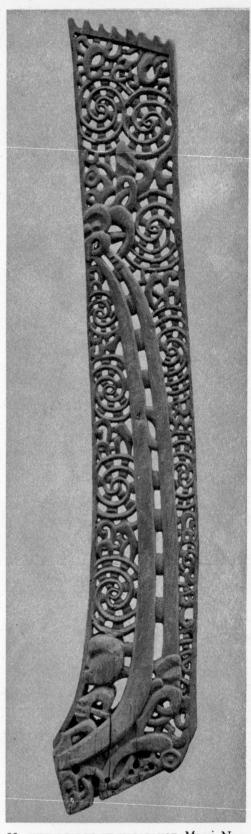

87. FIGURE. Maori, New Zealand. *Peabody Museum, Harvard University*

88. STERN-PIECE OF WAR CANOE. Maori, New Zealand. *de Young Memorial Museum, San Francisco.*

89 (*a, b and c*). CARVED CANOE PADDLE
HANDLE, DETAILS. Maori, New Zealand.
University Museum, Philadelphia.

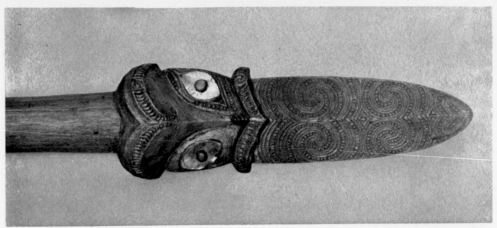

90. "TAIAHA", FIGHTING STAVE, DETAIL. Maori, New Zealand. *Peabody Museum, Salem, Mass.*

91. FEATHER-BOX. Maori, New Zealand. *Museum of Anthropology, University of California, Berkeley.*

92. FEATHER-BOX, BOTTOM VIEW. Maori, New Zealand. *Peabody Museum, Harvard University.*

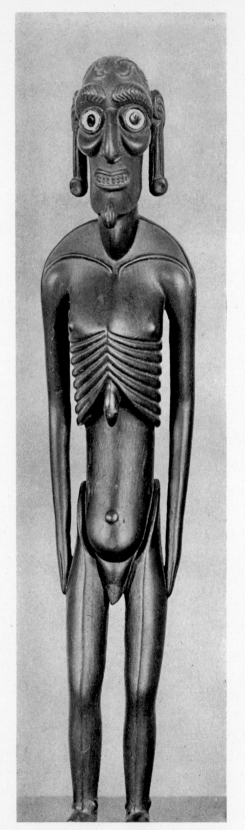

94. CLUB, DETAIL. Easter Island. *Collection Eliot Elisofon, New York.*

93. WOODEN FIGURE. Easter Island. *Peabody Museum, Salem, Mass.*

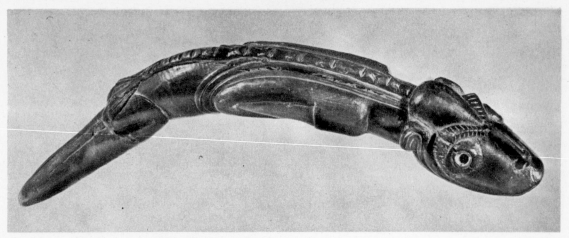

95. LIZARD FIGURE. Easter Island. *Brooklyn Museum.*

96. HEADDRESS OR MASK, PAINTED TAPA CLOTH. Easter Island. *Peabody Museum, Harvard University.*

97. FEMALE FIGURE. Hawaii. *Collection Mrs. Vaid McHattie Forbes, Honolulu, on loan to Honolulu Academy of Arts.*

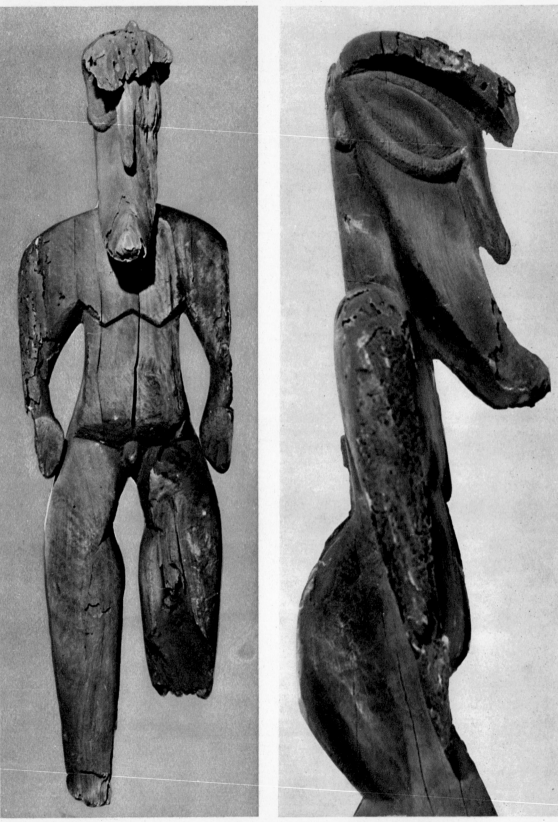

98 (*a and b*). MALE FIGURE AND DETAIL. Hawaii. *Bernice P. Bishop Museum, Honolulu.*

99. STANDING MALE FIGURE. Hawaii. *Bernice P. Bishop Museum, Honolulu.*

100. FRAGMENTARY CARVING. Hawaii. *Bernice P. Bishop Museum, Honolulu.*

101. SMALL AGGRESSIVE FIGURE. Hawaii. *Bernice P. Bishop Museum, Honolulu.*

102. "KONANE" GAME BOARD, WITH CARVED FIGURES. Hawaii. *Collection Mrs. Vaid McHattie Forbes, on loan to Honolulu Academy of Arts.*

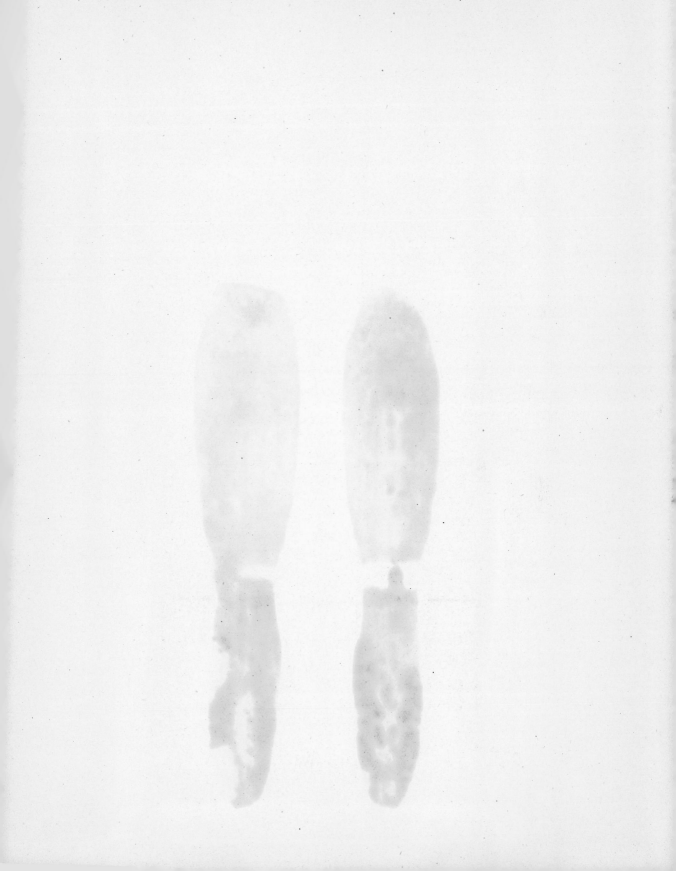